CAMILLE SAINT-SAËNS AND HIS WORLD

OTHER PRINCETON UNIVERSITY PRESS VOLUMES PUBLISHED
IN CONJUNCTION WITH THE BARD MUSIC FESTIVAL

Brahms and His World
edited by Walter Frisch (1990)

Mendelssohn and His World
edited by R. Larry Todd (1991)

Richard Strauss and His World
edited by Bryan Gilliam (1992)

Dvořák and His World
edited by Michael Beckerman (1993)

Schumann and His World
edited by R. Larry Todd (1994)

Bartók and His World
edited by Peter Laki (1995)

Charles Ives and His World
edited by J. Peter Burkholder (1996)

Haydn and His World
edited by Elaine R. Sisman (1997)

Tchaikovsky and His World
edited by Leslie Kearney (1998)

Schoenberg and His World
edited by Walter Frisch (1999)

Beethoven and His World
edited by Scott Burnham and
Michael P. Steinberg (2000)

Debussy and His World
edited by Jane F. Fulcher (2001)

Mahler and His World
edited by Karen Painter (2002)

Janáček and His World
edited by Michael Beckerman (2003)

Shostakovich and His World
edited by Laurel E. Fay (2004)

Aaron Copland and His World
edited by Carol J. Oja and
Judith Tick (2005)

Franz Liszt and His World
edited by Christopher H. Gibbs
and Dana Gooley (2006)

Edward Elgar and His World
edited by Byron Adams (2007)

Prokofiev and His World
edited by Simon Morrison (2008)

Brahms and His World (revised edition)
edited by Walter Frisch and
Kevin C. Karnes (2009)

Richard Wagner and His World
edited by Thomas S. Grey (2009)

Alban Berg and His World
edited by Christopher Hailey (2010)

Jean Sibelius and His World
edited by Daniel M. Grimley (2011)

CAMILLE SAINT-SAËNS
AND HIS WORLD

EDITED BY
JANN PASLER

PRINCETON UNIVERSITY PRESS
PRINCETON AND OXFORD

Copyright © 2012 by Princeton University Press

Published by Princeton University Press, 41 William Street,
Princeton, New Jersey 08540
In the United Kingdom: Princeton University Press,
6 Oxford Street, Woodstock, Oxfordshire OX20 1TW
press.princeton.edu

Library of Congress Control Number: 2012937254

ISBN: 978-0-691-15555-5 (cloth)
ISBN: 978-0-691-15556-2 (paperback)

British Library Cataloging-in-Publication Data is available

This publication has been produced by the Bard College Publications Office:
Ginger Shore, Director
Anita van de Ven, Cover design
Natalie Kelly, Design
Text edited by Paul De Angelis and Erin Clermont
Music typeset by Don Giller

This publication has been underwritten in part by grants from
Furthermore: a program of the J. M. Kaplan Fund and
Helen and Roger Alcaly.

Printed on acid-free paper. ∞

Printed in the United States of America

1 3 5 7 9 10 8 6 4 2

Contents

Contents

PART V
SAINT-SAËNS IN THE 20TH CENTURY

Acknowledgments and Permissions

My deep thanks go to the indefatigable and brilliant Leon Botstein for taking on the challenge of such a controversial and complex composer; Byron Adams and Christopher Gibbs for the foresight and tenacity to make it happen; Irene Zedlacher, for her administrative support and endless good cheer; Paul De Angelis for his careful editing; Ginger Shore for her art direction and help with the illustrations; Natalie Kelly for her book design; the translators, especially Mark DeVoto; and Jill Rogers for her conscientious research assistance.

I'm particularly grateful to Yves Gérard, Saint-Saëns's biographer, for his advice, enthusiastic support, and the two days we shared at the Saint-Saëns archives in Dieppe. Sabina Ratner, editor of the thematic catalogue of Saint-Saëns's instrumental works, helped me to understand the composer's stature among musicians today. Timothy Flynn's annotated bibliography and recent biographies by Stephen Studd and Brian Rees provided a firm foundation on which we have built. The staff at major archives offered their generous assistance and permission to reproduce illustrations, especially Sonia Popoff at the Médiathèque Musicale Mahler, Paris, and Pierre Ickowicz at the Château-Musée de Dieppe. All copyright holders and the works reproduced for which they granted us permission are listed in the permissions section below.

Most of all, I would like to thank my co-authors, an international group of experts from astronomy to film studies, performance to music history. With their generous collaboration, I hope that, taken as a whole, these essays and "documents" will bring new understanding and appreciation to Saint-Saëns and his music.

Permissions

The following copyright holders have graciously granted permission to reprint or reproduce the following copyrighted material:

Gallica Bibliothèque numérique, Paris, for Figure 1 in "Inspired by the Skies? Saint-Saëns, Amateur Astronomer" by Léo Houziaux.

Ville de Dieppe Collection, Château-Musée ©Ville de Dieppe, from *Lettres de compositeurs à Camille Saint-Saëns*, ed. Eurydice Jousse and Yves Gérard (Lyon: Symétrie 2009), for Figure 1 in "Rivals and Friends: Saint-Saëns, Massenet, and *Thaïs*" by Jean-Christophe Branger.

Ville de Dieppe Collection, Château-Musée ©Ville de Dieppe, photography by Jann Pasler, for Figure 2 in "Saint-Saëns's Improvisations on the Organ (1862)" by William Peterson.

Bibliothèque nationale, Département de musique, Paris, for Figure 1; Bibliothèque nationale et universitaire de Strasbourg for Figure 2 in "Providing Direction for French Music: Saint-Saëns and the Société Nationale" by Michael Strasser.

Bibliothèque nationale, Département de musique, Paris, for Figure 1 in "Saint-Saëns as President of the Société des Compositeurs (1887–1891)" by Laure Schnapper.

Bibliothèque nationale, Département de musique, Paris, for Figure 1 in "Saint-Saëns at the Société des Concerts du Conservatoire de Paris (1903–1904)" by D. Kern Holoman.

Ville de Dieppe Collection, Château-Musée ©Ville de Dieppe, photography by Jann Pasler, for Figure 1 in "Saint-Saëns: The Traveling Musician" by Stéphane Leteuré.

The Morgan Library & Museum, New York, for Figure 1 as well as the musical examples in the "Analytical and Historical Programme" in "Saint-Saëns in England: His *Organ* Symphony" by Sabina Teller Ratner.

Ville de Dieppe Collection, Château-Musée ©Ville de Dieppe, photography by Jann Pasler, for Figure 1 and Figure 2, Coll. Médiathèque Musicale Mahler, Paris, for Figure 3 in "Saint-Saëns, 'Algerian by Adoption'" by Jann Pasler.

Ville de Dieppe Collection, Château-Musée ©Ville de Dieppe, photography by Jann Pasler, for Figure 1 and Figure 2 in "Friendship and Music in Indochina" by Jann Pasler.

Carnegie Hall, New York, for Figure 1 in "Saint-Saëns in New York" by Carolyn Guzski.

Coll. Médiathèque Musicale Mahler, Paris, for Figure 1 in "Saint-Saëns and Latin America" by Carol A. Hess.

Ville de Dieppe Collection, Château-Musée ©Ville de Dieppe, photography by Jann Pasler, for Figure 1 and Figure 2 in "Saint-Saëns and the Ancient World: From Africa to Greece" by Jann Pasler.

Ville de Dieppe Collection, Château-Musée ©Ville de Dieppe, photography by Jann Pasler, for Figure 1 in "Saint-Saëns and Rameau's Keyboard Music" by Katherine Ellis.

Ville de Dieppe Collection, Château-Musée ©Ville de Dieppe, photography by Jann Pasler, for Figure 1; The Art Archive at Art Resource, New York, photography by Gianni Dagli Orti, for Figure 2 in "Lyres and Citharas of Antiquity" by Marie-Gabrielle Soret.

Durand & Cie., ©1931, copyright renewed 1959, for Example 12, Ravel's Left Hand Concerto, in "Saint-Saëns, Ravel, and Their Piano Concertos," by Michael J. Puri.

Photofest, Inc., New York, for Figure 1 and Figure 2 in "Saint-Saëns and Silent Film/Sound Film and Saint-Saëns" by Martin Marks.

Cover Caption and Credit:
Photograph of a portrait of Camille Saint-Saëns, 1880, Ville de Dieppe Collection, Château-Musée ©Ville de Dieppe.

The author and publishers have made every effort to trace holders of copyright. They much regret if any inadvertent omissions have been made.

Introduction:
Deconstructing Saint-Saëns

JANN PASLER

A composer whose career spanned seventy years and five continents, a virtuoso who performed, wrote, and excelled in nearly every musical genre, a writer almost as prolific in prose as in music, and a man who cultivated long friendships worldwide with astronomers, philosophers, botanists, and ordinary music lovers: it is no wonder that during his lifetime Saint-Saëns was so eminent, to some the quintessentially French musician. Music biography, however, is often a function of music history, linked to style, influence, legacy. When fashions change, agendas shift and historians elevate new heros; disenchantment can ensue. A life understood as valuable in one context can lose its meaning in another. Whether on account of his controversial positions on the future of music or his wartime rejection of German music, Saint-Saëns was pushed to the sidelines of history. At the same time, his music was never far from concert halls. What then are we to make of Saint-Saëns's double-sided reputation: on the one hand, as a monumental composer, the "French Beethoven,"[1] and on the other, as a crusty old reactionary, resentful and resistant to change? And why, almost a century after his passing, does his music continue to appeal?

This book deconstructs such a paradox and, in the tradition of the Bard Music Festivals, gives us reasons to reconsider Saint-Saëns and his world. Proposing a new approach to music biography, with a postmodern tolerance toward incongruities, it examines the ironies and contradictions within the composer and his reputation. With a kaleidoscopic approach to narrative, it presents a collection of micro-stories and analyses: seven longer articles and twenty-three short essays. The latter were commissioned to shed light on a particular musical event, scientific or philosophical idea, aesthetic interest, or personal relationship as represented by concert programs (both within France and abroad, by amateurs as well as professionals), scientific essays, letters, and poems. Pretexts for investigating important but lesser-known aspects of his personality, opinions, and career, these shed light on not only his musical activities, but also his private life, his playful as well as serious nature, his sense of adventure as well as his commitment to his nation. Saint-Saëns understood that Paris was a world driven by competition and rivalry over resources and prestige; to survive he needed time away and personal warmth, especially after his mother and two children passed away and he separated from his wife. Frequent concert tours and residencies abroad, especially in North Africa, provided both privacy and recognition. Through his correspondence, he kept in touch. A self-fashioned cosmopolitan, Saint-Saëns was perhaps the first truly global musician. As we look closer, we learn his legacy was not confined to the Western world, and that, contrary to what we may have presumed, more than thirty works continued to be performed in a wide variety of contexts.

While Saint-Saëns self-consciously contributed much to French glory, he also knew his limits and was capable of self-mockery, wit, and humor. In his personal collection in Dieppe is not only a bigger-than-life bronze likeness once offered to the composer, but also a tiny sculpture that, only a few inches in height, pokes fun at that grandeur. With one arm resting on a stack of his eight opera scores, the other on a small lyre, he stares upward as if possessed, his large head, bigger than his entire body, surrounded by a golden halo. Saint-Saëns had a close relationship with the prestigious Société des Concerts du Conservatoire, as Kern Holoman outlines, and was elected to the Institut de France in 1881—ironically, two years before he composed his opera *Henry VIII* and nine years before *Samson et Dalila* appeared on French stages. In fact, his most recent accomplishment had been his stewardship of a committee charged with reflecting on music instruction in elementary schools, a report reproduced here. Such recognition honored in part his remarkable public spirit, a commitment he bemoaned as noticeably lacking in the next generation. Not only did Saint-Saëns take seriously his role in judging the annual Prix de Rome in composition, making sure to be in Paris for the competitions; as a good republican, believing that all should have access to art music, he wrote innumerable works for worker choruses and students, conducted an amateur orchestra, and served on juries of *orphéon* competitions. He also dedicated many church organs, even late in life, as William Peterson explains in his contribution to this volume.

Saint-Saëns benefitted from this official status by writing frequently in the press and winning the attention of philosophers like Gustave Le Bon and astronomers like Flammarion, the former relationship explored here by myself, the latter by Léo Houziaux. The composer loved science. Early in life, he turned away from religious belief to embrace rational logic. But his combative nature, unafraid of controversy, and his love of polemics fueled debates. Such attributes, along with the reputation of being *peu mondain*,[2] not a socialite, were uncommon among those in official positions of power.

Counterbalancing this was Saint-Saëns's sense of humor, particularly evident in private. Playful and fun-loving, he would cross-dress, reputedly even with Tchaikovsky, though, as Mitchell Morris here explains, this did not mean he was necessarily homosexual. He loved travesty as a form of sociability. This also came out in piano performances. Once in East Prussia, when competing with other pianists in "funny tricks at the piano," he beat them all by playing the minuet from *Don Giovanni* with his right hand and, with his left hand on the strings of the piano, accompanying himself as if on the harp, thereby preceding Henry Cowell by more than two decades.[3] His letters abound with his imaginative wit, represented here in a letter to Durand about what to call his Suite, op. 90. So too his drawings that sometimes adorn them, such as an image of a pot cooking over a fire, signaling his ongoing work on the ballet in *Samson et Dalila*. Such playfulness also permeates some of his music. In the *Carnival of Animals*, he not only parodied Offenbach, Rossini, and other composers, he put himself among the fossils, with a bit of *Danse macabre* in the xylophone; in 1892 he wrote a one-act comedy, *La Crampe des écrivains* (Writers' cramp), for his friends in Algiers.

Also paradoxically, Saint-Saëns was both open and resistant to new trends in music. To understand this, we need the context, for the composer lived long enough to intersect with several generations. Leon Botstein sees Saint-Saëns (born 1835) as the "leading conservative" in French nineteenth-century music, certainly more so than Bizet (born 1838). Yet most of his music vigorously supported democratic republican ideals, left-of-center when the republicans came to power in 1879, albeit more centrist in the 1890s when republicans made alliances with conservative monarchists to fight anarchism and the spread of socialism.[4] To avoid falling back into civil war, republicans needed a new sense of history that incorporated the heritage of both the ancien regime and the Revolution. In response, Saint-Saëns sought ways to negotiate tradition and modernity. *Henry VIII* makes allusions to a five-act revolutionary tragedy, gives the common people a parliamentary role, and synthesizes the influence of Gounod and Wagner. *Les Barbares* shows how people can rise above conflict, as if art could reconcile Dreyfusards and anti-Dreyfusards.[5] With his *Organ Symphony* (1886), its original analytical program notes here introduced by Sabina Ratner, Saint-Saëns also forged "a fertile alliance between what does not die with what progresses."[6] And in *Phryné*, he returned to the humor, charm, and delicacy associated with opéra-comique, the quintessential French genre, reminding his contemporaries of certain values long associated with the French race.

At the same time, as Dana Gooley demonstrates, Saint-Saëns resembles Liszt, another child prodigy virtuoso-composer, in using his performances to impose "modern" pieces on audiences, especially abroad. Moreover, Marie-Gabrielle Soret, like Julien Tiersot before her, points out how the composer, with his independent spirit, curiosity, and frankness, used his press reviews to defend and promote progressive composers such as Liszt, Bizet, and Wagner, wielding warrior metaphors that suggest criticism as a form of combat. When it came to Wagner, what he first deemed progressive he later condemned as a threat to the very nature of French music, a position he took before Debussy too shifted from writing *d'après* to *après Wagner*. Less known is how concert organizers, such as Pasdeloup and Colonne, often placed his music next to their first performances of Wagnerian works, as if Orientalist timbres in works such as his *Bacchanale* presented a strong French counterpart to Wagner's innovations.

At the heart of this paradox is the word *classical*, often used to describe the composer's music. Throughout his life, he admired the "vigorous grace" of Mozart's concertos, learned all of them as early as 1863, and performed them continuously until his death. He was attracted to Beethoven for his music and "the idea of universal brotherhood," as Romain Rolland put it, and wrote his own Variations on a Theme of Beethoven for two pianos. Gooley and Michael Stegemann explore his reception in Germany. As Botstein points out, Rolland compared Saint-Saëns to Mendelssohn and Voltaire, the latter for his clarity of thought, elegance, and precision of expression. From the eighteenth century he also inherited his "love and need of liberty."[7] But Saint-Saëns was equally invested in the French Baroque, especially Rameau, performing the same pieces for decades and serving as general editor of a new edition of Rameau's music, a preface to which Katharine Ellis introduces in this volume.

The classicism of ancient Greece also became increasingly important to Saint-Saëns. He studied it on frescos, contemplated it through figures such as Hercules and Helen, and tried to reproduce it, almost literally, in his incidental music to *Antigone* (1893). This was not a reactionary turn, but rather a vision of France's future as rooted in the Mediterranean, as opposed to northern Europe, a source of recent cultural "decadence." In *Antigone*, imitating Pindar's choruses, he sought to create a modern equivalent for ancient Greek *mousiké*, thereby recapturing its power. If this experiment failed, it did not stop Saint-Saëns from continuing to study ancient Greek musical instruments (his essay is included here), perhaps as the key to making new kinds of sounds.

Saint-Saëns had other ideas about the future as well, especially involving assimilation, another republican ideal at home with the working classes, and abroad with the colonized. The first Frenchman to incorporate the pentatonic scale in *La Princesse jaune* (1872), he also explored the augmented seconds of Arabic music, imitated the sounds of Arab orchestras, and created musical heterogeneity and coexistence. I explore these, along with their racial, historical, and political implications, in his *Africa* fantasy. Through Orientalism, he even found common ground with his rival Jules Massenet, as Jean-Christophe Branger points out in their correspondence about Massenet's *Thaïs*. Saint-Saëns was also fascinated with "the idea of what America will eventually be," seeing it as a forerunner of the "new world" that lies ahead. And he got involved in the newest technologies, recording his music on the gramophone and writing music for an early film, analyzed here by Martin Marks.

Saint-Saëns's relationship to the avant-garde, post-1900, is perhaps least understood. Byron Adams and I reflect on his concept of evolution as the philosophical basis for his rejection of decadence and atonality. He could be utterly dismissive of newer musical trends, yet also warm and encouraging to young composers, such as Florent Schmitt, recent winner of the Prix de Rome; as another composer Charles Koechlin pointed out, he was "known for great generosity." For their part, this generation was ambivalent, though respectful. Michel Duchesneau examines the reasons why they may have included one of his fugues on a concert for the Société musicale indépendante, an organization they founded in 1909 to promote contemporary music. In a review just after he died, Emile Vuillermoz presented his late fugues as emblematic of Saint-Saëns's musical resistance to Wagner: "clarity, logic, measure, simplicity, lucidity, and reason."[8] Ravel was particularly drawn to Saint-Saëns. His personal library, now at the Bibliothèque nationale, was full of Saint-Saëns scores, many of them annotated; MS 17649 is his analysis of *La Jeunesse d'Hercule*. Koechlin, who never ceased defending Saint-Saëns's work despite the composer's sometimes offensive opinions, noted how Ravel learned orchestral balance from his music. Michael J. Puri shows that it was not only brilliant piano writing and orchestration, but also self-parody, ambiguation, and other dynamic aspects of Saint-Saëns's development sections that strongly influenced Ravel's music. Though more than one critic has remarked that Saint-Saëns's focus on abstract beauty was a precursor to Stravinsky's neoclassicism, this never proved a reason to rethink his legacy.

Still another paradox underlies Saint-Saëns's public image as cold and competitive, for, as we show, he had a great capacity for friendship. As René Thorel tells it, he had "three faults: to be too good, sometimes too frank, and always too modest." His frankness, in particular, earned him enemies as well as friends.[9] Impatient and never satisfied with his successes, always focused on the next work, he was forever hounding his publisher Auguste Durand to do more to promote his music. And, yes, he had rivals, especially Massenet, who was more successful in the theater, and César Franck, less successful in the concert hall, These rivalries also played out between and within French musical organizations, as suggested in the essays by Michael Strasser and Laure Schnapper. Yet even after cofounding the Société nationale for composers, Saint-Saëns appeared more often as performer than composer, using his considerable skills to promote the work of his colleagues, including Marie Jaëll and the Vicomtesse de Grandval, female composers who also studied with him (see my essay with Florence Launay). This generosity also emerges in his voluminous correspondence. In this volume we have chosen to highlight the interchanges not with his student Gabriel Fauré or his librettist Louis Gallet, the pianist Caroline de Montigny de Serres or his painter friends, but rather little-known relationships that also lasted several decades. Yves Gérard points to a lifelong friendship with the operetta composer Charles Lecocq, surprising in that the two wrote such different music. An essay reproduced here by Paul Viardot serves as a window on Saint-Saëns's close ties to Paul's mother Pauline and her family. I look at the composer's personal relationships with friends in the French colonies, where a shared passion for music, botany, acoustics, and animals sheds light on the composer's "indulgent heart" and lively sociability. Here we get an idea of how Saint-Saëns lived abroad, especially in Algiers on and off over fifty years, and in what forms his music reached audiences there.

If "this artist, essentially classical in his works, led the most fanciful of lives,"[10] his intellectual restlessness matched by his physical restlessness, still Saint-Saëns's ongoing health problems are another puzzling paradox. These sent him to North Africa, first in 1873 and so often thereafter, but they also did not make travel easy. When he finally made it to the United States for a two-month tour in 1906—after projecting this trip so many times, beginning in 1888—he caught a cold on the ship that developed into diphtheria and some paralysis. This forced him to cancel his first engagement in Boston. As Carolyn Guzski recounts, he performed in New York, despite continuing symptoms throughout the tour. Nonetheless, he never slowed down, as is clear in Stéphane Leteuré's essay. In 1916 he returned for his third tour in Latin America, discussed by Carol Hess, and concertized until days before he died in 1921. As the young French-Algerian composer Raoul de Galland put it, he was "eternally young, ardent, enthusiastic."[11]

Times did change. *Pierrot Lunaire* hit Paris in 1922. It became fashionable to "(1) flee charm and sweetness," "(2) seek violent rhythms," and eventually "(3) move toward atonal and serial music."[12] Yet, even without the numerous students and disciples enjoyed by fellow composers d'Indy and Fauré, Saint-Saëns was never forgotten, although increasingly he had to share the public sphere, particularly with Debussy. His music continued to be performed in France and worldwide. In Helsinki, for example, one of the rare capitals he never visited, the Philharmonic played it almost every year from 1882–1931, more than the music of any other French composer. Leopold Stokowski in Philadelphia and Piero Coppola in Paris recorded some of his works in the 1920s, and later many more. Radio-Paris, for example, broadcast *Samson et Dalila* in 1929 and in 1930 put on a Saint-Saëns festival. Radio orchestras in Algiers and Rabat performed more than thirty different Saint-Saëns works in 1928–1930, most of them multiple times and often something every day.[13] Listeners in Algiers specifically asked to hear a number of his works performed and broadcast in 1932. In a 1935 book for radio listeners, Vuillermoz and his collaborators, who otherwise reduced him to a "superior dilettante," began by illustrating the idea that "music is an art of thinking with sounds" with the theme of the *Organ* Symphony; in the weekly radio lectures this critic gave in the early 1940s four of the eight lectures in Vuillermoz's personal archives are on Saint-Saëns's music.[14] By the late 1940s and 1950s, Saint-Saëns's Christmas Oratorio made it all the way to equatorial Africa, where a protestant missionary music manual called for its final chorus to be sung to a Gabonese text in Fang.[15] Martin Marks has so far counted ninety-six film scores that borrow his music.

Given Saint-Saëns's eclecticism—compositions in all genres and collaborations with those representing the full range of society—no book about him can cover all facets of the composer and his work. Saint-Saëns's operas, little discussed here, deserve their own volume. Annegret Fauser uses his songs, not mere miniatures, to survey the stylistic variety of his oeuvre. We hope that the reader will agree with Koechlin that, like good apples that yield excellent calvados whose years in the bottle do nothing to alter the flavor, it is time to partake of his music anew.[16]

NOTES

1. Camille Bellaigue, "La Musique française au XIXe siècle," *La Musique des familles*, 19 October 1889, 5. Gounod also used this expression after hearing his *Organ* Symphony.

2. Charles Koechlin, "À propos de Camille Saint-Saëns," *La Pensée*, May–June 1949, 28.

3. Hugo Leichtentritt, unpublished memoir, in the chapter, "Back in Europe: London and Paris," Leroy Robertson Archive of the J. Willard Marriott Library at the University of Utah in Salt Lake City, kindly provided by Mark DeVoto.

4. See Jann Pasler, *Composing the Citizen: Music as Public Utility in Third Republic France* (Berkeley: University of California Press, 2009), especially chapters 5 and 11 and pp. 301–305 on the republican ideals underlying his *La Jeunesse d'Hercule* and *Etienne Marcel*.

5. Brian Rees, *Camille Saint-Saëns: A Life* (London: Chatto and Windus, 1999), 347, and Pasler, *Composing the Citizen*, 656.

6. A. Landely, *Art musical*, 30 June 1889, 92.

7. Romain Rolland, "Saint-Saëns," in *Musicians of Today*, trans. Mary Blaiklock (New York: Henry Holt, 1914), 102, 104.

8. Emile Vuillermoz, "Camille Saint-Saëns," in *Musiques d'aujourd'hui* (Paris: G. Crès, 1923), 102.

9. René Thorel, "Saint-Saëns intime," *Musica* 6/57 (1907): 92–94.

10. Maurice Emmanuel, Emile Vuillermoz, et al., eds., *L'Initiation à la musique* (Paris: Tambourinaire, 1935), 292.

11. Raoul de Galland, "Silhouettes de musiciens illustrés: Encore quelques notes sur Camille Saint-Saëns," *Revue musicale de l'Afrique du Nord*, 1 February 1912, 1.

12. Koechlin, "À propos de Camille Saint-Saëns," 33.

13. In fall 1928, for example, Radio-Maroc broadcast *Suite algérienne* (14 times), *Samson et Dalila* excerpts (12), *Danse macabre* (8), a ballet from *Henry VIII* (7), suites from *Ascanio* (7), *Javotte* (6), Prelude to *Le Déluge* (4), *Etienne Marcel* (4), *Serenade d'hiver* (4), etc.

14. *L'Initiation à la musique*, 3, and Emile Vuillermoz, "L'Initiation à la musique," grande emission radiophonique hebdomadaire, 1941–1944. Typescript lectures in the Coll. Médiathèque Musicale Mahler, Paris.

15. See hymn no. 25 in *Nten ô Bya e wume Nžame: Recueil de cantiques en fang* (Paris: Société des missions évangéliques de Paris, Mission du Gabon, 1947).

16. Koechlin, "À propos de Camille Saint-Saëns," 34.

PART I

SAINT-SAËNS THE PERSON

Saint-Saëns in (Semi-)Private

MITCHELL MORRIS

It is often said that when Saint-Saëns was asked on one occasion whether he was homosexual, he replied, "*Non! je suis un péderaste.*" This is one of those tales, widely reported but scantily documented (if that), that tends to collect around celebrated cultural figures. Surely so wispy (if witty) a bit of innuendo has no place in the accounts of responsible biographers? Not so. In fact, there are a cluster of reasons why an account of Saint-Saëns's life must take stock of such factually attenuated stories, not to mention the better supported tale in which the warm acquaintance between Saint-Saëns and Tchaikovsky, arising from their common interests in the arts as well as their network of acquaintances, reached a high point in their short balletic performance (without, importantly, an audience) of the myth of Pygmalion and Galatea.[1]

At stake in these stories is the way that narratives about Saint-Saëns as a person are likely to make sense in the framework of modern notions of sexual identity. We tend, in our heavily psychologized world, to read actions and statements, deliberate as well as accidental, as disclosures of interior states. Consequently, performing as a ballerina or claiming the label "pederast" are frivolous gestures with a serious self-revelatory point. On the strength of these anecdotes, some modern writers have taken Saint-Saëns to be, for all intents and purposes, gay. Other writers, either more skeptical or more resistant, have ignored such tales, leaving Saint-Saëns "heterosexual" by default, or actively argued against them. The pigeonholes of our everyday talk about sexual object choice, however, do not translate smoothly into the rich array of sexual desires and social identities that proliferated in nineteenth-century European culture. For instance, a quick glance at Richard von Krafft-Ebing's monumental sexual taxonomy *Psychopathia Sexualis*, first published in 1886, reveals a breathtaking carnival of desires—an array of divergent objects, actions, and attitudes—ranging far beyond the animal/vegetable/mineral commonplaces of the present's official categories. But of course those categories spilled out into extra-scientific life, where they became social labels; and though those labels could enable better control of society's sexual deviants, they could just as easily assist those sexual deviants by giving them a name with which to make wider sense of their lives.

Making sense of lives is the central task of biography. As in all other forms of historical writing, any biographical account selects from among the innumerable list of things that may be said to make a specific kind of coherence. When it comes to biographies of creative figures, there is commonly a persistent wish that the details of a life resonate in some way with the art made in that life. But how? In his *Lives* (1550) Vasari, modeling his aesthetic hagiographies on those in the Latin tradition, never thought twice about stylizing the life stories of his exemplary artists, adding fragments of fiction to support his sense of what they ought to have done or said; archives and dates were less important than what he judged to be the essence of the personalities and achievements worth praising. Modern standards for biographies are less accommodating. Biography is one species of history, and like all histories it prizes scrupulous attention to material reality—to documents and their contexts of meaning. Contemporary biographers must avoid blatant fictions or be unmasked as frauds. Particularly difficult to locate and explain are those moments in life where public appearances are broken by the unruly manifestations of the private.

What might it mean that Saint-Saëns may have declared himself *un péderaste,* or that he certainly did pirouette and plié onstage with Tchaikovsky behind him, and Nikolai Rubinstein providing the keyboard accompaniment? Do these moments reveal something important about Saint-Saëns's sense of himself? To leap to the conclusion that these moments speak directly to the composer's sexual identity is problematic, as is the assumption that they say nothing about the composer's sexual identity.[2] Such occasions call for reflecting more deeply on how Saint-Saëns made sense of his own life, and how we make our own kind of sense of his life.

This is where Paul Viardot's brief sketch of Saint-Saëns "off-duty," amusing himself and others *chez* Viardot, is especially significant.[3] Viardot declares at the outset that his aim is to set out a portrait of the artist, not as a young man (in the period described, Saint-Saëns would have been in his early forties), but as a successful composer at ease among his friends, before he became a kind of walking monument of French musical life. Dancing adroitly between the arch and the affectionate, Viardot's account is focused on the brilliant trifles of Saint-Saëns's performances, not in his parents' grand, "semi-official" Thursday soirees, where "the cream of Parisian intelligentsia" in all their gossipy array could be expected to appear, but rather in the "intimate" circumstances of the Viardot Sunday evening parties for special friends.[4]

A brief sketch of the social whirl in the Viardot household shows the layered complexity that allowed Saint-Saëns his expressive social space. The outer layer of visitors to the Viardot home was huge and extremely important; artists such as Delacroix and Doré, writers such as Renan, political figures, outstanding musicians, and a cavalcade of distinguished foreign guests (assumed to speak French), all were familiar figures at small dinner parties and large, as well as more formal social gatherings. The Thursday evenings—"rigidly musical," according to Henry James—would count as one of these events. The most intimate friends, who came on Sundays, experienced occasions equally musical but much looser in structure. And what a frothy riot those occasions were; charades were only the simplest kind of silly on the menu. Much more significant are Viardot's descriptions of Saint-Saëns lampooning celebrated scenes and roles from real operas and constructing clever spoofs of arias and romances.[5]

Plainly, Saint-Saëns had a gift for travesty in all senses. His parodic costuming as Gounod's Marguerite or Gluck's Armide, not to mention his range of ballerina turns, suggest a lively taste for performing femininity. And, like his painstaking dress, Saint-Saëns's care with the musical performance—"the jewel song with long pauses and trills that would have made Madame Carvalho and La Patti jealous!"—suggests that for all their hilarity there was something serious about their execution. "The Gluck aria . . . would have won approval of Madame Litvinne herself!" Viardot may seem to be minimizing the intensity and noteworthiness of these escapades by referring to them as "good, wholesome gaiety." But this kind of performance is not as simple a pleasure as he would have it seem. Crucially, the characterizations Viardot describes are not those portraying women as everyday beings; we are treated to no descriptions of the ordinary life of reproduction and householding when Saint-Saëns performs. Instead, these are women-on-stage, that is, theatrical representations of "the feminine," high-keyed stylizations whose impact is proportional to their distance from reality. What matters most in these performances is the awareness of layered irony they seem to presume in the audience. After all, the notion that "the feminine" is constructed through artifice is not new to the twentieth century.

To choose one example chronologically close to Saint-Saëns: no less an author than Baudelaire, in *The Painter of Modern Life* (1863), used large amounts of ink asserting the importance of artifice, particularly as it bore on fashion and cosmetics, and their inseparability from women's business. To be a woman—or at least a successful one à la Baudelaire—is to be artificial. And yet that artifice is supposed to be an external manifestation of presumed inner qualities of femininity. When femininity is on stage, what we might call the "natural artifice" of everyday womanhood is doubled.

We experience the artifice of an artifice. And the further disjunction created by a man playing at theatrical femininity—is that now the artifice of an artifice of an artifice? At this point, it may seem that fiction propagates in both directions simultaneously; there is no "natural" point of stability inward or outward, only the specific frame of performance, *faute de mieux*.

Complicating these nested layers of feigning is the ancient ambiguity at the heart of the notion of effeminacy. Since Plato's dialogues, effeminacy was accounted for in two incompatible ways. On the one hand, the effeminate man desires women (and not men) so intensely that he becomes like them; this assumes that desire moves toward sameness. On the other, he desires men (and not women) so intensely that he becomes like a woman; this assumes that desire moves toward difference. In the majority of definitions, beginning with Plato, both of these explanations tend to operate simultaneously, never mind the inherent contradiction between them. But there is a much larger problem, and it points back to the question of theatricality. Bluntly put, it is not the case that effeminate men "act like women"—it is the case, rather, that they do *not* quite "act like men." In the case of effeminacy there is another register—one at once more spacious and more erratic—where some kind of gender-ambivalent hyper-expressivity seems to occupy the space more frequently given to the typical rules of gender presentation. And to an important degree, this is what Saint-Saëns's carnivalesque theatricality accomplished on stage.

Such entangled "as ifs" play seriously at upending the customary values. By piling performance on performance, they point ironically at the way conventions so persuasively pretend to be "natural." This is not to say that these carefully self-undermined representations are actually "subversive"— in any case, that word has been so overused in contemporary life it has become little more than the glue used to plug the holes in the public presentation of our self-regard. Saint-Saëns's antic performances were never meant as high-minded critiques of social norms, nor as utopian gestures. They were too completely framed by their private venue for that. In fact, that rigorous framing is probably what allowed them to take place without causing any social discomfort; the alibi of "just playing" is no less potent for being transparently only half-truthful. Given the careful restriction of Saint-Saëns's performances to "safe" spaces, they might more usefully be regarded as semi-personal experiments in theatricality. What better way to game the system of conventions, though, than by working from the most overtly constructed point in the social system—the protocols of gender?

Why might such games have appealed to Saint-Saëns? It matters greatly that he had been raised in circumstances of intense feminine presence. He was born while his parents were living with his mother's aunt and uncle; his father died only three months after his birth, and his uncle died not long thereafter. Other than a brief stay in a sanitarium during his infancy, the child was reared by his mother and great aunt, a challenging but doting pair; their constant attention to the exceedingly precocious child quite probably contributed to the delicacy of comportment that could be exaggerated to such brilliant effect in his later stagey send-ups.[6] The mannerisms of most kinds of cross-dressed performance, whether taken "straight" or as ironic, commonly depend on abstracting and intensifying details of gesture and carriage held to be proper to women or men; and Saint-Saëns, a man of intense expressive desires and capacities, was by upbringing preadapted to just such a style.

Cross-dressing, of course, has been an important theatrical resource in a huge array of times and places, and France is no exception. Cross-dressing in both directions was a commonplace of light entertainment in the ancien régime, especially in venues such as the Comédie-Italienne, where it constantly showed up in satire, farce, and witty commentary on contemporary events. After the upheavals of the revolution and Napoleon's rule, French understandings of gender moved away from the older styles of *travesti* toward a more "serious" attitude toward the boundaries between male and female roles and identities. One major casualty of this was female impersonation, which became increasingly disreputable over the course of the nineteenth century; it was certainly still possible in the 1870s to don dress and wig and perform—at least in semi-private—without incurring universal wrath and possible legal repercussions; but tightening concern for preserving masculinity made for a steadily worsening popular clime. It is worth noting that this austerity tended to be put on hold during festive occasions like Mardi Gras, when the sight of a man in a dress could seem to be a recollection of the ancien régime: "the last echo of long-vanished gaieties from earlier times."[7] Male impersonation, by contrast, was a theatrical mainstay into the 1880s, though as women became more politically and socially visible, pants roles became more problematic.[8]

Despite the record of official disapproval, it is clear that theatrical cross-dressing continued its lively existence in less "respectable" capacities. Certainly this was the case in the anglophone world, where drag roles for both genders—but particularly vivid in the case of female impersonators—continued to hold a place on the stage into the twentieth century. Indeed, it has been widely noted that in North America, female impersonation was considered especially suitable entertainment for women and children, since it was taken to be a practice of great refinement. Saint-Saëns, that great world traveler, would have had numerous occasions to observe this. Closer study of performances in the theatrical demimonde (not to mention police records) might well turn up more evidence of the continuing existence of such performance styles.

But it is arguable that the twists on gender and sexual identity embodied in Saint-Saëns's drag roles were not simply valuable as experiments in self-reflection; on the contrary, this kind of theatricality was part of a broader project of creating a distinctive form of sociability. Note that Viardot includes a comic song improvised by Saint-Saëns at one of the Viardots' Sunday evenings. The song is a robust role-reversal number in a very popular style that would be perfectly at home in a charivari of almost any century. The overturned gender is obviously part of the fun— and note that, to have the rather dainty Saint-Saëns singing such a butch number would add yet another disorienting layer to the play of masculine and feminine—but that is not the entire story. The song was *improvised*, words and music alike, and the pleasure of the song comes as much from Saint-Saëns's musical and verbal agility and speed as it does from the broad humor of the characterization. This hearkens back to what may have seemed a throwaway remark about the "unexpected inventions" when Saint-Saëns played charades. All of these—the games, the drag performances, the singing stand-up—were features of the composer's admirable sociability. And it is precisely that sociability, such a contrast to the stony mien *à la grand maître*, that Viardot aims to invoke. As his account draws to a close, he brings us to his present (1904), with Saint-Saëns an emblem of French musical life. Viardot himself was by this time a widely known violinist, composer, and conductor, distinguished enough to meet with Saint-Saëns on thoroughly professional terms. Nevertheless, he quotes a wry little poem Saint-Saëns took from one of his stage plays to make up a thank-you note.[9] In doing so, Viardot seeks to persuade us that under all that granite or bronze we may still find the traces of Saint-Saëns the playful.

Figure 1. The "wagon lady" from Viardot's article as depicted in *Le Guide de concert* (1914).

PAUL VIARDOT
Saint-Saëns, the Playful
From *Le Guide de concert* (1914)

Those who had the misfortune of not having known Maestro Saint-Saëns forty years ago, and who see him now only as the great man, member of the Institute, recipient of medals from here or there, musician of genius, adored, celebrated, loved, criticized, feared, praised—in a word the greatest French composer—cannot imagine what this already celebrated master was like, with his ever-youthful ardor, his witty, often biting repartees, his passion for work, and his health that confounds time itself. When his work was accomplished, he let his flights of fancy run wild in a place more congenial to him than any other: my parents' town house, at the corner of the rue de Douai and rue de Bruxelles.

On Thursday evenings, which were devoted to music, the cream of Parisian intelligentsia (and one could say, of all the world) gathered there. Saint-Saëns never missed a soirée, unless his affairs called him away from the capital. He himself contributed much to these evenings, either as author, ready to accompany all his works, or as organist, since he was fond of the fourteen-pedal organ that Cavaillé-Coll had made especially for my mother.

But those quasi-official soirées did not equal the Sunday evening gatherings, intimate reunions devoted to good, wholesome gaiety. There, Saint-Saëns's surprising imagination appeared in all its beauty. Charades especially, a favorite pastime of these evenings, allowed him to astonish spectators with the most unexpected inventiveness. The gathering consisted of a number of intimate friends, all extremely funny and witty. As for me, still too young and stupid to give suitable responses to such subjects, I was generally happy with the modest role of stagehand. I would draw the curtain, allowing the limited but well-chosen audience to admire Marguerite-Saint-Saëns at her spinning wheel, in full costume, two immense plaits of blond hemp down her back, and to hear her/him sing the jewel song with long pauses and trills that would have made Madame Carvalho and La Patti jealous! Another time, I tied a long set of *plaisirs*, those horn-shaped wafers, to long strings, and made them dance across the stage at full speed while Saint-Saëns, our *prima donna assoluta*, dressed as Armide, sang the Glück aria "Fuyez, plaisirs, fuyez!" (accompanied at the piano by my mother) in such a way that he would have won the approval of Madame Litvinne herself!

And Saint-Saëns as a ballerina! Miming the various diabolical temptations offered to Robert the Devil, played by Romain Bussine! And Saint-Saëns snug in a "pink flannel jumpsuit," playing someone torn apart by love, as a white porcelain plate representing the moon, lifted little by little above a screen by the chief stagehand, shed light on a passionate duet with a female medical student!—and an English one, at that!

And the improvised arias and songs, with text and music! Here is an example, the words of which come from my memory. Couplets of a wagon lady [see Figure 1]:

Quand mon homme est en ribote *C'est moi qui conduis les ch'vaux.* *J'fourr' mes jambes dans ses boîtes* *Et j'tap' sur les animaux.*	When my man is on the booze I'm the one who drives the cart. I shove my legs into his shoes And whip the horses smart.
Refrain: *Hue! Dia. Hue! Dia.*	*Refrain:* Giddyup! Whoa. Giddyup! Whoa.
Gare là-dessous, gare les voitures,	Watch out for carts down there, watch out.
Hue! Dia. Hue! Dia. (Andante) *Ou j'te cass' la hu…re!*	Giddyup! Whoa. Giddyup! Whoa. *(Andante)* Or I'll bash in your snoooout!
J'suis pas un' d'cell' qui roucoule,	I'm not one of those ladies who bills and coos,
Et quand on m'dit des douceurs,	And if you call me sweet something or other,
Qu'on m'appell' ma chatt', ma poule, *J'leur z'y réponds: Et ta soeur!* . . .	If you call me sweetheart or honey, I'll answer: So's your mother!
Refrain: *Hue! Dia.* etc. . . .	*Refrain*: Giddyup! Whoa. etc…

Saint-Saëns, now, no longer dresses up as an Egyptian dancer, a Siamese organist, or as a wagon lady (although I'm not so sure!) but his spontaneous vivacity has remained the same. The author of the Symphony in C Minor, the *Organ* Symphony, continues to act toward his friends as the least affected, most straightforward "comrade" imaginable.

When I was leading the Classical Concerts in Marseille, I had to organize a Saint-Saëns festival [1901], and conduct that very symphony, in which the composer played the organ part.

The next day, I took the maestro on a little boat, a sort of freighter, casting off for Bône [Algeria]. He was the sole passenger. I placed him in the care of the captain, quite proud he could offer his services to such a passenger; the journey must not have been boring since, a few days later, the mail brought me the following letter, which I extract from my keepsakes:

Bône, 27 December 1904.

Des poissons, agitant leur redoutables queues,	Fish, waving their formidable tails,
Nous ont bien fait router pour le commencement,	Made us plot our course carefully at first,
Mais quel jour! quel soleil! les belles nappes bleues	But what daylight! What sunlight! The beautiful blue sails
De la mer et du ciel! Quel voyage charmant!	Of the sea and sky! What a charming journey!
Nous avons mangé du marsouin;	We ate *dolphin*;
Nous avons mangé de la dinde	We ate turkey
Truffée et cuite avec grand soin;	Stuffed and cooked with great care;
Je crois qu'Apollon sur le Pinde	I think Apollo on Pindus
Jamais ne s'est tant régalé!	Never ate better fare!
Ici, je loge à l'hôtel Bell'vue;	Here, I'm staying at the Bell'vue Hotel;
Il est "belle-vue" appelé	It is called "belle-vue"
Parce qu'il donne sur le port, et la revue	Because it looks out on the harbor, and you
Est facile de tous bateaux, petits et grands,	Can see all the boats, big and little,
Barques, navires et chalands	Dories, ships and scows
Qui passent devant ma fenêtre.	That pass my house.
Je suis en plein soleil, et je me sens renaître! . . .	I'm in bright sunshine, I feel reborn!

The author of this letter will certainly not be angry with me if I entrust posterity with a specimen of his poetic talent, which was not intended to be made public. Sensitive souls know the delightful lines from his play *Botriocéphale*, which enjoyed the honors of the footlights: in reproducing them here, I wanted only to bear witness to the extreme simplicity of one of the greatest men upon whom France prides itself, whose long-lasting, unalterable friendship is one of my greatest pride and joys.

—Translated by Jann Pasler

NOTES

1. The singer-composer Pauline Viardot-Garcia was a central link in this social network. The Russian writer Ivan Turgenev was in most respects a member of the Viardot household; he even brought his natural daughter Pelageia (renamed Paulette) to Paris to be brought up with the Viardot children. He was also an early admirer of Tchaikovsky and

acted as a conduit for exchanges of musical works between the composers. When Tchaikovsky and Saint-Saëns met in 1875, the Turgenev connection was part of the foundation of their mutual affinity. Although Tchaikovsky was actually reluctant to meet Viardot and Turgenev in person, when at last he paid a social call (in 1886, over a decade after occasional correspondence had begun) he was charmed by Viardot-Garcia's personal manner—as well as the autograph score of *Don Giovanni* in her possession—and made visits to her house whenever he was in Paris and not overly busy.

2. Extant evidence suggests that Saint-Saëns, though he may have had several liaisons with women, and though he married, may have had a larger number of sexual encounters with men. It is not simply coincidence that this period saw a tremendous increase in (homo-)sexual tourism in North Africa, the Near East, and parts of Southeast Asia—areas notoriously included in "the Sotadic zone," Richard Francis Burton's term for warm regions filled with people prone to sodomy. And Saint-Saëns's habits at times do suggest those of a sexual tourist. See Richard Francis Burton, "Terminal Essay" in *The Book of a Thousand Nights and One Night: A Plain and Literal Translation of the Arabian Nights Entertainments* ([S.l.]: Burton Ethnological Society, 1885). For a consideration of sexual tourism, see Joseph A. Boone, "Vacation Cruises; or, the Homoerotics of Orientalism," *PMLA* 110/1 (January 1995): 89–107.

3. Paul Viardot, "Saint-Saëns Gai," in *Le Guide de concert* (1914, repr. 1922): 13–14. Paul Viardot (1857–1942) was a violinist, composer, musicologist, and conductor. Saint-Saëns wrote a short preface to his *Histoire de la musique* (Paris: Ollendorff, 1905). [Ed.]

4. "Intimate" in this case does not necessarily mean entirely private, since on occasions private parties might be described in journals. On the question of public/private distinctions in late nineteenth-century social gatherings, see Anne Martin-Fugier, *Les Salons de la IIIe République: Art, littérature, politique* (Paris: Perrin, 2003), esp. 272–75.

5. Among the farrago of charades and musical performances we must count the genre of *saynète* or comic scena, usually translated as "sketch." See ibid., 275–78.

6. This upbringing is very similar to that of the young Alexander Scriabin—another composer of formidable musicianship who was distinctly epicene in manner.

7. See the article by the pseudonymous Masque de velours, "Le Travesti," *Revue illustrée* (Paris, 1885): 145–48.

8. Published research on cross-dressing and the nineteenth-century French stage has been limited. A useful discussion is found in Lenard R. Berlanstein, "Breeches and Breaches: Cross-Dress Theater and the Culture of Gender Ambiguity in Modern France," *Comparative Studies in Society and History* 38/2 (April 1996): 338–69. Jann Pasler offers a valuable overview of the situation in this period and its possible impact on the composer and his music in "Cross-Dressing in Saint-Saëns's *Le Rouet d'Omphale*," in *Queer Episodes in Music and Modern Identity*, ed. Sophie Fuller and Lloyd Whitesell (Urbana: University of Illinois Press, 2002): 191–215.

9. In addition to his illustrious career as a composer and organist, and his lively worldwide correspondence on a huge range of topics cultural and scientific, Saint-Saëns found the time to write several farcical stage plays including *Botriocéphale,* which he called a "bouffonerie antique." It is published in his *Rimes familières* (1902). He also wrote a parody of Italian opera, *Gabriella de Vergy*, performed at the home of Jules Barbier in 1884; *Les Odeurs de Paris* (n.d.), a parody for "private amusement"; a one-act comedy, *La Crampe des écrivains* (1892), involving disguise, which premiered at the Théâtre Municipal, Algiers, in 1892 and was published in an Algerian newspaper; and a comic play *Le Roi Apépis (1903)*, adapted from a novel. Saint-Saëns directed performances of *Botriocéphale* and *La Crampe* at the Béziers festival in 1902, after the premiere of his *Parysatis*. He brought *Le Roi Apépis* to Béziers in summer 1903. [Ed.]

Inspired by the Skies?

Saint-Saëns, Amateur Astronomer

LÉO HOUZIAUX

If we believe Camille Flammarion, at the end of his long life Camille Saint-Saëns confessed that when he was a young boy, he dreamed of becoming an astronomer.[1] He was precocious in many sciences such as botany, entomology, geology, and always regretted knowing too little mathematics.[2] Before he was ten, he was reported to have watched the phases of the moon through opera glasses, and found astronomy a very absorbing hobby.[3] A poetess friend of his mother obtained an invitation for him to visit the Paris Observatory, where he saw the sky through a professional telescope—an unforgettable experience. In his *Divagations sérieuses*, he writes that people thought he was foolish to give up his first royalties from published melodies to acquire an astronomical refractor from Sécrétan, the best Parisian optician of the time.[4] Such a decision shows that watching the stellar scene had become a passion. With planets and stars still visible after dusk during a stroll on the boulevards, for two sous at Place Vendôme people could look through the eyepieces of "astronomers" to see the moon or Saturn's rings while surrounded by merchants selling French fries and snails from Burgundy.

Saint-Saëns was an early adherent of the Société astronomique de France, registered as a regular member (No. 553) in 1893 when total membership was 640.[5] Flammarion founded the Société in June 1887 after the success of his book, *L'Astronomie populaire*, borrowing the title from one published posthumously by François Arago (1786–1853), another famous popularizer of astronomy and director of the Paris Observatory.[6] When he was a young boy, Saint-Saëns eagerly read Arago's book—"the alpha and omega of his astronomical knowledge."[7] In 1888, together with authorities of several scholarly societies, Flammarion purchased the former Hôtel des États de Blois on the rue Danton as home for the new society.[8]

· 12 ·

Because the astronomical circle needed an observatory, a dome was erected on top of the building along with a meeting room and library. When he lived on rue Marboeuf (1890–93), Saint-Saëns attended several meetings there.[9]

When the society was founded, the composer was already a recognized personality—a member of the Institut de France since 1881. Flammarion and his colleagues felt honored by having such a famous man at their meetings. At the yearly general assembly in 1894, Raymond Poincaré, minister of public instruction and fine arts, referred to his visit to the Juvisy Observatory where he met Saint-Saëns.[10] The composer told him that even in musical composition he had never found a thrill comparable to the one given by study of the sky. Such study could also profit politicians, he suggested, encouraging them to consider reality in more reasonable terms: "Thus they would come to understand better how little are things they believe to be grand, how momentary are what they see as eternal, and how contingent what seems absolute."[11]

Saint-Saëns's numerous writings suggest that science, both pure and applied, led him to philosophical reflection.[12] As early as 1902, although in Cairo, he wanted to contribute to the current debate on the possibilities of life on other planets, a discussion that had recently taken place at

Figure 1. Flammarion and Saint-Saëns.

a meeting of the Société astronomique. That year he wrote to Flammarion about the so-called aim of nature. Here he proposed, with some conviction, that planets must exist around other stars. He was also remarkably well advised in stating that the physical conditions needed for human beings are very severe and that these occurrences happen very rarely.[13] In general issues like these, Saint-Saëns's reasoning is accurate. Nowadays, we are quite inclined to interpret their spectroscopic observations as a proof of the existence of exoplanets.

We can better understand his close friendship with the astronomer Flammarion when we note that both were intrigued by the great philosophical issues of human life. Although an officially appointed organist in two Parisian Catholic churches, Saint-Saëns was called at the time a "materialist," that is, someone who believes that everything on Earth, including human beings, is made exclusively of matter. Yet, paradoxically, both he and Flammarion, who wrote books entitled *L'Inconnu et les problèmes psychiques* (1917) and *La Mort et son mystère* (1921), spent a lot of time investigating phenomena resulting from "table-tapping" séances and searching for scientific explanations for getting in touch with the souls of people dead for centuries, as well as other so-called spiritual activities. Victor Hugo, after the death of his wife, and upon hearing the composer's *Hymn to Victor Hugo*, invited Saint-Saëns to dinner, and as after-dinner entertainment they tried to get in touch with the souls of Molière and similar notable persons.[14] Flammarion also reported that Saint-Saëns was struck by certain coincidences. His friend, the painter Henri Regnault, was shot on the outskirts of Paris in late January 1871, and at that very instant, according to Saint-Saëns, the main theme of his *Requiem* came to him.[15]

Given his renown, Saint-Saëns was considered by many members of the French astronomical society, in particular by its secretary-general, as a means of attracting attention to their circle.[16] This is obvious from how Flammarion uses his friend's submissions to the group's journal. In an 1889 article (see document below), Saint-Saëns, reflecting on a remark by Arago and showing a capacity for critical thought in this domain, expresses his doubts about modifications of the lunar surface.[17] His main argument is that every month each point of the lunar surface gradually undergoes a very high increase in temperature, and this leads to expansion and contraction of the rocks, inducing cracks and ultimately the tumbling down of rocky material. This could affect minor aspects of the soil in the vicinity of lunar mountains and craters. The phenomenon is common on Earth, where the main cause of changes in landscape, besides earthquakes, is air motions in the atmosphere. But these motions cannot exist on the moon, which explains why Saint-Saëns was reluctant to admit changes in the lunar landscape. In response, Flammarion tries not to discourage him: "It is so marvelous to study [the moon] in the calm silence of starry nights, the hours of contemplation being so sweet and delightful." Neither Saint-Saëns nor Flammarion were aware that there could be lunar volcanoes, and that sixty-nine years later Russian astronomer Kosirev would observe from Poulkovo (St. Petersburg) a lunar eruption in the crater of Alfonsus.

Five years later, Flammarion inserted in his journal a personal letter from Saint-Saëns describing what he saw as a "problem" in the telescopic view of the moon.[18] Next to a diagram that depicted the situation, he speculated that the moon itself would be brought close to Earth by the telescope and that, if literally brought closer, it would not be possible to see the whole lunar hemisphere, only a restricted portion of it. This is quite clear, of course. When flying high in a plane, one sees only a tiny part of Earth's surface. But when looking through a telescope, one does not bring the whole moon close to the observer's eye; one sees an enlargement of only that part of the moon in the telescope's field of view, which becomes more and more restricted as the enlargement increases. The response to this letter, signed "C. F." (Camille Flammarion), is cautious. Recalling that the letter came from the illustrious composer of *Samson et Dalila*, C. F. again states that the question is interesting; in fact, important enough to be communicated to the members at the next meeting of the society. However, he realizes that such a "problem" is completely unrealistic (the celestial object is not really brought close to the observer by a telescope) and indicates that the writer does not understand what a telescopic image really is. Flammarion avoids an uncomfortable situation with Saint-Saëns by saying that although the effect is nearly impossible to detect, his remark shows he is not put off by difficult questions.

Saint-Saëns's interest in the stars grew ever more strong during his travels, especially in the Mediterranean region and on the Red Sea, where he could realize the curvature of the earth and discover the constellations people of the Northern Hemisphere do not see. He often mentioned to Flammarion ideas that came to him in the African darkness, where he had a gorgeous view of the southern skies of different star colors (specially in close double stars) and bright gaseous nebulae. To him, the stars shone as dazzling diamonds, and the firmament was divided by the wide luminous trace of the Milky Way.

In his "Questions d'optique" (1911), Saint-Saëns reports on mirages he saw near the Red Sea (see document below).[19] It is indeed one of the best places in the world to observe mirages almost every day during the dry season. Many visitors noticed their frequent occurrence. Consider what the painter Pol Stiévenart (1874–1960) reported while traveling in Egypt and the Middle East around 1920:

When we say that in moving from Djebel Mousa in the Sinai, we rolled the Red Sea backwards to the place where a mirage joined the extreme tip of the Gulf of Akaba—we are expressing an undeniable conviction. All the more so since a short time after, looking back on this, we notice that the sea blocked the way again, a clear proof that it had drowned the Egyptian troops sent to catch us.[20]

All who have seen mirages tend to have similar convictions, so it is easy to understand that this phenomenon left Saint-Saëns with an unforgettable sensation. Physically, mirages are very well explained by the heating of lower layers of the atmosphere. In reducing the density, the heat reduces the air's refractive index to a value that finally induces total reflection.[21] The image seems to move back when one walks in its direction. Various types of Fata Morganas are also explained in this way. Unfortunately, Saint-Saëns in his "Questions d'optique" comes to an explanation of his own that does not make sense. He imagines discontinuities of long duration in the air density. Furthermore, he worsens his case by confusing the mirage phenomenon with the flattening of fumes from the Stromboli volcano, which is due to a quite different cause, a temperature inversion. This can be seen when the atmospheric temperature, after diminishing as altitude increases, starts rising regularly, blocking the convection process and with it the cloud layer, which stops ascending.

In this article, Saint-Saëns also returns to the "problem" he wrote about in Flammarion's journal in 1894, of the moon and sun seeming larger close to the horizon and smaller when observed high in the sky. He talks about his experience of seeing boats on the horizon that seem larger than when they are seen on the ocean surface. The year after Saint-Saëns published this article, a distinguished physics teacher at the Lycée Henri IV in Paris refuted his ideas and offered an accurate explanation of the phenomenon.[22]

We know that Saint-Saëns regretted his *nullité mathématique*, but having had no regular schooling in science, he was unable to understand the formation of mirages and other luminous phenomena in the open air. The trajectory of light rays in a medium with changing density and refractive index (such as a variably heated air layer), giving rise to, among others, the mirage phenomenon, requires the use of Fermat's Principle, which applies differential equations to optics.

In the memoirs he writes about so elegantly in his *École buissonnière* under the title of "Les Astres" (see document below), Saint-Saëns tells us what sort of astronomer he thought he was: *le ver de terre amoureux des étoiles* (the earthworm in love with the stars). Being a very realistic man, Saint-Saëns doubted he could contribute anything of real substance to astronomical knowledge, though he spoke up at the meetings of the Société astronomique and published his ideas in the group's journal. Until about 1930, many people believed the "universe" was still limited to the solar system; in Flammarion's famous book, the starry sky occupies a very tiny portion at the end. This might explain why Saint-Saëns, admiring the diversity of the stars' aspects through his 8-cm diameter instrument, did not get especially interested in stellar variability in brightness, a domain in which, as he writes, "a naïve, conscientious observer can contribute something non-negligible."[23] But astrophysics was still in its infancy. Except for philosophers like Kant, few could imagine we were living in a stellar system of billions of suns, itself surrounded by billions of similar stellar systems showing all kinds of shapes.

Although he might not have noticed it himself, Saint-Saëns's most important contribution to astronomy was helping to spread a taste for astronomical science. Through his enthusiasm and writings, Saint-Saëns encouraged laymen to observe nature—lending, for example, his instruments to the young sons of his friend Gabriel Fauré and discussing the sky with their mother, Marie.[24] He allowed Flammarion to make use of his fame to attract public attention to the importance of astronomical research. In such outreach activities, Saint-Saëns was a true help to his dear friend as well as to scientists of his time.

CAMILLE SAINT-SAËNS
Changes on the Moon
From *Revue d'Astronomie populaire* (1889)

Concerning the new lunar observations, our illustrious friend Camille Saint-Saëns sends us the following reflections:

Arago noted that very serious minds let themselves pass into strange aberrations when they concerned themselves with the Moon. His remark comes to mind every time the so often troubled question of current lunar eruptions arises. In the state the lunar globe finds itself, there is nothing less probable than such facts; and if these occurred, appearances would be quite different from those that are ordinarily pointed out.

Changes on the Moon's surface must occur because perpetual transformation is the universal law; the changes in heat and cold, experienced by that surface, cannot fail to provoke successive dilations and contractions leading at length to the breaking up of rocks and consequently to those *collapses*, which produce the appearance of excavations of all shapes and are of great interest. A volcanic eruption would indeed be much more curious, but the Moon doesn't much care about the spectacle it offers us, and will certainly not have an eruption for our pleasure.

As for the state of mind that one could call *lunar overexcitement* and that all astrophiles are familiar with, it is easy to explain. The Moon is, astronomically speaking, quite close to us; it looks as if, with a little effort, one could touch it; and the impossibility of being completely informed about this globe, so nearby, causes a kind of mental torture with its own charm, and act strongly on the imagination.

—C. SAINT-SAËNS.

Yet, who knows? Let us not discourage research. In fact, the Moon is much less well known than we have imagined. We cannot get closer than a hundred leagues to it. Also, it is so marvelous to study in the calm silence of starry nights. The hours of this contemplation are sweet and delightful. It is beautiful, full of light, and extraterrestrial.

C[amille] F[lammarion]

CAMILLE SAINT-SAËNS
Optical Illusions
From *L'Écho de Paris*, 22 October 1911

A certain fear troubles me as I undertake this task: fear not of being wrong, of asserting erroneous things, or—we'll say the word—of saying silly things; the best, the most scholarly people have done that. The fear haunting me is that of passing for one of those pretentious characters who deal thoughtlessly with questions they know nothing about, thinking themselves more artistic than the artists; more scientific than the scientists; and self-assuredly playing the role of the fool who thinks he knows more than his betters. As a stranger to Science, I know it well enough to know with what sacred terror one should approach it, and that you cannot touch it, however lightly, without risking burning your fingers. Through conversations I've had with scientists, I know too that, understandably absorbed by their prodigious work, they do not always devote sufficient attention to the close, detailed observation of ordinary facts, and that sometimes a naïve, conscientious observer can contribute something non-negligible. Thus on his famous rock with its unbroken view, Victor Hugo, having observed all the phases of a storm without any scientific preconceptions and having described this in detail in *Toilers of the Sea*, destroyed without even realizing it a nascent theory on the formation of storms that was beginning to gain favor.

Not everyone is Victor Hugo. But the value of his observation lies not in the genius of the observer, but in the care he brought to his observation, the absence of any preconceived idea. This is difficult for scientists, who cannot remove themselves from their theories, and that is why we have seen them deny the existence of stones fallen from the sky and stubbornly persist in other famous mistakes that imbeciles take advantage of to deny the value of science and scientists. So it is in all humility, but strong in my naïveté and good faith, that I bring the result of patient observations, conducted over many years, to facts that have not yet been completely understood.

Let us begin with the phenomenon of the *mirage*. I spent an entire week walking around the Isthmus of Suez to observe these phenomena. I saw some surprising things, and I bitterly regret not having had a camera to record them, since they are difficult to describe and preserved only in my memory, as if they had never existed. So we will speak only of well-known phenomena: objects and the sky, reflected by the sand and giving it the aspect of a stretch of water.

The explanation given for this phenomenon is somewhat complicated.[25] As light rays, from high up, approach the ground and encounter progressively warmer, less dense layers of air, they bend more and more in the opposite direction, from down to up. There is nothing objectionable about this classic explanation. But another is possible. When two transparent media of different densities are superimposed, the surface that demarcates them forms a mirror. That is how air and water behave, and how the surface of water reflects objects. Here, the reflecting surface is that of the densest medium, but the effect is the same in the opposite case. Look from down to up in an aquarium and you will see that the fish, when close to the surface, are perfectly reflected there, along with the artificial rocks and plants around them.

We know that layers of air close to the earth are warmed by the sun that communicates its heat to them, but rapidly get cooler as they get farther away from it. Less known is that this cooling, when accompanied by a change in density, does not always occur progressively, and that the atmosphere is often made up of zones of different densities, which do not intermingle.

In the summer, with good weather, it is not unusual to see flotillas of white clouds above taking on the pretty aspect of cauliflowers or beaten egg whites, which we are familiar with, while their base is horizontal, as if cut with a knife. They are gliding, as if over a layer of air of different density. The opposite can also occur. One day, as I was passing by Stromboli, which was pouring out smoke, I was surprised to see the smoke from this volcano stop at a certain altitude and spread out as if it had encountered the surface of a ceiling; two clouds that were drifting some distance away behaved in the same way. The phenomenon lasted for about two hours. We are also familiar with the smoke of Vesuvius rising up in a straight line to a great height and then spreading horizontally, taking on that stone-pine shape so well described by Pliny. We could admire this beautiful phenomenon during the siege of Paris during the fire in the Buttes-Chaumont.

So it is not impossible that a thin layer of air, heated by contact from the burning, rarefied desert ground, could be followed *without transition* by a less hot, denser layer. In moments of absolute calm, the surface of transition would be flat and reflect objects, giving it the appearance of a layer of water. The strange phenomenon known by the name of Fata Morgana—objects reflected in the sky—might be explained in this way. We have seen it in Paris, where one day above the Eiffel Tower a second tower seemed to touch the first one, upside-down. The illustrated newspapers reproduced this.

But there is another problem long needing a solution. This is the apparent magnification of stars and constellations when they are close to the horizon. Who has not noticed the enormous size of the sun setting over the sea, of the moon rising, red and impressive, over the countryside? The clouds floating over our heads are obviously closer to us than the ones disappearing in the distance. It follows that the sky adorned with clouds seems to us like a ceiling curving on all sides over the horizon; in other words like a lowered vault. The same is not true for the stars. Since the distance separating us from them can be practically regarded as infinite, they should all seem to us equally distant. But we know that is not at all the case. Whereas those closer to the horizon seem distant to us, the stars at the zenith look quite close. In desert countries, the impression of closeness is great, and we can understand why simple people, completely ignorant of the reality of things, have the idea of reaching them by a high tower. Given this illusion, the cause for which escapes me, one can easily demonstrate how it leads to the magnification of constellations on the horizon and their shrinkage at the zenith. We might be satisfied with this explanation if the phenomenon was always alike, but it is not. Near the horizon, the sun and moon are far from always having the same magnification, moderately amplified on some days, enormously on others. Even very high above the horizon, the moon varies in size from one day to the next. So here is another cause for magnification, added to the first. This one gives the effect of a *magnifying glass* produced by the atmosphere in certain conditions when the air is calm, the mist light and transparent. This effect is not yet generally acknowledged.

One evening at twilight, I was enjoying the fresh air on the banks of Lake Geneva, gazing at the Swiss mountains on the other side of the lake, when, between two summits, a huge grayish globe *leapt* up that I did not at first recognize, so extraordinary was its volume and swiftness of ascension. It wasn't until three or four seconds had gone by that I could reco-gnize the moon with its familiar spots; then it resumed its tranquil movement. But let us leave the stars and come back down to Earth. How many times have I seen ships, after losing their shape and size as they grew distant, suddenly seem huge when they reach the horizon! Here the phe-nomenon is not constant, but intermittent, so there is no reason to liken it to that of the magnification of constellations.

Some pianists are familiar with a little fantasia called *Souvenir d'Ismaïlia*. It was written in that delightful little town during a two-day retreat I took in 1895, having as my companion a seahorse whose graceful movements were my only distraction. The pretty little animal caused indescribable horror to the maid serving me. To return to Port Saïd, I took a small steamer with a dozen passengers. We were drifting calmly on the famous canal when suddenly the town appeared quite close, and the passengers rejoiced at the idea of landing in a few minutes. Only I noticed that the houses didn't look natural . . . And then, suddenly, as if from the wave of a fairy's wand, the houses lost their size and looked small and far away, to the disappointment of everyone.

I could give even more examples, but will limit myself to the relation of what I observed not long ago at the Tuileries, during a competition of aerostats. The day was splendid, the air calm; a mist obscured the horizon on the northern side, where the very light breeze pushed the balloons. These seemed to diminish in volume, as should be expected as they grew distant, but only up to a certain point, past which one could see them get larger and resume the dimensions they had earlier.[26]

If I have dared to make these observations public, it is because I was en-couraged to do so. A letter with a few words about them, addressed to Mr. Flammarion and inserted by him into the *Bulletin de la Société astronomique*, earned me the great honor of receiving letters from scholars who agreed with me, accompanying their approbation with technical details impossi-ble to reproduce here. One scholar showed me how objects can be seen as if through a huge lens. He pointed out that, as reported in the treatise on optics by Brewster, the coasts of France can be seen from Hastings, a dis-tance of fifty or so miles, as distinctly as with the best spyglass. Another confessed that many of these seemingly paradoxical phenomena are so poorly explained that classical works limit themselves merely to their definition. Finally, I was told how a painter noticed in twilight "herds of sheep in which the groups in the middle got larger as they moved away." Now that's an appearance that could in no way be linked to the lowered vault of the sky!

Now it is up to the scientists to complete, to clarify these observations, to explain them by constructing theories. In our time, people become great painters or great musicians without study; as for becoming only slightly scientific, that is quite a different matter, and it is mere prudence not to hazard it. My timid explanations are presented here only as hypotheses, and offering a hypothesis—need one say?—is always allowed. It is the powerful lever that raises mountains when it does not break in one's hands. The most famous hands have known this adventure, and it has not dishonored them.

CAMILLE SAINT-SAËNS
The Stars
From *École buissonnière* (1913)

To return to what concerns me, I am an astronomer, the way one is a painter if one has gone to the Louvre or the Salon to look at paintings, or a musician, if one has heard Sunday concerts of Beethoven's symphonies. I have tried to understand the great laws of astronomy, I have contemplated the stars with passion, and that's it. But I couldn't do enough to encourage others to follow my example. You can't imagine the joys procured by studying the starry sky, even with a small instrument. With a telescope, the stars look completely different. They present the most varied tints. There are yellow ones, red ones, green ones, like brilliantly illumined precious stones; Castor is made up of two stars of a pale, delicate green, for many stars appear double in the telescope, and often the components are of different colors. What can we say about a great starstrewn nebulae like Orion? These are extraordinary splendors everyone should experience, and you need not be a scientist to do so.

As everyone knows, we can only see part of the sky, and for a long time I yearned for the day when I could see stars invisible in our northern latitude. Once, in the Canary Islands, I was able to admire the beautiful Canopus star, the brightest after Sirius, and to see above my head, at the zenith, constellations that I had always seen close to the horizon. But that was not enough. So, the first time I traveled down the Red Sea, I impatiently awaited the appearance of constellations I had not yet seen: Crux, Centaurus, and Argo Navis! Since the Red Sea stretches directly north to south, every day as we drifted toward the equator we saw the North Star set, and when it finally touched the horizon, we saw the Crux or Southern Cross rise, which is not a perfect cross. I was sailing down the Red Sea to go to the island of Ceylon. A few kilometers away from Colombo there is a delightful hotel near a forest, called the Mount Lavinia, where I stayed for some time. Every night I strolled on the terraces, unable to resist the desire to contemplate the dazzling sky where one could see, next to Crux, the

Argo Navis and Centaurus, whose largest star is the closest star to the Earth, or rather to the Sun. Compared to such distances, the distance of Earth to the Sun is an entirely negligible quantity. The Sun is for us a *star seen from up close*.

Despite my lack of scientific knowledge, I have sometimes dared to send letters to the *Bulletin* of the Astronomical Society and to take the floor during meetings of the Society. But I am not one of those people who think they know more than the scientists. I limited myself to reporting observations gathered during my voyages. I cannot resist the desire to speak of one made on the Red Sea. The northern part of this famous sea is very narrow, and when you go farther south, you can see, throughout the whole first day, a long mountain chain in tender pink, parallel to the Asiatic shore. This chain seems to describe a curve created by the very shape of that long series of summits. Naturally, that was my first impression. But the hours went by, the day advanced, and the mountains still presented the same shape. Looking attentively, I saw that the mountains were disappearing little by little beneath the horizon on the northern side, and that the curve still preserved a perfect regularity. Finally I understood that this harmonious curve was none other than the very curvature of Earth. Once I heard a simpleton say: "If Earth were round, we'd see it!" We can see it; it only takes knowing enough to observe it.

A phenomenon unknown to most of the public is the "zodiacal light," seen after dusk in the evening and early in the morning. Hard to make out in a brightly lit city, one can see it in the country, but it is very pale in our climates. In Africa it is admirable, even brighter than the Milky Way. In December of 1909, I found myself in Luxor, and through a window looking out exactly on the Levant, I could contemplate it in all its glory. It was Ramadan, and the Arabs interpreted the light as dawn, and every day as soon as it appeared, a muezzin began chanting in a wonderful voice with an extraordinarily high tessitura that the cold of the morning could not change, invulnerable as birdsong. This song was something between that of birds and men. The voice was fresh as bubbling spring water, unalterable and indefatigable. I never tired of hearing it. What it sang escapes all analysis and cannot be written.

Those neumes of Gregorian chant of which today we understand so little, now that our editions are only an attenuated reduction sung heavily by bass voices, neumes that Saint Isidore said were meant for a high, sweet, and clear voice: I wonder if originally they may have sounded, in their primitive execution, not unlike these nearly unreal vocalizations in which one hears, in a nascent state, the first stammerings of music.

—*Writings by Saint-Saëns translated by Jann Pasler*

Figure 2. Caricature of Saint-Saëns as astronomer by Van Hasseldt.

NOTES

I would like to express my sincere thanks to Jann Pasler for asking me to write this introduction and for providing me with most of the references cited in the text. Working closely with her on this essay has been a real pleasure.

1. Camille Flammarion, *Mémoires biographiques et philosophiques d'un astronome* (Paris: Flammarion, 1912), 82. In recounting this, Flammarion (1842–1925) noted that, for his part, he would have liked to have been a musician; he had even learned counterpoint and composed a few bagatelles. He worked from the age of sixteen as a technical aide (*aide-calculateur*) at the Paris Observatory. Having established his own observatory at Juvisy (south of Paris) he became a major promoter of astronomy and sciences in general in France during the Second Empire and Third Republic.

2. See James Harding, *Camille Saint-Saëns and His Circle* (London: Chapman & Hall, 1965), 19. For a summary of Saint-Saëns's scientific interests, see Remi Cellier, "Saint-Saëns, homme de science," *Guide du concert* (1914), 48–50; and Jean Lacroux, "Camille Saint-Saëns, amateur d'astronomie," *Cahiers Ivan Tourguéniev–Pauline Viardot–Maria Malibran* 9 (1985): 126–28.

3. Harding, *Camille Saint-Saëns*, 22.

4. Camille Saint-Saëns, "Une Lettre à l'astronome Hirn," in *Divagations sérieuses: Problèmes et mystères* (Paris: Flammarion, 1913), 144.

5. In his letter to Auguste Durand on 3 February 1892, Saint-Saëns asked Auguste's son Jacques to send the Société astronomique de France 15 francs. Coll. Médiathèque Musicale Mahler, Paris. [Ed.]

6. Camille Flammarion's book, *L'Astronomie populaire*, published by his brother, the Parisian bookseller Ernest Flammarion in 1879, had a very wide audience. A real "para-

gon" of the scientific outreach literature, it was often reprinted. Twenty-five years after Flammarion's death, the most distinguished French astronomers of the twentieth century rewrote *L'Astronomie populaire* in homage to his memory.

7. Camille Saint-Saëns, "Ce fut l'Alpha et l'Oméga de ma science astronomique," in *École buissonnière: Notes et souvenirs* (Paris: Pierre Lafitte & Cie, 1913), 329.

8. Before the French Revolution, all the *états* (provinces) maintained Paris houses where delegates handled provincial matters with the king's ministers.

9. Flammarion, obituary notice for Saint-Saëns, *L'Astronomie* (1922), 41.

10. Poincaré was later president of the French Republic (1913–1920).

11. "Discours de M. Poincaré, ministre de l'instruction publique, membre de la Société," *Bulletin de la Société astronomique de France* (1894): 130.

12. See the overview in Julien Tiersot, "Saint-Saëns écrivain," *Revue de musicologie* 4/7 (August 1923): 113–25. [Ed.]

13. Camille Saint-Saëns, "La Vie dans l'univers: Lettre à M. Camille Flammarion," *Bulletin de la Société astronomique de France* (1902): 281–82. *Revue d'astronomie populaire de météorologie, et de physique du globe* was published by Flammarion from 1882 until 1893, and was replaced in 1894 by *Bulletin de la S.A.F.* In 1922, the title became *Bulletin de la Société astronomique de France et Revue mensuelle d'astronomie, de météorologie et de physique du globe*. Today the journal bears the title *L'Astronomie: Société astronomique de France*.

14. Stephen Studd, *Saint-Saëns: A Critical Biography* (London: Cygnus Arts, 1999), 134.

15. *New York Times*, 6 June 1922, cited in ibid., 81.

16. In 1885, Saint-Saëns was elected as a foreign associate of the Académie royale des sciences, lettres et beaux-arts de Belgique. In 1907, the composer was also recognized by an honorary doctorate at Oxford and the Grand Cross of the Order of Saint Charles, presented to him by Albert, Prince Consort, in person.

17. Camille Saint-Saëns, "Changements sur la lune," *Revue d'astronomie populaire* (1889): 349–50.

18. Camille Saint-Saëns, "Un problème," *Bulletin de la Société astronomique de France et l'astronomie* (1894): 173.

19. *L'Écho de Paris*, 22 October 1911, also reproduced in Saint-Saëns, *École buissonnière*, 320–21, albeit with some alterations.

20. Pol Stiévenart, *Afrique du Nord, Sahara, Niger* (Brussels: La Renaissance du livre, 1955), 10.

21. Saint-Saëns gave a talk on mirage at the Société astronomique de France on 2 November 1904, summarized in the *Bulletin de la S.A.F.* (1904): 530–32, where the conventional explanation of the mirage phenomenon is recalled by the society's secretary, Touchet.

22. L. Benoist, "L'Agrandissement des astres à l'horizon," *Bulletin de la Société astronomique de France et l'Astronomie* (1912): 415–17.

23. Camille Saint-Saëns, "Questions d'optique," in *École buissonnière*, 319.

24. Camille Saint-Saëns and Gabriel Fauré, *Correspondance (1862–1920)*, ed. Jean-Michel Nectoux (Paris: Klincksieck, 1994), 58–59.

25. In fact, this explanation is not complicated, it is merely an application of the law of refraction and total reflection (as already noted by mathematician Monge). See my introduction for more details. Saint-Saëns invokes this so-called complication in order to propose his own theory.

26. This phenomenon is due to the atmospheric pressure that diminshes steeply with height; at those heights, the pressure of hydrogen or helium within the balloon shell inflates it.

Business and Politics, with Humor:

Saint-Saëns and Auguste Durand

JANN PASLER

Saint-Saëns's correspondence with his publishers, Auguste Durand and later his son Jacques—some 2,500 letters spanning almost fifty years, 1873 to 1921—reveal the man as complex, preoccupied with his career, but also witty and even humorous.[1] Besides documenting travels and residencies abroad, dates of performances and compositions, and interactions with various collaborators, the letters reveal his opinions, especially about musical life and politics in the capital. As such, they give a rare perspective on Saint-Saëns's state of mind and what mattered to him. If at times he seems frustrated and pushy, complaining or insisting on this or that from his publishers, he can also be poetic and insightful, creatively musing about his compositions or performances. When he needs support for his agendas, the writing is clear and declarative. But when he and Durand are bantering about a title or cover image, it turns charmingly playful, sometimes downright hilarious. These same attributes characterize the occasional drawings gracing these pages, whether of a scene contemplated as he composed or a pertinent image popping to mind to sum up his sentiment.

Given the relationship, most of Saint-Saëns's letters recount, not surprisingly, his musical experiences—the works and performers that did well in rehearsals and onstage, from St. Petersburg to Algiers—as well as his musical hopes and plans for which he needed Durand's help. Although *Samson et Dalila* would not be produced in Paris until 1890 and at the Opéra until November 1892, he was determined it would make its tour of Europe earlier. On 30 March 1878, Saint-Saëns tells Durand he had spoken of *Dalila* with Strasbourg's theater director: "You would do well to write to him. He seems well disposed." From Vienna in March 1879, "I think, especially with *Dalila*, that we'll be invited back again next spring. Get Levy working on it, he has a huge influence here." Similarly, for other major works, such as when he asks Durand on 4 March 1894 to send a score of *Phryné* to the head of government (résident supérieur) in Hanoi—"I think they need distractions in this distant city"; on 19 February 1895 he wonders, "When will they do *Phryné* at Covent Garden? I almost want to write the Duchess of Connaught." Saint-Saëns expected the Durands not only to back up his efforts to get his music performed, but also to deliver messages to colleagues. Once he asked Jacques to send money to the Société astronomique for a new membership (3 February 1892).

With Saint-Saëns abroad but closely following life in Paris through French newspapers, Auguste became a sounding board for his reactions, opinions, and dictums. After reading *Le Figaro* in Algiers, he explains, "You are right not to cede to Colonne's desires. It's for him to furnish his own performers to satisfy his public" (16 February 1888). On 26 December 1891 he asks Durand to push for *Prosperine* at the Opéra in 1893, proposing, among other changes, to add "a ballet to the beginning of Act 3 that could help it fit in the big house very well." Saint-Saëns grew increasingly anxious about *Dalila*: "What is needed now is to let the public know about the existence of *Dalila* everywhere in the world. . . . Performances and correspondence with theater directors, all that must reach the ears of the public" (18 December 1891). The temperature got heated between them, the language blunt, when it came to negotiating over the Opéra's *Samson* premiere. On 7 June 1891 in Algiers, Saint-Saëns worries, "You seem resigned in advance that [Massenet's] *Hérodiade* will be done before *Samson*. You must realize that I will absolutely not allow this. The Opéra cannot put on *Samson* without my authorization and I will not give it without this condition: production within one year and a ban on playing any other work on a biblical subject before it. . . . Take it or leave it. The Opéra will put on *Samson* before *Hérodiade* or it will not have the work at all." On 7 January 1892 he reiterates, "No *Hérodiade* before *Dalila*, or no *Dalila*. Besides, it's impossible to give two biblical works one after the other." On 22 January, frustrated that the press was writing about *Hérodiade* but still not *Dalila*, he whines, "This is the system I was used to. . . . But when I was young I had no one to support me. Now that I am a man and I have an intelligent, millionaire publisher, this is all the more difficult to swallow." As Durand also published the French edition of *Lohengrin*, a huge success in its Opéra premiere in 1891, Saint-Saëns peppers his letters with references to it as well. On 28 April 1891 in Naples, he observes, "In putting on *Lohengrin*, the Opéra is cutting the grass under the feet of the 'Société des grandes auditions'! So I'll bet she will do *Tristan*. *Tristan*, in French, with the terrible poetry of Wilder! Let's wait and see, it will be horrible."[2] Clearly a bit paranoid, he felt in competition with Wagner. On 25 January 1892 he points out, "They say that *Hérodiade*, *Sigurd*, and *Lohengrin* are everywhere, but *Dalila* has also made its tour de France";[3] and on 5 January 1893, again from Algiers, "Why are they playing *Lohengrin* and not *Samson* this week? This interruption in the middle of a successful run is not good." In this letter, Saint-Saëns acknowledges that music publishers could wield a great deal of power, especially when an opera was a commercial success.

Saint-Saëns also shared with Durand the status of his works and many compositional concerns. To indicate that he was working on the "ballet" of *Dalila*, he draws an image of a hot pan over a fire, cooking, so to speak (30 March 1876). From St. Petersburg, 15–27 November 1875, he puzzles over what to call *Le Déluge*: "An oratorio, lyrical poem, biblical cantata, or I don't know what. Biblical oratorio seems kind of redundant, oratorio subjects being generally taken from the Bible." The exact titles of works were also an ongoing question. If he is happy with *Africa* from the beginning for its "stylish sobriety" (21 November 1891), his title *Benvenuto* later morphes into *Ascanio* (30 November 1889). Over the years, *Dalila* is by far his most common name for his opera (and later his dog), except after 1892, when he mentions *Samson* or *Samson et Dalila* in reference to specific productions in Algiers and Paris.[4] In working through his instrumentation for *Ascanio*, he explains, "I want dancers to use castanets" and "natural trumpets" in the orchestra, as there would have been "no modern instruments in the court of François I" (30 November 1889). Letters from 1892 describe the instrumentation of *Nuit persane* (18 February) and fingering for *Africa* (30 April). In 1894, he attaches a preface for *Antigone*, explaining how his use of unison singing was meant to produce the "effect of the ancient Greek chorus." Through these letters, we follow the composer as he starts and finishes a work, undertakes its orchestration, reviews proofs, complains of errors in the scores, discusses possible performers, and finalizes the title and cover image.[5]

The Suite, op. 90, for piano, is a fascinating focal point for this correspondence, drawing in both serious and humorous allusions to contemporary politics. Though Saint-Saëns composed its minuet in France in September 1891, the prelude and fugue, gavotte, and gigue were written in Algiers that November as he worked on *Nuit persane* for Colonne (the first part mailed to Durand on 30 November). And, in late December, while focused on getting *Dalila* produced at the Opéra and preparing for its premiere in Algiers the next spring, he reviewed proofs not only for this suite but for *Africa*, *Rhapsodie bretonne*, and *Proserpine*. This suggests that his compositions may have had some mutual resonances.[6]

All the preoccupations discussed so far arise in Saint-Saëns's letter from Pointe Pescade, Algiers, on 21 November 1891. The tone and agenda are already set in his letter of 14 November in which the composer not only

Figure 1. Cover of Saint-Saëns's Suite, for piano,
op. 90, published by Durand.

establishes the order of the dances, following Baroque tradition, but also requests that the cover make specific reference to the period of Louis XV with an image of a female musician (*marquise*) playing the harpsichord.[7] (In a letter of 18 February 1892 he confesses that he was "positively in love" with the chosen *marquise* and "can't stop thinking about her.") Here, Saint-Saëns's visual imagination and literary prowess reach a high point and turn pointedly political.

The epithets in the 21 November letter begin with the plausible and end with the ridiculous. Saint-Saëns, giving free reign to his imagination, uses rhyme and alliteration to generate analogies ranging from the aesthetic and political, the medical and scientific, the culinary and botanical, to the "edifying" and "insignificant." In such successions, the most serious of subjects coexist alongside their questionable undersides: the luminary Socrates cast next to the occult, the Bible's sanctity tarnished by the erotic, the clarity of mathematics confused with the aquatic.

My dear friend,

The news that you give is excellent and I regret not going to the revival of *Étienne Marcel* in Lyon. As for *Samson*, if they are missing a main role [*titulaire*], [consider] Lougey à Sellier, who has worked a good deal on the part and whose voice was in good shape last summer.

I strongly approve your ideas on *Prosperine*. Please send me the proofs.

In a few days, I hope to send you the first part of *Nuit persane*, the first of four. From the perspective of the calligraphy, it's wonderful. Unfortunately, that's not the aspect that will interest the audience the most.

If you'd like an epithet for the Suite, I have more than one to propose: for example, Franco-Russian suite, ancient-modern suite, 18th-century suite or end-of-the-last-century suite; notorious suite, ambulatory suite; curly-haired suite, wavy-haired suite, candy box suite, rococo, Pompadour, DuBarry, Maréchale powder suite; fastidious, insidious, radiant, forgetful suite; anti-Wagnerian, anti-venereal suite; aristocratic suite, Socratic or autocratic; occult suite, amusing suite, annoying suite, ridiculous suite; astrological, pathological, demogogical suite, Ceylonese suite; Arcadian, Pasquierian or Magdalene suite; Bel-Abbèsian suite; aquatic suite; mathematical suite, clerical, monastic, wobbly or Lupercalian suite; old junk suite; chancroid or anthropoidean suite; flabelliform, labiate, composed suite, vegetal or vegetarian suite; tempered suite, biblical suite, erotic suite, mesenteric suite; typhoid suite; enophile, hydrophile, colombophile suite; Greek suite; opportunist, *fumiste* suite, philological suite, decadent, comical or culinary suite; angular suite, quadrangular suite; pointed suite; ridiculous suite, appalling, deplorable, prejudicial or censured suite; meritorious suite, Conservatoire suite, suite with apples, with small onions, fried suite, boiled suite, grilled suite, shriveled-up, stunted suite, insignificant suite, suite without sequel or purpose [*suite sans suite*], pharmaceutical suite, crystallized suite, perfumed suite; coquettish suite, . . . diabolical suite, divine, celestial, edifying suite; scandalous suite; limpid, lapidary, insipid suite; four-footed suite; insecticide suite; rhomboidal suite—you can choose, but I would prefer, quite simply, *suite*.

All I ask is that you don't put *Boulangist Suite* with the portrait that you have under the title. I'd rather have *Cyclist Suite*, with the portrait of Charles Terront.

The weather is wonderful here, with flowers everywhere—it's delightful!

In friendship
C. Saint-Saëns

It all begins in the most rational way, with an allusion to the Franco-Russian alliance, the first stage signed in August 1891. As French aristocrats had spearheaded the diplomacy, what better way to recognize this than by a suite recalling the ancien régime? Next, a reference to how the composer negotiates the *ancien/moderne* divide with dances that in their form recall the eighteenth century—with all those lovely powdered aristocrats—but in their harmonies the late nineteenth century. Under the *ralliement* (coalition) government of the early 1890s, formed to hold back anarchism and socialism, Saint-Saëns joined conservatives in exploring new relationships between the past and the present. Republicans and monarchists alike in the Union centrale des arts took the lead in promoting the rococo tradition as an important model for studying inherently French characteristics such as elegance and charm. Of course, nostalgia underlies any such "forgetful" suite, but lest the reader confuse his politics, Saint-Saëns follows "aristocratic suite" with an implicit question, "Socratic or autocratic?" The placement of Wagner here, whose music was embraced by many nineteenth-century aristocrats, is particularly appropriate: Saint-Saëns rejected Wagnerism as a dogma and, in rhyming "anti-wagnérienne" with "anti-vénerienne," he anticipates Max Nordau's association of Wagnerites with disease and degeneracy.[8]

With "astrological, pathological, demogogical suite" followed by "Ceylonese suite," Saint-Saëns leaps into the absurd.[9] Like the "fumistes" at the Chat Noir cabaret and the "Incohérents" whose exhibitions and costume balls from 1882 to 1896 critiqued all forms of solemnity, making fun of contemporary politics, society, and art, Saint-Saëns here looks beyond logic and common sense to amuse and delight his friend. Might Durand have caught an allusion here to their exhibitions in the lobby of the temple of high art, the Eden Théâtre, where Incohérent artists' satirical, incongruous, and even absurd images would have entertained audiences in 1889 and 1891 attending the Concerts Lamoureux's performances of Wagner? Might their humorous, but self-serious titles— such as a completely black painting titled *Negros Fighting in a Cellar, at Night*—have inspired some of these silly epithets, even anticipating titles of compositions by Erik Satie? After "meritorious suite, Conservatoire suite," Saint-Saëns leaps to a series of culinary-inspired suites, as if Conservatoire norms are merely one kind of taste. Then, after the culinary metamorphoses into the pharmaceutical, and eventually the chemical, the perfumed, the coquettish, and the diabolical, Saint-Saëns flips to its opposite: "divine, celestial, edifying suite," as if equally absurd. Perhaps the point was French gaiety versus Wagnerian pretentions to the sublime.

This succession comes to its most poignant in the sonorous sleight of hand that juxtaposes two stars of mass culture—General Boulanger, the charismatic political puppet on whom monarchists pinned their ambitions at returning to power in 1888–89, and Charles Terront, the French cyclist who in September 1891 had just won the Paris–Brest–Paris race, a predecessor to the Tour de France, which started in 1903. Saint-Saëns certainly did not want to be associated with monarchists such as the Duchesse d'Uzès who funded Boulanger's presidential campaigns. In a letter of 25 January 1892, he adds, "The big Wagnerian movement over the past ten years is not more spontaneous than the Boulanger movement: the reasons are, quite simply, Baron Hirsch and Madame d'Uzès." True to form for a composer who was later to be among the first to make recordings and write for a silent film, he would choose a representative of the newest technology, associated at the time with the "new woman" and female emancipation.[10] But then again, this, like the other epithets, would only be a distraction. In the end, Saint-Saëns preferred the word that said it all, and yet pinned him down the least: "quite simply, *suite*."

NOTES

1. These letters are currently in the Coll. Médiathèque Musicale Mahler, Paris. All letters cited come from this collection; all translations are my own.

2. On Countess Greffulhe, its director, and her attempt to produce *Tristan* in 1893, see my "Countess Greffulhe as Entrepreneur: Negotiating Class, Gender, and Nation" in *Writing Through Music: Essays on Music, Culture, and Politics* (Oxford and New York: Oxford University Press, 2008), 285-317.

3. Before its Opéra premiere, *Samson et Dalila* had been produced in Weimar (1877), Hamburg (1882), Brussels (1878 in concert), Liège (1888), Rouen (1890), Paris (1890), and then Geneva, Bordeaux, Toulouse, Nantes, Dijon, New York (in concert), Algiers, Montpellier, Florence, and Monte Carlo.

4. For an analysis of these gender implications in the 1890s reception of the work, see my "Contingencies of Meaning in Transcriptions and Excerpts: Popularizing *Samson et Dalila*," in *Approaches to Meaning in Music*, ed. Byron Almén and Edward Pearsall (Bloomington: Indiana University Press, 2006), 170–213.

5. In her remarkable *Camille Saint-Saëns, 1835–1921: A Thematic Catalogue of His Complete Works*, vol. 1 (Oxford: Oxford University Press, 2002), Sabina Teller Ratner includes a selection of this correspondence, though only in French, as it relates to each composition.

6. For a look at what other works Saint-Saëns was composing during 1891–92, see Table 2 in my essay in this volume, "Saint-Saëns and the Ancient World."

7. For a discussion of the music, see my *Composing the Citizen: Music as Public Utility in Third Republic France* (Berkeley and Los Angeles: University of California Press, 2009), 632–33.

8. Max Nordau, *Entartung* (1892); *Dégénérescence*, trans. Auguste Dietrich (Paris: Alcan, 1894).

9. A troupe of eighteen Ceylonese were exhibited at the Jardin zoologique d'acclimatation in Paris in 1883, and seventy appeared in 1886.

10. See, for example, Mary Louise Roberts, *Disruptive Acts: The New Woman in Fin-de-Siècle France* (Chicago and London: University of Chicago Press, 2002); and Peter Zheutlin, "Women on Wheels: The Bicycle and the Women's Movement of the 1890s," http://www.annielondonderry.com/womenWheels.html.

Rivals and Friends: Saint-Saëns,
Massenet, and *Thaïs*

JEAN-CHRISTOPHE BRANGER

Two months to the day after the death of Massenet, which occurred on 13 August 1912, Saint-Saëns published an article in *L'Écho de Paris* where he mentions bitterly his ties with the late composer:

> Much has been said about the friendship that joined us because of the attentions he lavished on me in public—but only in public. He could have had that friendship, and, if he had wanted it, it would have been as devoted as a solid friendship can be. But he did not want it. He has told people—though I told no one—how for one of his works I obtained access to the Weimar Theater, which had just produced *Samson*.[1] What he did not recount was the icy coldness with which he welcomed the news when I told him, I who was expecting a different reaction. From then on, I no longer insisted, and have often been content to delight at his successes, without expecting any reciprocity on his part—which I knew, from the confession he made to me one day, was impossible. My friends, my comrades, were Bizet, Guiraud, Delibes; they were my brothers in arms. Massenet was a rival.[2]

This obituary, written relatively late, came after an even more unequivocal—not to say violent—reaction that Saint-Saëns recorded when he learned of Massenet's death. In a letter dated 15 August 1912, he wrote to his publisher:

> Your news did not reach me, but I heard it from *Musica* and *Excelsior*, which asked me for articles. I declined the honor. Massenet behaved despicably toward me; he managed to hold back my career by many years [. . .], not to mention all the tricks he played on me whenever he could. There are enough other people around to sing his praises

and speak of the goodness of the abominable being who refused to go see Gallet[3] near his end (the poor man had charged me with asking him) because the sight of a dying man made him ill!

Selfishness, lies, and avarice have never had a better incarnation! Still his death, which I was expecting, was very difficult for me [. . .]. But writing his eulogy is beyond me. They will attribute my silence to envy, in which they will be quite mistaken! Envy was among the finest of his qualities, not mine. I never stopped defending him against those who foolishly denied his talent. That talent was not without defects; but who does not have faults?[4]

These few lines of profound resentment continue to surprise us when we read the correspondence between Saint-Saëns and Massenet, in which no reciprocal animosity is perceptible.[5] On the contrary, the two composers show a constant friendliness toward each other, and both express their feelings of friendship or admiration. About *Le Cid* (1885), Saint-Saëns asserts: "I can only find one word: dazzling! That orgy of life and sun gave me a pleasure I cannot express, and I am going to enjoy it as much as I can. Long life to your work and to you so you can write more. / Your admirer and friend / C. Saint-Saëns."[6] Twenty years later, Massenet received another long letter from Saint-Saëns about their authors' rights in Egypt that ended with hieroglyphs next to a hypothetical translation: "Rejoice / and triumph, / Son of the sun!"[7] Massenet was not to be outdone in this chorus of praises. After receiving a copy of the Third Symphony, he wrote to Saint-Saëns: "I am filled with wonder for this *unique* work! / Yours, dear friend, and great maestro, for you are a great, *a very great maestro.*"[8]

Comparing several sources allows one to untangle the complex web of their relationship. Since both men came from the same generation, Saint-Saëns and Massenet quickly settled into a form of rivalry on both an artistic and institutional level. On the one hand Massenet, winner of the Grand Prix de Rome in 1863, was elected to the Institut de France in 1878 over Saint-Saëns, who nevertheless entered in 1881, but without ever having won the famous prize for composition. On the other hand, both men were jointly made *grand officier* of the Legion of Honor in December 1900, giving rise to an exchange of polite remarks beneath which simmered a profound rivalry as yet undeclared:

I embrace you and rejoice at the thought that we are going to wear the same ornament.

—C. Saint-Saëns[9]

Yes, dear, great friend, it is indeed the "same ornament," as you say so kindly and wittily . . . *only* . . . I did not write your *admirable Third Symphony in C minor*:

not counting the rest!!!
From my wife and me, our *affection and our admiration*.
And thank you, thank you again.

J. Massenet[10]

However, the competition between the two composers erupted publicly in 1910 when the periodical *Musica* published a photomontage showing Saint-Saëns and Massenet with the caption: "In the beginning of this month, a governmental decree will raise one of these two so justly famous maestros to the rank of *grand-croix* of the Legion of Honor. Equally admired, equally beloved: which of these two renowned composers will be named, and who will be the first to be surprised at finding himself in the photograph illustrating this page?"[11] Yet, neither would be rewarded at that time,[12] which no doubt provoked the statements in a 14 September 1910 speech Massenet made a few months later celebrating the memory of Emmanuel Frémiet, but probably with himself in mind: "He lacked none of the honors awarded to the living; perhaps the *grand-croix* of the Legion of Honor, in which he was only *grand officier*, but if he lacked that supreme honor, public opinion had awarded it to him long ago."[13] As for Saint-Saëns, he wrote to his friend Charles Lecocq in a peremptory tone:

You also mention the *grand-croix*: it is my turn to have it, but since I will remain absolutely neutral, as I have done all my life, and since the other one [Massenet] will pull all the strings within his reach, he is quite capable of going over my head. That will be one more bitter pill to swallow after so many others. I will console myself by thinking that the other one, despite his wonderful talent, was not able to achieve the *Symphony in C Minor* in the concert hall or *Samson* in the theater.[14]

We see in this letter another aspect of the rivalry of the two composers, for while citing, understandably, his two chief masterpieces, Saint-Saëns takes no note of his numerous failures in the lyric theater, which must have distressed him even more in view of Massenet's multiple successes in this domain. Inversely, Massenet probably felt a sort of frustration at never having distinguished himself in the concert hall aside from his orchestral suites. In 1903, after panning his Concerto for Piano, a genre in which Saint-Saëns excelled, critics urged him to take up music for the stage again. They thought Massenet inept at constructing the kind of symphonic developments that at the time only a composer like Saint-Saëns could create. Saint-Saëns's publisher, Jacques Durand, returned to this apparent dichotomy and the reciprocal jealousy of the two composers when he told of his final meeting with Massenet in 1909, just before the premiere of *Bacchus*:

> [Massenet] spoke to me of his music, especially of a symphonic passage from his opera entitled *La Bataille des singes*. He described the musical development he had given to this part of his work, the careful writing he had put into it, and, bringing his thoughts to a more concrete point, he added that he would be happy if I drew this symphony to the attention of Saint-Saëns, whose appreciation, as it happens, was very important to him. I promised the maestro what he asked of me, and left him, thinking of the symphonic worries that troubled him and comparing them to Saint-Saëns's concerns when it came to the theater.
>
> Massenet would have keenly wanted to be a great symphonist, and Saint-Saëns a great dramatic composer. They were jealous of each other artistically on that occasion—for the rest, entirely mistakenly.[15]

The two composers did, however, feel a reciprocal admiration that could lead them to more discernment in which sincere reflections were nonetheless intermingled with biting or self-interested statements. A professor of composition at the Conservatory, Massenet enthusiastically urged his students to consult scores by Saint-Saëns, for which Saint-Saëns was grateful.[16] He also did not hesitate to praise his talent, though sometimes perhaps with an ulterior motive. On the eve of the dress rehearsal of *Samson et Dalila*, which had been at the heart of a bitter competition with *Hérodiade* over which was premiered first,[17] Massenet wrote to the director of the Opéra de Paris: "Triumph is certain—*it is a recognized masterpiece.*"[18] Similarly, Liszt received an unexpected *confidence* from Massenet, whose talent he appreciated, although he did not place him on the same level as Saint-Saëns: "Having been told that Massenet and Saint-Saëns were not on very good personal terms, I avoided mentioning Saint-Saëns until he assured me that he considers him the most important French musician since Gounod."[19] The artistic and personal intimacy between the Hungarian composer and Saint-Saëns may have encouraged Massenet to make this joke, reported by Reynaldo Hahn: "I told him that Bizet, despite his great talent, was not original, and pointed out that no one says 'That's like Bizet,' whereas they do say 'That's like Gounod,' 'That's like Massenet,' 'That's like Liszt.' 'But sometimes,' Massenet answered me, 'when listening to Liszt, people say: That's like Saint-Saëns.'"[20]

As for Saint-Saëns, although he criticized *Marie-Magdeleine* (1873)[21] and *Hérodiade* (1881) in veiled terms in his articles,[22] he also demonstrated his admiration for their author's skill. The day after the production of *Don César de Bazan* (1872), he exclaimed:

> Massenet has a wonderful musical organization. He has the gift of melody, a feeling for the picturesque, a vivacity of rhythm; he has his own way to deal with the orchestra that makes him stand out from a thousand others; he is a mixture of refined searching and violent brilliance, with exquisitely soft touches that recall certain embroidered and sequined fabrics from the Orient. In short, he gathers together all that seduces and charms, adding a prodigious ease. He would be the man to give us ten operas a year if he could find the opportunity.[23]

Similarly, Saint-Saëns was severe with some of his rival's works, like *Don Quichotte* (1910) and *La Navarraise* (1894), which "horrified" him in 1903,[24] though he unreservedly admired *Le Roi de Lahore* (1877), *Manon* (1884), and *Thérèse* (1907).[25] His favorite work, though, remained *Thaïs* (1894)[26]— to such an extent that he composed a "paraphrase for piano" of Lisztian inspiration, based on motives from the last scene, which ends with the heroine's death. This piece, *La Mort de Thaïs*, Saint-Saëns dedicated to Massenet's wife, whose elegance he admired.[27] The work condenses, as the end of the opera does, the most prominent instrumental motives, especially that of the famous "Meditation," transformed in extremis into an intensely lyrical motive. But, before that episode, Saint-Saëns introduces his paraphrase with the frenzied motive of "La Course dans la nuit" (The ride into the night), which he mistakenly calls "La Course à l'abîme" (The ride to the abyss) in his letter to Massenet dated 16 October 1895.[28] This *lapsus calami*, which refers to the penultimate scene in *La Damnation de Faust*, sheds light on Saint-Saëns's infatuation with *Thaïs*: Massenet's opera is an eminently Lisztian, even Berlioz-like, work because of its harmonic writing and the little symphonic poems that link certain scenes together.[29] It is not by chance, then, that Saint-Saëns built his paraphrase on motives that were, above all, instrumental and *a fortiori* from pieces belonging to a genre that he himself introduced into France under the influence of Liszt and Berlioz, two composers he profoundly admired.

The correspondence included at the end of this essay gathers together most of the letters exchanged between Saint-Saëns and Massenet from this period, from the premiere of Massenet's "lyric comedy" on 16 March 1894 to the performance by Saint-Saëns of his paraphrase during the anniversary concert of his first (1846) recital on 2 June 1896.[30] Composed in October 1895[31] and published by Heugel (Massenet's publisher),[32] *La Mort de Thaïs* undoubtedly marks a point of equilibrium in the tumultuous relationship between the two composers. Massenet invited his rival to lunch so that Saint-Saëns could perform his transcription for him and his wife. In a letter dated 9 November 1895, the author of *Manon* takes the liberty of composing a contrapuntal work on a motive Saint-Saëns had notated in his last letter (see Figure 1). Can we not fail to see in this academic exercise as much an allusion to his correspondent's talent, as the display of an author wishing to show aptitudes people denied he had?[33]

Thus the complex relationship that Saint-Saëns maintained with Massenet remains an interesting index of the two composers' psychology. In the case of Massenet, it reveals a conflicted composer probably sincere in the displays of admiration shown Saint-Saëns, who nonetheless attributed the most cowardly actions to him—still unproven today. His incessant affability remains more the mark of a psychologically fragile personality, as outlined perfectly by Charles Lecocq after he read the obituary written by Saint-Saëns:

> [Massenet] was essentially a man who liked no one but who wanted to be liked by everyone. During his life he was amiable on the surface, and in conversation always avoided giving any opinion about things or people [. . .]. Essentially, he was not a mean man, but a fearful, pusillanimous, nervous one who feared strong emotions. The proof is that he never attended his own premieres.[34]

As for Saint-Saëns, his correspondence with Massenet sometimes shows an evolution in his thinking. For example, in a letter to Massenet of 1 November 1895[35] he could praise *La Navarraise*—the same piece he unequivocally criticized several years later, as we've seen, in addressing someone else.[36] Also, three years after Massenet's death, he recounted to Charles Lecocq two dreams in which Massenet and Gounod appeared successively, with the conclusion that Massenet, "annoying and unbearable," was endowed with a "great talent" but lacked the "elevation" and "scope" of Gounod.[37]

It is reasonable to wonder about the contrasting reactions of an author known for his frankness and not much given to this sort of fickleness. Did Saint-Saëns fear the so-called sinister behavior of Massenet, whose influence and image were unquestionably important? Or should we see in this behavior, in which animosity mingles with admiration, the reactions of a composer who found in Massenet's music a reflection of his own aesthetic preoccupations, despite a personality that not only repelled him but stood in the way of his own quest for success.

In the obituary Saint-Saëns wrote about Massenet, he praises Massenet's style in terms that can unarguably define the sensibility he himself expressed in *Samson et Dalila*: rejection of the blind influence of Wagner, of

Figure 1. Letter to Saint-Saëns from Jules and Louise Massenet, 9 November 1885.

unrestrained modernity, of the overweening influence of Italian vocalism; subtlety of symphonic construction, ensured by leitmotifs [*motifs de rappel*], but also a persistence of vocal forms in which song preserves its rights.

> In these times of aesthetic anarchy [. . .] Massenet provided an example of impeccable writing, knowing how to link modernism to respect for tradition at a time when to rank as a genius it was enough to trample on tradition. Unparalleled master of his profession, broken of all his difficulties, possessing all the deepest secrets of his art, he scorned the acrobatics and exaggerations that the naïve confuse with musical science and went his own way, one he had outlined himself without regard for what people might say. Knowing how to profit, rightly, from the novelties brought us from abroad, but assimilating them perfectly, he gave us the comforting spectacle of a truly French artist whom neither Rhine maidens nor Mediterranean sirens could seduce. Virtuoso of the orchestra, he did not sacrifice the voice on its account, and as a lover of voice, he did not sacrifice orchestral color to it. Finally, he had this superior gift: life, the gift that cannot be defined but which an audience does not mistake, and which ensures fortune to works inferior to his own.[38]

The essence of Massenet's music, then, remains eminently French—in Saint-Saëns's opinion, its true value. After a 1910 meeting with Massenet who was now weak from illness, Saint-Saëns confided to Charles Lecocq feelings beyond the contradictions already outlined, in which a form of compassion cropped up: "He is very changed, older, thinner, he trembles ominously. That is very difficult for me, for although it is impossible for me to think of him as a friend (it's he who didn't want to be), I am grateful to him for the brilliance he casts on the French school, and for that I forgive him everything."[39]

Massenet–Saint-Saëns Correspondence

Camille Saint-Saëns, letter to Jules Massenet, on stationery with the letterhead "Bedford Hotel/Paris/17 rue de l'Arcade."[40]

Paris, 3 April 1894
My dear friend,
    You must already have heard that I have seen *Thaïs*, and was utterly charmed by it. Colonne, who attended the same performance,

agreed with me. He came to see me the next day and we shared our enthusiasm. We are not complete idiots about music, and I am quite certain that idiots are those who don't think as we do today—they will think like this tomorrow, I have no doubt about it.

The last scene is a pure diamond. I think about it all the time, and can't get enough of it.

And the first scene! And the incantation to *Vénus enchantement de l'ombre*!

And everything!!

Thank you for these artistic pleasures that you have given me.

C. Saint-Saëns

Jules Massenet, letter to Camille Saint-Saëns. The allusion below to "these difficult past few days" is no doubt a reference to the dress rehearsal and the opening night for Thaïs *on 16 March 1894 at the Palais Garnier. The dress rehearsal was full of multiple problems, and both performances received a lukewarm reception.*[41]

Paris, 3 May 94

Ah! My dear, great friend, if only you'd been there at the premiere! Your presence would have consoled me in *these difficult last few days*. Your letter erases *the memory* of that, and is for me the dearest and finest evidence of esteem I have ever received.

My wife and I thank you from the bottom of our hearts.

I admire and love you.

Massenet

Jules Massenet, letter to Camille Saint-Saëns. Saint-Saëns had just composed his "concert paraphrase for piano," La Mort de Thaïs, *and wanted to dedicate it to Mme Massenet.*[42]

Lyon, 14 October 1895

Dear great friend,

You could not have touched my heart more and, after the honor you've done me, your attention to my wife fulfills my wildest dreams.

With affectionate thanks!
Massenet

Camille Saint-Saëns, unpublished letter to Jules Massenet.[43]

Paris, 16 October 1895

All the honor is mine, dear colleague and friend, for I have had too much pleasure in . . . messing around with your exquisite music (will you forgive me?) to have any right to thanks. I never tire of playing this *Mort de Thaïs*, at the risk of infuriating my neighbors; I hope others besides me will play it, too. It was truly vexing for us pianists to abandon it wholly to the violinists; they've been gloating over it for long enough now.

As an introduction, I've used Athanaël's "Ride to the abyss" [*course à l'abîme*].

With all my friendship and my respects to Mme Massenet

C. Saint-Saëns

Louise Massenet, letter to Camille Saint-Saëns.[44]

20 October 1895
My dear Maestro,

My husband tells me you would like to put my name on your transcription of *La Mort de Thaïs*. I want to tell you how touched I am. It is a great honor for the work and a joy to me; thank you for remembering your old friend who has remained your great admirer.

Louise Massenet

Jules Massenet, letter to Camille Saint-Saëns.[45]

46 rue du Général Foy [Paris]
31 October 1895
Dear friend,

How we would love to hear your beautiful paraphrase! What an honor and a pleasure it would be if you chose a day to come to lunch—*any morning*—I would make myself free if I'm not already!

Yours, with admiration and from my heart.

Massenet

Camille Saint-Saëns, unpublished letter to Jules Massenet.[46]

1 November 1895,
My dear friend,

One of my fingers has been hurt, I've stopped playing the piano and I've lost whatever performance skills I had gained! . . . Give me a week to get the rust out and next week we will *arrange* it whatever day you like.

I finally saw *La Navarraise* before the 5th[47] and I think you have done a surprising thing; [the critics?] had not at all given me that impression. I had prudently reserved my judgment and I see that I was right to do so. In terms of the picturesque, I know nothing like it.

Among a thousand things, there are low notes on the harp that pleased me greatly . . . yet I'm not sure if it's the harp that plays them, but what is certain is that the effect is wonderful.

But why have them say Ara*qouil*? "*qui*" is pronounced the same in Spanish as in French.[48]

Cordially yours
C. Saint-Saëns

Jules Massenet, letter to Camille Saint-Saëns.[49]

Paris, 7 November 1895
Dear friend,

I know how busy you are now—what a triumphant month![50] Ah! How joyful we are, we love you and admire you so deeply.

I don't dare ask you which day you can come to lunch. As soon as you decide, we will be so happy.

Yours with all my heart
Massenet

Jules Massenet, letter to Camille Saint-Saëns (see Figure 1).[51]

Melody composed by C. Saint-Saëns in his letter of 8 November:[52]

Wed – nes – day! On Wednesday for lunch at our place. You will be free at one o'clock for your Opéra rehearsal. Eleven-thirty, rue du général Foy! [Lyrics set to music.]

Paris, Saturday morning 9 Nov./95
M

We will be so happy to have you over on Wednesday morning.

L M

Jules Massenet, visiting card "Massenet/46 rue du Général Foy," sent to Camille Saint-Saëns immediately prior to 20 November 1895.[53]

Till next Wednesday, 20 November 1895 at 11:30 in the morning, at home, dear *great friend!*

Jules Massenet, letter to Camille Saint-Saëns. The reference to 2 June concerns Saint-Saëns's upcoming concert at the Salle Pleyel that would celebrate the fiftieth anniversary of his first concert there on 6 May 1846. Notable on the program besides his Concerto for Piano no. 5, op. 103, under the direction of Taffanel, was a solo performance of La Mort de Thaïs.[54]

[Néris-les-bains] 27 May 1896
Dear friend,
    We are taking the waters, my wife and I, and we have just learned of the program on 2 June!
    My wife is as moved as I am, thinking solely of you.
    What a disappointment for us not to be able to leave here—I would like to run over but that would leave my wife alone during that absence.
    We are with you with all our hearts and we applaud the triumph of your fifty years of admirable productivity and recognized glory!
Your affectionate and grateful
Massenet

Camille Saint-Saëns, letter to Jules Massenet.[55]

3 June 1896
My dear friend
    La Mort de Thaïs was praised to the skies, as always.
    My hands were in form and I didn't perform it too badly.
    A thousand affectionate thoughts for Madame Massenet and my friendship to you.
C. Saint-Saëns
—Translated by Jann Pasler

NOTES

1. In *Mes Souvenirs* (Paris: Pierre Lafitte, 1912), 80, published serially in 1911–12 then in book form just after his death, Massenet did in fact mention this episode before adding: "Great men alone have these generous impulses!" The two testimonials differ, however, in chronology, with Saint-Saëns placing it in 1877 and Massenet in 1867: on that date, the two men had participated in three composition competitions—a cantata, an opéra comique, and a grand opera. According to Massenet, Saint-Saëns, who won with his cantata *Prométhée*, recommended Massenet's *La Coupe du roi de Thulé* when Saint-Saëns's work was not chosen in the opera competition. Massenet reworked and completed this material in *Le Roi de Lahore*.

2. Camille Saint-Saëns, "Jules Massenet," *L'Écho de Paris*, 13 October 1912, reprinted in *École buissonnière* (Paris: Pierre Lafitte, 1913), 274–75.

3. Louis Gallet (1835–1898), librettist for both Massenet (*Marie-Magdeleine, Thaïs*, etc.) and Saint-Saëns (*Ascanio, Proserpine*, etc.).

4. Saint-Saëns to Jacques Durand, Aix-les-Bains, 15 August 1912, Coll. Médiathèque Musicale Mahler, Paris, cited in Yves Gérard, "Massenet à travers les écrits de Saint-Saëns," in *Massenet en son temps*, proceedings of Actes du colloque de l'Opéra de Saint-Étienne (1992), ed. Gérard Condé (Saint-Étienne: L'Esplanade Saint-Étienne Opéra, 1999), 100.

5. Most of Massenet's letters to Saint-Saëns are kept at the Château-Musée de Dieppe, though Saint-Saëns's letters to Massenet have been dispersed. Some are preserved at the Beinecke Rare Book and Manuscript Collection at Yale, and others, in the collection of the Bessand-Massenet family, were sold in Paris (Hôtel Drouot) in 2002 and have not since been located. My warm thanks go to Noël Lee for providing me with photocopies of the documents owned by Patrick Gillis.

6. Saint-Saëns to Massenet, 26 December 1885, formerly in the Bessand-Massenet Collection; in Anne Bessand-Massenet, *Jules Massenet en toutes lettres* (Paris: Éditions de Fallois, 2001), 88.

7. Saint-Saëns, unpublished letter to Massenet, [Egypt], 4 February 1896, formerly in the Bessand-Massenet Collection.

8. Massenet to Saint-Saëns, Paris, 25 January 1887, in *Lettres de compositeurs à Camille Saint-Saëns*, ed. Eurydice Jousse and Yves Gérard (Lyon: Symétrie, 2009), 419.

9. Saint-Saëns, unpublished letter to Massenet, 15 December 1900, former Bessand-Massenet Collection.

10. Massenet to Saint-Saëns, Paris, 16 December 1900, in *Lettres de compositeurs à Camille Saint-Saëns*, 429. The motive reproduced in Massenet's letter is a musical citation of the ornamented motive played initially by the strings in Saint-Saëns's *Organ* Symphony, no. 3.

11. See *Musica* 88 (January 1910): 5.

12. Saint-Saëns would be decorated in 1913, unlike Massenet, who died without having obtained the highest honor.

13. Jules Massenet, "Funérailles de M. Frémiet," in *Mes Souvenirs*, 322.

14. Saint-Saëns to Charles Lecocq, [?] January 1910, in Gérard, "Massenet à travers les écrits de Saint-Saëns," 101.

15. Jacques Durand, *Quelques Souvenirs d'un éditeur de musique*, 2nd series (1910–24) (Paris: Durand, 1925), 6.

16. See C. Saint-Saëns, "Jules Massenet," *L'Écho de Paris*, 13 October 1912, 1; rpt. in *École buissonnière*, 275.

17. In its final version, *Hérodiade* was not staged at the Palais Garnier until 1921. On this competition, see Marie-Gabrielle Soret, "*Samson et Dalila* ou comment ébranler les colonnes du temple," in *Opéra et religion sous la IIIe République*, ed. Jean-Christophe Branger and Alban Ramaut (Saint-Étienne: Publications de l'Université de Saint-Étienne, 2006), 117–19.

18. Massenet, unpublished letter to Eugène Bertrand, Paris, 14 November 1892, Staatsbibliothek zu Berlin, SS Nachl. 31, 99.

19. Franz Liszt to Olga von Meyendorff, 31 January 1879, in *The Letters of Franz Liszt to Olga von Meyendorff 1871–1886 in the Mildred Bliss Collection at Dumbarton Oaks*, trans. William R. Tyler, intro. and notes by Edward N. Waters (Washington, D.C.: Dumbarton Oaks Research Library and Collection, 1979), 336.

20. Reynaldo Hahn, "Journal d'un musicien," *Candide*, 19 August 1935, 3.

21. Phémius [Camille Saint-Saëns], *La Renaissance littéraire*, 12 April 1873, cited in Eugène de Solenière, *Massenet: Étude critique et documentaire* (Paris: Bibliothèque d'art de "la Critique," 1897), 105: "The music of M. Massenet is original without being baroque and

amusing without being trivial; that's more than you need to succeed. By examining it attentively one discovers, not without surprise, that it stems from the music of M. Gounod, which it does not at all give the impression of doing. At bottom it is Gounod, but condensed, refined, and crystallized; M. Massenet is to Gounod as Schumann is to Mendelssohn."

22. Camille Saint-Saëns, "Hérodiade," *Le Voltaire*, 22 December 1881.

23. *La Renaissance littéraire*, 7 December 1872, reproduced in Julien Tiersot, "Les Premiers Articles de Saint-Saëns (suite et fin)," *Revue de musicologie* 5/9 (February 1924): 18–19.

24. See Gérard, "Massenet à travers les écrits de Saint-Saëns," 106.

25. Ibid., 109.

26. Henri Busser, in "Anatole France et la musique," *Ménestrel*, 24 October 1924, 438–39, states that Louis Gallet had first wanted to give his libretto to Saint-Saëns, who declined, before offering it to Massenet.

27. In a letter to Auguste and Jacques Durand on 8 February 1906, Saint-Saëns wrote: "He [Massenet] says in front of his wife, quietly, but so that she can hear, that she is 'always the same.' That is not true, but it is certain that she is as charming as one can be at her age, and she dresses beautifully." Cited in Sabina Ratner, *Camille Saint-Saëns 1835–1921: A Thematic Catalogue of His Complete Works* (Oxford and New York: Oxford University Press, 2002), 1:477.

28. See the letters section at the end of this article.

29. This is even truer in the original 1894 version, from which Saint-Saëns worked to write his paraphrase. The three scenes in Act 2 ("Alexandrie," the "Chambre de Thaïs," and the "Place publique") are closely linked by two symphonic interludes played with the curtain down—the "Symphonie des amours d'Aphrodite" and the famous "Méditation"—while "La Course dans la nuit" links the two scenes in Act 3 (the second "Thébaïde" and "La Mort de Thaïs"). Unusual in the lyric theater by their number and length, these orchestral pages call for choreography and prolong speech by conveying the conscious or unconscious thoughts of the characters. Thus, the "Méditation" illustrates the courtesan's conversion to religion; the "Course dans la nuit" portrays the storm—internal and external—that accompanies Athanaël in his frantic race to find Thaïs; the "Symphonie des amours d'Aphrodite" (removed in 1898) is a dance of seduction which, as the stage directions indicate, anticipates Salomé's Dance of the Seven Veils: "Slaves prepare to remove Thaïs's clothes, whose gestures become more and more animated. Athanaël has fled, with a horrified gesture. The curtains close. The music continues until the next scene. It's a sort of symphonic poem on the affairs of Aphrodite and the young Syrian god Adonis."

30. Saint-Saëns himself had given his work its first performance on 8 May 1896 at the Music Conservatory of Milan, then on 22 May 1896 at La Trompette. See Ratner, *Camille Saint-Saëns*, 1:477.

31. See ibid., 1:476. The manuscript is preserved at the Château-Musée de Dieppe. Soon after composing it, Saint-Saëns confided to a friend: "I have just written a pretty piece on *Thaïs* [. . .]." Saint-Saëns to Philippe Bellenot, October 1895, Bibliothèque nationale de France, NLA-254 (021).

32. Camille Saint-Saëns, *La Mort de Thaïs* (Paris: Heugel, 1895). Probably because of this piece, Massenet would dedicate his four-hand suite for piano, *Année passée* (1897) to Saint-Saëns after already dedicating his First Suite, for four-hand piano, op. 11 (1867?) to him.

33. Both composers were apparently used to these ambiguous playful exercises: the Bessand-Massenet archives preserve a fugue theme written by Saint-Saëns with the following dedication: "To my dear colleague Massenet to teach him how not to write fugue themes." Another fugue exercise by Saint-Saëns is also accompanied by a note handwritten by Massenet: "Saint-Saëns / Souvenir of a meeting at the Institut (Grand Prix)."

34. Charles Lecocq to Saint-Saëns, 21 October 1912, in Gérard, "Massenet à travers les écrits de Saint-Saëns," 102.

35. See the letter dated 1 November 1895 in the letters section below.

36. See Gérard, "Massenet à travers les écrits de Saint-Saëns," 106.

37. Ibid., 102–4.

38. Saint-Saëns, "Jules Massenet," 273–74.

39. Saint-Saëns to Lecocq, 30 March 1910, in Gérard, "Massenet à travers les écrits de Saint-Saëns," 104.

40. From the former Bessand-Massenet Collection, repr. in Massenet, *Jules Massenet en toutes lettres*, 125.

41. Jousse and Gérard, *Lettres de compositeurs à Camille Saint-Saëns*, 422.

42. Ibid., 423.

43. From the former Bessand-Massenet Collection.

44. *Lettres de compositeurs à Camille Saint-Saëns*, 423.

45. Ibid., 424.

46. From the former Bessand-Massenet Collection.

47. On 30 October, the famous soprano Emma Calvé sang for the last time in Paris the title role she created in London in June 1894 and then the next year at the Opéra-Comique where she was replaced by Mme de Nuovina, a singer of lesser caliber.

48. Saint-Saëns is referring to the masculine character of Araquil, whose pronunciation, "Araqouil," is given in a footnote in Massenet's score (for voice and piano), *La Navarraise* (Paris: Heugel, 1894), 11.

49. *Lettres de compositeurs à Camille Saint-Saëns*, 424.

50. Before supervising the Opéra rehearsals of *Frédégonde*, which premiered 18 December 1895, Saint-Saëns conducted the second act of *Proserpine* at the Concerts Colonne on 3 and 10 November. Concurrently Lamoureux successfully performed his Third Symphony.

51. *Lettres de compositeurs à Camille Saint-Saëns*, 425.

52. This letter has not survived.

53. *Lettres de compositeurs à Camille Saint-Saëns*, 425.

54. Ibid., 427.

55. From the former Bessand-Massenet Collection, partially repr. in Massenet, *Jules Massenet en toutes lettres* 125.

Saint-Saëns and Lecocq:
An Unwavering Friendship

YVES GÉRARD

The relationship between Camille Saint-Saëns and Charles Lecocq is surprising. Did they not build their reputations by successfully representing two completely different, almost antagonistic areas of music? Lecocq focused on opéra-comique and, especially, operetta, with his triumphant *La Fille de Madame Angot*, demonstrating the link between these two genres. For his part, Saint-Saëns explored all types of instrumental music and, moreover, wrote a series of theatrical works representative of the various aspects of lyric music in the nineteenth century, from historical grand opera to naturalist drama. *Samson et Dalila*, a biblical opera, was successful worldwide and embodied the quintessence of both French aesthetics through *tragédie lyrique* and German aesthetics through Wagnerian symphonic drama.

At the moment of Lecocq's death, on 24 October 1918, Saint-Saëns revealed the sources of this unexpected friendship. One explanation appeared in a letter dated 25 October 1918 to one of his close friends, Dr. Félix Regnault:

> Newspapers probably informed you of the death of my old friend, Charles Lecocq. I met him at the Conservatoire when I was 16; that was 67 years ago. Afterward, we lost touch for quite a while, but then reconnected; since then we have been good friends, despite our careers being so different. For some time, I watched him decline; his graceful handwriting became heavy and sloppy, and his usual wittiness disappeared from his letters. The end came as no shock, so I am not as devastated as I would be by an unexpected death—there was forewarning! He began to have choking spells and took to his bed for two or three days only. All in all, it was a peaceful end.[1]

Indeed, the two young men attended the Paris Conservatoire at the same time. Saint-Saëns was a student in Benoist's organ class from October 1838 to July 1851, when he won first prize. Lecocq, in the same class, was a mere second runner-up in 1852. However, Lecocq earned first prize in harmony and accompaniment in 1850, and was second runner-up in the counterpoint and fugue class in 1851, winning second prize in 1852. The two composers met in Halévy's composition class in 1851. Halévy was more concerned with his own work than with teaching student composers. Consequently, both had few good memories—more generous in Saint-Saëns's case, more grudging in Lecocq's—but their friendship was formed. With their careers taking different paths, they lost track of each other until 1881, when they grew closer again. Given Saint-Saëns's way of life—taking off for warm climates each winter for reasons of health, and rushing to ever more concerts and other events during the remaining seasons—their correspondence evolved from a simple exchange of viewpoints, on music or poetry, for example, into a real chronicle of Parisian musical life, as related by the stoic Lecocq. In turn, the reactions to Lecocq by Saint-Saëns, who was almost always abroad, transformed the description of individual musical events into real discussions on general problems.

After the premiere of Gustave Charpentier's *Louise* at the Paris Opéra-Comique on 2 February 1900, Lecocq wrote to Saint-Saëns in Las Palmas:

Dear friend,

Now that you are away, we can chat a little. Yesterday I attended the dress rehearsal of *Louise*, which I want to talk to you about before reading reviews that could affect my opinion.

The action takes place in Montmartre (you see already that Charpentier's Muse flies no higher than the suburban hill). There is a family of laborers, a father, a mother, and a daughter. The father works outside the home, the mother cooks, and the daughter dreams of marrying a young man from Montmartre, an artist. When the curtain rises, Louise is at the window talking with Julien, who is outside. They have a long conversation about their romantic plans. The mother enters and overhears the two lovers. She listens in, and when she realizes what they are discussing, she slams the window shut, runs the suitor off, and causes a scene with her daughter, who is headstrong. The father returns from work. I don't know what kind of work, but it must be tiring because he appears exhausted. He pulls a letter out of his pocket and reads it. The letter is from Julien asking for his daughter's hand. A meek father, he tries to please his child, and is so imprudent as to sing these two verses to her, the only ones in the play:

Every creature has the right to be free,
Every heart has the right to love.

Not that badly said, and not that badly thought, and the daughter takes advantage of it. Mother lights the lamp, and while the wick is being lit and the lampshade adjusted, the orchestra plays a beautiful orchestral interlude [*symphonie*]. There is another interlude for the evening soup. Then they talk, and everything falls apart since the mother will hear nothing of the young artist. The daughter adores the arts and has already told her father as much, who responds, "If everyone made art, no one would be left to do real work (literal)." The mother turns red with fury, the father lowers his head, and the daughter sobs and rebels.

In the second act, we're still in Montmartre, not far from Sacré Cœur, which is partly visible in the background. There are ragpickers, thieves, merchants, passersby, policemen, etc. Louise is headed for work, as a seamstress. Julien spies her, and they engage in conversation. Louise is determined to move out of her parents' home, but still hesitant. At the beginning of the act, there is a lovely fog effect, and two ragpickers appear. One recounts to the other stories of past loves. Then someone enters and sings something I didn't quite understand. Suddenly he opens his fine coat and his chest is lit up by electric lights. I thought I was going crazy. The ragpicker says he saw this good fellow once when he was twenty. It apparently is the spirit of love. Once this figure closes his coat he disappears, and a number of bit characters parade by, each with something to say.

The third act takes place at the seamstresses' workshop. Everyone is cheerful except Louise. Suddenly, they hear singing in the courtyard. All the women run to the window. It's Julien singing a serenade. The workers are delighted. Louise recognizes Julien's voice and is filled with emotion, but does not move. But then, his serenade over, Julien starts on about the lamentable parts of his love life and the seamstresses, who have been cheering him on, now boo and throw things on top of him. During this time, Louise goes out to join him, and the women look on in astonishment as they take off together. This act is very entertaining and very well staged.

In the fourth act we are still in Montmartre, on a balcony overlooking Paris. It is dusk. Julien and Louise are in a little house. They sing a long duet backed by a bass drum and brass, finishing in an extremely loud way. Night falls during the duet, and in the distance we see lights come on in houses, then the Eiffel Tower, illuminated.

There are even electric signs that flash on and off. Very beautiful. Hardly has the duet ended when we see something like a rocket rising in the distance, then another and another. It's the fireworks. Then we hear joyous cheering; a parade of happy Montmartre citizens in costume is carrying Japanese lanterns. They are coming to crown the Muse. The Muse is Louise, crowned now with roses. A lively ballet ensues. When the clamor reaches its peak, Louise's mother enters, to tell her daughter that her father is sick, stricken actually, and that he will not recover until she comes home. Yielding, the daughter follows her mother home.

We are back at the house. Father's doing better, mother's still cooking, and Louise is sad. The three have a long conversation. Louise stands her ground stubbornly and reminds her father that a creature should be free and a heart should love. The scene becomes tense, and the father, sweet up till then, becomes enraged and says to his daughter, "Well, if it's free marriage you want, get away from me!" With that, he seizes a chair and hurls it at Louise, who ducks and quickly flees. As soon as she's gone, the father is filled with remorse and desperately calls after her. But Louise does not return. Devastated, he collapses into his chair, and the play ends.

I don't have time to tell you about the music, which I thought unfit for the subject and the completely low class characters who develop during the course of the action. It's a poem in purposely prosaic prose, which contrasts oddly with the luxurious orchestration used by the composer. His supporters clamored for him, and he came out twice to wave to the audience. There were wildly enthusiastic people and others who were entirely disappointed. I was merely tired because it was so long, and stunned by what I'd seen and heard. I still don't know what to think of the merits of the play, but I still remain impervious to realism in music, which I believe is a false genre.

Best regards, and write back soon with your news,

Ch. Lecocq[2]

This humorous, anecdotal story of what Lecocq saw on stage ends with his general stance on realism in music. In Las Palmas on 6 March, Saint-Saëns wrote back, seizing on this aspect:

Your review of *Louise* was all the more important since it was the first I'd heard of the event, which was famous long before its birth. I don't know what I would think if I saw it, but I can only assume the combination of vulgar prose and transcendent music would strike my palate as a cuisine hard to get used to. What characterizes eras of decadence is the imbalance between methods used and goals being pursued, and I think that's what's happening here. In the fifteenth century, they made marvels of architecture that bucked commonsense and men of taste who make the comparison prefer thirteenth century works, which are logical and often just as whimsically charming.

The debate soon turned into an assessment of Charpentier as composer and his work *Louise*, which Saint-Saëns finally saw when he returned to Paris from the Canary Islands around 10 April. At the beginning of August 1900, Lecocq wrote:

I must say that since G. Charpentier was declared the leader of French music, I have realized that I do not know music and am too old to relearn it. Have you noticed the number of leaders of French music we've had the last several years? First there was Chabrier with *Gwendoline*, Bruneau with *Le Rêve*, d'Indy with *Fervaal*, and finally the one and only illustrious Charpentier with his triumphant *Louise*. Massenet is nothing now (have you read his latest Oratorio? Parts of it are superb).[3] Saint-Saëns, who only writes concertos, symphonies, chamber music, masses, and operas, counts for very little. Fortunately, Lady Posterity, with her common sense, has a way of putting everything back into place.

Saint-Saëns, who finally saw *Louise* in Paris, gave his assessment, dated 18 August:

With respect to *Louise*, I must admit that, setting aside my biases against the work—the singing of vulgar prose, the incomprehensible mixture of realism and symbolism, transcendent music accompanying simple characters, all things that displease me—many parts were charming and utterly seduced me.

Lecocq responded soon after (20 August):

To bring up Charpentier again, I don't deny his talent, but this undeniable talent is flawed by the audacity of strong biases and lauded too much by the mass of snobs who don't understand anything and proclaim it a work of genius, when it would have been a resounding dud if directed by some Carvalho or other.[4] The performers and staging were perfect (I know well that without staging there can be no success); they were very lucky to have found such an excellent cast. And Charpentier was on track, I'll say, when he called Carré his collaborator.[5]

Thus ended the conversation born of the premiere of *Louise*. It reveals the correspondents' interaction: Lecocq related to Saint-Saëns important current events happening in Paris and Saint-Saëns recounted the salient stories from his life on the road. The two streams of local news joined with more technical and aesthetic discussions, ranging from the use of trumpets in the works of Bach or Handel to the question of Wagner's music, from the writing of a libretto for which music was to be composed, with all the inherent problems of accentuation imposed by language, to the symbolist literature that annoyed both of them, from operas by Gluck to those by Verdi or Massenet.

This kaleidoscope of endlessly circulating facts and ideas brought together two artists with distinct careers, whose aesthetic ideals never coincided. Saint-Saëns wrote this disturbing letter to Jacques Durand on 25 October 1918 about the last days of Lecocq's life:

The day before yesterday, Lecocq talked to me, smiled at me—he was the same as ever, which gave me hope. But yesterday I left the Concert Interallié reception in a hurry; he was no longer conscious and looked terrible. I knew he would not make it through the night and I was right. He was still breathing, but in reality he was already gone. He died with the illusion—one that I carefully maintained—that I admired his works. Sometimes he made things that were charming in their naïveté, and his operettas were much better than the *Veuves joyeuses* operettas we have imported from Austria or England.[6]

Indeed, what brought them together, besides this infinitely nuanced friendship, was a common passion for "the illustration and defense" of a typically French musical art. Echoing in a different way the words of Saint-Saëns, Lecocq once defended his territory in these words:

The poor operetta, mistreated and abused, slandered and scorned! But the discontented and jealous have not succeeded in killing it outright. They have tried to drown it, but it always rises to the surface again, perhaps because of its lightness. Those who say that light music is an insult to great art are talking rubbish. Neither you nor I invented it; it has always existed under other names, and it will always exist, like all things that have a *raison d'être*. In France, the gaily free French spirit will never die.[7]

Saint-Saëns never "insulted" the operettas of his friend Lecocq—another key to the two minds coming together despite their differences. For thirty-seven years, and especially after 1900, these two comrades never ceased delighting each other with their epistolary exchanges. Consequently, they continue to interest us today, whether or not one follows them in their alternating dialogue.

—Translated by Anna Henderson and Jann Pasler

NOTES

This article is taken from two works I am preparing: *Saint-Saëns: Sa vie, son œuvre* (Fayard) and *La Correspondance Saint-Saëns–Lecocq: Une anthologie*.

1. Fonds Saint-Saëns, Château-Musée de Dieppe.
2. In the Fonds Saint-Saëns, the correspondence between Saint-Saëns and Lecocq totals almost 1,400 letters. Unless otherwise indicated, excerpts of writings by Saint-Saëns and Lecocq are taken from 500 letters I have selected for my forthcoming anthology.
   See also Georges Lebas, "Lettres inédites de Lecocq à Saint-Saëns," *Revue musicale* 4 (1924): 119–31 and 5 (1924): 121–46. [Ed.]
3. Referring to Massenet's *La Terre promise*.
4. Léon Carvalho, director of various theaters, was known for his habit of wanting to alter works he was producing. Saint-Saëns and Lecocq both had experiences with this, recounted wittily by Saint-Saëns concerning *Le Timbre d'argent* and bitterly as well by Lecocq concerning *Plutus*.
5. Albert Carré, director of the Opéra-Comique since 1898, directed *Louise*.
6. Saint-Saëns to Durand, Coll. Médiathèque Musicale Mahler, Paris.
7. Charles Lecocq, Preface, in Albert Van Loo, *Sur le Plateau—Souvenirs d'un librettiste* (Paris: Ollendorf, ca. 1910).

PART II

SAINT-SAËNS THE MUSICIAN

Saint-Saëns and the Performer's Prestige

DANA GOOLEY

In an 1884 address to an assembly of the five academies Saint-Saëns reflected on the "battle" between Germany and France for musical influence. He credited Germany with developing the arts of polyphony, orchestration, and harmony so richly that "Germany, in our time, has arrived at the apogee of musical development."[1] "At the same time," he continued, "Germany seems to be taken with a growing disdain for melody. . . . What will happen? Will France, which never lets itself be taken to extremes, at least in music, have enough influence to brake the momentum?"[2] This, he answered, would be settled by history. However, if France wanted to acquire comparable power and influence, it could not afford to wait for good compositions. It needed performers, committed disseminators: "How much further the influence of our school would extend if our young musicians could be persuaded to cross continents and oceans and make themselves pioneers of French art for a few years, at the same time acquiring experience and renown from which they would amply profit when they returned!"[3]

This call for young musicians to travel abroad and advance the cause of French music suggests that Saint-Saëns, in 1884, thought the French national school of music would benefit from a stronger international presence. Over the previous fourteen years, the combined forces of the Conservatoire and the Société nationale had stimulated the composition of chamber music, orchestral works, cantatas, and *mélodies*—a surge in French musical creativity. Yet the international penetration of these compositions was another matter, and the recent influence of Wagner on young composers looked like a unidirectional wave of German influence, lacking a French counterweight. The kind of musician Saint-Saëns called for—the touring musician who promotes French works internationally—hardly existed in France. In the 1840s Berlioz had conducted his own works in various parts of Europe, but no one was following in his footsteps. The only musician in France who fit Saint-Saëns's performer-pioneer to perfection was . . . Saint-Saëns. For nearly twenty years, both at home and abroad, he had been performing his own works alongside German classics, at the piano, organ, and conductor's podium. He had built up an international reputation and created a place for his own compositions in the repertoire of concert institutions in Germany, England, Russia, Austria, and the United States. Now, in 1884, he was looking for younger musicians who would do the same and hold back the hegemony of German musical values.

Saint-Saëns's conviction that itinerant performers wielded indispensable taste-making power and influence was based on close observation of how "progressive" musical works had worked themselves into the European repertory. Three musicians of differing nationalities—Franz Liszt, Hans von Bülow, and Anton Rubinstein—had succeeded in using their power as performers to impose new, unfamiliar, sometimes riskily "modern" pieces on audiences that were not always ready to welcome them. All three had started as child prodigies, and had built up credibility and influence through years of international concertizing as accomplished piano virtuosos. Liszt and Rubinstein, furthermore, had always promoted their own compositions from the concert platform, thus perpetuating the tradition of the virtuoso-composer. Not only did Saint-Saëns benefit from their support, but he also wrote essays in their defense and promoted their works in Paris. For all of the differences between Saint-Saëns and the virtuoso-composers in terms of temperament and experience, there was a great deal of common ground.

This essay draws on over a dozen periodicals from France, Germany, England, and the United States to flesh out Saint-Saëns's early career as a performer, delineating it in terms of venues, reception, and repertoire. The press reception clearly documents widespread admiration for his identity as performer matching, and sometimes even exceeding, his recognition as composer. His performing experience and prestige provided the foundation for his affinity with the figure of the virtuoso-composer. Studies of Saint-Saëns have given ample attention to his compositions, biography, and writings, but his activities as a performer have rarely been spotlighted. A focus on his keyboard performances helps sharpen our perspective on some of the more unusual aspects of his career and reputation. Before 1870, he was known to the French musical elite as a composer of distinction, but to the broader public as an organist and concert pianist. With a storehouse of prestige based on his performances, what I call "performance capital," he could advance his own works and aesthetic causes. This pragmatic interweaving of performance and composition became more significant in 1868, when he became close friends with Anton Rubinstein, renewed his connection with Franz Liszt, and composed his second piano concerto, whose style differed noticeably from his previous compositions.

His identification with Rubinstein and Liszt added a "philosophical" dimension to his identity as a performer. It catalyzed his commitment to "modern" musical directions (especially the Lisztian symphonic poem) and inspired the composition of virtuosic piano concertos for his tours. Saint-Saëns thus revived and revalidated the role of the international composer-virtuoso at a period when it seemed to be in decline.

In 1862, as the virtuoso-composer identity was losing relevance, Oscar Comettant distinguished eight categories of pianists, noting that the first category, "the virtuoso-pianist who composes . . . has become an extreme rarity in our time."[4] Pianists had not ceased composing entirely, but few wrote bravura concert pieces and opera fantasies in the manner of Sigismond Thalberg. Of the living French exemplars of the virtuoso-pianist, Comettant singled out Henri Herz and Émile Prudent. Both still toured widely as international concert artists, playing brilliant opera fantasies and concertos of their own composition to the near total exclusion of other repertoire. But few followed their example. In 1860, a German correspondent in Paris noticed the change: "Even in Paris . . . good music is starting to become fashionable. Even completely mediocre virtuosos consider it necessary to include a sonata or a trio by Mozart, Beethoven, or Mendelssohn on their programs."[5]

The rewards of international renown motivating Prudent and Herz to tour were eclipsed in the 1850s by the new prestige attached to instrumental pedagogy and classical repertoire. Performing and teaching had always been closely allied, but the prestige of teaching was higher than ever. Most pianists graduating from the Conservatoire as composers eventually belonged to the group Comettant called "pianist-teachers who compose."[6] Comettant described the emergence of a new type, "the pianist-virtuoso who does not compose," and welcomed it as a positive product of modern specialization.[7] The pianist who played compositions by others exclusively, Comettant argued, freed himself from invidious comparisons between his playing and his composing. Moreover, the non-composing pianist could more easily develop a sense of the various styles and schools, give better performances of the works of masters, and thus contribute to "the popularization of the piano works of all the great classical masters."[8] Among Saint-Saëns's peers, Francis Planté incarnated this trend most clearly. In choosing *not* to study counterpoint, organ, and free composition (*composition idéale*) alongside piano at the Conservatoire, Planté had foreclosed a future in composition and the interplay of performance, composition, and teaching that characterized most pianist-teachers.[9] Yet his career thrived in the 1850s through an association with the strictly classical concerts of Jean-Delphin Alard.

Saint-Saëns's piano teacher, Camille Stamaty, represents a break in the tradition of the virtuoso-composer. Following early successes as a performer, Stamaty devoted himself mainly to teaching, and laid great emphasis on classical repertoire. He rejected the generous use of the sustain pedal central to the "modern" bravura style of his teacher Kalkbrenner, and further rejected Kalkbrenner's refined, dandyish persona. Stamaty, with "manners reflecting Puritanism, holding that severe bearing that pious or elevated persons indefinably maintain in religious establishments," passed on these musical and personal values to his young protégé.[10] Indeed, Saint-Saëns's mother had asked Stamaty to act not only as a teacher but also as a surrogate father, and the possessive attitude Stamaty demonstrated toward his student suggests that he willingly accepted the charge.[11]

For various reasons, then, the young Saint-Saëns had only the faintest connection to the figure of the traditional virtuoso-composer. His pianistic activities pulled him toward an affinity with the new model: the pianist-interpreter of classical inclination. In 1850s Paris, this was the surest way to mark oneself as a modern musician. In the years preceding his organ appointment at Saint-Merri (1853), he was something like a "house pianist" at the symphony concerts of the Société de Saint-Cécile, devoted to classical repertoire and to music by living French composers. In 1850, the year of the society's debut, he played a Mozart Concerto in E-flat and Beethoven's Fantasy for Piano, Chorus, and Orchestra. The next year he played the piano part in Beethoven's Triple Concerto and again the Beethoven Fantasy. In 1852 he played the Mozart Concerto in G Major, and in 1853 the Beethoven Fantasy once again. This propaganda for the Beethoven Fantasy, previously unknown to French audiences, was a coup for the Société de Saint-Cécile, since it competed with the venerable Société des Concerts du Conservatoire, which had long prided itself on performances of Beethoven's symphonic music. Saint-Saëns could take partial credit for broadening the repertory of classic works, an effort praised by critics. The Société eventually invited Saint-Saëns to play the Beethoven Fantasy in its concert series of 1862, 1863, and 1867, although he was not invited to play another concerto with that organization until 1869, when he presented his newly composed Piano Concerto no. 3.[12]

While he was organist at the church of Saint-Merri (1853–58), Saint-Saëns gave few concerts at the piano. His brilliant organ playing, which had won him his only first prize from the Conservatoire in 1851, garnered more prestige. In 1858 he was appointed organist at the Église de la Madeleine, a prestigious position that gave him more exposure than Saint-Merri because of the church's size and the elite social profile of the parishioners. The *Revue de Paris* welcomed the newly appointed organist as "a young man who will be, we hope, one of the glories of the French school."[13] At services he improvised nearly everything he played, and his style reflected a deep absorption of counterpoint, earning passing references as "the young and learned organist."[14] Because organ concerts were rare, the French public heard Saint-Saëns play during organ inaugurations, grand festive occasions in which he participated several times.[15] He also appeared at concerts of religious music societies and in halls that possessed organs. For decades, the organ played a large role in maintaining Saint-Saëns's high status as a musician.

Shortly after his appointment to the Madeleine, Saint-Saëns entered more decisively into the Parisian concert world, where chamber music concerts had become à la mode. In the 1850s, a number of chamber music societies began to pursue "classics only" programming even more strictly than the trend-setting Société des Concerts du Conservatoire. Some cultivated regular associations with pianists. The Alard-Franchomme concerts for example (founded 1847), used Francis Planté until 1861, when the young pianist temporarily retired and was replaced by Louis Diémer. When violinist Charles Lamoureux started his own classics-oriented chamber music series in 1860, he realized that guest pianists could help him compete with other societies and made a minor star of Henri Fissot.[16] Between 1857 and 1861, Saint-Saëns participated in the Séances de musique classique et historique of cellist Charles Lebouc and the Concerts de musique classique of violinist Antoine Bessems, where he played a Beethoven sonata with violinist Achille Dien. In 1863 he made a cameo appearance at Lamoureux's Séances populaires de musique de chambre, playing Beethoven's Sonata in B-flat Major, op. 22. Between 1867 and 1870, he played annually with the Maurin string quartet, a group devoted to Beethoven and classical repertoire. At a Maurin soirée of 1867, for example, he collaborated in one of the Schubert piano trios and performed Beethoven's Variations in C Minor as a soloist. In 1869 the Maurin quartet featured the rarely heard late quartets of Beethoven, and Saint-Saëns contributed his part by playing Beethoven's late sonatas, opp. 101 and 109. Through these various associations, Saint-Saëns consolidated a strong relationship to the classical repertoire reaching all the way back to his 1846 debut, when he had played Mozart and Beethoven concertos.

Saint-Saëns also joined the concert scene of the 1860s as an entrepreneur. Like most leading instrumentalists, he gave one or two annual "benefit" concerts for his own profit. In 1864 he announced a six-concert series between January and May with a thematic focus on Mozart's piano concertos, championed by very few pianists at the time. The next season he announced a six-concert chamber series with Sarasate, discontinued after its first installment because the pianist and violinist conflicted over "classic" versus "virtuoso" repertoire. Saint-Saëns's most interesting and unusual entrepreneurial concerts were those consisting only of his own compositions (1860, 1862, 1863, and 1866). In France there was virtually no precedent for such concerts, with the exception of Berlioz and of Rubinstein who, during his 1857–58 visit to Paris, gave chamber music soirées consisting almost exclusively of his own compositions and arrangements. To simplify logistics for these concerts, Rubinstein had relied on the assistance of the Société Armingaud. It is telling that Saint-Saëns, likewise, hired Armingaud's group for the pioneering concert of his own works of 1860.

While Saint-Saëns was mounting his own concerts, he also generously lent his services to other performers, visiting and native, at their benefit concerts. Violinists Joseph Telesinski, Sarasate, Joachim, and Wilhelmji all used him as an accompanist, as did cellist Jules Lasserre. He was heard frequently at concerts of numerous societies supporting composers: the Société des quatuors français, Société des beaux-arts, Institut musical, Société de musique sacrée, Société de Saint-Cécile, and others. The repertoire Saint-Saëns played here was diverse, but Beethoven was central, especially the piano sonatas: the *Waldstein* (1856), a Sonata in G Major (probably op. 79, 1857), the Sonata in B-flat Major, op. 22 (1863), and the Sonata in C-sharp Minor (1864) in addition to the late sonatas mentioned above. His solo repertoire further included one of Beethoven's C-major sets of variations (ca. 1846), the 32 Variations in C Minor (1866 and 1867), *Eroica* Variations (1866), and Polonaise, op. 89 (1868). Surprisingly, he did not play solo piano sonatas by Mozart and Haydn. The only other sonata-like piece in his repertoire was Bach's Italian Concerto, which he revived in 1864 and continued to play well into the 1870s. Chamber music works played in this period include Beethoven's Quintet for Piano and Winds (1863), the *Kreutzer* Sonata (1862, 1865), Trio in E-flat, op. 70/1 (1865), and Cello Sonata in A (1865).

Concert reviewers in the 1850s and 1860s did not describe Saint-Saëns's pianistic manner in much detail, but expressed discontent with the dryness and emotive restraint in his playing.[17] Henri Blanchard, longtime reviewer for the *Revue et gazette musicale*, criticized the sixteen-year-old for "leaving the public impassive and cold" in his performance of Mozart's Concerto in G Major.[18] Two years later Léon Kreutzer wrote in relation to a Saint-Saëns performance of the Beethoven Choral Fantasy: "I would wish for more ardor and energy from this young man . . . [and] the character of the piece reflected a little in he who plays it."[19] To judge from an 1863 review of the Fantasy, his playing had not changed much a decade later: "Mr. Saint-Saëns played his part with magisterial aplomb and a perfect neatness. Such calm and resolute sangfroid in interpreting Beethoven!"[20] The consistency of these and other, similar critiques make it all the more surprising that Saint-Saëns featured Beethoven's music so prominently in his repertoire.

In the mid-1860s, as his thirtieth year approached, Saint-Saëns began to break the exclusive alignment with Beethoven, Mozart, Bach and the "classics," modernizing his repertoire and, with it, his approach to sound and expression. When he performed the Beethoven Choral Fantasy at the Conservatoire in 1867, the *Revue et gazette musicale* could now praise "the truly poetic manner in which he played the piano part. . . . Until now this eminent artist has been reproached, and not without reason, for dryness and harshness; to judge from the evidence of last Sunday, these faults seem to have disappeared completely."[21] A second performance of the Fantasy that season, this time at the Athénée, drew similar remarks: "The progress he has made in his manner of phrasing, and the delicacy of touch he has acquired, place him today in the first rank of virtuosos."[22] Critics occasionally complained about his "dryness" afterward, but changes in his repertoire suggest that Saint-Saëns did modernize his approach in significant ways. At an 1864 recital of cellist Jules Laserre he played a Hungarian Rhapsody by Liszt, a composer new to his repertoire, and delivered it "à la Liszt."[23] He launched his 1865 concert series with the Schumann Piano Concerto in A Minor, previously unknown to Parisian audiences, its solo part demanding a poetic, subjective or "interior" attitude from the performer. Earlier he had played other Schumann "poetic" pieces—some *Fantasiestücke* (1862) and the Piano Trio no. 1 (1864)—and had started adding Mendelssohn's character pieces to his repertoire. After this, he gravitated to bolder, more dramatic pieces, requiring more virtuosity than his previous repertoire: Beethoven's *Eroica* Variations (1866), transcriptions by himself of Meyerbeer's *Marche aux flambeaux* (1864) and Wagner's *Lohengrin* (1865), Weber's *Konzertstück* (1867), a Polonaise and the Barcarolle of Chopin (1867 and 1868), and Liszt's *St. Francis Walking on the Waves*, in both the piano version and his transcription for organ (1866). The trend toward modern repertoire and style, however, did not keep Saint-Saëns from simultaneously broadening his repertoire with pieces by Rameau and Bach.

When Saint-Saëns ended his five-year stint teaching piano at the École Niedermeyer in 1865—where he also composed and taught religious music— he wasted no time planning his first concerts outside of France. In the fall he went to Leipzig with his Piano Concerto no. 1 in D Major (composed 1858) and tried to make an impact abroad through both performance and composition. The Paris correspondent of Leipzig's *Allgemeine musikalische Zeitung* had heard him play Beethoven's Choral Fantasy in 1863 and called him "one of the most serious and worthy French artists": "Seldom have we heard this piece played with such fine penetration into its spirit and with so much energy."[24] Critical response in Leipzig and Frankfurt was much more generous to the pianist than to the composer.[25] The Leipzig reviewer, identifying him as "organist at La Madeleine in Paris," dismissed the first piano concerto as a "heaping up of French effects," but lauded the "impressive technique" (*überraschende Technik*) on display in Saint-Saëns's solo-piano transcriptions of Bach pieces. Yet the critic questioned whether it should be permissible "to make instrumental church music concert-friendly and subservient to virtuosity through *Presto-Tempo*."[26] The Frankfurt reviewer voiced similar reservations: his performance of Mozart's Concerto in E-flat Major demonstrated "great dexterity, but left us cold"; the Bach transcriptions were "inappropriate" (*ungeeignet*); and "a brilliant composition of Mr. Saint-Saëns on themes by Gounod put the virtuosity of the player into the brightest light, but less his taste."[27] These responses were filtered through a German bias against the supposedly "French" taste for virtuosity and effect, a bias well documented in Michael Stegemann's essay in this volume. What matters most here is that Saint-Saëns—by playing his own concerto, Bach transcriptions at a rapid pace, and a brilliant opera fantasy—was judged a "virtuoso." His pianism was very much up front during this first foray beyond the French border. In France, on the other hand, his reputation remained that of the composer-pianist.

During these years as a concert pianist and organist, Saint-Saëns also sought to establish himself as a composer of chamber music, concertos, and symphonies. Yet he faced three significant obstacles. First, he had never won the Prix de Rome, the prestigious award that was the clearest path in France to success as a composer, especially in opera. Second, his compositions encountered significant resistance, or sheer indifference, from music critics. The recurrent complaints, voiced by writers of different persuasions and biases, was that his compositions lacked inspiration, melodic invention, originality, and the communicative warmth necessary to reach a public audience. Critics could not easily ascribe these problems to youth or immaturity, since his music was totally accomplished at the level of compositional technique, and was recognized for its polish. Third, his compositions lacked significant exposure. Ensembles that gave instrumental music a broad public hearing—Pasdeloup's Concerts populaires de musique classique (starting in 1861) or Lamoureux's Concerts populaires de musique de chambre (starting in 1863)—were fixated on a "classic" German repertoire. In the 1860s Pasdeloup programmed only one orchestral piece by Saint-Saëns: the Marche-Scherzo movement from the Symphony in A Minor (no. 2). Chamber music societies, too, were quite exclusively devoted to classic works and rarely picked up Saint-Saëns's compositions. The exceptions were performances of his Piano Quintet in A Minor by Lamoureux's quartet society in 1860 and his Piano Trio no. 1 in 1865 by the Société des trios anciens et modernes.[28]

In these unfavorable conditions Saint-Saëns mounted his own concerts, where his performance skills proved a critical means of gathering exposure and prestige. The manner in which he "imposed" and "exhibited" his works was observed by contemporaries as an exception to the rule for aspiring composers. Critic Paul Scudo wrote in 1862:

> M. Saint-Saëns, a pianist and organist who lacks neither ambition nor talent, held two musical soirées where he exhibited all sorts of compositions in his manner: sonatas, concertos, and symphonies. M. Saint-Saëns, who has studied well and lives in a starchy, somewhat pedantic world . . . has not managed to convince us that he was destined by God to compose music. . . . Whether tending the organ at the Church of the Madeleine, or playing a concerto of Beethoven at the Conservatoire, or in one of his compositions . . . M. Saint-Saëns remains quite simply a highly distinguished artist who does honor to the masters who gave him such fine lessons.[29]

From Scudo's perspective, coming out of opera criticism and belles lettres rather than specialist music criticism, Saint-Saëns was first and foremost an instrumentalist: organist, interpreter of classics, and pianist-composer. In 1868, after several years of such concerts, including the highly publicized 1867 concert featuring *Les Noces de Prométhée*, Saint-Saëns's self-promoting concerts were recognized as a personal trademark: "This composer is not the kind to willingly stay still. He is, as we say colloquially, a *digger*, and each year he has made a habit of putting on his own musical exhibition."[30]

Saint-Saëns's way of executing these concerts closely resembled certain long-standing conventions of traveling virtuosi. They relied on the generous reciprocity of assisting artists such as Sarasate and Laserre. They were held in the low-cost venue of the Salle Pleyel-Wolff. They presented the artist as a free agent operating outside of any particular institution, in a double capacity as pianist and composer. The main difference was that these concerts were *intended* to highlight Saint-Saëns's qualities as a composer of symphonic music, not especially as a player. A reviewer of his April 1866 concert explicitly referred to the imbalance between Saint-Saëns's reputation as performer and composer: "I do not think the young and learned organist was looking for appreciation of his talent as a performer, long known to everyone in the audience. . . . He thus presented himself as a composer, and he can congratulate himself on the reception he was given."[31] Counting many luminaries in the audience—Berlioz, Gounod, Hiller, and Liszt—this concert featured several of Saint-Saëns's chamber works: the Suite for Cello and Piano, the Piano Quintet in A Minor, and the Serenade in E-flat Major for organ, piano, violin, and viola. But though

Saint-Saëns's identity as composer was up front, the performer was hardly in retreat. At the piano he played some short pieces by Schumann and Liszt's bravura-laden *St. Francis Walking on the Waves*, and he held the piano part in all three chamber works, two of which incorporate conspicuous moments of virtuoso display.[32] Indeed, the Quintet was originally conceived as a quasi-symphonic concerto to be performed with string orchestra.[33]

An important breakthrough to broader recognition as a composer finally came one year later, when Saint-Saëns's cantata *Les Noces de Prométhée* won the competition for a composition at the 1867 Universal Exhibition. This grand cantata earned him "official" prestige, and it was widely interpreted as compensation for the Prix de Rome he never received.[34] The "triumph" soon became a debacle because the planned premiere had to be cancelled. But Saint-Saëns was granted a subsidy to perform the cantata on his own. At the concert he arranged for this purpose, he played no piano—a unique occurrence. Instead he conducted an orchestra, choir, and vocal soloists in the cantata as well as his Ave Verum, the finale of his Christmas Oratorio, and his "Symphony in D." That the latter piece was actually an orchestral suite with movements titled "Prélude-Sarabande-Gavotte-Romanze-Finale," and was published as such—Suite for Orchestra (op. 49, pub. 1877)— suggests a deliberate attempt to spin the event as a "symphonic" concert.[35] Saint-Saëns's removal of the piano from the scene may have had a similar motivation, as there was a certain symbolic incommensurability between the piano and the "higher" genres. As his friend Arthur Hervey later wrote, an association with the piano could inhibit a composer's prospects at succeeding in symphony and opera: "The very successes [Saint-Saëns] had obtained as a composer of symphonic works went against him. What could a writer of symphonies know about operas? The fact of his being an organist and a pianist made matters worse, *particularly the last of these qualifications.* 'Bizet,' he writes, 'who played the piano admirably, never dared to play in public for fear of aggravating his situation.'"[36] Such a separation of "pianist" from "composer" was not typical of Saint-Saëns's outlook, but it did not hurt him to have staged it for this brief moment, as the cantata figured prominently in his successful nomination to the Legion of Honor in 1868.[37]

With this milestone, it appeared that Saint-Saëns had acquired a new status that would enable him to transcend the identity of pianist and break into the "higher" sphere of opera, thus following the career trajectory of his contemporaries Bizet and Massenet. But Anton Rubinstein's visit to Paris that year, 1868, reawakened his affinity for the role of international virtuoso-composer and pulled him in a different direction.

"The race of piano-gods seemed to have vanished forever, when one lovely day there appeared on the walls of Paris a small, narrow poster bearing this name: Antoine Rubinstein."[38] With these words, Saint-Saëns captured the sense of surprise and awe that came over him, and over the public, when Rubinstein first appeared in Paris in 1858. Rubinstein featured his first two piano concertos (in F and G), as well as solo piano pieces by himself, Schumann, Mendelssohn, Weber, Chopin, and Beethoven.[39] His power as a performer resided in a seemingly inexhaustible wellspring of sonic energy that hit listeners like waves of torrential sound, combined with an equally forceful personality and a mysterious, otherworldly look, enhanced by his supposed resemblance to Beethoven. The two musicians did not get to know each other on this first visit. But Saint-Saëns did contact him in late April, after Rubinstein's concerts came to an end, expressing hope he might play a fragment of his newly composed concerto for the Russian.[40] The meeting apparently never took place, but Saint-Saëns completed the Concerto no. 1 in D Major in August–November 1858.[41] Since Saint-Saëns had not previously tried his hand at composing a piano concerto, Rubinstein's impressive concerts and concertos may have served as a stimulus to its production or completion.

Rubinstein's role in the genesis of Saint-Saëns's Piano Concerto no. 2 in G Minor was more direct. During Rubinstein's 1868 return to Paris, the two musicians quickly developed a close bond: "Rubinstein and myself, we were almost inseparable in Paris, and many people were surprised by it."[42] On 19 March Saint-Saëns conducted the orchestra for Rubinstein's Piano Concerto no. 4 in D Minor. The success of this partnership motivated them to reverse roles for Saint-Saëns's benefit concert several weeks later. Saint-Saëns played not only his first concerto and some solo pieces, but also his new concerto, written in the frenzied seventeen days after Rubinstein's concert.[43] Some aspects of the new concerto, though original and unmistakably personal, betray the influence of his colleague: the intensely dramatic cast of the outer movements, the awesome, tidal wave–like climax of the first movement, the driving, demonic intensity of the last movement, and the free form of the first movement (Saint-Saëns commented on the irregular construction of Rubinstein's concertos in his article). The anonymous reviewer for the *Revue et gazette musicale* thought that this concerto might better be called "Fantaisie for piano and orchestra," its first movement "in the style of Rubinstein."[44] *Ménestrel*'s reviewers concurred and named it a breakthrough composition: "Saint-Saëns, stimulated by the famous Russian pianist's example, has enriched his interesting oeuvre with a new concerto showing notable progress over his earlier works";[45] "this work would suffice on its own to rank M. Saint-Saëns among the best composers of our time."[46]

If the composer-virtuoso Rubinstein awakened in Saint-Saëns a sense of personal and artistic affinity, Saint-Saëns made light of their antithetical temperaments and, in a revealing comment, compared their relationship to the unusual intimacy between Liszt and Chopin. They could easily bond over the steady stream of negative criticism their compositions had received. Saint-Saëns spoke frankly about the weaknesses he perceived in Rubinstein's compositions and defended him, saying that a musician should not be measured by his compositional achievement alone: "Like Liszt, Rubinstein knew the disappointment of not seeing his successes as a composer match those of his successes as a virtuoso."[47] The contemporary music world seemed incapable of recognizing a great keyboardist as a great composer. There were other affinities too. Like Saint-Saëns, Rubinstein composed in an exceptionally wide range of genres—concertos, symphonies, songs, operas, chamber music, and piano works—thus resisting the tendency to specialization. And through his leadership of the St. Petersburg Conservatory, Rubinstein was spearheading a "Russian school" of musicians that could stand comparison with the Germans, a project paralleling Saint-Saëns's efforts to advance the "French school." A striking difference was that Rubinstein had traveled the world and successfully disseminated his own compositions on the international stage—a full-fledged cosmopolitan composer-virtuoso. Saint-Saëns, though only six years younger, had only recently risen to prominence in France, and his compositions were barely known abroad.

Over the next two decades Saint-Saëns, whose career had previously centered on Paris, evolved into a regularly touring composer-pianist and symbolic leader of the "French school" in instrumental composition. The decisive shift in this direction came after his bonding with Rubinstein and the success of the G-minor concerto. In October 1868, about five months after its premiere in Paris, he returned to Leipzig for the first time since 1865, performing his new concerto as well as Beethoven's Polonaise, Chopin's Barcarolle, and his arrangement of Bach's Bourrée from Violin Sonata no. 2 (BWV 1003). Critical response to his playing was positive, but not his compositions.[48] On this trip he also brought the concerto to two German cities not previously visited: Berlin and Cologne. In Paris after the tour, Pasdeloup, who had previously shown considerable reserve toward Saint-Saëns's compositions, invited him to play the G-minor concerto at the Concerts populaires. This was his first appearance as a pianist there and it was easily his largest audience to date.[49] One reviewer took note of Saint-Saëns's pianism and his growing international reputation: "The young master played his concerto with those strong qualities and the authority that recently earned him an enthusiastic success among our neighbors, the Germans."[50]

Saint-Saëns returned to Leipzig in November 1869 with his newly composed third piano concerto. Reactions to this composition recalled heated debates over new music in Germany, in which Saint-Saëns was aligned with the modern school. But his status as a pianist was clear. The *Neue Zeitschrift* review opened with the statement: "[Saint-Saëns] belongs unquestionably to the greater pianists of the present."[51] The careful choice of the word "greater" (*hervorragenderen*) rather than "greatest" shows that this critic was placing Saint-Saëns short of the very highest class of virtuosi. It is nevertheless a stronger statement than was normally heard in earlier years. On the second half of this concert Saint-Saëns played a set of solo-piano pieces, following his custom for Gewandhaus appearances. But in contrast to the Bach arrangements used in 1865 were Romantic character pieces by Mendelssohn, Chopin, Schumann, and Paladilhe, ending with a solo-piano transcription of the "Dervish Chorus" from Beethoven's *Ruins of Athens*. This latter programming choice not only announced his orientation toward more modern piano repertory, but *The Ruins of Athens* transcription was apparently made expressly for the tour. Among his piano transcriptions it makes exceptional bravura demands that, as a reviewer noted, "gave Mr. Saint-Saëns an opportunity to show his endurance and virtuosity in the brightest light."[52] The unusual choice of Beethoven's "Dervish Chorus" for transcription may well have to do with Saint-Saëns's intensive study of Liszt's music in this period. Liszt's Fantasy on Motives from *The Ruins of Athens* had been published in Leipzig in 1865, its first half devoted to elaborations on the "Dervish Chorus" (see Examples 1a and 1b). (Saint-Saëns probably heard Rubinstein's transcription of the "Turkish March" from *The Ruins of Athens* when Rubinstein played it in Paris in 1858. The "Turkish March" is the other theme Liszt develops in his fantasy.) Clearly, Saint-Saëns's piano playing was evolving along with his increasing affiliation with progressive musicians.[53]

The strength of Saint-Saëns's reputation as pianist, especially outside France, is clear in an invitation from Anton Rubinstein. In 1871 Rubinstein, as head of the St. Petersburg Conservatory, wrote to Saint-Saëns asking if he might be interested in accepting "a position as professor of piano at the conservatory, playing when needed at quartet concerts of the Society, and being the pianist of Her Imperial Highness . . . the *maestro* of her palace."[54] He would be replacing Alexander Dreyshock, a virtuoso-composer who wrote almost exclusively for piano and served the empress in the 1860s. The offer was flattering, recognizing Saint-Saëns as a pianist of international stature. But it is difficult to imagine Saint-Saëns taking this offer seriously since it included nothing that might appeal to his ambitions as a composer. Although Rubinstein knew Saint-Saëns reasonably well, his invitation reveals that, from an outsider's perspective (in 1871), Saint-Saëns looked first and foremost like a performer, and only secondarily a composer. The most likely reason is that Saint-Saëns had not yet had an opera

Example 1a. Elaborations on the "Dervish Chorus" from Liszt's Fantasy on Motives from *The Ruins of Athens*.

produced on the stage, and his chamber music and symphonic composi-tions had not made a cumulative impact.

When writing of Rubinstein's difficulty in finding acceptance as a com-poser, Saint-Saëns tended to treat Liszt and Rubinstein as twin manifestations of a single phenomenon: "Liszt and Rubinstein remained great, without trying to be, through the greatness of their intransigent character."[55] What Saint-Saëns recognized and explicitly defended in them was their breadth—intellectual, instrumental, compositional, perhaps also spiritual or personal—which made "composition" in the narrow sense an inap-propriate measure of their overall worth. Liszt and Rubinstein were both virtuoso-composers with completely international reputations and spheres

Example 1b. Excerpt from Saint-Saëns's solo-piano transcription of the "Dervish Chorus" from *The Ruins of Athens*.

Example 1b continued

of influence. Both were controversial, known for their "modern" orientation, and both projected an aristocratic, high-minded air in their artistic
pursuits. Saint-Saëns had already looked up to Liszt for some time. In
1855 he had sent Liszt a newly composed mass, receiving a brief, avun-
cular note of praise from the Weimar Kapellmeister. In 1866, when Liszt
was in Paris for a performance of his *Graner Messe*, he graced Saint-Saëns's
concert with his presence. Saint-Saëns reciprocated with a performance
of Liszt's *St. Francis Walking on the Waves*, perhaps in tribute to Liszt's transformation into an *abbé*.[56]

A more substantial investment in Liszt and his music becomes noticeable
from 1868, when Saint-Saëns sent Liszt the newly composed, Rubinstein-
influenced piano concerto. This time Liszt sent a more extensive reply
praising the concerto's novel formal concept and suggesting additional
figurative lines superimposed upon what Saint-Saëns had already written.[57] Saint-Saëns then began promoting Liszt's works from the piano. At
a chamber music soirée of pianist Jean-Henri Bonewitz he played the
four-hand arrangement of Liszt's symphonic poem *Mazeppa*, soon to be
followed by the arrangement of *Festklänge*.[58] He also joined pianist Louise
Langhans in Liszt's extremely difficult *Concerto pathétique*. A far more sig-

nificant, highly virtuosic addition to his repertoire was Liszt's *Fantaisie sur des airs hongroises* for piano and orchestra, which he placed alongside his Third Concerto at a 12 March 1870 concert in Paris. He played it again in 1874 at the Concerts Colonne, after *Le Rouet d'Omphale*, and "earned a brilliant virtuoso success."[59] During the 1876 season he played Liszt's piano-orchestra arrangement of Schubert's *Wanderer* Fantasy, another tour de force.

Saint-Saëns was attracted not just to Liszt's compositions and to the novel idea of the symphonic poem, but also to the aura of indefinable superiority that Liszt carried with him. In a letter from around 1880 Liszt wrote to Saint-Saëns, "*As you once said insightfully*, it is an established matter that we are two musicians of a superior caste, given to understanding one another with open heart. My activity is declining, yours is rising."[60] An anecdote by Henri Duparc confirms Liszt's close artistic affinity for his young admirer: "Liszt once spoke the following words in my presence . . . 'There are today very skillful people, capable of playing true tours de force; but there are only two pianists who completely understand the entire extent of their art: they are Liszt and Saint-Saëns.'"[61] If Liszt felt uncommonly close to Saint-Saëns, and vice versa, it is because their lives had multiple parallels. Both had been through the trials and triumphs of the child prodigy. Both possessed phenomenal musical memories, improvised with great fluency, and cultivated their intellects through reading. Liszt and Saint-Saëns both matured late as composers, in part because of precocious early success in performance. Both absorbed multiple styles with such facility that their compositions sometimes sounded eclectic and fragmented, and both faced difficulties gaining critical acceptance as composers. But what Liszt signaled most clearly with his comment to Duparc is that Saint-Saëns commands not just the piano but also the organ, improvisation, and composition, "the entire extent of his art." In a period marked by specialization, they belonged to an aristocracy of musicians who excelled in multiple branches.

As Saint-Saëns incorporated Liszt's works and those of other Romantic composers into his repertory, comments on his "dryness" more or less disappeared, and observers noted the acquisition of qualities more characteristic of modern pianism. There are signs that in 1868–69 he was working out certain problems in his piano playing, after having botched performances of his Second and Third piano concertos (something that was hardly ever observed earlier or later). Both concertos make technical and rhetorical demands of a distinctly "modern" sort, including virtuoso flourishes, heroic assertions, and extreme rapidity. Possibly he had not yet mastered his own idiom. In this phase, his metronomic regularity and lack of coloristic variety, earlier faulted, were drawing fewer complaints, perhaps even erring too far in the other direction.[62] Over time these technical wrinkles were evidently ironed out and his variegation of sound developed further. A report on his performance of the Liszt arrangement of the *Wanderer* Fantasy claimed it was "the great success of the event. . . . The famous pianist draws from his instrument sonorities and soft effects that are truly amazing."[63] On the audio recordings he made in his late years, he consistently breaks chords and asynchronizes the hands, reflecting the influence of pianistic practices that were "modern" in the 1860s. We cannot be sure exactly when he adopted these practices, but we can be relatively certain they were absent from his playing in his youth.

The greater breadth of sound and sonority Saint-Saëns exhibited in his playing helped him succeed with the larger audiences of Paris's popular concert series, evading the complaints of "coldness" that had previously dogged him. Both the Concerts Colonne, where he played the "Wanderer Fantasy," and the Concerts Pasdeloup, where he played his Fourth Piano Concerto in 1878, were distinguished by audience participation and immediate, active response.[64] At the latter, Saint-Saëns was interrupted several times by applause, the "compositeur-virtuose" brought back for three warm curtain calls.[65] Scenes like this, in which every bravura climax leads to audience acclamation, are reminiscent of Liszt's glory days and of a virtuoso tradition that had been interrupted, in France, by the didactic, classics-oriented initiatives in the 1850s and 1860s. In 1877 Henri Duparc evoked the Liszt-Rubinstein horizon of reference most explicitly: "The playing of Saint-Saëns has marvelous purity, grace, energy, and nobility. But in my opinion these essential qualities, so rarely united in a single artist, do not constitute his principal merit; what makes Saint-Saëns the best of our French pianists and the often fortunate emulator of Liszt and Rubinstein is *personality*, sometimes so indefinable."[66]

Before he produced his symphonic poems in the mid-1870s, the three piano concertos Saint-Saëns composed between 1868 and 1870 served as the best vehicles for launching his reputation as a symphonic composer and pianist in Germany. (In France he was concentrating on his first operatic projects, *Le Timbre d'argent* and *La Princesse jaune*.) In Germany he played the First Concerto in 1865, followed by the Second in 1868, the Third in 1869, and the Fourth in 1870. For some time German and Austrian audiences heard no other pieces by Saint-Saëns. In the 1870s, the concerto he played most often in Germany was the Fourth, perhaps because of its more experimental and symphonic character, which confirmed his association with progressive musicians. As his symphonic poems, concertos, and especially *Samson et Dalila* became known, German concert organizations and major conductors, including Liszt and Hans von Bülow, were eager to add him to their rosters. German critics also gave high praise for his playing, calling him "a pianist of a rare order, a virtuoso of the greatest kind, who manages to combine the greatest self-awareness and the highest nobility with his extraordinary virtuosity."[67]

Saint-Saëns's pianism and strategic choice of the concertos likewise characterized his penetration of England, mainly in the later 1870s. Beyond France, Saint-Saëns eventually acquired more celebrity in England than anywhere else, and the process of building his reputation was clearly related to his performances of his own music at many concerts. Although he had briefly appeared in 1871 and 1874, the year 1876 marked his first participation in the serious-minded chamber music concerts of John Ella's Musical Union,[68] where he performed his Piano Quartet in A Minor, Bach transcriptions for solo piano, and together with Alfred Jaëll, his *Variations sur un thème de Beethoven*, op. 35, "the climax of the matinee," albeit poorly attended because it was late in the season.[69] The *Musical Standard* reviewer identified Saint-Saëns as "organist of La Madeleine, and in high repute on the Continent both as an organist and as a pianoforte player," with no mention of his status as a composer.[70] Shortly thereafter Saint-Saëns gave an even more sparsely attended piano recital in which he played his own piano pieces as well as his Bach transcriptions and Beethoven's *Waldstein* Sonata. The critic for the *Musical World* was impressed neither by the playing nor by the piano compositions. Though noting that Saint-Saëns was "recognized as a composer of merit," he wrote, "we were only afforded the opportunity of judging M. Saint-Saëns as a composer for the pianoforte, in which capacity we are unable to rate him as anything much above the ordinary stamp."[71] Saint-Saëns returned to Ella's series the next year (1877) to play his Piano Trio no. 1, but the exposure among the serious musical audience was not yet translating into widespread recognition.

This situation changed suddenly in 1878, the year after he left his post at the Madeleine. Already in March he was being described as "a French musician now greatly in vogue, as a composer of both instrumental music and operatic music," although English audiences barely knew his music.[72] A comment in the *Musical World* suggested that British audiences were eager to catch up with Saint-Saëns's rising star now that he had established himself on the Continent: "For several years past M. Saint-Saëns has been a regular visitor to London, but till quite recently has only found an asylum at the *matinées* of Professor Ella, so slow are we in England to recognize merit in a composer until he has established a reputation abroad. This Saint-Saëns has done, both in France and in Germany."[73] In June 1878 he appeared as a guest artist at the New Philharmonic Society concerts, conducted by Wilhelm Ganz, playing the solo part of his Second Piano Concerto. The unusually strong attendance at this concert "was due in large measure to M. Saint-Saëns, the eminent French composer, organist, and pianist . . . [who] not only took part in the concert as solo pianist, but introduced one of his most important works."[74] Saint-Saëns was invited back to the New Philharmonic the next season to play his Piano Concerto no. 4, this time raising the stakes by adding his second symphony and conducting it himself.[75] Before the year was out he had returned to play his Third Piano Concerto and introduce his symphonic poem *Le Rouet d'Omphale*. Because he had played his Second, Third, and Fourth concertos in a relatively short space of time, Saint-Saëns was compelled to revive his much older First Piano Concerto for his 1880 appearance at the New Philharmonic Society (now renamed "Mr. Ganz's Concerts").[76] During this same season, Saint-Saëns played his Fourth Concerto at Carl Richter's symphonic series.[77]

With this flurry of concerto appearances in 1878–80, Saint-Saëns had become familiar on the London concert scene and anchored the spread of his compositions there. In June 1878 his publisher Auguste Durand took out a full-page advertisement in the *Monthly Musical Review* listing Saint-Saëns's entire published oeuvre, including all the arrangements for solo piano, four-hand piano, and chamber ensembles. Then he began to diversify his profile, pairing the First Concerto with his Beethoven Variations, rendered by himself and pianist Caroline Montigny-Rémaury. At a benefit concert of pianist Jenny Viard-Louis, he introduced London audiences to his *Danse macabre*, followed by performances on the organ of his *Bénédiction nuptiale* and Bach's Fugue in G Minor (the fugue was encored).[78] In 1880 he gave a full organ recital at the Albert Hall.

The climax of this period in Britain was the premiere of his oratorio *La Lyre et la harpe* at the Birmingham Festival (1879). But the pattern of British critical reception, as previously in Germany, was to express more admiration for the performer than the oeuvre. The same biases against program music and "modern" musical directions marring his reception in France and Germany were found in England as well. A detailed review of his Piano Concerto no. 3 and *Le Rouet d'Omphale* found plenty of faults with the compositions, yet fully confirmed Saint-Saëns's high status as a keyboardist: "The merits of M. Saint-Saëns as an executant on the organ and the pianoforte are well known to English amateurs, and a better interpreter of his own works could not be desired."[79] The critic "D.T." at the *Musical World*, who had a moderate aesthetic viewpoint, reviewed numerous concert performances of Saint-Saëns's works in this period, but often strained to praise them. Reviewing an 1879 performance of the Piano Quartet (in Saint-Saëns's absence), he wrote: "It is in many respects very strange, and it is the work of an eminent man—reasons amply sufficient in themselves to justify reticence as to whatever may not command prompt admiration."[80] In 1880 the same writer claimed that the First

Piano Concerto "has no pretensions to rank with the greatest examples of its class," but felt that this mattered little because "the pianist was M. Saint-Saëns himself, who . . . played his own music in a manner possible to no one else."[81] Saint-Saëns had become popular, and was recognized as "eminent," without gaining full critical approbation for his compositions per se.

In the 1880s Saint-Saëns returned to London regularly to play and conduct, and pieces such as the Piano Concerto no. 2, the Beethoven Variations, and *Danse macabre* had entered the repertory of several performers. But the canonization of his works over time did not suppress attention to his superior reputation as a keyboardist. On the occasion of a concert he put on in London in 1887, the *Musical World* reported:

> His admirable qualities as a performer, both on the organ and the pianoforte, are so well known both here and abroad that it will suffice to say that his reputation previously gained in the last named capacity, by exceptional crispness of touch, brilliant execution, and conspicuous intellectuality, was fully maintained on the present occasion. Indeed, it must be owned that M. Saint-Saëns shone far more prominently as an executant than as a composer, since the transcription of his choral and orchestral Hymn to Victor Hugo produced little effect, whilst his sonata for piano and violin . . . proved on the whole an unequal work.[82]

The artistic capital Saint-Saëns built up through regular and consistent performances in London played an indirect role in the genesis of his Symphony no. 3.[83] In 1885 Francesco Berger, secretary of the prestigious Philharmonic Society, invited him

> either to play one of your Concertos, or to compose a new one and play it, or to play a Concerto by some other master, whichever you prefer. But, I need scarcely add, they would prefer you to appear in one of your *own* compositions. . . . I sincerely hope . . . that the wish of the Directors may be agreeable to you, of presenting you to their celebrated Society *in the double capacity of Pianiste and Composer*.[84]

Saint-Saëns suggested programming either of two pairings: his Piano Concerto no. 4 with his *Rhapsodie d'Auvergne* (for piano and orchestra), or Beethoven's Piano Concerto no. 4 with his Septet in E-flat Major. The ensuing negotiations led to his commission for his Symphony no. 3, a work that linked the tradition of large-scale classical forms with the tradition of the practicing church organist, thereby merging his "double capacities" in a way that Berger could never have imagined. British audiences, then,

came to know Saint-Saëns's music in performances at which he was normally present, and thus linked his identity as composer to that as pianist,
organist, or conductor.

Saint-Saëns's strategic deployment of his concertos and his pianism in
Germany and England brought him very close to the model musician he described in 1885: the international, touring promoter of the "French school."
This was hardly the way he had begun. Saint-Saëns's early career as a pianist
had aligned him strongly with the "classical" camp in Paris—that is, those
professional musicians, many associated with the Conservatoire, who wanted
to make the works of Mozart, Haydn, Beethoven, and Mendelssohn better
known through repeated exposure, better quality performances, and an extension of the repertoire beyond the well-known symphonies into chamber
music and piano sonatas. His dry, *détaché* touch and ascetic deportment at
the instrument, his near-exclusive choice of Beethoven sonatas for solo performances and of concertos by Mozart and Beethoven for orchestral
appearances, and his close ties to fledgling, "classics-only" chamber music
societies make him highly representative of the classicizing drive of the 1850s
and 1860s. In this elite, relatively insular milieu, there was little room for
positive validation of the traditional virtuoso-composer, an identity either
irrelevant or actively resisted by those seeking the progress of "serious" musical values. From this relatively parochial "classic" position, Saint-Saëns
evolved into a touring performer featuring newly composed concertos,
piano-centered chamber works, a few original bravura pieces and arrangements, and even the occasional piano-orchestra work by Liszt, alongside his
own original works for orchestra. This evolution, which took place gradually
over the 1860s, entailed a gradual embrace of modern repertory and,
through this, an enrichment of his piano technique and expressive rhetoric
to keep pace with the demands of modern instruments, halls, and audiences.
    The transformative turning point in this evolution was his encounter
with Rubinstein in 1868 and the ensuing renewal of contact with Liszt.
Rubinstein and Liszt gave Saint-Saëns a new point of identification. They
demonstrated the unique power wielded by the musician in whom compositional and performative identities are fully intertwined—a power that
is both ethical or spiritual, because it marks a rare breadth of perspective,
and pragmatic, because it enables the musician to advance his "causes"
efficaciously on the international stage. They validated the virtuoso-
composer as a contemporary, relevant agent of musical progress. As a
musician with an exceptional range of skills—organist and pianist, interpreter and improviser, composer of religious, symphonic, and vocal
works—Saint-Saëns had many reasons to feel an affinity with Rubinstein
and Liszt, despite vast differences of temperament. There were ante-

cedents to his reclamation of the virtuoso-composer identity: notably the 1865 concerts in Leipzig and Frankfurt and the periodic benefit concerts consisting exclusively of his own works. But the encounter with Rubinstein acted as a kind of mirror, reflecting back aspects of his identity previously left unrecognized, and suggesting paths for his future. It spurred him on to compose new concertos, take them to Germany on tours, and start disseminating Liszt's "modern" music vigorously. Ironically, this shift of focus took place during the period 1868–70, when he was preparing for a belated breakthrough into opera with *Le Timbre d'argent*. It is no accident that the Second Piano Concerto stood at the center of Saint-Saëns's transformation. His link to the concerto genre reached all the way back to his 1846 debut, when he was first exposed to the public playing concertos by Mozart and Beethoven, and was sustained through periodic performances of the Beethoven Choral Fantasy, the Mozart concerto series of 1864, the 1865 premiere of Schumann's Piano Concerto, and occasional performances of his own concertos in France and Germany. Rubinstein had shown how a performer's presence can summon an ethical and personal force to enhance the overall impact of a composition, and the impact was felt in Saint-Saëns's breakthrough concerto. The genre's unique balance of performative and symphonic values, its aspiration to both "serious" compositional craftsmanship and to efficacious audience communication, gave it new relevance as French musicians and organizations increasingly devoted themselves to the popularization of "serious" works.

Saint-Saëns's affinity for the composer-virtuoso, the concerto genre, and the values associated with them came into the open later, during a 1904 controversy known as the "war of the concertos."[85] Saint-Saëns's position in the heated controversy, which went as far as the courtroom, would have been unthinkable without his attachment to the unique virtues of the composer-virtuoso and the concerto. At the heart of the debate was the idea, aired vociferously by French Wagnerians, that concertos were superficial, regressive, and individualistic, and therefore did not belong on serious concert programs. At the symphonic concerts of Colonne and Lamoureux, impassioned Wagnerians protested by booing and hissing every concerto played—whether by Liszt, Saint-Saëns, or Beethoven. In the ensuing debates, Saint-Saëns defended the concerto in a highly original manner. After citing the impressive precedents for the genre in Mozart, Beethoven, and Schumann, he wrote:

> It is virtuosity itself that I want to defend. It is the source of the picturesque in music, it gives the artist wings with whose help he escapes platitudes and the everyday. The conquered difficulty is in itself a beautiful thing; Théophile Gautier, in *Émaux et camées*, con-

sidered this issue in immortal verses. . . . Virtuosity triumphs in all the arts. . . . On the matter of the concerto, this supposedly inferior genre is superior in that it permits the performer to manifest his personality, an invaluable thing when this personality is interesting.[86]

Saint-Saëns reiterated his defense of the concerto in *Le Gaulois*: "One cannot deny that, in principle, this form took performative display as its goal. Where was the problem? No one saw any problem, as they were free from the Puritanism with which we have been invaded in recent times."[87] He again argued the benefits of virtuosity for musical progress in his centennial essay on Liszt (1911).[88]

By aligning virtuosity with charm, verve, and freshness, and defending the performer's personality for its potential enrichment of music, Saint-Saëns was speaking against the grain of nearly all of his contemporaries, spinning the virtuoso as an agent of musical progress rather than a remnant of a superseded past. The key element of his vindication may have been his attention to audience response and the importance of the public. Virtuosos and their concertos embodied a certain healthy, audience-friendly hedonism that resisted the pull of excessive compositional severity and ponderousness. Saint-Saëns objected to critics and composers who "suppose that the public is, by its nature, averse to art, and that every work that succeeds in pleasing is the result of regrettable concessions."[89] In his opinion, master composers of the past had always worked within canons of the "correct" and their works "were not in contradiction with public sentiment."[90] Appealing to the public, he believed, was not a concession but a response to the urge to communicate. Liszt, whose virtuoso career was a profound education in what works and does not work with the public, demonstrated this knack for popular address in his symphonic poems, "popular in Russia and will become so in France."[91] The only resistance to them came "not from the public, but from conductors."[92] The composer of symphonic inclinations could not afford to lose contact with the public, and the concert pianist could take advantage of the concerto to give a popular articulation to elevated compositional ideas.

Camille Saint-Saëns continued to play piano and organ in public long after his reputation would have enabled him to concentrate on composition exclusively.[93] In the early 1890s, after over a decade of restless itinerancy, he seriously considered giving up piano performances, but the invitations kept pouring in and some inner resistance prevented him from stopping.[94] To the perpetual amazement of his admirers, he continued to perform at a high level the rest of his life. His "artistic cinquentennial" of 1896 commemorated not only his major works, but also his pianistic debut of 1846.[95] In 1910 the *Musical Times* reported on a gala concert "marking the 25th anniversary of his first appearance as a performer in England" that, recalling his 1876 debut at the Musical Union, featured him playing his Piano Quartet.[96] While he was alive, he was always recognized and honored in this "double capacity" as pianist and composer. Small wonder that Busoni—himself an international, all-embracing virtuoso-composer with an equal reverence for Bach and Liszt—drew attention to this increasingly rare, enlarged sense of musicianship in his obituary:

> The logical development of this generation is that it has again brought forth a group of composers who do not trouble themselves at all as to whether, or in what way, their creations can be performed. If we look back from this present state . . . to Saint-Saëns's personality, we see in him a figure that is well rounded from every side.[97]

NOTES

1. Camille Saint-Saëns, "Causerie sur le passé, le présent et l'avenir de la musique," in *Harmonie et mélodie* (Paris: Calmann–Lévy, 1885), 274–75.

2. Ibid., 275.

3. Ibid., 276.

4. Oscar Comettant, *Musique et musiciens* (Paris: Pagnerre, 1862), 134.

5. B. Damcke, "Aus Paris: den 20 April 1860," *Allgemeine musikalische Zeitung*, 5 May 1860, 150.

6. Henri Ravina was a standout representative of this class. Marmontel recalled that Ravina "did not have the passion for travel of Herz, Thalberg, and Prudent," but made many private appearances at the salons of the emperor and the aristocracy. He published hundreds of salon pieces that "remained gracious, songful, effective, without ever veering into extreme difficulty." A. Marmontel, *Virtuoses contemporains* (Paris: Heugel, 1882), 96–97.

7. Comettant, *Musique et musiciens*, 153.

8. Ibid., 155.

9. Marmontel, *Virtuoses contemporains*, 126. Marmontel regretted Planté's choice. It was apparently an unfortunate consequence of a cabal that had kept Planté from receiving the top prize in the annual piano competition, leaving him embittered about competing in other categories. Theodore Ritter was another such pianist specializing in the classics.

10. Ibid., 219.

11. See the exchanges between Camille Stamaty and Saint-Saëns's mother in *Lettres de compositeurs à Camille Saint-Saëns*, ed. Eurydice Jousse and Yves Gérard (Lyon: Symétrie, 2009), 575ff.

12. Indeed, the next time he was invited to play at the Société des Concerts du Conservatoire, in 1876, he was once again asked to play the Beethoven Choral Fantasy. By this point he was playing Beethoven's Fourth Concerto with the other symphonic organizations, those of Pasdeloup (1877) and Colonne (1874). He played the Choral Fantasy again in 1878 with Pasdeloup. There is a striking rhetorical parallel between Beethoven's Fantasy and the finale of Saint-Saëns's Third Symphony. In the Beethoven, the hymn-like tune is first stated by vocal soloists with the piano playing high-register broken chords be-

hind them; this tune is then immediately repeated *fortissimo* by the choir. Saint-Saëns, in his finale, introduces the hymn-like tune first quietly, with the piano (brought into the symphony solely for this moment) playing shimmering arpeggios around it, before repeating it *fortissimo* with full organ and orchestra.

13. L. Girard, "Chronique de la quinzaine," *Revue de Paris,* 1 January 1858, 147.

14. Wilhelm, "Revue musicale," *Revue contemporaine et Athenaeum français,* 15 December 1857, 197.

15. See William Peterson's essay in this volume.

16. Joël-Marie Fauquet, *Les Sociétés de musique de chambre à Paris de la Restauration à 1870* (Paris: Aux Amateurs de livres, 1986), 160. This is the best source of information on chamber music repertoire in France before 1870.

17. Critic Maurice Bourges wrote of Saint-Saëns's 1850 debut of the Beethoven Choral Fantasy: "It was surprising to find some coldness in his style, all the more since his renown did not wait for an official public appearance to advance a reputation for this precocious talent." Bourges, "Union musicale: Deuxième concert," *Revue et gazette musicale,* 17 February 1850, 55.

18. Henri Blanchard, "Société Sainte-Cécile, premier concert," *Revue et gazette musicale,* 25 January 1852, 25.

19. Léon Kreutzer, "Auditions musicales," *Revue et gazette musicale,* 24 April 1853, 150.

20. Léon Durocher, "Société des Concerts du Conservatoire . . . ," *Revue et gazette musicale,* 22 February 1863, 60.

21. "Concerts de la semaine," *Revue et gazette musicale,* 13 January 1867, 13.

22. "Concerts et auditions musicales de la semaine," *Revue et gazette musicale,* 7 April 1867, 108.

23. Joseph d'Ortigue, "Septième Concert du Conservatoire," *Ménestrel,* 10 April 1864, 149.

24. R. J., "Berichte: Paris," *Allgemeine musikalische Zeitung: Neue Folge,* 25 March 1863, col. 238.

25. "Music Abroad," *Dwight's Journal of Music,* 9 December 1865, 150. "If not as a composer, yet as an executant in every case, especially as an interpreter of the works of Bach, his reception was flattering at Leipzig, as it had been a few days before [actually a few days after] at Frankfort."

26. *Allgemeine musikalische Zeitung: Neue Folge,* 4 November 1865, col. 725.

27. D. L., "Frankfurt a. M.," *Allgemeine musikalische Zeitung: Neue Folge,* 15 November 1865, col. 753.

28. B. P., "Pariser Briefe," *Niederrheinische Musik-Zeitung,* 18 August 1860, 268–69. The German correspondent who noted the performance of Saint-Saëns's Quintet—he calls it a "quartet," but this must be an error—said that Adolphe Blanc also had a quintet performed that season, and that Blanc had overall succeeded better in imposing his compositions than Saint-Saëns.

29. Paul Scudo, *La Musique en l'année 1862 ou Revue annuelle des théâtres lyriques et des concerts* (Hetzel, 1862), 109–10. This article also appeared in *Revue de Paris.*

30. Albert l'Hote, "Concert de M. Saint-Saëns," *France musicale,* 10 May 1868, 144. The French original for *digger* is *piocheur*; emphasis in original.

31. "Concerts et auditions musicales," *Revue et gazette musicale,* 29 April 1866, 130.

32. The finale of the Suite includes a rather abrupt shift toward the end in which the pianist suddenly displays dexterity with astonishingly rapid runs. The finales of many of his other chamber music pieces, including the Sonata for Violin and Piano, the Septet, and the Piano Quintet, likewise build into their finales passages of conspicuous piano virtuosity. In the Piano Quintet especially (1855–56, published 1865), the piano nearly always plays the leading role and is written in a highly virtuosic fashion.

33. Elizabeth R. Harkins, "The Chamber Music of Camille Saint-Saëns" (PhD diss., New York University, 1976), 87–90.

34. Biographer Arthur Hervey saw the 1867 prize as compensation for the failure to win the Prix de Rome. See his book *Saint-Saëns* (New York: Dodd, Mead, 1922), 6.

35. At the next Paris performance of this piece, on the first of a series of Concerts de l'Opéra that Henri Litolff launched in 1869, it was called "Suite d'orchestre."

36. Hervey, *Saint-Saëns*, 8–9. Emphasis added. The original source of Saint-Saëns's words is his essay "Histoire d'un opéra comique," in the collection *École buissonière*. Busoni, in his brief 1921 on essay on Saint-Saëns, claimed that "he had already acquired fame as a brilliant pianist and organist quite early in life. . . . From the very first his fame as pianist stood in the way of the young Saint-Saëns as a composer." Ferruccio Busoni, *The Essence of Music and Other Papers*, trans. Rosamond Ley (London: Rockliff, 1957), 171.

37. See Arthur Pougin's report on musicians awarded the Legion d'honneur in *La France musicale*, 23 August 1868, 263. Pougin did not think Saint-Saëns was a distinguished composer and went to some length to suggest that his success was a highly "orchestrated" affair. In the report he wrote that "the work that drew the most attention, due to the circumstances of its birth, is the Exposition Cantata, played last year at the Palace of Industry." Pougin referred ironically to "the young organist, decorated as 'composer,'" and claimed that his musical ability was matched by a "talent, no less great, for putting himself forward and having himself discussed at every opportunity and sometimes without the opportunity" (263). Pougin voiced his resentment again in 1869, referring to Saint-Saëns as an "artist whose value is enormously exaggerated by a small, specialized coterie" in "Auditions musicales," *La France musicale*, 28 November 1869, 377. *La France musicale* reported that Saint-Saëns was decorated as "composer of music" (23 August 1868, 1), and the *Ménestrel* explicitly linked the Legion of Honor award to the Exposition cantata (23 August 1868, 310). See also Jean Bonnerot, *C. Saint-Saëns: Sa vie et son oeuvre* (Paris: Durand, 1923), 55. The journal *Orchestre*, 10 September 1867, noted that there were several musical luminaries in the audience at the *Noces de Prométhée* concert, but attendance by the general public was somewhat thin.

38. Camille Saint-Saëns, "Antoine Rubinstein," in *Portraits et souvenirs* (Paris: Société d'édition artistique, 1909), 144.

39. S. D., "Concerts d'A. Rubinstein," *Revue et gazette musicale*, 21 March 1858, 92.

40. Rubinstein to Saint-Saëns, 30 April 1858, in *Lettres de compositeurs à Camille Saint-Saëns*, 552.

41. Ibid., 552n2.

42. Saint-Saëns, "Antoine Rubinstein," 147.

43. Brian Rees, *Camille Saint-Saëns: A Life* (London: Chatto and Windus, 1999), 142.

44. "Concerts et auditions musicales de la semaine," *Revue et gazette musicale*, 17 May 1868, 157.

45. Frédéric Szarvady, "Une Lettre allemande sur la musique française," *Ménestrel*, 30 August 1868, 317. This opinion became standard. In a 1905 overview of Saint-Saëns's music, Emile Baumann highlighted the pivotal importance of the concerto in his compositional development, and contemporary commentators have generally agreed. Emile Baumann, *Les Grandes Formes de la musique: L'Œuvre de Camille Saint-Saëns* (Paris: Ollendorff, 1905). Biographer James Harding asserted that the Second Piano Concerto "marked his emergence as a fully formed musical personality and was also of historical significance, for it was the first important native work in this genre and provided a model for the French composers who came afterward." *Camille Saint-Saëns and His Circle* (London: Chapman & Hall, 1965), 105. See also Rees, *Camille Saint-Saëns*, 142–44.

46. *Ménestrel*, 10 May 1868, 192.

47. Saint-Saëns, "Antoine Rubinstein," 152.

48. St., "Correspondenz: Leipzig," *Neue Zeitschrift für Musik*, 23 October 1868, 376. "As a pianist Saint-Saëns belongs decidedly to the greatest artists. He has a strong, firm touch, a well-trained, impeccable technique, especially great dexterity in octaves . . . [etc.]." This Gewandhaus concert and the previous one were conducted by the orchestra's first violin-

ist, Ferdinand David, a Frenchman, who was filling in for the usual conductor, Reinicke. For the previous concert David programmed Saint-Saëns's "Concertstück," op. 20, and played the solo part himself. "Correspondenz: Leipzig," *Neue Zeitschrift für Musik*, 16 October 1868, 366–67.

49. Albert l'Hote, "Concerts populaires," *La France musicale*, 13 December 1868, 400.

50. *Ménestrel*, 20 December 1868, 23.

51. *Neue Zeitschrift für Musik*, 10 December 1869, 429.

52. "Leipzig," *Allgemeine musikalische Zeitung*, 15 December 1869, 399.

53. A French review of his Third Piano Concerto from 1870, otherwise very favorable toward Saint-Saëns and his music, took note of a new strain of Lisztian influence: "With the exception of the finale, which is bold, it is difficult to see in this piece anything but a regrettable aberration; it can be compared with everything that the recent style of Liszt possesses in incoherence and tormentedness." *Revue et gazette musicale*, 13 March 1870, 100.

54. Rubinstein to Saint-Saëns, 21 May 1871, in *Lettres de compositeurs à Camille Saint-Saëns*, 553.

55. Saint-Saëns, "Antoine Rubinstein," 149.

56. Saint-Saëns also played Liszt's *St. Francis Legend* in a Parisian concert featuring the Müller brothers. See Charles Beauquier, "Pariser Briefe," *Allgemeine musikalische Zeitung*, 16 May 1866, 162.

57. Liszt to Saint-Saëns, 4 August 1869, in "Lettres inédites de Liszt à Saint-Saëns," *Revue musicale* 9 (May 1828): 60–61.

58. "Matinées pour musique de chambre, sous la direction de M. Bonewitz," *L'Europe artiste*, 15 March 1868, n.p. On the same program Saint-Saëns played one of his Bach transcriptions, which "did not fail to achieve its brilliant effect."

59. H. Marcello, "Concert National," *Chronique musicale*, 15 March 1874, 267.

60. "Lettres inédites de Liszt à Saint-Saëns," 66–67. Emphasis added. The editor surmises this letter is from 1882–84.

61. Henri Duparc is quoted in "Saint-Saëns," *Journal de musique*, 3 March 1877, 1.

62. Marmontel noted Saint-Saëns's "excess of rhythmic precision" in his *Virtuoses contemporaines*, 19.

63. Ch. De Rozio, "Musique, " *Le Petit Parisien*, 15 December 1876, 3.

64. Jann Pasler, *Composing the Citizen: Music as Public Utility in Third Republic France* (Berkeley, Los Angeles, and London: University of California Press), 159–61 and 469–70.

65. "Concerts: Nouvelles diverses," *Revue et gazette musicale*, 10 March 1878, 77.

66. Duparc is quoted in "Saint-Saëns," *Journal de musique*, 2. Emphasis in original.

67. "Berichte: Leipzig," *Allgemeine musikalische Zeitung*, 12 December 1877, 797.

68. On the Musical Society see Christina Bashford, *The Pursuit of High Culture: John Ella and Chamber Music in Victorian London* (Woodbridge: Boydell Press, 2007).

69. *Musical Standard*, 8 July 1876, as reprinted in "London," *Dwight's Journal of Music*, 5 August 1876, 278.

70. Ibid. According to Rees (*Camille Saint-Saëns,* 216), Saint-Saëns wrote a letter to Durand saying that both the Piano Trio and Piano Quartet had been well received on this visit.

71. "M. Saint-Saëns," *Musical World*, 22 July 1876, 499. In 1878 Saint-Saëns's Cello Sonata, op. 32, was also played at the Musical Union matinées by Hans von Bülow and Lasserre.

72. "Popular concerts," *Musical World*, 30 March 1878, 213.

73. C. A. B., [no title], *Musical World*, 20 July 1878, 463.

74. D. T., "New Philharmonic Concerts," *Musical World*, 22 June 1878, 405.

75. "The Third New Philharmonic Concert," *Times* (London), 27 May 1879, 5.

76. In his memoirs Wilhelm Ganz wrote that he was "naturally proud to have been the first to enable him [Saint-Saëns] to play his splendid concertos in England." Ganz, *Memories of a Musician: Reminiscences of Seventy Years of Musical Life* (London: John Murray, 1913), 264; see also 135–36.

77. *The Daily Telegraph*, 12 June 1880, reproduced in "The Richter Concerts," *Musical World*, 19 June 1880, 385.

78. D. T., "Madame Viard–Louis's Concerts," *Musical World*, 7 June 1879, 349. A report on this concert from the New York *Daily News*, 3 June 1879, said that the audience liked the piece in spite of the fact that critics objected to its "anti-ideal" content. See *Musical World* of 7 June 1879, 353, which reproduces the *Daily News* article.

79. "M. Saint-Saëns," *Times* (London), 8 December 1879, 10. It appears that many *Musical World* reviews of Saint-Saëns from this period were to some extent plagiarized, though altered, from the lengthier, more detailed, and somewhat less positive reviews in the *Times*.

80. D. T., "The Popular Concerts," *Musical World*, 11 January 1879, 23. For a further critique less inclined to excuse him on the basis of his reputation, see "Monday popular concert," *Times* (London), 7 January 1879, 3.

81. D. T., "Mr. Ganz's Orchestral Concerts," *Musical World*, 8 May 1880, 289.

82. "M. Saint-Saëns's Concert," *Musical World*, 28 May 1887, 416–17.

83. For more about this process, see Sabina Ratner's essay in this volume.

84. Letter from Francesco Berger to Camille Saint-Saëns, 3 August 1885. Cited in Daniel Martin Fallon, "The Symphonies and Symphonic Poems of Camille Saint-Saëns" (PhD diss., Yale University, 1973), 450. Emphasis added.

85. On the *Guerre des concertos* see Marc Pincherle, *Le Monde des virtuoses* (Paris: Flammarion, 1961), 21. A more complete account of the event, together with a dossier of contemporary press articles, is in Jean-Christophe Branger, "'La Guerre du concerto' dans la presse française," in *Le Concerto pour piano français: Entre romantisme et modernité*, ed. Alexandre Dratwicki (Lyon: Symétrie, forthcoming). I wish to thank Professor Branger for sharing his article with me.

86. These lines were penned by Saint-Saëns during the 1904 debate but were not published at the time. They were first published by Fernand Baldensperger in "Une Consultation de Saint-Saëns sur le concerto," *Ménestrel*, 6 July 1934, 255.

87. *Le Gaulois*, 29 October 1904. This article can be seen at the Bibliothèque nationale de France, Arts du spectacle, in the file "Saint-Saëns: Dossier des articles" (RO–4309).

88. Camille Saint-Saëns, *Au courant de la vie* (Paris: Dorbon-Aîné, 1914), 26.

89. Saint-Saëns, *Harmonie et mélodie*, 279.

90. Ibid., 280.

91. Ibid., 172.

92. Ibid.

93. "Mr. Saint-Saëns, whose activity is remarkable, has not let his compositional work dominate him entirely; *he has not ceased to present himself as a virtuoso*, even making frequent artistic trips whether to Germany, Austria, or all the way to Russia. At the same time he has fulfilled his organist duties at the church of the Madeleine." F.-J. Fétis, *Biographie universelle des musiciens et bibliographie générale de musique, supplément et complément*, ed. Arthur Pougin (Paris: Firmin-Didot, 1880), 2:472. Emphasis added.

94. Letter from Saint-Saëns to Francesco Berger, the secretary of the London Philharmonic Society. Cited in Rees, *Camille Saint-Saëns*, 301.

95. *C. Saint-Saëns et son cinquantenaire artistique* (Paris: Durand, 1896).

96. The concert was held in Queen's Hall on 7 June 1910, according to the *Musical Times*, 1 July 1910. Cited in Harkins, "The Chamber Music of Camille Saint-Saëns," 72.

97. Busoni, *The Essence of Music*, 172.

Le Maître and the "Strange Woman," Marie Jaëll: Two Virtuoso-Composers in Resonance

FLORENCE LAUNAY AND JANN PASLER

Muse who with your fingers can make a soul tremble,
Even in the ashes of a heart burnt out and devoured,
Strange woman, why try to reignite a flame?
I have lived too much, suffered too much, loved too much.

The tree has felt the wind of dreary prairies
The daystar's rays, the storm's wet tears
Turn by turn have battered it; on twisted branches
Its scorched foliage knows no more flowers.

—Camille Saint-Saëns, "Poem for Marie Jaëll," 10 November 1887

Translated by Charlotte Mandell and Robert Kelly

Camille Saint-Saëns never published these verses dedicated to Marie Jaëll (1846–1925).[1] Yet he did pay homage to two other female musicians in his book *Rimes familières* (1890): the composer Augusta Holmès, with two poems, "L'Irlande t'a donnée à nous. Ta gloire est telle . . ." (Ireland gave you to us. Your glory is such . . .) and "Il est beau de passer la stature commune . . ." (It is great to rise above the common state . . .), and the singer-composer Pauline Viardot, with "Gloire de la musique et de la tragédie . . ." (Glory of music and tragedy . . .).[2] His poem to Marie Jaëll was probably too intimate for public disclosure.

A "strange woman" Marie Jaëll must have been; she was a superb pianist, ambitious composer, and charismatic teacher. In her *Lisztiania*, Lina Ramann points out several times that, while serving as Franz Liszt's secretary during her three stays in Weimar in 1883, 1884, and 1885, she baffled the horde of admirers that clustered around the Hungarian composer. On 29 May 1884, for instance, when she played her own Concerto no. 2 in C Minor, "Saint-Saëns conducted it, with her at the piano looking like a drunk maenad."[3] Though Ramann's deep antipathy for Marie Jaëll, apparent in several of her remarks, should prompt caution, it is nevertheless obvious that Jaëll was unconventional and unusual if only because she composed in large forms, shunning the salon piano pieces and *mélodies* often associated with creative female talent, and performing her works alongside those of the greatest composers of the period.

In many ways, what probably attracted Saint-Saëns to Jaëll was what they shared. Both began as child prodigy pianists with a taste for "the most difficult works" of Mozart and Beethoven. In her first concert at age nine, reviewers appreciated not only Jaëll's "extraordinary technique and perfect performance" but also her "rare comprehension" of the music and "profoundly musical feeling."[4] Both also composed, even though Jaëll's vocation as a composer, as opposed to that of Saint-Saëns, blossomed only in adulthood. Both were close to Liszt, another virtuoso-composer, and, like him, appreciated what could be understood and expressed through virtuosity.[5] Both wrote concertos as well as poetry and shared an interest in science and the mysteries of life. They also dedicated works to each other and showed mutual esteem by performing and promoting each other's music. For thirty years, beginning in 1871, Camille also gave Marie composition lessons and advice. When his two children died, she wrote a touching composition in their memory. However, as their correspondence from 1876 to 1901 suggests, the teacher was not always in favor of the pupil's experimentation, an attitude that eventually led her to turn away from composition. When one considers the many ways that Camille supported Marie, such a portrait conflicts with the usual image of him as a misogynist. On the contrary, Camille Saint-Saëns is among the musicians who most supported female composers in the second half of the nineteenth century.

Performing Camille Saint-Saëns/Performing Marie Jaëll

As a performer, Marie Jaëll's career deserves far more attention than it has heretofore received. After performing the complete works of Schumann (1889) and Chopin (1890), she was the first to play the complete works of Liszt (1889–92) in Paris, as well as the thirty-two sonatas of Beethoven (1893), and this even before Édouard Risler and Blanche Selva.[6] Marie also played a major role in popularizing the music of Saint-Saëns, along with the pianist Alfred Jaëll (1832–1882), her elder by fourteen years, whom she had married in 1866.[7] Called "the prominent pianist of the 1865 season" in London and "the cosmopolitan virtuoso par excellence in Paris," Alfred's considerable reputation all over Europe meant frequent concert tours. Three months before they married, Marie joined him on the concert stage in London where they thrilled audiences with their two-piano transcriptions of Schumann's *Manfred*.[8] The following April Marie also accompanied him at the Philharmonic Society and the Crystal Palace in London, and that July, before the King of Prussia in Ems, Germany, to audiences' delight.[9] In August, they had the opportunity to perform with the famous singer Carlotta Patti and the violinist Sarasate on the northern French coast. This pace seems not to have let up for years, and in 1872 their concerts took them as far as St. Petersburg.

Besides Liszt's music, which she performed frequently in Paris as well as on tour,[10] Marie eventually became associated with the music of Saint-Saëns, more so than Alfred, perhaps because he had once been a rival when they both toured Germany as soloists in the 1860s. Saint-Saëns dedicated his *Variations on a Theme of Beethoven,* op. 35, for two pianos, to the couple. He knew that, with their "skill and incredible technique," they could rise to the challenge of its extraordinary technical requirements (the fourth of its ten variations was inspired by Liszt).[11] They premiered it in Paris at Colonne's Concert National on 28 March 1874 when the music was still unpublished. Four weeks earlier, on 4 March 1874, Marie and Alfred performed a two-piano transcription of Saint-Saëns's *Phaeton,* three months after its orchestral premiere. The couple also played it twice in April 1875 at the Salle Érard, the second time at the public's request.[12] They then presented Saint-Saëns's *Fantaisie* for two pianos, possibly a premiere, on 18 May 1875 in a benefit concert at the Salle Ventadour.[13] On 10 February 1876, they performed a two-piano transcription of the *Danse macabre,* a year after its premiere. After giving his *Variations* again at the Concerts Colonne on 2 April 1876, followed by *Danse macabre* as an encore, Marie began to play Saint-Saëns's music with the composer himself. On 29 April 1876 at the Société nationale de musique, they premiered his transcription for two pianos of Henri Duparc's symphonic ballade, *Léonore,* programmed after her Quartet.[14] Then on 4 July 1876, Marie and the composer played his *Variations* in London at the Musical Union (where Alfred appeared regularly). Marie did it again with Alfred just after the 1878 Paris Exposition and with Louis Diemer in 1887.

Saint-Saëns greatly appreciated this effort. When it came to finally publishing his Piano Concerto no. 1 in 1875, he dedicated it to Mme Jaëll, perhaps because of the rave reviews given to her performance of his Concerto no. 2 (1868) at the Concerts Colonne on 13 December 1874, when critics claimed, "Never have people applauded so much at Colonne's performances"—a real feather in the cap also for the young orchestra in the fall of its first full-time season.[15] Marie also repeated the Second Concerto at Pasdeloup's Concerts populaires on 14 February.

Marie soon became known for her renditions of Saint-Saëns's concertos, performing the third with the Concerts Colonne on 5 November 1876, the first again under Colonne on 12 January 1879 as well as at the Salle Érard on 19 January 1889, and the second on 4 May 1882 and 23 and 30 November 1884. On a single concert held on 27 February 1890, she presented, in order, his four piano concertos, with Colonne conducting, and "captivated the audience at times with charm, at times with the power of an interpretation that is devoid of vulgarity and knows how to respect the work, while never ceasing to be personal and constantly awakening new and unexpected sensations, presenting it to us as attractive throughout and marvelously balanced."[16] She also helped popularize Saint-Saëns's *Danse macabre* (again in March 1877) and his *Souvenir d'Italie* (1887) in Paris in 1890, 1891, and 1897.

Whether or not Jaëll's playing style changed over the years, critical reviews of her performances did. In the 1870s, she was praised for her "vigorous, energetic, and powerful playing," "great technical skill," "charac-terized more by virile strength than by feminine grace"—characteristics that allowed her to take on the most difficult of pieces.[17] Her "stunning technique" enabled her to stand up to these "strenuous ordeals."[18] However, in the mid-1880s these attributes began to count against her. In 1884 came the comment that perhaps her virtuosity and "fieriness" were "a bit too impulsive," and in 1885, along with recognizing her as a "great artist," some wanted her to show more "*feminisme*" (here meaning femininity).[19] In 1889 reviewers instead focused on how her interpretation of the Con-certo no. 2 had "purity, ease, style, and charm" as well as "exquisite tact," "the most befitting nuances," and "a particularly delicate feeling."[20] When she presented the complete Beethoven sonatas in 1893, she was praised specifically for *not* drawing attention to her own considerable virtuosity or personal success, but rather for losing herself while elevating Beethoven.[21]

What interested her increasingly were the piano's musical timbres, which led to writing a series of pedagogical books on the subject, beginning with *Le Toucher* (the first version of which was published in 1893–94). Saint-Saëns admired her pedagogical works greatly and in December 1895 wrote to her in reference to her upcoming publication *La Musique et la psychophysiologie* (1896), "This little book will go with me everywhere."[22] This focus on timbre, together with her "superb authority," made her an ideal performer of Saint-Saëns's *Africa* (1891), which she played at the Concerts Lamoureux on 27 November 1892 and 22 and 29 January 1893.

First, the *Ménestrel* critic praised her understanding of the work and what was needed for an ideal performance:

> Here, the art of reconstruction is striking. We do not just hear the notes, but the composer's whole set of impressions that give rise to the notes, so much so that each motive, each phrase, each line gives us a sense of the work's general outline. The time and dimensions needed for the performance no longer count. The listener sees the whole at once, as if at a glance. It follows that the entire composition imprints itself on the mind with a living intensity and splendid depth, which are the most beautiful results to which a creative artist and his interpreter can aspire.[23]

Second, Marie was able to produce "new effects, full of surprises" from "personal, entirely personal techniques," which she had just written about in *Le Toucher*. As a result, "She played with exquisite discretion, and with such assured virtuosity that she was able to subtly color even extended and difficult passages, lending them a delightful transparency."[24] Audiences demanded three curtain calls.

Compositional Resonances

If Marie Jaëll's first composition, the Piano Quartet performed at the Société nationale on 29 April 1876, did not stand up to her reputation as a pianist despite the excellent performance,[25] her First Piano Concerto, which she performed there on 13 May 1877, "threw completely new light" on her music. Eclipsing mention of all other works on the program (by Dubois, Franck, Castillon, Duparc, and Lefebvre), *Ménestrel*'s reviewer wrote: "Her Concerto in D Minor is much more of a symphony than a piano piece with orchestra. The virtuoso has stepped aside in order to foreground the symphonist." Colonne, the conductor, said that one day Jaëll could turn out to be the "French Schumann."[26] Perhaps not surprisingly, she dedicated this concerto to Saint-Saëns.

Marie went on to compose *mélodies* that she and her husband performed in Paris and London. Then, on 13 May 1879, she organized a soirée of her unpublished music at the Salle Érard, hiring Colonne's orchestra. She performed her first concerto again, and this time her music of "unexpected but pleasing timbral combinations" and her Wagnerian preference for "endless modulations" proved that she was capable of "anything, in terms of difficulties, that could possibly be imagined."[27] Increasingly, Marie's music drew attention both abroad (in Ghent and

Liège in 1879, Leipzig in 1883, Weimar in 1884) and among composers who, moreover, endorsed her overwhelmingly. Referring to her Second Piano Concerto, Liszt wrote to her on 5 March 1884: "When can we expect your superb concerto which you were supposed to perfom in Paris?"[28] She premiered it shortly thereafter at the Salle Pleyel on 19 April during a concert of the Société nationale de musique with the Orchestre Colonne, conducted by André Messager.[29] On 2 May, before she joined him in Weimar, Liszt requested that Marie Jaëll bring the score and orchestral parts of her Concerto in C Minor—"a major and brilliant work," he added.[30] In Paris *Ménestrel* reported the great "success as a virtuoso and composer" attained by Marie Jaëll with her new concerto in Weimar.[31] She performed this work, seemingly for the last time, on 1 February 1885 in Paris, along with Liszt's Concerto in E-flat Major, conducted by Benjamin Godard. Arthur Pougin was in attendance and gave an enthusiastic review of the work, albeit tinged with the male-centered view typical of the period:

> The concert given these last few days by Mme Jaëll has highlighted once again the rare and precious qualities of this powerful, passionate, poetic artist, for whom one could only wish a bit more femininity [*féminisme*].[32] Whether as a virtuoso or as a composer,[33] interpreter or creator, Mme Jaëll is certainly a great artist in the full meaning of the word, who gives to the listener the entire gamut of emotion and passion. Her Concerto in C Minor is a major work, and she performed it superbly, as she did Liszt's Concerto in E-flat. Between these two powerful compositions, she chose to let us hear a few pieces by Chopin, Schumann, Hans von Bülow, and herself, which she played with a musical and poetic sense one rarely encounters.[34]

Her Concerto in F Major for cello was first performed at the Salle Érard in May 1882 by Jules Delsart and conducted by Charles Lamoureux on the same concert in which Marie played Saint-Saëns's Concerto in G Minor. Critics praised her cello concerto for its "originality and rich instrumentation," and her performance for the virtuosity and style she brought to the Saint-Saens.[35] This concerto was played several more times, notably on 4 May 1884, once again at the Salle Érard on a concert of her new works that again included her performance of Saint-Saëns's Concerto in G Minor. Camille Saint-Saëns's influence can certainly be seen in her interest in concertos, for he was both Marie Jaëll's composition teacher and the champion of this form in the musical life of late nineteenth-century France.[36]

Marie Jaëll's first compositions were piano pieces that clearly revealed the influence of Liszt, of whom she was one of the great interpreters. This resemblance was greeted amiably by Johannes Brahms: "How insipid the young pianists who always play the same pieces by Liszt! But talk about Jaëll! Now there's an intelligent, witty person: she invents her own things for the piano, just as bad as Liszt's!"[37] This first creative period came to an end in 1874 with *Valses*, op. 8, for piano four hands, played by Saint-Saëns and Liszt together in Bayreuth during the summer of 1876[38] and by Marie Jaëll with Saint-Saëns during a concert at the Société nationale on 2 March 1878.[39] Perhaps in recognition of her waltzes, in 1877 Saint-Saëns dedicated to her his Étude no. 6, op. 52, "in the form of a waltz." Later she wrote *Valses mélancoliques* and *Valses mignonnes*, both published in *Ménestrel* (1888 and 1889), and for Saint-Saëns, a kind of counterpart to their more serious music of "transcendental difficulty."

The limited success of her Piano Quartet was perhaps a response to an identity crisis expressed therein. In this quartet, she distances herself from the Lisztian harmonic compositional style of her first works and embraces a more resolutely Germanic mood, with some themes and contrapuntal treatments inspired by Johann Sebastian Bach, and a last movement that shows a strong kinship with Brahms, both in theme and piano style. Born Marie Trautmann in French Alsace, she spoke German fluently enough to write poems and opera libretti in German.[40] The German annexation of Alsace as a result of the Franco-Prussian War profoundly affected her. She chose French citizenship in 1872 and for several years refused to perform in Germany, though it was the site of her first successes as a child prodigy. Her correspondence and intimate writings reflect this conflict, and her choice of Saint-Saëns as mentor in 1871 takes on a special importance. He was not only a founding member of a specifically French institution, the Société nationale de musique, he was also a composer and performer thoroughly steeped in the German musical heritage, himself torn by deep aesthetic-nationalist conflicts.

In any case, there were many bonds between the two musicians. As noted earlier, Saint-Saëns dedicated his Concerto no. 1 in D Major to Marie Jaëll and she dedicated her own First Piano Concerto to him, as well as her piano pieces *Sphinx* and *Prisme, Problèmes en musique* (1888). She composed a *Paraphrase* for piano based on his choral work, *La Lyre et la harpe*, op. 57 (1894), as well as a melodrama on his poem "Les Heures" (undated).[41] Both composers set to music poems by Victor Hugo. Even more revealing of their close ties is *Am Grabe eines Kindes/Au Tombeau d'un enfant* (1879) for contralto, chorus, and orchestra, a work inspired by the death of Saint-Saëns's sons, for which Marie Jaëll wrote both the music and the libretto.[42]

This work in three parts—"Das Grab," "Chor des Erdgeistes," and "Chor des Engels"—caused a stir at the Antwerp Cercle artistique on 26 January 1880 and was enthusiastically acclaimed in a review by the correspondent of the *Revue et gazette musicale de Paris*:

The first [movement], with its soft and solemn coloring, contains beautiful effects depicting the early years and life of a child in characteristic fashion. . . . The child's death is described in a truly dramatic way. Daring, lugubrious dissonances clash and collide until they reach gradations and developments of striking effect. The third chorus, more melodic than the preceding ones, impressed the public most deeply. The rich vocal sonorities, orchestral contrasts, and powerful peroration contribute to a grandiose whole that prompted prolonged applause. The composer was called back to the stage and warmly acclaimed.[43]

But what direct stylistic influence did Camille have upon Marie and her inspiration? He was her professor; she played his music. Though an in-depth study of this influence has yet to be written, audible similarities of theme, harmony, and structure clearly exist between the two works for cello and orchestra, Jaëll's Concerto in F Major (1882) and Saint-Saëns's - Concerto no.1, op. 33 (1873).[44] The two pieces present many passages of harmonic immobility, where the soloist plays a series of arpeggio patterns on tonic or dominant chords extended over several measures. Saint-Saëns's work has no pauses between the movements and presents itself in extended sonata form, with another exposition of the first theme in the final episode of the piece. Though Jaëll's concerto is clearly in three short movements, her first movement, Moderato, presents a mixed sonata and lied form, a kind of condensed reproduction of the Saint-Saëns piece. After the second movement, Lento, in lied form, the Jaëll concerto concludes with a Vivace molto movement in sonata form on a boisterious tarantella rhythm that includes an expansive second theme "*à la* Saint-Saëns." (See Example 1).

Example 1. Second theme from the last movement, Vivace molto, of Marie Jaëll's Concerto in F Major.

The Correspondence

Especially revealing of the affinities between the two artists are their frank epistolary exchanges in which their temperaments are both drawn together and clash, revealing, often with humor, the torments of inspiration. One of Marie's undated letters, probably written shortly before Liszt's death in 1886, sheds light on this clearly emotive relationship:

> Mon cher maître,
> How happy Liszt was when he succeeded in putting us together at the piano. The generous solicitude of this friend, whom we revere and who loves us both, must not be squandered. Forgive me if I've offended you and don't confuse the woman with the artist, for in the depth of her soul the woman has all the peace and calm lacking in the artist. If I've been thoughtless to the point of causing pain without knowing it, it's because I saw no harm. Is that such a huge crime? When you'll have forgiven me, let me hear from you; as for me, I'll remain silent since this will make you happy and I've never wanted anything else.
> As always, your most grateful pupil, Marie Jaëll[45]

But Marie cannot be silent, and the year 1887 marks a climax in their relationship. In a series of letters at the beginning of the year, she expresses her admiration for his Symphony in C Minor (*Organ*) with growing exaltation: "*Mon maître*, I came out of the Conservatoire bursting with raucous, wild cries.[46] Brühnhilde had awakened so frighteningly that I thought I would die,"[47] etc. In November came Saint-Saëns's response in verse, reproduced at the beginning of this article: "Strange woman, why try to reignite a flame? / I have lived too much, suffered too much, loved too much." We might think that Saint-Saëns sought to distance himself from her. On the second of December, entirely absorbed in the composition of his opera *Ascanio,* he sent Marie this ambiguous message:

> Do not torment yourself and be good. . . . I think of you all the time in depicting my Scozzone, who is all passion and devotion and is loved, but not as she would like to be.
> Only Scozzone represents Italian music, and that's not it at all.
> Your friend, C. Saint-Saëns[48]

Their passionate relationship would gradually wane, for musical reasons. Just as his composition was entering a period of withdrawal into the past, she was pursuing a progressive creative path. Her piano piece *Sphinx* had appeared in the *Album du Gaulois* (1885), foreshadowing a turning point toward experimentation in sound and rhythm that moved away from the post-Romantic style she had previously employed. Could she have been inspired along these lines by a much earlier Saint-Saëns *mélodie*, "Tournoiement, songe d'opium" (Swirling, dream of opium), the sixth of his *Mélodies persanes* (1870–72), based entirely on repetitive sixteenth-note patterns? The idea took shape in works she dedicated to him: *Prisme, Problèmes en musique (Reflets dansants, Reflets chantants)*, published by Heugel in 1888. Like *Sphinx*, these pieces are based on short motives, repeated in numerous variations, with rhythmic changes and transpositions. On 2 August 1893, she wrote to her teacher:

> Cher maître,
>   Ideas, in such profusion and so funny, came to me in a work that I am about to finish that I cannot fail to send to you. It is *Enfer, Purgatoire* and *Paradis*. One doesn't come across music of this kind every day. May it lead you to excuse inconsistencies in behavior that I regret immediately afterward.
>
> M. Jaëll
>
>   I started this work a few weeks ago. *Phryné* had something to do with it, though it doesn't resemble your work.[49]

During this period Marie composed her monumental *Pièces* for piano, referred to above, inspired by Dante's *Inferno*: I. *Ce qu'on entend dans l'enfer;* II. *Ce qu'on entend dans le purgatoire;* III. *Ce qu'on entend dans le paradis.* (What is heard in hell . . . purgatory . . . paradise.) Heugel published them in 1894. Some harmonic elements, inspired by Liszt and Richard Wagner, are still apparent, particularly in the meditative pieces of the third part of the tryptic. Some repeating melodic and rhythmic elements foreshadow aspects of the impressionist musical language but without its harmonic sensuality, notably the lushness of the juxtaposed chords. In contrast, harmony stays in the background to bring attention to the accumulations of succinct motives, repeated to the point of obsession.[50] It is no over-statement to say that, with these pieces, Marie Jaëll created an original langage that allows us, with hindsight, to situate her among the precursors of minimalist music.

Saint-Saëns must have reacted immediately and negatively. As if to avoid passing judgment on her composition, we find in several of his letters a harsh critique of aspects of Marie's piano playing. For instance, writing to Auguste Durand from Algiers on 24 April 1894, he says, "Mme Jaëll gave a concert here last night; as always she played much too fast and used too much pedal, making the music incommunicable and incomprehensible.

But what phenomenal playing. How can I put it to good use, and how can she?"[51] Indeed, Marie wrote to him on 7 August:

What point is there in my sending you my manuscripts?
They contain *very new* ideas. If Liszt were still among us, he would have been enormously pleased by them; he would have gladly said to me: *Forge ahead!* I thought you were similar!

Marie Jaëll

With her *Pièces,* which were apparently never played in concert, Marie Jaëll's inspiration came to an end, except for a short orchestral piece with the moving title *Harmonies d'Alsace* (1917) and her *Paraphrase* for piano of Saint-Saëns's choral piece, *La Lyre et la harpe,* op. 57, which she sent to the composer in 1894 with a message that betrays her fear of him at the time:

Cher maître, I very much wanted to come and see you at home yesterday. But I never dared. I wrote this as a form of greeting.

M. J.[52]

From this we may conclude that Marie Jaëll's creative period corresponded to the time of her close ties to Camille Saint-Saëns. Thus we see how vital the esteem of her venerated *maître* was in stimulating her creative abilities.

Saint-Saëns, a Feminist?

It is surprising, then, that the deep, lasting relationship between Saint-Saëns and Jaëll has been overlooked by the composer's biographers. Although there may not have been physical relations between the two, there was certainly an intense relationship on multiple levels.[53] Both Marie Jaëll and, before her, Clémence de Grandval (1828–1907), were among the few composition students of Saint-Saëns. Born Clémence de Reiset, Grandval was a childhood friend and became Saint-Saëns's student around 1850. The composer's biographers claim he had tender feelings for her. In any event, she benefited from his teaching, as can be seen from the impeccable compositional style of her Trio de salon for oboe, bassoon, and piano, published by Schonenberger in 1851. This highly original work initiated a creative period in all musical genres, especially in sacred music for orchestra, for which Grandval can be placed, with Cécile Chaminade, Augusta Holmès, and Marie Jaëll, as one of the four important French female composers in the latter half of the nineteenth century. As with Jaëll, Saint-Saëns showed his support for Grandval on many occasions, in particular by conducting her symphonic works and opening wide the doors of the Société nationale to her. It was certainly thanks to his influence, along with that of César Franck and Vincent d'Indy (both also famously generous to female musicians), that the Société welcomed no less than fourteen woman composers between 1872 and 1900.[54] When Grandval was awarded the Rossini Prize in 1881, Saint-Saëns, aware of the difficulties women had in attaining recognition, wrote in the press: "[Her *mélodies*] would certainly be famous if their author had not made the mistake— irreparable in the eyes of many—of being a woman."[55] In 1887, along with Gabriel Fauré, he backed Jaëll's admission to the Société des compositeurs de musique in 1887.[56] From its founding in 1862 until 1911, this institution counted in its ranks twenty-eight women out of 395 active members.[57] In 1910, another female composer, Mel (Melanie) Bonis (1858–1937), became one of its secretaries, and the first woman to hold this post, at a time when Camille Saint-Saëns was one of its honorary presidents.[58]

Yet, it is said that after hearing Mel Bonis's Quartet no. 1 in 1906, Saint-Saëns said with surprise, "I never would have thought a woman capable of writing that. She knows all the tricks of the trade."[59] And the following statement about the composer Louise Héritte-Viardot (1841– 1918), Pauline Viardot's eldest daughter, has also been attributed to him:

What a blunder the good Lord committed when he made Louise a woman! She has all the natural gifts, enlighted intelligence, broadness of outlook, erudition, and determination of an altogether superior man. And as an artist! And composer! . . . What inspiration, what talent, what power, what technique, what deep knowledge, what originality (subversive at times), emanate from each of her works! Really, the good Lord made a strange mistake; for if Louise were a man, her genius would bring about a true revolution in music.[60]

This essentialist view of sexual difference is similar to the one he expressed about Augusta Holmès, whose hand in marriage he purportedly sought at least twice.[61] She succeeded in getting recognized by the Paris public with her dramatic symphony *Les Argonautes,* a work that was played not only at the Concerts Pasdeloup but also three times at the Société des Concerts du Conservatoire (in 1880 the press favored it not for the second prize, which it won, but for the first prize of the City of Paris). In his review, however, Saint-Saëns seems very ambiguous about his friend, envious of her courage, perhaps, but also troubled by her independence:

Women are odd when they get seriously involved in art: their primary concern seems to be making people forget they are women and showing a boundless virility, without realizing that this very preoccupation betrays them as women. Like children, women know no obstacles, and their willpower breaks all barriers. Mademoiselle Holmès is certainly a woman: she is outrageous."[62]

Saint-Saëns was not mistaken about Holmès's attraction to elements of music then regarded as masculine, and his generalizations about other female composers are hardly surprising.[63] Both attitudes represent the extreme polarization of the sexes at the time that ascribed essentially different "natures" to men and women. This polarization also influenced writing on music—consider the works of Bernhard Marx, Hugo Riemann, and Vincent d'Indy—and even the very concept of musical language, as recent feminist musicology has shown so convincingly. Such essentialism developed in parallel to the feminist movement, whose adherents were sometimes just as essentialist as their opponents. In reality, the musical world had included women professionally for several centuries, but now was fraught with turmoil. Increasing in their numbers due to the admission of women into the Conservatoire's composition classes in the second half of the nineteenth century, female composers were like other women then gaining access to jobs in competition with male counterparts. The "threat" became even more concrete with the founding of associations and unions of female musicians, such as the Association des femmes artistes et professeurs in 1877 or the Union des femmes professeurs et compositeurs in 1904.[64] Saint-Saëns, incidentally, was a member of the honorary committee of the Union des femmes artistes musiciennes, founded in 1910, along with Jules Massenet, Gabriel Fauré, and Claude Debussy.[65] Occasionally, there were concerts reserved exclusively for works by women. With the controversial admission of women to the Prix de Rome competition in 1903, fear set in.[66] In 1912 Émile Vuillermoz expressed the deep anxieties of his contemporaries in an article titled "Le Péril rose" (The pink peril). A year later, when Lili Boulanger triumphed as the first woman to win the Premier Grand Prix de Rome,[67] he described the situation as, "La Guerre en dentelles" (The War in Lace).

Indeed, the Prix de Rome competition and the 1908 "fugue affair" connected to Nadia Boulanger are perhaps responsible for the image of Saint-Saëns as hostile to women musicians, misleading up till then. In the first round of the competition, Nadia Boulanger, Lili's sister, had written the required fugue for string quartet rather than for voice. Saint-Saëns reacted violently to this failure to comply with the rules and wanted to disqualify her, but the rest of the jury overrode him and allowed her to enter the second round.[68] She went on to obtain only the second grand prize, and also failed to win in 1909. She remained convinced that her being a woman cost her the Premier Grand Prix, a claim supported by Amédée Boutarel who wrote in 1913 about Boulanger's 1908 prize: "She never entered competitions after that, knowing that juries were subject to hostile influences against female candidates."[69] But was it her gender that elicited a hostile response, or her music? In his reply to a letter from Nadia Boulanger in which she denied wanting to "draw attention to herself by a willful pursuit of originality,"[70] Saint-Saëns accused her of having wanted to "dazzle." He concluded:

> You should have been disqualified. Since you weren't, take advantage of the jury's leniency. With your natural gifts, your experience, you have everything you need to succeed. If only you would understand that overshooting the goal is not reaching it, and that the natural and the simple are usually more profitable than the pursuit of an effect.[71]

We could interpret this as the visceral reaction of an established composer, anxious to protect the venerable institution to which he belongs from the flaunted ambition of a young composer eager to break down barriers. But in some ways, it echoes his resistence to a similar ambition in Augusta Holmès, whom he otherwise supported. An element of misogny, thus present in his earlier life, may have increased with the passing of time. We can deduce this aspect of his personalty from a letter to Fauré in 1920. Writing about his resignation from the Board of the Conservatoire, Saint-Saëns explained it was "because it's full of journalists, theater directors, women, because it is no longer composed exclusively of competent people."[72]

Saint-Saëns, like many of his contemporaries, could not bear the transition from exception to rule, represented by the rise of more and more women to highly qualified professions in the early twentieth century. In the nineteenth century, the few woman composers posed no challenge to the "natural" order. Their gender may even have worked in their favor, which explains why, in retrospect, the last third of the century looks like a moment of grace in their difficult history. Marie Jaëll understood well her exceptionalism:

> By the will of God, I am among the chosen ones. It is a responsibility, all the more sacred in that the number of chosen women is negligible. How many others could do as well as me, might even outdo me? But nobody knows what it's like to "be a woman" and become something. It's almost impossible, and it might well turn out to be impossible for me too. I'll only lay down my arms when I'm unable to bear them, when I'm lying beneath them.[73]

—Translated by Catherine Temerson, Jann Pasler, and Alice Teyssier

NOTES

1. The poem is at the Bibliothèque nationale et universitaire de Strasbourg (BnuS), Fonds Marie Jaëll (BnuS, MRS JAËLL 322, Dossier 240) as are all the works by Marie Jaëll mentioned here, except for the *Paraphrase* for piano based on the Camille Saint-Saëns chorus piece, *La Lyre et la harpe*, op. 57, which is at the Bibliothèque nationale de France (BnF) MS. 11925.

2. Camille Saint-Saëns, *Rimes familières* (Paris: Calmann-Lévy, 1890), 21, 39, 43.

3. "Saint-Saëns dirigierte es—sie selbst glich vor dem Klavier einer trunkenen Mänade." Lisa Ramann, *Lisztiana: Erinnerungen an Franz Liszt in Tagebuchblättern, Briefen und Dokumenten aus den Jahren 1873–1886/87* (Mainz: Schott, 1983), 256.

4. Jean Gallois, *Camille Saint-Saëns* (Sprimont, Belgium: Mardaga, 2004), 153.

5. Saint-Saëns and Marie Jaëll were in Liszt's box at the Trocadéro for a performance of his oratorio, *Sainte Elizabeth*, on 8 May 1886, only months before he died. Ibid., 258.

6. Ibid., 154, and *Ménestrel* during these years.

7. Alfred Jaëll, who was of Austrian origin, was also a child prodigy. By 1850, he was considered one of the best pianists of the period, and toured constantly and tirelessly, mastering a large repertoire that ranged from Bach to his contemporaries. With his unfailing virtuosity (he is depicted in caricatures as having ten fingers on each hand), he was praised for his ability to "make the piano sing" in a great variety of colorful sonorities. See Marie-Laure Ingelaere, "Alfred Jaëll, ami de Brahms et de Liszt: Un pionnier," in *Marie Jaëll: Un Cerveau de philosophe,* ed. Laurent Hurpeau (Lyon: Symétrie, 2004), 33–53.

8. *Ménestrel*, 4 June 1865, 215; 24 June 1866, 238; and 5 August 1866, 286.

9. *Ménestrel*, 28 April 1867, 176; and 28 July 1867, 280.

10. Liszt thanked Marie publicly in Rome for her performance of his music there. *Ménestrel*, 2 January 1876, 39.

11. "Puissance de mécanisme," *Ménestrel*, 9 April 1876, 151.

12. *Ménestrel*, 11 April 1875, 152.

13. *Ménestrel*, 9 May 1875, 183. In her *Thematic Catalogue*, Ratner thinks the premiere of this work was not until 1898. Sabina Teller Ratner, *Camille Saint-Saëns, 1835–1921: A Thematic Catalogue of His Complete Works* (Oxford and New York: Oxford University Press, 2002), 87.

14. *Ménestrel*, 7 May 1876, 183. Note that both Michel Duchesneau, working from the printed programs in his *L'Avant-garde musicale et ses sociétés à Paris de 1871 à 1939* (Liège: Mardaga, 1997), 232, and Ratner in her *Thematic Catalogue*, 455, have assumed that the work was premiered at the Société nationale de musique on 13 January 1877.

15. *Ménestrel*, 20 December 1874, 22.

16. *Ménestrel*, 26 January 1890, 32; and 23 February 1890, 63; and Amédée Boutarel, *Ménestrel*, 9 March 1890, 77.

17. *Ménestrel*, 22 February 1876, 102.

18. *Ménestrel*, 19 January 1879, 63.

19. *Ménestrel*, 30 November 1884, 420; and 2 January 1885, 72.

20. *Ménestrel*, 27 January 1889, 31.

21. H. Barbedette, *Ménestrel*, 29 January 1893, 37.

22. Saint-Saëns to Marie Jaëll, 3 December 1895, BnuS, MRS JAËLL 322, Dossier 240.

23. Amédée Boutarel, "Concerts Lamoureux," *Ménestrel*, 27 November 1892, 383.

24. Ibid.

25. *Ménestrel*, 7 May 1876, 183.

26. *Ménestrel*, 20 May 1877, 198. A critic for the *Revue et gazette musicale*, 20 May 1877, 157, commented similarly.

27. *Ménestrel*, 18 May 1879, 200.

28. Correspondence between Franz Liszt and Marie Jaëll, cited in Marie-Laure Ingelaere, "Marie Jaëll, concertiste-compositrice (1870–1917)," *Revue d'Alsace* 125 (1999): 171. This article by Marie-Laure Ingelaere, who supervised the Fonds Jaëll of the BnuS for many years, is the first large-scale study devoted to Marie Jaëll's activities as a composer, along with Marie-Hélène Cautain's master's thesis, "Marie Jaëll interprète et compositeur," Université Paris-Sorbonne (1987).

29. Duchesneau, *L'Avant-garde musicale,* 242.
30. Ingelaere, "Marie Jaëll," 171.
31. *Ménestrel,* 1 June 1884, 215.
32. The meaning here, "femininity," certainly ironic, contrasts with the usual use of the term, increasingly apparent in the fin de siècle.
33. Contrary to Germany, which used the term "Komponistin" starting in the eighteenth century, France would only officially adopt "compositrice" with the 1932–35 edition of the *Dictionnaire de l'Académie Française.* Yet Adrien de La Fage had suggested the usage as early as 1847 in *Revue et gazette musicale de Paris,* in an article titled "Supplément aux deux articles, 'Des Femmes-compositeurs,'" 3 October 1847, 323–25, in response to two articles by Maurice Bourges of 19 September 1847, 305–7, and 26 September 1847, 313–15.
34. *Ménestrel,* 1 February 1885, 72.
35. *Ménestrel,* 7 May 1884, 182.
36. See Michael Stegemann's research on this subject, *Camille Saint-Saëns und das französische Solokonzert von 1850 bis 1920* (Mainz: Schott, 1984).
37. Ernst Burger, *Franz Liszt: Chronique biographique en images et documents* (Paris: Fayard, 1988), 332.
38. Laurent Hurpeau, "Liszt–Jaëll: Une correspondance méconnue," in *Marie Jaëll: Un Cerveau de philosophe,* 92.
39. Alfred Jaëll asked Franz Liszt to help him find an editor for *Valses* in Germany— "Marie would be *so happy!*"—and he added, "I would love to get her Quartet, which you know, published, but that would be more *difficult.*" Letter of 9 June 1876, cited in ibid., 94.
40. Jaëll is author of the poems of her five lieder and of her cycle of *mélodies, Bärenlieder,* and she also wrote the libretti of her symphonic poem with voice, *Ossiane,* her work for chorus and orchestra, *Am Grabe eines Kindes,* and her unfinished opera, *Runéa.* Except for *Ossiane,* whose French version is by Charles Grandmougin, Marie Jaëll authored the French versions of her German-language works as well.
41. This poem was published in the collection *Rimes familières,* 57–59.
42. Camille Saint-Saëns lost his two sons in 1878 in the space of a few weeks: the eldest, André, aged two and a half, fell to his death in his parents' apartment and the younger boy, Jean-François, died of a pulmonary disease at the age of seven months.
43. *Revue et gazette musicale de Paris,* 1 February 1880, 39. This work was first performed in Strasbourg in early 1879, conducted by Franz Stockhausen.
44. Florence Launay, *Les Compositrices en France au XIXe siècle* (Paris: Fayard, 2006), 334–35.
45. Letter quoted by Hurpeau, "Correspondance Jaëll–Saint-Saëns: Une Alsacienne et un maître à penser de la musique française," in *Marie Jaëll: Un Cerveau de philosophe,* 120.
46. The orchestra of the Société des Concerts du Conservatoire performed the work on 9 and 16 January 1887.
47. Letter of January 1887, Fonds Saint-Saëns, Marie Jaëll no. 6, Château-Musée de Dieppe.
48. Letter quoted by Hurpeau, "Correspondance Jaëll–Saint-Saëns," 114. Scozzone, passionately in love with Benvenuto Cellini and deeply jealous of the young Colombe, with whom Cellini and his apprentice Ascanio are both in love, will be stricken with remorse and will sacrifice herself by taking Colombe's place in the coffin where, in a plot devised by herself and the duchess (in love with Ascanio), Colombe was supposed to have suffocated to death. Camille Saint-Saëns dedicated his opera to Pauline Viardot.
49. Letter quoted in ibid., 121. Saint-Saëns's opéra-comique *Phryné* had been premiered in Paris at the Théâtre-Lyrique on the previous 24 May.
50. For more details about these pieces, see Launay, *Les Compositrices,* 224–28; Marie Jaëll, "Le Divin dans la musique," *Ménestrel,* 10 October 1886, 361–62, and 7 November 1886, 391–93. This multi-part article provides the keys to understanding the turning point in her inspiration at that time. Her style of accumulation seems meant to illustrate the "movement of the unitary rhythm of the mute and divine vibrations of light" and "the infinite in the life of rhythm" that she perceived in observing nature; see *Ménestrel,* 7 November 1886, 392.
51. Florence Launay thanks Jann Pasler for providing a copy of this letter from the Médiathèque Musicale Mahler, Paris. See also the letter of 3 December 1895, quoted in note 22 above.

52. Marie-Laure Ingelaere, "Catalogue des œuvres," in Hurpeau, *Marie Jaëll: Un Cerveau de philosophe*, 203, points out that Saint-Saëns gave this piece to Auguste Durand who personally passed it on to Charles Malherbe for his collection of musical scores in manuscript. Currently it is at the BnF Musique, MS. 11925.

53. See Launay, "Les Alliés des compositrices françaises du XIXe siècle," Actes du colloque international et pluridisciplinaire: L'Engagement des hommes pour l'égalité des sexes, February 2010, Institut Émilie du Châtelet, Paris.

54. For a list of the female composers whose works were performed at the Société - nationale de musique between 1872 and 1914, see Launay, *Les Compositrices*, 454–62. Discrimination toward female musicians was nonetheless written into the rules of the Société: "Women will have all the privileges granted to Active, Associate and Honorary Members, but under no circumstances may they be Committee members," BnF Musique, Rés. F. 994 (D, 14). Nadia Boulanger became the first woman member of the Committee in 1919.

55. Camille Saint-Saëns, "Le Prix Rossini," *Journal de musique*, 26 February 1881, 2.

56. The letter of admission is reproduced in Hurpeau, *Marie Jaëll: Un Cerveau de philosophe*, n.p.

57. For a list of the female members of the Société des compositeurs de musique, see Launay, *Les Compositrices*, 465–66.

58. Laure Schnapper, *La Société des compositeurs de musique* (Paris: Université Paris IV-Sorbonne, 1981), 193.

59. Christine Géliot, *Mel Bonis: Femme et "compositeur" (1858–1937)* (Paris: L'Harmattan, 2009), 202.

60. Louis Héritte de La Tour, *Une Famille de grands musiciens: Notes et souvenirs anecdotiques sur Garcia, Pauline Viardot-Garcia, La Malibran, Louise Héritte-Viardot et leur entourage* (Paris: Stock, 1922), vi–vii. This book is a translation of Louise Héritte-Viardot's *Memories and Adventures* (London: Mills & Boon, 1913). The composer's son added a preface to the French edition.

61. Gallois, *Saint-Saëns*, 104.

62. Camille Saint-Saëns, "Les Argonautes," in *Harmonie et mélodie* (Paris: Calmann-Lévy, 1885), 228.

63. See Jann Pasler, "The Ironies of Gender, or Virility and Politics in the Music of Augusta Holmès," *Women & Music* 2 (Fall 1998): 1–25; repr. in *Writing Through Music: Essays on Music, Culture, and Politics* (Oxford and New York: Oxford University Press, 2008), 213–48.

64. See the chapter "Conscience féministe," in Launay, *Les Compositrices*, 144–61. See also Michel (Marie) Daubresse, "Associations et syndicats," *Le Musicien dans la société moderne (1914)* (Paris: Le Monde musical, 1935), 95–113.

65. Marcel-Jean Vilcosqui, *La Femme dans la musique française de 1871 à 1946* (Paris: Université de Paris IV-Sorbonne, 1987), 526.

66. See Annegret Fauser's important article, "*La Guerre en dentelles*: Women and the Prix de Rome in French Cultural Politics," *Journal of the American Musicological Society* 51/1 (Spring 1998): 83–129. See also Launay, *Les Compositrices*, 40–47, 130–33.

67. Émile Vuillermoz, "Le Péril rose," *Musica* 114 (March 1912): 45; and Émile Vuillermoz, "La Guerre en dentelles," *Musica* 131 (August 1913): 153.

68. Lili Boulanger describes this in her *Agenda*, 2 May 1908, quoted in Annegret Fauser, "Comment devenir compositeur? Les Stratégies de Lili Boulanger et de ses contemporaines," in *Nadia Boulanger et Lili Boulanger: Témoignages et études*, ed. Alexandra Laederich and Karol Beffa (Lyon: Symétrie, 2007), 284–85.

69. *Ménestrel*, 15 February 1913, 53.

70. Jérôme Spycket, *Nadia Boulanger* (Lausanne: Payot, 1987), 28.

71. Letter of 10 May 1908, London, quoted and reproduced in ibid., 28–29.

72. Correspondance Saint-Saëns–Fauré, no. 124, 31 July 1920, cited in Jean-Michel Nectoux, *Gabriel Fauré: Les Voix du clair-obscur* (Paris: Flammarion, 1990), 274.

73. Letter to Anna Sandherr, 27 November 1878, BnuS, MRS JAËLL 322, Dossier 244.

Saint-Saëns's Improvisations on the Organ (1862)

WILLIAM PETERSON

As an organist in Paris, Camille Saint-Saëns held positions at Saint-Merri (1853–1858) and La Madeleine (1858–1877). The organs at both churches were constructed by the great organ builder, Aristide Cavaillé-Coll. The one at Saint-Merri (rebuilt in 1857) had three manuals and a pedal division (39 stops). The organ at La Madeleine (1846) had four manuals and a pedal division (48 stops).[1] As a concert organist, Saint-Saëns's reputation extended both inside and outside France. He also published compositions for organ between 1857 and 1919 in various genres: Fantaisie, Prélude et fugue, Sept Improvisations, *Marche réligieuse, Bénédiction nuptiale*.

In 1862 Cavaillé-Coll completed a 36-stop organ for Notre-Dame de Saint-Dizier, 120 miles east of Paris in the Champagne-Ardenne region, with three manual divisions and a pedal division, replacing a 1792 organ by Jean Richard.[2] In the inaugural concert, Saint-Saëns improvised, presenting a formal display of the organ's resources, alongside an organ work

---

PREMIÈRE PARTIE.

1. Improvisations sur les différents jeux de l'orgue	
2. "L'Ascension"	Luigi Bordese
3. Improvisation sur l'orgue ("Pastorale")	
4. "Cantique de Noël"	Adolphe Adam
5. Improvisation sur l'orgue	

SECONDE PARTIE.

6. Improvisations sur les différents jeux de l'orgue	
7. "Ave Maria"	Luigi Cherubini
8. Improvisation sur l'orgue ("Orage")	
9. "Lauda Sion"	
10. Prélude en mi bémol	Sébastien Bach

Figure 1. Program for 1862 Inauguration of the organ built by Cavaillé-Coll for Notre-Dame de Saint-Dizier.

by J. S. Bach and vocal pieces by soloists and the choir.[3] Saint-Saëns often performed at such occasions in Paris: inaugurating organs at Saint-Merri (1857), Saint-Sulpice (1862), Saint-Thomas-d'Aquin (1862), Notre-Dame-de-Paris (1868), and La Trinité (1869).[4]

In 1863, A. Bourdon published a long, detailed commentary on the Saint-Dizier concert, also reflecting on the nature and purpose of improvisations on the program. In conjunction with the blessing of the organ, Saint-Saëns's music seemed like a prayer—"une prière plaintive." Bourdon points to individual organ stops and the musical context in which these stops were heard. In the opening improvisation, Saint-Saëns began with two flutes (the Flute and Bourdon) then added stops to make a crescendo. Saint-Saëns revealed both the soft and the powerful aspects of the organ; Bourdon noted: "You are frightened and transported." In the second improvisation, a kind of "pastorale," the stops seemed all from the string family, beginning with the Viole de gambe. Here the listener could hear a "string quintet," a striking imitation of actual string instruments within a musical context characterized by "delicate" emotions. The third improvisation, just before intermission, struck the writer as a "symphony" of reed stops: initially the Oboe and Clarinet—presumably the Cromorne on the Positif—and eventually the powerful, Trumpets and Les Bombardes.[6]

Particularly valuable is Bourdon's account of the final "Storm" improvisation, a well-known genre at the time:

> The piece was sung . . . a strange noise is heard! It seems that a storm is beginning. It is in the distance now, but one feels that it is approaching . . . *Lightning flashes and thunder rolls in the expanse* . . . and soon the elements, unchained, one against another, no longer seem to obey the voice that holds them captive. The storm bursts—the impetuous wind blows under the vaults of the church. We are all witnesses to one of nature's great cataclysms and we are all transported under the spell of the artist's prodigious talent. It is he who controls the storm . . . It is he who holds the lightning! . . . His rage subsides! Hear the prayer that ascends to heaven! You who have heard these marvelous phenomena, these frightening effects, tell us if it is possible to translate this magnificent improvisation into words![7]

The sequence of episodes closely resembles that found in many published storm pieces from the nineteenth century. Almost always they included the threat of the storm, increasingly violent winds, explosive elements with thunder and lightning, and its aftermath, typically associated with a prayer for recovery from the powerful storm.[8]

If storm fantasies in this period drew on certain stylistic discoveries and achievements from earlier decades (including the *Tè Deum*), these works are with good reason associated with the development of organ building in France, as exemplified by Cavaillé-Coll's growing list of important instruments ready to be inaugurated. There were abundant opportunities for organists to demonstrate these instruments by means of improvisations and composed pieces. By all accounts, Louis James Alfred Lefébure-Wély (1817–1869), well known for improvising storm fantasies, was one of the most important figures within this scene, and a model in some ways for Saint-Saëns's improvisations at the time. Having held the position of organist at Saint-Roch, Lefébure-Wély was appointed to La Madeleine in 1847. From 1863 until his death he served as organist at Saint-Sulpice. Lefébure-Wély turned his attention again and again to the possibilities of presenting scenographic spectacles on the organ. A plan for an organ piece titled "Ocean Voyage" or "Voyage at Sea" centered on a storm at sea and the disruption it brought to the ship's voyage and to its crew. In this plan he delineates the narrative with references to fluctuating dynamic levels on the organ, and he also connects certain moments to specific organ stops: at a pivotal point the "sailors' prayers" ought to be presented, he writes, with a "soft, reverent melody" on the Voix humaine stop.[9] On one memorable occasion, as Lefébure-Wély improvised a storm on the new Cavaillé-Coll organ in Ghent in 1856, the gas lights were dimmed, presumably to heighten the listener's experience of the storm.[10] Lefébure-Wély was heard at inaugural recitals for seven Cavaillé-Coll instruments between 1855 and 1863.[11]

A notable repertoire of substantial published storm pieces connected directly or indirectly to the organ arose in the second half of the century in France.[12] The mid-nineteenth-century storm fantasy, improvised or composed, was a spectacle in sound, providing listeners with a literally astonishing experience. Though it depends on an elaborate sequence of distinctive and contrasting sounds arranged in an episodic formal structure, the technological innovation of the thunder pedal was, for better or worse, an important triggering mechanism facilitating the storm music. Often referred to as *effet d'orage* or *tonnerre* (storm effect or thunder), the thunder pedal was a combination pedal—one of several *pédales de combinaisons*—usually at the extreme left above the bottom pedal keys and thus often listed as the first of the combination pedals in a stop list.[13] The use of the thunder pedal was one of several techniques that aimed to produce special effects in the bass register. In some musical scores, composers of storm fantasies supplied directions describing performing techniques that had become well established by the middle of the century. For example, at the end of the score of his *La Procession de la fête d'un village, surprise par un orage* (Village festival procession surprised by a storm) of 1863, Blanc supplies an explanation of how to create the wind and thunder effects.[14] First, the organist should place the feet across the pedal keys, using varying numbers of keys. Then, on organs lacking a pedal keyboard, one should use the forearm, allowing it to roll back and forth, depending on the effect desired.

In simplest terms, the storm fantasy is an extended, episodic composition that depicts in music the power—even the threatening power—of nature. One episode leads magically to another, in part because the resources of the Cavaillé-Coll organs are ready to be deployed, as needed, for the fluctuating dynamic levels—a dramatic decrescendo could be produced within just one measure.[15] The fantasy, then, offers both the player and the listener an opportunity to hear sharply contrasting timbres and dynamic levels characteristic of the instrument—from the individual flute, perhaps supporting an oboe melody (in a pastoral passage), to the thunderous full organ ensemble that might well be used for the climactic storm episode.

In his concert at Saint-Dizier in 1862, Saint-Saëns found the improvised storm an appropriate vehicle for demonstrating the resources of their new Cavaillé-Coll instrument. The improvisation, to judge from the published account, was both vivid and successful. The improvised storm found its place near the end of his program, after the improvisations in other genres. Indeed, a consideration of the order of improvisations in the two-part inaugural concert raises a number of issues with regard to Saint-Saëns's overall plan. He obviously intended to provide demonstrations of both individual stops and small combinations of stops, as well as the full-organ sonority in both parts of the concert. The crescendo and decrescendo possibilities explored in the opening improvisation revealed to listeners the power of the three-manual organ. Yet, in the second improvisation, a kind of pastoral fantasy, he explored the string stops in an improvisation that would have been, from a timbral perspective, monochromatic. The second half of the concert was planned, it seems, to demonstrate other—more colorful—sonorities and how the new organ presented a wide variety of textures. In the opening improvisation, Saint-Saëns started with the individual Flute stop followed by an exploration of string stops within modulatory passages, revealing to listeners "a new harmonic world." He then presented gentle sounds not yet heard in the concert: the Voix céleste, which would have been coupled with the Viole de gambe on the Récit division, and the Unda Maris stop. The shimmering effect created by these stops led Bourdon to think of "a sweet prayer about the waves of the ocean."[16] The final improvisation, the storm fantasy, was the traditional vehicle for demonstrating the full range of sonic possibilities within the framework of a single musical statement (here, a single improvisation) and in the service of a well-known musical program. With good reason, Bourdon praised Saint-Saëns for bringing to listeners "improvisations that were not only brilliant but highly varied."[17]

Saint-Saëns obviously treasured the opportunities he found for exploring the art of improvisation, not only in inaugural concerts but also in church services. As a functioning organist, Saint-Saëns dedicated himself to improvisation. "During the twenty years I played the organ at the Madeleine, I improvised constantly, giving my fancy the widest range. That was one of the joys of life."[18] As we have seen, the organ itself was part of the appeal of improvisation. "To play freely with the colors on his vast palette, there is but one way—he must plunge boldly into improvisation,"[19] he once explained. "It is improvisation alone which permits one to employ all the resources of a large instrument, and to adapt oneself to the infinite variety of organs."[20] And, "Between the *pianissimo* which almost reaches the limit where sound ceases and silence begins, down to a range of formidable and terrifying power, every degree of intensity can be obtained from this magical instrument."[21]

The importance of improvisation for Saint-Saëns, however, went beyond the challenge offered by the organ as an instrument. As he observed, "The practice of improvisation frequently develops faculties of invention which, without it, would have remained latent."[22] For him, "Necessity, and the inspiring character of the instrument, sometimes accomplishes what meditation is unable to achieve."[23] Although Saint-Saëns never published any storm fantasies for the organ, his improvisations were sometimes a stimulus for composition: "It may excite surprise to learn that the Andante of my first Sonata for piano and violoncello, and the conclusion of my Symphony in C Minor, were created on the manuals of the organ."[24]

From time to time in his writings, Saint-Saëns stressed broader issues associated with improvisation. First, he underlined the importance of preparation and education to facilitate the art of improvisation. A. M. Henderson, a visiting organist at Saint-Merri in 1906, recalled a remark Saint-Saëns made on the need for improvisatory skills: "You have many fine organists in England, but few good improvisers. It is an art you do not sufficiently practice or study, and it needs to be practiced and studied."[25] In his article on "Music in the Church," Saint-Saëns also spoke with pride of the important place improvisation held in the program of organ studies at the Conservatoire. To him an ideal program was one that allowed organ students to study not only technique and "execution" but also improvisation.[26]

Second, Saint-Saëns acknowledged the importance of working with models of improvisation and endeavoring to develop one's own style or aesthetic. On several occasions he pointed to the improvisations of Lefébure-Wély as a model. While acknowledging that these had many fine qualities, Saint-Saëns felt they could be marred by a "frivolous and secular style." The style that Saint-Saëns developed was one that depended, in part, on the use of chant melodies and on contrapuntal procedures. In one of his essays, he explained that sometimes within the Mass he focused his improvisation on plainchant. Saint-Saëns, for whom Bach's music was a model throughout his career, also improvised on the organ in church using fugues and counterpoint in two, three, and four voices—aspects of his music associated with a more severe style.[27]

Joseph Bonnet, one of the greatest organists of his day to hear Saint-Saëns improvise, explains the appeal of this music for his contemporaries: "No one who has had the pleasure of hearing him will ever forget his extraordinary improvisations, so authentically classic in style and so dazzling in their virtuosity."[28]

Figure 2. Caricature of Saint-Saëns with organ pipe legs, keyboard waistline, and full organ headpiece.

NOTES

1. For stoplists of these organs, see Jesse Eschbach, *Aristide Cavaillé-Coll: Aspects of his Life and Work: A Compendium of Known Stoplists by Aristide Cavaillé-Coll: 1838–1898*, vol. 1 (Paderborn: Verlag Peter Ewers, 2005).

2. For an account of the organ at Saint-Dizier, see Kurt Lueders, "Rappel historique," in *L'Orgue Aristide Cavaillé-Coll de l'église Notre-Dame de Saint-Dizier: Relevé technique par Laurent Plet, facteur d'orgues*. Published by *La Flûte harmonique*, special number 66/67/68 (1993) 2–8. For stoplists, see Eschbach's *Compendium*.

3. The program in Figure 1 is reconstructed from one in Rollin Smith's *Saint-Saëns and the Organ* (Stuyvesant, NY: Pendragon Press, 1992). Consideration has also been given to similar programs in A. Bourdon's *Notice sur le Grand Orgue de Notre-Dame de Saint-Dizier construit par M. Cavaillé-Coll* [sic], *facteur d'orgues à Paris* (Bar-le-Duc: N. Rolin, 1863), Orpha Ochse's *Organists and Organ Playing in Nineteenth-Century France and Belgium* (Bloomington & Indianapolis: Indiana University Press, 1994), and my recent article "Stormfantasieën voor het 19de-eeuwse orgel" as edited by Luk Bastiaens in *Orgelkunst* 33/2 (2010): 52–68. Bourdon reports that the Adam and Cherubini pieces on this program were sung by soloists and that both "L'Ascension" and "Lauda Sion" were sung by the choir of Notre-Dame de Saint-Dizier.

4. See Rollin Smith, *Saint-Saëns and the Organ*, for a discussion of the events at Saint-Merri (35–36), Saint-Sulpice (66–69), Saint-Thomas-d'Aquin (71–73), Saint-Dizier (73–75), Notre-Dame de Paris (87–90), and La Trinité (93–96).

5. A. Bourdon, *Notice sur le grand orgue de Notre-Dame*, 29–33. Thanks to Kurt Lueders for providing access to the reprint of this book. See Smith, *Saint-Saëns and the Organ*, for a reconstruction in English of the 1862 program (73).

6. Ibid., 29–31.

7. Ibid., 32–33. Translation adapted from Smith, *Saint-Saëns and the Organ*, 75.

8. See William J. Peterson, "Storm Fantasies for the Nineteenth-Century Organ in France," *Keyboard Perspectives: Yearbook of the Westfield Center for Historical Keyboard Studies* 2 (2009): 1–29. For a discussion of the development of the storm fantasy and how the resources of the Cavaillé-Coll organ are used in published compositions by Clément Loret, Louis James Alfred Lefébure-Wély, and Jaak Nikolaas Lemmens, see esp. 18–29.

9. Fenner Douglass, *Cavaillé-Coll and the Musicians*, 2 vols. (Raleigh, NC: Sunbury, 1980), 1:110.

10. See Peterson, "Storm Fantasies," 1.

11. Kurt Lueders, "Louis-James-Alfred Lefébure-Wély," in *Le Grand-Orgue de Saint-Sulpice et ses organistes*. Published by *La Flûte harmonique*, special number 59/60 (1991): 41.

12. The following five representative works were published, for the most part, in the 1860s and 1870s: Georges Schmitt, *Offertoire pour la Pentecôte* (*Le Musée de l'organiste* 1/15, probably 1857); J. Blanc, *La Procession de la fête d'un village surprise par un orage* ("Tableau musical") (1863); Louis-James-Alfred Lefébure-Wély, *Scène pastorale (pour une inauguration d'orgue ou messe de minuit)* (ca. 1867); Jacques-Nicolas Lemmens, Grand Fantasia in E Minor ("The Storm") (1866); and Clément Loret, *Fantaisie pastorale* (probably 1877).

13. For a thumbnail description of the device, see Peter Williams and Barbara Owen, *The New Grove Musical Instruments Series: The Organ* (New York: W. W. Norton, 1988), 315. See also Kurt Lueders, "Reflections on the Esthetic Evolution of the Cavaillé-Coll Organ," in *Charles Brenton Fisk: Organ Builder*, 2 vols. (Easthampton, MA: Westfield Center for Early Keyboard Studies, 1986), 1:137.

14. Here is written "Manière d'imiter le tonnerre" (Method for imitating thunder).

15. The system of ventil pedals (*pédales de combinaisons*) made a decrescendo a fairly simple operation. In one measure of his *Fantaisie pastorale* Loret calls for the organist to remove the grand orgue reeds, the Positif reeds, and the pedal reeds on three of the successive beats, which could be done by pressing three ventil pedals in succession (measure 166).

16. Bourdon, *Notice sur le grand orgue*, 32.

17. Ibid., 32–33.

18. Camille Saint-Saëns, "The Organ," in *Musical Memories* (London: John Murray, 1921), 107.

19. Ibid., 104.

20. Camille Saint-Saëns, "Music in the Church," *Musical Quarterly* 2 (1916): 8.

21. Saint-Saëns, "The Organ," 101–2.

22. Saint-Saëns, "Music in the Church," 8.

23. Ibid.

24. Ibid.

25. A. M. Henderson, "Memories of Some Distinguished French Organists: Saint-Saëns," *Musical Times* 78 (1937): 535–36.

26. Saint-Saëns, "Music in the Church," 8.

27. Ibid., 7. Reports on performances from the 1850s (the inaugural concert at Saint-Merri) to the 1890s (improvisations at Saint-Séverin) provide detailed accounts of Saint-Saëns's improvisations of fugues. See Smith, *Saint-Saëns and the Organ*, 35–36, for critical commentary on the improvisations "in fugal style" in 1857 at Saint-Merri; and see 191–92, for the improvisation of "counterpoint in two, three or four voices" and fugues at Saint-Séverin, presumably in the 1890s.

28. Joseph Bonnet, *Historical Organ-Recitals: In Six Volumes* (New York: Schirmer, 1929), 5:viii–ix. See also the Duchesneau essay in this volume for a description of the role Bonnet may have played regarding Saint-Saëns and the Société musicale indépendante.

Providing Direction for French Music: Saint-Saëns and the Société Nationale

MICHAEL STRASSER

Throughout the first two decades of his career, Camille Saint-Saëns, like many other French composers of his generation, was continually frustrated by public and critical indifference to his musical creations. Adolphe Botte, writing in *Revue et gazette musicale*, described the situation confronted by serious young composers in Second Empire Paris. "Everyone tells you that M. Saint-Saëns is a serious, educated artist; but no one will play his works for you. It is like that in Paris—a dozen young musicians about whom people speak only with a certain gravity, and whom the public does not know, and perhaps never will."[1]

Although interest in "serious"—that is, non-theatrical—music showed signs of increasing during the 1860s, it was only after the twin catastrophes of the Franco-Prussian War and the Commune uprising prompted a period of national self-examination that French audiences began to embrace the musical values represented by concert and chamber music, together with the young French composers who wrote such music. In December 1872, Saint-Saëns lauded the emergence of a new school of French music that, he argued, deserved encouragement. "But," he added, "it is young, subject to lose its way, and is in need of direction."[2]

To provide such direction to the emerging national school of young French musicians, Saint-Saëns banded together in 1871 with his good friend Romain Bussine, Alexis de Castillon, and several other French musicians to found the Société nationale de musique (SN).[3] The statutes clearly spelled out its philosophy: "The goal of the society is to further the production and popularization of all serious musical works. To encourage and to bring to light, as much as is in its power, all musical endeavors, in whatever form may take, on condition that they reveal elevated and artistic aspirations on the part of the author."[4]

The emphasis on "serious musical works" that would "reveal elevated and artistic aspirations on the part of the author" was a conscious response to the mood of reform and renewal permeating French intellectual life just after the Franco-Prussian War. It speaks to the high moral purpose behind the establishment of the SN. This would not merely be a forum for the introduction of new works, but an instrument for national renewal through art.

The founders envisioned their new organization as a private association rather than a public concert society—a refuge where members would participate in the study and performance of one another's compositions as a kind of "brotherhood, with absolute disregard for self-interest."[5] The SN would be governed by an elected committee, responsible for examining new works submitted by members, composing concert programs, and managing finances, logistics, and other administrative details. In one of the first official acts of the newly formed organization, Bussine was elected

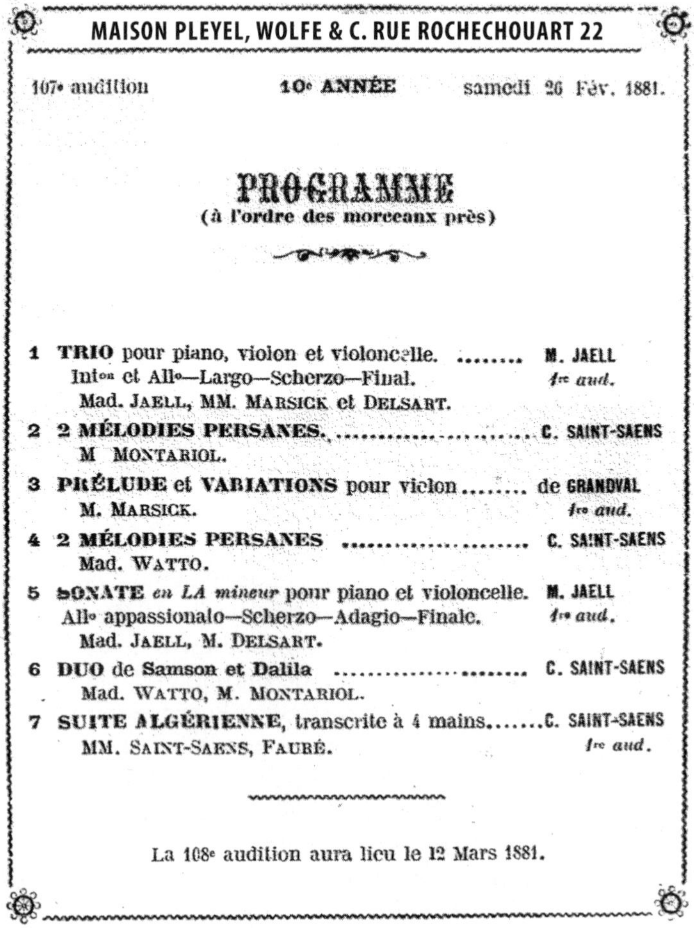

MAISON PLEYEL, WOLFE & C. RUE ROCHECHOUART 22

107ᵉ audition   **10ᵉ ANNÉE**   samedi 26 Fév. 1881.

PROGRAMME
(à l'ordre des morceaux près)

1 **TRIO** pour piano, violon et violoncelle. .... M. JAELL
     Intᵒⁿ et Allᵒ—Largo—Scherzo—Final.   1ᵉ aud.
     Mad. JAELL, MM. MARSICK et DELSART.
2 **2 MÉLODIES PERSANES.** .... C. SAINT-SAENS
     M MONTARIOL.
3 **PRÉLUDE et VARIATIONS** pour violon .... de GRANDVAL
     M. MARSICK.   1ᵉ aud.
4 **2 MÉLODIES PERSANES** .... C. SAINT-SAENS
     Mad. WATTO.
5 **SONATE** en *LA mineur* pour piano et violoncelle. M. JAELL
     Allᵒ appassionato—Scherzo—Adagio—Finale.   1ᵉ aud.
     Mad. JAELL, M. DELSART.
6 **DUO** de Samson et Dalila .... C. SAINT-SAENS
     Mad. WATTO, M. MONTARIOL.
7 **SUITE ALGÉRIENNE**, transcrite à 4 mains....... C. SAINT-SAENS
     MM. SAINT-SAENS, FAURÉ.   1ᵉ aud.

La 108ᵉ audition aura lieu le 12 Mars 1881.

Figure 1. Société nationale, Program for Concert no. 107, 26 February 1881.

president, and Saint-Saëns vice president. Both men would retain their positions for the organization's first fifteen years.

During the 1870s, the SN grew in stature and prestige, garnering much praise from the more open-minded critics in the musical press for its efforts to promote the music of young French composers. In contrast, conservative critics, notably those writing in Léon Escudier's *L'Art musical*, viewed it, with some justification, as a veritable nest of Wagnerians, intent on subverting what they perceived as the traditional values of French music.[6]

Saint-Saëns, who was often accused by these same conservative critics of pro-Wagnerian tendencies, was the SN's most vocal defender during the 1870s, using his position as the most visible and respected of his nation's young composers to counter critics' accusations, notably in an article which appeared in *Harmonie et mélodie*.[7] He protested that the conservatives' portrayal of the SN as a "coterie of intolerance and mutual admiration" was false, and insisted that intolerance was impossible there because "the members come together on one point only, the cult of serious music, and separate on all others."[8] He pointed out that the Committee contained both "reactionary classicists and advanced Wagnerians, who are no less intelligent for that. It's a *cénacle*, if you wish; it is scarcely a *coterie*."[9]

Saint-Saëns' use of the words *cult* and *cénacle* to describe the SN's membership is revealing, and somewhat undermines his claim to tolerance. The "cult of serious music" did constitute a sort of artistic religion, and though there was indeed a certain degree of receptivity among the faithful to different interpretations of the scriptures, there was at the same time a marked disdain for those unwashed heathens who insisted on dwelling in the lower reaches of vulgarity and simple-mindedness.

Over the first several decades of its existence, the SN hosted around eleven concerts per year, most of which could be classified as chamber concerts, held on Saturday evenings at Salle Pleyel, the small concert hall operated by the piano firm Pleyel, Wolff, et Cie on rue de Rochechouart. Beginning in 1874, the SN also staged an average of two orchestral concerts per year, one at the more spacious Salle Érard and the other, featuring a smaller ensemble, at Salle Pleyel.

Concert no. 107, of 26 February 1881, fell near the middle of the SN's tenth season. The audience for this and other chamber concerts would have consisted of members of the SN—composers, other musicians, and interested amateurs—their invited guests, and critics. Attendance at chamber concerts probably averaged between one and two hundred, and that for orchestral concerts might be twice as large.[10]

For those who think of the SN primarily as a chamber music society, the program offers an unexpected mix of chamber music, *mélodies*, a vocal excerpt from an opera, and a transcription of an orchestral work. The SN indeed played a large role in the growth of a viable school of French chamber music in the late nineteenth century. Fauré, for one, acknowledged that he might not have written chamber music but for the stimulus provided by the SN,[11] and sometimes composers were actively encouraged to compose new chamber works for SN concerts.[12] One can speculate that perhaps some of the masterpieces of late nineteenth-century French chamber music might not have been composed except for the opportunity provided by the organization. Yet chamber works did not dominate the programs, and at some concerts, no chamber music was performed.

From 1871 to 1881, works by Saint-Saëns appeared ninety-nine times on SN programs; no other composer even approached this total.[13] During the 1870s, he was clearly the most popular of the new generation of French composers, not only at the SN but at Sunday orchestral concerts as well.[14] Thus it is not surprising to see that his name figures prominently on this program.

Also noteworthy, but not unusual, is the appearance here of works by two women composers. Over the first two decades of the organization's existence, works by women composers were performed at eighty-two, or roughly 38 percent of the 215 concerts, and thirty-one of those concerts included more than one work by a female composer. Compositions by Augusta Holmès, Cécile Chaminade, Marie Renaud, Pauline Viardot and her daughter Louise Héritte-Viardot were heard at SN concerts during the 1870s and '80s, as well as music by the two women listed on the program of Concert no. 107: Marie Jaëll and the Vicomtesse de Grandval (née Marie Rieset). A string quartet by Jaëll had been programmed in 1876, and she had performed her Piano Concerto in D Minor at an SN orchestral concert in May 1877.[15] Grandval's suite for flute and piano had been heard at one of the organization's first concerts, on 13 January 1872, and since then her name had appeared over fifty times on its SN programs. The statutes drawn up in 1871 had stipulated that women would be eligible for all the privileges of membership in the SN (although they were specifically excluded from service on their Committee), and it is clear that women composers were indeed welcomed and treated as equals at SN concerts.

As both Jaëll and Grandval had studied with Saint-Saëns, he undoubtedly offered them encouragement and, possibly, support when the Committee was considering one of their works for possible performance. The fact that the Vicomtesse de Grandval often offered additional financial support to the SN above and beyond the amount of her yearly dues probably made the Committee more inclined to program her compositions. But both of these women had achieved the status of serious composers, with their works occasionally performed on the city's orchestral concerts. Grandval, who was the more

Figure 2. Marie Jaëll.

prolific of the two, also appeared with some regularity on programs of chamber music societies. If her works did not meet with the enthusiastic approbation that was often showered on those of Augusta Holmès (the most prominent female composer on the Parisian scene), she was certainly accorded the status of a respected musician by the critics.

The program for Concert no. 107 offers some insight into the extent to which member composers participated in performances (see Figure 1). Works performed at the SN often featured the composer at the keyboard as part of a chamber ensemble or as accompanist for a soloist, as in the performance of Marie Jaëll's new piano trio. As was stipulated in the statutes, members often assisted one another with performances, and thus we find Saint-Saëns accompanying the violinist Martin Marsick in the premiere of Grandval's *Prélude et variations* at Concert no. 107. Works calling for piano four-hands or two pianos were often performed by the composer and other SN members. Saint-Saëns frequently joined with Fauré and others in such collaborations, as he did in this performance of an arrangement of the *Suite algérienne*.

Saint-Saëns appeared fairly often as a performer at SN concerts, playing his own works (thirty-two times over fifteen years) and those of other members, both the famous—Fauré, d'Indy, and Franck, for example—and the unknown. Among the lesser-known figures whose works Saint-Saëns performed were Paul Lacombe (in 1872), Victor Sieg and Octave Fouque (1876), and Emile Bernard (1877). In sum, he participated as soloist or member of an ensemble in performances of forty-two works by other composers during his time as an SN member. In addition, he conducted two of his works at SN orchestral concerts.

Members also participated in larger ensembles. They banded together to perform choral works, although the quality of the SN chorus evidently left something to be desired. It was often singled out for criticism, as in an anonymous review from 1876, which stated that the chorus was "composed of members who were endowed with any kind of voice, and among whom the vice president and soul of the Committee, M. Saint-Saëns, bravely took his part."[16] Although the SN contracted with professionals to perform in orchestral concerts, even here members could sometimes be counted upon to participate, primarily to save money. In a 1910 letter concerning a proposed concert series, d'Indy informed Paul-Marie Masson that he could minimize costs if he and some friends played percussion parts, "as we used to do at the Société nationale, where there were always composers who could play triangle or cymbals."[17]

When their works were chosen for inclusion on an SN program composers were responsible for providing performers, and the prestige of performing before an audience that included many of the most esteemed figures in the Parisian music world enticed the city's finest instrumentalists and singers. Martin Marsick and Jules Delsart, who appeared several times on Concert no. 107, would certainly have been included on any list of the finest string players in Paris. In addition to their solo performances, they had founded a quartet in 1876 that featured on its programs works by young French composers.[18]

Many of the singers who appeared on SN programs were familiar to Parisian audiences. Some were fixtures in Parisian opera houses since before the war, and others were just beginning their careers, having won Conservatoire prizes during the early 1870s and then moving on to establish their names on the city's lyric stages.

Though some of the works performed on Concert no. 107 were new, others would have been familiar to listeners from other venues. For example, *Suite algérienne* had been premiered at the Concerts Colonne on 19 December 1880 and several times at the Sunday orchestral concerts before it was heard in a transcription for piano four-hands at the SN. This was not unusual. Many of the orchestral works heard in piano reduction at SN chamber concerts were staples of the orchestral repertoire in Paris. Saint-Saëns's *Marche héroïque*, for example, was performed at the first SN concert, and on three subsequent occasions, and his *Le Rouet d'Omphale* was played three times during the 1870s.

Because such works were performed often in Paris, their composers obviously had no need to hear them performed at the SN to judge the results of their efforts, and they were probably well known to SN members. The inclusion of piano reductions of such popular compositions on SN chamber programs may thus have been motivated by a desire by composers or their publishers to advertise the availability of piano reductions for the home market. Or these pieces may have been included simply because the Committee occasionally had trouble filling out a program with appropriate chamber works, a supposition supported by statements made by Saint-Saëns in his 1880 article on the SN. "[French] composers have a marked tendency to neglect chamber music in favor of orchestral music. . . . And the Committee of the Société nationale, which does not receive enough duos, trios, and quartets to fill the programs of the ordinary concerts, must address itself to a pile of [orchestral] scores of which it can execute only a small number."[19]

Throughout the 1870s Saint-Saëns was clearly an active and enthusiastic participant in the activities of the organization he had helped to found; his works were programmed often, he performed there frequently, and he was heavily involved in the society's administration. But by the end of the tenth SN season, it was clear that the sense of common purpose that had motivated the membership during the postwar period had begun to dissipate, and the philosophical and stylistic differences between the group's "reactionary classicists and advanced Wagnerians" had become more pronounced. At the end of the 1880–81 season the Franckists—that is, the "advanced Wagnerians"—took complete control of the Committee and there is evidence that Saint-Saëns began to reduce his involvement in SN affairs at this point. Although there had always been times when he was unable to attend Committee meetings due to the demands of his performing career, with each passing year, beginning in the early 1880s, Saint-Saëns's absences became much more frequent.[20]

The final and decisive break came in November 1886, when d'Indy and his allies succeeded in amending the statutes to allow for the performance of chamber works by foreign composers. (Orchestral concerts would continue to be restricted to works by French composers.) It is difficult to understand how Saint-Saëns could have objected to this proposal on its face. He had always allied himself with the idea of artistic freedom and openness, and was certainly receptive to the music and ideas of non-French composers. In the name of artistic freedom, he had vigorously defended Wagner against narrow-minded and jingoistic critics during the 1870s, and had put his ideals into practice through his occasional participation in performances of works by d'Indy and other "advanced" composers at SN concerts.[21]

As enthusiasm for Wagner's music grew in the 1880s, however, Saint-Saëns became ever more disturbed by the increasing arrogance and self-righteousness of the Wagnerians. Their successful push to admit foreign music at SN chamber concerts must have seemed one more galling indication that the Franckists were determined to impose their will. The "cult of pure music" to which Saint-Saëns had so enthusiastically subscribed in the previous decade had been taken over by a priesthood that brooked no disagreement on matters of aesthetic faith. His beloved Société nationale had been taken over by young musicians he classified as "sectarians."[22] It is little wonder he felt increasingly alienated from them. In the end, both Saint-Saëns and Bussine, rather than follow the increasingly narrow path laid out by the organization's younger members, decided to abandon the organization they had founded and worked so tirelessly to nurture for some fifteen years.[23]

Given the circumstances of his departure, it might seem surprising to find that Saint-Saëns's works were occasionally performed at SN concerts for the next fifteen years. One might reasonably conclude that Gabriel Fauré, who was a respected member of the Committee throughout this period, might have been largely responsible for the continued inclusion of Saint-Saëns's music on SN programs. On 21 January 1887, Fauré wrote to his old friend asking him if he would attend the premiere of his new piano quartet (no. 2 in G Minor), which would occur the following night at an SN concert. Two days later, Saint-Saëns replied, stating that he had not attended the concert "1. Because I will never go there again. 2. Because I had to spend the evening working."[24] In one of the saddest ironies of his career, Saint-Saëns's bitterness over the the Franckists and other French Wagnerians eventually led him to adapt some of the same Wagnerphobic attitudes against which he had once fought so valiantly, violating his own deeply held principles of artistic freedom in the process.[25]

Unfortunately, the events that led to his resignation from the SN and an increasingly acrimonious conflict with the Franckists tend to overshadow Saint-Saëns's contributions to the cause of new French music during the crucial years after the Franco-Prussian War. Throughout the 1870s, in the face of withering attacks by conservative critics, he valiantly and eloquently defended the ideas and music of young French composers. The Société nationale was infused from the beginning by his artistic ideals, and it was in no small part due to his efforts that the SN became an important vehicle for the promotion of a new style of serious French music. Even after his departure, the organization continued to provide a forum for the most adventurous new French music, and set the stage for the leading role that French composers would play in the century to come.

NOTES

1. Adolphe Botte, "Auditions musicales," *Revue et gazette musicale* (15 April 1860): 162.

2. Phémius [Camille Saint-Saëns], "Musique," *La Renaissance littéraire et artistique* (28 December 1872): 285.

3. Bussine, a singer, was appointed professor of voice at the Conservatoire in 1872 and retained that post for the rest of his career. Castillon was one of Franck's earliest composition students. Others involved in the creation of the SN included César Franck, Jules Massenet, Gabriel Fauré, Henri Duparc, and Théodore Dubois. See Michael C. Strasser, "Ars Gallica: The Société nationale de musique and Its Role in French Musical Life, 1871–1891" (PhD diss., University of Illinois at Urbana-Champaign, 1998), 125–42, for details about the society's founding.

4. The original statutes, written in the hand of Alexis de Castillon and signed by him, Saint-Saëns, and Jules Garcin, are located in Bibliothèque nationale de France (BnF), Musique, Rés. 994, D3.

5. Ibid., "fraternellement, avec l'oubli absolu de soi-même."

6. See Michael Strasser, "The Société Nationale and Its Adversaries: The Musical Politics of *l'Invasion germanique* in the 1870s," *19th-Century Music* 24/3 (Spring 2001): 225–51.

7. Camille Saint-Saëns, "La Société nationale de musique," in *Harmonie et mélodie* (Paris: Calmann-Lévy, 1885), 207–15.

8. Ibid., 213.

9. Ibid. A cenacle is, literally, an upper room, and the term is often used to refer to the room in which the Last Supper took place. It is sometimes used to describe a literary group. A coterie implies a clique. Saint-Saëns is hinting at the almost sacred—and certainly serious-minded— character of the SN and pointedly denying that it was a shallow and self-interested clique, as conservatives suggested.

10. See Strasser, "Ars Gallica," 146–68, for information on the membership of the SN, and 205–9 for information on attendance at SN concerts.

11. Jean-Michel Nectoux, *Gabriel Fauré: A Musical Life*, trans. Roger Nichols (Cambridge: Cambridge University Press, 1991), 80.

12. Strasser, "Ars Gallica," 395–96.

13. Fauré was next, with fifty-seven performances. Other composers whose names appeared at least thirty times on SN programs from 1871 to 1881 included the Vicomtesse de Grandval (54), Charles Lefebvre (50), Théodore Dubois (49), Édouard Lalo (41), César Franck (39), and Georges Pfeiffer (30).

14. During that decade, his works were played thirty-nine times at Pasdeloup's Concerts populaires, sixty-four times at the Concerts Colonne, and six times at the staid Société des Concerts du Conservatoire, where new French music was still considered exotic fare. No other French composer received more than two performances at the Conservatoire concerts during the 1870s.

15. See the Launay-Pasler essay on Jaëll in this volume.

16. "Concerts et auditions musicales," *Revue et gazette musicale de Paris* (17 May 1876): 150.

17. Vincent d'Indy to Paul-Marie Masson, 29 December 1910, BnF Musique.

18. Beginning with the 1880–81 season, the SN engaged the Marsick-Delsart Quartet as its "official" quartet, a move that increased the organization's stature while relieving composers of the necessity of securing their own performers for chamber works. See Michael Strasser, "Grieg, the Société nationale, and the Origins of Debussy's String Quartet," in *Berlioz and Debussy: Sources, Contexts and Legacies: Essays in Honour of François Lesure*, ed. Barbara L. Kelly and Kerry Murphy (Aldershot, Eng.: Ashgate Publishing, 2007), 108–9.

19. Saint- Saëns, "La Société nationale de musique," 214.

20. During the 1881–82 season Saint-Saëns attended only seventeen of thirty-three Committee meetings. In the following two seasons, he was counted as present at twenty of thirty and sixteen of thirty-two meetings, respectively. In 1884–85, however, Saint-Saëns was present at only eight of the twenty-five meetings, and during his last season with the SN (1885–86), he attended only three of the twenty-seven Committee meetings.

21. For example, on 10 March 1877, Saint-Saëns joined d'Indy in performing a piano four-hands arrangement of the latter's *Ouverture d'Antoine et Cléopâtre*. He also played the piano part in the premiere of Franck's Quintet on 17 January 1880.

22. Saint-Saëns, *Harmonie et mélodie*, xx–xxi.

23. For information on the internal politics of the Société nationale during the early 1880s, see Strasser, "Ars Gallica," 369–466.

24. Camille Saint-Saëns and Gabriel Fauré, *Correspondance (1862–1920)*, ed. Jean-Michel Nectoux (Paris: Editions Klincksieck, 1994), 53.

25. See, in particular, Camille Saint-Saëns, *Germanophilie* (Paris: Dorbon-Ainé, 1916).

Saint-Saëns as President of the Société des Compositeurs (1887–1891)

LAURE SCHNAPPER

In November 1886, Vincent d'Indy succeeded in reforming the Société nationale de musique, founded originally to promote French composers who belonged to the association. Opening it to programs with classical works and, to a smaller extent, to foreign composers provoked the resignation of Romain Bussine, its president, as well as that of Saint-Saëns, another Société nationale founder and its honorary president since 1872. Saint-Saëns then turned to the Société des compositeurs de musique, the Society of Composers, to which he had belonged for many years.[1] Already greatly renowned, he was elected its president, taking the place of Victorin Joncières (1839–1903).

The Société des compositeurs was a learned society that, since its foundation in 1862, had organized conferences and lecture-concerts for its members. It also sought to promote instrumental music, and in 1873 created a composition competition whose award-winning works were played during an annual concert at the Salle Pleyel, the association's headquarters since its creation and the usual venue for its activities. Saint-Saëns persuaded the members to initiate a series of public concerts and lecture-concerts there. During a special general assembly on 20 October 1887, which Gabriel Fauré attended as a member, Saint-Saëns presented the orientation he wanted henceforth for the Société des compositeurs:

> Gentlemen, we are not merely a friendly group of died-in-the-wool artists, a sort of small-time musical academy where we exchange our ideas about Art. No. We are above all creators who want to live, that is, to be heard, judged, and. . . . Our Society is an association of mutual defense, a cluster of intelligent minds struggling against all-too-many difficulties, endlessly *in search of ways to present our works before the public*. This is the inalienable but, we have to admit, almost utopian right of all artists.[2]

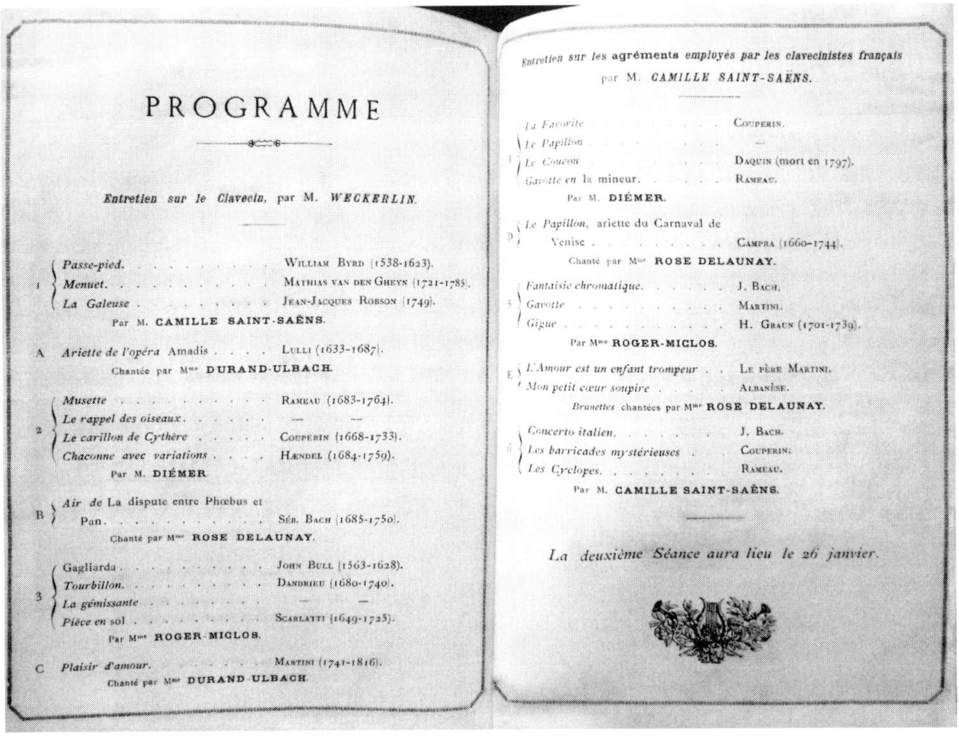

PROGRAMME

Entretien sur le Clavecin, par M. *WECKERLIN.*

1 *Passe-pied.* . . . . William Byrd (1538-1623).
Menuet. . . . . Mathias van den Gheyn (1721-1785).
La Galeuse . . . . Jean-Jacques Robson (1749).
Par M. **CAMILLE SAINT-SAËNS.**

A *Ariette de l'opéra* Amadis . . . . Lulli (1633-1687).
Chantée par Mme **DURAND-ULBACH.**

2 *Musette* . . . . Rameau (1683-1764).
Le rappel des oiseaux. . . . . . — —
Le carillon de Cythère . . . . . Couperin (1668-1733).
Chaconne avec variations . . . . Hændel (1684-1759).
Par M. **DIÉMER.**

B *Air de* La dispute entre Phœbus et Pan. . . . . Séb. Bach (1685-1750).
Chanté par Mme **ROSE DELAUNAY.**

3 Gagliarda . . . . John Bull (1563-1628).
Tourbillon. . . . . Dandrieu (1680-1740).
La gémissante . . . . — —
Pièce en sol . . . . Scarlatti (1649-1725).
Par Mme **ROGER-MICLOS.**

C *Plaisir d'amour.* . . . . Martini (1741-1816).
Chanté par Mme **DURAND-ULBACH.**

Entretien sur les **agréments** *employés par les clavecinistes français*
par M. *CAMILLE SAINT-SAËNS.*

4 *La Favorite* . . . . Couperin.
Le Papillon . . . . —
Le Coucou . . . . Daquin (mort en 1797).
Gavotte en la mineur. . . . . . . Rameau.
Par M. **DIÉMER.**

D *Le Papillon,* ariette du Carnaval de Venise . . . . Campra (1660-1744).
Chanté par Mme **ROSE DELAUNAY.**

5 *Fantaisie chromatique.* . . . . . . J. Bach.
Gavotte . . . . Martini.
Gigue . . . . H. Graun (1701-1739).
Par Mme **ROGER-MICLOS.**

E *L'Amour est un enfant trompeur* . . Le père Martini.
Mon petit cœur soupire . . . . . Albanèse.
Brunettes chantées par Mme **ROSE DELAUNAY.**

6 *Concerto italien.* . . . . J. Bach.
Les barricades mystérieuses . . . . Couperin.
Les Cyclopes. . . . . Rameau.
Par M. **CAMILLE SAINT-SAËNS.**

La deuxième Séance aura lieu le 26 janvier.

Figure 1. Program for the lecture-concert on the harpsichord at the Société des compositeurs de musique on 12 January 1888.

The assembly unanimously gave him full power to carry out this plan, and, even if the adventure lasted only a short time, it lets us establish Saint-Saëns's position toward the reforms brought about under the aegis of d'Indy.

The rules of the Société nationale stipulated that "works by dead French composers and living or dead foreign composers can take their place in concerts." In contrast, the rules that the Société des compositeurs adopted on 20 October 1887 held that works by French composers of the past could be included in their concerts, but all works by foreigners would be rejected:

> Art. 5. Works by foreign composers *can never* be included in the Société's concert programs.
>
> Art. 6. Works by *dead* French composers *may*[3] figure in the programs of the concerts in question.

The Société des compositeurs did maintain ties with several foreign composers for many years, however, creating for them the status of "correspondent members." These numbered six in 1877,[4] increasing to around twenty composers, "chosen from the elite of European artists."[5] Such correspondents were excluded de facto from concerts, although the Belgian Charles de Bériot attended some general meetings.

Saint-Saëns attacked the internal functioning of the Société nationale not only for its embrace of foreign repertoire, but also for its partiality to César Franck and his students. Meanwhile, Saint-Saëns advocated "the free manifestation of all ways of musical thinking."[6] Furthermore, unlike the Société nationale, whose examination committee chose the programs for its concerts, Saint-Saëns decided to limit this committee's power at the Société des compositeurs and give priority to the principle of choosing by lot, letting the public be the principal judge:

> Most of the pieces are chosen by lot from the pieces presented by society members; the rest are chosen by committee. From this emerge two good things to remember:
>
> 1. The absolute independence of the composers who are responsible for their own works, without having to undergo the examination of a jury;
>
> 2. The liberal, wise abstention of the Committee, unwilling to serve as an intermediary between the artist and the public, its true judge.[7]

On a practical level, the institution of these concerts, scheduled every other Thursday, required a few adjustments. Because until then performances had been reserved exclusively for members of the Société des compositeurs, it became necessary to create a new category of "listener-member." By paying 20 francs, a "listener-member" received a yearly subscription card that permitted attendance to the eight concerts in each season, running from January to June.[8]

In 1888 four concerts alternated with four lecture-concerts, which the Société des compositeurs was accustomed to organizing. The first lecture-concert, on 12 January 1888 (see program reproduced in Figure 1), was devoted to the harpsichord and, after a presentation by Jean-Baptiste Weckerlin, librarian of both the Conservatory and the Société des compositeurs, Saint-Saëns delivered a lecture, "Entretien sur les agréments employé par les clavecinistes français" (Discussion of the ornaments used by French harpsichordists). It is notable, however, that, in the context of lecture-concerts, he did not hesitate to perform foreign works, such as a *Passepied* by William Byrd or the Italian Concerto by Bach. Next came a session on 9 February: Adolphe Populus talking on the use of the quarter tone and Henri de Lapommeraye on Berlioz as a writer. The meeting on 8 March, featuring Louis-Albert Bourgault-Ducoudray and Oscar Comettant, was devoted to popular song, and the one on 19 April, with Weckerlin and Gustave Lyon, dealt with organology.[9] In 1889, the number of concerts increased to six, and there were only two lecture-concerts: one devoted to the use of the orchestral horn by A. Limagne (21 February), the other to "digressions on Richard Wagner" by Laurent de Rillé (18 April). In 1890, there was only one concert.

This policy had the result of presenting, over the course of the sixteen meetings in 1888 and 1889, a large variety of composers—some, like the Vicomtesse de Grandval, Alexandre Guilmant, Georges Pfeiffer, Paul Lacombe, César Franck, and Saint-Saëns himself, played in 1888 at both the Société nationale and the Société des compositeurs.[10] It should be noted, however, that Saint-Saëns, who was the most often performed composer at the Société nationale until his departure,[11] only appeared there twice from late 1887 to 1890 ("La Solitaire," a song performed on 7 January 1888, and Prelude for piano on 15 February 1890), whereas during this specific period his pieces were played six times at the Société des compositeurs, even though they put on fewer concerts (seventeen for the three seasons, as compared with thirty-one at the Société nationale).[12] Saint-Saëns's works performed in Société des compositeurs' concerts at the Salle Pleyel are as follows:

1888

Introduction et Rondo capriccioso for violin, with Paul Viardot (26 January)

Souvenir d'Italie, op. 80 (written in 1887) for piano, with Marie Jaëll (3 May)

1889

Septet in E-flat Major for trumpet, two violins, alto, cello, double bass, and piano, op. 65 (written in 1880), with Isidor Philipp at the piano (10 January)

L'Enlèvement, melody with orchestral accompaniment, with Mme Duvernoy-Viardot, orchestra conducted by F. Altès (4 April)

Marche héroïque for two pianos, with Blas Colomer and Ferdinand de La Tombelle (lecture-concert of 18 April)

1890

Grand duet from *Samson et Dalila*, with Mlle Lyonel and M. Piroia (27 March)

Though the system of choosing by lot may have pleased Société members, it did not attract the public, as the lack of selectivity could not guarantee the value of the works presented. In reacting against d'Indy, Saint-Saëns no doubt made the mistake of refusing all aesthetic authority [*revendication*]. In any case, that was the opinion of Georges Pfeiffer who, in 1890, noted the failure of this initiative:

We are studying how to solve, practically, the question of concerts. It is true that that we can hardly praise ourselves, either artistically or financially, for the success of the concerts we've given the past two years. [. . .] By adopting this absolute law, we wanted the Society to call freely on all schools, to open its doors to all musicians. . . . But, wanting to be too big, we have often become lost in the void. The Society[13] that has taken up the banner of the avant-garde—valiantly but exclusively—succeeds and prospers. Meanwhile, for lack of a well-defined banner, we have no regiment to follow us.[14]

Given the conditions imposed on itself, the Société des compositeurs could not compete with the Société nationale,[15] then experiencing its moment of glory and, thanks to subsidies from the Ministry of Fine Arts, able to recruit better artists.[16] What's more, Saint-Saëns did not seem to involve himself much in the undertaking, and his absence as president at general meetings was regularly deplored:

Again this year, in the absence of our eminent and dear president Saint-Saëns, one of our vice presidents, regretful to us all, must replace him at today's General Meeting.[17]

In 1891, after only three years, Saint-Saëns resigned the presidency, turning it back over, ironically, to that admirer of Wagner and César Franck, Victorin Joncières, who went on to hold it for another thirteen years. After his departure, only two concerts were planned per year, and programs would be only partially devoted to Société members:

The program for these two evenings has not yet been decided. But I can tell you that there is discussion of presenting an old work,[18] plus a few modern compositions, limiting expense as much as possible.[19]

Such intentions are far from those proclaimed four years earlier; there was even question of again taking up the group's initial activities as a "circle" and learned society.[20] The intervention of Saint-Saëns was ephemeral, and it was not until the creation of the Société musicale indépendante (SMI) in 1909 that the Société nationale de musique had any real competition.

—*Translated by Jann Pasler*

NOTES

1. Saint-Saëns's name appeared on a list of potential members for the new association (Bibliothèque nationale de France, Musique, Rés. F F995 [henceforth BnF Musique]), but there is no list printed at the end of the Société des compositeurs de musique bulletins before 1877. He does appear on the list, however, from 1877 to 1879, and after 1883. See Laure Schnapper, "Membres, présidents et lauréats de la Société des compositeurs de musique," available at http://www.irpmf.cnrs.fr/ under "Association des artistes musiciens," then "Autour de l'association," http://www.irpmf.cnrs.fr/spip.php?article298.

2. Emphasis added. "Rapport lu par le secrétaire Gustave Canoby à l'assemblée générale extraordinaire du 20 October 1887," 5, included at the end of the volume in which are published the Société des compositeurs annual reports, 1889–96 (BnF Musique, Vmc 4293). The French original of the last sentence reads: "Droit incontestable de tous les artistes, mais aussi, disons-le, terriblement chimérique."

3. Emphasis in the original. Ibid., 10.

4. I have not found a list of members before that date.

5. *Annuaire de la Société des compositeurs de musique* (1879), 28, BnF Musique, This included several Germans, like Stephen Heller, Ferdinand Hiller, Friedrich Kiel, and Friedrich Gernsheim, with the addition of Carl Reinecke in 1883.

6. From a letter by Saint-Saëns to solicit new members, dated 5 November 1888, BnF Musique, at the end of the volume of annual reports of the Société des compositeurs (1889–96).

7. Ibid. See also Article 4 of the rules for concerts adopted by the special session of the Société on 20 October 1887, ibid.

8. As for the Société nationale, it gave eleven concerts during the 1887–88 season, and ten in 1888–89. See the programs in Michel Duchesneau, *L'Avant-garde musicale et ses sociétés à Paris de 1871 à 1939* (Sprimont, Belgium: Mardaga, 1997), 246–49.

9. Jean-Baptiste Weckerlin, "Entretien sur le clavecin, la viole d'amour, la viola di gamba et la mandoline"; Gustave Lyon (director of the Pleyel et Cie, the piano company), "Entretien sur les transformations successives du mécanisme du clavecin et du piano"; and J. Carpentier (engineer at the École Polytechnique), "Le mélographe et le mélotrope."

10. In two seasons alone pieces by these composers, among others, were performed: Hector Berlioz, Émile Bernard, Georges Bizet, Léon Boëllmann, Gustave Canoby, Félicien David, Adolphe Deslandres, Louis Diémer, Théodore Dubois, César Franck, Benjamin Godard, Charles Gounod, the Vicomtesse de Grandval, Alexandre Guilmant, Victorin Joncières, Édouard Lalo, Albert Lavignac, Jules Massenet, Raoul de Montalent, Louis Niedermeyer, Jean-Grégoire Pénavaire, Georges Pfeiffer, Henri Reber, M. Renaud-Maury, Camille Saint-Saëns, Ambroise Thomas, Ferdinand de la Tombelle, and Jean-Baptiste Weckerlin.

11. At the Société nationale, Saint-Saëns had 131 works performed from 1871 to 1886, that is, an average of 8.7 works per year. (see Duchesneau, *L'Avant-garde musicale*, 23). See also Michael Strasser's essay on the Société nationale de musique in this volume.

12. Still, even without his presence, Saint-Saëns's music continued to be performed at the Société nationale both before and after this period, that is, his Sonata no. 1 for violin and piano on 22 January 1887, his Valse-caprice (*Wedding Cake*) on 5 February 1887, his Étude-valse and Overture to *La Princesse jaune*, this one in a two-piano, four-hands transcription and performed by d'Indy, Fauré, Messager and Raymonde Blanc on 19 February 1887, and a song on 7 February 1891. Also, from 1887 to 1892, Saint-Saëns was frequently absent from Paris, often in Algeria and Egypt. See Jann Pasler's essays on the composer and his music in North Africa in this volume. [Ed.]

13 Referring probably to the Société nationale.

14. Georges Pfeiffer, "Allocution du président," Assemblée générale of 16 January 1890, *Annuaire de la Société des compositeurs* (1890), 25–26. BnF Musique.

15. A handwritten letter by J.-B. Weckerlin demonstrates this: "If you make a program only with music, we become a weak imitation of the Romain Bussine meetings; for there was [Mme] Viardot, [Mme] Grandval, Taffanel, Fissot, Rémaury etc., and we only have Lefort who is very worn out, and very young for classical music." BnF Musique, Fonds Weckerlin.

16. As for subsidies, in 1889, the Société nationale obtained the sum of 2,000 francs, in addition to the Pleyel subsidy of 1,704 francs. See Duchesneau, *L'Avant-garde musicale*, 27.

17. Pfeiffer, "Allocution du président," 25.

18. *Jeu de Robin et Marion*, edited by Weckerlin.

19. *Annuaire de la Société des compositeurs* (1891), 11. BnF Musique.

20. Arthur Pougin, "Rapport annuel sur les travaux du Comité,"*Annuaire de la Société des compositeurs* (1892),19. BnF Musique.

Saint-Saëns at the Société des Concerts
du Conservatoire de Paris (1903–1904)

D. KERN HOLOMAN

The 77th season of the Société des Concerts du Conservatoire, nine pairs of concerts presented by the nation's most prestigious orchestra on Sundays at two o'clock in the hallowed old Salle du Conservatoire, concluded on 17 and 24 April 1904 with a program built around Camille Saint-Saëns, then sixty-eight years old (see Figure 1). It was hardly daring but certain to please. The *Organ* Symphony had been introduced in France by the Société in January 1887, shortly after its London premiere, and had become a signature work at the Conservatoire. *Le Déluge* (The flood), a "biblical poem" consisting of a prelude and three multi-part movements, had been in the repertoire since February 1891. Saint-Saëns was always a welcome soloist at the Conservatoire concerts, most often choosing, when allowed to play a work other than his own, a Mozart concerto. (His prodigious gifts had long been compared, in France, to Mozart's.) The Mozart D-Minor Concerto, K. 466, was a substitute for Saint-Saëns's own *Africa,* op. 89, a concerto-like fantasy for piano and orchestra completed in 1891 in Cairo.[1] In French parlance such a one-composer program would be considered a true Festival Saint-Saëns.

Each work emphasized a particular strength of the Conservatoire concerts. Though comparatively small after its 1897–98 remodeling (842 seats), the Salle du Conservatoire had seen the installation of a pipe organ by Aristide Cavaillé-Coll, completed ca. 1870 and inaugurated at the start of the forty-sixth season, 1872–73, with César Franck playing the E-Minor Prelude and Fugue, BWV 548. From its console the titular organist, Alexandre Guilmant, oversaw the revival of interest in the Baroque repertoire (Handel organ concertos from 1875, the B-Minor Mass from 1891); for this concert he was honored to yield his place to the composer of the day. *Le Déluge* brought focus on the eighty-voice house chorus, a constituent of the Société des Concerts from its founding. The chorus had made possible and then established any number of major works in Paris, from Beethoven's Ninth and *Missa solemnis* through Berlioz's *Roméo et*

GRANDE SALLE DES CONCERTS, RUE DU CONSERVATOIRE, 2

CONSERVATOIRE NATIONAL DE MUSIQUE

Société des Concerts

77e ANNÉE

19e CONCERT

Le Dimanche ***17 Avril 1904****, à* ***2*** *heures.*

PROGRAMME

1° **Symphonie** en *ut* mineur (n° 3) . . . . M. C. Saint-Saëns.

I. — Adagio; Allegro moderato; Poco Adagio.
II. — Allegro moderato; Maestoso; Allegro.

2° **Concerto** en *ré* mineur, pour piano . . . . Mozart.

Allegro. — Romance. — Rondo.

M. Camille SAINT-SAËNS.

3° **LE DÉLUGE** . . . . M. C. Saint-Saëns.

Poème biblique de Louis GALLET.

Soli : Mlle Jeanne LECLERC, de l'Opéra-Comique.
Mme Maria GAY.
MM. Léon LAFFITTE, de l'Opéra, et Charles W. CLARK.

Le Concert sera dirigé par M. GEORGES MARTY

On est INSTAMMENT prié de ne pas ENTRER ni SORTIR pendant l'exécution des morceaux.

LES PROGRAMMES DOIVENT ÊTRE DÉLIVRÉS GRATIS

Figure 1. Program of Société des Concerts du Conservatoire concert held on Sunday, 17 April 1904, featuring both works and piano performance by Saint-Saëns.

Juliette—even in the early twentieth century, the Société des Concerts was thought to be the only organization technically and structurally capable of presenting that work correctly—and later, a proper "Sirènes" from Debussy's *Nocturnes*. With Saint-Saëns as piano soloist, the Société was admired for performances of Beethoven's Choral Fantasy. Indeed the Société des Concerts had fostered the vogue for concertos in Paris, having systematically presented all the French virtuosi as well as Chopin, Mendelssohn, and Mme Schumann during the first decades. If attention in Paris was momentarily diverted in 1904 by a brouhaha following the hissing, across town, of Paderewski in Beethoven's *Emperor* Concerto,[2] the Conservatoire was equally embroiled in the frenzy to contract headliners: in those years, for instance, Ricardo Viñes, Ferruccio Busoni, Pablo Casals, Emile von Sauer, and of course Jacques Thibaud and Marguerite Long. Like every other European orchestra, the Conservatoire was seeing ever greater measures of its time and money spent on cultivating star concerto artists.

The confection of programs, one of the mission-critical tasks of any philharmonic society, fell at the Société des Concerts to its executive committee of nine or ten, of whom the leading members were the vice-president/conductor and the secretary-general. Typically, the committee would begin to deliberate in September on programming for the season that would open at the end of November and run just past Easter, endeavoring to establish an attractive, balanced pace to their offerings: a steady stream of inviting concerto soloists, premieres (mostly French, mostly established composers, in the case of the Conservatoire concerts), bread-and-butter repertoire—all leading up to the Holy Week *concerts spirituels* and season finale the following week. The 1903–04 season needed to recognize the Berlioz centenary, which it did on 6 and 13 December 1903, the concerts closest to his birthday, with a complete *Roméo et Juliette* and a first performance of the *Rob-Roy* Overture.[3] It would feature a complete *The Seasons* of Haydn during Christmas week and culminate on Maundy Thursday and Good Friday with the *St. John Passion* of Bach.

First performances, first modern performances, and first performances at the Conservatoire were carefully woven into the season's fabric: Liszt's symphonic poem *Orphée* and a cappella vocal works of the French Renaissance in late December; Henri Duparc's symphonic poem *Lénore* in January; and a remarkable group of three premieres on the same concert in February —Brahms's Tragic Overture, Dukas's *L'Apprenti sorcier*, and excerpts from Rameau's *Les Indes galantes* as recently edited by Dukas and Saint-Saëns (with Charles W. Clark in the role of Huascar).[4] In late February and early March came a Fantasy for Harp and Orchestra by Théodore Dubois (director of the Conservatoire and hence president of the Société des Concerts), Grieg's *Peer Gynt* Suite, and the Bach *Magnificat*; in mid-March, Borodin's First Symphony and the famous *La Bataille* of Clément Jannequin.

This was a robust offering, a strong third year for the conductor George Marty (see Table 1), who had, unusually, risen into the position from his work as a chorusmaster, and whose taste ran especially to large orchestra-chorus works. What it lacked was the draw of star soloists: a Mozart concerto had used Isidor Philipp from the Conservatoire (20, 27 December 1903),[5] and for Saint-Saëns's Cello Concerto no. 1, used Cornélis Liégeois, another local (10, 17 January 1904). The executive committee was even more concerned, for one of the first times since the founding of the concerts, that there would be unsold subscriptions as the season opener approached. It was decided to put out a call of distress to Saint-Saëns, tempting him with the same formula used by the previous conductor, Paul Taffanel, and woo him back to the hall of the Conservatoire: a concerto and, if desired, a first performance. Saint-Saëns proved well disposed to the invitation, and the season, to judge from the press and the secretary-general's *rapport moral*, concluded on the desired high note.[6]

Table 1. Conductors of the Société des Concerts during the Saint-Saëns era

Théophile Tilmant	1860–63
François George-Hainl	1863–72
E.-M.-E. Deldevez	1872–85
Jules Garcin	1885–92
Paul Taffanel	1892–1901
Georges Marty	1901–8
André Messager	1908–19
Philippe Gaubert	1919–38

By 1904 Saint-Saëns and the Société des Concerts had enjoyed a very long history together. The orchestra at his 1846 debut in the (old) Salle Pleyel, when he was ten, was under the direction of Théophile Tilmant, who was to become second conductor of the Société des Concerts. As a student at the Conservatoire Saint-Saëns had crept into the concert hall to listen to the rehearsals:

It was Paradise, guarded by an angel with a gleaming sword in the person of Lescot, the doorkeeper in the rue Bergère whose duty it was to prevent the impious from entering the sanctuary. . . . He went on his rounds as slowly as possible so as not to have to throw me out until the very last minute. . . . I tiptoed through corridors, squatted low in boxes, and always managed to snatch a few shreds of music, taking back to class with me an odor of Beethoven and Mozart, a strong taint of heresy.[7]

It is Saint-Saëns who tells us how the disposition of the chorus, in front of the orchestra, so that the conductor's back was typically to the singers, often caused singers and players to diverge during performances. On these occasions, he recalled, the founding conductor Habeneck would turn toward the unfortunate choristers, and thus also to the public, and make faces. "Since he was very ugly, the only result he got was bursts of laughter from the audience."[8]

On 27 April 1862, under Tilmant, Saint-Saëns appeared as piano soloist with the Société des Concerts for the first of many concerts. He was the first of the major nineteenth-century French composers to gain traction in Conservatoire concerts, so tradition-bound as to have been routinely described already for a decade as the "Louvre of Music." The enthusiastic reception of the *Organ* Symphony in 1887 confirmed his position, at least as the Société saw it, at the head of the French compositional enterprise. After the pair of scheduled performances, the director of the Conservatoire, Ambroise Thomas, himself a fine composer, came in person to the committee to promote a third hearing: "It is powerful and exceptionally noteworthy, and given the invasion of German music, it would be well to offer another performance of this work that so honors the French school."[9] Accordingly, a supplementary concert with single-ticket sales, unusually, and open to the public at large, was offered on 13 March 1887. (Later the committee sent a delegation to invite Saint-Saëns to compose a new symphony for the Société des Concerts, but he was instead to abandon the genre altogether.) By contrast, the reception of César Franck's D-Minor Symphony, in February 1889, was guarded and in some quarters outright hostile.

The *Organ* Symphony—and not the Franck—headed the program of the official Paris Centennial Exhibition concert on 20 June 1889, with 220 performers in an all-French repertoire that featured works by composers the Société considered of signal importance in France.[10] The bond between Saint-Saëns and the Société des Concerts continued strong and permanent, enriched by the composer's personal affection for the leadership (including his students André Messager, conductor from 1908, and Gabriel Fauré, president from 1905). Virtually Saint-Saëns's entire orchestral output was played during his lifetime, with some three dozen works—about a third more than Beethoven—in the active repertoire before 1900.

With Paul Taffanel, the flute virtuoso and seventh conductor of the Société des Concerts, the relationship was especially close. Saint-Saëns's Romance for Flute and Piano was, to judge from his programs, Taffanel's favorite recital piece,[11] and Saint-Saëns, having lost two children of his own, stood as godfather to Taffanel's second daughter, born in 1882. (Taffanel was the flutist at the birth of *Le Carnaval des animaux*, organized by the Société's principal cellist, Charles Lebouc—who was thus the first to play "The Swan.") "They say that the Société des Concerts is becoming the Concert

Saint-Saëns," the press muttered at the close of 1897. But it was only proper, the secretary-general responded, "to bring the work of a country-man to light where it concerned an artist of such recognized value already well played abroad; audience reception is the better measure."[12]

The Société des Concerts naturally shared enthusiasm for the new com-plete edition of the works of Rameau, published by Auguste Durand beginning in 1894 with Saint-Saëns as supervising editor. Saint-Saëns drew together a notable editorial staff, including Dukas for *Les Indes galantes*, d'Indy for *Dardanus*, and Debussy for *Les Fêtes de Polymnie*.[13] The Société had been actively cultivating the Baroque repertoire for some time: Lamoureux's fixation on the Bach-and-Handel masterpieces for orchestra and chorus began in the early 1870s, while he was still a *sociétaire*, and led to his leaving the society in 1877 to found his own, now called the Concerts Lamoureux. Marty's chorus and chorusmaster, Émil Schvartz, simultane-ously kept an eye on the French Renaissance; the works they premiered in 1903–4 had been published in Henry Expert's *Les Maîtres musiciens de la renaissance française* (1892–1908) and extracted in a published reprint en-titled *Répertoire de la Société des Concerts du Conservatoire de Paris extrait des Maîtres musiciens de la renaissance française* (Paris: 1906). Saint-Saëns himself went on to develop interests in Lully and Charpentier, while the orchestral suites drawn from Rameau, like those from Handel, were eventually ab-sorbed into the twentieth-century symphonic repertoire.[14]

Both Saint-Saëns and the Société des Concerts were, in short, cultural barometers, and it is instructive to observe their intersections in the new cen-tury, since each occasion was, in its way, a moment that defined what was imagined by many to be the pinnacle of French art music. When Georges Marty died unexpectedly in office, on 11 October 1908, Saint-Saëns, seconded by Dubois and Fauré, was called to chair the organizing committee for the *con-cert extraordinaire* in Marty's memory to benefit his widow, and himself appeared at the piano for Mozart's Concerto in C Minor, K. 491 (15 November 1908). When the orchestra began to appear beyond Paris, always in signature pro-grams, a work of Saint-Saëns was typically included on the program and, when it was possible to convince him, Saint-Saëns himself. At the Brussels Exhibition Universelle et Internationale in 1910, *Phaéton* figured alongside works of Dukas, Debussy, Franck, Fauré, and Berlioz as evidence of the Parisians' "re-fined good taste," appropriate for playing before Elizabeth, queen of the Belgians. In Lille in 1911, the orchestra welcomed Saint-Saëns as pianist in his Fifth Piano Concerto, with *Le Rouet d'Omphale*, *L'Apprenti sorcier*, Franck's *Rédemption*, and Beethoven's *Eroica*. The first salvo in a campaign, led by the impresario Gabriel Astruc, to relocate the Société des Concerts to a more mod-ern facility came on 11 February 1912 with a monster concert at the Trocadéro. There, to an audience of 4,500, the *Organ* Symphony was offered with its mighty Cavaillé-Coll instrument, followed by Richard Strauss's *Taillefer* (as first offered to the Parisians) and Beethoven's Ninth.

Saint-Saëns appears to have played with the Société des Concerts for the last time during one of the wartime *matinéees musicales* at the Sorbonne during the 1915–16 season. His music naturally figured in the "propaganda tours" organized for the orchestra (by Alfred Cortot and his staff in the Ministry of Public Instruction and Fine Arts) to Switzerland in 1917 and to the United States in 1918.[15] Repertoire for the American tour included *Le Rouet d'Omphale,* the prelude to *Le Déluge* (recorded for Columbia in New York, as was the Bacchanale from *Samson et Dalila*),[16] Symphonies nos. 2 and 3, Violin Concerto no. 3, and Piano Concertos nos. 2, 3, 4, and 5. Peace was celebrated at another Trocadéro concert, 11 May 1919, with Beethoven's Ninth and the *Organ* Symphony.

When news was received of Saint-Saën's death in Algiers, 16 December 1921, the society's postwar conductor, Philippe Gaubert, was immediately summoned to the Office of Fine Arts to discuss funeral arrangements. The orchestra and members of the chorus thus appeared for the state funeral, and the Sunday concert following began with the composer's *Marche héroïque,* labeled "à la mémoire de Saint-Saëns." By 12 February 1922 the committee had been able to arrange an all-Saint-Saëns commemorative concert: the *Organ* Symphony, the third violin concerto with George Enescu, the symphonic poem *La Jeunesse d'Hercule,* two excerpts from the song cycle *La Nuit persane,* and the *Suite algérienne.* A second memorial concert was offered on the Sunday of the first anniversary of the composer's death, 17 December 1922, with the *Organ* Symphony and *Danse macabre* featuring the concertmaster Alfred Brun as soloist. *Le Carnaval des animaux,* publication of which was forbidden by Saint-Saëns until after his death, was added to the repertoire in February 1925.

Though he was never officially a *sociétaire,* Saint-Saëns figured prominently in the affairs of the Société des Concerts du Conservatoire de Paris for an astonishing fifty-some years, carrying away six of the orchestra's medals for distinguished service. This was altogether natural. Composer and orchestra were not so different in age or upbringing, spontaneously returning to their roots in Beethoven and Mozart as the source of all that followed. And it was fitting, since they had much in common: impeccable technique, for instance, and firm commitment to that portion of new music that met their narrow, often conservative, measures of excellence.

NOTES

1. See Sabina Teller Ratner, *Camille Saint-Saëns (1835–1921): A Thematic Catalogue of His Complete Works: The Instrumental Works* (New York: Oxford University Press, 2002), 1:396; and Jann Pasler, "Saint-Saëns and the Ancient World: From Africa to Greece," in this vo-

lume. This would have been a first performance at the Conservatoire; after previous performances Saint-Saëns had written of the difficulty of capturing the appropriate style and on this occasion most likely was not feeling up to its demands.

2. Pierre Sérié, "La 'Guerre du concerto' dans la presse française (December 1904)," in *Le Concerto pour piano français: Entre romantisme et modernité*, Alexandre Dratwicki, ed. (Lyon: Symétrie, forthcoming).

3. *Rob-Roy* had recently been published for the first time, in *Hector Berlioz: Werke*, ed. Charles Malherbe and Felix Weingartner (Leipzig: Breitkopf & Härtel, 1900).

4. The baritone Charles W. Clark (1865–1925), sojourning in Paris (as was the Canadian baritone Charles Edward Clark), was from Chicago. On one occasion his voice was described as a "typical American voice, a voice full, strong, manly, [a man] with agricultural background and high art ambitions"; see *Philharmonic* 3 (1903): 104. In 1909 a visitor to Paris described him as "probably the greatest concert baritone in the world;" see *The Lyceumite and Talent* 3/26 (1909): 28.

5. Isidor Philipp (1863–1958) had been a student of Saint-Saëns.

6. Albert Vernaelde, secretary, in minutes of the Assemblée Générale, 26 May and 9 June 1904, Bibliothèque nationale de France, Musique, D 17342 (1), 19–37 (henceforth BnF Musique).

7. Camille Saint-Saëns, "Le Vieux conservatoire," in *École buissonnière* (Paris: Pierre Lafitte, 1913), 43 (first two sentences). Saint-Saëns, "La Société des Concerts," in *Harmonie et mélodie* (Paris: Calmann Lévy, 1885), 194 (last sentence). I use the translation of James Harding, *Saint-Saëns and His Circle* (London: Chapman & Hall, 1965), 40.

8. Camille Saint-Saëns, "La Salle de la rue Bergère," in *École buissonnière*, 35.

9. Minutes of the executive committee, 25 January 1887, BnF Musique, D 17344 (11).

10. In addition to the *Organ* Symphony: Cherubini's Air from *Les Abencérages*, two movements from a symphony by Henri Réber, excerpts from Ambroise Thomas's *Psyché*, excerpts from Ernest Reyer's *Sigurd*, the then-famous prayer from Auber's *La Muette de Portici*, a suite from *Le Roi s'amuse* of Léo Delibes, and excerpts from the oratorio *Mors et vita* of Charles Gounod.

11. Edward Blakeman, *Paul Taffanel: Genius of the Flute* (New York: Oxford University Press, 2005), 45.

12. Pierre Chavy, secretary-general, in *rapport moral* for the Assemblée Générale, 24 May 1897, BnF Musique, D 1734, cited the press, "On a semblé dire que la Société des Concerts deviendrait le Concert St.-Saëns" and responded, "Quand une nation a le bonheur de posséder un artiste de cette valeur, à qui appartient-il donc le plus de le mettre en lumière, si ce n'est à ses compatriots eux-mêmes? Et nous, Société essentiellement française, lui refuserons-nous la place que l'étranger lui accorde?"

13. See Anya Suchitzky, "Debussy's Rameau: French Music and Its Others," *Musical Quarterly* 86/3 (2002): 398–448.

14. The *Dardanus* Suite, arranged by Vincent d'Indy, was a favorite of Charles Munch; the suite from *Les Indes galantes* was orchestrated by Théodore Dubois and Saint-Saëns. Hamilton Harty's version of Handel's *Water Music* and Thomas Beecham's suite from Handel's *The Faithful Shepherd* were familiar and popular with symphony audiences in the second half of the twentieth century.

15. The tour itineraries and repertoire are summarized online in my transcription of the published programs of the Société des Concerts: http://hector.ucdavis.edu/SdC/ Programs/ Pr090.htm for Swiss tour, 1917; http://hector.ucdavis.edu/SdC/Programs/Pr092.htm for U.S. tour, 1918. Of Beethoven's Fifth in Los Angeles, the reviewer wrote: "To have given us the greatest work of the greatest composer was a piece of French subtlety hard to surpass. . . . There was no knocking here, but a suave and smoothly presented work of art." Jeanne Redman, *Los Angeles Daily Times*, 4 December 1918.

16. The New York recordings are enumerated as the first entries in my discography of the Société des Concerts: http://hector.ucdavis.edu/SdC/Recordings; and see "Note on the 1918 Recording Sessions in New York." The excerpt from *Le Déluge* appears in the commemorative CD, *Société des Concerts*, Vogue 665001, CD 1, track 7 (1990).

PART III

SAINT-SAËNS
THE GLOBETROTTER

Saint-Saëns: The Traveling Musician

STÉPHANE LETEURÉ

Camille Saint-Saëns's travels were cause for conjecture, analysis, and questioning during and after his lifetime. Take one example: in winter of 1888 the Parisian press wondered about the mysterious disappearance of the artist, who had quietly left the city because of his deep sorrow over his mother's death on 18 December. Speculation ran rampant. Some imagined a kidnapping linked to his inheritance, others pictured Saint-Saëns's boat sinking in the middle of the ocean. That the musician entrusted organization of the performances of his opera *Ascanio* to the librettist Louis Gallet disconcerted commentators, who knew how the composer made a point of supervising rehearsals for his operas, especially their premieres.

Thirty years later, following his death, *Le Guide du concert* commissioned an article from Jean Bonnerot, "Saint-Saëns the Traveler."[1] Pointing out that the composer was present in Paris more often than people thought, Saint-Saëns's former secretary lists the reasons that motivated him to travel: obvious health concerns,[2] a pronounced taste for exoticism (regarded as a source of inspiration), the promotion of his twofold career as performer and composer, his intellectual interest in archaeology, and finally, the need to flee France and enjoy anonymity. Saint-Saëns often traveled under an assumed name (Charles Sannois, see Figure 1). The musician's nomadic existence, then, was a subject studied by both his contemporaries and his biographers. What portrait can we paint of Saint-Saëns's nomadism? What geography and chronology were shaped by his peregrinations? What significance can be attributed to this habit that lasted for half a century?

Europe: Promoting His Work

In 1857, at age twenty-two, Saint-Saëns left for Rome with a priest from Saint-Merri, Abbé Gabriel. If we are to believe Bonnerot, the object of this trip was to initiate the young Camille into Italian art. This first trip, part of the tradition of the Italian tour, did not really begin the composer's no-madism. All his life Saint-Saëns saw Italy as both a rival and a land that shared Latin roots with France—thus a counterweight to Germany. Italy was a musical model to be surpassed. Saint-Saëns visited the country seven-teen times, sometimes to get away from the winter cold. Coming to a dozen cities along the peninsula was justified not only by concert tours but also personal motives: his taste for art and archaeology and the presence of the École française de Rome. Saint-Saëns would wait eight years after his first Italian visit to begin a series of tours in Germany, in 1865, 1868, and 1869 respectively, until the Franco-Prussian War.

Starting in the 1870s the musician took a number of land and sea routes over the course of 179 trips to 27 countries.[3] He discovered Algeria just after its pacification in 1873, but his journeys to Russia (St. Petersburg and Moscow) and Belgium in 1875 inaugurated an accelerated habit of travel-ing. In 1879 he went to Brussels, Germany, the Austro-Hungarian Empire, Italy, Switzerland, and England. This period corresponds with leaving the église de la Madeleine, where he had been organist from 1857 to 1877.

Saint-Saëns spent the most time on his travels in Germany and the United Kingdom, followed by Austria. He went to Vienna in 1876, 1879,

Figure 1. Envelopes addressed to Charles Sannois, the pseudonym Saint-Saëns adopted on his numerous voyages.

and 1886 for concerts that were greatly appreciated by the Viennese aristocracy. In the German Reich, where he made seventeen trips between 1865 and 1913, he made himself known as a pianist and as one of the rediscoverers of Bach. In Weimar, he found support from Franz Liszt. The previous year, Saint-Saëns was among fifty-two French celebrities at the inauguration of the Bayreuth Festspielhaus. A guest of Wagner, Saint-Saëns attended the performance of the *Ring* Cycle. He belonged to the circle of close friends received at Wahnfried. Vengeful arguments provoked by the French defeat in the Franco-Prussian war of 1870–71 held no sway over his motivation to visit Germany. Saint-Saëns waited until 1885 to criticize Wagner's work in *Harmonie et mélodie*,[4] and then recognized as many merits as faults. This criticism caused him to be booed during his German tour in 1886 and the General Association of German Music temporarily crossed him off their list of honorary members. The real break with Germany, though, dates to 1914 when he accused the Germans of using a brutal strategy to destroy the national heritage in occupied territory in Belgium and France. Although he could be found in the entourage of the Kaiser in Berlin in 1913, by the following year Saint-Saëns had definitively ended his habit of visiting Germany.

Saint-Saëns experienced his first trip to England (of twenty-two) as an absolute necessity. He took refuge in London in 1871 to flee the repression that followed the Commune uprising. As an organist at the Madeleine and a former soldier of the Fourth Battalion of the Seine National Guard, Saint-Saëns feared for his life, so he obtained an engagement at the Royal Albert Hall, where he found his friend Charles Gounod. Three years later Saint-Saëns returned to England by choice—for professional reasons, to make himself known as an organist. In 1879, he managed to put *La Lyre et la harpe* on the program of the famous festival in Birmingham. Full recognition of his talent as a composer by British opinion was won after the production in London of his famous Symphony in C Minor (the *Organ* Symphony) on 19 May 1886, in the presence of the Prince of Wales, the future Edward VII. During a ceremony on 13 June 1893 Saint-Saëns, along with Edvard Grieg, Piotr Tchaikovsky, Arrigo Boïto, and Max Bruch, obtained the title of Doctor of Music from the University of Cambridge. The production at Covent Garden of his opera *Henry VIII* on the symbolic date of 14 July 1893 crowned the career of the French composer, who was received several times by Queen Victoria and her close entourage. It was Saint-Saëns who was given the honor of composing the *March for the Coronation of Edward VII* during the ceremony at Westminster Abbey on 12 August 1902. Saint-Saëns's jubilee, celebrated in London in 1913 under the aegis of Queen Mary, marked the official appreciation of British authorities for the composer's work. The homeland of the oratorio was a major stage for Saint-Saëns, and contributed to his international renown almost as much as Germany had.

Although he greatly enjoyed visiting the musical heartland of Europe, Saint-Saëns did not hesitate to travel to northern and eastern fringes. During the winter of 1875–76, braving the cold, which he feared above all else, he gave recitals in Moscow and St. Petersburg. He took advantage of his Russian visit to meet his friend Antonin Rubinstein, and Tchaikovsky with whom he also formed a friendship. In Moscow in April 1887, he conducted the Orchestre de l'Opéra for seven concerts in support of the Red Cross. This charitable gesture placed him in contact with a Russian aristocracy eager to discover works with musical instruments not often used in Russia, like the clarinet and oboe. The composer dedicated his *Caprice sur des airs danois et russes* to the Czarina Maria Feodorovna. At the end of summer 1897, Saint-Saëns conducted a series of concerts in Stockholm and Copenhagen. Before he left, Queen Louise of Denmark requested a private concert in her Bernstorff Palace.

Twelve visits to Belgium allowed Saint-Saëns to become close to the royal family. His correspondence attests to the friendship and esteem formed during those times. Brussels offered Saint-Saëns the possibility of introducing his principal works, like the Piano Concerto no. 2, which he performed on 14 March 1875. With a theater as prestigious as La Monnaie, the Belgian capital often provided the musician the opportunity to have his works heard. Like Monte Carlo, where he went at least nine times, Brussels, and to a lesser extent Liège, were for Saint-Saëns an extension of Paris, a similar chance for international recognition.

Switzerland guaranteed Saint-Saëns a similar warm welcome. From 1877 to 1920, during multiple tours that also brought him to Germany or Austria, the composer crossed the Swiss border fifteen times for visits to Basel, Geneva, Lausanne, Montreux, and Vevey. From 18 to 21 May 1913, Vevey paid him homage with a festival dedicated to his compositions. Worried he might not be up to the task because of his advanced age, Saint-Saëns performed works for two pianos with the virtuoso Paderewski. The success of those four days testifies to Switzerland's wish to be part of the obligatory stopovers on the international tours of the French maestro.[5]

The Mediterranean and the East: An Exploration of the Old World

Saint-Saëns took advantage of the revolution in transportation and France's vast colonial empire to explore distant lands and to feed his taste for Orientalism. From 1889 to 1909, he was tempted nine times by the

Canary Islands. Italy and Spain, which he visited seventeen and twelve times, respectively, served as springboards for his travels through the Mediterranean basin, in particular on the European and Algerian coasts. His passage through the Suez Canal in 1889 led him as far as Ceylon, in 1895 to Indochina.

Yves Gérard has counted nineteen trips made by Saint-Saëns to Algeria, from 1873 to 1921. The geographical proximity, sunny climate, and spa facilities all agreed with him. He spent in total about four to five years of his life in Algeria,[6] enough time to allow him to compose a large number of works there, whether completely or partially.[7] He did not, however, write the famous *Suite algérienne* there—it was composed partly in Boulogne-sur-Mer—nor did he compose exclusively Orientalist works in Algeria.[8]

Egypt was one of his favorite destinations, visited sixteen times between 1890 and 1914. Saint-Saëns took advantage of these trips to tour the archaeological sites of Karnac and Luxor, and he shared with the archaeologist Georges Legrain an interest in ancient Egyptian music. Not only did he compose his Piano Concerto no. 5—*The Egyptian*—while visiting that country, but also the orchestral pieces *La Foi,* in which he used Egyptian scales deemed authentic; the song, "Le Lever du soleil sur le Nil" (Sunrise over the Nile); as well as *Sur les bords du Nil* (By the shores of the Nile), dedicated to the Khedive Abbas II Hilmi in 1908.[9] If Saint-Saëns visited Egypt almost as often as Algeria, it was because he benefited from a warm welcome by the reigning family, especially Mohammed Ali Pasha, brother of the Khedive. Saint-Saëns's bust was officially unveiled at the Khedivial Opera House in Cairo in November 1911.

During the last five years of his life, the composer assiduously visited the Mediterranean area. His stay in Athens in May 1920 marked both an intellectual and emotional culmination. Invited by George Nazos, the director of the Athens Conservatory, he was accorded the same reception as a head of state. He was received by King Alexander I as a major contributor to the revival of ancient art, which encouraged Greek nationalism exacerbated by the end of the world war and during the territorial disputes with Turkey.[10] Saint-Saëns had long embodied philhellenic classicism, and he attached profound meaning to climbing the Acropolis. In the twilight of his years, he finally touched those age-old columns that, to him, had allowed the entire edifice of European civilization to be constructed over the past two thousand years. The official nature given to this Athenian stay made Saint-Saëns an agent of diplomatic rapprochement between the two nations, emerging from five years of war victorious and reconciled. He rejoiced at hearing the crowd greet him with shouts of "Long live France!" and no doubt left Athens with the feeling of having finally managed not just to go back in time, but also to be a link between past and present.

For Saint-Saëns, the ancient remains of such Mediterranean destinations seemed to preserve a past protected from turmoil in the West since the Industrial Revolution. Traveling through Greece, Egypt, or Algeria was like declaring love for the preindustrial age. Traveling was paradoxically akin to a quest for immobility, or a nostalgia for the past.

Saint-Saëns's Preoccupation with the Future: Journeys to the Americas

Saint-Saëns first came to the United States in 1906. He began a series of concerts in New York and conducted *Le Rouet d'Omphale* at Carnegie Hall.[11] He continued his tour in Philadelphia, Chicago, and Washington, and on 3 November played his Piano Concerto in G Minor before President Theodore Roosevelt. The First World War did not put an end to this wish to discover the New World. At peril of his life, he crossed the Atlantic in 1915 to go to San Francisco, where the Panama-Pacific Exposition was under way. For the occasion he composed *Hail! California* for orchestra, organ, and military band, and gave concerts and lectures. On 5 June, he attended the official inauguration of the Palais de la France. His bust, by the sculptor Injalbert, was among the collections exhibited in this temporary building, which faithfully reproduced the Palace of the Legion of Honor on the Seine in Paris. In the United States, Saint-Saëns hoped to promote French music and diminish German musical influence. He wanted to aid in the rapprochement under way between France and the United States, which was still unsure about entering the war. What is more, this mission allowed him to see in America a future for art music, which he feared was drifting off course in Europe. Witnessing the United States' rise in power and the exceptional vitality of its unfolding musical life, Saint-Saëns joined those who thought of America as a land of the future for art and Western civilization.

The following year Saint-Saëns, like many French musicians, chose South America. In Brazil, Argentina, and Uruguay, he hoped to help reinforce the place occupied by French music in competition with its Italian and especially German counterparts.[12] In June 1916 diplomatic relations between France and Uruguay, during the middle of the war, led him to compose the national anthem, *Partido colorado*, dedicated to the Uruguayan government. Convincing white elites to regard France as a strong cultural model implied winning the competition with Germany on the music level. Saint-Saëns took advantage of not only the support of French expatriates but also the French diplomatic network.[13] Buenos Aires and Montevideo seem to have been the most important stages of his journey. Accompanied by several French singers,

Saint-Saëns participated in the collective effort to convince the higher social classes to identify with France. In this, he was an *artisan de la francophonie*. Foreign countries' recognition of Saint-Saëns's "typically French" values contributed greatly to elevating the composer-performer to the status of a representative of "national musical genius" from 1900 to 1921. Other factors also contributed. His performances of Bach brought him respect not just for his pianism but also for helping Germans rediscover their Baroque heritage; his skill as an organist confirmed his appeal for German music lovers. His impressive number of tours, concerts, and festivals turned Saint-Saëns into a major figure of European musical life, even when he was unable to convince the Opéra de Paris to include his music in its repertory and as a result gave provincial or foreign theaters the honor of premiering his lyrical works.[14]

Furthermore, the composer's adherence to republican ideals, his institutionalization by the Third Republic as well as by pre-republican academic institutions such as the Institut de France,[15] procured him official recognition, signifying national character in a time when this was most important. Saint-Saëns's fame abroad was fed by this recognition, which in turn was enhanced by his successes throughout the world. French identity was thus part of intercultural exchanges, though not devoid of arguments for national preference like those that governed the founding of the Société nationale de musique in 1871.[16] Saint-Saëns, then, needed to prove himself abroad to succeed in France and embody the ideal of the French musician to succeed abroad. Saint-Saëns's nomadism, as documented in his passport, was thus a metaphor of his identity.

The geography of his journeys brings several of Saint-Saëns's preoccupations to the fore: going back in time and finding nourishment in the sources of European culture, especially in North Africa and the Near East, lands perceived as cradles and preservers of antiquity; making himself known professionally in the great musical theaters of Europe; and extending the influence of French music to the Americas. Besides being one of the first contributors to cultural exchange on an international or even intercontinental scale, Saint-Saëns was also one of the first beneficiaries of cultural globalization. His taste for travel sheds light on two complementary motivations. On the one hand, travel reinforced his celebrity and amplified his renown. On the other hand, visits to North Africa or the Canary Islands allowed for withdrawal into self, artistic freedom, and escape from the throes of celebrity.

A quintessential figure of French musical nationalism, Saint-Saëns was both an agent for the spreading of French music throughout the world and a highly regarded intercultural mediator. His vocation as globetrotter allowed him to interact with the social, cultural, and political elites of other nations. With his close ties to several reigning families—such as the Belgian and Monte Carlo sovereigns—Saint-Saëns received many honorific decorations.[17] His proximity to the heads of state of several countries raised him to the status of an ambassador of French culture. Aware that cultural stakes were now being played out on a global scale, Saint-Saëns presented himself as one of the main figures of French cultural messianism at the beginning of the twentieth century.

—Translated by Jann Pasler

NOTES

1. Jean Bonnerot, "Saint-Saëns voyageur," *Le Guide du concert*, special issue (1922): 20–24.

2. Saint-Saëns suffered all his life from weakness in his lungs, which forced him to avoid the cold.

3. I have compiled this list based on the rigorous biography by Jean Bonnerot, *C. Saint-Saëns (1835–1921): Sa vie et son œuvre* (Paris: Durand, 1923).

4. Camille Saint-Saëns, *Harmonie et mélodie* (Paris: Calmann-Lévy, 1885).

5. *La Patrie Suisse*, 7 May 1913; *Feuille d'avis de Vevey*, 22 May 1913; *À la Veillée*, supp., 21 May 1913.

6. This calculation is based on the exhibition catalogue *Camille Saint-Saëns et l'Algérie*, Château-Musée de Dieppe, 4 October 2003 to 19 January 2004, Dieppe, Les Amis du Vieux Dieppe. Emilie Leroy, Yves Gérard, and Pierre Ickowicz (chief curator at the Château-Musée de Dieppe) contributed greatly to the catalogue and exhibition.

7. The third act of *Samson et Dalila*; the first two acts of *Ascanio*; *Nuit persane,* adaptation of *Mélodies persanes*; *Phryné*; *Chant saphique*; Méditation for violin with piano accompaniment; part of the second trio, *Frédégonde*; Fantaisie for harp; the second act of *Les Barbares*; a draft of *L'Ancêtre*; Sonata no. 2 for cello and piano; *La Terre promise*; *Cyprès et lauriers*; Élégie for violin and piano; Six Fugues for piano; *Odelette* for flute; *Marche dédiée aux étudiants d'Alger*; sonatas for clarinet and piano, oboe and piano, bassoon and piano; as well as various songs.

8. See Jann Pasler's "Saint-Saëns and the Ancient World" in this volume.

9. Saint-Saëns finished *Africa* and composed his *Valse mignonne* in Cairo, respectively in March 1891 and 1896. Saint-Saëns dedicated his *Valse mignonne* to Princess Badia, daughter of the Khedive.

10. Greece hoped to profit from peace treaties and its close relationship to France by enlarging its territory.

11. See Carolyn Guzski's "Saint-Saëns in New York" in this volume.

12. Saint-Saëns went to South America in 1899, 1904, and 1916. See Carol Hess's "Saint-Saëns and Latin America" in this volume.

13. This inference is based on documents stored in the diplomatic archives in Nantes.

14. Saint-Saëns's availability for performances can be linked to the absence of children (his two children died in infancy) and the break with his wife.

15. Saint-Saëns entered the Académie des Beaux-Arts of the Institut de France in 1881. During that period he frequented the Élysée Palace, and later on took part in important official ceremonies, such as the funeral of President Sadi Carnot in 1892 and the Universal Exhibition of 1900.

16. Symbolized by the motto "Ars gallica."

17. As documents of the Médiathèque Jean Renoir de Dieppe attest.

Saint-Saëns in Germany

MICHAEL STEGEMANN

"The old world and the new celebrate his fame," wrote the Cologne music critic Otto Neitzel in November 1898 in the foreword to his Saint-Saëns biography, which shortly thereafter appeared in the Famous Musicians series published in Berlin. "In Germany he shines brilliantly, and this brilliance is then reflected in France, quickly lighting up the whole musical world."[1] In fact, Saint-Saëns, in his aesthetic and his works, was distinctly more indebted to the German musical tradition than to the French one: "From earliest childhood on, [I] grew up in the spirit of Haydn and Mozart," he explained, late in life, to Camille Bellaigue.[2] He might have added the names of Bach, Handel, Beethoven, and Schumann. Above all in his contributions to instrumental music—symphony, solo concerto, and chamber music (quintet, quartet, trio, or sonata for two instruments)—Saint-Saëns was at home as the inheritor of the classical Austro-German tradition. So great indeed were the historical paths that Saint-Saëns followed in these categories—above all in his symphonies[3] and his piano concertos[4]—that they all lead back to the very models that had mostly disappeared in France after 1789. Such a character runs like a thread through Saint-Saëns's life as a composer and pianist, and is manifest in the earliest repertory of the gifted Wunderkind. In his first public appearance (in July 1840, in the salon of a certain Mme Violet), not yet five years old, he accompanied the violinist Antoine Bessems in a Beethoven sonata,[5] and at his official debut concert in the Salle Pleyel in Paris (6 May 1846), Mozart's B-flat Major Concerto (KV 450, with Saint-Saëns's own cadenza) and Beethoven's C-Minor Concerto, op. 37, were among the works on the program.[6] His emphatic insistence on the music of "Beethoven, Mozart, Weber, and Schumann, who at that time were more or less unknown to many in the city on the Seine,"[7] was and remained notorious, and was repeatedly and sharply commented on in the French press.[8] Throughout Paris there were performances of orchestral and chamber music from among the Viennese classics, including the Beethoven symphonies conducted by

François-Antoine Habeneck at the Conservatoire concerts, and the quartet evenings that Pierre Baillot and others established in the various chamber music societies. But their significance for Parisian musical life, and above all for the public, remained marginal.

Despite his choice of repertoire, perceived as eccentric by his contemporaries, Saint-Saëns was recognized as one of the outstanding French pianists of his generation. Yet he could hope for little understanding of his firm commitment to instrumental genres. In France of the Second Empire, and especially Paris, such an aesthetic orientation was practically the last thing that brought success to an up-and-coming young musician. Next to the world of the virtuoso, which flourished in the fashionable salons, it was in theaters that the blossoming or the withering of a composer was decided. From the echoes of the bel canto operas of Rossini, Donizetti, and Bellini, through the grand opera of Meyerbeer and *opéra lyrique* of Gounod, all the way to *wagnérisme*—only with such endeavors did one ever get noticed by the public. Until the February 1871 founding of the Société nationale de musique, authoritatively promoted by Saint-Saëns, a French composer interested in the central genres of Viennese classicism such as symphony, solo concerto, string quartet, piano trio, duo and solo sonata had little chance of getting heard:

> A French composer who had the audacity to venture into the territory of instrumental music had no means of getting his works performed unless he put on his own concert and invited his friends and critics. As for the public, the real public was not interested; just seeing the name of a living French composer on a poster was enough to drive everyone away.[9]

The fact that Saint-Saëns was committed to nourishing these genres of instrumental music, scorned by much of the French public, gives him an exceptional position among the French composers of the nineteenth century. Up to his thirtieth year he had completed, among larger instrumental works in the classical sense, the (unnumbered) symphonies in A major (ca. 1850) and F major (*Urbs Roma*, 1856); the Symphony no. 1 in E-flat Major, op. 2 (1853) and Symphony no. 2 in A Minor, op. 55 (1859); the Suite for Orchestra, op. 49 (1862/63): his Piano Concerto no. 1 in D Major, op. 17 (1858); and his first two violin concertos, in A major, op. 20 (1859) and C major, op. 58 (1858); as well as the Piano Quintet in A Minor, op. 14 (1855); the Piano Quartet in E Major (1853); and the first Piano Trio in F Major, op. 18 (1864). None of these works came close to success with the Parisian public, not only because of their forms and genres but also because of their musical style, as an unnamed critic warned:

There is definitely anarchy about in the realm of sound; sonorous strangeness aspires to a dictatorship of which one must beware. Some young composers scorn melody with a lamentable affectation, and haughtily disdain everything that one loves and respects. To begin with, they break the rhythms, the periods; they jerk their phrases; they lay waste to everything. And if, by chance, a few lyrical measures are promising and make one hope for a beautiful thought, they quickly vanish, while trying to make believe they could have continued—as indeed logical and vigorous minds would have. Were one to believe this new school, that would have been decidedly old-fashioned. Is this deliberate, is it impotence? Be that as it may, the public is evidently on the side of the critic. It receives these works coldly, and knows perfectly how to distinguish where there is merit in the performance, and where there is nothingness in the inspiration.[10]

Saint-Saëns, in the 1860s, was doubtless one of the most advanced of "some young composers," and with each work he provoked his public anew: "M. Saint-Saëns, who has studied well and who is in a stuck-up, rather pedantic world, imagines that it is enough to work a formula to death and bang out noisy chords on the piano to lead the knowing ones astray," as the influential critic Pierre Scudo wrote.[11] "He definitely has not managed to convince us that he is destined by God to compose music." In view of such comments by those in France who constantly and vehemently disapproved of Saint-Saëns's multi-movement instrumental works, it was clear why the composer would turn for support to the country where these genres had their roots: Germany.

Different studies have shown that the relationship between the German music world and Camille Saint-Saëns—particularly in the context of the Franco-Prussian War of 1870–71 and the First World War—was just as conflicted and strained, as was acceptance in his native France on account of his belief in the German musical tradition (and, for a time, in Richard Wagner's ideas).[12] However, if one looks at early reactions to Saint-Saëns's appearance in Germany one sees that in the 1860s basic reservations about his music were already being raised—long before musico-political aspects burdened the relationship. We see this as early as his first visit to Germany on 26 October 1865—a few weeks after his thirtieth birthday—in the fourth Gewandhaus concert in Leipzig under Carl Reinecke's direction. Saint-Saëns had chosen for his German debut as pianist and composer his Piano Concerto no. 1 in D Major, op. 17, as well as several of his Bach transcriptions, surely in honor of the city of the great and honored cantor of the Thomaskirche. At its only other performance, the world premiere in Paris on 28 February 1862 in the Salle Pleyel (with the Orchestre des

Italiens, conducted by François Seghers), this concerto had, astonishingly enough, even found some approval, though in the report in the *Revue et gazette musicale de Paris* it was unclear whether the work or its performance was being praised: "M. Saint-Saëns knew better than anyone how to make the most of those qualities of seriousness, energy, ardor, impetuosity, and slightly austere charm that characterize his Concerto in D. He has been welcomed as one welcomes only great talents."[13] If Saint-Saëns had hoped that his concerto would find a favorable echo in Germany—above all in Leipzig, the city of Bach, Felix Mendelssohn-Bartholdy, and Robert Schumann, the home of the time-honored Gewandhaus Orchestra—he was disappointed. The judgment of the *Allgemeine musikalische Zeitung* was laudatory about his piano playing, but had nothing good to say about the concerto:

> The concert offered the opportunity of getting to know the Parisian pianist, Mr. Saint-Saëns, who introduced himself with his own three-movement Concerto in D Major and several of his own arrangements for piano of Bach's instrumental works. If we, along with the public, could find nothing to our taste about the *composer* whose concerto was lacking in every melodic invention and can be spoken of only as a piling-up of French effects in standard concerto form, nevertheless we found his playing of Bach's pieces very exciting on account of his surprising technique—which these works allowed him to demonstrate.[14]

Friedrich Wilhelm Stade in the *Neue Zeitschrift für Musik* was somewhat less harsh, recognizing and praising the concerto's symphonic character and the originality of its instrumentation:

> As a soloist Mr. Camille Saint-Saëns, organist at La Madeleine church in Paris, performed a concerto of his own composition as well as his own arrangements of pieces by Bach (Overture to Cantata no. 29, Adagio from Cantata no. 3, and Fugue from the C-Major Violin Sonata), and, as an encore, by thunderous [*stürmisches*] demand, a Bourrée (B minor) by the same composer. As a composer S[aint-Saëns] presented a virtuoso piece in symphonic form. However much recognition he deserves for this effort, he has carried out this self-imposed task rather unfortunately, and in one respect actually overshot the mark. The orchestra generally dominated throughout, even if exposed passages were regularly given to the piano. Still, regarding the musical thinking as a whole, there is only praise to be made. Though it is sometimes suffused with much that is ordinary, and though a strict organic connection is missing, the work, in general, is nevertheless noble and the composition rich in interesting

harmony, original turns and combinations, and an independent and characteristic instrumentation.[15]

How could a composer like Saint-Saëns, so thoroughly indebted to the German tradition, be so undermined in Germany?

Saint-Saëns made one of his first and most important connections to Germany as a sixteen-year-old when, in 1851 or 1852, at the home of the violinist and conductor François Seghers, he met Franz Liszt. It was the beginning of a deep and lifelong friendship binding the two composers. Liszt followed Saint-Saëns's musical development with great interest and recommended him to the German musical press early on: "Among excellent artists, virtuosi, and composers in Paris especially deserving of mention, there is Camille Saint-Saëns. As he mentioned, he was in Leipzig last year and played his concerto there with the Gewandhaus. But they didn't know what was in him and let him come and go with remarkable ignorance [*mit vornehmer Ignoranz*]."[16] Indeed, the *Neue Zeitschrift für Musik*, under its editor-in-chief Franz Brendel, had been much more indulgent than the conservative *Allgemeine musikalische Zeitung* in its report of Saint-Saëns's debut in Leipzig—unsurprisingly, since it was the authoritative mouthpiece of the "New German School," which Liszt had set in motion during his term as grand-ducal Kapellmeister of the Weimar Altenburg. Liszt's letter of recommendation to Brendel underlined *NZfM*'s interest in Saint-Saëns, as exemplified, for instance, in its issue of 18 May 1866 about a Paris performance of his Piano Quintet, "in which the composer has poured out his rich storehouse of melodious invention and thematic combinations to his heart's content, so much so that here and there the listener wishes that he might in the future proceed somewhat more economically."[17] Liszt also emphatically recommended the works of the twenty-four-years-younger Frenchman to his students and friends:

> I have requested the Countess de Mercy to ask you for a list of your published works, in particular those for several instruments.[18] What I have heard about them in Paris gives me the strong desire to hear them again, and I also wish to send them to some friends capable of appreciating them and making them properly known by playing them *correctly*: notably to M. [Giovanni] Sgambati here [in Rome] and M. [Hans] de Bülow in Munich.[19]

When Saint-Saëns arrived in Leipzig for his debut in October 1865, the so-called Battle of the Romantics was at its height. The struggle, originally touched off by Robert Schumann, between conservative-reactionary opponents of program music led by Johannes Brahms, Ferdinand Hiller, Joseph Joachim, and the Viennese critics' "pope," Eduard Hanslick, and the champions of "Music of the Future" as promoted by Liszt and Wagner, had split German musical life into two irreconcilable enemy camps. Just four years after Liszt's departure, Weimar counted as much as ever as the high fortress of the New German School, whereas Leipzig was the center for its most embittered opponents. For the most part, the public here remained decidedly hostile to the "New Music," even though Carl Reinecke, director of the Gewandhaus, had been making a sincere effort to maintain a balance between the two currents in his programs since 1860.

One can ask how well informed Camille Saint-Saëns was about the quarrel between the two sides, or, conversely, whether (and how) those in Leipzig knew that the Frenchman was a protégé of Liszt and embraced his principles. In any case, Saint-Saëns's failure probably had something to do with his being perceived in Leipzig as a partisan of the New German School. A wording such as "piling-up of French effects" suggests that the concerto may have been implicated in the tensions between the German and French, "Teutonic" versus "Romantic" musical aesthetic, whose roots reach far back into the eighteenth century. Above all, it was the conservative circles of German musical life, and not only in Leipzig, that insisted upon this distinction. Here too it had been Robert Schumann who, in his famous review of the *Symphonie fantastique* of Hector Berlioz, had drawn the battle lines along which the program music of the "French School" and the "absolute music" of the Germans would be considered as opposites:

> The German, of delicate feelings and averse to anything personal, does not wish to be diverted so crudely in his thoughts. [. . .] Berlioz wrote for his Frenchmen, for those who with ethereal modesty are difficult to impress. I can just imagine them, reading the program they hold in their hands and applauding their countryman, who hit the mark so precisely; the music alone won't suffice for them.[20]

In his Leipzig debut Saint-Saëns was thus caught up in the "quarrel of the Romantics" without wishing to be, a situation that became even more pronounced when he returned to Leipzig in 1869 to play the world premiere of his Piano Concerto no. 3 in E-flat Major, op. 29, once again under the direction of Carl Reinecke.

If the D-Major Concerto had been tolerated by the Leipzig public four years earlier "with remarkable ignorance," this time there was almost a scandal: "A rather odd chord at the beginning of the Adagio almost touched off a battle in the corridors of the Gewandhaus"[21] (whereas the harmonic subtleties of this Andante were as far-reaching for their time as were comparable passages in Liszt or Wagner.) As for the press, reviews can again be clearly differentiated according to tendencies and schools. The conservative *AMZ*'s judgment, as expected, was devastating, and this time the paper made no secret of its opinion that Saint-Saëns amounted to a French partisan of the New German School:

> The new piano concerto of this artist, who is highly regarded in the French capital, was not able to excite our sympathy. It belongs throughout to that so-called interesting genre and gives evidence of a talent less for really original creation than for assembling different styles. Individual, significant beginnings fail to hold to their promise, and despite strongly presented orchestral effects that have a re-markable flavor of Music-of-the-Future, the work does not overcome a phrase-heavy rhetoric [*Phrasenhaftigkeit*]. At best the last movement succeeds through a compact form and a certain fiery temperament. The piano, as played by M. Saint-Saëns, took up the struggle with the orchestral demons he himself conjured up. [. . .] The remaining solo pieces he offered[22] suffered from a certain pretentious and calculated character that was able to dazzle, but not create warmth.[23]

Meanwhile, as expected, the review in the *NZfM* turned out distinctly more positive, though it was no unbounded hymn of praise. Interestingly, "the rather banal theme of the last movement"—the movement the *AMZ* had singled out for partial praise—was the one criticized by the *NZfM*:

> S[aint-Saëns] belongs indisputably to the more distinguished pianists of the present time and has won our sympathy as well for his incli-nation, as a Frenchman, toward a more dignified German taste. Just as talented and ingenious as his playing is the range of his com-positions, and what especially captivates us about these is their prominent tendency to lively progress, to being part of the *newer* school. This striving is still impaired, to be sure, by the lack of a more mature structuring and a more unified style. The most varied germs of thought, like a collection of clever *aperçus*, are lined up unsteadily one upon another. Now and then one notices a certain adherence to particular motives; these motives, however, are not consolidated into real phrases and periods, but shove themselves restlessly forward. Interest stirred up at first by the completely fiery, energetic exertion of significant means and ideas is not concentrated, but is gradually scattered. Still, his new concerto deserves by no means the unfavor-able reception and detrimental judgment received here (at most excepting the rather banal theme of the last movement); on the con-

trary, we have found quite valuable ideas (in the Andante, even really soulful thoughts) and a noteworthy talent for modulations and original harmonic effects. Yet the whole work stands in need of the most basic rewriting so that, as already mentioned, the layout can be brought into more unified clarity and the better kernels of thought into a degree of consequence through a more solid formal architecture. As a player, on the other hand, S[aint-Saëns] earned the richest applause, and rightly so, though in the choice of works he leaned too much, as is his wont, on small forms that belong more properly in the drawing room.[24]

The exhaustiveness of this concert review substantiates the position that the *NZfM* conceded to Saint-Saëns. The "lack [. . .] of a more unified style" was a point addressed and criticized over and over in Saint-Saëns's case, just as in Liszt's. This was similar to the position of the *AMZ* review of a performance of Liszt's Christmas Oratorio, which Anton Rubinstein conducted in Vienna on 31 December 1871: "I believe that there never was a composer who had less 'style' than Liszt."[25] Several more decades were required before Saint-Saëns's striving for a balanced tension between content and form in a musical work could be recognized as a quality and referred to with the attribute "Atticism." Thus Alfred Mortier wrote, in an obituary in *Le Guide musical*:

Saint-Saëns is a traditional type [of musician], which is why the younger generation looked at him critically. He knew how to mix wisdom with boldness and, in many ways was an innovator. But he had too much taste to go too far and venture into unknown territory. Musically, his trademark was Atticism, the search for perfection in form.[26]

The Leipzig concert was also discussed in other newspapers, and always negatively. In the *Neue Berliner Zeitung*, for example:

Mr. Saint-Saëns, as a composer, has suffered a serious fiasco in his new piano concerto, which he performed himself, for it possesses no content whatever, and for the lack of such content one was repaid not even by a single formal closure. Even as a pianist, Mr. Saint-Saëns did not do well.[27]

That may well have been the case, for even the *Signale für die Musikalische Welt* took on Saint-Saëns's playing—its reviewer, Eduard Bernsdorf, was a recognized opponent of Music of the Future: "His musical conception is rooted in the works of Viennese classicism and the early Romantics, which serve as models for his own compositions. As an adherent of the formal aesthetic of E[duard] Hanslick, Bernsdorf, in his own music criticism, opposed the composers of the New German School."[28] Clearly Saint-Saëns and his E-flat major Concerto could expect nothing positive from this side. Bernsdorf wrote in 1869:

> At the outset and without further ado, we declare that the focus of enjoyment in yesterday's seventh Gewandhaus concert lay for us (and perhaps others in the audience) in the two orchestral pieces. The other works met our expectations only slightly or not at all and thus brought us disappointment. But should we call it disappointment to suppose that Mr. Saint-Saëns would perform a concerto at least no worse than the one offered at his first appearance here? And to find now that this new concerto was inferior to the older one in every respect, that only in its last movement did we apprehend some fairly tasteful elements, while the first and second overdo themselves in endless passage work, setting it out in no orderly formation, no well-wrought fabric, and striving to conceal their inner hollowness and emptiness behind all kinds of exterior flourishes, decorations, coquetries, and simperings? And to see, further, that Mr. Saint-Saëns came up short as a technician of the piano—the very thing we were entitled to expect from him in light of his earlier achievements— namely, that he conducted himself even more contrary to correctness than before, in a nonchalant and cavalier manner? And now to pass from questioning to a different tone, we wish to take note that of the smaller pieces Mr. Saint-Saëns performed, only the Chopin Nocturne gave us genuine pleasure; all the others, especially Mendelssohn's "Gondola Song," were too affected and too refined in their performance, and the most difficult of them—the transcribed [Beethoven] "Dervish Chorus"—even suffered, it seemed to us, from various mistakes and missed notes. The rather strong protests raised after the concert—in the form of hisses—should not, for the sake of completeness, go unremarked.[29]

Even if one can distinctly make out the camps of adherents and opponents of Music of the Future from these reviews, it would be wrong to classify and interpret reactions to Saint-Saëns exclusively from this perspective. After all, even the *NZfM* was not uncritical of the composition—as had been the case already with the D-Major Concerto—and caviled at the formal weaknesses that could be overcome only by the "most basic rewriting."

The apparent indecisiveness of this verdict fits with the style of the concerto: while on the one hand Saint-Saëns's E-flat-Major Concerto follows the classical three-movement model of fast-slow-fast and its internal formal structure (unlike his G-Minor Concerto no. 2, op. 22, or C-Minor Concerto no. 4, op. 44), on the other hand the quasi-symphonic relationship between solo and orchestra and above all the joyful harmonic experimentation are distinct declarations of the musical avant-garde of their time. To say it another way: for the conservatives his music was always too modern, but for Music of the Future adherents he did not go far enough. Or was he, in the end, simply too French for the Germans?

In Weimar on 27 May 1870, under the auspices of the Beethoven ceremonies and the Tonkünstlerversammlung, Franz Liszt launched Saint-Saëns's cantata *Les Noces de Prométhée*, op. 19, for the 1867 Universal Exhibition. The world premiere in Paris had been wrecked by various intrigues, and in the *NZfM*, reviewer Otto Blauhuth, though an informed follower of Liszt, was anything but enthusiastic:

> To render a final judgment on this composition after hearing it for the first time does not seem advisable. If one cannot brush aside the fact that the work contains a number of significant interesting features and skillfully lays claim to the listener's attention and expectation, still much else appears rather naïve and strange, as well as decked out with French effects that lie far from our German taste. Saint-Saëns possesses a genuine talent, but it needs to be clarified, and as long as this does not occur, it will remain only a risky effort trying to unite the achievements of the New German School with French taste.[30]

That the *AMZ* devoted no more than a single sentence to the performance and otherwise sneered that Weimar, on account of Liszt, had become the "playground of Music of the Future" is indicative of its basic attitude. But it would really be interesting one day to investigate what was actually meant by these "French effects" that so much agitated the music pages of the German press and were criticized over and over from different quarters. The question about the specific Frenchness of this music remained a theme well into the twentieth century. To take one example: as late as 1950 one finds in a study by the Viennese musicologist Andreas Liess, *German and French Music in the Intellectual History of the 19th Century*, that "small motives and short themes" are typical of French music:

> One must "feel oneself" into this "more shallow" character and into these—by German taste less characteristic—formations of thematic process. Even so, they have something "artificial" about them and

lack the fulfillment of the immediate, their upward-rising source. These distinguishing features are found in individual gradations among all French composers of instrumental music. Saint-Saëns shows a distinct coolness in his works, crystal-clear forms of high spiritualization.[31]

After the Franco-Prussian War the attitude of the German musical scene toward Saint-Saëns did not fundamentally change. Then as earlier he was seen as an outstanding pianist, and then as earlier his works met incomprehension or rejection. True, isolated voices spoke up to demand a revision of this prejudice, astonishingly even in the *AMZ* (1876):

> Saint-Saëns has long been known in Germany for his excellent piano playing. And as a composer one finds account is taken in programs here and there. Yet he has not found the recognition that, in my view, he deserves. In part the reason may be found in his works, which from the beginning appear quite foreign to one who thinks and feels German. But this ignorance seems unjust to me because his works contain quite characteristic beauties which, if they do not always captivate with inner warmth, nevertheless are definitely to be recognized as significant for their technical perfection and their profound execution.[32]

The opponents of the New German School continued to brand Saint-Saëns an adherent of Music of the Future, the more so since Franz Liszt emphatically continued to promote his music in Germany, up to the world premiere he initiated of the opera *Samson et Dalila,* at the Weimar Court Theater on 2 December 1877. "Among today's French composers I know of none who deserves the attention of an intelligent and musically cultivated public as much as Mr. Saint-Saëns."[33]

Saint-Saëns refused to be put off by all this and regularly visited Germany, where the "Battle of the Romantics" eventually took a somewhat calmer turn. The passionate zeal with which the opponents attacked one another in the press during the 1860s settled into a position of firm, though less polemical commitment. Only Eduard Hanslick, of the *Neue Freie Presse* in Vienna, continued to spout his pungent venom against Liszt and his followers. Even the Leipzig public had obviously become accustomed to welcoming the Frenchman as a regular visitor, especially his piano playing, which was "celebrated in a manner as seldom happens here" according to the *AMZ* after a concert on 24 November 1877 where Saint-Saëns performed, among other things, his Piano Quintet, op. 14, and Bach's Italian

Concerto in F Major, BWV 971. "Mr. Saint-Saëns is indeed a pianist such as we possess few, a virtuoso of the most excellent kind, who with his extraordinary virtuosity knows how to combine the greatest composure and the highest nobility."[34] Even such advanced works as the Fourth Piano Concerto or the symphonic poem *Danse macabre*, op. 40—with which Saint-Saëns, as harbinger of the new genus established by Liszt, had made plenty of enemies in France—were tolerated at the Gewandhaus without scandal (program of 4 November 1877). At best, he drew comparison with German musicians, such as this judgment: "One should not begrudge this ingenious composer, a creativity that, like Schumann's, emanates from the deepest wellspring of feeling."[35]

As far as Saint-Saëns's solo concertos are concerned, the originality of these works was unique not only in France but also in Germany, where no composer would have sought a similar "squaring of the circle" between classical tradition and contemporary musical language.[36] The depth of irritation provoked by these works can be seen in two reviews of performances in Stuttgart, of the Fourth Piano Concerto in May 1879 and the First Cello Concerto, op. 33, on 22 March 1881:

> In the pieces heard on Palm Sunday there is no lack of meaningful ideas, only they are seldom properly worked out and indeed proceed in a trivial manner. The piano concerto, introduced by a briefly varied theme, is like a strange [*sic*] mosaic as it proceeds; but one hopes that no claim will be put forth that this establishes a new style for piano concertos.[37]

That Saint-Saëns had established a "new style" in his C-Minor Concerto —for German standards no less than for French—was not clear until much later, not even until the second half of the twentieth century. Nonetheless, the original formal construction of his concertos was repeatedly criticized:

> The composition itself failed to arouse our artistic interest in the slightest; it is a mosaic-like, formless entity. In his works, Saint-Saëns disavows nothing of the thoroughly educated musician, but his artistic fantasy is titillating, restless; it wanders unsteadily here and there from one extreme to the other; Saint-Saëns finds no firm ground; to create organic structures is denied him. Yet he overwhelms us with a veritable rocket barrage of ingenious inspirations and piquant details, in a word, he "macabrizes." We do not know any more recent compositions, in which the famous—many would say the notorious—*Danse*

macabre does not throw its shadow; the spectral call surprised us even in his symphonic ballet music [*sic*] *La Jeunesse d'Hercule*.[38]

In this regard, it is noteworthy that in the late 1870s and early 1880s Saint-Saëns experienced in France recognition that had long been withheld from him. His election to the Académie des Beaux-Arts (on 19 February 1881) and his nomination as an officer of the Légion d'honneur (on 14 July 1884) reflect an esteem on the part of the official French musical world that corresponds to a gradually altered view of his music.[39] From the young revolutionary, as he was considered in the 1860s and 1870s, he had imperceptibly become an official composer of the French Republic. Later, many composers of the younger generation (such as Claude Debussy) saw in him a representative of the old school. Not that he had fundamentally altered his style, just that in the altered musical environment his works were judged otherwise.

In Germany, on the other hand, his music was regarded as skeptically as ever, if not with such open hostility. After the Symphony no. 2 in A Minor, op. 55, was performed by Hans von Bülow and the Hofkapelle in Meiningen in December 1888, an anonymous author in the *Musikalisches Wochenblatt* grumbled:

> There can hardly be found a harsher contrast to [Anton Bruckner's Symphony no. 3 in D Minor] than the A-Minor Symphony by Saint-Saëns played in the second concert of the Meiningen Hofcapelle under Dr. von Bülow's direction. To Frenchmen this work may appear to be a symphony, but in Germany such a creation will not be conceded to have the significance of a symphonic work in either form or content. In the most favorable light it will be considered a suite dependent on virtuosity; its tightly proportioned four movements, like most of this composer's works, stand out only through their studied piquancy, not through depth or monumental size. The themes are downright trivial, genre painting with narrowly limited horizons. The shocking paltriness of this work could not have been more drastically illustrated than in contrast with the A-Major Symphony of Beethoven, which followed it.[40]

Here again the apparent discrepancy between content and form—or was it yet again the old hostility toward Franz Liszt (and his star pupil von Bülow) with their Music of the Future that guided the pen of the reviewer of the *Musikalisches Wochenblatt*? The concept of "piquant" ("piquant details" or "studied piquancy") was now the obvious stand-in for "French effects"—but meant the same thing in principle.

When Otto Neitzel 's biography of Saint-Saëns (cited earlier) appeared in 1899, the "Battle of the Romantics" was at last history. Thus Neitzel's appraisal of the instrumental works should be regarded as a validating voice, as far as the renown of the Frenchman in fin-de-siècle Germany is concerned:

> The concessions to the taste of the greater public that we encountered several times in Saint-Saëns's operas do not concern us in the domain of concert and chamber music. He is revealed here at his most significant, most original, and most elegant. There may well have taken place in him a certain change in the way the first naturally bubbling flow of invention was replaced by the ripeness and glow of effort and a more considered use of themes, whose earlier freshness is relieved by greater characterization and conformity to mood. In this area he really stands as one of the most significant lights in modern music in Germany, and—because France and Germany dominate the world of music—in the whole world.[41]

Saint-Saëns was barely sixty-five when Neitzel's biography was published. He still had twenty-two years to live and continued to be considered the doyen of French music. His significance was praised, directly and repeatedly, for the development of the solo concerto, particularly in Germany. Take, for example, this excerpt from Arnold Schering's 1905 *History of the Instrumental Concerto*:

> Saint-Saëns is a master in the invention of pungent passages [once more the old "French effects" and "piquancy"?], a modern representative of the old, brilliant concerto school of the Romantic era. Particularly when it is a matter of spinning out graceful themes, his composing for the piano shows a clarity without peer; he touches us like the tone of silver bells, but touches not so much the mind as the ear. Indeed his art turns first of all toward the listener's sense of sound and what sound is capable of, pursuing at length an ingenious conversation about a short theme and its possibilities for coloristic change. But Saint-Saëns descends even deeper into the life of feeling and occasionally gives us movements of gripping power and soulfulness. [. . .] For this he possesses a talent for fortunate invention commanded by none of his tribal relatives. Among these, it is not rare to see cleverness replace depth of feeling.[42]

What reservations about Saint-Saëns remained in Germany no longer concerned aesthetic positioning, but musical-political and sociopolitical controversies. The depth of these resentments and revanchism reemerged on 15 October 1906 at the first Philharmonic concert in Berlin under Artur Nikisch; among other pieces on the program were the Piano Concerto no. 5 in F Major, op. 103, the Prelude to the opera *Les Barbares*, and the concert fantasy *Africa*, op. 89. Saint-Saëns had not appeared in Germany for twenty-two years. Reactions were rather mixed. Ernst Eduard Taubert wrote in *Die Musik*:

> Naturally, the old master Saint-Saëns was received with friendly applause when he stepped on the podium, and the applause he received when he left it was just as friendly. But it is likely that nobody was genuinely warmed by this French music; it was much too empty of ideas, too lacking in feeling. If one wanted to honor the old French master, one would have done better to put on the program one of his older piano compositions or orchestral works. These African-Arabian motives, this geographical music, delivered especially in such large doses, really are of less interest to the public who attend these concerts.[43]

Likewise the *Allgemeine Musikzeitung*:

> It would be inappropriate to point again to the reasons one of the most prominent artists of France has stayed away so long from German soil, though so many of his much less significant countrymen have been received here with more or less deserved enthusiasm. Welcome to Mr. Saint-Saëns, and we would be delighted to have him bring or perform good music for us. [. . .] The two piano works are already known here; that they would be performed in the most consummate manner imaginable under the composer's masterful hands was to be expected; nevertheless they did not become more interesting.[44]

For Saint-Saëns, the return to "enemy" Germany had been both a serious gesture and one of rapprochement, if not reconciliation. This is shown in a contribution to *Le Figaro* in Paris, republished in the *Neue Freie Presse* in Vienna and appearing eventually in the *Allgemeine Zeitung*:

> Mr. Saint-Saëns, following his return to Germany, has struck up a "political song," in which, according to a telegram in *Le Figaro* that was picked up by the *N. F. Presse* in Vienna, he offered his opinion as follows about what a rapprochement between France and German would require:
>
> "One cannot depend on France's forgetting the two lost provinces [Alsace and Lorraine]. The reproaches that are made against me at

this time because of my tour in Germany are nonsense, but they are prompted by a feeling of irreparable pain from an open wound. I share that pain. Will Germany ever give back our provinces? I do not dare to hope for it. And if we took them back by force, can one believe that Germany would forgive us? Prior to the calamitous works of Bismarck, all of Europe loved the fatherland of Beethoven and Goethe. It played a role in the modern world, the role that Greece occupied in the ancient world. With that Germany one could live in peace. Today, Germany is an armored Amazon with fist on sword. One fears it, one admires it; but except in Austria, Germany finds love nowhere. And yet, are France and Germany supposed to live like the gingham dog and the calico cat? Two large neighboring nations cannot renounce each other independently. Science, the arts, commerce, and industry bring them unceasingly together. France, in greeting German musicians heartily and in hailing the works of Richard Wagner, who had grossly insulted her, has been a model of politeness. May this politeness be mutual and may it grow from day to day. One can only wish and hope for it; more cannot be demanded."

(We should offer the opinion, that in the area of art, with respect to politeness to France, Germany has remained not the least bit guilty, but indeed has taken the lead in providing a good example. —The Editors.)[45]

It is difficult to estimate whether the tensions, which come to unconcealed expression here, really were still an echo of the war of 1870–71 (which at the time already lay thirty-five years in the past), or whether they gave utterance to anxiety about the political and military predominance of Germany—the gloomy premonition of the drift toward a new and catastrophic war in Europe. In any case, Saint-Saëns's plea for "mutual politeness" was not shared by all Frenchmen. A composer like Claude Debussy, who thought and felt as a confirmed nationalist, was full of scorn and refusal when he spoke just four years later about a "Week of French Music" in Munich:

What are we going to do there? Have they begged us to go there? No! So, what does this endeavor mean? [. . .]

The Germans do not have to understand us, any more than we must seek to become pervaded by them.

Besides, Munich, though well chosen from the "political" point of view, as *Le Figaro* says, is indifferent to our art.

Concerts of modern music are attended there only by rare amateurs. One comes to hear French music out of politeness. One will applaud, perhaps, with that Germanic courtesy that is so difficult to endure. I am convinced that our art will never conquer the German nation.

Now, one sees perhaps, under the circumstances, a means of rapprochement in the circulation of our works! Music is not made for that . . . and the hour is certainly poorly chosen![46]

Once again, in these comments by Debussy, we see that Saint-Saëns's supranational European thinking was neither understood nor accepted on either side of the Rhine. Nothing had changed a few years later when he returned to Berlin. On 28 September 1913 the Berlin Philharmonic put on a celebratory concert in his honor and when "the graying composer appeared, the public rose to its feet and gave him a thunderous ovation."[47] But there was also subliminal criticism:

With his name are connected several unpleasant personal-poetic incidents, of which one is now reminded once more. But [. . .] at this concert he experienced honors upon honors. The German musical world will now be as happy about this as it was at one of the last music festivals, when he was honored in Heidelberg—he who unswervingly broke so many lances on behalf of new German art despite occasional political fits. We honor in him an outstanding spirit and rather than point out occasional willfulness, we wish to follow along contemplatively on the path of art, sometimes willingly, sometimes hesitantly.[48]

Concerning the reception and echoes of Saint-Saëns's music in Germany, his once so revolutionary aesthetic became more and more out of fashion, overtaken by ever newer stylistic currents, and finally overrun by them. (One should always remember that Saint-Saëns was born eight years after Beethoven's death and died eight years after the premiere of Igor Stravinsky's *Rite of Spring*.) Performances of Saint-Saëns's symphonies, concertos, and chamber music had become less and less frequent even before his death, and in 1927 Emil Naumann ascertained, somewhat perplexed: "Unfortunately, the instrumental works of Saint-Saëns are performed in Germany so seldom and in such isolation that one can hardly form a secure judgment of his position and his absolute significance."[49] In the next fifty to sixty years Saint-Saëns was considered a charming, agreeable composer of salon pieces and virtuoso studies—and naturally so as the composer of the *Carnaval des animaux*, whose deadly popularity overshadowed almost all of the rest of his creations. Not until the 1970s does an altered interpretation of the composer begin to emerge in the country whose music had been so important to him, especially in his earlier years.

—Translated by Mark DeVoto

NOTES

1. Otto Neitzel, *Camille Saint-Saëns* (Berlin: "Harmonie" Verlagsgesellschaft für Literatur und Kunst, 1899), Foreword.

2. Saint-Saëns to Camille Bellaigue, 18 June 1921, cited in "Lettres de Saint-Saëns et Camille Bellaigue," *Revue des deux mondes* 4 (1926): 533–58.

3. See Daniel Martin Fallon, "The Symphonies and Symphonic Poems of Camille Saint-Saëns" (PhD diss., Yale University, 1973).

4. See Michael Stegemann, *Camille Saint-Saëns and the French Solo Concerto from 1850 to 1920* (Portland, OR: Amadeus Press, 1991).

5. See Jean Bonnerot, *C. Saint-Saëns (1835–1921): Sa vie et son oeuvre* (Paris: Durand, 1923).

6. Ibid., 21.

7. *Neue Musik Zeitung* 27/19 (May 1906): 424

8. See D. Kern Holoman, *The Société des Concerts du Conservatoire, 1828–1967* (Berkeley: University of California Press, 2004) [Ed.]; Joël-Marie Fauquet, *Les Sociétés de la musique de chambre à Paris de la Restauration à 1870* (Paris: Aux Amateurs de Livres, 1986).

9. Camille Saint-Saëns, "La Société nationale de musique," *Le Voltaire*, 27 September 1880; Saint-Saëns, *Harmonie et mélodie* (Paris: Calmann-Lévy, 1885); Saint-Saëns, *Regards sur mes contemporains*, ed. Yves Gérard (Arles: Éditions Bernard Coutaz, 1990), 213.

10. *Revue et gazette musicale de Paris*, 8 April 1860, 2.

11. Pierre Scudo, *La Revue des deux mondes*, 15 June 1862, cited in Bonnerot, *C. Saint-Saëns (1835–1921)*, 41.

12. See Michael Stegemann, "Camille Saint-Saëns und Deutschland," *Neue Zeitschrift für Musik* 137/4 (July/August 1976): 267–70; *Camille Saint-Saëns* (Reinbek: Rowohlt, 1988); and "Camille Saint-Saëns, 'Germanophilie': Hintergründe einer musikpolitischen Affäre," in *Échos de France et d'Italie: Liber amicorum Yves Gérard*, ed. Marie-Claire Mussat, Jean Mongrédien, and Jean-Michel Nectoux (Paris: Buchet/Chastel, Société française de musicologie, 1997), 257–68.

13. "Auditions musicales," *Revue et gazette musicale de Paris*, 9 March 1862, 3.

14. *Allgemeine musikalische Zeitung* 3/44 (4 November 1865): 725.

15. [Friedrich Wilhelm] St[ade], *Neue Zeitschrift für Musik* 32/45 (3 November 1865): 395.

16. Franz Liszt to Franz Brendel, Rome, 19 June 1866, in *Franz Liszts Briefe*, vol. 2: *Von Rom bis ans Ende*, ed. La Mara (Leipzig: Breitkopf & Härtel, 1893), 91.

17. W[ilhelm] L[anghans], "Correspondenz," *Neue Zeitschrift für Musik* 33/21 (18 May 1866): 177.

18. Marie-Clotilde-Elisabeth Louise de Riquet, Comtesse de Mercy-Argenteau, pianist friend of Liszt and Napoleon III.

19. Liszt to Saint-Saëns, Rome, 5 July 1867, in *Lettres de compositeurs à Camille Saint-Saëns*, ed. Eurydice Jousse and Yves Gérard (Lyon: Symétrie, 2009), 388.

20. Robert Schumann, "Symphonie von H. Berlioz" (1835), in Robert Schumann, *Gesammelte Schriften über Musik und Musiker* (Leipzig: Georg Wigand, 1854), 1:141.

21. Bonnerot, *C. Saint-Saëns*, 56.

22. "At the end of Part 2, Saint-Saëns played a) *Venetianisches Gondellied* (F-sharp minor) by Mendelssohn [from *Lieder ohne Worte*]; b) Nocturne in F-sharp Minor [op. 48, no. 2] by Chopin; c) *Des Abends* [from *Fantasiestücke*, op. 12, no. 1] by Schumann; d) "La Mandolinata" by Paladilhe; and e) the Chorus of Dervishes from Beethoven's *Ruins of Athens*, transcribed by C. Saint-Saëns." *Signale für die musikalische Welt* 27/64 (26 November 1869): 1013.

23. *Allgemeine musikalische Zeitung* 4/50 (15 December 1869): 398.

24. *Neue Zeitschrift für Musik* 36/50 (10 December 1869): 429.

25. *Allgemeine musikalische Zeitung* 7/5 (31 January 1872): 86.

26. Alfred Mortier, "D'un siècle à l'autre," *Guide musical* 24/1 (1 January 1922): 4.

27. *Neue Berliner Musikzeitung* 23/49 (8 December 1869): 404.

28. Peter Andraschke, "Bernsdorf," in *Die Musik in Geschichte und Gegenwart*, ed. Friedrich Blume (Kassel: Bärenreiter, 1973), 15:710.

29. E[duard] Bernsdorf, *Signale für die musikalische Welt* 27/64 (26 November 1869): 1013.

30. Otto Blauhuth, "Die Tonkünstlerversammlung in Weimar," *Neue Zeitschrift für Musik* 37/20 (10 June 1870): 226.

31. Andreas Liess, *Deutsche und französische Musik in der Geistesgeschichte des neunzehnten Jahrhunderts* (Vienna: Berglandverlag, 1950), 57.

32. S. de Lange, "Aus Paris," *Allgemeine musiklaische Zeitung* 11/22 (31 May 1876): 345.

33. Liszt to Grand Duke Carl Alexander of Saxony and Weimar, Villa d'Este, 27 December 1875, in *Briefwechsel zwischen Franz Liszt und Carl Alexander Großherzog von Sachsen*, ed. La Mara (Leipzig: Breitkopf & Härtel, 1909), 172.

34. *Allgemeine musikalische Zeitung* 12/50 (12 December 1877): 797.

35. *Allgemeine musikalische Zeitung* 12/46 (14 November 1877): 733.

36. See Michael Stegemann, *Camille Saint-Saëns und das französische Solokonzert 1850–1920* (Mainz: Schott, 1984); or Stegemann, *Camille Saint-Saëns and the French Solo Concerto*.

37. *Allgemeine musikalische Zeitung* 14/22 (28 May 1879): 347.

38. *Allgemeine musikalische Zeitung* 16/22 (20 April 1881): 252.

39. Note that he was first honored with the Legion of Honor in 1868 [Ed.].

40. *Musikalisches Wochenblatt* 17/2 (7 January 1886): 22.

41. Neitzel, *Camille Saint-Saëns*, 69.

42. Arnold Schering, *Geschichte des Instrumentalkonzerts* (Leipzig: Breitkopf & Härtel, 1905), 199.

43. Ernst Eduard Taubert, *Die Musik* 21 (1906/1907): 183.

44. *Allgemeine Musikzeitung* (October 1906), cited in Peter Muck, *Einhundert Jahre Berliner Philharmonisches Orchester*, vol. 1: *1882–1922* (Tutzing: Hans Schneider, 1982), 340.

45. *Allgemeine Musikzeitung* (December 1906), cited in ibid.

46. Claude Debussy, "Une Semaine de musique française à Munich," *Paris-Journal*, 11 August 1910, cited in *Claude Debussy: Monsieur Croche et autres écrits*, ed. François Lesure (Paris: Gallimard, 1971), 286ff.

47. *Neue Zeitschrift für Musik* 80/40 (2 October 1913): 555.

48. Walter Paetow, cited in Muck, *Einhundert Jahre Berliner Philharmonisches Orchester*, 417.

49. Emil Naumann, *Allgemeine Musikgeschichte* (Berlin: Eigenbrödler, 1927), 840.

Saint-Saëns in England:
His *Organ* Symphony

SABINA TELLER RATNER

Saint-Saëns's fertile association with England was long and illustrious. It all started after the conclusion of the Franco-Prussian War in 1870, when civil war broke out in Paris. Saint-Saëns had served in the National Guard, and his mother and aunt, anxious about his vulnerability, urged him to leave. The next day he landed in England and made his way to London. He was hoping to play at some of the concerts at the International Exposition, but the season had already begun. His Paris mail during the Commune did not reach him and some of the London engagements escaped him. As his francs were scarce, he left to sing in the courts of London. Felix Levy lent him money and, in gratitude, Saint-Saëns dedicated his newly composed *Menuet et valse* for piano to Levy's wife, Sarah. After Gounod's great biblical elegy *Gallia* was performed on 1 May 1871 at Albert Hall, Gounod allowed Saint-Saëns to transcribe the work for the British publisher Novello for five guineas. He also composed a *mélodie* on Tennyson's poem "A Voice by the Cedar Tree," sold to Augener, and another *mélodie* on T. Davis's "My Land" for Boosey. George Grove arranged for him to give an organ recital at the Crystal Palace, followed by a chamber concert as pianist at St. James's Hall. Pauline Viardot introduced him to London society at her musical evenings. The Commune finally ended on 28 May and Saint-Saëns resumed his work in France. Nevertheless, he returned for several London recitals in October to inaugurate the organ of the newly opened Royal Albert Hall, with great success. He was described as an exceptional and distinguished performer. From that point onward, he became a frequent, increasingly popular, and respected visitor to England.[1]

The most successful of Saint-Saëns's English commissions remains his Symphony in C Minor, op. 78, for the Royal Philharmonic Society. Although it is called no. 3, it is actually the fifth symphony by Saint-Saëns. His first, the Symphony in A Major, was written around 1850 but never published during his lifetime. The second, Symphony in E-flat Major, op. 2, was composed from 8 June to 24 July 1853 and published two years later in October 1855, with the premiere on 18 December 1853 at the Société

Sainte-Cécile in Paris, directed by François Seghers (the work's dedicatee). The third, Symphonie en Fa (*Urbs Roma*), composed between 2 June and 25 July 1856, won the *concours* of the Société Sainte-Cecile de Bordeaux, on 26 January 1857. On 15 February 1857 the Société des jeunes artistes du Conservatoire under Jules Pasdeloup premiered it, and on 10 June 1857 Saint-Saëns conducted it at the Société Sainte-Cécile. However, it too was never published during Saint-Saëns's lifetime.[2] On 25 March 1860 the Société des jeunes artistes du Conservatoire under Jules Pasdeloup also

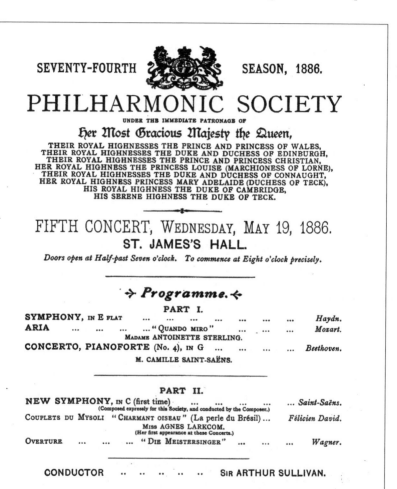

Figure 1. Cover of analytical program for the Royal Philharmonic Society concert of 19 May 1886, featuring the premiere of Saint-Saëns's *Organ* Symphony.

premiered his fourth symphony, in A minor, op. 55, written by Saint-Saëns from July to September 1859, but only published in November 1878.

With his Symphony no. 3, Saint-Saëns intended to "renew the symphonic form" with its cyclical structure, two movements with two subdivisions each, and a distinctive sound including the organ[3] and the piano for two and four hands.[4] Later called the *Organ* Symphony, it was first conceived in London. The director's minutes of the Philharmonic Society for 1 August 1885 reveal that Saint-Saëns was to be invited to play a concerto. The following correspondence chronicles the sequence of events that resulted in the work and the rationale for its analytical program.[5]

On 3 August 1885 Francesco Berger, honorary secretary of the Philharmonic Society, contacted Saint-Saëns "either to play one of your concertos, or to compose a new one and play it, or to play a concerto by some other master, whichever you prefer. But I need scarcely add, they would prefer you to appear in one of your *own* compositions. The dates I can offer you are (at present) March 18, April 1 and 15, May 19 and June 2. I sincerely hope that one of these may suit you, and that the wish of the Directors may be agreeable to you, of presenting you to their celebrated Society in the double capacity of Pianist and Composer. We have the finest Orchestra in England, and in Sir Arthur Sullivan an accomplished and amiable Conductor."[6] A second letter soon followed: "Would you be able to compose some Symphonic Work expressly for next season? instead of recommending one that is not new. We should, I think, prefer to produce *quite a new work* if you have time to prepare one." Saint-Saëns responded by promising to make every effort to fulfill their desire and write a new symphony specifically for the Philharmonic Society.[7]

Six months later, on 19 February 1886, Saint-Saëns wrote to his publisher Auguste Durand: "You will have the first half 15 March and the second at the end of that month. I think that it will be best to have it copied, because I am going to experiment a great deal in this formidable thing and it is possible I will make changes after the first performance."[8] The following month Saint-Saëns confirmed to Berger:

The symphony is in the works. I am warning you that it will be formidable. Here is the instrumentation: 3 flutes, 2 oboes, 1 English horn, 2 clarinets, 1 bass clarinet, 2 bassoons, 1 contrabassoon, 2 natural horns, 2 chromatic horns, 2 chromatic trumpets, 1 natural trumpet, 3 trombones, 1 tuba, 3 kettledrums, organ, a piano played by four hands and the strings, naturally. Fortunately there are no harps. But, unfortunately, it will be difficult. I am doing what I can to attenuate the difficulties.

As in my Fourth Concerto and my Sonata for Violin, it appears to have only two parts: the Allegro and the Adagio, the Scherzo and the Finale, are each fused together.

This devil of a symphony has risen by a semitone; it didn't want to remain in B minor, it is now in C minor.[9]

I am looking forward to conducting this symphony. Will the others look forward to hearing it? *That is the question.*[10] It is you who wanted it, I am washing my hands of it.

I shall bring the orchestral parts well corrected, and if you are willing to give me a good rehearsal of the symphony apart from the final rehearsal, all will go well.[11]

The Philharmonic Society required the score in advance as they traditionally prepared an analytical program for their concerts.[12] Questioning whether it would arrive in time, as it was still in the hands of the copyists, Saint-Saëns volunteered to write an analysis that could be arranged to suit them. He intimates: "I am very happy to have this symphony performed, I would like to be there already."[13]

Saint-Saëns informed Durand on 18 May that they had rehearsed the symphony and he was right, it was truly formidable. Happily, he was dealing with a first-class orchestra. As for the effect produced by the symphony, it was impossible to predict. But he was satisfied.[14] On 20 May 1886, a day after this performance, he wrote to Durand from London:

I have intentionally made you wait, out of spite [*méchanceté*]. The symphony was a colossal success, with some expected resistance making it still more intense. Probably it will be violently challenged, people take me on for everything with impunity! Otherwise, a magnificent performance. The Prince and Princess of Wales attended the concert; they must have been terribly bored.

I have some small corrections to make, but nothing much. The coda of the Finale is truly extraordinary. I am going to do an arrangement for two pianos next—but how can we have it performed in Paris? I only see one possibility, the Conservatoire, and I fear that it will make the walls crack! We will see if Cavaillé or someone else can put a portable organ in the hall where Colonne performs. As for a harmonium, that seems absurd to me after yesterday's performance. Ultimately you can always have it played in America, where there are organs everywhere.[15]

The next day, 21 May 1886, Saint-Saëns alerted Durand: "There will be only one change to make in the symphony, but it is an important one.

It's at the end of the Adagio; I am forced to renege on the effect of the *soli* and to use half of the instruments for the melody, the other half to pluck [*pincer*] the accompaniment. That would be inconsequential, but this new combination necessitates dividing the second violins instead of the violas; it's a complete upheaval—my music has not as yet been sent back to me."[16] This modification accounts for the slight difference in Saint-Saëns's analysis as it appears in its English and French versions.

After its successful premiere on 19 May 1886 at the fifth concert of the Philharmonic Society at St. James's Hall in London conducted by Saint-Saëns (see Figure 1), the symphony took off on its unique trajectory: 5 August 1886 at Aix-la-Chapelle; 9 and 16 January 1887 at the Société des Concerts du Conservatoire de Paris, conducted by Jules Garcin and repeated on 13 March 1887; the New York Philharmonic Society conducted by Theodore Thomas on 19 February 1887; followed at the Société des Concerts du Conservatoire, Lyon, conducted by Alexander Luigini on 20 March 1887; and on 19 April 1888, again in Paris where Édouard Colonne conducted the Adagio with Alexandre Guilmant at the organ.

The power and magistral effect of the orchestration and the innovative structure of the work enthralled early audiences. The scoring for the organ is especially effective in the Adagio, and the treatment of the organ and the piano as members of the orchestra rather than solo instruments anticipates twentieth-century practice. Saint-Saëns's skillful use of fugal techniques and his development and transformation of a single theme to unify this abstract symphonic work also distinguish his notable achievement.

Saint-Saëns's English biographer Arthur Hervey has called the Symphony no. 3 one of the most remarkable symphonies of modern times.[17] Arthur Pougin echoed his French compatriots in his enthusiasm for the work.[18] Liszt, even before he was honored with the dedication to this work, confided that he considered Saint-Saëns the ablest and most gifted among modern composers.[19] The success of Saint-Saëns's symphony gave him great pleasure. He thought it would continue "crescendo" into Paris and elsewhere.[20] Gabriel Fauré joined the laudatory chorus: he had followed the music with the score at the January 1877 performance so that he didn't miss a single note of this symphony, which he expected to live much longer than the sum of both their ages.[21]

Saint-Saëns remained ever popular in Britain. On 26 June 1907 he went to Oxford to receive an honorary doctorate in music from the new chancellor, Lord Curzon. His Fantaisie, op. 124, for violin and harp was performed for the first time on 3 July 1907 at Aeolian Hall in London. On 29 September 1909 His Majesty's Theater in London mounted *La Foi*, an Egyptian drama by Eugène Brieux, with incidental music set by Saint-

Saëns. Soon thereafter Saint-Saëns composed a grand duo for violin and cello, *La Muse et le poète*, in which the instruments are meant to converse rather than compete. It was first played by Ysaÿe, violin, and Hollmann, cello, with Saint-Saëns at the piano, at Queen's Hall in London on 7 June 1910. And on 11 September 1913, Saint-Saëns came to the sumptuous Gothic cathedral in Gloucester for the premiere of his oratorio *La Terre promise* (*The Promised Land*), setting a text by Hermann Klein and sung by three hundred local choristers.

The *Organ* Symphony did not receive much further exposure in England until 2 June 1913. Saint-Saëns celebrated the seventy-fifth anniversary of his musical career at a Jubilee Festival in Queen's Hall, Langham Place in London, under the patronage of Her Majesty Queen Mary and the Queen Mother. Along with *Africa*, excerpts from his Piano Concertos nos. 2 and 5, and other works, it included the *Organ* Symphony performed by the Beecham Symphony Orchestra. Frederick B. Kiddle played the organ, Charlton Keith and Thomas Chapman the piano.

Today Symphony no. 3 enjoys a multitude of recordings by the world's most prestigious orchestras. In 2011 alone, 125 years after its creation, the *Organ* Symphony was played by the Toronto Symphony Orchestra, the Seattle Symphony Orchestra, the New York Philharmonic, the Geneva Symphony, the London Philharmonic, the Winnipeg Symphony Orchestra and the Baltimore Symphony Orchestra, among others!

Analytical and Historical Programme for His New Symphony in C Minor and Major

[The score of this work includes a four-handed pianoforte part, which has been kindly undertaken by Mr. H. R. BIRD and Mr. EATON FANING.]

The Score of this work not being at hand for analysis in the usual course, M. Saint-Saëns has kindly forwarded some remarks of his own, in elucidation of its aim and structure. Here follows a close translation:—

"This Symphony, like its author's fourth Pianoforte Concerto, and Sonata for Piano and Violin, is divided into two movements. Nevertheless, it contains, in principle, the four traditional movements; but the first, arrested in development, serves as an Introduction to the *Adagio,* and the *Scherzo* is linked by the same process to the *Finale.* The composer has sought to avoid thus the endless resumptions and repetitions which more and more tend to disappear from instrumental music under the influence of increasingly developed musical culture.

"The composer, believing that symphonic works should now be allowed to benefit by the progess of modern instrumentation, has made up his orchestra in manner following: 3 flutes, 2 oboes, 1 English horn, 2 clarinets, 1 bass clarinet, 2 bassoons, 1 double bassoon, 2 horns, 2 valve horns, 1 trumpet, 2 valve trumpets, 3 trombones, 1 tuba, 3 drums, organ, pianoforte (sometimes played by two hands, sometimes by four), 1 triangle, 1 pair cymbals, 1 bass drum, and the usual strings.

"After a slow introduction consisting of a few plaintive bars:—

the initial theme, sombre and agitated in character, is stated by the strings, in C minor—

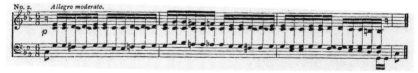

A first transformation of this theme—

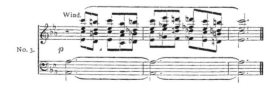

leads to a second subject—

marked by a greater tranquillity. This, after a short development presenting the two themes simultaneously, appears in a striking form—

which, however, is of brief duration. A second transformation of the initial theme follows—

Uncertain and restless in itself, it allows the plaintive notes of the introduction to be heard at intervals. Various episodes bring with them an increasing calm, and so lead to the

Adagio,

in D flat; the theme of which, extremely quiet and contemplative, is stated by the violins, violas, and celli, sustained by the chords of the organ—

This subject is next taken up by a clarinet, horn, and trombone, accompanied by the strings divided into a great many parts.

"After a variation (*en arabesques*) executed by the violins, the second transformation of the initial theme for the *Allegro* reappears, bringing back a vague feeling of unrest, augmented by dissonant harmonies—

which soon give place to the theme of the *Adagio*, this time played by a violin, viola, and violoncello *soli*, accompanied by the chords of the organ and the persistent rhythm in triplets of the preceding episode.

"The first movement ends with a *Coda*, mystical in sentiment, presenting in alternation the two chords of D-flat major and E minor, and resolving itself in the following manner—

"The second movement opens with an energetic figure, *Allegro moderato*—

immediately follwed by a third transformation of the initial theme of the first movement—

more agitated than its predecessors, and limited to a fantastic character which frankly declares itself in the *Presto*—

where appear from time to time, transient as lightning, the arpeggios and rapid scale passages of the pianoforte, accompanied by a syncopated rhythm in the orchestra, and occurring each time in a different key (F, E, E-flat, G). These playful flashes are interrupted by an expressive phrase—

To the repetition of the *Allegro moderato* succeeds a second *Presto,* which makes as though to repeat the first, but scarcely has it begun before there appears a new figure, calm, grave, austere—

and quite the opposite of fantastic in character. A conflict ensues, ending with the defeat of the agitated and fantastic element. The new idea soars aloft, as in the blue of a clear sky, to the heights of the orchestra, and after a vague reminiscence of the initial theme of the first movement—

a *maestoso* (C minor) announces the ultimate triumph of the idea calm and elevated. The initial theme of the first movement, now completely transformed, is next stated by the strings (divided) and pianoforte (four hands)—

and taken up by the organ with all the forces of the orchestra. Development follows, almost entirely constructed, it should be observed, in three-bar rhythm—

An episode, quiet and somewhat pastoral in character, is twice repeated—

and a brilliant *Coda,* in which the initial theme, by a final transformation, takes the form of a violin passage—

finishes the work; the three-bar rhythm here becoming, by natural logic, one vast measure in triple time, of a semibreve each, or twelve crotchets in the bar."

—Translated and prepared by Joseph Bennett

NOTES

1. On 15 June 1878 Wilhelm Ganz engaged Saint-Saëns to play his Piano Concerto no. 2. Its success led to Saint-Saëns being engaged for three consecutive seasons. On 31 May 1879 he conducted his Symphony in A and performed his Piano Concerto no. 4. A month later he appeared at the London Philharmonic with his Piano Concerto no. 2. In 1879 the city of Birmingham commissioned Saint-Saëns to write a symphonic work for its festival.

La Lyre et la harpe, with poetry by Victor Hugo, was premiered there on 28 August and in Paris the following January. Living in the midst of noble memories of England that evoked its kings and queens, Saint-Saëns later created the opera *Henry VIII*, with its variations from Byrd's *Carman's Whistle*, another theme from Byrd's *Medley*, as well as many Irish and Scottish melodies.

2. The two symphonies, Symphonie en la and Symphonie en fa (*Urbs Roma*) were finally published posthumously in Paris by Éditions françaises de musique, Technisonor, in 1974.

3. Saint-Saëns probably included the organ because he was familiar with the instrument in St. James's Hall where the Philharmonic Society performed. In that hall, on 2 July 1879, Saint-Saëns played the Prelude and Fugue in A Minor for organ by Bach, along with his Piano Concerto no. 2.

4. Saint-Saëns wrote on 25 October 1918 to Pierre Aguétant: "If any symphony could lay claim to the honor of renewing the symphonic form, it should be my symphony in C, for its unusual division, and for the use of the organ." Pierre Aguétant, *Saint-Saëns par lui-même* (Paris: Éditions Alsatia, 1938), 41. Note: all French texts in this essay have been translated by Sabina Teller Ratner.

5. Exchange of letters between Saint-Saëns and the Philharmonic Society, London, who commissioned this symphony. British Library Loan 48, 13/29 Royal Philharmonic Society Letters, vol. 29 (BL); and Fonds Saint-Saëns, Château-Musée de Dieppe (FS).

6. Berger's letters can be found in FS.

7. At the same time, Saint-Saëns did not make a formal commitment to produce such a work. Saint-Saëns to Berger, Paris, 25 August 1885, BL.

8. Saint-Saëns to Durand, Prague, 19 February 1886, Coll. Médiathèque Musicale Mahler (MMM).

9. A short score sketch in B minor of the symphony includes an Andante section followed by Allegro moderato with some instrumentation indicated. See Bibliothèque nationale de France, Musique, MS 916(8).

10. Quotation from Shakespeare's *Hamlet*, in English in this letter.

11. Saint-Saëns to Berger, Paris, 19 March 1886, BL.

12. See Myles Birket Foster, *History of the Philharmonic Society of London: 1813–1912* (London: John Lane, The Bodley Head, 1912). The tradition of analytical programs started in 1869 (304). In 1885 the programs were annotated by Francis Hueffer and Charles E. Stephens, and later by Joseph Bennett, critic of the *Daily Telegraph* (398). Bennett translated Saint-Saëns's analysis and prepared the program.

13. Saint-Saëns to Berger, Paris, 21 April 1886, BL.

14. Saint-Saëns to Durand, London, 18 May 1886, MMM.

15. Saint-Saëns to Durand, London, 20 May 1886, MMM.

16. Saint-Saëns to Durand, London, 21 May 1886, MMM.

17. Arthur Hervey, *Saint-Saëns* (New York: Dodd, Mead, 1922), 98.

18. Writing about the Conservatoire performance, Arthur Pougin wrote in *Ménestrel*, 16 January 1887: "The work had a great success in England; it also brought its author a veritable triumph; as far as I'm concerned I don't recall ever having seen the public of the Conservatoire, usually little inclined toward enthusiasm, applaud with such frenzy anyone other than a virtuoso. It was as if the bravos would never end. One must say that the work was quite beautiful, strong, constructed and written in magisterial way, and that it merited on every point the reception it received."

19. Franz Liszt to Carl Riedel, Pest, 5 May 1874, in *Letters of Franz Liszt*, ed. La Mara, trans. Constance Bache (New York: Charles Scribner's Sons, 1894; repr. New York: Greenwood Press, 1969), 2:250.

20. Liszt to Saint-Saëns, Weimar, 19 June 1886, FS.

21. Gabriel Fauré to Saint-Saëns, 21 January 1887, FS.

Saint-Saëns, "Algerian by Adoption"

JANN PASLER

Saint-Saëns's long relationship with Algeria, in numerous residencies over almost fifty years, provides a unique window on Western music's presence, role, and meaning beyond the West. For the adventurous, the context was rich and inviting. Throughout the French Empire, colonial towns created replicas of Parisian life through not just architecture and urban design, but also theaters, orchestras, and military band concerts. Just after arriving in 1830, the new government in Algiers subsidized a theater for opera, ballet, and comedy; in 1853 it built the magnificent Théâtre Impérial on the waterfront, later incorporating plans borrowed from the Théâtre de Châtelet in Paris to permit large, spectacular works.[1] The theater brought together both French settlers and other Europeans, with shared musical tastes and experiences ideally bridging their differences. In 1833 French settlers in Algeria founded a Philharmonic Society and in 1850 the Société des Beaux-Arts, an organization for which Saint-Saëns later served as honorary president.[2]

Here, as in France, Western music reached a larger public through military bands that performed regularly in public parks. Each regiment had its ensemble.[3] These brought the sounds of contemporary Paris to the empire, including opera fantasies based on recently staged works, such as *Samson et Dalila*. While challenging performers with the rhythms, melodies, and harmonies of art music, military bands educated the local people about tastes on the mainland and gave settlers a palpable sense of current Parisian fashion.

Saint-Saëns arrived in Algiers in October 1873, just after the shift from military control to civilian government and a substantial influx of French settlers from Alsace and Lorraine fleeing the aftermath of the Franco-Prussian War. By 1876 there were roughly 200,000 French in Algeria and 190,000 other foreigners (many became naturalized French in 1889). Saint-Saëns often wintered in Algeria to escape the weather and stresses of Parisian life, whether at his old Moorish villa at Pointe Pescade, 4 kilometers from Algiers, the mineral baths at Hamman-Righa and Blida, or

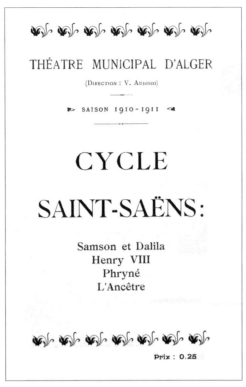

Figure 1. Cover of program from the 1910–11 season at the Théâtre Municipal in Algiers.

Biskra, Oran, Philippeville, and Mustapha. He made friends easily, especially with well-placed French music lovers such as Amédée Guillemin, mayor of Algiers in the 1890s, with whom he discussed acoustics.[4] Some have claimed that he listened to a lot of Arabic music while in Algeria, that his "Bacchanale" from *Samson et Dalila* contains music based on a melody in the Zidane scale of an Arabo-Andalousian Touchiat he once heard in the Kasbah.[5] However, the composer rarely commented on Algerian music or even indigenous Algerians.[6] Saint-Saëns's article "Algérie" in *L'Echo de Paris* (24 December 1911) is mostly a tribute to the tranquil beauty of Algerian nature. As Charles de Galland, mayor of Algiers ca. 1910, put it, the composer looked to "the sources of nature itself for his inspiration, to the rhythm of the sea."[7] With Galland, who had undying support, respect, and affection for him, he shared an interest in acoustics as well as a friendship that lasted almost twenty years, as documented in letters on many subjects—family, local events, plants, and music. Galland's family considered the composer "one of ours because of the exquisite goodness" that he so often showed them. In return, they "lived closely with him in their thoughts and followed him in the course of his travels," always happy to hear of his successes.[8]

But Saint-Saëns was in Algeria to compose. From letters to his publisher Auguste Durand, Galland and his composer son, Raoul, and the Spanish pianist Llorca, with whom Saint-Saëns often performed in Algiers, we learn that the composer kept to himself as much as he could, and that he valued isolation and independence except when it came to performing his own music or helping out with rehearsals. He had a convivial life when he so chose—socializing with friends, playing Chopin on the piano in his hotels, and in 1905 accepting membership on the Committee for Old Algiers. But in 1888 Saint-Saëns asked Durand not to mention to anyone that he was still in Algiers, lest news travel back: "Here they think I've left . . . which gives me complete freedom."[9] Returning to Algiers in March 1889, he requested that mail be sent to him under the pseudonym Charles Sannois. As much as he enjoyed the composer's presence, Galland understood that Saint-Saëns did not come to Algeria "to walk around in a dream-like state, because he was not interested in sterile reverie. . . . Rather he came to think, to work, and to produce something in contact with the vibrations that rise from the soil and the water, from the waves of sound and light."[10.]

Nonetheless, Saint-Saëns's presence had a profound impact on the musical tastes and practices of the European settlers in Algeria. After his first visit in 1873, Algerian musicians performed *Danse macabre* for violin and voice—only two years after its composition and even before it became an orchestral tone poem.[11] In May 1874, an Algerian deputy sent him a scenario for an Algerian *grand opéra* that had been entrusted to him, a proposal that apparently went nowhere.[12] Two residencies related to Algerian performances of his *Samson et Dalila* were particularly significant. First, Algerians gave their premiere of this opera on 8 February 1892, ten months before its Paris Opéra premiere in November. Second, Algiers presented five major theatrical works by Saint-Saëns in 1911, including local premieres of *Henry VIII*, *Phryné*, and *L'Ancêtre*.

Concert organizers, perhaps even more than critics, played an important role in shaping how these works were heard. In 1892 they prepared audiences for *Samson et Dalila* through the works they performed before it as well as during its run, as we see below. In 1911, when the public had become accustomed to premieres of new works, then regularly part of each season, the director drew attention to Saint-Saëns's importance by producing an unprecedented number of works by one composer. Such decisions encourage us to reflect on how the reception of a musical work can be influenced by what is heard before or after it. Moreover, performances of Saint-Saëns's music in non-theatrical genres and venues around the same time suggest we look beyond the theater to understand the meanings that may have been associated with Saint-Saëns's music and to the cumulative impact these performances may have had on the reception of his operas. In Algeria, as elsewhere, Saint-Saëns's reputation benefited greatly from the visibility brought to him by performances in all genres.

On 4 January 1892, a month before *Samson et Dalila* was premiered at the Algiers Théâtre Municipal, one of the major newspapers, *Le Moniteur de l'Algérie*, featured on its front page a lithograph image of Saint-Saëns with a short biography. Critics had been clamoring for something new, as Meyerbeer and Halévy, Charles Lecocq and Offenbach, had long dominated its programs. Saint-Saëns had wanted to propose *Étienne Marcel* in 1888, but the grand opera troupe there had not done well with *Hérodiade* and *Le Tribut de Zamora* that year.[13] For the 1892 season, the director had hired an excellent baritone and promised that, if all went well, he might even put on *Ascanio* later that spring.[14] To help build excitement and educate audiences, Saint-Saëns's chamber music was performed on 24 and 28 January and the First Regiment of Zouaves played military band tran-

Figure 2. Lyse Charney, singer from Algeria, performed at the Algiers Théâtre Municipal as Dalila beginning on 20 January 1911, and as Anne Boleyn beginning on 31 January.

scriptions of *Danse macabre* on 24 January and his *Gavotte* on 30 January (see Table 1). Some Zouaves already knew Saint-Saëns personally, as he had brought them in to play the "Tuba Mirum" in a performance of his *Requiem* at the Algiers cathedral in December and found their performance "marvelous."[15] Meanwhile, Saint-Saëns rehearsed the first act of his opera on 27 January, which went pretty well, the orchestra showing "lots of ardor" and the singers, with "pretty voices" seeming to "understand what they were singing."[16] With the hall sold out, journalists positively predisposed, and enthusiasm growing among music lovers, the Zouaves performed a fantasy on *Samson et Dalila*, featuring its most famous tunes, on 31 January at the Place du Gouvernement. Band performances not only preceded theatrical ones, here as elsewhere, but also offered to those without the means to attend theater the opportunity to enjoy new sounds and musical experiences.

Above all, theater and concert organizers prepared their audiences for *Samson et Dalila* by programming explicitly Orientalist music. In the weeks leading up to the premiere on 8 February 1892 and thereafter in juxtaposition with Saint-Saëns's opera, the director J. Guillien presented Bazin's *Le Voyage en Chine*, Verdi's *Aida*, and Meyerbeer's *L'Africaine*, a local favorite (see Table 1). Also, on 3 February the orchestra performed a concert with two works inspired specifically by Algeria: Félicien David's *Le Désert* and Saint-Saëns's *Suite algérienne*. After its premiere, more performances of *Samson* alternated with Delibes's *Lakmé,* set in colonial India (20, 23 February).

If the point was to accustom audiences in the "Orient" to Orientalist dreaming—a strategy that went without comment in the press—critics were not impressed. *Le Voyage en Chine* had "only one pretention: to make one laugh and relax pleasantly"; as for *Aida* on 21 January, it had its "usual effect"; and *L'Africaine*, with its tired singers, was "very mediocre." Only David's *Le Désert*, a work strangely little known in Algiers, had an "exotic and penetrating charm" that plunged the listener's soul into "tranquil dreaming and a delightful *langueur*."[17]

In a colony where anti-Semitism was rampant, Orientalist power struggles associated with such works sometimes collapsed into religious ones. When it came to *Samson et Dalila*, Algerian critics focused on the "religious character" of the work—"something of the archaic and the sacred that gives it a particular quality and a very biblical color"—and on Dalila's hatred of her enemy rather than on her seductive charms.[18] One critic even heard in it "plainchants and several pieces that resemble psalms." The earliest reviews also made other points that would have appealed to the local population: the opera was conceived in 1870, that "terrible year" of the Franco-Prussian War, the memory of which was so important to many Algerian settlers. Moreover, if Algiers saw itself as an extension of the

Table 1. Saint-Saëns's Music and Other Western Opera in Algiers, 1892

DATE	OPERA	INSTRUMENTAL MUSIC	MILITARY BAND
7, 9, 14 Jan.	*Le Voyage en Chine*		
21, 23 Jan.	*Aida*		
24 Jan.	*Le Voyage en Chine*	SS, *Rhapsodie d'Auvergne*	SS, *Danse macabre*; *Carmen*
27 Jan.	*Faust*		
28 Jan.	*Aida*	SS, *Allegro appassionato*	
30 Jan.	*La Traviata*		SS, *Gavotte*
31 Jan.	*L'Africaine*		SS, *Samson et Dalila*; *Le Trouvère*
2 Feb.	*Mignon*		
3 Feb.		*Le Désert*; SS, *Romance*, *Suite algérienne*	
4 Feb.	*Aida*		
7 Feb.	*Le Grand Mogol*; *Faust*		SS, *Hymne à Victor Hugo*; *Rigoletto*
8, 9 Feb.	*Samson et Dalila*		
11 Feb.	*Si j'étais roi*		
13 Feb.	*Aida*		
14 Feb.	*Le Voyage en Chine*; *Miss Helyett*		SS, *Danse macabre*; *Sigurd*
16 Feb.	*Samson et Dalila*		
17 Feb.	*La Traviata*		
18 Feb.	*Samson et Dalila*		
20 Feb.	*Lakmé*		
21 Feb.	*Samson et Dalila*		SS, *Hymne à Victor Hugo*; *L'Africaine*
23 Feb.	*Lakmé*		
25 Feb.	*Aida*		
26 Feb.		SS performance: *Danse macabre*, *Beethoven Variations*	
7, 8, 10, 19, 26, 30 March	*Sigurd*		
20 March			SS, *Ascanio*
1, 4, 5, 7 April	*Lohengrin*		*Robert le diable*
8 April		All Saint-Saëns: *Wedding Cake, Septet, Une Nuit à Lisbonne, Romance, Chanson à boire*	
10, 12 April	*Faust, Lohengrin*		*Faust*; *Samson et Dalila*
19 April			*Lakmé; Samson et Dalila; Sigurd*
21 April			*Lakmé*
18 December	*Samson et Dalila*		*Samson et Dalila*
19 December			*Samson et Dalila*

Note: Cairo premiered *Samson et Dalila* on 26 March 1893. In 1893, the Algiers military band performed the fantasy on *Samson et Dalila* on 5 March, 6 April, 22 June, and 17 August, and a fantasy on his *Ascanio* on 6 April. Chamber ensembles also continued to perform his music that year, including *Pas redoublé* (9 March), *Hymne à Victor Hugo* (30 March), *Danse macabre* (3 May), and *Le Rouet d'Omphale* (4 June).

French provinces, mention that the opera had been produced in Marseille the previous year (in a production that, incidentally, "greatly satisfied" the composer, en route to Algiers)[19] and recently in Bordeaux would have called on Algerians' competitive spirit.[20]

If on 17 February Saint-Saëns wrote to Durand that his opera had been "the great success of the season" and he was very happy with it, he must have been disappointed when two singers got sick and had to be replaced for the fourth performance on 18 February.[21] When attendance went down, a critic blamed this on mounting *La Traviata* the previous day, an Algerian favorite that always attracted a full house. The critic found the empty seats "truly regrettable" but acknowledged that, to be understood, *Samson et Dalila* needed time. Its exquisite elements and beauties were waiting to be discovered, and the performance itself was "very respectable," the orchestra as good as one could hope for.[22] For the fifth and final performance, the hall was again full, and the reception, according to Saint-Saëns, "very warm."[23] But then the bass got laryngitis and, in March and April, the theater moved on to Wagnerian music—Ernest Reyer's *Sigurd* (first performed in Algiers in 1890, its performance on 7 March 1892 was prepared by the fantasy based on *Sigurd* performed by the Zouaves on 14 February) and the Algerian premiere of Wagner's *Lohengrin* on 1 April, less than a year after its Parisian premiere. Such works may have encouraged listeners of *Samson et Dalila* to focus on its Wagnerian influences.

Yet even when his opera left the theater, interest stayed focused on Saint-Saëns. Multiple times the Zouaves played a work that they themselves introduced to the Algerian public, *Hymne à Victor Hugo*. They also continued to give the fantasy based on *Samson et Dalila*, sometimes on the same concert with fantasies based on *Sigurd* and *Lakmé*. In 1893 the Zouaves repeated *Samson et Dalila* five more times, along with other Saint-Saëns works. His chamber music as well continued to be performed at the Société des Beaux-Arts, where on 26 February "the hall was too small to hold all those who wanted to attend the concert with Saint-Saëns and Llorca." There, after hearing a work well known to Algerians, *Danse macabre*, albeit played on two pianos where it seemed "brand new," no one wanted to leave.[24] Saint-Saëns performed there again on 8 April 1892, with Galland in the orchestra. On 30 April, he graced the front page of another major newspaper, *La Coulisse algérienne*, this time with a photograph taken locally, and a full-page article on his life, works, and writings. Reviews of *Samson et Dalila* followed, reprinted from *Revue algérienne*, *Annales algériennes*, and the Milanese press on the triumph of the opera's premiere in Florence. This time Algerians called him a brother, like other settlers an "Algerian by adoption." Summarizing his "genius as more Greek than Italian" in its "clarity, taste, and delicacy," one critic noted that it "does not exclude strength when the style calls for it."[25] Another commented, "The man has the heart and soul of a youth that never dies. His regard penetrates the mysterious harmony of things." If you see him in town, "salute him. It's French Music that passes by."[26]

In 1893 critics continued to complain that they had heard Halévy's *La Juive* 17 times, Meyerbeer's *Huguenots* 13 times, and Gounod's *Faust* 25 times —if the theater is a museum, one of them wrote, it should be free! Increasingly, Algiers's Théâtre Municipal began to add new works to their repertoire—Bruneau's *L'Attaque du moulin* (1895), Godard/Vidal's *La Vivandière* (1896), Reyer's *Salammbô* (1896), and even the Algerian composer Marius Lambert's *Le Songe du berger* (1896). Of special note was Charpentier's *Louise* in 1901. Algiers was the first town to mount it after Paris, and the composer came to direct the rehearsals. Then came Puccini's *Tosca* (1903–4), Erlanger's *Aphrodite* (1903–4), Messager's *Fortunio* (1907–8), Xavier Leroux's *Le Chemineau* (1907–8), Dukas's *Ariane et Barbe-bleu* (1909), and numerous Massenet operas: *Le Portrait de Manon* (1901), *Le Jongleur de Notre-Dame* (1903–4), *Thérèse* (1907–8), and *Ariane* (1908–9). Some of these also traveled to other Algerian towns and Tunis; some had reprises over the years. From 1905 to 1911 Algerians chose to produce 39 percent of the Opéra-Comique premieres in Paris. Of the four produced there in 1911, Victor Audisio, director of Algiers's Théâtre Municipal, chose Saint-Saëns's *L'Ancêtre* and Massenet's *Thérèse* over Magnard's *Bérénice* and Ravel's *L'Heure espagnole*. All this was important because theaters in North Africa were reported on in the Parisian press, at least in terms of their repertoire.

In summer 1910 Audisio was busy negotiating with singers for a "Saint-Saëns Festival" at the Théâtre Municipal the following season (see Figure 1). Mayor Galland wrote to Saint-Saëns of his "profound joy" at hearing the news: "How much you have contributed to the education of this Mediterranean people, intelligent, alert, but ever changing, without discipline and without tradition."[27] By November, both local newspapers and Raoul de Galland began to spread the word. The latter, who had benefited from the composer's compositional advice and practical help over the years, considered him "the greatest pianist and the most perfect French organist," and noted that his presence in Algiers for this festival would have an "enormous influence on the artistic evolution of Algiers."[28]

Audisio's 1910–11 season, with singers, chorus, and an orchestra of the first order, was extraordinary for the number of new works produced: seven *drames lyriques*, including a reprise of *Samson et Dalila* (20 January) then Saint-Saëns's *Henry VIII* (31 January) and *L'Ancêtre* (23 February), and two opéra-comiques, Puccini's *Madame Butterfly* and Saint-Saëns's *Phryné* (7 February); two shorter new operas; four new operettas; and five new ballets, plus the reprise of Saint-Saëns's *Javotte*.[29] Saint-Saëns was thus represented by three genres. Of course, he was present to help rehearse these works, as were Charles-Marie Widor and Henri Février who also came for their Algerian premieres that season. Acknowledging the composer's status in Algiers by that time, the program notes began, "Saint-Saëns is the purest glory of the French musical school. It is superfluous to give a biography for this illustrious composer."

As in 1892–93, many concerts of Saint-Saëns's music preceded these theatrical productions. The composer himself performed in an orchestral concert on 18 January, and the first Concert populaire of the year offered an all-Saint-Saëns program "that could not have been more brilliant."[30] From his perspective, most of these went well, though it was quite demanding to rehearse and prepare one work after the other. If the costumes for the Philistines resembled those of "Iroquois" and the set for *L'Ancêtre* was "horrible," more important was the singing of Mlle Lyse Charney, whose voice he adored (see Figure 2). The success of *Henry VIII* and *Phryné*, with Charney in the leading roles, suggested these would be performed again at the end of the season.[31]

Saint-Saëns remained extremely active as a composer and performer in Algeria, even the year he died there, on 16 December 1921. On 11 March the Société des Beaux-Arts put on a Mozart–Saint-Saëns concert with the composer performing his *Variations on a Theme of Beethoven* with Llorca. In Oran the Théâtre Municipal, calling Saint-Saëns back after his concert there on 9 February 1920, put on an all-Saint-Saëns festival on 16 March 1921, with an orchestra of eighty musicians joining the composer in his *Rhapsodie d'Auvergne*, Valse-caprice (*Wedding Cake*), and Menuet-valse and conducting an orchestral performance of his *Marche héroïque*. On 21 March, back in Algiers, he presented a concert with the twenty-two-year-old violinist Jean Noceti, whom he had mentored, including Rameau's *Tourbillons* and *Cyclopes*, his Violin and Piano Sonata, op. 75, and the Algerian premiere of his *Élégie*, op. 160, dedicated to Charles de Galland. Then on 6 April he played again with Noceti in Tunis before an audience of 1,500. Evidently neither the extensive travel nor the heavy performance schedule tired him; as Galland observed, the "brilliant success" in Tunis again confirmed the "eternal youth in his fingers and in his works."[32]

Although reviews and his voluminous correspondence suggest that Saint-Saëns was universally beloved in Algeria among Francophile settlers, not everyone agreed. In a 1914 lecture, a professor at the Oran *lycée*, more sympathetic to Franck, d'Indy, and Debussy, deemed Saint-Saëns the "Célibitaire de la Musique," a composer who could have been the Monteverdi of France, but instead was its Mendelssohn.[33] It's true that Debussy's music had been performed in Oran in 1914, but this professor's tastes were not that common: d'Indy did not come with his music until 1923; Debussy's

Pelléas et Mélisande did not grace an Algerian stage until 1927, and his *Faune* most likely premiered in 1929, when Inghelbrecht conducted it there. Even then, the people of Algiers did not forget Saint-Saëns. While continuing to perform his music, in 1927 the city named one of the longest and most beautiful boulevards after him and, in 1934, a park.

Figure 3. Saint-Saëns's sketch of his house, Château Vert, near Algiers, from a letter to Durand, February 1888.

NOTES

1. The Théâtre de Châtelet was known for large exotic spectacles, such as Jules Verne's *Around the World in Eighty Days*, and on Sunday afternoons the Concerts Colonne. Already in 1877 Algiers' theater orchestra had 38 musicians; by 1900 there were 50 performers, along with 40 choristers.

2. The concert hall of the Société des Beaux-Arts had 600 seats and good acoustics.

3. There were also bands of indigenous soldiers, such as the Algerian *nouba*, who played their own instruments.

4. Guillemin's letters to Saint-Saëns in 1893–94 discuss acoustics in preparation for an essay Guillemin was writing on the subject. Saint-Saëns honored other Algerian friends by dedicating his scores to them, such as the optician Dr. A. Kopff (*Suite algérienne*) and the insurance agent, Eugène Béguet (*Caprice arabe*). Fonds Saint-Saëns, Château-Musée de Dieppe (FS).

5. A Touchiat is an instrumental piece, often an overture to a suite of pieces, this one in the Zidane scale. For details of Saint-Saëns's various stays in Algeria and the various pieces he composed while there, see his correspondence with Auguste and Jacques Durand, Coll. Médiathèque Musicale Mahler, Paris (MMM); Léo-Louis Barbès, "Les Séjours de Saint-Saëns en Algérie," *Société agricole, scientifique, et littéraire* 82 (1970): 83–96; and the Raoul de Galland and Léo-Louis Barbès account in "Camille Saint-Saëns algérien," *Alger, Algérie: Documents algériens* no. 42 (20 December 1949), which can be found at http://alger-roi.fr/Alger/documents_algeriens/culturel/pages/42_saint_saens.htm.

It is of note that the main theme of the *Bacchanale* reuses a fully orchestrated *Marche turque* (Bibliothèque nationale de France, Musique, Ms 545). This was most likely composed in 1859 or 1869, around the time of his *Orient et Occident*.

6. An exception to Saint-Saëns's distance from indigenous musicians was his contact with Edmond Yafil, who in 1919 proposed to collaborate with him on "lyrical adaptations" of some of the two thousand Arabic airs he had collected. Yafil was coeditor, with Jules

Rouanet, of *Répertoire de musique arabe et maure* (Algiers: Yafil, 1904–23). See his letter to Saint-Saëns of 24 January 1919, FS.

7. Charles de Galland, "Camille Saint-Saëns," *La Revue Nord-Africaine*, 19 February 1905, 197–98. Galland (1851–1923) grew up in Algiers and had been a professor at the *lycée* there. He was also an amateur musician and the promoter of the Grands Concerts populaires that aimed to bring art music to the masses in Algiers.

8. For example, see Galland's letter to Saint-Saëns of 28 April 1920, FS.

9. Saint-Saëns to Durand, Isly, 9 April 1888, MMM.

10. Galland, "Camille Saint-Saëns," 198.

11. H., "Le Concert de M. Stern," *Moniteur de l'Algérie*, 19 February 1874.

12. Paul Samary, note on calling card to Saint-Saëns, 9 May 1874, FS.

13. Saint-Saëns to Durand, Algiers, 28 February and 30 February 1888, MMM.

14. Saint-Saëns to Durand, Pointe Pescade, 9 December 1891, MMM.

15. Saint-Saëns to Durand, Pointe Pescade, 15 December 1891, MMM.

16. Saint-Saëns to Durand, Pointe Pescade, 28 January 1892, MMM.

17. V. R. L., "Chronique théâtrale: *Le Désert*," *Moniteur de l'Algérie*, 3 February 1892.

18. Whereas in the 1870s, when the opera was written, Parisian audiences were taken with Dalila's seductive charms in excerpts performed in concerts, in the 1890s, with misogyny directed at the rising feminist movement and a secure alliance between France and Russia, Parisian critics focused more on the opera's virile qualities, as in its Handelian choruses, and on the hatred of Dalila, priestess of Dagon, god of the Philistines, for her enemy. See Jann Pasler, *Composing the Citizen: Music as Public Utility in Third Republic France* (Berkeley and Los Angeles: University of California Press, 2009), 665; and "Contingencies of Meaning in Transcriptions and Excerpts: Popularizing *Samson et Dalila*," in *Approaches to Meaning in Music*, ed. Byron Almén and Edward Pearsall (Bloomington: Indiana University Press 2006), 170–213.

19. Saint-Saëns to Durand, Marseille, 24 October 1891, MMM.

20. These reviews come from *Moniteur de l'Algérie*, esp. V. R. L., "Chronique théâtrale," *Moniteur de l'Algérie*, 10 February 1892.

21. Saint-Saëns to Durand, Pointe Pescade, 18 February 1892, MMM.

22. V. R. L., "Chronique théâtrale," *Moniteur de l'Algérie*, 17 February 1892.

23. Saint-Saëns to Durand, Pointe Pescade, 24 February 1892, MMM.

24. "La Vie à Alger," *Moniteur de l'Algérie*, 27 February 1892.

25. Pierre Loys, "Nos Gloires artistiques, Camille Saint-Saëns," *Coulisse algérienne*, 30 April 1892, 1.

26. Raoul d'Artenac, "L'Actualité. Saint-Saëns," *Revue algérienne*, repr. in ibid., 3.

27. Charles de Galland to Saint-Saëns, 22 August 1910, FS.

28. Raoul de Galland, "Saint-Saëns à Alger," *Revue musicale de l'Afrique du Nord*, 1 November 1910, 1.

29. Here is a list of first performances in Algiers of contemporary opera/drames lyriques in 1910–11, followed in each case by location and year of their premieres: Saint-Saëns, *Henry VIII* (Opéra, Paris 1883); Saint-Saëns, *Phryné* (Opéra-Comique, Paris 1893); Saint-Saëns, *L'Ancêtre* (Monte Carlo 1906; Paris 1911); also, a revival of *Samson et Dalila*; Henri Février, *Monna Vanna* (Opéra, Paris 1909); André Gaillard, *La Fille du soleil* (Béziers, 1910); Alexandre Georges, *Miarka* (Opéra-Comique, Paris 1905); Jean Nouges, *Quo Vadis?* (Nice, 1909; Gaîté, Paris 1909); Giacomo Puccini, *Madame Butterfly* (Paris, 1907); Charles-Marie Widor, *Les Pêcheurs de St-Jean* (Opéra-Comique, Paris 1904).

30. Saint-Saëns to Durand, Algiers, 3 February 1911, MMM.

31. Saint-Saëns to Durand, Algiers, 22 and 25 February 1911, MMM.

32. Charles de Galland to Saint-Saëns, 28 May 1921, FS. Saint-Saëns also played the organ for a Galland family wedding that year.

33. R. Lalou, "La Musique française contemporaine: Œuvres et influences," *Annales universitaires de l'Algérie* 3 (1914): 26–27.

Friendship and Music in Indochina

JANN PASLER

Saint-Saëns made many friends aboard the ship he took for Ceylon in December 1889. The captain thought he was a "Jewish diamond merchant from Holland." In fact, no one suspected his true identity until he shared the truth when he arrived at his destination.[1] Among those he befriended was Louis Jacquet, who declared himself "charmed" by the way the composer traveled incognito under the name "Charles Sannois."[2] Jacquet used this first encounter to begin a long-lasting correspondance with the composer, whom he referred to as "my dear uncle." In letter after letter Jacquet thanked Saint-Saëns for his "amiability and courtesy," sent warm wishes from their friends on the ship, and asked him not to forget the invitation to come to Poulo Condore, a chain of small islands south of Saigon.[3]

For years, Jacquet would reextend this invitation—in 1892 he even suggested that they travel there together, with Jacquet as his "nephew, M. de Poulo." The island housed a penitentiary for political prisoners where Jacquet was an administrator. He explained, "Our isolation from the rest of the world is complete, news about the great events of the century never make it out here. For company, I have only the lieutenant in charge of the navy regiment here, the doctor, the secretary/accountant and his wife . . . all of them charming. Under me I have 460 Annamites or Cambodians. . . . Everything is happy and cheerful." The next year, Jacquet wrote, "You can work here, as among the soldiers some have very nice voices that you could use, as necessary, for rehearsals. I even have an instrument in my salon." Jacquet later reassured him, "Don't worry about a thing. You'll have a table, housing [near the beach], and the tranquility you need to work."[4]

Some five years after their meeting, Saint-Saëns agreed to take up Jacquet's invitation. On 11 January 1895 he left Port Said, Egypt, for the month-long journey to Indochina—"the unknown."[5] He stayed in Saigon from 13 February to 20 March, where he saw his old friend Armand Rousseau, recently appointed governor of Cochinchina, and heard French music performed in the theater, perhaps planting the seeds for the performance of his *Samson et Dalila* in Saigon in 1901. He spent the month that followed writing music as Jacquet's guest in Poulo Condore, before

·

returning to Marseille via Singapore in late May. The main allure of Poulo Condore for Saint-Saëns was most likely the same as it was with North Africa: the weather and the isolation. Durand was waiting for him to finish Guiraud's opera, *Brunnhilde* (later called *Frédégonde*), left incomplete when his colleague died. In letters Jacquet would later remind Saint-Saëns of how, in Poulo Condore, the sea could be "calm as a pond" . . . how he'd "never seen so many stars . . . like a vast coat of ermine fur."[6]

If originally the composer saw the trip as the opportunity to visit Japan and North America on the way back to France, he soon realized that it would be too cold to cross the Pacific at that time.[7] Nonetheless Jacquet returned

Figure 1. Program from the Tenth Colonial Regiment Military Band concert in Hué, Indochina, on 14 September 1901. Featured on the program is music by both Saint-Saëns and Jacquet.

to this idea in 1897, 1901, and 1902 while trying to lure Saint-Saëns for another visit, proposing to travel from Indochina back to France with him, via Japan and America.[8] Saint-Saëns may also have wanted to go to Cambodia, the site of exciting archaeological work by his compatriots in Angkor Wat. In Indochina as in Algeria, he had a modest interest in indigenous music, and just after his arrival he wrote to Durand, "I've heard some music here with its own charm, but that charm is purely Asian and I'll leave it to someone more clever to make a Cochinchinoise rhapsody." A month later, he changed his mind: "It seems there is something to be made with Cambodian music." However, an outbreak of cholera and then the season of high waters made this impossible.[9] Saint-Saëns said he would come back in winter 1896, when Jacquet promised to introduce him to a young Cambodian whose sister was in the entourage of King Norodom, but he never made it.[10] Nonetheless, as he wrote to Durand, his time in Poulo Condore was one of "bliss"—"this equatorial stay has positively rejuvenated me."[11]

The story of Saint-Saëns's visit to Indochina is a window onto one of his many personal relationships, emerging from a chance encounter, yet, as with Charles de Galland in Algiers, lasting over twenty years. It also provides a glimpse into the musical life of the settlers and the role Saint-Saëns's music played in it. Although the composer's letters to Jacquet are apparently lost, in his personal archives Saint-Saëns saved those he received from his friend. The letters followed him around the world from 1890 to 1909. What did the two men share? And what does this tell us about the composer and his experiences in Indochina?

Both had a keen interest in plants, animals, and music. Jacquet's love of nature permeates his descriptions of the region and constitutes much of what he used to tempt the composer back. Here was no amateur informed only by his passions. In 1891 Jacquet wrote of wanting to be director of the botanical gardens in Saigon. Failing to get the job, he nonetheless became principal administrator of farming (*culture*) in Poulo Condore and later inspector of agriculture in Cochinchina. Just after Saint-Saëns left, Jacquet wrote of some rare flowers they had admired together and described a violet with round, velvety petals that grew in the rocks of the island hills, reminding him of his youth in the Alps.[12]

Jacquet regularly updated Saint-Saëns on developments in his flower and vegetable gardens and reported on the unusual species he saw on various excursions, documented with his camera. In November 1895, after his return to France, Saint-Saëns sent Jacquet some tulip, hyacinth, and narcissus bulbs to go alongside his roses, geraniums, and lotus. They arrived in perfect shape for December planting.[13] Botanical descriptions are particularly strong in letters Jacquet wrote from the hill country outside Hué, inhabited by the indigenous Moïs where, in March 1897, he was sent on a mission by the governor, Paul Doumer, to collect plant species. He also wrote from Hué, the Annamite capital, where he settled in 1899 to establish a new agricultural and horticultural institution for the study of colonial farming and local animals. In his letters, Jacquet even sent Saint-Saëns some strong cinnamon from the area and a dried orchid, which is still attached to the letter.[14] In 1901, he became director of agriculture for the protectorate of Annam and Tonkin and then finally director of the botanical gardens in Hanoi, his ultimate ambition.

Was it Saint-Saëns's encouragement that first led Jacquet to apply for this job in 1890? Most likely Jacquet knew that Saint-Saëns's friendship with the governor could help him. Moreover, in 1896 Saint-Saëns lent Jacquet 6,000 francs to cover farming expenses, perhaps the planting of 84 hectares of rice.[15] The composer was probably fascinated with what Jacquet knew and observed. As a young boy, Saint-Saëns had planted seeds in his windowbox to observe their growth. When reading about Jacquet's description of the bamboo varieties outside Hué, he would have been able to compare these to those he had seen in the botanical gardens of Algiers, where he enjoyed spending hours.[16] Like Jacquet, he collected specimens, once promising Durand he would bring back seeds from Brazil.[17] He also made drawings of flowers in his correspondence. His letter of 28 March 1895 to Durand from Poulo Condore ends with his colored pencil drawing of an orange lotus with red tips and three lotus pods.[18]

Jacquet and Saint-Saëns were also drawn to animals, especially those that "sang" or otherwise produced interesting sounds. As he expanded his estate, Jacquet wrote of his chickens, ducks, pigs, fish aquarium, and cows, building shacks for them all, then, among the Moïs, of the "amusing" chickens he "never heard so talkative, having a repertoire more varied than that of the roosters." The latter, "even more ridiculous," resembled "bad singers from the provinces who force their voices to be successful. The first vibrations of the notes are pure, even fresh . . . then the voice shakes, the note breaks down, nothing more disagreeable for the ear than that."[19] In Hué, he wrote of huge frogs that sang for him each evening. For his part, when Saint-Saëns got back to France, he sent Jacquet some snails.[20] And in his essay, "Observations of a Friend of Animals," in which he reflects on animal intelligence, Saint-Saëns recounts how the enormous spiders of Cochinchina took advantage of the telegraph wires to "spin the woof on which they watched for their prey . . . the result of observation and reflection."[21] In his essay on the ideas of Vincent d'Indy, he refers to an enormous beetle there whose flight produced a powerful sounding chord, which led him to conclude, "What an enchanted fairyland are these tropical regions."[22]

Finally, Jacquet, apparently a novice, shared with Saint-Saëns a love for music. Upon returning to Poulo Condore after his first encounter with the composer, he ordered a piano from Saigon to learn to play and rehearse the amateurs who gave performances on the island.[23] Attached to the letter he wrote Saint-Saëns about his efforts was the program of a concert there on 23 April 1891. Seven singers presented romances, monologues, and songs (some excerpted from operas such as *Mignon* and *La Fille du tambour-major*), a trio, and a chorus from *Le Cigale et la fourmi*. Jacquet admitted that their repertoire could use some more variety, implying that perhaps they could do some Saint-Saëns. Most likely Jacquet learned a great deal from listening to Saint-Saëns practice the piano every day during the composer's month in Poulo Condore, even the Isidor Philipp exercises and chromatic scales in thirds.[24] After he left, Jacquet apparently began to write music, sending Saint-Saëns some small branches of a bush pasted on a colored ink drawing with the note *la* on a musical stave.

To a letter sent from Hué in 1901, Jacquet attached a program for a concert on 14 September in which he as well as Saint-Saëns were featured as composers alongside popular band composers Wettge, Waldteufel, and Corbin —Jacquet with a "concert" work, Saint-Saëns with a fantasy based on *Samson et Dalila* (see Figure 1). The image on the program features Indochinese musicians—some, if not all, women playing indigenous instruments, an analogue to the metaphorical females that adorned the programs of Parisian orchestras at the time. Handwritten at the top is the name of the ensemble, the military band of the Tenth Colonial Regiment. This was one of the few "mixed" ensembles including both Indochinese and French soldiers, unlike those with only French, or the *tirailleurs annamites* or *tirailleurs tonkinois*, with only locals. The Tenth Colonial, based in Haiphong, was visiting Hué at the time, which makes the inclusion of Jacquet's music on their program, published in Hanoi, all the more remarkable. Perhaps this came about after Jacquet met one of its new officers, a sous-lieutenant from Béziers, France, "black as the night," who "sang admirably" and knew Saint-Saëns's *Déjanire* by heart (*sur le bout des doigts*). The work had been written for the huge Béziers arena and premiered there in August 1898. Military and local bands played it in transcription each summer when Saint-Saëns returned for subsequent performances.[25] Naturally, as Jacquet noted, he and the sous-lieutenant "became very good friends immediately."[26]

Saint-Saëns's Music in Indochina

Probably because of Jacquet, Saint-Saëns began to think of Indochina as an outlet for his music. A year before his visit, he asked Durand to send a score of *Phryné* to Emile Sieffert, the résident supérieur in Hanoi. Saigon had produced its first Western opera, Offenbach's *Les Deux Aveugles*, just after the French arrived in 1864. Each year the city council published a

Figure 2. Louis Jacquet and his friends, c.1895-96.

Cahier de charges, indicating budget and other requirements for the theatrical season and chose a director, responsible for assembling a troupe of singers and orchestra players in France. Often local military band performers were added, although as Jacquet once reported to Saint-Saëns, this sometimes led to disputes between a director and the regiment. The repertoire was fairly conservative, but in 1894, of the twelve scores the director purchased from Choudens, seven works—including Bruneau's *L'Attaque du moulin*, Messager's *La Basoche* and *Madame Chrysanthème*—had only recently been premiered in Paris. Beginning in 1898 the *Cahier de charges* required "a minimum of five opéra-comiques and five operettes" that had not been done in Saigon in the past three years" or "works that are renowned and just appeared in France."

When Saint-Saëns attended the Saigon theater in 1895, he was a little disappointed: "I've just heard *Mignon* and *Manon*, very well sung I might add, but the orchestra is terrible." Again thinking that his own *Phryné* might be ideal in this context, he wrote to Durand, "There is a young light singer, Mlle Dupenet, who vocalizes with a stunning brilliance and would sing *Phryné* very well, if she only weren't so thin . . . with a nose that never ends."[27] Two years later Jacquet, visiting Saigon, wrote that the troupe was horrible and the public had even whistled at the tenor.[28] But locals were hopeful when a magnificent new theater was built, modeled on the Petit Palais in Paris. It opened in January 1901 with a first performance of Massenet's *La Navarraise* and had an "enormous success," especially with the soldiers who had just returned from their campaign in China. The 1900–1901 season was full of new works, including Puccini's *La Bohème* and Saint-Saëns's *Samson et Dalila*. Two new sets—the Dagon temple and the scene with the millstone—were built for the Saint-Saëns production, which apparently remained in their repertoire through 1910 along with *Hamlet*, *Carmen*, *Lohengrin*, *Lakmé*, and *Werther*, among dozens of others. By 1913, the opera was also in repertoire at the Hanoi theater.

The military band program from September 1901 typifies the way such works reached wide audiences in the colonies and entered the popular mainstream. Such performances suggest that even as far as Indochina, there was receptivity to new works, a desire to stay in touch with Parisian fashions perhaps because the west was associated with progress. What better emblem of this than new music?

NOTES

1. Jean Bonnerot, *C. Saint-Saëns, sa vie et son oeuvre* (Paris: Durand, 1923), 146–47.

2. See Figure 1 in Stéphane Leteuré's essay in this volume.

3. Louis Jacquet to Saint-Saëns, Singapore, 8 January 1890, Fonds Saint-Saëns, Chateau-Musée de Dieppe (FS). Saint-Saëns also corresponded with others from that ship, such as Mme Ricoux. She lived in Hanoi and invited him to visit.

4. Jacquet to Saint-Saëns, 8 December 1892, 1 April 1893, 18 January 1895, FS.

5. Saint-Saëns to Auguste Durand, Port Said, 10 January 1895, Coll. Médiathèque Musicale Mahler, Paris (MMM).

6. Jacquet to Saint-Saëns, Poulo Condore, 23 April 1895, FS.

7. Ibid. Evidently Saint-Saëns did meet some Japanese women in Saigon. See Jacquet's letter to him, Saigon, 1 March 1897, FS.

8. Jacquet to Saint-Saëns, 23 April 1895, 25 November 1901, 18 September 1902, FS.

9. Saint-Saëns to Auguste Durand, Saigon, 19 February, 5 March, 20 March 1895, MMM.

10. Jacquet to Saint-Saëns, Poulo Condore, 12 September 1895, FS.

11. Saint-Saëns to Auguste Durand, Poulo Condore, 20 March, 28 March 1895, MMM.

12. Jacquet to Saint-Saëns, Poulo Condore, 24 May 1895, FS.

13. Jacquet to Saint-Saëns, Iles de Poulo Condore, 4 November 1895, FS.

14. Jacquet to Saint-Saëns, Hué, 5 May 1899, FS.

15. Jacquet to Saint-Saëns, Poulo Condore, 21 April 1895, 4 July 1896, FS.

16. James Harding, *Saint-Saëns and His Circle* (London: Chapman & Hall, 1965), 22, 128.

17. Saint-Saëns to Durand, Petropolis, 9 June 1899, MMM.

18. See flower drawings also in his letters to Durand from Algiers, 18 February 1892, and Avignon, 12 August 1894, MMM, and to Louis Gallet, some of which are reproduced in J. L. Croze, "Camille Saint-Saëns: Fantaisies et pages intimes,"*Revue illustrée* 9 (1890): 272–74.

19. Jacquet to Saint-Saëns, Le Lang-Bian (Moïs country), 18 February 1898, FS.

20. Jacquet to Saint-Saëns, Poulo Condore, 2 May 1891, FS.

21. *Outspoken Essays on Music*, trans. Fred Rothwell (Freeport, NY: Books for Libraries Press, 1922), 128–29.

22. See Jann Pasler's essay on Saint-Saëns and d'Indy in this volume.

23. Jacquet to Saint-Saëns, Poulo Condore, 2 May 1891, FS.

24. Saint-Saëns to Durand, Poulo Condore, 28 March 1895, MMM.

25. The Fonds Saint-Saëns includes an all-Saint-Saëns program presented on 21 and 25 June 1903 by the Seventeenth Infantry Regiment in Béziers. The concert featured not only a fantasy on *Samson et Dalila*, but also a prelude and march from *Le Déluge*, a ballet from *Étienne Marcel*, and a waltz from *Le Timbre d'argent*.

26. Jacquet to Saint-Saëns, Hué, 25 May 1901, FS.

27. Saint-Saëns to Durand, Saigon, 19 February 1895, MMM.

28. Jacquet to Saint-Saëns, Saigon, 1 March 1897, FS.

Saint-Saëns in New York

CAROLYN GUZSKI

Camille Saint-Saëns arrived on American shores in 1906 only after prolonged deliberation. *New York Tribune* critic Henry E. Krehbiel recalled an anticipated visit at least fourteen years prior, and further negotiations at the turn of the century also proved fruitless. Yet the septuagenarian's ultimate decision to embark on an arduous two-month debut tour of the United States was emblematic of the cultural authority the nation had achieved by the opening decade of the twentieth century. Preceded by an enviable artistic reputation in America, Saint-Saëns rode the crest of a wave of European musical visitors seeking to promote their careers in the New World during the Gilded Age and Progressive Era.[1]

In the vanguard of historic arrivals were eighteenth-century British dramatic troupes who had introduced the London sensation of ballad opera to the colonies. The Federal period brought Continental musical celebrity to the young nation when the Spanish tenor Manuel del Pópolo Vicente García (1775–1832) and his family imported Italian opera to New York in 1825, but it was the 1850 tour of Jenny Lind (1820–1887) that revealed the potentially lucrative rewards available to the Europeans. After the Swedish soprano's inaugural concerts yielded an unprecedented $15,000 under the astute promotion of P. T. Barnum, virtuoso instrumentalists began to arrive in profusion. Rapid economic expansion in the Gilded Age encouraged musical instrument purveyors to entice the burgeoning middle-class market with figures of international prestige, and the 1872–73 Steinway-sponsored tour of the Ukrainian pianist Anton Rubinstein (1829–1894), an inseparable friend of Saint-Saëns in Paris, resulted in an astounding 215 concerts in 239 days, including seven farewell recitals in New York.[2]

Composers were comparatively late arrivals. Johann Strauss II (1825–1899), the "Waltz King," overcame his aversion to the long sea voyage to make an 1872 visit to New York and Boston, host of the World's Peace Jubilee and International Music Festival; and Jacques Offenbach (1819–1880) endeavored to offset unexpected bankruptcy proceedings in Paris by importing the opéra-

Figure 1. Program for the Saint-Saëns concert at Carnegie Hall, 18 November 1907.

PROGRAMME—Continued

3. Algerian Suite,   *Saint-Saens*
   a. Arrival in the Harbor
   b. Moorish Rhapsody
   c. Evening Reverie
   d. French Military March

4. Soli for Piano—
   a. Valse mignonne
   b. Valse nonchalante   } *Saint-Saens*
   c. Valse Canariote
      Played by the Composer

5. a. Le Rouet d'Omphale, Poeme Symphonique,
                                       Saint-Saens
      (By general request)
   b. Phaeton, Poeme Symphonique,   *Saint-Saens*

KNABE PIANO USED

For special announcements see second page following

Figure 1 continued

bouffe vogue to the 1876 Centennial International Exhibition in Philadelphia. The appearance of Pyotr Il'yich Tchaikovsky (1840–1893) at the 1891 opening of Andrew Carnegie's new hall for music raised the artistic bar: the composer conducted several performances of his music in New York, including the Piano Concerto no. 1 in B-flat, op. 23, whose first performance in 1875 Boston was a rare example of a major European world premiere in nineteenth-century America.[3] An apex was reached with the advent of Antonín Dvořák (1841–1904) as director of New York's National Conservatory of Music from 1892 to 1895. The distinguished Bohemian made artistic contributions in his new surroundings that continue to reverberate on the American cultural scene—notably, the 1893 world premiere of the Symphony no. 9 in E minor, op. 95 (*New World*) at Carnegie Hall.[4]

Saint-Saëns's timing seemed impeccable: his October–December 1906 visit, placed between the 1904 tour of Richard Strauss (1864–1949) and the imminent arrival of Giacomo Puccini (1858–1924) in January 1907, presented a luminous constellation of American debuts to the New York public within a three-year span. The unprecedented cluster of the pre-eminent composers of Germany, France, and Italy reflected the cosmopolitan atmosphere that had developed in the East Coast cultural centers, but the reality of German hegemony in New York symphonic circles and growing Italian dominance at the opera presented a unique artistic challenge. French influence had historically served as a counterweight to the sustained influence of *Kultur*, as Americans remained in thrall to the German emigrants who had educated the country musically. Fresh developments in the national sphere, however, began to impinge on the German legacy by the turn of the new century: a prolonged student exodus bleeding talent to the Leipzig Conservatory (the nineteenth-century educational institution of choice) began to dissipate, the musical generation inspired by Dvořák promoted indigenous materials and training, and popular trends—typified by the dramatic rise of ragtime—were vividly in the ascendant.[5]

Franco-American cultural relations remained in flux, yet French music in New York drew on an extensive nineteenth-century symphonic performance tradition that had ironically received impetus from three German-born conductors—Carl Bergmann (1821–1876), Theodore Thomas (1835–1905), and Leopold Damrosch (1832–1885)—who successively introduced America to the music of Hector Berlioz, a radical stance at midcentury.[6] A heated rivalry for new scores that had developed between Thomas and Damrosch extended naturally to those of Saint-Saëns; the three were almost exact contemporaries, and Damrosch's acquaintance with the composer dated from 1857, when the pair were young associates of Liszt at Weimar.[7] British critic Hermann Klein, who heard Saint-Saëns play in London just as his music was achieving prominence in New York during the 1870s, remembered, "His music at that period had about it a strange, exotic ring, a touch of newness that suggested Berlioz rather than the modern German school, yet not exactly reminiscent of either. In short, it sounded original."[8]

New York audiences first heard major works of Saint-Saëns when the Theodore Thomas Orchestra gave the American premieres of the symphonic poems *Le Rouet d'Omphale*, op. 31, in 1875 and *Danse macabre*, op. 40, in 1876.[9] In 1879 Damrosch's competing New York Symphony Society offered his Symphony no. 2, op. 55, and before long Boston, the "Athens of America," entered the fray, chiefly under Carl Zerrahn (1826–1909), director of the Handel and Haydn Society and Harvard Musical Association. The two cities shared an impressive string of Saint-Saëns premieres across the final quarter of the nineteenth century.[10]

With Leopold Damrosch's untimely death in 1885, the torch passed to his son Walter, who at twenty-three exhibited sufficient expertise to take on his father's founding legacy with the New York orchestra (if not his masterful conducting skills). The necessity of maintaining a competitive edge against the unassailable German repertoire dominance of the New York Philharmonic required supremacy in the French realm, a strategy that redounded immediately to Saint-Saëns's benefit when his new barcarolle for small orchestra and harp (*Une Nuit à Lisbonne*, op. 63) appeared on the debut concert of the new music director.[11] After Theodore Thomas left the city in 1891 to helm the new Chicago Symphony, Damrosch easily dominated the field with over three-quarters of the Saint-Saëns performances heard in New York. Two particularly high-profile events furthered the composer's already considerable reputation: the 1891 American debut of Ignacy Jan Paderewski (1860–1941), catapulted to celebrity with a performance of the Piano Concerto no. 4 in C minor, op. 44 (the first Saint-Saëns score heard at Carnegie Hall); and the first U.S. presentation of *Samson et Dalila*, a March 1892 concert version at Carnegie Hall that anticipated its Paris Opéra staging by eight months. The firm position held by Saint-Saëns in the symphonic repertory also garnered critical respect from the exigent critic of the *New York Post*, Henry T. Finck, who noted the composer's infiltration of historically Austro-German territory by commending him as "the first Frenchman who may be said to have successfully competed with German composers on their own ground."[12]

Renewed plans for an American tour appear to have coalesced during the summer of 1906, as Damrosch received a formal proposal from Knabe Pianos representative Bernhard Ulrich in July that offered Saint-Saëns's engagement as conductor, pianist, or organist.[13] The overture came at an auspicious juncture. Damrosch had only recently won a hard-fought battle with New York's formidable Musical Mutual Protective Union to reconfigure his woodwind section with French-Belgian principals, a strategy designed to counter the superiority of the Boston Symphony Orchestra in its appearances at Carnegie Hall.[14] Despite the surprisingly late arrangements—negotiations for the November concerts extended into late September—the conductor seized the opportunity to showcase his revitalized ensemble by engaging France's greatest living composer. In 1905–6, Damrosch's French repertoire component rose to a 22 percent share of his programming, in contrast to 6 percent at the New York Philharmonic, during a season that included the New York premiere of Debussy's *Prélude à l'après-midi d'un faune* as well as works by Berlioz, Lalo, Dukas, and d'Indy.[15] When Ulrich requested a steep $1,200 per appearance, Damrosch responded creatively by engaging Saint-Saëns as pianist to open the 1906–7 season (no fee details are extant), then scheduled two non-subscription concerts of the composer's music for which he and Ulrich would privately share expenses and profit.[16]

Repertoire considerations emerged as a crucial element of the American scene as composers' visits grew increasingly dependent on the *réclame* associated with premieres. Pietro Mascagni (1863–1945) had planned his 1902 American debut around the U.S. premieres of *Iris* and *Guglielmo Ratcliff*, his latest essays in verismo; Richard Strauss was "treated like a visiting head of state" during a tour in which he conducted the world premiere of the *Symphonia Domestica* at Carnegie Hall on 21 March 1904; and the Metropolitan Opera had already invited Puccini to supervise the first staging in Italian in America of his three-year-old *Madama Butterfly* during the 1906–7 season.[17] Concern was also posed by potential comparison with the 1905 visit of Vincent d'Indy (1851–1931), who made a notable U.S. debut as the first musician invited to guest conduct the Boston Symphony Orchestra at Carnegie Hall. Viewed as an influential if controversial figure in the burgeoning French modernist school that captured the imagination of the musical public, the composer provoked wide discussion with programs focused on French works of the preceding decade.[18]

Damrosch acknowledged the audience fascination with novelty by successfully suggesting Saint-Saëns's *Africa*, for piano and orchestra, op. 89 (1891), as the debut's centerpiece because "it has never been played here." The New York premieres of the orchestrated Allegro Appassionato, op. 70 (1884), and Valse-caprice (*Wedding Cake*), op. 76 (1885), were soon added to the program.[19] Extant promotional materials also reveal that the original description of the composer as "distinguished" was changed to "famous," and that his work was positioned to reflect its pathbreaking origins:

Curiously enough, Saint-Saëns, looked up to as the dean of the French composers, is today considered a conservative force. In his younger years, as a disciple of Liszt, he was viewed as a great revolutionist. Thus wags the world.[20]

Enthusiastically received by a large and demonstrative audience at the debut performance, the seventy-one-year-old soloist retained a virtuoso command of the keyboard, as his historic 1904 Paris recordings testify. Moreover, the performance represented a physical triumph in light of the pianist's continuing struggle with the lingering symptoms of a near-fatal case of influenza contracted on the Atlantic crossing.[21] But the repertoire strategy misfired with the city's leading critics, who were unimpressed by "pretty trifles" with "small claim to be set forth as really representative of his quality as a composer." The two subsequent all-Saint-Saëns programs on 15 and 18 November (see Figure 1) embodied a largely retrospective approach that returned the composer to solid ground with the press: "The greeting to him in person has been none the less heartily given because he comes as the composer of what has been so long known here and not as one making a new propaganda for his art."[22] Saint-Saëns evidently proposed to perform the Piano Concerto no. 5, op. 103 (*Egyptian*; 1896), which he considered the New York premiere, unaware that Raoul Pugno had performed it there in 1898. But no composition after 1886 was included among the other major works given: the Piano Concerto no. 2, op. 22; Symphonies no. 2 and 3 (*Organ*); ballet music from *Henry VIII*; the symphonic poem *Phaéton*, op. 39; and a repetition of *Le Rouet d'Omphale*.[23]

Attendance at the special concerts was lower than expected, with Carnegie Hall reaching two-thirds of its capacity by the second program.[24] The New York season was thick with notable visitors—Ruggero Leoncavallo (1857–1919), Alexander Scriabin (1872–1915), virtuoso pianists Moriz Rosenthal (1862–1946), Josef Lhévinne (1874–1944), and Ossip Gabrilovich (1878–1936)—but Saint-Saëns avoided being drawn into open competition with his colleagues, particularly when interviewed on the potentially incendiary topic of musical modernism. After Leoncavallo had unwisely criticized Wagnerian music drama on the record, the French composer maintained a diplomatic approach: "My position is what it was from the first. I admired and praised the Wagner music dramas and still do so. But I could not go with the Wagnerites." When it came to contemporary French music, he explained, "I am not here to criticize others. I am here to interpret my own works, and must let others interpret theirs, if they wish. I particularly do not wish to criticize the younger men. I am perfectly willing that they should do their work."[25] In his final accounting to Ulrich, Damrosch acknowledged a classic *succès d'estime*: "I regret for both our sakes that the financial results were not as brilliant as the artistic, but personally I gladly contribute my share towards the deficiency because of the pleasure that these very dignified concerts have been to me."[26]

Invigorated by his New York reception, the composer traveled to Philadelphia and Chicago, where he performed the popular Piano Concerto no. 2 in G Minor with the Chicago Symphony Orchestra, before continuing on to Washington, D.C. The capital's historic New National Theater was the venue for Saint-Saëns's belated Boston Symphony Orchestra debut, at which he repeated the G-Minor Concerto under Karl Muck in the presence of President Theodore Roosevelt. Saint-Saëns was delighted by the attendance of the chief executive, who hosted a distinguished party that included French ambassador Jean Jules Jusserand, Secretary of War William Howard Taft, Massachusetts Senator Henry Cabot Lodge, and first daughter Alice Roosevelt escorted by her new husband, Ohio Congressman Nicholas Longworth IV.[27] On the pianist's return to New York, a solo recital at Carnegie Hall arranged at the request of his admirers, followed by a farewell concert at the Metropolitan Opera on Christmas Day 1906, brought the arduous sojourn to a festive conclusion.

Saint-Saëns reflected on his memorable North American experiences (he returned only once to the United States, in 1915) in the charming essay "Impressions of America." With characteristic elegance, the composer offered a poetic valediction: "What pleased me abroad was not so much the present America as the idea of what America will eventually be. I seemed to behold a mighty crucible in which a thousand ingredients are mixed to form an unknown substance. . . . Everything one sees in America appears, from a distance, as a kind of mirage, for we are still in a transition period, preparing for a new world."[28]

NOTES

I gratefully acknowledge the assistance of archivists Robert Hudson (Carnegie Hall), Richard Wandel (New York Philharmonic), and Robert Kosovsky (New York Public Library) in navigating the extant documentation on Saint-Saëns in New York. I thank Sylvia Kahan and John Graziano of the CUNY Graduate School and Ivan Docenko of SUNY College at Buffalo for their invaluable contributions.

1. Henry E. Krehbiel, "Charles Camille Saint-Saëns: A Representative of French Music," *The Etude* 25 (June 1907): 369. In correspondence, the composer mentioned several times the possibility of coming to America prior to 1906. In 1893, invited both to the Universal Exhibition in Chicago and to the University of Cambridge to receive an honorary doctorate, he felt obliged to accept the latter.

2. John Dizikes, *Opera in America: A Cultural History* (New Haven and London: Yale University Press, 1993), 18; Vera Brodsky Lawrence, "First Fling," *Opera News* 53 (September 1988): 22–23; William Brooks, "Jenny Lind," *The New Grove Dictionary of American Music*, ed. H. Wiley Hitchcock and Stanley Sadie (London and New York: Macmillan, 1986), 3:87–88; Harold C. Schonberg, *The Great Pianists*, rev. ed. (New York: Simon and Schuster, 1987), 272, 276.

3. "Herr Strauss' Concerts," *New York Times*, 9 July 1872, 5; Andrew Lamb, "Jacques Offenbach," in *Grove Music Online, Oxford Music Online*, http://www.oxfordmusiconline.com/ subscriber/article/grove/ music/20271; George Martin, *The Damrosch Dynasty: America's First Family of Music* (Boston: Houghton Mifflin, 1983), 113–19.

4. John C. Tibbetts, ed., *Dvořák in America, 1892–1895* (Portland, OR: Amadeus Press, 1993); Jack Sullivan, *New World Symphonies: How American Culture Changed European Music* (New Haven and London: Yale University Press, 1999).

5. E. Douglas Bomberger, "The German Musical Training of American Students, 1850–1900" (PhD diss., University of Maryland, College Park, 1991); Lawrence Gilman, "The New American Music," *North American Review* 179 (December 1904): 868–72. Dvořák's views were originally quoted in "Real Value of Negro Melodies," *New York Herald*, 21 May 1893, which became a sensation and was reprinted abroad.

6. Ora Frishberg Saloman, "Presenting Berlioz's Music in New York, 1846–1890," in *European Music and Musicians in New York City, 1840–1900*, ed. John Graziano (Rochester, NY: University of Rochester Press, 2006), 29.

7. Walter Damrosch, *My Musical Life* (New York: Charles Scribner's Sons, 1923), 154.

8. Hermann Klein, "Saint-Saëns As I Knew Him," *Musical Times*, 1 February 1922, 91.

9. The first known Saint-Saëns New York orchestral performance occurred in July 1867, when Thomas programmed the Tarantelle, op. 6, for his Terrace Garden outdoor concert series. *New York Herald*, 5 July 1867.

10. H. Earle Johnson, *First Performances in America to 1900: Works with Orchestra* (Detroit: Information Coordinators, 1979), 305–16. An astonishing number appeared shortly after their Paris premieres: *Le Rouet d'Omphale*, op. 31 (Paris 1873, New York 1875); *Phaéton*, op. 39 (Paris 1873, Boston 1876); Cello Concerto no. 1, op. 33 (Paris 1873, Boston 1876); *Danse macabre*, op. 40 (Paris 1875, New York 1876); *La Jeunesse d'Hercule*, op. 50 (Paris and Boston, 1877); Piano Concerto no. 4, op. 44 (Paris 1875, Boston 1878); *Le Déluge*, op. 45 (Paris 1876, Boston 1880); *Suite algérienne*, op. 60 (Paris 1880, Boston 1881); *Rhapsodie d'Auvergne*, op. 73 (Paris 1884, Boston 1886); Symphony no. 3 (*Organ*), op. 78 (London 1886, New York 1887); and Piano Concerto no. 5 (*Egyptian*), op. 103 (Paris 1896, New York 1898).

11. "Amusements: The Symphony Society," *New York Times*, 28 March 1885. The work was formally identified when Damrosch repeated the program on the occasion of his twenty-fifth anniversary performance with the ensemble; "Music: The Damrosch Jubilee," *New-York Tribune*, 16 March 1910.

12. Finck, *New York Evening Post*, 27 October 1906, quoted in Robert L. Carter, "Sidelights on Saint-Saëns," *Musical Courier*, 31 October 1906, 21.

13. Bernhard Ulrich to Walter Damrosch, 6 July 1906, Walter Damrosch Papers, New York Public Library for the Performing Arts, Series 3, Box 8, "Saint-Saëns"; hereafter Damrosch Papers. The brevity of the document suggests that Damrosch had preliminary knowledge of the project.

14. Damrosch was fined a substantial $1,000 but ultimately was permitted to import Georges Barrère (flute), Marcel Tabuteau (oboe/English horn), Leon Leroy (clarinet), and Auguste Mesnard (bassoon) together with Adolph Dubois (trumpet) to the orchestra. Martin, *Damrosch Dynasty*, 131, 189–90.

15. The New York Philharmonic Archives, http://nyphil.org/about/archives.cfm, contains comprehensive performance information for both orchestras, which merged in 1928.

16. The New York Philharmonic had refused to exceed its $750 ceiling for Eugène Ysaÿe in 1904–5; see Howard Shanet, *Philharmonic: A History of New York's Orchestra* (Garden

City, NY: Doubleday, 1975), 202–3. Damrosch to Ulrich, 29 September 1906, Damrosch Papers, Series 5, Box 13, "1904–1909 (Part B)."

17. Alan Mallach, "The Mascagni Tour of 1902," *Opera Quarterly* 7 (Winter 1990): 14; Bryan Gilliam, *The Life of Richard Strauss* (Cambridge and New York: Cambridge University Press, 1999), 82. The trend continued across the following decade: Gustav Mahler (1860–1911) conducted the 1908 U.S. premiere of his Symphony no. 2 (*Resurrection*) in the first year of his American career; Sergei Rachmaninoff (1873–1943) composed the Piano Concerto no. 3, op. 30, for his U.S. debut at Carnegie Hall in November 1909; and Jean Sibelius brought the world premiere commission of his tone poem *The Oceanides* to the Norfolk Music Festival in June 1914.

18. The composers represented were Fauré (Saint-Saëns's most renowned pupil), Chausson, Dukas, Franck, Debussy, Albéric Magnard, and d'Indy himself. "The Boston Symphony Orchestra Again: A New Symphony by Vincent d'Indy Given," *New York Times*, 13 December 1905.

19. Damrosch to Saint-Saëns, 26 September 1906, Damrosch Papers, Series 3, Box 8, "Saint-Saëns." The correspondence belies the suggestion of biographer Stephen Studd that the content of the debut program may have represented a late substitution for more substantial works originally planned. Studd, *Saint-Saëns: A Critical Biography* (London: Cygnus Arts; and Madison, NJ: Fairleigh Dickinson University Press, 1999), 245.

20. Press releases, New York Symphony Society, Season 1906–1907; Damrosch Papers, Series 3, Box 8, "Saint-Saëns."

21. *Legendary Piano Recordings: The Complete Grieg, Saint-Saëns, Pugno, and Diémer* (Swarthmore, PA: Marston Records, 2008); "Saint-Saëns Ill at Sea," *New York Times*, 25 October 1906; Studd, *Saint-Saëns*, 244–46.

22. Henry E. Krehbiel, "The Coming of M. Saint-Saëns," *New York Tribune*, 4 November 1906; [Richard Aldrich], "Dr. Saint-Saëns's First Appearance," *New York Times*, 4 November 1906; [Aldrich], "Dr. Saint-Saëns Again Appears in Concert: Shows to More Advantage in His Second Programme," *New York Times*, 16 November 1906.

23. The programs were largely comprised of works heard most frequently by New York audiences in the preceding decades. The Pugno performance (which included the U.S. premiere of Franck's Symphonic Variations), conducted by Theodore Thomas with the Chicago Symphony Orchestra at Carnegie Hall, was evidently unknown to both Damrosch and Saint-Saëns. "A Concert of French Music," *New York Tribune*, 8 March 1898; letter from Saint-Saëns to Johannès Wolff, 19 November 1906: "Yesterday I gave the premiere of the Fifth Concerto. People always want to hear the G Minor and have me play it in spite of myself. The Fifth was very well received despite its novelty. I am delighted with Damrosch and his orchestra." My translation; cited in French in Sabina Teller Ratner, *Camille Saint-Saëns 1835–1921: A Thematic Catalogue of His Complete Works* (Oxford and New York: Oxford University Press, 2002), 1:401.

24. Carnegie Hall box office statements, 15/18 November 1906, Damrosch Papers, Series 5, Box 13, "1904–1909 (Part B)."

25. Konrad Dryden, *Leoncavallo: Life and Works* (Lanham, MD, and Toronto: Scarecrow Press, 2007), 103–4; "Dr. Camille Saint-Saëns Discusses Modern Music," *New York Times*, 25 November 1906.

26. Letter and account summary from Damrosch to Ulrich, 24 November 1906, Damrosch Papers, Series 5, Box 13, "1904–1909 (Part B)."

27. "President at Concert," *Washington Post*, 5 December 1906, 13. The composer was originally scheduled to make his American debut with the Boston Symphony Orchestra in Boston, but postponed the date due to his illness.

28. In *Outspoken Essays on Music*, trans. Fred Rothwell (London: Kegan Paul; and New York: E. P. Dutton, 1922), 150–51.

Saint-Saëns and Latin America

CAROL A. HESS

A musical citizen of the world, Camille Saint-Saëns traveled to Latin America in 1899, 1904, and 1916, visiting Brazil, Argentina, and Uruguay in various combinations. In this essay, I briefly invite further reflection on these trips and suggest ways that a Latin Americanist perspective can enhance our understanding of French music on the international stage during Saint-Saëns's times. All three of his visits cry out for more hard data, especially the 1899 journey. For example, Jean Bonnerot tells us that performances by Saint-Saëns and various string players accrued "two months of triumphs" in Argentina.[1] Stephen Studd, on the other hand, contends that Saint-Saëns actually went to Rio de Janeiro and São Paulo, blaming "ignoran[ce] of South American geography" for prior faulty reports.[2] Indeed, recently discovered data provide new evidence of Saint-Saëns having visited Rio and performed there (see Figure 1).[3]

Lack of information about South America extends beyond geography. Although Latin American musical research has seen considerable activity in recent years, scholars have yet to undertake the sort of work essential to understanding Saint-Saëns's experience there—namely, assessing the agendas of the various critics and the political orientations of the papers for which they wrote. Yet an undocumented statement can beckon, such as Studd's assertion that during the 1899 trip "Saint-Saëns caused some bad feeling by admitting that he did not know any South American composers or their music."[4] To whom did Saint-Saëns address this remark? Was it reported in the press? If so, by whom, and what was the newspaper's political slant? If the anecdote is true, Saint-Saëns's confession neatly crystallizes the interplay between local and international influence that has been reenacted in so many contexts throughout Latin American history. To be sure, Saint-Saëns's Latin American contemporaries sought recognition for themselves and the musical traditions of their respective countries, most notably Carlos Gomes of Brazil, whose opera *Il Guarany* had triumphed in 1870 at La Scala. Yet these composers embraced both the

THEATRO S. PEDRO DE ALCANTARA

Domingo, 2 de Julho de 1899, á 1 hora da tarde

Concerto de Despedida

DE

CAMILLE SAINT-SAËNS

Com o valioso concurso dos Srs. Arthur Napoleão, V. Cernicchiaro e F. Cordiglia Lavalle

PROGRAMMA

PRIMEIRA PARTE

1 BALLET DE HENRY VIII (a pedido)........ **Saint-Saëns**
1 *Introduction. Entrée des Clans*—2 *Idylle Ecossaise* —3 *Danse de la Gipsy*—4 *Gigue et Final.*

2 2ᵉ SYMPHONIE, (la mineur) (a pedido) n. 2 et n. 3 »

3 SCHERZO, pour deux pianos............. »

Saint-Saëns—Arthur Napoleão

SEGUNDA PARTE

1 HENRY VIII, Entr'acte du 2ᵉ acte......... »

2 3ᵉ CONCERT, pour violon et orchestre....... »

V. Cernicchiaro

3 *a*) NUIT A LISBONNE, dediée à S. M. D. Luiz, Roi de Portugal.... *b*) RIGAUDON................. »

TERCEIRA PARTE

1 DANSE MACABRE, poême symphonique...... »

2 RAPSODIE D'AUVERGNE, piano et orchestre... »

Saint-Saëns

3 VARIATIONS, sur un thême de Beethoven (a pedido).......................... »

Saint-Saëns—Arthur Napoleão

NOTA—Na 2ª parte e na RAPSODIE D'AUVERGNE a orchestra é regida pelo Sr. *Cordiglia Lavalle.*

TYP. DO JORNAL DO COMMERCIO

Figure 1. The composer performed at this all-Saint-Saëns concert in Rio de Janeiro in July 1899.

national *and* the cosmopolitan. Far from resisting the latter, they often deliberately set out to cultivate it, favoring Italian and, mainly, French models. Their outlook reminds us that globalization is with us not only today but also shaped the art music of the past.

Approaching Saint-Saëns's Latin American experience in these terms corresponds to recent trends in both historical musicology and Latin American studies. Whereas scholars once evaluated European music within a surprisingly narrow geographic range (that is, within Europe itself), many now probe its reach in Asia, Africa, and the Americas.[5] Consequently, labels such as "French," "German," or "Latin American" music, although still useful in certain contexts, may seem cramped, or at least redolent of once-potent nationalist frameworks. A similar non-nationalist orientation has taken shape in Latin American studies. Preoccupied in recent decades by questions of difference, scholars nowadays acknowledge this important construct but also some of the excesses that have been committed in its name, including what we might call—*pace* Benedict Anderson —"imagined nationalisms."[6]

As for Saint-Saëns, two of the cities he visited, Rio de Janeiro and Buenos Aires, have been dubbed "the Paris of Latin America." Leaving aside the question of which had the more valid claim, we can sketch out some parameters of this French-tinged aesthetic agenda in Rio de Janeiro, thanks to a fine recent study by Cristina Magaldi. Upper-class *cariocas* (residents of Rio) read French-language music magazines and bought pianos from Paris, such as those by the pianist and piano manufacturer Henri Herz, marketed as especially "suitable for the Brazilian climate."[7] By the 1880s, *cariocas* were flocking to the Eldorado, a local version of the Alcazar d'Été in the Champs-Élysées, and to mass concerts modeled on Jules Pasdeloup's Concerts populaires. In 1887, Carlos de Mesquita initiated the Sociedade de Concertos Populares, a showcase for Brazilian nationalism that featured works by Arthur Napoleão, Francisco Braga, and Alberto Neopomuceno, just as Saint-Saëns's own Société nationale de musique had initially promoted French music. Works by Massenet, Chabrier, and Saint-Saëns himself were also programmed at the Sociedade to satisfy Francophile appetites.[8]

To be sure, this phenomenon was especially strong before 1889, when Pedro II quietly left the country amid Republican fervor and the time-honored image of a refined "Tropical Versailles" began to rapidly lose its luster.[9] Yet cosmopolitanism continued to compel. More than a mere craving, Magaldi observes, Paris "served as a filter" through which many European musical styles passed before they were reshaped by Brazilians, a phenomenon whose effects were felt for decades.[10] These reshapings bear out Néstor García Canclini's oft-cited theories of hybridity, accord-ing to which cultural representations arise through networks of practices and agendas that reconstitute themselves in the public imagination, often in surprising ways.[11] For example, after Offenbach's *L'Orphée aux enfers* premiered in 1865 at the Alcazar Lyrique (managed by a Frenchman), the cancan, with its air of *scandale*, came to influence Carnaval, contributing to the bacchanalian spirit that remains one of that extravaganza's chief attractions today.[12] Yet Brazilians cherished their cosmopolitanism. We might assume that a 1937 Portuguese translation of the Italian-language *Il Guarany*, which appeared during the intense official nationalism of dictator Getúlio Vargas, would be warmly greeted. But as Magaldi argues, the translation was rejected because it "clashed with the work's very foundation," namely, the premise that locally trained composers could satisfy both local and inter-national publics.[13]

What of the other "Paris of Latin America," Buenos Aires? Interested in Latin American musical genres (the *Havanaise* for violin and orchestra dates from 1887), Saint-Saëns in 1901 assayed an even better-known genre, the Argentine tango, in *Lola*, a *scène dramatique*, which some believe to be the first European rendering of that dance.[14] Given the complex ety-mology of the term, along with obvious overlaps between the tango and the *habanera* and a paucity of sources on the turn-of-the-century tango, such a claim must be viewed with caution.[15] Three years later, in July, Saint-Saëns arrived in Buenos Aires, the home of the tango, and possibly performed throughout Argentina.[16]

But it was not until his visit of 1916 that Saint-Saëns became acquainted with the most compelling symbol of Argentine cosmopolitanism, the Teatro Colón. Finished in 1908 in the heart of Buenos Aires, the seven-tiered, acoustically perfect Colón was more than an example of neo-French Renaissance architecture transplanted to the Americas. With its great hall and marble staircase reminiscent of the Opéra, the Colón has served as a monument to elite culture, a potent topic in a country that had debated "civilization versus barbarism" since 1854, when essayist and politician Domingo Sarmiento published his hard-hitting essay, "Civilización y bar-barie o vida de Juan Facundo Quiroga," which refers to the eponymous Argentine military man and politician but is actually a pamphlet against dictator Juan Manuel de Rosas. The Colón was also a site of critical debate over musical *argentinidad* (Argentine identity), which some believed should proclaim its cosmopolitanism while others advocated folklore, an espe-cially heated topic at the turn of the twentieth century when *argentinidad* itself seemed to be threatened by waves of immigration.[17] In addition, the Colón represented economic well-being: from Saint-Saëns's 1916 visit and throughout the 1920s, Argentina was the wealthiest country in Latin America.[18]

At the height of the Great War, Latin America was a target of propaganda from both the Allies and Central Powers. As contemporaneous author Gaston Gaillard noted, German banks, commercial enterprises, cultural associations, and growing populations empowered pan-Germanism in "all its brutality" despite whatever spiritual ties of *latinité* existed between Latin America and France.[19] Stéphane Leteuré argues persuasively that Saint-Saëns himself practiced cultural diplomacy during the 1916 trip, albeit in an unofficial capacity.[20] He arrived in Buenos Aires on 15 May, where audiences would have known some of his orchestral works from performances at the Colón: in 1909, *Le Déluge*, Symphony no. 3, repeated in 1915; in 1911, *Marche héroïque*; in 1915, *Danse macabre*, *La Rouet d'Omphale*, *Introduction et Rondo capriccioso*; and in 1916, *La Jeunesse d'Hercule* and Piano Concerto no. 4.[21] In 1910 and 1914, the Colón had heard *Samson et Dalila*, both times in Italian. Saint-Saëns would conduct the 1916 *Samson* and the three singers who had made the long journey with him would sing (in French) the roles of Dalila (Jacqueline Royer), Samson (Léon Lafitte), and the High Priest (Marcel Journet). One critic at opening night (probably Ernesto de la Guardia) offered a veritable catalogue of *latinité*'s aesthetic qualities, noting in Saint-Saëns's "Gallic art" a "perfect balance and harmony of proportions, craftsmanship as secure as it is subtle, nobility of declamation . . . a pure and elevated melodic sentiment . . . the supreme elegance of style."[22]

If the Colón welcomed Saint-Saëns with open arms so, too, did the neo-classical Teatro Solís across the River Plate in Montevideo. One of the oldest still-functioning theaters in the Americas, it opened on 25 August 1856 (Independence Day), presenting *Ernani* to a public already acquainted with Italian opera and European culture in general. The European heritage, specifically its "Latin" dimension, was taken up in Uruguay by José Enrique Rodó in his essay of 1900, "Ariel," which would be widely read for some four decades.[23] An allegory of Shakespeare's *The Tempest*, written in the aftermath of the effortless *yanqui* victory in the Spanish-American War, "Ariel" upholds the Southern Hemisphere's intrinsically Latin sensibility as an antidote to the materialism of Caliban (the United States). In short, what became known in Latin America as *arielismo* rested on the same values as those associated with *latinité*.

Accompanied by the conductor-composer André Messager and the composer Xavier Leroux, Saint-Saëns traveled in July to Montevideo, performing his fifth piano concerto and Mozart's Concerto in A Major, K. 488, and conducting his *Rhapsodie d'Auvergne* at the Solís. Some propose that

Saint-Saëns forged even closer bonds in Uruguay: imbued with "liberté, egalité, fraternité," the country had declared 14 July a national holiday.[24] To be sure, the circumstances under which Saint-Saëns composed a *Hymne pour le 14 juillet* as a new national anthem require further study.[25] Surely the idea of Saint-Saëns leaving his mark in Uruguay in this way has its appeal, as does the playing of *La Marseillaise* when the Grand Old Man of French music bid farewell to Latin America for the last time, risking the same fate on his return trip as that of Spanish composer Enrique Granados, who died in the English Channel on the last leg of a trip from the United States when his ship was torpedoed by a German U-boat.

Was Latin American admiration for Saint-Saëns and for cosmopolitanism in general rooted in a cultural inferiority complex? As I have pointed out elsewhere, inflated comparisons such as the "Paris of Latin America" often do little more than seal peripheral status.[26] Magaldi proposes that social realities in Rio de Janeiro (poor sewage, lack of basic infrastructure, and outright filth) were sufficiently overwhelming that *cariocas* listened to concert music "to imagine they were somewhere else."[27] Also complicating Francophile fantasies in Latin America was the region's racial diversity. Given Brazil's large African population, many viewed the country as essentially African—even after slavery was abolished in 1888. In a country such as Peru, where elites have long exploited a large indigenous population, any sense of cultural advancement enjoyed by composers such as José María Valle Riestra (1859–1925) or Luis Lavalle (1874–1922) was inevitably counterbalanced by the bleak conditions of everyday life.

With these realities in mind, we can examine another expression of French patriotism in Latin America. In May 1910, Saint-Saëns's *Marche heroïque* (*Marcha heróica*) was performed at Lima's Teatro Municipal.[28] Saint-Saëns, immortalized in the Peruvian capital today with a street sign, wrote the march for his friend Henri Regnault, who died in the siege of Paris in 1870. There, the work had resounded in Good Friday concerts of 1879 and 1881, ensuring that love of country assumed sacred connotations, as Jann Pasler has observed.[29] In Peru, the march was more generally construed as a promise of victory in the midst of ongoing struggle against poverty, political unrest, and military conflicts. The anonymous program annotator gives pride of place to Regnault's own words: "We have lost many men and must replace them with other ones, better and stronger," but adds "pain is not a principle of annihilation but a fruitful motive for action." Thus, a first-world composer's homage to a European tragedy is sufficiently ample to hint at local "pain" and serve as a call to action. Surely Saint-Saëns's Latin American experience involves many more such correspondences among cosmopolitanism, local expression, and the actual conditions of day-to-day life, all waiting to be illuminated.

NOTES

1. Jean Bonnerot, *Camille Saint-Saëns, 1835–1921* (Paris: Durand, 1922), 169.

2. Stephen Studd, *Saint-Saëns: A Critical Biography* (London: Cygnus Arts; Madison, NJ: Fairleigh Dickinson University Press, 1999), 222.

3. On 24 May 1899 Saint-Saëns wrote Durand about possibly writing a Brazilian suite for piano with six movements: "1. La Baie de Rio, prelude; 2. Petrópolis, allegro maestoso; 3. Le Singe et le perroqué, scherzo; 4. La Foret vierge, reverie; 5. L'Araignée et le scorpion, 2e scherzo; and 6. Les Nègres libres, finale." He would ask Clairin for illustrations. Then, on 9 June 1899, from the Hotel d'Europa, Petrópolis (Rio de Janeiro state), he discussed his stay in Brazil, including programs for two of his five concerts there— all-Saint-Saëns concerts at the Theatro S. Pedro de Alcantara on 25 June and 2 July 1899, in which the composer performed. He also mentions chamber music concerts there, the first on Sunday the 18th. He planned to return to Europe on 12 July. The letter is housed at the Médiathèque Musicale Mahler (MMM), Paris. [Ed.]

4. Studd, *Saint-Saëns,* 222.

5. For example, Edward Said's "The Empire at Work: Verdi's *Aida,*" which considers Verdi's opera in its Egyptian context and challenges the assumption that "the West and its culture are largely independent of other cultures." Said, *Culture and Imperialism* (New York: Vintage Books, 1994), 111.

6. Camilla Fojas, *Cosmopolitanism in the Americas* (West Lafayette, IN: Purdue University Press, 2005); Akhil Gupta and James Ferguson, "Beyond Culture: Space, Identity, and the Politics of Difference," in *Culture, Power, and Place: Explorations in Critical Anthropology*, ed. Akhil Gupta and James Ferguson (Durham, NC: Duke University Press, 1997), 33–51.

7. Cristina Magaldi, *Music in Imperial Rio de Janeiro: European Culture in a Tropical Milieu* (Lanham, MD, Toronto, and Oxford: Scarecrow Press, 2004), 8.

8. Ibid., 3–4, 83.

9. Kristen Schultz, *Tropical Versailles: Empire, Monarchy, and the Portuguese Royal Court in Rio de Janeiro, 1808–1821* (New York: Routledge, 2001).

10. Magaldi, *Music in Imperial Rio de Janeiro,* 1.

11. Néstor García Canclini, *Hybrid Cultures: Strategies for Entering and Leaving Modernity*, trans. Christopher L. Chippari and Silvia L. López (Minneapolis: University of Minnesota Press, 1995).

12. See, for example, press commentary from February 1889 cited in Leonardo Affonso de Miranda Pereira, *O carnaval das letras* (Rio de Janeiro: Coleção Biblioteca Carioca, 1994), 121.

13. Magaldi, *Music in Imperial Rio de Janeiro,* 153.

14. Irénée Mauget, *Avec les gloires de mon temps* (La Celle-Saint-Cloud: La Maison des Intellectuels, 1963), 87, cited in Stéphane Leteuré, "Le Drapeau et la lyre: Camille Saint-Saëns et la politique, 1870–1921" (PhD diss., Université François-Rabelais, Tours, 2011), 344. Note that Saint-Saens did refer to this work as having a "Tango" in his letter from Bône, Algeria, to Durand on 22 and 24 January 1901; thinking that it might be popular at casinos and the Jardin d'acclimation, on 31 January he encouraged Durand to hire Henri Rabaud to transcribe it for orchestra. On 7 February 1901, it appears that Fauré

was willing to take on this task and Saint-Saëns wrote to his editor, "you'll see that *Lola* will become the great success of modern times!!!" [Ed.]

15. Primary source material on tango dating from before 1910 is almost nonexistent. See Jo Baim, *Tango* (Bloomington and Indianapolis: Indiana University Press, 2007), 3.

16. On 23 July 1904, *Le Figaro* states that Saint-Saëns had telegraphed from Buenos Aires: http://gallica.bnf.fr/ark:/12148/bpt6k2867085.r=Saint-Saens.langEN. I thank Jann Pasler for references to *Le Figaro* in this article. Bonnerot's account of the trip (*Camille Saint-Saëns*, 181) remains undocumented.

17. See Deborah Schwartz-Kates, "The *Gauchesco* Tradition as a Source of National Identity in Argentine Art Music (ca. 1890–1955)" (PhD diss., University of Texas, 1997).

18. Nicolas Shumway, *The Invention of Argentina* (Berkeley, Los Angeles, London: University of California Press, 1991), x–xi.

19. Gaston Gaillard, *Amérique Latine et l'Europe occidental: L'Amérique Latine et la guerre* (Paris: Berger-Levrault, 1918), 19.

20. Leteuré, "Le Drapeau et la lyre," 343–52.

21. Robert Camaaño, *La historia del Teatro Colón: 1908–1968*, 3 vols. (Buenos Aires: Editorial Cinetea, 1969) 2:15, 26, 50, 55.

22. [Ernesto de la Guardia ?], "Arte y Teatro: Colón," *La Prensa*, 22 May 1916.

23. Carlos Fuentes, "Ariel," trans. with reader's reference and annotated bibliography by Margaret Sayers Peden, with a prologue by José Enrique Rodó (Austin: University of Texas Press, 1988), 14.

24. Letter from Albert Dalimier, French under-secretary of state for fine arts, cited in Leteuré, "Le Drapeau et la lyre," 350.

25. When Saint-Saëns returned to France, he reported to the under-secretary of state on the 5,000 francs he had received as an honorarium for the composition of a patriotic hymn during his visit to Uruguay (*Le Figaro*, 27 August 1916). [Ed.] Studd proposes that Saint-Saëns wrote the work on the request of the Uruguayan president. Because Feliciano Viera belonged to the centrist Colorado Party, others suggest that Saint-Saëns's work was called *Partido Colorado*. Neither title appears in the *New Grove* catalogue of Saint-Saëns's works. The current Uruguayan anthem, by Fernando Quijano, was adopted in 1848.

26. Carol A. Hess, *Manuel de Falla and Modernism in Spain, 1989–1936* (Chicago and London: University of Chicago Press, 2001), 6.

27. Magaldi, *Music in Imperial Rio*, 97.

28. I thank Jann Pasler for making this program and Figure 1 available to me.

29. Jann Pasler, *Composing the Citizen: Music as Public Utility in Third Republic France* (Berkeley, Los Angeles, London: University of California Press, 2009), 307.

PART IV

SAINT-SAËNS, AESTHETICS PAST AND PRESENT

What's in a Song?

Camille Saint-Saëns's *Mélodies*

ANNEGRET FAUSER

Too easily relegated as mere miniatures to the margins of a composer's oeuvre, *mélodies*—as songs are called in France—can nevertheless provide a fascinating entry into a composer's musical, aesthetic, social, and political world. Camille Saint-Saëns's *mélodies* are no exception. They were among his first works when, at the age of six, he composed a handful of *romances*. Songs still formed part of his output in the last year of his life with the *Vieilles chansons* based on French Renaissance poetry. There are over 140 songs in his total output.[1] Some are mere trifles, written quickly as an offering for a music-loving hostess; others are substantial compositions in both scale and aesthetic weight. Each, however, reflects the genre's expressive and formal fluidity that allowed it to span the intricate web of musical life in France, for *mélodies* were at home as much in the parlor as in the concert hall. As a genre originating in the nineteenth century, *mélodies* not only stood for art song (as we understand the term nowadays) but encompassed a range of more specific vocal forms that—even when they had their own, earlier history—were now subsumed under this category, whether ballads, *romances, chansons*, or even, appropriating the German word, *lieds*. Moreover, although they could carry the stigma of effeminacy through their association with female performers and listeners, the celebrated role of poetry in *mélodies* simultaneously underscored their proud embodiment of French nationality in ways few other musical genres could match.

Contradictory and multifaceted, the genre poses its own challenges to historiography, and even within the output of a single composer, *mélodies* resist clear-cut taxonomies. Approaching Saint-Saëns's songs thus demands several lines of inquiry: the roles of the composer and poet; the aesthetic framework of the *mélodie*; and Saint-Saëns's poetic and musical choices in the context of French music and society. Thus there emerges a composite view of the genre in Saint-Saëns's compositional output as an attractive form suited to any number of purposes, from intimate moments through musical travelogues to patriotic statements, and one stylistically more varied than any other aspect of his oeuvre.

The Myth of the Bard

True poetry, Saint-Saëns wrote in 1885, must be sung. "Sing!" he exhorted poets, quoting Victor Hugo's "À un poète aveugle" and its reference to Milton and Homer. Hugo was almost certainly using the verb *chanter* in its generic poetic sense. But Saint-Saëns read it differently. In times of yore "the poet sang," but now, he continued, "the poet sings no more."[2] Modern artists, he declared, lived in a fractured world in which each art claimed its own impoverished singularity. Salvation lay in a return to the earlier union of poetry and music. Indeed, the mythical figure of the ancient bard—whether the Greek Homer or the Celtic Ossian—had fired the imagination of nineteenth-century musicians from Hector Berlioz to Richard Wagner, and the concept of the musician/poet as the genuine, original artist pervaded aesthetic discourse throughout the nineteenth century and well into the twentieth. In contrast to Wagner and his followers, however, Saint-Saëns did not conceive of the singular embodiment of poet and musician as the utopian ideal; rather, his epitome of the modern bard lay in the persona of the poetically minded composer who restored music to verse, and to French verse at that.

So far as Saint-Saëns was concerned, the composer stood above the poet, provided true poetic expression was served. Poetry, he asserted, was not created for silence: "It must be spoken lyrically. To speak lyrically is to sing." Yet "whereas one must sing the verses, poets have no means to indicate how one has to sing them."[3] The ability to shape song, therefore, remained the sole domain of musicians. Of course, the composer also had to respect language: Saint-Saëns admonished the young Lili Boulanger, whom he had caught making a mistake in text setting. "You are a perfect musician, now study the French language in depth, it is indispensable."[4] It was this kind of intimate linguistic sensitivity that could turn a mere musician into a Homeric bard, for only a composer had the power to deliver true expressive greatness to French poetry. Saint-Saëns explained that "through music, the French language can acquire the rhythmic verses and all the combinations of antique poetry."[5] Even so banal a text as two lines from an operetta by Charles Lecocq could take on the quality of a Greek distich in Saint-Saëns's reckoning if the composer made this intrinsic rhythmical quality audible.[6] For that reason, an educated composer might even venture to write his own poetry. Thus the Wagnerian musician/poet entered Saint-Saëns's artistic world through the back door, remaining simply only one possible incarnation of the modern bard who, because he was a musician by trade, could realize any poetry, including his own, to its full potential solely through his compositional craft. In turn, he could teach poets what might seem impossible in their own art without music in the frame.[7]

Saint-Saëns emerged in some of his songs as both poet and composer, though most of the *mélodies* that set his own poems were clustered in the 1890s—the high point of French Wagnerism—with such works as "Guitares et mandolines" (1890), "La Libellule" (The dragonfly, 1893), "Le Lever de soleil sur le Nil" (Sunrise over the Nile, 1898), "Sonnet" (1898), and "Les Cloches de la mer" (The bells of the sea, 1900). The title of "Sonnet" poses some mystery, because the poem—with its four quatrains in alternating rhyme set in a modified strophic form—is anything but a traditional sonnet. With its slightly irregular verses, both poem and setting seem to foreground the expression of a love hidden but burning beyond death, pushing emotional expressivity at the expense of a more artful formal structure.

Clearly Saint-Saëns cared much about his next song, "Les Cloches de la mer," a dramatic and sonically evocative *mélodie* about the eerie echoes across the sea of death knells for perished sailors. This was one of the few songs he sent to his friend and colleague Gabriel Fauré immediately after completion, and Fauré was so impressed with the poem that he asked to keep Saint-Saëns's autograph and returned a copy of the text in his own handwriting.[8] The song is built on a bell motive, the offbeat rhythms of which capture the distorted quality of sound traveling across the water, while the contour outlines the retrograde of the "Dies irae." The quasi-ostinato repetitions of this motive are superimposed in a multilayered texture with a slowly moving pedal in the middle voice, wave-like arpeggios in the left hand, and a melodic line in the voice that mostly circles in chromatic half steps (Example 1).

The song is in modified strophic form: the middle section breaks away from the almost oppressive quality of the first three strophes with a passionate accusation of nature's cruelty before the musical elements of the beginning gradually return. It is a dramatic song, rich in tone-painting, that translated well into its orchestrated incarnation ten years later, when the composer arranged it for one Mlle Ravaut.

Yet in an earlier poem with the title "ΓΝΩΤΙ ΣΕΑΥΤΟΝ" (Know yourself), Saint-Saëns had worried whether—as a modern bard—he could ever do justice to the ocean:

La mer tente ma lyre avec ses épouvantes	The ocean tempts my lyre with its terrors,
Ses caresses de femme et ses goëmons verts.	Its female caresses and its green seaweeds.

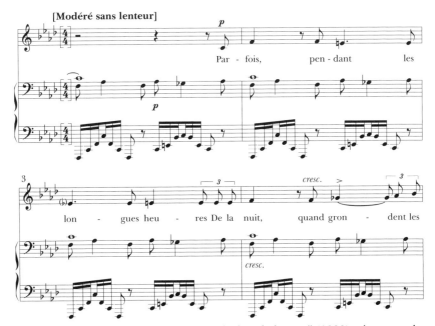

Example 1. Camille Saint-Saëns, "Les Cloches de la mer" (1900), piano-vocal score, mm. 6–9.

Though he might consider rhyming about its waves and its vastness like other artists, he cannot dare:

Mais non, je suis trop peu pour cette rude tâche;	But no, I am too small for this hard task;
Tu m'as découragé par ton immensité.	You have discouraged me with your immensity.[9]

His song, "Les Cloches de la mer," can in effect be seen as an answer to this earlier quest for artistic self-understanding, for the composer's verses in the song echo "ΓΝΩΤΙ ΣΕΑΥΤΟΝ" in some vocabulary, and the terrifying quality of the ocean stands at the center of both the song's text and its music in a poetic and sonic exploration of the antagonistic relationship between human frailty and immensely powerful natural worlds.

Similarly, "Le Lever de soleil sur le Nil"—written directly for voice and orchestra—fuses an evocative text with musical tone-painting into a striking, through-composed *mélodie* that juxtaposes the eternal renewal of sunrise over the flowing waters of the Nile against the ruins of human endeavor. (Those remains "tell us," so the final line says, "that the Gods are dead.")[10] From the luscious, shimmering sonorities of the first part, culminating in a *fortissimo* climax, to the muted sonorities of the conclusion, the song's expressivity draws on the world of the late nineteenth-century symphonic poem as its generic framework. Two letters to his friend and publisher Auguste Durand reflect the importance Saint-Saëns attributed to this work. He wrote that he had "conceived of it in Egypt," where Saint-Saëns sometimes spent the winter for the sake of his health, yet "had not dared" to create it then; even in its current incarnation, he considered it "unfortunately quite short."[11] The second letter explains Saint-Saëns's compositional intentions: the singer "should do the indicated nuances, sing piano when needed—especially at the beginning. You must prevent her from singing the words *are . . . dead!* with a beautiful *portato* between them; this would be awfully banal, and would furthermore substitute the expression of passionate regret for that of *implacable fate* which is the one of the work."[12] Though words were indeed important in this and other *mélodies* of Saint-Saëns, this letter shows that, in the end, he believed that true poetic expression was achieved primarily through music and its performance in song.

The Aesthetic Framework of the *Mélodie*

By reconfiguring the ancient bard as a poetic composer who manifests (French) poetry in and through sound, Saint-Saëns thus claimed victory for music in the *paragone* of the nineteenth century, which revived the famous Renaissance debate over the superiority of artistic expression by broadening its parameters from painting and sculpture to include music and other arts.[13] If opera was the genre that was ultimately at stake in this contest, *mélodies* were nonetheless at the heart of the debate, for songs were considered the musical embodiment of French poetry, especially in the late nineteenth century.[14] After all, as Saint-Saëns asked in a discussion of Victor Hugo's poetry, did "the rhythms and sonorities of the verse not call naturally for song to bring them to light?"[15] Saint-Saëns was not alone in thinking thus. Fauré, following in the footsteps of his teacher and friend, considered the role of music in a *mélodie* as "highlighting the profound emotion that inhabits the soul of the poet and that words are unable to render exactly."[16] Indeed, for all the importance of poetry within song, so the composer Charles Koechlin wrote, music alone could bring out the unsuspected beauty of verse.[17]

These comments formed part of two intersecting discussions on song composition. Many nineteenth-century French poets had claimed the inherent musicality of language as an integral aspect of poetry, the holistic lyric quality of which could only be destroyed through musical setting. This view gained particular popularity with Parnassian and Symbolist poets in the wake of the French Wagner reception, with Charles Baudelaire's landmark essay, "Richard Wagner et *Tannhäuser* à Paris" (1861), serving quite literally as a fanfare for the poetic avant-garde.[18] As poets laid claim to the musical dimension of language, it became vital, therefore, for French musicians to reclaim the sonic dimension of poetic lyricism lest they lose the aesthetic justification for song composition entirely. Indeed, when Saint-Saëns quoted Victor Hugo's admonition that the poet should be singing—"Chante!"—and then translated the well-known phrase "dire un poème" as to sing (not recite) the text, he not only usurped the role of bard for modern musicians but also staked his claim as a modern composer to surpass poetry through music.

In his delightful 1885 setting of Hugo's poem, "Une Flûte invisible," Saint-Saëns even went a step further. The obbligato flute allows us actually to experience the "invisible flute" merely evoked by Hugo's verse and thus demonstrates the added value of composition. Any poet might have thought this a statement of the obvious. But by mimicking birdsong in the flute's playful appoggiaturas, Saint-Saëns attributes music not just to the shepherds in the fields (Hugo's first strophe) but also to the birds whose song brings joy to an otherwise more sinister nature (second strophe). Though the most charming song is that of love—at least according to Hugo's third strophe—the flute, with its birdlike chirping, has the last word in Saint-Saëns's setting (Example 2).[19]

Formalist as he may be, Saint-Saëns routinely turned to sonic mimicry and word-painting in his *mélodies* to strengthen poetic expression as, for example, in "La Libellule"—where the piano liberally uses the familiar tropes associated with insects since Berlioz's "Queen Mab Scherzo."[20] In "Une Flûte invisible," however, the musician transformed a poetic metaphor into a musical reality. Yet another resonance here plays on musical genre and its meaning. Drawing on the distinct idiom of the French *romance* in the song's texture, phrase structure, and tone, Saint-Saëns's seemingly innocuous song turns into an aesthetic statement of the first order: not only has music primacy in poetic expression, but it is also first and foremost French because—as we shall see below—the *romance* had a long history of signifying Frenchness during the nineteenth century.

Saint-Saëns's self-conscious musical reference to such an indubitably French genre as the *romance* reflects the second tenet of the aesthetic debate on song composition in late nineteenth-century France. As was the case with numerous other genres—from the symphony to the music drama—French aesthetic discourse in the nineteenth century was often shaped in contrast to rival musical cultures, most prominently that of Germany. In other genres like opera or ballet for example, such dichotomies were often inflected or even fractured by the acknowledged influence of other national tradi-

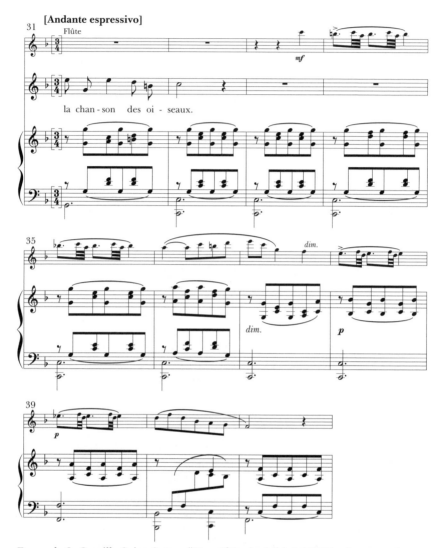

Example 2. Camille Saint-Saëns, "Une Flûte invisible" (1885), piano-vocal score, mm. 31–41.

tions, whether Italian or Russian. With song, however, French aesthetics was shaped through the binary construction of a competition between *mélodie* and lied. On the one hand, French musicians and music theorists created a pedigree for the genre that claimed the *romance* as an eminently French song form with roots firmly entrenched in the ancien régime. Even though the *romance* was associated with the feminine world of the salon and thus often denigrated for its musical and technical simplicity, these same elements of clarity, regularity, and immediate appeal turned it into a prime candidate for a genre characterized as "eminently French."[21] Famous *romances* could therefore have considerable shelf lives, with pieces such as Martini's "Plaisir d'amour" (1785) part of a musical experience that continued throughout the nineteenth century. Even though French song developed increasingly more complex formal and textural structures through the nineteenth and early twentieth centuries, the *romance* had staying power precisely because of its nationalist significance, and was subsumed under the broader umbrella of *mélodie française* in the oeuvre of, among others, Hector Berlioz, Charles Gounod, Léo Delibes, Jules Massenet, Gabriel Fauré, and, of course, Saint-Saëns.[22]

One the other side of the binary was the German lied. Though songs from other nations such as Norway or Russia would filter into French musical life by the fin de siècle, French nineteenth-century discussions on the song as genre were dominated by the need to demarcate French song from the German tradition. This was not only because of the intrinsic pride associated with the autochthonous tradition of the *romance*, but also due to worries about Franz Schubert's influence on the development of the French genre.[23] Composers and performers alike had brought Schubert's songs into the French sphere in the 1830s, with Adolphe Nourrit, Berlioz, and Franz Liszt as leading champions. French adaptations in the early 1830s—such as "La Jeune Religieuse" ("Die junge Nonne") or "Le Roi des Aulnes" ("Der Erlkönig")—became staples of the Parisian salon and concert repertoire. Indeed, despite the widely proclaimed roots of the French *mélodie* in the *romance*, anxiety over such Germanic influence was increasingly rampant, especially in the later decades of the century. For it was Schubert who was perceived as having shown the way to a song type in which the piano as much as the voice conveyed "the summary of the poetry, its character, its various sentiments, in a word, the colour of the poetic thought."[24] The attribution to Schubert of what French critics came to associate with one of the key aspects of the *mélodie*—the genre's poetic use of the piano—thus led to fraught engagement with both Schubert specifically and with the German lied more generally. Saint-Saëns was not immune from this kind of concern. It shines through, for example, in a remark he penned in 1896 where he denied any influence of Schubert's songs on his early "La Feuille du peuplier" (The leaf of the poplar, 1853), because, he said, he had known none of them: he chalked up any resemblance with Schubert's "Die Krähe" (The crow) to "bizarre coincidence."[25] Even his early songs, he assured his readers, were French through and through.

In order to exorcize the influence of Schubert, and then Schumann, on French song—and at the same time claim national superiority in this aesthetics contest—French writers routinely characterized German song as unrefined, heavy, lacking in prosody (which may have had to do more with bad translations into French than the original German word setting), and as based on strophic folksong. In contrast, the *mélodie* counted as an aristocratic, refined genre that embodied poetry in its musical manifestation.[26] This nationalist perspective hardly took into account Germany's own long-standing debates over the lied, which were highly complex and explored similar tropes with respect to how French critics viewed the *mélodie française*.[27] Rather, it set the poetic qualities and richness of French *mélodies* against a somewhat distorted and self-serving depiction of German song as limited by its national roots in the *Volkslied*. One relatively late and somewhat extreme example crystallizes how French polemics caricaturized the German rival when, in the politically charged years around World War I, Koechlin published the following blunt comparison: "The majority of French *mélodies* bear no resemblance to German lieder. The latter—relatively short, naïve, in a popular vein, with a sometimes touching but often also banal or falsely profound sentiment—have no particular color. . . . Almost all German songs, from Schubert to R. Strauss, resemble each other; and it is always sub-Schumann or sub-Brahms; for us (and I don't think that I am wrong)—from Berlioz and Gounod to Ravel via Massenet, de Castillon, Duparc, Franck, Fauré, and Debussy—it is all about variety."[28] Though Saint-Saëns is missing in this list, Koechlin discussed his *mélodies* in a different context, where he characterized them as influenced in their aesthetic stance by Victor Hugo. The poet, Koechlin claimed, shaped the ideas about song of Bizet and the young Fauré as well.[29] Koechlin also tapped into a well-established rhetorical gambit in French musical aesthetics that appropriated aristocratic heritage and artistic refinement as a national virtue against what he described as the more boorish and uncultured German neighbor.[30]

Besides Schubert, the specter of Wagner hovered over vocal music in France, not only because numerous modern poets professed Wagner to be their aesthetic guide, but also because his broader concepts about word–music relationships had an impact well beyond opera and were intensely debated among French musicians and music critics.[31] Yet because French poetry was so unquestionably and self-consciously national, and song forms became increasingly fluid in response to both poetic developments on the one hand and musical changes on the other, Wagner could be easily co-opted for the aesthetics of song, in contrast to the field of French opera, where anxiety over Wagner's influence remained very high indeed.[32] Composers and poets both appropriated Wagnerian rhetoric in discussing song—we have already seen Saint-Saëns turning to the figure of the bard—though few were as explicit as the Wagnerian Camille Mauclair, who declared that song was the "hyphen between music and letters, the precursor of the fusion of the arts. It is at least curious to consider that the ancient *romance* will bring to realization what Wagner has tried in the field of drama."[33] This rhetorical strategy crowned the *mélodie* as the most advanced vocal genre in a discursive field whose competitiveness ran along nationalist divides by shifting the ground from the dangers of direct competition in opera to one where national pride could run unfettered. Mauclair's triumphalism was thus not far from Koechlin's claim of aristocratic superiority.

At first glance, Saint-Saëns's songs seem unlikely candidates for such lofty claims. Although he had participated intensely and throughout his life in the public debate about Wagner and his (nefarious) influence on French music, his few comments on song composition addressed practical issues more than theoretical ones. Thus we learn most about Saint-Saëns's ideas about song from his compositional output itself. Some of his *mélodies*, especially those that hark back to the *romance* as generic mold—even so enchanting a setting as "Une Flûte invisible"—differ quite strongly in their musical and aesthetic scope from, for example, Debussy's and Fauré's through-composed Verlaine settings (with their emphasis on the piano). This plus Saint-Saëns's catholic taste in poetry have caused his *mélodies* to receive their share of criticism.[34] Yet the aristocratic flair and self-conscious engagement with nuanced poetic expression we encountered in, for example, an orchestral song such as "Le Lever de soleil sur le Nil" are not to be dismissed so easily. We find them, too, in a number of his Hugo settings, including "Si vous n'avez rien à me dire" (If you have nothing to tell me; 1870), and also in his 1912 song, "Le Vent dans la plaine" (The wind on the plain), the first of Paul Verlaine's *Ariettes oubliées*. Saint-Saëns had chosen for the title of this last song the epigraph (by Charles Favart) that Verlaine had placed above the poem, "C'est l'extase langoureuse" (It is the langorous ecstasy). Our ears may be more familiar with Debussy's languid, somewhat episodic, and through-composed setting of this poem about the sounds of nature and love, but Saint-Saëns's lighter touch—especially in the piano—produces a striking treatment of the strophic structure of the poem. This is most noticeable in the enjambment from the third to the fourth stanza, where the extended cadence places the emphasis on the deictic personal pronoun *tu*, directing the listener to what becomes the focal (and indeed musical) point of the poem: "le chœur des petites voix" (the chorus of little voices). Repeated at the end of the song for emphasis—and the sole moment in the *mélodie* in which the accompaniment assumes a melodic profile by way of an imitative "chorus" with the singer—the final line focuses on the voice pure and simple as the piano pauses, the voice sustains the highest note of the piece, and the piano reenters to turn the singular into the plural (*voix* is both in French). Saint-Saëns's decision to set the four stanzas, then repeat the first two in a more intense setting, renders the poem an embodiment of music itself, the sound of nature—"frissons des bois"— merging with the song of sensuality. Just like "Une Flûte invisible," this *mélodie* foregrounds musical over poetic expression, distilling the sonorities encapsulated in the verse into musical gestures grounded in a long history of French song.

Content and Context

Saint-Saëns's songs cut across a wide range of poetic themes, musical forms, and even languages if one takes into account his 1854 setting of Ludwig Uhland's "Ruhethal" or his two English songs from 1871, "A Voice by the Cedar Tree" (Tennyson) and "My Land" (T. Davis). In contrast to such contemporaries as Jules Massenet and Gabriel Fauré, Saint-Saëns wrote only two song cycles: *Mélodies persanes*, op. 26, on poems by Armand Renaud (1870), and *La Cendre rouge* (The red ash), op. 146, by Georges Docquois (1914) and dedicated to Fauré. The latter cycle is a finely honed setting of ten poems that takes the voice sometimes even close to *Sprechgesang*. Saint-Saëns explained to Fauré: "I do not dare call them *mélodies* because they are something else which I should not know how to define. There is something both of the amusing and of the harsh in them, something for most tastes, not all."[35] Two more collections of songs, though not cycles, mark the end of his career and, in their archaic elegance, conjure unequivocally the glory of the French past: his *Cinq Poèmes de Ronsard* and his *Vieilles Chansons*, both published in 1921, though two of the Ronsard songs were written earlier: "L'Amour oiseau" (Love bird) in 1907 and "Grasselette et Maigrelette" in 1920. By harking back to the era of the Pléiade, Saint-Saëns's choice of poetry here brings him closer to Debussy—who had turned to the Renaissance *chanson* in his *Trois Chansons de France* (1904) and the *Trois Ballades de François Villon* (1910), for example—than Fauré in these final years. This is somewhat ironic given that Saint-Saëns and Debussy were rarely mentioned in the same breath—and we have already seen their very different settings of "C'est l'extase amoureuse."

The rest of Saint-Saëns's *mélodies*, however, were conceived as individual compositions, even though he sometimes focused his attention on a small number of texts by one poet, whether Victor Hugo in 1868, Théodore de Banville in 1892, his own poetry in 1898, or the Comtesse de Noailles in 1907. Until the late 1880s, the poet most dominant in his output was Hugo (1802–1885), his first poetic love. The composer remembered how as a child he formed "instantly an intimate relationship" with Hugo's poems, and because of his own profoundly musical nature, "started to sing them."[36] As he grew older, his "hugolâtrie" only increased, and he devoured the poet's works as soon as they appeared. And he was not alone: Berlioz's "admiration for Hugo equaled" that of Saint-Saëns.[37] In his early decades, Saint-Saëns composed a number of his best-known songs on texts by the poet: "Rêverie" (1851), "Le Pas d'armes du roi Jean" (The tournament of King John, 1852), "L'Attente" (The wait, 1855), and "Extase" (1860). In the case of "Rêverie," and for all its Schubertian flavor in particular in the piano writing (not that Saint-Saëns would ever have admitted it), the song nevertheless stays formally indebted to the French *romance*, with its clear-cut form and sequential melodic phrasing. Similarly, "Le Pas d'armes du roi Jean," written when Saint-Saëns was seventeen years old, sets Hugo's medievalist ballad in a Schubertian idiom, though, as Stephen Studd puts it, the song can be considered "a small masterpiece comparable to those of Schubert at the same age, an evocative blend of bravado and tenderness."[38] Saint-Saëns orchestrated this ballad in 1855 (the year before Berlioz orchestrated his *Nuits d'été*), turning it into a colorful concert work for voice and orchestra with careful attention to a wide range of orchestral effects—from the brass and drums conjuring the sound of the tournament to the harps, divided strings, and high winds associated with the beautiful Yseult. It became a favorite for concert performance in Paris and elsewhere throughout Saint-Saëns's life.

Song orchestrations and songs written directly for voice and orchestra were an important manifestation of a genre with which French composers led the way in European compositional practice. Early examples include Louise Farrenc's *Andréa* (ca. 1838), Berlioz's *Les Nuits d'été* (1856), César Franck's *Paris!* (1870), and Henri Duparc's *La Vague et la cloche* (1871). As in the case of the *mélodie* for voice and piano, the poetry that composers set as orchestral songs was varied and ranged from ballads and lyrical poems to odes and hymns. Both Franck's and Duparc's compositions were *poèmes pour voix et orchestre*, as these works were termed in France. Such compositions fused the *mélodie française* with Lisztian aesthetics of the symphonic poem (whose "invention" Saint-Saëns celebrated, in 1885, as a French contribution to symphonic composition) to bring song into the concert hall.[39] Works in the genre by other composers include, for example, Alfred Bruneau's *Penthésilée, reine des Amazones* (Penthesilea, queen of the Amazons, 1892), Ernest Chausson's *Le Poème de l'amour et de la mer* (The poem of love and the sea, 1893), and Maurice Ravel's *Shéhérazade* (1904). Saint-Saëns himself was one of the most prolific composers of such orchestral songs, ranging from orchestrated piano songs such as "Rêverie," "Extase," and "Papillons" (Butterflies) to such substantial works for voice and orchestra as the evocative "Le Lever de soleil sur le Nil," the folklike "Les Vendanges" (The harvests, 1898), and the explicitly nationalist "Hymne à la paix" (Hymn to peace, 1920).

In 1887, Saint-Saëns returned to Hugo's ballads for another large-scale orchestral song, "La Fiancée du timbalier" (The drummer-boy's fiancée). Though he later created a reduction for voice and piano, Saint-Saëns conceived this vibrant setting for a large orchestra and an excellent (female) bard. Years later, he wrote to Durand: "'La Fiancée du timbalier' has a future. It is strongly sustained by the poem of Victor Hugo. But an excellent orchestra is necessary, and the piano is insufficient. And then, it is not enough to be sung, it must be recounted."[40] The tale is told by the drummer-boy's fiancée who is waiting for his return from war as a musician in the Duke of Brittany's army. She was warned the previous night by an Egyptian augur that one drummer would be missing. While the triumphant pageant of soldiers files through the streets of the city and the musicians march past, she sinks dying as she realizes that her beloved is indeed not there. Saint-Saëns's setting reveals the experienced composer of symphonic poems as well as of songs in its taut and careful musical organization and in the range of orchestral effects. Balladic strophes are interspersed with descriptive episodes, whether the heroine's lyrical call to her sisters to join her in waiting for her beloved's return, the ominous foretelling of death, or the sonic representation of the pageant. Saint-Saëns explained that when the text calls out "Voici les timbaliers," he "wanted to render the effect of a military band bursting out from around a street corner."[41]

Saint-Saëns wrote the strikingly dramatic orchestral song, "Pallas Athénée," op. 98 (text by Jean-Louis Croze), for the glorious new star of the Paris Opéra, Lucienne Bréval, who premiered the work in the 1894 summer festival in the ancient Roman theater of Orange, for which the piece was commissioned.[42] As he would four years later in "Le Lever de soleil sur le Nil," Saint-Saëns set a text speaking of the death of the ancient gods. It opens with the same line with which he closed the later song: "Les Dieux sont morts" (The gods are dead). However, in this hymn, the goddess Athena rises from her grave and leaves the Parthenon to come to Provence, "the sister of Greece" (and where Orange is located), as a divine protector.[43] Not surprisingly, the work was a major success with its Provençal audience, but it also became popular in Parisian concert halls. The celebration of French culture as rooted in Greek antiquity was a trope that, as Jann Pasler shows in her essay in this volume, pervaded both Saint-Saëns's cultural world and that of France. Yet this noble culture of the past needed a soil in which to thrive, and Occitania was not only the most Mediterranean part of France but also the area that had been celebrated by the influential regionalist author Frédéric Mistral as representing the heart of Greco-Latin culture. Indeed, Mistral described himself—again in a turn to the figure of the bard—as a humble student of Homer. This movement of Provençal regionalism, called the Félibrige, celebrated the language and culture of the region in festivals such as the one in Orange for which Saint-Saëns wrote his celebratory hymn.

If "Pallas Athénée" evoked Félibrige tenets in its celebration of the French South, Saint-Saëns's *Mélodies persanes* for voice and piano (several were later orchestrated) are unmistakable in their poetic evocation of the Orient. This cycle of six *mélodies* was set to verses by Armand Renaud, a Parnassian poet who was among the circle of Saint-Saëns's friends that included the painter Henri Regnault and the composer Augusta Holmès. In the preface to his *Nuits persanes* (Persian nights, 1870), the poet explained that not all oriental poetry was the same. Arabic poetry, for example, had "fallen into decadence." Yet Persian poetry was, above all others, "the most original and the most complete."[44] Saint-Saëns selected the six poems from various chapters of the collection but kept them roughly in the order in which they appeared.[45] With three songs each for female and male voices, *Les Mélodies persanes* speaks to the genre's place in French society as much as to its aesthetic purpose, for each song seems to embody the character of its dedicatee. The opening song, "La Brise" (The breeze), for example, is written for a contralto and dedicated to Pauline Viardot, the famous singer/composer of Spanish descent. Its habanera rhythm, which underlies the entire setting (save for a short interruption in the final eight measures), characterize it more as a Spanish song (in homage to Viardot) than a Persian one, though the turning melismas in the melody and the Dorian flavor add more explicitly orientalist signifiers into the mix. The third song ("La Solitaire")—dedicated to Augusta Holmès—is a fast-moving, passionate call to an absent lover, its dominant musical gesture distant from the melancholy that Renaud's original title (and part of the text) suggests. Rather, the setting seems to have taken its cue from the first stanza in which the young woman asks the "proud young man" to take her on his horse toward the "heaven of love." The chromatic writing in the melodic line could still be interpreted as a hint of musical orientalism, but—as with Regnault's orientalist paintings—it is the subject matter more than the technique that reflects its orientalist side.[46] The painter himself is the dedicatee of the fourth song, "Sabre en main" (Sword in hand). Saint-Saëns thought highly of Regnault's musical ability and described his voice as "enchanting" and "irresistibly seductive."[47] Again, the song shows few obvious markers of musical orientalism, save perhaps the prominent melismas in the opening unaccompanied vocal line and their repetition toward the end of the song that were also clearly intended to showcase Regnault's prowess (Example 3). Most of the song, however, is dominated and finally overwhelmed by the chordal piano writing in urgent dotted rhythms that are closely related to the idiom and thematic world of "Le

Pas d'armes du roi Jean," portraying the soundscape of a medieval tournament (Example 4).

The other three songs similarly avoid any deliberate Orientalisms, and
instead set the text in a contemporary Western idiom with the lightest
touches of musical exoticism. Indeed, the only song that foregrounds
exoticism as a marked difference is the opening song; once established
sonically as a cycle about another culture, the remaining songs barely
engage with acoustic signifiers that were associated with the Orient, in contrast to Saint-Saëns's later Orientalism, which draws on non-Western music
as sonic markers of exoticism.

This cycle gained popularity, however, not just because of its musical
and topical appeal. It also carried aspects of a musical memorial because
of Regnault's death in the battle of Buzenval during the 1871 siege of Paris
in the Franco-Prussian War. As the poet Renaud recalled later, he would
return from battle and meet up with Regnault and other friends in the
evening when the painter often "sang in his beautiful voice several poems
from the *Nuits persanes*, set to music by Saint-Saëns."[48] On the night before
his death, so his friends recalled, Regnault performed "Au Cimétière" (At
the cemetery) from *Les Mélodies persanes* in Augusta Holmès's drawing

Example 3. Camille Saint-Saëns, "Sabre en main," *from Mélodies persanes*, op. 26,
no. 4, mm. 49–55.

Example 4. Camille Saint-Saëns, "Sabre en main," *from Mélodies persanes*, op. 26, no. 4, piano-vocal score, mm. 68–80.

room, and during the painter's funeral, Saint-Saëns played it on the organ.[49] After the war, numerous friends promoted the song cycle in Regnault's memory.[50] Thus a painter famous for his Orientalist topics became associated with an Orientalist song cycle that—in one of the songs—embodied his voice in the melodic line. Here private music making became the object of public consumption: buying the score and performing the songs gave vicarious access to a group of artist-heroes and their music.

Mélodies did indeed travel from private into public spaces, and vice versa. Thus "Le Bonheur est chose légère" (Happiness is a light thing), a *romance* from Saint-Saëns's 1877 opera, *Le Timbre d'argent* (*The Silver Bell*), was published separately as a song for voice and piano. Saint-Saëns's *mélodies* also had a malleable quality in that a song could, for example, be transformed into a symphonic poem, as was the case with his "Danse macabre" (1872). The *mélodie*—to a text describing the infernal dance of the dead— was a varied strophic song that Saint-Saëns expanded, in 1874, into a major symphonic composition with some of the song intact (especially its opening strophes). When Saint-Saëns later orchestrated the original piano song in 1903, he retained the emblematic *scordatura* solo violin from the symphonic poem, but stuck to a smaller, less colorful orchestra (Example 5). Among friends and colleagues, the infernal quality of the melody could even be playfully repurposed for a memorandum, as when Emmanuel Chabrier sent a letter that underlaid the opening motive of "La Danse macabre" with the words: "A Memorandum, on Thursday morning" (Example 6).[51]

Indeed, musical motives—whether from songs or other musical genres—formed part of the day-to-day exchange among musicians in Paris, a shared musical language that allowed, in composition, for the play with allusion and quotation that was so characteristic of fin-de-siècle France.[52]

Yet not all songs could move with such ease, even for Saint-Saëns. As we have seen, the composer considered the orchestra vital for his "La Fiancée du timbalier." The later piano reduction was, to his mind, a pale reflection of the original. It seems that adding orchestral color to piano songs was a step easily taken by the composer because it supported the craft of the modern bard by adding further expressive qualities to the music, especially for a larger, public space. It also gave singers a self-contained work to perform on the concert stage, rather than the less satisfactory opera excerpts that, around 1900, started to carry the stigma of misplacement and routine.[53] Just like concertos for instrumental soloists, some orchestral songs could be written specifically for a singer's strengths: "La Libellule," for example, was written for the fêted coloratura soprano, Sibyl Sanderson. Few other performers, Saint-Saëns joked, "are able to climb the heights in which this insect flies."[54] Other song orchestrations were offerings to individual singers who had sung the piano version and wanted to take the *mélodie* into the concert hall.[55] Some orchestrations, however, were highly demanding not so much for the singer as for the instrumentalists: in the case of "Les Fées" (The fairies, 1892), as Saint-Saëns wrote to his publisher, "I had to be inventive, and this will be inaccessible to second-rate orchestras."[56] Still, Saint-Saëns crafted these orchestrations carefully to frame the singer's voice without drowning it, while exploiting the coloristic possibilities of the orchestra to underline the poetic qualities of the *mélodie*.

Song composition accompanied Saint-Saëns from his earliest musical steps —where the text could provide a structural skeleton for his musical expression—to the end of his life, when the *chansons* he composed harked back to the glorious days of the Pléiade. Through their variety, Saint-Saëns's songs offer a unique window onto both the *mélodie* as a genre and the musical, poetic, social, and political worlds of Saint-Saëns. Each song fascinates by way of its intrinsic themes, with words and music an invita-

Example 5. Camille Saint-Saëns, "La Danse macabre," song orchestration, mm. 1–11.

Un mé - mo - ran - dum, Le jeu - di ma - tin,

Example 6. Emmanuel Chabrier, text underlay for Saint-Saëns's *Danse macabre* motive, in Chabrier to Saint-Saëns, n.d., in Eurydice Jousse and Yves Gérard, eds., *Lettres de compositeurs à Camille Saint-Saëns* (Lyon: Symétrie, 2009), 104.

tion to the listener to explore their meanings. As varied as his songs are, however, Saint-Saëns's approach to song composition remained shaped by his overall compositional concern about formal clarity as a signifier of French music. Even when he pushed the envelope, for example in "Le Vent dans la plaine," he remained firmly grounded in the aesthetic matrix of that "eminently French" genre the *romance*, whose structural restraint mitigated against the freer musical prose of younger contemporaries such as Debussy. To compare him with these contemporaries, however, is to miss an important point by way of a misplaced aesthetic prejudice. It has become commonplace to describe Saint-Saëns's *mélodies* as old-fashioned and lacking in "individual expressivity" when compared to those using more "advanced" compositional techniques such as the *mélodies* of, for example, Debussy, Fauré, or Reynaldo Hahn. For Saint-Saëns himself, however, this apparent lack would be high praise indeed, for it would show that he had done his work well as a national bard by sounding, in his *mélodies*, the poetry of France—not for his own sake but for the nation's greater glory.

NOTES

1. Pending the publication of the volume of the catalogue of Saint-Saëns's complete works that includes his songs, the most detailed list can be found in Frits Noske, *French Song from Berlioz to Duparc*, trans. Rita Benton, rev. 2nd ed. (New York: Dover, 1970), 387–96.

2. Camille Saint-Saëns, "La Poésie et la musique," in *Harmonie et mélodie* (Paris: Calman-Lévy, 1885), 257–66. Unattributed epigraph quotes Victor Hugo: "Chante! Milton chantait! Chante! Homère a chanté!" Saint-Saëns: "Oui, le poète chantait; mais le poète ne chante plus" (257).

3. Saint-Saëns, "La Poésie et la musique," 259. Katherine Bergeron discusses French concepts of declamation and song in *Voice Lessons: French Mélodie in the Belle Epoque* (New York and Oxford: Oxford University Press, 2010).

4. Saint-Saëns to Lili Boulanger, 10 March 1914, Bibliothèque nationale de France (BnF), Musique, Fonds Boulanger.

5. Saint-Saëns, "La Poésie et la musique," 265.

6. Ibid.

7. Ibid., 264.

8. Gabriel Fauré to Saint-Saëns, postmarked 28 June 1900, in Camille Saint-Saëns and Gabriel Fauré, *Correspondance (1862–1920)*, ed. Jean-Michel Nectoux (Paris: Éditions Klincksieck, 1994), 71–72.

9. "ΓΝΩΤΙ ΣΕΑΥΤΟΝ," Camille Saint-Saëns, *Rimes familières* (Paris: Calman-Lévy, 1890), 45–46.

10. Camille Saint-Saëns, "Le Lever de soleil sur le Nil," for voice and orchestra, text by Camille Saint-Saëns, autograph manuscript, BnF Musique, MS. 2485: "Nous disent que les Dieux sont morts."

11. Saint-Saëns to Auguste Durand, 16 March 1898, Coll. Mediathèque Musicale Mahler, Paris (henceforth MMM), courtesy of Yves Gérard.

12. Saint-Saëns to Auguste Durand, 15 April 1898, MMM, courtesy of Yves Gérard.

13. Lydia Goehr discusses the nineteenth-century incarnation of the paragone and its stakes with respect to Richard Wagner in "—*wie ihn uns Meister Dürer gemalt!* Contest, Myth, and Prophecy in Wagner's *Die Meistersinger von Nürnberg*," *Journal of the American Musicological Society* 64 (2011): 51–117. Matthias Waschek addresses the paragone in the context of French Wagner reception in "Zum *Wagnérisme* in den bildenden Künsten," in *Von Wagner zum Wagnérisme: Musik-Literatur-Kunst-Politik*, ed. Annegret Fauser and Manuela Schwartz, Transfer: Die deutsch-französische Kulturbibliothek, vol. 12 (Leipzig: Leipziger Universitäts-Verlag, 1999), 535–46.

14. For a discussion of the aesthetics of French song, see Noske, *French Song*, and Annegret Fauser, *Der Orchestergesang in Frankreich zwischen 1870 und 1920*, Freiburger Beiträge zur Musikwissenschaft, vol. 2 (Laaber: Laaber Verlag, 1994), 59–76.

15. Camille Saint-Saëns, "Victor Hugo" (1911), in *École buissonnière* (Paris: Pierre Lafitte, 1913), 49–55, at 50.

16. Gabriel Fauré, "Sous la musique que faut-il mettre?" *Musica* 9 (1911): 38.

17. Charles Koechlin, "La Mélodie," in *Cinquante ans de musique française de 1874 à 1925*, ed. Ladislas Rohozinski, 2 vols. (Paris: Les Éditions Musicales de la Librairie de France, 1925), 2:1–62. "Une beauté virtuelle apparaît que l'on ne soupçonnait pas" (2).

18. This became commonplace rhetoric among French fin-de-siècle poets. See, for example, Henri de Régnier's comment: "Il me semble que la poésie est un art complet et qu'un poème se suffit à tout seul." For Fauré, see "Sous la musique que faut-il mettre?" 39. See also Fauser, *Der Orchestergesang*, 60–67. Wagner's influence on French literature and painting has been subject to a significant body of literature. For a short survey on Wagnerism as a European cultural phenomenon, see Annegret Fauser, "Wagnerism: Responses to Wagner in Music and the Arts," in *The Cambridge Companion to Wagner*, ed. Thomas S. Grey (Cambridge: Cambridge University Press, 2008), 221–34.

19. On the role of birdsong in Western music theory, see Matthew Head, "Birdsong and the Origins of Music," *Journal of the Royal Musical Association* 122 (1997): 1–23.

20. On the musical representation of insects in the context of the *Scherzo fantastique*, see Francesca Brittan, "On Microscopic Hearing: Fairy Magic, Natural Science, and the *Scherzo fantastique*," *Journal of the American Musicological Society* 64 (2011): 527–600.

21. On the *romance* as genre and its nationalist credentials, see, for example, Rainer Gstrein, *Die vokale Romance in der Zeit von 1750–1850* (Innsbruck: Edition Helbing, 1989); Andreas Ballstaedt and Tobias Widmaier, *Salonmusik: Zur Geschichte und Funktion einer bürgerlichen Musikpraxis* (Stuttgart and Wiesbaden: Franz Steiner Verlag, 1989); David Charlton, "The *Romance* and Its Cognates: Narrative, Irony, and *Vraisemblence* in Early Opéra Comique," in *Die Opéra Comique und ihr Einfluß auf das europäische Musiktheater im 19. Jahrhundert*, ed. Herbert Schneider and Nicole Wild (Hildesheim: Olms, 1997), 43–92; and David Tunley, *Salons, Singers, and Songs: A Background to Romantic French Song, 1830–1870* (Aldershot: Ashgate, 2002), 58–88.

22. Tunley, *Salons, Singers, and Songs*, 102–18. On the role of the *romance* in Berlioz's song composition, see Annegret Fauser, "The Songs," in *The Cambridge Companion to Berlioz*, ed. Peter Bloom (Cambridge: Cambridge University Press, 2000), 109–24, esp. 109–12.

23. Noske, *French Song*, 22–35; Katharine Ellis, *Music Criticism in Nineteenth-Century France: La Revue et Gazette musicale de Paris, 1834–80* (Cambridge: Cambridge University Press, 1995), 131–34; Tunley, *Salons, Singers, and Songs*, 89–101.

24. Henri Panofka in the *Revue et gazette musicale de Paris* (1836), cited in Ellis, *Music Criticism*, 132.

25. Camille Saint-Saëns, preface for a 1896 edition of his *Mélodie de jeunesse*, BnF Musique, Rés.F.1644(14): "cette bizarre coïncidence."

26. Koechlin writes in "La Mélodie" that "la *mélodie* française pour piano et chant reste bien différente du *lied* allemand. Non seulement dans la structure . . . mais dans l'*esprit* même, qui très vite a cessé être celui de la chanson populaire, pour au contraire s'affirmer comme une des manifestations les plus 'aristocratiques' de la musique" (1).

27. On the German debates about song, see for example Walther Dürr, *Das deutsche Sololied im 19. Jahrhundert: Untersuchungen zu Sprache und Musik* (Wilhelmshaven: Heinrichshofen, 1984); and the excellent overview in the introductory chapter of Elisabeth Schmierer, *Die Orchesterlieder Gustav Mahlers*, Kieler Schriften zur Musikwissenschaft, vol. 38 (Kassel and New York: Bärenreiter, 1991). For a broadly conceived perspective on song over Western music history, see the two-volume *Musikalische Lyrik*, ed. Hermann Danuser (Laaber: Laaber Verlag, 2004).

28. Charles Koechlin, "Commentaires sur mes compositions" (ca. 1918), manuscript, extract published in Fauser, *Der Orchestergesang*, 180–84, at 180.

29. Koechlin, "La Mélodie," 9.

30. Jann Pasler, *Composing the Citizen: Music as Public Utility in Third Republic France* (Berkeley, Los Angeles, and London: University of California Press, 2009), 629–41. On the use of this strategy during the 1861 Parisian *Tannhäuser* scandal, see Annegret Fauser, "'Cette musique sans tradition': Wagner's *Tannhäuser* and Its French Critics," in *Music, Theater, and Cultural Transfer: Paris, 1830–1914*, ed. Annegret Fauser and Mark Everist (Chicago: University of Chicago Press, 2009), 228–55.

31. For an early discussion in the 1860s, see Fauser, "'Cette musique sans tradition'"; see also Jean-Louis Jam and Gérard Loubinoux, "D'une Walkyrie à l'autre . . . Querelles et traductions," in *Von Wagner zum Wagnérisme*, 401–30.

32. For an in-depth discussion of Wagnerism, including its contradictions, in French fin-de-siècle opera, see Steven Huebner, *French Opera at the Fin de Siècle: Wagnerism, Nationalism, and Style* (Oxford and New York: Oxford University Press, 1999). With respect to the confrontations earlier in the century that contrasted clear-cut French forms with Wagner's suspected attack on form, see Hervé Lacombe, *The Keys to French Opera*, trans. Edward Schneider (Berkeley, Los Angeles, and London: University of California Press, 2001).

33. Camille Mauclair, "Le 'Lied' français contemporain," *Musica* 7 (1908): 163–64, at 164.

34. See, for example, Noske, *French Song*, 231; Michael Stegemann, *Camille Saint-Saëns* (Reinbek: Rowohlt, 1988), 93–96.

35. Saint-Saëns to Fauré, 3 June 1914, cited in Stephen Studd, *Saint-Saëns: A Critical Biography* (London: Cygnus Arts; and Madison, NJ: Fairleigh Dickinson University Press, 1999), 264.

36. Camille Saint-Saëns, "Victor Hugo," 49: "Avec les vers d'Hugo, je me trouvais d'emblée en communion intime, et, ma nature essentiellement musicale primant le tout, je me mis à les chanter."

37. Ibid., 50: "dont l'admiration pour Hugo égalait la mienne."

38. Studd, *Saint-Saëns*, 26.

39. Camille Saint-Saëns, *Harmonie et mélodie*, 159, cited in Fauser, *Der Orchestergesang*, 114.

40. Saint-Saëns to Jacques Durand, 31 March 1918, MMM, courtesy of Yves Gérard.

41. Saint-Saëns to Auguste Durand, 21 February 1888, MMM, courtesy of Yves Gérard.

42. On the festival, see Pasler, *Composing the Citizen*, 649–51.

43. Camille Saint-Saëns, "Pallas Athénée," words by Jean-Louis Croze, orchestral score (Paris: Durand & Fils, 1894). The autograph score (BnF Musique, MS. 2457) is dated 7 September 1894 and titled "ΠΑΛΛΑΣ ΑΘΗΝΗ."

44. *Poésies de Armand Renaud: Les Nuits persanes, idylles japonaises, Orient* (Paris: Alphonse Lemaire, 1896), 4: "Avant de parler d'Orient, if faut d'abord bien définir de quel Orient on entend parler. . . . De toutes, c'est la forme persane qui, en poésie surtout, est la plus originale et la plus complète. L'Arabie tombe en décadence."

45. In the collection of poems, the order is "La Brise," "Mélancolie" (titled "La Solitaire" by Saint-Saëns), "Splendeur vide," "Au Cimetière," "Sabre en main," and "Tournoiement." In the cycle, Saint-Saëns switched the order to "La Brise," "Splendeur vide," "La Solitaire," "Sabre en main," "Au Cimetière," and "Tournoiement."

46. Ralph Locke discusses the complex and contradictory manifestations of musical exoticism in his book, *Musical Exoticism: Images and Reflections* (Cambridge: Cambridge University Press, 2009). One of Locke's foundational texts in this research area addresses more specifically Saint-Saëns and Regnault; see "Constructing the oriental 'Other': Camille Saint-Saëns's *Samson et Dalila*," *Cambridge Opera Journal* 3 (1991): 261–302.

47. Camille Saint-Saëns, cited in Brian Rees, *Camille Saint-Saëns: A Life* (London: Chatto & Windus, 1999), 153.

48. *Poésies de Armand Renaud*, v.

49. Rees, *Camille Saint-Saëns*, 159.

50. *Poésies de Armand Renaud*, v–vi.

51. Emmanuel Chabrier to Saint-Saëns, undated, in *Lettres de compositeurs à Camille Saint-Saëns*, ed. Eurydice Jousse and Yves Gérard (Lyon: Symétrie, 2009), 103–4, at 104.

52. On musical allusion in fin-de-siècle France, see Annegret Fauser, "Musik als 'Lesehilfe': Zur Rolle der Allusion in den Opern von Jules Massenet," in *Musik als Text: Bericht über den Internationalen Kongreß der Gesellschaft für Musikforschung Freiburg im Breisgau 1993*, ed. Hermann Danuser and Tobias Plebuch (Kassel: Bärenreiter-Verlag, 1999), 462–64.

53. Although operatic extracts were common fare in European concerts throughout the eighteenth and nineteenth centuries, by the fin de siècle and with the transfer of Wagnerian work concepts onto opera this practice became increasingly suspect. The composer Florent Schmitt spoke for many in this exasperated comment: "And what should one give this soloist to sing? Eternally those fragments of operas by Gluck, Mozart, Wagner, or that air of the Archangel from [César Franck's] *La Rédemption*?" See Florent Schmitt, cited in Fauser, *Der Orchestergesang*, 141.

54. Saint-Saëns to Jacques Durand, 1 February 1915, MMM, courtesy of Yves Gérard.

55. For a detailed discussion of song orchestration and French concert practice, see Fauser, *Der Orchestergesang*, 140–65.

56. Saint-Saëns to Auguste Durand, 31 December 1892, MMM, courtesy of Yves Gérard.

Saint-Saëns and the Ancient World:

From Africa to Greece

JANN PASLER

In March 1891, just after finishing *Africa*, for piano and orchestra, Saint-Saëns wrote from Cairo to his publisher Auguste Durand, "I've tried to put on display an Africa that is original [*inédit*]." Five years later, again from Cairo, he whetted Durand's appetite for the second movement of his Piano Concerto no. 5 in similar terms: "You're going to see things that are unheard-of [*inouies*]. . . . It's possible that this part will only please its author."[1] What was so unusual, so unprecedented about these works? Did they build on impressions from Saint-Saëns's first stay in Algeria in 1873, as expressed in his *Suite algérienne* (1880)? If so, what did he choose to borrow and assimilate from African music, and to what end? And why use the piano, an instrument of equal temperament incapable of reproducing the complex sounds of African music?

To understand such works, we must examine how Saint-Saëns interpreted not only the differences but also the similarities and possible relationships between Europe and North Africa since French colonists had begun to settle there in greater numbers in the 1870s. When he compared *Africa* with a "Hungarian rhapsody," saying in jest that perhaps "Hungarian gypsies came from Africa," he may have been referring to the migrations that linked these regions during various epochs, leaving traces in their music.[2] With many at the turn of the century preoccupied with the search for racial and cultural origins, North Africa, as part of the Mediterranean diaspora, could prove a rich font of knowledge about ancient Greece and Rome. Experimenting with musical heterogeneity and coexistence thus had not only colonial meanings but also racial, historical, and political implications.

Africa in 1891

The appeal of Africa to the composer and his audiences in the 1890s was complex. First, the final effort to return France to monarchy had failed in the late 1880s, and in 1891, after the first stage of the Franco-Russian alliance was signed, republicans felt empowered to expand their imperialism, especially in Africa. As Jules Ferry had presented it a decade earlier, the utility of the colonies was practical, strategic, psychological, symbolic, and above all economic. The colonies offered primary materials to enhance French productivity, expanded markets for French products, and new contexts for asserting French glory. In 1891, parts of Guinea and the French Sudan (Upper Senegal) became distinct French colonies. Dahomey became a French protectorate in 1892 (part of French West Africa in 1904), and Madagascar, a protectorate since 1885, a colony in 1896.

Figure 1. Saint-Saëns in Algerian clothes, with his statue of Phryné.

Works such as *Africa* and the Fifth Concerto beg certain questions. Was the composer attempting to stimulate curiosity and interest in the continent, or merely paying tribute to his own impressions? Was he writing to encourage escape, albeit an imaginary or vicarious one, creating a fantasy onto which listeners could project their own desires? Or was he pointing to racial differences? In some ways, these works addressed the objection that writers in the colonial press often expressed: France was good at collecting colonies, but it did not always know how to take advantage of them (*les mettre en valeur*).[3] African music presented to Western composers and audiences new scales, sonorities, and rhythms as potentially rich in implications as the continent's natural resources. Engaging with the Other's difference could push on the boundaries of Western sound, a musical benefit of colonial expansion.

Yet, after significant difficulties in Dahomey and fierce resistance by the Tuaregs in what would become French Sudan, anticolonialist sentiment in France began to grow.[4] By 1895, support for the Madagascar expedition was limited, even if the soldiers most affected came mostly from other African colonies. From this perspective, feeding the French desire for exotic fantasies in music and the other arts might have contributed to simplified positions on complicated issues, adding to prejudice, arrogance, and support for unenlightened policies. Was Saint-Saëns, as someone who frequently lived in North Africa and traveled widely, sensitive to this? Between *Africa* and the Fifth Concerto, Saint-Saëns composed *Caprice Arabe* for two pianos (1894)—which he called "a little *Africa* for two pianos"[5]—and *Souvenir d'Ismaïlia* for piano (1895), but thereafter little colonial-inspired music.[6]

A second factor influencing the composer and his public were conflicting attitudes toward race and racial origins, which grew heated in the 1890s. As divided as they were on how to accomplish their political goals, most republicans endorsed monogenism, the idea that all races descended from one. Consequently, they ardently believed in the potential of the environment to influence people and in the ability of colonized peoples, through education and reason, to adapt and change, including those in their colonies.[7] Also, the Universal Exhibition of 1889 had posed the question of a world culture, as monogenists sought to understand universal traits throughout the globe. Non-Western music, considered by many an inferior art, seemed to reflect earlier stages of the evolution in which all cultures participated. Monarchists, in contrast, tended to embrace polygenism, the idea that each human race has a separate origin. Refuting the idea that man is everywhere equal, this concept served to preserve inherited privileges. At the International Colonial Congress in 1889 and in his book *Les Lois psychologiques de l'évolution des peuples* (1894), Gustave Le Bon proposed that the nature of a people, as manifested in its arts, is fixed and homogenous, not alterable by education or intelligence—an argument against any beneficial impact of Westerners and Western education in Africa. Music scholars were divided on whether they could perceive universal traits in African music, but tended to agree, when it came to music, that cultural as well as racial differences were primordial.

Third, these attitudes toward race implied different colonial policies. At home republicans considered France the product of ancient Greek and Roman traditions assimilated through the Gauls and German traditions passed down through the Franks. In 1893, just after the French premiere of Wagner's *Die Walküre*, a writer for the populist newspaper *Le Petit Journal* explained French enthusiasm for Wagner by pointing out that "we, more sophisticated descendants of the Latins, have retained the greatest and brightest ability, that of assimilation."[8] Abroad, republicans in principle sought not to ignore racial and religious differences but to build some kind of "moral community" based on living under the same economic and social regime. Sympathetic musicians saw music and musical practices as languages to be shared; music was a way to help "solve the problem of assimilation," whether this meant indigenous people identifying as French or other Europeans living in French North Africa. Some saw music as not just part of the "civilizing mission," but as the only thing that could prepare "a fusion of the races." Saint-Saëns was known for his incredible capacity for assimilation, his ability to incorporate and use for his own purposes all kinds of music, suggesting sympathy for republican colonialism.

However, many colonizers did not want their power usurped by indigenous voters. And few Algerian Muslims were willing to repudiate their rights to Islamic law in order to become French citizens. Problems in attempting to impose French institutions in Indochina at the end of the century led to all-out attacks on assimilationist policy. Some looked to the British system of association, which embodied a more distanced relationship between colonizer and colonized: cooperation by native peoples in their own administration, but little expectation of assimilation of European values and customs. Associationist colonial policies, eventually adapted by French administrators, encouraged more recognition of difference. In the musical world this shift of focus had its greatest impact in the use of the phonograph in lieu of Western notation to record indigenous music, a recommendation of the Music History Congress during the Paris Exhibition of 1900. Although Saint-Saëns apparently did not collect recordings of non-Western music or use them in his music, the fact that he never shared with others his notation of indigenous tunes—at least to our knowledge—and may have destroyed most of them, suggests that perhaps he was all too aware of the limitations of Western transcription.[9]

Fourth, significant tourism by Westerners in North Africa and popular interest in archaeology were an important part of the context for Saint-Saëns's African experiences. In the 1890s, the French magazine *À travers le monde* published "Advice to Travelers," a series that described organized tours of Algeria and Tunisia lasting twenty-five days and costing 850 francs in first class. These articles suggest what the typical tourist would need and might expect. In Algeria, besides Algiers, Blidah was among the proposed destinations; venturing a little farther was Biskra, and finally Tunis. Perhaps the reflection of experiences he may have shared with other tourists, Saint-Saëns devoted one of the movements in his *Suite algérienne* to Blidah. The opening theme of *Africa* is from a tune he heard in Biskra, and one of its final themes, a Tunisian song. Still, if he ventured into more distant and unusual destinations, apparently he was less adventurous than others who wrote about their tourism in North Africa.

Egypt, where Saint-Saëns sketched *Africa* and wrote the Fifth Concerto, was especially popular with tourists, particularly after the Paris exhibitions, the Egyptian caravan of 123 people on display at the Paris zoo in August 1891, and new archaeological discoveries there. Any visit inevitably included a trip down the Nile. As many tourists noted, the Valley of the Nile was a "very fashionable winter destination" with railroads and "luxurious boats."[10] In 1895, it was even difficult to find a room in a hotel, and the Guide Joanne was fast sold out.[11] Albert Gayet, in Egypt to collect objects for the Musée Guimet in Paris, wrote of his ten trips in the 1890s: "It's on a tourist boat that one is best situated to see the monuments and archaeological discoveries."[12] On one such visit, he shared meals with Greeks, Italians, Americans, Germans, Austrians, Hungarians, Spaniards, Swedes, the English, and even Russians. Many published their memoirs, some noting that, perhaps like cruise ships today, tourists were entertained nightly with a "belly dance," an entertainment popularized during the universal exhibitions. This suggests that Saint-Saëns's experiences in North Africa, and especially on the Nile in 1896, were undoubtedly shaped not just by the land, its people, and whatever music he may have heard there, but also by the presence of other Westerners he traveled with, such as the painter Georges Clairin, and those he met on the trip, such as Georges Legrain, director of restoration at Karnak. Besides taking notes on the pyramids, photographing them, and writing about mirages, did he perhaps collect tunes as he would archaeological artifacts, fascinated with what they might suggest about the distant past or as evidence of connections between Arab music and that of ancient Greece? When he wrote works like *Africa* and his Concerto no. 5, did he have in mind a kind of musical souvenir for his fellow travelers and Egyptomanes back home—or was it something more serious?[13]

Composing In and About Africa

We know that Saint-Saëns was drawn to North Africa not just for the climate, good for his health, but also for the calm that allowed him to work without the stresses and distractions of Paris.[14] As Camille Bellaigue and others have pointed out, Saint-Saëns had "a taste for representing distant and rare things."[15] His attitude toward difference can be gleaned early on from the musical presentation in *Orient et occident* (1868) and *Suite algérienne* (1881). Although *Orient et occident* does not suggest anything specifically French about the West, the march articulates a French ideology of Western superiority and progress. Saint-Saëns used an ABA form: the music coded as Western—the A sections—serves as the framework for understanding, containing, and dominating the B section, the music coded as Eastern. The structure is far more complex than the typical military march, however. Saint-Saëns does not merely juxtapose the differences between the Western and Eastern sections, underlined by the use of counterpoint and thematic development in the first and static harmonies in the second, but instead deploys an arsenal of compositional and formal devices to make his point. In the A section, for example, a Western theme, beginning with four half notes moving in deliberate steps outward to fill the sound space with discipline and control, adapts to different contexts and endures change. The incorporation of a dance-like second theme suggests that the West is not just assertive but also capable of lyricism and grace, and that these contrasts can coexist. In the B section, heavily articulated bar lines contain the energy of different melodies, instruments, and rhythms, as if within prison bars, the melismas of its oscillating theme squeezed into upbeats to emphasize the downbeats of each measure. In a quasi-recapitulation, Saint-Saëns brings back the Orientalist B theme, but slows its 64th-note melismas to eighth notes to accommodate the pace and duple meter of the A theme. In the final minutes of the march, the rhythmic and timbral diversity disappears and the whole orchestra marches together. Saint-Saëns thus posits the Orient as a stereotyped Other only to take it over, neutralize its difference, and assimilate it by virtue of Western skill. By the end of this march, the juxtaposition and binary opposition of East and West seem an illusion.

In the *Suite algérienne*, Saint-Saëns likewise frames the oriental material in the middle with an opening prelude, signaling the arrival of the listener in Algiers, and finishes with a French military march, its "warrior accents" an explicit contrast to the "bizarre rhythms and "languorous oriental melodies" they follow. One critic saw the march as embodying the "justice and benefits of our domination,"[16] perhaps a reference to the disciplined coordination and coherent structure that the French may have perceived as their contribution to colonial life, here represented by the march's closed form, ABA.[17] Another heard no "violence or brutality" in it, "just plain gaiety."[18]

In contrast, there are no marches in *Africa* and his Piano Concerto no. 5. Neither is about domination. In the former, the composer tries to come to grips with the enormous diversity within Africa, as manifested by its musical traditions. Biskra, where Saint-Saëns heard *Africa*'s opening tune, is a gateway to the Sahara Desert.[19] It was settled by desert nomads in the Middle Ages and later became a tourist destination.[20] Most of the Chaoui population was black and their music, as performed on the double-reed *raita*, often expressed their warrior nature. Biskra means instability, which is precisely the nature of *Africa*'s opening theme A (see Example 1). As in certain Chaoui music in which the wind players insist on the upper note of a melodic motive, theme A in *Africa* begins in the oboe and emphasizes E♭, over and over. Turning round and round on the same pitches, the theme's first downbeat lands on an augmented second, melodically and harmonically, and its syncopated rhythms avoid any regular beats, giving rise to unusual metric patterns of 2 + 3 + 2 + 3, as Michael Stegemann points out.[21] Moreover, even if the work starts softly, the insistent accents on offbeats have an aggressive, threatening quality. After spinning out a long cadenza ad libitum, the composer uses it in a thoroughly Western manner to modulate to another key and to create Western counterpoint between the piano and other instruments. The result is a kind of musical hybridity in which the instability of the theme serves as a pretext for Western development.

Saint-Saëns also incorporated African rhythms and rhythmic ostinati. His interest in the latter is clear in his sketches for the work in Ms 916 (10–11), where five of the seven melodic fragments are so accompanied, three of them with two ostinati patterns. In the Meno allegretto (p. 6 of

Example 1. Saint-Saëns, *Africa*, theme A, mm. 1–10.

Table 1a. Thematic Succession in *Africa*.

A / piano cad. / A' / piano / B / A'' / piano / c / D / D' / piano cad. / A

E / $\frac{E}{A}$ / E' / piano / F

G / G / B' / H / G' / H / I / F / G

piano G / $\frac{G}{A}$ / E / F' / piano

the piano score), an ostinato, the work's third theme c (the lowercase a reference to its rhythmic rather than melodic nature), creates a structure over which Saint-Saëns expresses himself freely. Rapid two-octave descents are played over this rhythm, then two times these descents in thirds, followed by arpeggios twice spanning two octaves. In some ways, this outcry resembles war songs from French Sudan as recorded on wax cylinders currently in the Berlin Phonogramm-Archiv (Archiv Sénégambie). Other rhythmic ostinati accompany theme D. Saint-Saëns's sketch for theme D is unusual in that it appears in *Africa* with the same notes, rhythms, tonality, and phrase length. Theme D is characterized not only by its dance-like melody, but also by the oboe's high A, with its melismas, and the rhythmic ostinato on weak beats in the low register. By "theme" here, I mean the musical aspect that renders each section distinct—usually a melody that repeats and develops in various instruments. However, as with theme D, a theme can also involve textural and temporal elements. I will discuss these according to type rather than order of appearance.

The first part of the work, as Table 1a suggests, consists of a kind of rondo, ABAcDA. What gives the sense of a quasi-closed structure is, after a series of contrasting themes, the return of not only theme A and the initial tempo, but also the piano cadenza with *rapido* and non-measured arabesques and arpeggios that almost stop time. From this alternation in the work between thematic and improvisatory material comes *Africa*'s subtitle: fantasy, a work based on a mosaic of themes.[22]

Five new themes appear in the second and third parts of the work, themes E, F, G, H, and I. Themes E and G are aggressive, to be played *marcato* and *fortissimo*. The former (p. 10), which dominates part 2, is a close variant of one in his sketches indicated as "Danse des almées" and possibly heard at the Paris 1889 Exhibition.[23] It is characterized by the Arabic scale Maia (D♭, E♭, F, A♭, B♭, C) with an oscillation of eighth notes around D♭ (at the octave, the unison, in thirds, and in sixths) ending on two accented weak beats. Perhaps this aspect inspired Saint-Saëns to bring back theme A momentarily in counterpoint with it. The aggressivity, however, dissipates as the theme modulates to G major and transforms into a variant, E',

Table 1b. Themes in *Africa*.

leggiero e tranquillo, before disappearing into chromatic arabesques and a long chromatic scale rising more than three octaves in preparation for the five-scale rising line at the end of the work. Theme G (p. 13), again in *fortissimo* octaves, plays a major role thereafter. The return of this theme, its tempo, and its scale (with an augmented second, B♭–C♯) give rise to a second, rondo-like arch form in the middle of the work (see line 3 of Table 1a). With its binary, well-balanced rhythms (2 + 2 + 2 + 4 + 4) and its accents on strong beats, theme G is perhaps the easiest to remember (and, with its bombastic quality, the most fun to play). Like theme E, G becomes more lyrical later in G'. Theme A returns superimposed on themes E and G, as if to take them on, however momentarily.

Two other themes, H (p. 14, bottom two staves), and I (p. 16, bottom two staves), are more folklike.[24] The first, developed almost as if by Bach, evokes a dance. The second, played only in the orchestra, turns in place within a fourth, its difference underlined with a bare tremoli accompaniment and a simple repeating rhythm in the low bass.[25] Like theme D, themes H and I pass quickly, without consequence, but contribute to the atmosphere.

Saint-Saëns called *Africa* an "outgrowth of the *Suite algérienne*."[26] There are three ways to understand this. Both works were inspired by "the contrasts in the African countryside."[27] The succession of themes, with their different scales and moods, also recalls Arabic Nuba, multi-movement music that inspired the "Rhapsodie mauresque" of *Suite algérienne*, even if most Nuba music remains in one scale. And if there is no march at the end of *Africa*, no Western music framing perception of African materials, the work is nevertheless dominated by the aggressive, assertive themes A, E, and G; the more lyrical and dance-like themes come only in the middle and for the sake of contrast. Significantly, Saint-Saëns treats these two types of themes differently, as if the aggressive aspects of North Africa need to be taken on—not subverted but developed for Western ends, whereas the peaceful, playful ones can be acknowledged but left aside.

The Pastoral Theme: Indigenous Music in France and Africa

The second (or B) theme of *Africa* (p. 4), a folklike tonal melody of sweep and grace, raises not the issue of difference with Western music, but similarity. The theme appears twice in his sketches, first with quite different rhythms and a different shape after the first two bars, but later in a form very similar to that in *Africa* (compare Table 1b, theme B, with Examples 2a and 2b). However, in the second sketch the form theme B takes is marked *vivace* and has an *ostinato* accompaniment, with each downbeat

Example 2a. *Africa*, first sketch for theme B.

accented, whereas in *Africa*, it is more lyrical and played much slower, *andantino espressivo*. In *Africa*, moreover, theme B is in E flat major, accompanied by rolled chords in simple harmonic progressions (I-I⁷-I, I-III-I, and III-III⁷-I). As such, it presents a stark contrast of tempo, mood, character, and especially scale with the rest of the piece. This suggests that Saint-Saëns was not averse to transforming the character of what was most likely an indigenous tune, perhaps to underline its compatibility with Western music.

Was Saint-Saëns commenting here on the impact that Westerners can have on such an environment? In his hands, theme B becomes a nicely balanced eight-measure melody, alternating with two variations, to form a well-proportioned and self-contained interlude in the piece. Or, in juxtaposing it to the other themes, was he attempting to capture the difference in feeling between the desert and North African cities, nomad and sedentary peoples, or "vengeance and love," the two great passions expressed in Arab music? In its "languor," Emile Baumann heard it as "tinged with the calm associated with nighttime in Algiers."[28] The use of tonality supports the notion that the coastal cities were, in a certain way, "the continuation of Europe with which they were long in touch."[29] Theme B never returns in *Africa*, but like the lyrical middle section of military marches—nostalgic, perhaps, for the peaceful life back home—its presence is nevertheless salient. So what are we to make of this?

Consider what Saint-Saëns was composing and performing around the same time (see Table 2).

Africa was completed in Cairo on 1 April 1891, but he was still working on the orchestration in Algiers in June. Saint-Saëns published a version for two pianos that October, just before the first performances on 25 October and 8 November 1891 in Paris. In Algiers in November, while correcting the proofs for the piano version of *Africa*, he orchestrated some of his earlier Orientalist songs, transforming them into *Nuit persane*. Then, from September through November, he wrote a Suite for piano, op. 90,

Example 2b. *Africa*, second sketch for theme B.

with a minuet, gavotte, and gigue.[30] In the gavotte, Saint-Saëns adopts the
meter and upbeats associated with eighteenth-century gavottes, but introduces seventh and ninth chords, as if to modernize it. Such musical
references to eighteenth-century forms suggest that he was interested in
using music to bridge a link to the distant French past. In summer 1891,
he arranged some music by Lully for a revival of Molière's *Le Sicilien* in
Paris and, in 1892, composed a Sarabande and Rigaudon for a new edition of Charpentier's *Le Malade imaginaire*, performing them in Algiers in
March 1893.[31] As I have argued elsewhere, these works should be understood in the context of the republican desire for a history that included
not only the Revolution but also the ancien régime.[32]

At the same, Saint-Saëns became interested in the oldest parts of France,
Brittany and Auvergne. There, where the Celts retreated from Romans and
their influence, folksongs were thought to embody the customs and values
of the earliest French. As music scholars began to draw attention to these
songs as documenting a time before assimilation and hybridization, Saint-
Saëns returned to this repertoire.[33] In November 1891 he wrote a new
Rhapsodie bretonne for orchestra, based on Breton motives previously used
in his *Trois Rhapsodies sur des cantiques bretons* for organ (1866), which premiered on 17 January 1892. And in his March 1891 letter to Durand, cited
earlier, he explicitly compared *Africa* to his own *Rhapsodie d'Auvergne* (1884),
which "it's destined to overshadow because it is much more developed."
Like *Africa*, this rhapsody is also a succession of folklike themes that are
developed and interpenetrate; it also ends with a chromatic scale that

Table 2. Saint-Saëns's Works in Three Genres, Composed 1891–92

	AFRICA	EARLY MUSIC	RHAPSODIES
1891			
MARCH–APRIL	Composition		Letter on *Africa* and *Rhapsodie d'Auvergne*
SEPTEMBER		Suite for piano, op. 90	
OCTOBER	Score for 2 pianos Premiere		
NOVEMBER	Orchestral parts		*Rhapsodie bretonne*
DECEMBER	Piano solo score		*Rhapsodie d'Auvergne* performed by Saint-Saëns in Algiers
1892			
JANUARY			*Rhapsodie bretonne* premiere
FEBRUARY	Orchestral score	Sarabande, Rigaudon	

stretches the entire length of the keyboard, followed by accented chords. While correcting proofs of *Africa*, the composer performed *Rhapsodie d'Auvergne* at the seminary of Notre Dame d'Afrique for the missionary order Pères Blancs (White Fathers) and black Sudanese. Moreover, he often proposed to perform these rhapsodies together with his *Africa*.

It is possible that the composer was attracted by the fantasy and the rhapsody as similar genres. But his reasons for working simultaneously with indigenous music in France and in Africa probably went beyond the question of genre. Amateurs as well as professionals shared the belief that there were similarities between these regions of France and North Africa, as well as between their music. Whereas Mohammed Hassan compared the mountains of North Africa to the plateau of Auvergne, with its villages and farms, Raymond Pilet heard explicit resemblances between an Arab song and one from Auvergne, which he attributed to similar life conditions, similar feelings, and similarly limited means.[34] From Villoteau to Tiersot, musicologists had argued for similarities in the musical repertoire of these two regions—simple melodic formulas that repeat, but never in the same way twice, which they explained in various ways. When Villoteau suggested that two Egyptian airs resembled French folksongs, he assumed that the French *chansons* had been brought to Egypt by Greek merchants.[35] Salvador Daniel, a musician based in Algiers, pointed out similarities between North African scales and Greek scales, especially the Phrygian.[36] Tiersot observed that an Arab air he heard at one of the universal expositions began like a well-known Breton song. He admitted that Breton sailors could have made their music known on the African coasts, yet he preferred to explain this not as documenting influence, but rather in the nature of "primitive song in all times and all places."[37]

So, perhaps it should not surprise us that, though Saint-Saëns bragged about his *Africa* as "*inédite*," he should refer to the Hungarian gypsies that some believed were originally from Egypt. Ralph Locke describes the improvised musical tradition of gypsy music that Liszt emulated with his Hungarian rhapsodies:

> A typical Hungarian-Gypsy performance . . . might begin with slow, heavily improvised passages in free rhythm . . . that alternated with lyrical or melancholy melodies. These melodies were sometimes repeated many times, each time differently embellished. Sooner or later, the performance would move to a second, culminating phase, in which one or several uptempo tunes were likewise repeated with increasingly elaborate ornamentation and at an increasingly frantic tempo.[38]

With its syncopations, augmented seconds, cadenzas, multiple tunes, and frenetic ending, this could also describe *Africa*. Indeed, a reviewer in 1893 called the work "a kind of rhapsody, conceived and written with unquestionable mastery."[39] The comparison is also apt in that Saint-Saëns was an "internal outsider" in North Africa, as gypsies were "internal outsiders" in Hungary.[40]

The Theme in Triplets: Western Virtuosity

One last theme in *Africa* remains to be discussed, theme F (p. 11), which is almost entirely in triplet sixteenth notes in G major. In the first part of the work, triplets appear in the accompaniment or elaboration of other themes. In theme F, they are different. Baumann hears them as "a swarm of drunken wasps,"[41] maybe because the second time we hear them, toward the end (p. 17), the motive is off by one sixteenth note; that is, the first of the repeated sixteenth notes begins on a weak beat instead of a strong beat. One can also hear this theme as very Western. There is the chromaticism, the semitone movement that connects the triplet pairs (D♯ to E, C♯ to D, etc.). More important, theme F is intimately tied to the nature of the piano. Writing a theme in thirds also entails playing with the equal temperament of the piano, without which these thirds would not be harmonious. Theme

F also draws attention to the challenge of light, agile playing, marked *leggierissimo* throughout, as the composer once pointed out to Durand.[42]

Theme F appears only three times, but these are significant moments, related to the surrounding music. If, the first time, the theme arises out of and disappears into a long, quick, chromatic ascent of four octaves, in the middle of the work it changes into octaves and chords that also rise chromatically more than two octaves. The result is a local structure of X Y X' Y'. At the end of *Africa*, theme F' is followed by a similar chromatic ascent, but in thirty-second notes and spanning almost the entire keyboard. This return creates another rondo-like arch structure within the work, framed by F. Except in the work's conclusion, each time that it ends—in octaves that build in intensity, descending to the piano's lowest register—theme F serves to prepare the assertive theme G, also in octaves.

The work is thus full of all kinds of virtuosity—Saint-Saëns clearly had the Western pianist in mind—but the pianism required by the thirds suggests a commentary on his conception of French music, music that is beyond conventional gender binarisms. Alongside the aggressive themes (perhaps inspired by certain African music) as well as lyrical or pastoral themes (suggesting a connection between France and North Africa in the distant past), theme F helps the music to escape these binary oppositions and leads the work toward the realm of "pure" sonority. In a work that begins with a scale on G with an augmented second and ends on G major, theme F, the only theme in G major, also plays a structural role. By its pianism and its tonality, it announces the end, prepares it in a certain way, and creates it, an ending that emerges out of virtuosity.

This theme and its pianistic virtuosity add an important political dimension to *Africa*. It suggests that North Africa was not just inhabited by many kinds of indigenous people, but also by a motley collection of Jews and Westerners: Italians, Spanish, Maltese, and Greeks, all naturalized in 1889. To the extent that the theme is playful and easy, providing moments of repose from the challenges of surrounding music, it points to the tastes and customs of the coastal cities, which one tourist characterized as "effeminate."[43] There Western music was played regularly. A theater for opera opened in Algiers in 1853 and later in Cairo (1869), Oran, Constantine, Mascara, Tlemcen, Tunis and other towns. Each year the city councils hired theater directors, who formed their troupes in Paris before returning to give six months of performances. In addition, settlers played in their own orchestras (philharmonic societies), choruses, and wind bands; military bands played regularly in public parks. As we have seen in my essay on Saint-Saëns, "Algerian by Adoption," the composer was part of this community and highly appreciated. When *Africa* was played in April 1893, Algerians called for an encore.[44] Performing and listening to Western music served an important purpose: it provided settlers with a sense of the culture they shared and an ongoing connection to the outside world.

Perpetual Motion

Besides its succession of themes, it is equally important to note the succession of timbres, textures, and tempi in *Africa*—a virtuosity perhaps inspired by African music. Each section is also characterized by its own relationship among the instruments, essential to its sound. In several parts, the piano and orchestra alternate in their articulation of the theme or its fragments, but not always. Theme I appears only in the orchestra, while the thirds of theme F are played mostly on the piano.

Africa begins with a relatively thin texture of woodwinds and strings. Theme A's timbre intensifies in moving to the orchestra and returns to the piano to finish up *fortissimo* in its extreme registers. After the timbral and temporal juxtapositions of the aggressive themes A, E, and G come an Andante espressivo (theme B), an Allegretto pesante (theme c), a percussive, then tranquil passage (theme D), an animated one (D'), a scherzando, and a very light section (theme F). The fourth part of *Africa* begins and ends with pianistic virtuosity. First, there is an Animato, with sixteenth notes in oscillating octaves played very high on the piano, *fortissimo*. As that dissipates, theme G returns in the bass, *marcato*; then A can be heard under G, and next E, *fortissimo*, in thick chords. The effect of this rapid and brutal succession of thematic fragments of A, E, and G is counterbalanced momentarily by a return to the thirds of theme F, *leggierissimo*, before a chromatic scale, *fff*, traverses the piano rapidly from its lowest to highest register. The frenzy finally comes to an end with seven G-major chords, struck percussively as if to break the spell of the work. The effect of such successions resembles not only that of Hungarian rhapsodies but also Arab music, as described in 1890:

> Perpetual movement: slow at first, then with less solemnity; gradually it becomes more animated, soon follows lightness, rapidity, brilliance, driving force, and fury. Finally, a swirling vortex, vertigo, then . . . silence.[45]

Listening to *Africa*, an Algerian critic nonetheless found it and the composer quintessentially French: "The most complete expression and the most stunning manifestation of his talent as the most important harmonizer and orchestrator of the French school."[46]

The Piano Concerto No. 5

This concerto, also incorporating African music and written in Egypt, likewise requires extraordinary virtuosity and ends in a frenzy. Saint-Saëns explained to his publisher: "The piano part is formidable: there are superimpositions of thirds to make one tremble."[47] But, so that the concerto would not be taken for just another *Africa*, he explained, it should be understood as a long sea voyage, its second movement a kind of memoir of his trip from Egypt to Saigon in winter 1895. In the middle of his second movement we hear a song of boatsmen on the Nile. This time there is nothing particularly new or unusual about this choice, nor in the nature of the song. Villoteau had noted numerous such songs on his visit to Egypt eighty years earlier.[48] By the 1890s they were part and parcel of the tourist experience, described in terms that resembled reviewers' perception of the Nubian theme in Saint-Saëns's concerto: "Melancholic song, but resigned and fatal, harmonizing marvelously well with the panorama of the Nile . . . the monotony seems made to sooth sorrow and give rise to dreaming," wrote Mag Dalah in 1892.[49] Without access to Saint-Saëns's transcription of what he heard, we will never know if the song's many forms in the concerto, however subtly different, are of an Egyptian origin or the result of the composer's imagination. In the concerto, the melody appears in G major, introduced by the piano, *cantabile*, accompanied by delicately oscillating octaves—a musical gesture signifying water since Liszt. With the orchestra "always *pianissimo*," the piano harmonizes, accompanies, and develops this theme more than any others in *Africa*. "In drawing out consequences and exquisite deductions" and with "beauty that emerges from its transformation"—"its transfiguration" more than its melodic essence—Bellaigue suggests that Saint-Saëns "opens the theme to a new way of being: he enlarges it, opens it out to pure music, and the humble cantilena from Egypt thus enters into the order, and as if within the divine circle, of universal beauty."[50]

Saint-Saëns also incorporates a pentatonic melody in the second movement. Possibly he heard this tune in Cochinchina, where he had spent a month that spring.[51] Like the Nubian theme, the piano again introduces the melody accompanied by repeated octaves, this time ornamented with delicate grace notes. Saint-Saëns adapted it to the Western context in choosing to emphasize, from among its five notes, the three that make a tonal chord (F♯, A♯, and C♯). Bellaigue heard it as quite different from the Nubian theme: "not dreamlike, but lively, bouncy, *et piqué de notes de crystal*."[52] In putting it near the Nubian theme, was Saint-Saëns perhaps trying to suggest an inherent affinity between Asian and Arab music (as per Villoteau) or, as the ethnomusicologists Hornbostel and Lachmann later suggested, between Javanese and Berber music?[53] Or was the point merely the hetereogeneity of a traveler's experience? In the Fifth Concerto, the Nubian and pentatonic themes never come back, nor do they interact with other material. And, even more than themes B and I in *Africa*, the pentatonic one comes and goes like a flash of memory. After a long pause at the end of its section, the piano picks up its tonality only to fill in the gap between the D♯ and F♯ of the pentatonic scale with E and F, thereby shifting from pentatonicism to chromaticism.

The structure of this movement is another mosaic of themes, with the Arabic-sounding *capriccioso* theme A, with its augmented seconds, the sublimely calm Nubian theme B, the *dolce et grazia* theme C, and the *cantabile* pentatonic theme D in twenty-four absolutely static measures, followed by a Spanish guitar-like cadenza, *capricciosamente*. The second movement thus features static, but mysterious and attractive aspects of the Orient, albeit framed by its more troublesome aspects as in *Africa*, here connoted by the agitated rhythmic *ostinato*, with furious pianistic passages over it.

Placed between two fully Western outer movements in F major, the concerto recalls the structure of *Orient et Occident* and *Suite algérienne*. However, the treatment of movements 1 and 3 suggests an evolution in Saint-Saëns's thinking. Growing weary of too much change back home—Wagnerism, impressionism, and "hybrid" genres—Saint-Saëns was beginning to rethink Western music, chiding "its instability, its incapacity to hold on to a form, a style, for any length of time, and its obsession with seeking the new at all cost."[54] Baumann characterizes moments of struggle in these movements as "a witty jousting between two reconciled forces," as in a Haydn middle movement.[55] Perhaps to upset the typical binarisms, the outer movements also have extremely calm moments, thanks to long passages in F major and themes emphasizing the tonic and dominant. The first movement, especially its final theme, revels in perfect consonance, as if to suggest that change in the West, too, is momentary and that beauty lies elsewhere. Ravel borrowed for the end of his *Jeux d'eau* its final ascending passages: the move toward white sound and the concluding harmonic progression from VI to I. Bellaigue, ever the classicist, calls the concerto "true music, pure music."[56]

Mediterranean Connections: Ancient Greece,
Past and Future

Associating the "pure" with something so hybrid suggests that more was going on in the Fifth Concerto, at least for some French listeners, than a musical travelogue. Bellaigue probably meant that the music, for him, transcended its referentiality. But such an effect also makes one wonder whether Saint-Saëns was aiming for a quality that rose above cultural differences, not for the sake of abstraction, but to hark back to the classical purity associated with the proportions and refinement of ancient Greek and Roman art. At the French premiere of *Samson et Dalila* in 1890, reviewers who praised its "purity of lines" and compared its Handelian choruses of "grand allure" to those of ancient Greece were thinking about notions of beauty embodied in the ancient world. *Le Rouet d'Omphale*, frequently performed in the early 1890s, was also appreciated for its "clarity and simplicity that constitute the Greek genius."[57] In this sense, Saint-Saëns was perceived as being like Puvis de Chavannes, whose paintings recalled the classical beauty of the Greeks. In 1893, the stakes of this classicism got higher when French archaeologists made spectacular discoveries at Delphi, including that of the first notated song. Renewed attention to the ancient world underlined the origins of Western culture and, therefore, of France. It also served as a counterforce to widespread fascination with new currents coming from the North: not only Wagner but also Ibsen, popular at the Théâtre Libre beginning in 1890; Grieg, frequently performed on concerts that decade; and Russian music, promoted as part of the Franco-Russian alliance (1891–96).

In fact, between 1891 and 1896, Saint-Saëns's African-inspired music was composed alongside a good number of Greek-inspired works: his revisions of *Prosperine*, lyric drama based on a character from Greek mythology; *Chant Saphique* for cello and piano (1892); incidental music for *Antigone* (1893); the opéra-comique *Phryné* (1893); "Pallas Athénée" for voice and orchestra (1894); and the vocal duet *Vénus* (1896). Later came incidental music for *Déjanire* (1898) and the one-act opera, *Hélène* (1903).[58] And, according to his correspondence with Durand, many of these were written in Algeria and Egypt. In spring 1891, as he was composing *Africa*, he revised *Prosperine* in Cairo and Algiers.[59] While in Algiers just after finishing *Africa*, he began to read Augé de Lassus's libretto *Phryné*. By February 1892 he was already into the second act of his new Greek opus. He worked on it in Algiers again in January 1893 and during his tour of North Africa.

Brian Rees implies that Saint-Saëns chose Phryné as part of the period's attraction to "the sexual freedoms of the classical Greeks."[60] But Saint-Saëns's secretary, Jean Bonnerot, saw *Phryné*, premiered at the Opéra-Comique on 24 May 1893 with Sybil Sanderson, as Saint-Saëns's "French revenge" to *Die Walküre* staged only days before at the Opéra.[61] With Verdi's *Aïda* popular there that year, Saint-Saëns did not have the option of challenging Wagner with another Orientalist opera. As Louis Gallet put it, "Next to the religious grandeur of *Die Walküre*, nothing is more healthy than the aerial lightness of *Phryné*."[62] Opéra-comiques were long considered quintessentially French, and this one was traditional in every way, from the alternation of dialogue and music, to the graceful melodies and the reduced, almost Mozartean orchestra. This two-act comedy from fourth-century BCE Athens centers on a courtesan associated with the cult of beauty and her young lover, who plots to ensnare his uncle to settle a score. When Phryné appears like a statue of Aphrodite, the stodgy Greek magistrate, commemorated on his own bust nearby, is overwhelmed and becomes the prey of the femme fatale. (The image included with the score is of the statue that Saint-Saëns later kept in his apartment, as can be seen in Figure 1.) All is in good fun. As Rees points out, the music is full of mockery and parodies—of municipal bands commemorating busts, "Sullivan-like references to Handel," and even the "sugary harmonies" of Massenet's music.[63] In March 1894 Saint-Saëns, thinking it would be a good distraction, asked Durand to send a copy of the score to the résident supérieur in Hanoi for performance there.[64]

With archaeological discoveries drawing attention to what could be learned from vases, sarcophagi, and frescos, in April 1891, just after finishing the orchestration of *Africa*, Saint-Saëns traveled to Naples and Pompeii, a Roman town he considered "essentially Greek."[65] Then, not surprisingly, to accompany the dancers in *Phryné*, the composer called for flutes and citharas. In a letter about his *Chant saphique* in January 1892, he included his drawing of a cithara.[66] His interest in the ancient world also drew him to the rhythm of Greek poetry. He compares Sapphic stanzas to those in Russian music, wondering if these too were inspired by ancient Greek rhythms.[67] In *Antigone*, he went furthest in trying to replicate ancient Greek music, especially its chantlike declamation (*mousiké*) and choral unison singing. In a letter to Durand, he comments not only on how the melodies follow rigorously the rhythm of the verses, but also on how he modeled certain sections on actual Greek tunes: the "Hymne to Eros" on a Greek popular song that Bourgault-Ducoudray had brought back from Athens; the instrumental ritornellos on Gevaert's research on Greek music; and the final chorus on a Pindar hymn. He also insists that the instruments support the voices, ornamenting them as Gevaert had understood. Not wanting anything "shimmering" like modern art, its "extreme simplicity is responsible for all its charm."[68] Through simplicity of means and the beauty of forms, Saint-Saëns suggested the importance of Greek culture and its ongoing relevance to contemporary French society.

In the years that followed, Saint-Saëns composed a third work about Hercules, *Déjanire* (1898), music for a tragedy by Louis Gallet based on Sophocles and Seneca. Baumann compared its melodies to "the anonymous songs coming from the beginning of the race," the music "pure and wise," although he does not accept the idea that Greek music could inject "new blood," being too tied to "the soul of the old Orient." Saint-Saëns uses the Aeolian mode in the first act and borrows popular tunes from contemporary Greece for Hercules' wedding; however, other themes are "so nobly balanced that they become the image of order and strength." As Baumann sees it, Saint-Saëns is thoroughly "Gallo-Roman."[69] The composer aimed not to "revive antique art" or express nostalgia for ancient times but to create an "ideal, symbolic, and spontaneous adaptation."[70] Gustave Larroumet, who had attended the first Olympics in modern times and toured Greece, found the work infused with "Greco-Roman spirit." In uniting "Greek sobriety with Latin splendor," the work resembled the region where it was premiered, "Narbonnaise Gaule, where the civilizations of Athens and Rome were united."[71] Later, in Algiers, Saint-Saëns wrote the third act of his opera *Les Barbares* (1901), on the conflict between the Gauls and the Romans in first-century Orange. The work has been called a response to Wagner's "declaration of war on the Latin races which he saw in the finale of *Die Meistersinger*."[72] Saint-Saëns returned to another Greek subject on feminine seduction with his one-act opera *Hélène* (1903), this one written largely in Egypt.

Why would Saint-Saëns be so focused on ancient subjects while living in North Africa? The area was full of Roman ruins, not only in Carthage outside Tunis but also in Tipasa near Algiers and elsewhere. *Revue africaine*, based in Algiers, published a regular column on archaeology in the area, such as the Roman ruins at Henchir-el-Hammam in 1892, the Kouali site in Tipasa in 1893, and antiquities near Algiers in 1894. It also published historical accounts of Romans in the region—on an expedition in 49 BCE and on vases as clues to culture (1900), and on Caesar in Africa (1903). Other North African journals published similar material.[73] Through his friend Augé de Lassus's book, *Spectacles antiques* (1888), dedicated to Saint-Saëns, the composer was drawn to similar archaeological sites in France. With his *Phryné* and *Les Barbares* performed at the ancient Roman theater in Orange, and *Déjanire* put on in Béziers—a summer festival conceived as the Latin equivalent of Wagnerians' Bayreuth—the composer helped to revive interest in the ancient theaters in southern France. As such, he drew attention to the heritage North Africa shared with France.

Conclusions

Four general remarks can be made about this oeuvre. First, *Africa* and the Fifth Concerto challenged with new forms of virtuosity, clearly written to show off the talents of the pianist, including Saint-Saëns. Maybe because *Africa* "fits me like a glove, I play it effortlessly, without worry," the composer took it everywhere, from Algiers to the concert celebrating his honorary doctorate in Cambridge (1893), London (1913), Rio de Janeiro (1903), and New York (1906). Ironically for a work full of aggressive themes and calling for muscular, even percussive playing, another kind of virtuosity made the biggest impression. Mme Roger-Miclos, to whom the work was dedicated, was praised for "her delicate and light hands" in the finale, "*pianissimos* of an exquisite velvety-softness," and "elements kept in the shadows needed for preserving the quasi-dreamlike, even veiled character of certain Moorish songs."[74] Commenting to Durand, Saint-Saëns also noted the "lightness" and "suppleness" required to play *Africa*.[75] An interesting example in the Fifth Concerto is the treatment of the octaves in the accompaniment to the Nubian and pentatonic themes. Even if such techniques possibly influenced Ravel, the very association of Saint-Saëns's music with virtuosity led to his disdain among the younger generation, some of whom preferred Scholist restraint. In *Mercure de France* (1907) Jean Marnold wrote, while attacking Saint-Saëns's Fourth Concerto, "The concerto is dead and so be it since pure virtuosity now leaves us indifferent."[76] After a "colonial concert" in 1934, a critic again described *Africa* as "stunning in its virtuosity." Was it perhaps for this reason that it seemed to him "as little African as possible"?[77]

Second, despite notions of fusion and assimilation between East and West associated with this music, Wagnerians, such as the music critic Willy, heard *Africa* as a model of resistance to fusion within European traditions, that is, between French and German music. In his review of its premiere, Willy suggests that Saint-Saëns, a "stern patriot," wrote "this brilliant fantasy" both as a kind of tribute to colonialism "that should be dedicated to General Dodds," head of the Dahomey expedition, and as a kind of countermodel to Wagnerism, "those who admire *Tristan* too much."[78] When it came to the Fifth Concerto, he criticized the composer for not exploring new harmonies. But perhaps with the Arab scales in *Africa* and the pentatonic one in the Fifth Concerto, Saint-Saëns simply had a different kind of musical progress in mind, or one more global in its perspective on progress.

Third, as one of its early reviewers remarked, *Africa* showed that the composer was "not only one of the undisputed leaders of the French symphonic school, he is a seeker, a scholar, in search of exotic elements to increase the artistic heritage." In this sense, Saint-Saëns resembled archaeologists of the period who scoured African cultures looking for typical (and sometimes primitive) elements to then study and bring back to France. The composer, however, made art with these fragments. And *Africa* resembles the *Suite algérienne* in an important way: the work does not have the "dreamy sentimentality associated with love in the country of Goethe and our own sweet country of France. Werthers and Jocelynes are unknown there."[79] His African-inspired music is "interesting more than moving," as one critic put it.[80] The mosaic of themes allows both him and his listeners to come to grips with and even take pleasure in difference rather than intimacy. At the same time, the fruits of Saint-Saëns's research lie in the hidden affinities his music invites us to consider, affinities between north and south, east and west, past and present that music was perhaps uniquely capable of suggesting.

Yet, ironically, other than a few times late in life when he asked the famous Arab tenor Bachtarzi to sing for him, apparently Saint-Saëns had little significant contact with Arabs.[81] If he took down transcriptions of local tunes, as is suggested in Ms 916 (10–11), he was not among those who published them and he once even expressed anxiety toward what "primitive men" lose "in contact with civilization."[82] Moreover, a work initiated after he had met a French Egyptologist in Egypt in 1896 who wrote him two years later offering not only a libretto, *Isis*, set in ancient Egypt, but also his transcriptions of Egyptian tunes and a phonograph to record others, never came to fruition, probably due to disagreements over the libretto.[83] In an article on Africa, published on the front page of *Echo de Paris* (1911), Saint-Saëns writes not a word about African music, but instead about changes in Algeria since his first visit in 1873, decrying the destruction of indigenous architecture by settlers—a protest with its own irony, given Bellaigue's praise for the composer's "transfiguration" of the Nubian melody in his Fifth Piano Concerto. Still, Saint-Saëns indicates that tourists might enjoy Algiers now as "a splendid European city, admirably well situated, brilliant, and gay. . . . Happily there are electric tramways and automobiles. But if you want to taste the charm of Algeria, you must take the train from Algiers to Oran and see the countryside."[84] As in Louis Bertrand's novel, *Le Sang des races* (1899), in which the main characters "realize their full potential only by abandoning the city in favour of a wider, grander arena, the as yet unsettled interior [*le Sud*],"[85] the main attraction to Algeria for Saint-Saëns was its nature—the sea outside his windows, its warm springs as in Auvergne, and its "absolute silence," so precious for rest and work. As a Tunisian composer-scholar saw it in 1899, "the beauty he was seeking found its source in the harmony of nature."[86]

Fourth, if Saint-Saëns increasingly chose to live in North Africa and build a career there, I argue he also used it as a refuge into a kind of

Greco-Roman past, a place associated with the sun, clarity, purity, and ideal beauty as expressed in *Phryné*, "Pallas Athénée," *Antigone*, *Déjanire*, and *Hélène*. While the young generation back home was struggling with "crisis" and "chaos," Saint-Saëns turned increasingly to the contemplative beauty of the Greco-Roman heritage. And he was not alone. Noting the Roman ruins in North Africa, Bertrand, a native of Lorraine who arrived in 1891 to teach at the Algiers *lycée*, believed that North Africa was first, before the arrival of the Arabs, a Latin Africa. Saint-Saëns may not have gone as far as Bertrand, who believed that because Latin civilization had flourished there in ancient times "France was merely repossessing what was hers by hereditary right."[87] However, having apparently few relationships with Algerians outside his musical friends and several officials (the mayor of Algiers), Saint-Saëns was part of the settler culture that remained largely distinct from the Arab world. It was also very diverse: anthropologists interested in the settler culture in North Africa began to write about the region as giving birth to a "new Mediterranean race," a vigorous and

Figure 2. Saint-Saëns sitting at the Parthenon, which he visited in May 1920 on the occasion of a Saint-Saëns festival with five concerts.

virile product of the intermingling of Europeans and locals willing to embrace France.[88] The composer's experiences in North Africa and beyond gave him a sense of France as part of a larger world, even beyond the French empire, one rooted in the ancient interconnectedness of the regions bordering on the Mediterranean.

In the greater Mediterranean basin, Saint-Saëns saw himself as heir to a lineage with not only traditions,[89] but also consequence. Fearful, like Bertrand, of the decline of Western civilization, Saint-Saëns saw the West as moving "in an anti-artistic direction."[90] From this perspective, his embrace of Greco-Roman beauty and simplicity should not be understood as a reactionary return to the past, but rather as drenching himself in the source of Western civilization to inspire a new vision of the future. At the end of his essay on *Hélène*, he echoes what he would write soon thereafter about America:

It may be that the civilization of which we are so proud, young enough in comparison with the age of humanity, is but transitory, a progress toward a higher state wherein that which now seems obscure will become clear, and certain things that appear to us as essential will be nothing but words. Let us hope so.[91]

NOTES

1. Camille Saint-Saëns to Auguste Durand, Cairo, 23 March 1891 and 30 March 1896, Coll. Médiathèque Musicale Mahler, Paris; henceforth MMM.

2. Saint-Saëns to Durand, Cairo, 23 March 1891. Ralph Locke addresses the theory that gypsies originated in Egypt in his *Musical Exoticism: Images and Reflections* (Cambridge: Cambridge University Press, 2009), 136.

3. "À quoi servent les colonies," *Á travers le monde*, 3 December 1898, 388.

4. Even though aristocrats joined the Groupe colonial in the Chambre des députés during the 1890s, resistance to colonial expansion was, ironically, far stronger than in the 1880s when it was led by the monarchist Right and focused on reclaiming Alsace and Lorraine.

5. Saint-Saëns to Durand, Las Palmas, 10 January 1894, MMM.

6. Later Saint-Saëns wrote incidental music for *La Foi* (1909), a drama set in Egypt, and two works for military band (1908, 1921).

7. In practice, some indigenous people accepted French education and became participants, bureaucrats, even citizens, though others did not, remaining subjects, not citizens.

8. Léon Kerst, "Paris au théâtre: Académie nationale de musique: Première représentation de *La Valkyrie*," *Le Petit Journal*, 13 May 1893.

9. In his *Camille Saint-Saëns and the French Solo Concerto from 1850 to 1920*, trans. Anne Sherwin (Portland, OR: Amadeus Press, 1991), Michael Stegemann discusses a transcription of a "danse des almées" possibly made in Paris in 1890 (Ms. 916 [10], Bibliothèque

Jann Pasler

nationale de France [henceforth BnF], Musique), but also points out that the sketches for the Fifth Concerto, however extensive, contain "no thematic references to oriental folk melodies" except a "grasshopper cry" (151–52). On the aims and limitations of musical transcriptions in North Africa, see Jann Pasler, "Musical Hybridity in Flux: Representing Race, Colonial Policy, and Modernity in French North Africa, 1860s–1930s," *Afrika Zamani* (Journal of the Association of African Historians), in press.

10. Albert Gayet, "Un Tour en Egypte," *À travers le monde*, 3 December 1898, 387. See also E. Cotteau, "Six semaines sur le Nil," *À travers le monde*, 3 March 1894 and 10 March 1894; and Harry Alis, *Promenade en Egypt* (Paris: Hachette, 1895), 20–21.

11. Alis, *Promenade en Egypt*, 20.

12. Gayet, "Un Tour en Egypte," 387.

13. That Saint-Saëns was able to return to the Nile several times thereafter, and stay in a palace belonging to the brother of the Khedive, suggests that he later benefited from being a famous, well-connected composer in a way few others could.

14. The Château-Musée de Dieppe has produced two exhibitions and catalogues related to Saint-Saëns's visits: *Camille Saint-Saëns et l'Algérie* (Dieppe: Le Château-Musée de Dieppe, 2004); and *Égypte, égyptologie, égyptomanie: Un Musée et ses collectionneurs* (Dieppe: Le Château-Musée de Dieppe, 1998).

15. Camille Bellaigue, "De l'exotisme en musique: À propos d'un nouveau concerto de M. Camille Saint-Saëns," *Revue des deux mondes* (1897): 462–63.

16. Emile Baumann, *Les Grandes Formes de la musique: L'Œuvre de Saint-Saëns* (Paris: Éditions littéraires et artistiques, 1905), 299.

17. See the analysis in my *Composing the Citizen: Music as Public Utility in Third Republic France* (Berkeley, Los Angeles, and London: University of California Press, 2009), 402–6, 431–32.

18. *Ménestrel*, 21 November 1891, 367.

19. Baumann, *Les Grandes Formes de la musique*, 232.

20. There, Gide wrote some of his novel *Si le grain ne meurt* (1924).

21. Stegemann, *Saint-Saëns and the French Solo Concerto*, 154.

22. In the 1890s, the composer also composed fantaisies for harp (1893), organ (1895), and two pianos with organ (1897).

23. Ms. 916 (11). In his *Saint-Saëns and the French Solo Piano Concerto*, see Stegemann's discussion of this "danse des almées," which follows the sketches in my Example 2a.

24. In his letter to Durand of 1 April 1891, Saint-Saëns indicates a "Tunisian national air" in the finale. However, as Tunisia's national anthem does not appear in *Africa*, it is possible he is referring to theme H or I as originating in Tunisia or a tune he heard there.

25. In his *Saint-Saëns and the French Solo Concerto*, Stegemann points out: "Though this melody moves only in the range of the augmented fourth, the scale on which it is based gets its oriental coloring from the flatted fifths, which causes the tonality to vacillate between B minor and D minor" (154).

26. Saint-Saëns to Durand, Cairo, 23 March 1891, MMM.

27. Baumann, *Les Grandes Formes de la musique*, 232.

28. Ibid.

29. Mohammed Hassan, "Les Arts de la musique en Orient" (1880), manuscript, Musée des instruments de musique, Brussels.

30. See Annegret Fauser's essay and mine on Saint-Saëns and Durand in this volume.

31. "Had much pleasure yesterday in playing the Sarabande and the Rigaudon with Mme Guillemin." Saint-Saëns to Durand, Algiers, 19 March 1893, MMM.

32. See my *Composing the Citizen*, chaps. 5 and 9.

33. See my "Race and Nation: Musical Acclimatization and the Chansons Populaires in Third Republic France," *Western Music and Race*, ed. Julie Brown (Cambridge: Cambridge University Press, 2007), 147–67.

34. Hassan, "Les Arts de la musique en Orient"; Pilet cited by Julien Tiersot, *Notes d'ethnographie musicale* (Paris: Fischbacher, 1903), 129.

35. Villoteau, "De L'État actuel de l'art musical en Égypte, ou Relation historique et descriptive des recherches et observations faites sur la musique en ce pays," in Edme-François Jomard, *Description de l'Egypte ou Recueil des observations et des recherches qui ont été faites en Egypte pendant l'expédition de l'armée française* (Paris: Panckoucke, 1821–1830), 14:131, 142.

36. Salvador Daniel, *La Musique arabe, ses rapports avec la musique grecque et le chant grégorien* (Algiers: Bastide, 1863). See also my "Theorizing Race in 19th-Century France: Music as Emblem of Identity," *Musical Quarterly* 89/4 (Winter 2006): 472–74; and "Musical Hybridity in Flux," in *Afrika Zamani*.

37. Tiersot, *Notes d'ethnographie musicale*, 127–30.

38. Locke, *Musical Exoticism*, 144.

39. H. Barbedette, "Concerts Lamoureux," *Ménestrel*, 29 January 1893, 37. In this review, he was praising the second of two performances of *Africa* by Marie Jaëll.

40. This concept comes from Locke, *Musical Exoticism*, 136.

41. Baumann, *Les Grandes Formes de la musique*, 233.

42. Saint-Saëns to Durand, 27 October 1903, MMM.

43. Isabelle Eberhardt, *Notes de route: Maroc, Algérie, Tunisie* (Paris: Charpentier, 1908), 217.

44. Saint-Saëns to Durand, 2 April 1893, MMM.

45. E. Pannier, "La Musique chez les orientaux," *Revue de Lille*, 1 October 1890, 687. Tourists in Egypt described whirling dervish performances in analogous terms. See Mag Dalah, *Un Hiver en Orient* (Paris: Delagrave, 1892), 123–26.

46. Raoul d'Artenac, "L'Actualité: C. Saint-Saëns," *La Gazette algérienne*, 17 February 1892.

47. Saint-Saëns to Durand, Cairo, 11 April 1896; see also his letter to Durand of 27 October 1903, MMM.

48. Villoteau, "De L'État actuel de l'art musical en Egypte," 243.

49. Dalah, *Un Hiver en Orient*, 27.

50. Bellaigue, "De l'Exotisme en musique," 467.

51. See my essay on Saint-Saëns in Indochina in this volume.

52. Bellaigue, "De l'Exotisme en musique," 468.

53. Villoteau, "De L'État actuel de l'art musical en Egypte," 12; Erich Hornbostel and Robert Lachmann, "Asiatische Parallelen zur Berbermusik," *Zeitschrift für vergleichende Musikwissenschaft* (1933): 4–11, 97–99.

54. Camille Saint-Saëns, "Le Mouvement musical," *Revue d'art ancien et moderne*, 10 December 1897, 388.

55. Baumann, *Les Grandes Formes de la musique*, 234.

56. Bellaigue, "De l'Exotisme en musique," 468.

57. Review of a Concert Lamoureux, *Ménestrel*, 21 February 1892, 62. Concerts Colonne performed *Le Rouet d'Omphale* five times from 1890 to 1892.

58. Moreover, in the 1870s, Saint-Saëns composed *Le Rouet d'Omphale* two years before his first trip to Algeria, then *La Jeunesse d'Hercule* three years before his *Suite algérienne*.

59. Saint-Saëns discusses his revisions of *Proserpine* in letters to Durand of 19 March 1891, 1 April 1891, and 11 June 1891, MMM.

60. Brian Rees, *Camille Saint-Saëns: A Life* (London: Chatto & Windus, 1999), 295.

61. Jean Bonnerot, *C. Saint-Saëns: Sa vie et son oeuvre* (Paris: Durand, 1922), 155–56.

62. Louis Gallet, "Musique," *La Nouvelle Revue* (June 1893): 875.

63. Rees, *Saint-Saëns*, 298.

64. Saint-Saëns to Durand, 4 March 1894, MMM.

65. Camille Saint-Saëns, "Egypte," in *École buissonière* (Paris: Pierre Laffitte, 1913), 82.

66. See the Soret essay in this volume on Saint-Saëns's thinking about these instruments.

67. Saint-Saëns to Durand, PPA (Pointe Pescade, Algiers), 14 January 1892, MMM.

68. Undated page in Saint-Saëns letters to Durand, late 1893, MMM.

69. Emile Baumann, *Camille Saint-Saëns et "Déjanire"* (brochure extracted from the *Nouvelle Revue*; Paris: Durand, 1900) 2–4, 7, 11, 18.

70. C. Saint-Saëns, "Les Choeurs d'Antigone," *Le Figaro*, 28 September 1893.

71. Gustave Larroumet, "Chronique théâtrale," *Le Temps*, 4 September 1899.

72. Stephen Studd, *Saint-Saëns: A Critical Biography* (London: Cygnus Arts, 1999), 225.

73. *Revue de l'Afrique française et des antiquités africaines* (1886–88), *Revue tunisienne* (founded 1894), and *Annales africaines* (Algiers, 1904–7),

74. Amédée Boutarel, "Revue des grands concerts," *Ménestrel*, 1 December 1901, 381.

75. Saint-Saëns to Durand, 27 October 1903 and 9 June 1904, MMM.

76. Jean Marnold, "Musiques," *Mercure de France*, 16 December 1907, 724.

77. Maurice Bouvier-Ajam, "Concerts divers: Orchestre national," *Ménestrel*, 8 June 1934, 214.

78. L'Ouvreuse du Cirque d'été (Willy), *Rythmes et rires* (Paris: La Plume, 1894), 31.

79. Louis de Romain, "Premier Concert populaire," *Angers-Artiste*, 22 October 1892, 36.

80. Barbedette, "Concerts Lamoureux," 37.

81. In his *Mémoires (1919–39)* (Algiers: S.N.E.D. 1968), Mahieddine Bachtarzi recounts that on a number of occasions Saint-Saëns asked him to sing Arab folksongs that the composer tried to transcribe, at times frustrated that the famous tenor performed his songs differently each time. I'm grateful to Anissa Bouayed for drawing my attention to this.

82. Saint-Saëns, *École buissonniere*, 13.

83. Emile Amélineau to Saint-Saëns, letters of 25 January 1898 and 19 September 1899, in Château-Musée de Dieppe, *Égypte, égyptologie, égyptomanie*, 72–74. See also Bonnerot's explanation of what went wrong in *C. Saint-Saëns*, 162.

84. C. Saint-Saëns, "Algérie," *L'Écho de Paris*, 24 December 1911.

85. Peter Dunwoodie, "Colonizing Space: Louis Bertrand's Algeria in *Le Sang des races* and *Sur les routes du sud*," *Modern Language Review* 105/4 (2010): 1006.

86. Antonin Laffage, "Saint-Saëns et son œuvre," newspaper clipping, Correspondence, box 647, Archives diplomatiques françaises, Nantes.

87. Patricia M. E. Lorcin, *Imperial Identities; Stereotyping, Prejudice, and Race in Colonial Algeria* (London: Tauris, 1995), 200–201.

88. In discussing the appeal of Africa to Saint-Saëns in his *Les Grandes Formes de la musique*, Baumann mentions Bertrand's "very beautiful" book, *Le Sang des races*, on "this mixture of peoples undergoing fusion" (103).

89. Saint-Saëns also wrote *L'Ancêtre* (1906), a Romeo and Juliet story set in Corsica.

90. Saint-Saëns, "Egypte," 82.

91. Camille Saint-Saëns, *Outspoken Essays on Music*, trans. Fred Rothwell (Freeport, NY: Books for Libraries, 1922), 112. See also the end of Carolyn Guzski's essay in this volume.

Saint-Saëns, Writer

MARIE-GABRIELLE SORET

Camille Saint-Saëns was a master musician in every way. But as a man of action and ideas, he wanted to express his artistic passions in words, whether to defend or promote them. According to one of his contemporaries, "He wrote because he had something to say. Something quite personal, that he held dearly. He would say it directly and concisely, with spirit and ease and a natural spontaneity that recalled the elegance and Attic style of Voltaire's letters."[1]

In his writing, Saint-Saëns comes across as musician, composer, performer, and dynamic force in a musical world that expressed itself through a medium undergoing great expansion, the press. His brilliant career as a virtuoso and his international renown opened doors for him at newspapers, which he used to spread his ideas. But his independent streak, his curiosity, and his bluntness led him to take on a large variety of subjects without worrying about the controversy they might provoke. For over fifty years, he cast an acute eye on his times. At first he wrote mainly music criticism in the form of articles and news columns. Then he turned to other forms of writing: reviews, letters, exposés, speeches, responses to interviews or investigations, holding forth about a diverse array of subjects from the most serious to the most unexpected. This voluminous body of work is abundant and heterogeneous, "a quirky, Protean achievement" consisting of almost five hundred articles published in more than a hundred different publications between 1870 and 1921, with some periods more intensely productive than others.[2] Saint-Saëns was already thirty-five years old when he first took up writing. If his lyrical compositions had yet to find a large audience, his reputation as a virtuoso performer was well established and his renown at both the piano and at the organ had spread well beyond the French borders. Why did he turn to the press? In fact, he had wanted to write for quite some time, but hesitated, no doubt for political and strategic reasons. With the beginning of the Third Republic, whose values he espoused, came a new opportunity: in 1872 he took up music criticism in one of the first publications authorized by the new regime, *La Renaissance littéraire et artistique*.

Although Saint-Saëns was a leader in the musical world, he was also something of an agitator, and wanting to write a column about music seemed suspect. Some speculated that because he could not get hired at the Opéra he would get even by promoting his views about his music in the newspapers.[3] Others thought that having a regular column in the press would allow him to promote his friends and his editors. Still others wondered if he was too musical and too partisan to be able to judge works that were not to his liking. "Why does Saint-Saëns need to write a weekly column? Isn't his real column his performance at the Madeleine every Sunday, his improvisations on Cavaillé-Coll's great organ?"[4]

Saint-Saëns's relations with the press were somewhat unusual. To begin with, he never dreamed of making a viable career of music criticism. He lived off his talents as a performer and a composer, which provided his principal sources of income. Although he was paid for his writing, he was never financially dependent on the press. This explains the freedom of his tone and his mobility among the newspapers in which he published. In addition, as author and musician, Saint-Saëns knew the press from the inside. A precocious musician, he had long known that criticism is a powerful tool that can make or break a career. From having been judged, he turned into a judge himself when he took up writing, not unaware of the obstacles that would present themselves before him: "Nothing is more difficult than to talk about music. It is already tricky enough for musicians, but almost impossible for others: even the strongest, most subtle minds lose their way."[5] One of Saint-Saëns's most pronounced characteristics as a writer was his frankness and his pronounced taste for polemics. The abundance of warrior metaphors he employs indicates that he considered music criticism a kind of combat. He knew he would need to convince and persuade, and it was this that motivated him, as he pointed out in 1879, when he began to write for *Le Voltaire*:

> It is not without hesitation that I decided to take up criticism. If I join the fray, it is because it seems to me—excuse the illusion, if it is indeed one—that I must. . . . Progress cannot make itself, and where would we be, I ask you, if no one had pushed the wheel? We would have been stuck in a rut down all these centuries. So I venture forth, at my own risk and peril. If, encouraged by my example, others join me on this path . . . I will have been compensated for my efforts, my aim will have been achieved.[6]

Saint-Saëns wrote to be published and to reach the greatest possible number of readers. Pedagogue and proselyte, he wanted to be sure his ideas would spread. This is why he preferred the mainstream press to the specialized press, oriented to a more limited public. He reserved his longest collaborations for the large dailies: *L'Estafette*, the republican newspaper *Le Voltaire*, then *La France* and *L'Echo de Paris*. This did not prevent him from occasionally writing for well-known journals such as *La Nouvelle Revue*, *La Revue de Paris*, *Le Monde musical*, to cite just a few. To give them some permanence, he collected some of his articles in anthologies: *Harmonie et mélodie*, *École buissonnière*, *Portraits et souvenirs*, and *Au Courant de la vie* are still cited. But hundreds of other articles he wrote have been forgotten as a result of their ephemeral publication in the press.[7]

Reading these texts, one is seduced by the writer's style—his concision, clarity, and way of putting things. As Adolphe Boschot points out, "His vision was very clear. His mind was so cultured, so well balanced, that he was able to analyze and bring clarity to his subject. In his memory, images, ideas, and judgments were placed with precisely the right words; he knew how to assign just the right labels to them. That is why he wrote so well. The neatness of his style, the charm and spontaneity of his turn of phrase, are reminiscent of the nervous sparkle of Voltaire as a writer."[8]

In his journalism, Saint-Saëns pulled off the difficult feat of preserving his independence. This is also what makes his texts so valuable: they are such a true reflection of his own views, and not dictated by exterior concerns. His judgment is resolutely impartial, and he can as easily cast an uncompromising eye on the works of his closest friends, such as Charles Lecocq or Augusta Holmès, as he can praise the achievements of rivals, such as Jules Massenet or Richard Strauss.

His touchy character and pugnacity have often been reproached. His contemporaries feared him, and controversy was never far off. Alfred Bruneau said he had the temperament of a fighter, and that "as soon as a subject attracted him, he would grab his polemicist's pen and use it harshly, furiously, courageously, wielding it like a fearful, vindictive sword."[9] Jean Bonnerot, his last secretary, also noted, concerning his writings, that "he loved freedom passionately: the reliable frankness of his judgments was a sign of his independence. He didn't bother to disguise what he thought and he said succinctly what he wanted to say without wasting time with empty phrases. He was occasionally wrong, but he never lied. . . . Until the last night of his life, he battled, fighting, with his face uncovered, courageously, without thinking that his terrible joking could come back to hurt him."[10]

His particular position as a musician-writer was sometimes difficult to maintain. In his writing as well as his music, his enemies tried to portray him as eclectic and opportunistic, unstable and fickle, mainly on the basis of his nationalism and his diatribes against Wagner. Saint-Saëns ardently defended Wagner when he first started out, but later violently criticized Wagnerism and its spread when it began to take up too much room on the French stage and young French composers had difficulty getting their work performed. He also tried to make his countrymen aware of music coming from beyond the Rhine—the works of Schumann, Mendelssohn, Liszt, and the Russian School. But this open-minded attitude was undermined by the rigidity of his nationalist positions during the First World War. Indeed, he was one of the first to call for a ban against German music on French territory, sacrificing some of his favorite composers on the altar of patriotism, justifying his position this way: "The music of Beethoven is sublime, that of Schumann is delightful, and this is precisely why we need no more of it. How can we not see that in enjoying this music, we are drawn into the idea that there exists a lovable Germany, kind, agreeable, artistic."[11] His positions would be soundly reproached and provoke heated debate in the press.

Nevertheless, reading his writing we see that although Saint-Saëns's ideas evolved, in reality they did not change very much. In over fifty years of writing for the press, he was loyal to the principles that nourished his entire approach to the arts. However, after the optimism of the early years of the Third Republic, he gradually gave in to the pessimism associated with a certain echelon of the intellectual elite in the period preceding the First World War. And even though he did not exactly approve of the new experiments being carried out by the younger composers, he was not impervious to the spirit these experiments conveyed. In this pivotal period, when solidly academic music coexisted with a thriving avant-garde—its voices heard clearly, thanks to the press—Saint-Saëns kept on in the same direction he had set for himself early on, going against fashion, ever faithful to his own aesthetic principles:

> I've spent my life daring to do what others did not, at my own risk and peril. If now, in music and in literature, I seem reactionary, it is because I do not think it necessary always to press forward, *no matter what*! Otherwise, you might as well find yourself saying that two and two do not make four, but five.[12]

Saint-Saëns's reflections on his art often went beyond purely musical considerations. Although the majority of his articles concern music, he also wrote on a surprising variety of other subjects. He was always interested in the sciences, and his passion for astronomy was well known to his friends.[13] For this reason, he published several articles on the gradual occultation of the planets, the repulsive force of the atmosphere, the objective existence of space and time, and the stars. His love of nature and animals informs numerous publications on such topics as the blindness of snails, the intelligence of bees, the kinship between animals and plants, the running of the bulls, etc. He was not indifferent to the goings-on of society and published reflections on soccer, repopulation, the rise in rents, the uses of wild blackberries, going through customs—to give only a few examples. In other writings, such as those collected in the two volumes, *Problèmes et mystères* and *Divagations sérieuses*, he considered aesthetics, philosophy, and the place of science and religion in society. More numerous still are the texts in which he brings together his criticism of how the French language evolved, noting grammatical deviations and its susceptibility to English expressions. For Saint-Saëns this was such a subject of ongoing interest that some suggested he should put forward his candidacy for the Académie française. To relax from composing, he also wrote poems for his friends, some of which he published in a collection, *Rimes familières*, or in plays, such as *Botriocéphale* or *La Crampe des écrivains*. His contemporaries noted that the eclecticism and frequency of these essays left him open to criticism. However, this diverse field of endeavor suggests how much Saint-Saëns was truly a figure of his era and the world that surrounded him. Bonnerot sums this up well:

> Interested in everything, at any given moment he had something to say on any subject. He was human, and nothing that concerned man or citizen was foreign to him. He took part in debates because it was impossible for him to stay quiet, because he refused to isolate himself in an ivory tower plugging up his ears against the noises of the street and life itself.[14]

Beyond these public essays, his abundant private correspondence—estimated at around 20,000 letters—has been largely unexplored. The recently published volume of composers' letters to Saint-Saëns partly fills this void, but represents only a fraction of his epistolary exchanges.[15] This enormous body of private writing, on which so much work remains to be done, will one day be studied as an indispensable complement to the musician's published writing. Indeed, a study of the correspondence quickly shows that Saint-Saëns frequently practiced a form of self-censorship. He chose the subjects he wanted to address intentionally, avoiding others for aesthetic, political, or personal reasons. These blanks are deliberate—and so we notice strange omissions. At no moment, for example, does he mention the names Debussy, Ravel, Dukas, Stravinsky, or Mahler, although he knew their works. Beginning in the 1890s, the names of his contemporaries are increasingly rare in his articles. Thus we can get a better sense of his opinion on certain subjects through his correspondence.

Saint-Saëns was a privileged witness to the evolution of artistic currents in his seventy years spent in French musical life; through his writing, he proved himself to be more an actor than a spectator. In the tumultuous period at the end of the Second Empire and the beginning of the Third Republic, he played a progressive role. Later he was more of a moderator, a reference point, whose importance is underestimated still today. He influenced not only the aesthetics but also the cultural politics of his day. His actions were, as chemists say, the "action of presence." "Everyone knew that Saint-Saëns 'was there.' Through his polemics and his masterpieces, which continue to be played, contested, and admired, he never let it be forgotten that in music, as in all arts, there is an obvious and necessary perfection."[16]

Expressing himself as he did in the press, Saint-Saëns took a courageous and perilous stance, one he maintained throughout his life and for which he never won anyone's approval—not from reactionaries, who found him audacious, nor from the forward-looking, who found him timorous. But in the end, thanks to his long associations with the theater and artists and his active participation in musical life, he knew (perhaps better than anyone else) how to feel and express the enthusiasm and the anguish of his contemporaries, gathering opinion and focusing debate around forceful ideas, putting viewpoints into perspective and acting as a go-between: a link between generations and a mediator between cultures.

—Translated by Lauren Elkin and Jann Pasler

NOTES

1. Léon Bérard, "Les Funérailles de Saint-Saëns à Paris," *Le Monde musical* 23–24 (December 1921): 378.

2. Yves Gérard, *Saint-Saëns: Regards sur mes contemporains* (Arles: B. Coutaz, 1990), 14.

3. Albert Dayrolles, "Saint-Saëns littérateur," *Le Figaro*, 4 March 1883.

4. Henri Moreno [Henri Heugel], "Semaine théâtrale," *Ménestrel*, 2 July 1876, 243.

5. Camille Saint-Saëns, "L'Illusion wagnérienne," *La Revue de Paris*, 1 April 1899.

6. Camille Saint-Saëns, "Musique," *Le Voltaire*, 18 July 1879, 1.

7. My edition of Saint-Saëns's writings on music is currently in press (Vrin, 2012).

8. Adolphe Boschot, *Maîtres d'hier et de jadis* (Paris: Plon, 1935), 104.

9. Alfred Bruneau, "Les Funérailles de Saint-Saëns à Paris," 377.

10. Jean Bonnerot, "Saint-Saëns," *La Vie des peuples*, 10 January–10 February 1922, 60.

11. Camille Saint-Saëns, " Aux amateurs de musique, " *L'Écho de Paris*, 28 May 1918, 2.

12. Saint-Saëns to Jean Bonnerot, Cannes, 18 January 1918. Bonnerot Collection, Château-Musée de Dieppe

13. See Leo Houziaux on Saint-Saëns's writings on astronomy in this volume.

14. Bonnerot, "Saint-Saëns," 60.

15. Eurydice Jousse and Yves Gérard, eds., *Lettres de compositeurs à Camille Saint-Saëns: Lettres conservées au Château-Musée de Dieppe* (Lyon: Symétrie, 2009).

16. Boschot, *Maîtres d'hier et de jadis*, 102.

Saint-Saëns and Rameau's Keyboard Music

KATHARINE ELLIS

When Camille Saint-Saëns sat down to write a brief but pithy introduction to his 1895 edition of Rameau's *Pièces de clavecin* he was able to draw on several decades' experience of the composer's music;[1] a month before his death he was still playing Rameau in public—flawlessly.[2] And though toward the end of his life he paid tribute to the work of Wanda Landowska as a champion of early harpsichord performance, his own contribution to Rameau's cause—as a performer and editor of the keyboard music, and as a more general figurehead (he was Honorary President of the Société Rameau on its foundation in 1901)—was widely recognized.[3] Perhaps, given the popularity of pieces such as the Second Piano Concerto, we tend to see more of Bach than Rameau in Saint-Saëns's compositional toolkit; but Rameau was no less a musical companion for life.

That said, as a child pianist Saint-Saëns came to Rameau relatively late— well after Bach and Handel, for instance, which he was playing in public by 1844, age eight.[4] The opportunity was there to hear a fair amount of Rameau in Paris before embarking on any himself. He might, for instance, have attended when pianist Amédée Méreaux played Rameau in the capital on 5 May 1844—the first known nineteenth-century performance of his keyboard music in Paris as professional concert fare; and the 1850s and early 1860s saw a good half-dozen pianists putting Rameau's music into their Paris programs.[5] Some of them, such as Méreaux's pupil Charlotte Tardieu de Malleville, or Marie Mongin, were true early music specialists; others, such as Wilhelmine Szarvády or the Norwegian pianist-composer Thomas Tellefsen, ranged more widely. Szarvády was celebrated for her Beethoven, Schumann, and eventually Brahms; Tellefsen was a Chopin pupil highly regarded as an interpreter of his teacher's music.[6] And though none of these concerts had the institutional heft or regularity of the most august series, headed by the Société des Concerts du Conservatoire (where operatic extracts by Lully and Rameau were featured regularly), they were routinely well attended and reviewed in the press. Many were organized by influential or like-minded musicians such as the Farrencs (publisher Aristide and composer Louise, whom Saint-Saëns did not apparently know personally) or the Delsartes (singer/ actor François and pianist Rosine, who took Saint-Saëns under their wing). Among these musicians were no fewer than three editors of Rameau's keyboard music, whose publications preceded that which Saint-Saëns prepared for Auguste Durand: Méreaux, Szarvády, and the team of Aristide and Louise Farrenc.[7]

A fourth Rameau editor became another friend. In the mid-1860s Saint-Saëns worked alongside Charles Poisot as fellow accompanist for a choral society of high-minded, high-bourgeois, and aristocratic Parisians— the Société académique de musique sacrée.[8] Unsung though he remains, Poisot, also a writer and arranger, was perhaps the composer's most tenacious nineteenth-century champion overall, and had by this time already set the fund-raising wheels in motion to erect a statue of his musical hero in their shared home town of Dijon. Saint-Saëns was to perform at two and possibly three events connected with the project, which did not finally come to fruition until 1880. Although he took no part in the organization, he was so committed to the Rameau venture that he opted to attend only the second Bayreuth *Ring* performance in August 1876 so that he could go to Dijon and play *Les Cyclopes*, *Les Niais de Sologne*, and a selection of *Pièces de clavecin en concert* at Poisot's hugely ambitious Rameau festival, which clashed with the Bayreuth premiere. In the meantime, in 1864 Schonenberger of Paris published an extra volume (no. 25) in the Bibliothèque classique des pianistes series, featuring Poisot's edition of Rameau's first two keyboard suites, and other works. Poisot's own preface ended with an audacious call for government funding for a complete Rameau edition—the very project (though still not publicly underwritten) with which Saint-Saëns would become engaged thirty years later.

All this suggests that where Rameau revivalism was concerned we can consider Saint-Saëns a relatively late entrant. But it is worth remembering just how much earlier these performances were than those nevertheless substantial early twentieth-century contributions of Wanda Landowska to the keyboard music revival, or of Charles Bordes and Vincent d'Indy for the operas. And in any case, what an entry it was. Where Tellefsen's signature pieces were the delicate trios, the *Pièces de clavecin en concert*, and Malleville's the solo gavottes and musettes, on 31 January 1863 Saint-Saëns burst onto the scene with a four-piece group, including *Les Cyclopes* and *La Joyeuse*. And he did so to an audience of seasoned professionals, at a meeting of the Société des compositeurs de musique—a group to which Poisot would also, in due course, play Rameau solos and arrangements. The Saint-Saëns contribution was undoubtedly an attempt to impress, if not to shock, and it made clear from the outset his conviction that a love of early music was perfectly compatible with being a composer and concert pianist, and appreciating new music. For, with the exception of *Les Tourbillons* and the *doubles* to *Les Niais de Sologne*, Rameau's solo output provided no better riposte than *Les Cyclopes* to those—numerous and vocal—who reckoned that early keyboard music was child's play and therefore not worth bothering with. Tongue-twister passages of hand crossing, left-hand figuration based first around tenths but widening with alarming rapidity to minor thirteenths, precipitate gestures involving descending arpeggios—all requiring pinpoint accuracy, often across spans of the keyboard so wide as to make good hand-eye coordination irrelevant—these ingredients played to Saint-Saëns's performing strengths. In short, he dazzled. Did *Les Cyclopes* ever—metaphorically at least—leave the music desk of his piano? I doubt it, and since for many decades he was almost the only pianist who dared execute its exhilarating tricks, one can see why. It was his way of tapping into the continuing visceral appeal of virtuoso display. It was surely in this spirit that in 1893, presiding over the prize-giving ceremony at the École de musique classique (the old École Niedermeyer), he delighted everyone by abandoning any idea of delivering a formal speech to the students; he simply played *Les Tourbillons* and *Les Cyclopes* for them instead.[9] We should not be surprised, then, to find him highlighting this latter piece in the introduction to his 1895 edition as one of those suitable for first-rank pianists only, those gifted few who having worked out how to finger the piece will easily solve what he calls the "*mystère*" of the music—the riddle of its meaning.

Nevertheless, the emphasis he places in this preface on technique and problem solving probably holds another of the keys to understanding why Rameau appealed so much to him: Rameau was what one might call a composer's composer. For Saint-Saëns it was, as his 1895 introduction indicates, of prime importance that in addition to writing music of great originality Rameau had been a theorist capable of revolutionizing harmony teaching. Saint-Saëns applauded the intellectual in music and saw it as something of an editorial duty to try to decode and faithfully represent the musician's thought. On an aesthetic level, craft, formal beauty, and purity of line and of tone mattered greatly to him. If all that seems rather cool for a man brought up in the nineteenth century, then yes, we should admit that the headier aspects of Romanticism all but passed him by and that the sublime was not his preferred territory. Closer in spirit to Gounod and Bizet than to the earlier generation of Berlioz or Liszt, he always prioritized clarity over emotion in music, and was disoriented to find, in the last decade of his life, that musical beauty was under threat not only from music of super-saturated emotion (Strauss, *verismo* opera) but also from the primitivism and studied banality represented by *The Rite of Spring* or

Parade. "Don't talk about beauty," was his waspish response to a journalist's question in 1920, "it's no longer fashionable."[10]

Concern with beauty and purity spilled over into editing and brought Saint-Saëns head to head with questions of authenticity. His preface still seems shocking, so direct is its opening challenge to the complacent. In the name of "fidelity" he poured scorn on the "parasitical luxury of added markings" in "puffed-up" editions. His target: those heavily edited texts that used to be the cheap standard fare for keyboard music from Bach to Beethoven, issued by publishers such as Peters, Litolff, or Breitkopf. To Saint-Saëns's consternation, they had flooded the French market with *espressivo* (and, as he later lamented, inaccurate) interpretations of early and classic music. His speech of 1915 on early music performance to the Panama-Pacific International Exposition in San Francisco rammed home this point, the message doubtless rendered especially urgent by being delivered just three weeks after the sinking of the *Lusitania* by a German U-boat.[11] Editorially he may well have viewed France as ahead of the game, even in 1895. Méreaux's *Les Clavecinistes* of the 1860s, just as *espressivo* and heavily fingered as anything that would come out of Germany, had already been countered by the less intrusive approach of pianist Louis Diémer from 1887; and repertoire within the Farrencs' *Trésor des pianistes* had always been free of such markings.[12] Where the musical text was concerned, for Saint-Saëns less was potentially more: what he wanted was openings for performative freedom, not prescriptions for playing by numbers— a standpoint that could only have been encouraged by his recognition (especially where "sketched" passages of Mozart's piano concertos were concerned) that there might be considerable distance between a composer's thought as published and as translated into a finished performance.[13]

With Rameau he could not give himself the same latitude as with Mozart, but we do not have to look too hard to see where he is heading. His interest in *L'Enharmonique* is piqued by internal evidence that might support a theory of tempo flexibility as a norm in Rameau performance; it is surely no coincidence, then, that *Les Tourbillons*, with its rondeau alternation of strict and looser sections and its prelude-like cascades descending in free fall toward the end, was another favorite piece. In this light the paradox Saint-Saëns offered in his preface—that by retaining flexibility "according to performance needs" one is maintaining fidelity to the music's spirit—is a precious insight into his own interpretive practice. Moreover, although Diémer was playing French Baroque repertoire on the harpsichord by at least 1889, Saint-Saëns was still unusually sensitive in this 1895 preface to the potential difference between playing Rameau on a harpsichord and on a piano. The instrument, he says, helps define the interpretive approach: a harpsichord communicates tranquility to the hands; the piano does the opposite, and thus one has to guard against losing the music's delicacy.

Perhaps we should stop and ponder the implications of this description of the kinds of interpretation a particular instrument induces in a performer, not least because Saint-Saëns presents it as a reflex rather than a willed action. Firstly, his response reveals a deeper musical physicality than comes through from critiques by writers who applaud the clarity and finish of his playing while typecasting him as rather detached and unemotional at the keyboard. It invites us to reconsider some of those critiques with more historical sensitivity.[14] Secondly, in philosophical terms, his distinction grasps the very problems that those working within the original instrument movement of the later twentieth century faced. But it does more: it leapfrogs a succession of "pioneer" generations and deposits the reader amid the questions that have been more common only in the last decade or so—of how best to adapt aspects of historically informed performance to a new style of interpretation on modern instruments. More important, with a certain lightness of touch Saint-Saëns reaches to the central question of what the "work" is. Where do its boundaries lie? What is essential (and what is its essence)? Where does the responsibility of the performer begin and end?

Nor does he forget that performers are also audiences. How should a listener respond to the fact that the conventional boundaries of a "work" are different for Rameau working in the eighteenth century as opposed to Saint-Saëns himself, composing on the cusp of the twentieth? Put in anachronistic terms his question is indeed astoundingly modern: Is there such a thing, he asks, as an "authentic" listener? If in the final analysis his answer seems equivocal, it is nevertheless very different from that expounded in the 1830s and 1840s, for instance, when early music enthusiasts mired in progress theories tried to persuade listeners to value what they heard by making allowances for the unsophisticated tools the composer had at hand.[15] Saint-Saëns's point is not so much about value, whether relative or absolute (that battle had been largely won in 1895), as about enjoyment of the "unusual" taking just a bit more effort in the form of a compact of historical imagination established between performer and listener.

Over a century on from Saint-Saëns's preface, we might consider that we have put many of these questions behind us. I would argue rather that we should not forget how prescient it was to ask them. In addition we might ask ourselves whether, in 2012, Saint-Saëns has been judged on such a small proportion of his output that he himself warrants the kind of extra listener effort he exhorts in Ramiste performers and audiences of 1895. Perhaps that is what the 2012 Bard Music Festival will bring about. Assuming, of course, that we really do want to get to know Saint-Saëns beyond "The Swan."

Preface
Rameau's *Pièces de Clavecin* (Durand, 1895)

Since the present edition aims above all at faithful reproduction of the composer's thinking, you will not find that superfluous wealth of inter-polations—indications of tempi, nuances, fingerings—on which so many editions of older works pride themselves. In compensation, perhaps a few words are in order.

On the subject of tempi to be used in performance, it should first be noted that the absence of indications, widespread in the music of the past, might suggest that until the middle of the last century the degree of ra-pidity or slowness, so important in our era, probably did not have the importance it does today. What's more, the distance between extreme tempi was quite small. All tempi must have been understood as between what we now call Allegro moderato and Andante. The Largos of Handel and Bach are not very slow; their Prestos are not very fast. Above all one should be prudent when it comes to speed: modern fast tempi were un-known to these older generations. As for the harpsichord in particular: though the action of this instrument is light and does not ask the per-former to expend the same muscular strength as required by a modern keyboard, we have only to place our fingers on a harpsichord to feel a de-sire for tranquility in interpretation inspired by the instrument's character, a character closer to the organ than the piano. Transferring music writ-ten for the harpsichord to the piano produces the opposite effect, and a little more rapidity becomes necessary. But we must resist this urge, at least in part, if we do not want to distort this delicate music, whose charm could not survive a violent performance.

What we call "nuance" was unknown in the world of the harpsichord. Large instruments were furnished with two keyboards and several regis-ters, allowing a considerable wealth of effects. Thanks to these resources, one could go from *soft* [*doux*] to *semi-loud* [*demi-fort*] to *loud* [*fort*], but this loudness was nothing like the formidable explosions that emerge from the cases of our concert grand pianos: it was purely relative. With some rare exceptions, the use of varying degrees of sonority was left to the per-former's taste, and it was impossible to proceed gradually from one to the other or to practice the learned art of infinite nuance and variety of touch that makes the modern piano so attractive.

An additional detail to be noted: along the way one may encounter stumbling blocks in the form of very short notes, sixteenth or thirty-second notes, the performance of which seems to require a tempo otherwise incompatible with the character of the piece, even considering the moderation associated with previous habits.

This difficulty comes from the preconceived idea that this music must be performed throughout in the same way, without changing tempo. But nothing proves this was the case; an indication placed by Rameau in one of his *pièces* ("The Enharmonic"), seems to prove the contrary. As precious as it is rare, this indication—*"without changing the speed"*—would have no meaning if the performers were not in the habit of changing the tempo from time to time. Moreover, consider that Rameau lived during the Rococo period, mannered in all things; add to this idea the excessive use of ornamentation that characterizes the music of the period and you will be led naturally to think that in interpreting the pieces in question one would be much more faithful to the spirit of the time by adopting a certain freedom of tempo [*allure*], speeding up and slowing down according to the needs of the performance, than by the opposite. But these fluctuations, like nuances one can add to take advantage of the piano and its resources, do not have the necessary or fixed quality they would have in modern music, where they form part of the [musical] idea itself. They are essentially accessory, depending on the whim of the performer, and can be modified ad infinitum without altering the work. The music of these older times draws its value from *form*, whereas *sensation*, which is sometimes everything, or almost everything, in modern music, is nothing, or almost nothing, in eighteenth-century music. According to this principle, Handel could write a concerto for organ or harp, and whether the concertizing part is performed by one or the other instrument or, alternatively, by the harpsichord, makes no difference. This situation gives rise to unusual perspectives on the various ideas and judgments that can be elicited by the same art in different eras. It shows us that in experiencing the music of past centuries, as in looking at the paintings of the pre-Moderns (*Primitifs*) we must restrain ourselves from seeking in works of art from earlier times effects and expressions of feeling that could not have existed in them. We must make clean slates of our daily habits as much as possible, and allow for whatever impressions these unusual forms produce. In this way, we will expand the range of our aesthetic enjoyment. Indeed the result is well worth a little effort.

On the subject of fingering: in Rameau's time it had little of the beautiful regularity it has today. One used one's thumb all the time, one fingered in the most elaborate [*baroque*] way. The author of *Castor et Pollux* was as revolutionary in that as in everything (we know that Rameau completely reformed the teaching of harmony). He worked to make fingering more rational, as is shown in the five-note exercise on page 19, so natural that it does not seem possible one could ever use any other, and yet this was a novelty at the time. Certain pieces are difficult to finger: *Les Cyclopes*, *Les Niais de Sologne*, for instance; but they should be approached only by first-class performers, who will easily find the key to their riddle [*mystère*]. As for the many easy pieces, finger them as you can and you will slip unwittingly into the style of the era.

—Translated by Jann Pasler

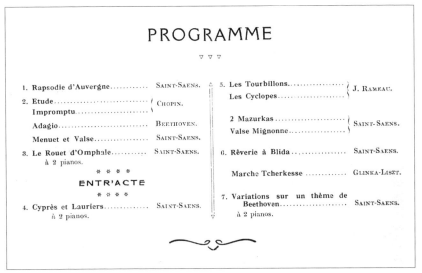

Figure 1. Second Concert (of two) given by Saint-Saëns with V. Llorca, Salle des Beaux-Arts, Algiers, 20 January 1920.

NOTES

1. Éditions Durand. This was the first volume of the *Œuvres complètes* of which Saint-Saëns was general editor, and for which he also edited the motets.

2. Stephen Studd, *Saint-Saëns: A Critical Biography* (London and Madison, NJ: Cygnus Arts and Fairleigh Dickinson University Press), 281.

3. Saint-Saëns mentioned Landowska in a 1915 speech to the Panama-Pacific International Exposition in San Francisco. See Camille Saint-Saëns, *On the Execution of Music, and Principally of Ancient Music*, trans. Henry P. Bowie (San Francisco: Blair-Murdoch, 1915), 7.

4. Studd, *Saint-Saëns*, 13. At this concert of July 1844 Saint-Saëns also played the music of John Field and a Mozart piano concerto.

5. Amédée Méreaux organized two *concerts historiques* (educational recitals of early music) at his salon in Rouen in March 1842. It is possible that he played a harpsichord,

rather than piano; the Paris concert was a charity event with a similar mixture of choral and keyboard works including Jannequin, Mozart, and Rameau.

6. Among this list even Tellefsen (1823–1874) is hardly a household name; for the female pianists, brief biographies appear in Katharine Ellis, "Female Pianists and Their Male Critics in Nineteenth-Century Paris," *Journal of the American Musicological Society* 50/2–3 (1997): 353–85.

7. Amédée Méreaux, *Les Clavecinistes de 1637 à 1790: Histoire du clavecin: Portraits et biographies des célèbres clavecinistes avec exemples et notes sur le style et l'exécution de leurs œuvres* (Paris: Heugel, 1864–67); Aristide [and Louise] Farrenc, *Le Trésor des pianistes* (Paris: A. Farrenc, 1861–74); Wilhelmine Szarvády, *Trois Morceaux de piano tirés des programmes de concert de Mme W. Szarvády*, 3 vols. (Paris: J. Maho, 1863–64).

8. The society functioned from 1861 to 1872, but its first concert was not until April 1863. Especially in the early years, its repertoire was strongly slanted toward early music. Concerts were conducted by a former choirmaster of Rouen Cathedral, Charles Vervoitte. Poisot played piano; Saint-Saëns played organ, from at least 1864, including a Rameau memorial concert of 1 May 1865, at which Méreaux played Rameau solo pieces from the 1731 and 1740 books, and three of the trios.

9. Reported, probably by a member of the school, in *Ménestrel* (6 August 1893), 256. From what we can tell in the press, Paris saw a fair amount of Saint-Saëns as an exponent of this repertory in the 1860s and 1870s, alongside several other pianists. By the 1880s however, it was Louis Diémer who dominated the Parisian concert market in French Baroque miniatures. Moreover, for Saint-Saëns as pianist the French Baroque meant Rameau and precious little else—and, within that, selected *Pièces de clavecin en concert* and the solo showpieces alone. From 1874 he routinely paired *Les Tourbillons* and *Les Cyclopes* (Concerts Danbé of 22 and 29 January, cited in *Ménestrel* previews of 18 and 25 January 1874, 54, 63, respectively). And he played them both at the Société nationale (8 March 1884). He also used the pairing when in ambassadorial mode, playing them internationally to the end of his life. Three late programs of 1920 see him presenting these two pieces in Algiers and Oran (16 January and 9 February 1920, respectively), and in Liège at the Conservatoire on 26 October. Thanks to Jann Pasler for supplying this information.

10. James Harding, *Saint-Saëns and His Circle* (London: Chapman & Hall, 1965), 222.

11. Saint-Saëns, *On the Execution of Music*, 8.

12. Nevertheless, Diémer was significantly more prescriptive than Saint-Saëns within the musical text of the score, especially in the writing out of ornaments down to the last alternation of a trill. Louis Diémer, ed., *Les Clavecinistes français*, 4 vols. (Paris: Durand & Schoenewerk, 1887–1912). The final volume, however, was edited not by Diémer but by a team of six, including both Saint-Saëns and d'Indy.

13. Saint-Saëns, *On the Execution of Music*, 16. This point constitutes the final flourish of his 1915 speech at the Panama-Pacific International Exposition.

14. To take just one example from many possibilities, an unsigned writer for the *Revue et gazette musicale* found his Schubert *Wanderer* Fantasy admirably clear and showing great purity of taste—but lacking sensuality (*séduction*) (review of 26 October 1879, 350). Studd gathers together more examples in his *Saint-Saëns*, 59–61.

15. One of the most respected music theorists and early music revivalists, François-Joseph Fétis, found himself trapped by precisely these tensions, even as he evangelized for a new appreciation of early music via his series of Paris *concerts historiques*.

Lyres and Citharas of Antiquity

MARIE-GABRIELLE SORET

Saint-Saëns's curiosity was piqued by images of the lyres and citharas of antiquity, so much so that he wrote an essay on them, revising it several times, adding to it, and illustrating it. These texts, each different from the next, were printed in various publications and were among the most widely distributed of his writings during his lifetime. Why was he so taken by this subject? He was drawn to archaeology and antiquity, enchanted by Orientalism and exoticism, and took a deep interest in organology, the study of musical instruments. The three areas of study intersect in both Saint-Saëns's musical compositions and written texts, appearing in various forms and drawing their inspiration, in part, from similar sources. His essay on ancient lyres and citharas, begun in the 1890s and modified continually for almost thirty years, is one of the most striking examples of these intersecting interests.

Saint-Saëns's affinity for ancient history is evident in his choice of subjects for symphonic poems (*La Jeunesse d'Hercule*, *Le Rouet d'Omphale*, *Phaéton*), certain hymns ("Pallas Athénée," *Hymne à Vénus*), as well as libretti (*Samson et Dalila*, *Hélène*, *Déjanire*, *Phryné*, *Parysatis*) and theater music (*Andromaque*, *Antigone*). He took great pains to re-create the feel of antiquity, researching and studying sources and emphasizing historical accuracy. Several times he gave reasons for this insistence, for example, in the texts about the choruses of *Antigone* (1893)[1] or the score of *Déjanire* (1898).[2]

Saint-Saëns's marked interest in re-creating antiquity emerged in his 1886 essay, "Note on the Theater Sets of Roman Antiquity."[3] Viewing ancient Pompeian frescoes and paintings at the museum in Naples gave Saint-Saëns the idea of trying to transpose such representations—which everyone else deemed merely fanciful—into a more or less objective reality.[4] Archaeologists wanted to see nothing but "purely inventive motifs, without any foundation other than that of an elegant fantasy and no grounding in any reality whatsoever."[5] However, Saint-Saëns was convinced that "it was not in keeping with the spirit of antiquity to ignore reality completely; its fantasy hewed close to nature and was well defined."[6] He wanted to prove that these images depicted reality, that what was considered the product of the painter's imagination was actually an image barely reshaped from reality and useful as a basis for concrete study. He analyzed images of theater sets through this lens, referring to the works of archaeologist and historian Léon Heuzey (1831–1922), and developing hypotheses on the use of *periaktoi*, a type of Greek revolving stage.[7] During the course of this study he noted "this beautiful woman playing the cithara among the carvings on the Pantheon, with her fiery eyes and mouth agape, clearly intent on declaiming or singing."[8]

Saint-Saëns's interest in instruments of the past extended to the Orient (defined principally as the Middle East and North Africa) as well as antiquity; Oriental musicians had preserved the knowledge of how to play these instruments and transmitted it through the centuries.[9] Saint-Saëns's study of organology expressed itself in many ways, in performances of his own works as well as in some of his correspondence and writing. For example, when he finished his opera *Parysatis* in Cairo in 1902, Saint-Saëns announced that he would try to "find some little Egyptian crotal bells for my dancers. I have a friend here who speaks Arabic and is willing to set aside his work to help me find them. I believe this will interest audiences in a way that is as yet unrivaled in our country."[10] When he composed the theater music for Eugène Brieux's drama, *La Foi*, which takes place in Upper Egypt during the Middle Kingdom, he had a set of instruments made which he wanted to be as accurate as possible: "This music is unlike anything I've ever done, and I will have the right components to make it happen. Before leaving Paris, I saw all the instruments that I had had made: tiny timpanis, temple bells, a special harp, giant sistrums etc."[11] In 1911 in Algiers, Saint-Saëns was received by Ham Nghi—the Prince of Annam (now Vietnam), who had been exiled to North Africa since 1889. Ham Nghi showed him a long zither: "He demonstrated how to play this grand instrument, with its thin metal strings and its little movable bridges, invented by the Chinese and played frequently in the Far East. It is not as I would have imagined: you do not press the strings between the bridges, but between the bridges and the end of the instrument, using little metal rings fitted onto the fingers of the right hand. The left hand presses on the strings between the bridges and touches them along their length, making them produce caterwauls and wailing that are not without charm."[12]

For a long time, Saint-Saëns's interest in organology satisfied his love of archaeology, research, and scientific speculation. He touched on these in some of his lectures at meetings of the Institut de France after his election in 1881. These lectures addressed such topics as descriptions of medieval instruments shown in manuscript miniatures at the Angers library (1883); a commentary on photographs of a terra-cotta organ discovered in Carthage (1885); and a talk on images of an organ and a "guitar" found on a sarcophagus in the church of the Minimes in Arles (1900).[13]

His visit to the 1889 Paris Universal Exhibition, about which *Le Rappel* had him write a series of articles, was for Saint-Saëns the perfect opportunity to comment on his discoveries. He was attracted to the novelties by makers of the harp-piano, for example, and inventions such as Gontard's harmonium, which played quarter tones and was considered by Saint-Saëns "the true music of the future."[14] He also saw instruments from beyond Europe, and attempted to describe their design and ways of being played. He was intrigued by a double flute being played by a Somali employing circular breathing techniques and "using a kind of mouthband commonly used by flutists of antiquity."[15] All this came to mind when he thought about the scenery and staging of *Les Barbares*, and he suggested to his collaborators, Pierre-Barthélémy Gheusi and Victorien Sardou, that they bring in "women playing double flutes attached behind their heads with straps."[16] At the 1889 Paris Exhibition he remarked as well on the little Chinese drums that were "notable for the extreme tension of their drumheads, on which neither time nor moisture had any effect." He mused, "I would have liked to have seen how these people managed to create such large drums, as it takes a man's entire strength to stretch a drum no larger than my hand."[17] He was also interested in Congolese harps—"beautiful little harps adorned with pegs. The sight of these pegs would have reassured Berlioz, who did not believe in oriental music and who concluded, after seeing Burmese harps that had no pegs for stretching the strings, that they were never tuned. This is a major mistake: like Greek lyres that also have no pegs, Burmese harps are tuned by friction, the strings being held in a small roll of cloth pressed tightly against the wood of the instrument."[18]

Saint-Saëns expanded on his observations during voyages abroad. After his visits to the Naples museum and numerous journeys to Egypt,[19] he came up with the idea of "researching whether it would be possible to have a precise idea of the construction of lyres, based on the many examples of lyres held by figures represented in statues."[20] Having observed that the shapes of lyres and citharas shown in modern paintings and in statuary were more or less unrealistic, he sought to find whether the same was true in the art of antiquity. So he studied the shapes of these instruments in antique statuary and murals, and on vases, and concluded that classical representations of the instruments were probably closer to reality than more modern ones, which to him appeared deformed. He then wrote notes on the design of lyres and citharas, especially the way strings were attached to the upper part of the instruments, as well as on the various methods of pegging and tuning. He also developed hypotheses on how accessories, pegs, and plectra were used. His research was meticulous.

A first reading of his essay on ancient lyres and citharas was given at the Institut de France on 15 October 1892, and was published the next week in *Le Monde artiste*.[21] But Saint-Saëns felt he had not yet exhausted the subject, as he confided to Jacques Durand in 1899: "I assume that you have been to see the new Pompeii excavation that I want so much to see. But when would I find the time to go to Naples? Nevertheless, I have begun a study on the construction of ancient lyres that I would have liked to continue."[22] He conducted further research during his later trips to Egypt and Italy and got information from the Egyptologist Victor Loret, who was "in the process of writing a history of ancient Egyptian music."[23] In the end, he returned to Naples in December 1901 and April 1902 and continued collecting information: "I've given up on Pompeii, which I'd meant to see again, and am returning to the museum to write a short essay on lyres that I will read to my colleagues at the Académie to bore them to tears."[24] On 25 October 1902, a second lecture at the Institut expanded on the results of the first one. The text was published in the *Bulletin de l'Institut*[25] and incited some interest because it was picked up by *Le Journal des débats*,[26] then in part by *Les Annales politiques et littéraires*[27] and in 1903 by *La Revue de l'art ancien et moderne*, the latter supplemented by several photos, the taking of which Saint-Saëns had directed with detailed instructions during another trip to Naples in December 1902. As he wrote to Auguste Durand: "I took advantage of my trip here to have some photographs of the marble Apollo taken for my essay, which will again be published, this time in J[ules] Comte's *La Revue illustrée*. Since the existing photograph had been taken of the artwork as a whole, I needed one showing the front of the cithara."[28] He also bought photos of Pompeian frescoes at the museum in Naples (see Figure 1). His friend, the Egyptologist Georges Legrain,[29] put Saint-Saëns into contact with the scholar Gustave Seguier, who was preparing a dictionary of Egyptian archaeology. Seguier gave him information on Egyptian harps. "Since harps are considered archaeological objects, I already collected quite a few; I would be happy to send you a copy of my sketches in the hope that you will find them useful. As for instruments that are almost intact, I made some rubbings for you, which you will find in the roll enclosed with this letter."[30] In another lecture, to the Académie on 4 July 1903, Saint-Saëns gave further information on the techniques used to play the instrument, which he had been able to observe during his previous trip to Egypt: "While walking through the Arab quarter of Ismaïla, I was attracted by the sounds of extraordinary music. I entered into a small building where strange and incomprehensible rites were taking place. There, a musician playing an enormous lyre sat in the position so often shown in classical paintings: with his right hand, he swiftly plucked the base of the strings with a plectrum; the left hand was placed up higher, nearer the middle of the instrument, behind the strings, with the fingers fanned out. I was extremely intrigued and could not understand how the musician could play this way, vigorously rubbing all the strings, and creating a motive of several notes that repeated indefinitely. I had to look closer, and that's when I saw what I could not have imagined: using the fingers of the left hand, the musician deftly brushed the strings, which he had to prevent from vibrating; the other strings, left untouched, vibrated alone while the plectrum struck them all at the same time."[31]

In 1912, Saint-Saëns wrote a third version of his essay for Lavignac and La Laurencie's *Encyclopédie*.[32] Still, he continued his research after publication and returned to visit the museum of Alexandria, "which has been very much improved and is of great interest. In the old museum, there was a very well preserved Roman cithara. It is not in the new museum; it must have been stolen during the move."[33] Finally, a fourth revised version of the essay was published in the *Bulletin de la Société française de musicologie* (1919).[34]

In May 1920, during a festival in his honor, Saint-Saëns, who by this time was very old and in ill health, nevertheless traveled to Athens to fulfill his dream of visiting the Acropolis and the archaeological museum: "I have already seen the museum, but I must see it again with an antiquities expert who will explain to me what I cannot understand and make me see that which I would miss. But it would take a very long time to study it all in depth: just these marble stelae, painted vases, and engraved stones . . . imagine learning everything about them! What's more, it is very well presented. I saw things there that I'd never seen before."[35] Once again, he wondered whether "these vase paintings were realistic." Undoubtedly, these new discoveries would have inspired another article.

We have chosen to reproduce the second version of the essay that first appeared in the *Bulletin de l'Institut* (1902), that is, the one a year later with some additions and a number of photographs in the *Revue de l'art ancien et moderne*.[36]

—Translated by Anna Henderson

Ancient Lyres and Citharas
From *La Revue de l'art ancien et moderne* (1903)

The construction of lyres and citharas of antiquity and their use seems not to have been the object of definitive study up to now. For a long time, my attention has been drawn to this subject, and wherever I have been able to find representations of these instruments—on vases, statues, murals—I have scrutinized them carefully, and have made some rather unexpected discoveries.

In its general outline, the structure of the lyre is well known: a skin stretched over a tortoise shell, which forms the sounding body, serves as

Figure 1. *The Concert*. Saint-Saëns commissioned this photograph of a Pompeian fresco that depicts a woman playing a lyre with her left hand and a second instrument with her right.

soundboard; strings, attached to the lower part of the instrument, are strung over a crossbar distant from the sounding body and supported by two arms that are often goat or antelope horns. In the cithara, the tortoise shell is replaced by a sort of box, more resonant than the shell and stretched skin; sometimes the strings are attached to the front side, sometimes to the inside of the box, from which they emerge through a central opening and are strung over the crossbar.

So far, everything is clear. But how were the strings attached to the upper crossbar, and how were they tuned? How were these instruments made to resound? Here things become more obscure.

The ancient Greeks seem not to have known about the use of tuning pegs, in general use now, and known in the East since antiquity.

In simple, primitive lyres, strings were attached to rolls, made of leather or cloth, whose crossbar formed the axis, and which turned by friction around it. This procedure, still in use among the Berbers, does not allow strong tension to be applied to the strings, which would produce greater resonance. The need for a more perfected system was soon felt, and pegs were invented; but these pegs differed greatly from those we are familiar with now.

A few years ago, I saw a very interesting object at the museum in Naples: a little bronze Apollo, about ten centimeters high, whose cithara had been taken apart. It had silver strings, made of two strands twisted together; the pegs, taken out of their holes, were scattered at the god's feet, and I noticed their unexpected shape: instead of being straight and cylindrical, they were cut square, and had a very angular, pronounced zigzag shape. Since then, this statuette has been repaired; they forced the pegs back into the crossbar holes, deforming them, without realizing they were destroying a highly important museum piece, probably unique in the world. This, however, remains an established fact: the string, after having been passed through the hole in the crossbar and strung by hand, was attached by the friction peg introduced from top downward into the same hole, normally into the crossbar, in the direction of the string. It should be said in passing that it was this arrangement that produced, in ornamental lyres, those rigid rods that pierce the crossbar and continue beyond it.

One also finds pegs placed perpendicularly to the instrument, as in our modern stringed instruments. The great marble Apollo, playing (plucking) the lyre, in the museum in Naples, offers a magnificent example of this. Here, the strings penetrate the front side of the crossbar and the pegs, four-sided, are placed above, but sideways to it, which must have meant the strings ran obliquely or at right angles within the crossbar, with the ends emerging freely on the opposite side.

These methods of attachment, where friction is made as great as possible, have the effect of allowing the artist to firmly secure the strings using the degree of tension he gives them at the outset; they do not allow him to tune the strings later.

How, then, were these lyres and citharas played? This we will now examine.

In most cases, the musician attacks the lower part of the strings with the π (plectrum) held in the right hand, while with the left hand he directly touches the strings in a higher region. This particularity has been noted and the reason for it has been sought. Several authors have expressed the opinion that the artist played the main song with the plectrum, and created a counter-melody with the left hand. This is an elegant and ingenious explanation; but although it draws support from texts, it is only a hypothesis, which can be contradicted by others. We will see later on how one might reconcile all these arguments.

If it is established that precise tuning could not be obtained with the system of pegs used by the ancients, why not suppose that the left hand was used to rectify the tuning and thus determine the note?

To support this new hypothesis with a fact, it was necessary to find a lyre-player who used both his left hand and the plectrum on the same string. I sought this for a long time; finally I found a convincing example in the famous painting in the Naples museum, *The Education of Achilles* (Figure 2).

The instrument shown is remarkable. It is large in size; the base descends below Achilles's hip and the upper end rises above his head. Since the strings are long, it is relatively easy to study them.

As Achilles, attentive, his eyes fixed on his master, touches a string with his left hand, the Centaur makes the same string resound in its lower part with the aid of a plectrum; the string has bent markedly from the vertical position the other strings are in, so there is no possible doubt about this.

This way of making the strings vibrate is not of a nature to give them much resonance, which explains the use of the plectrum: the latter does not at all resemble the little piece of shell our mandolin players use. Most often the form is that of a cylindrical handle, held with the whole hand, the extremities of which are equipped with two appendages in the shape of small leaves, thick at the base, the tip slightly curved, and probably sculpted from ivory. Other forms have been used, but they all seem conceived with the aim of allowing the artist to attack the string vigorously. The resonance thus obtained was certainly much more intense than that produced with the finger; as for the quality of the sound, it must have been poor: this should not overly surprise us. These days, the Japanese construct instruments that are wonders of stringed-instrument manufacture and of decorative art, where you pluck the strings with large shell or ivory plectra; their sound is pitiful. Let's not forget, moreover, that the lyres and citharas of the ancient Greeks were intended less "to make music," as we understand it, than to guide the voice, to support it in the desired tone and mode. If our hypothesis is correct, this could never have been anything but very difficult, and we can readily understand the expressions of profound attention on the faces of Achilles and the Centaur, student and teacher.

It remains for us to examine a strange appendage, apparently reserved for luxury instruments, a strange bridge attached to the crossbar, pro-

Figure 2. *The Education of Achilles*, Chiron and Achilles, fresco, Herculaneum, Italy.

jecting forward diagonally, slanting downward. I thought at first it was a way to distance the strings from the soundboard; the most knowledgeable archaeologists have adopted this viewpoint; we read in the *Dictionnaire des antiquités grecques et romaines*: "a bridge, a square piece of wood, slightly convex and parallel to the crossbar, on which the strings rest; it serves to isolate them from the soundboard." An attentive examination, however, led me to realize that this was a mistake; this bridge, not as wide as the crossbar, projects above the strings. What's more, looking at it close up, I saw that it seemed made from tubes placed side by side and closed above with knobs that must be the heads of pegs, since they are, to all appearances, equal in number to the strings; when there are many strings the bridge, which is narrower than the crossbar, becomes thicker, and the knobs are arranged on two rows. Thus in the lyre in *The Education of Achilles*, where one can make out eleven strings and allowably infer twelve, the appendage or bridge consists of two rows, one on top of the other, of six knobs each. Since no similar arrangement of this type exists in modern instruments, it is not easy to understand its function or use. One might imagine that its aim was to increase the length of the pegs and thus ensure the tension and fastness of the strings with a more extensive surface friction. The lyre shown in the painting clearly shows the position of this so-called bridge above the strings, its division into tubes, and the knobs that close them; the picture even shows separate tubes, perpendicular to the crossbar.

Coming to the system of rolls in large, relatively modern citharas, the crossbar is angled to allow the use of strings of different lengths, which makes these instruments a kind of transition between the lyre and the harp; here and there this crossbar bears transverse grooves meant to prevent the rolls from sliding on a slanting bar. Since these instruments, perfectly constructed, have sound boxes of some amplitude and no longer require such great tension on the strings, the friction pegs were abandoned, in a return to the old system, where the handling is easier, and which allows the instrument to be tuned. The cithara thus came into its own and became a true musical instrument, and the left hand remained free to be used as a performance aid. To this instrument are related, from all appearances, the descriptions of modes and scales we find in the texts, and which the example of *The Education of Achilles* does not allow us to apply to lyres with pegs, or lyres with the mysterious appendage taken till now as a bridge. By the above hypothesis, only lyres whose strings are attached to rolls could be tuned like citharas.

A curious fresco in the Naples museum shows a woman plucking the strings of a lyre with her left hand, while with her right she is causing a small instrument placed on a stand to resonate [see Figure 1]. The instrument is seen from the side, and its shape is hard to make out. Is this musician performing a song and counter-melody, a melody and a bass? Is she simply executing the same theme in two different octaves, as the Chinese and Japanese do on the *chen*, the most resonant of their plucked-string instruments? It would be rash to say one way or the other. What is certain is that this musician is doing something unusual, a sort of tour de force, since the three personages who surround her evince extreme surprise, almost trepidation. It should be noted that the instruments are constructed on the system of rolls, allowing them to be tuned and played with one hand.

The author of these remarks does not flatter himself on having completely elucidated the questions about the nature and use of these mysterious instruments. The question of the attachment of the strings to the lower part of the instrument still has to be studied; to this question are related the appendages that one sometimes sees fixed on the front part of the tortoise shell, especially in the group of the *Farnese Bull*. This field remains open for study and conjecture, which we leave to more capable scholars, and to professional archaeologists.

—Translated by Anna Henderson

NOTES

1. Camille Saint-Saëns, "Les Chœurs d'*Antigone*," *Le Figaro*, 28 November 1893, 1.

2. Camille Saint-Saëns, "*Déjanire* et M. Camille Saint-Saëns," *Le Figaro*, 11 November 1898, 1.

3. Camille Saint-Saëns, *Note sur les décors de théâtre dans l'antiquité romaine* (Paris: L. Baschet, 1886).

4. Saint-Saëns made eleven visits to Naples between 1884 and 1913, the first visit in January 1884 and the second in April 1891.

5. Saint-Saëns, *Note sur les décors de théâtre*, 8.

6. Ibid.

7. A triangular prism that pivots on a vertical axis. Each of the three faces shows a different set. Theater sets can be changed simply by rotating the device around its axis.

8. Saint-Saëns, *Note sur les décors de théâtre*, 24.

9. As Saint-Saëns himself admitted, with the "ballets in *Samson*, the *Suite algérienne*, *Caprice arabe*, *Africa*, *Souvenir d'Ismaïlia*, *Nuit persane*, *Parysatis* . . . I became the most important Orientalist in music." Camille Saint-Saëns, letter to Auguste Durand, Cairo, 1 February 1902, Médiathèque Musicale Mahler, Paris (MMM). One could also add the marches *Orient et occident* and *Sur les Bords du Nil*; songs including *Mélodies persanes*, "Désir de l'Orient," and "Lever de soleil sur le Nil"; theater music composed for *La Foi*; the *scène lyrique*, *Antoine et Cléopâtre*; his Piano Concerto no. 5; *La Princesse jaune*, inspired by the Far East, and, of course, *Africa*. See also Jann Pasler's article analyzing this work, in this volume.

10. Saint-Saëns to Auguste Durand, Cairo, 8 April 1902, MMM.

11. Saint-Saëns to Jacques Durand, Elche, 15 December 1908, MMM. A sistrum is a percussion instrument of ancient Iraq and Egypt.

12. Saint-Saëns to Jacques Durand, Algiers, 13 February 1911. The letter from Saint-Saëns is illustrated with a drawing showing the placement of the frets.

13. These details come from minutes of the Institut de France's meetings as discussed by Stéphane Leteuré in his doctoral thesis, "Le Drapeau et la lyre: Camille Saint-Saëns et le politique, 1870–1921" (PhD diss., Université François-Rabelais, Tours, 2011).

14. Camille Saint-Saëns, "*Le Rappel* à l'exposition: Les Instruments de musique," *Le Rappel*, 10 October 1889, 1.

15. Camille Saint-Saëns, "Torino," *L'Écho de Paris*, 25 June 1911, 1.

16. Saint-Saëns to an unidentified recipient (Victorien Sardou or Pierre-Barthélémy Gheusi), Bône, Algeria, 27 December 1900, Pierpont Morgan Library, New York.

17. Saint-Saëns, "*Le Rappel* à l'exposition," 2.

18. Ibid., 1.

19. Around fifteen trips to Egypt between 1891 and 1914 were recorded.

20. Camille Saint-Saëns, "Note sur la lyre antique," *Le Monde artiste*, 23 October 1892.

21. Ibid.

22. Saint-Saëns to Jacques Durand, 16 April 1899, MMM.

23. Victor Loret to Saint-Saëns, 3 October 1892, cited in *Égypte, égyptologie, égyptomanie: Un Musée et ses collectionneurs* (Dieppe: Château-Musée de Dieppe, 1998), 85.

24. Saint-Saëns to Auguste Durand, Naples, 17 April 1902, MMM.

25. Camille Saint-Saëns, "Essai sur les lyres et les cithares antiques," lecture to the annual public meeting of the five Académies, *Bulletin de l'Institut*, Institut de France (Paris: Firmin-Didot, 1902), 45–52.

26. Camille Saint-Saëns, "Essai sur les lyres et les cithares antiques," *Le Journal des débats*, supplement, 26 October 1902.

27. Camille Saint-Saëns, "La Lyre antique," *Les Annales politiques et littéraires*, 2 November 1902, 285–86.

28. Saint-Saëns to Auguste Durand, Naples, 13 December 1902, MMM.

29. Georges Legrain (1865–1917), Egyptologist and chief inspector of antiquities in Luxor, took over as director of the Karnak excavation in 1895.

30. Gustave Séguier to Saint-Saëns, Champagne, Vaud, 8 April 1908, Fonds Saint-Saëns, Château-Musée de Dieppe. These documents are kept in the Fonds Saint-Saëns, dossier Bonnerot no. 124.

31. Camille Saint-Saëns, lecture at Institut de France, 4 July 1903, cited in Leteuré, "Le Drapeau et la lyre," Annexes, 2: 78-79.

32. Camille Saint-Saëns, "Lyres et cithares antiques," in Albert Lavignac and L. de la Laurencie, *Encyclopédie de la musique*, vol. 1: *Antiquité-Moyen-Age* (Paris: Delagrave, 1913), 538–40.

33. Saint-Saëns to Jacques Durand, Alexandria, 5 January 1914, MMM.

34. Camille Saint-Saëns, "Lyres et cithares," *Bulletin de la Société française de musicologie* 3/4 (April 1919): 170–74.

35. Saint-Saëns to Jacques Durand, Athens, 29 May 1920, MMM.

36. *Revue de l'art ancien et moderne* 70 (1 January 1903): 23–30. Thanks to Florence Gétreau for her advice in selecting the text.

Saint-Saëns and d'Indy in Dialogue

JANN PASLER

Since their falling out in 1886 over the direction of the composer-run Société nationale de musique, we've long assumed that irreconcilable differences must have kept Camille Saint-Saëns and Vincent d'Indy estranged from each other.[1] Yes, after being good friends in the 1870s, the two locked horns over Wagner's importance for French musicians and notions of musical progress associated with his music. And yes, their politics, at least on the surface, were antithetical, with Saint-Saëns an anticlerical republican and d'Indy a Catholic monarchist. Moreover, Saint-Saëns was the quintessential insider, not only a member of the Académie des Beaux-Arts, but also its president in 1901. D'Indy was a self-fashioned outsider, co-founder of the Schola Cantorum as a private, religious alternative to the state-supported, secular Paris Conservatoire.

But the story is more complex. The Société nationale under d'Indy's leadership, and even d'Indy himself, continued to perform Saint-Saëns's music after he left, albeit without the presence of the composer.[2] And, as I've shown elsewhere, d'Indy was a man of alliance as well as opposition. Not only were his differences useful to the state in helping to bridge conflicts within the Republic and promote growth and change in the musical world, he actively collaborated with the government on various committees, even writing music for *orphéon* competitions and official state ceremonies, which earned him the Legion of Honor.[3] Saint-Saëns was similarly involved in excavating, studying, and building on the French aristocratic past—from the sixteenth-century pavanes that inspired dances in his operas *Étienne Marcel* (1878), *Prosperine* (1886), and *Ascanio* (1888) to the Baroque dances given modern clothes in his Piano Suite (1891), to the new Rameau edition he spearheaded (1895–1918), with d'Indy as one of his collaborators.[4] And, when it came to friends and patrons, Saint-Saëns did not require an allegiance to the Revolution, especially in England, Belgium, Spain, Portugal, and Monaco.[5]

Such overlapping concerns may have led to rivalry through the medium of music. As Saint-Saëns's *Organ* Symphony was being premiered in London, d'Indy, with a different approach to the form, worked on his own Symphony on a French Mountain Air. But, whether inspired by Saint-Saëns's long analysis of his Symphony no. 3, written for the English,[6] or coveting the prestige associated with such an extended analysis, or wanting to pit his work directly against that of Saint-Saëns, d'Indy wrote his own seven-page "Analytical and Thematic Notice" with extensive musical examples for his *Wallenstein* Trilogy. This was distributed at the Concerts Lamoureux premiere on 26 February 1888—to my knowledge the only other composition to receive such treatment in Paris. Another parallel can also be found. In 1886 while the Comte de Paris was plotting a return to power, d'Indy composed the minuet and sarabande for his *Suite en ré dans le style ancien* for trumpet, two flutes, and strings. In 1891, after the threat of a monarchical restoration had passed, Saint-Saëns composed his own minuet in his Piano Suite and an orchestral Sarabande and Rigaudon.[7]

The two composers' lifestyles would certainly have kept them apart. Saint-Saëns began to live regularly in North Africa and traveled often abroad.[8] Meanwhile, although d'Indy also conducted his music beyond Paris, he became deeply involved with Parisian musical life, especially as director of the Schola Cantorum beginning in 1900. The two most likely had few occasions to collaborate, though they probably kept an eye on each other's activities through the press. But, as time went on, they spoke out publicly in ways that drew them into dialogue, whether articulating their differences over the merits of the pope's *Motu proprio* (1903) on what music should and should not be performed in church as well as over how Latin is pronounced in its services, or their common attitudes toward Gluck and interpretation of his music.[9]

During World War I, Saint-Saëns, furious with Germany and still seething at the impact of Wagner on French music, fueled debate on its future with a series of articles published in the *Grande Revue* and *L'Echo de Paris*, some later collected in the short book *Germanophilie* (1916). Here he took aim particularly at *Parsifal*, a French favorite. The little book ends with his frequently quoted letter from 1881:

I shall always be heart and soul for Wagner against Brahms, for Wagner against the Philistines, but for Germany against France— never! My musical predilections will never make me forget that, even if art has no country, artists have one, and that it is not well for the French school of music to shelter itself in France under the protection of foreigners.[10]

While some colleagues thought Saint-Saëns had lived so long in Cairo he had not realized that "French music today owes less to Wagner than Saint-Saëns does to Liszt and the German classics,"[11] d'Indy responded with his own polemics, such as articles in *Courrier musical* and *L'Echo de Paris*.[12] Still, whatever their divergent perspectives on Wagner, both composers saw themselves as patriots and wrote war music.[13] Both also agreed on the importance of protecting French concert halls during the war from contemporary German and Austrian music not yet in the public domain.[14]

In early fall 1917, Saint-Saëns wrote another small book, *Les Idées de Vincent d'Indy*, an analysis of d'Indy's published notes for his *Cours de Composition* (the first two volumes, 1903–9), used to teach composition at the Schola. Ironically, he barely mentions Wagner, religion, or even what it means to write French music, a hot topic during this period. Instead, he turns to fundamental issues in all music: form, expression, the elements of music (rhythm, melody, and harmony), as well as musical editions, criticizing German approaches. Saint-Saëns's words foreshadow not only neoclassical values—Stravinsky's "music is powerless to express"—but also the early music movement's later preoccupation with authenticity, the postmodern critique of progress, and he even seems to foresee the atomic bomb. Returning to the particularities of personal taste, Saint-Saëns ends with the differences responsible for his break with d'Indy in 1886: his aesthetic resistance to the music of César Franck.

Read in conjunction with d'Indy's response, as expressed in a long letter to Saint-Saëns on 10 April 1919, a month after the book was published, these texts suggest that, except in their attitudes toward Franck and Catholicism, the two shared more than they perhaps previously realized, especially when it came to serious art. Perhaps both felt it under siege by the younger generation. When Saint-Saëns sounds conservative, discussing the need for artistic training, for respecting "rules and restrictions" so as not to fall into anarchy, when he defines the nature of harmony and the vitality of fugues, d'Indy is silent. Perhaps his agreement would have been obvious to them both. In his letter of reply, Saint-Saëns defends his positions: "You have your ideas, I have mine, and I don't pretend to change yours." But besides their shared pleasure in expressing, or at least representing, difference, underlying the dialogue is mutual respect. Moreover, the tone in their correspondence is light, almost bemused, like two old men looking in the mirror at each other, grateful they're both still alive, waiting for music to bring them together again.

Saint-Saëns to d'Indy, 4 February 1919, note attached to the proofs of Les Idées de M. Vincent d'Indy.[15]

My dear colleague,

　If I were like you, surrounded by disciples, I would not have written this little book. But, not enjoying such a situation, I can't think of any other way to draw attention to the ideas of yours that differ from my own, in the interest of musical education. If you do me the honor of reading this little book, you will see that I attach great importance to everything that comes from you.

With my highest esteem, C. Saint-Saëns

Musical Origins and Form

Saint-Saëns, from Les Idées de M. Vincent d'Indy *(1919), 1–4.*

On opening M. d'Indy's book one is immediately struck with admiration at the loftiness of his conceptions. We see how careful the author is—an attitude that cannot be too greatly admired—to look upon Art as one of the most serious things in life. . . .

　All those mythological scenes painted on the walls of Pompeii[16]—all that art, which we regard as secular—is religious art. . . . Such considerations make it easy to imagine that Art has its source in Religion. All the same, its origin is an even more modest one. Art came into being on the day that man, instead of being solely concerned with the utility of an object he had made, concerned himself with its form, and made up his mind that this form should satisfy a need peculiar to human nature, a mysterious need to which the name of *aesthetic sense* has been given.

　Afterward form was enriched by ornament, or decoration, which serves no other purpose than to satisfy this aesthetic need. . . . Here is the starting point in the radical difference between nature and Art, which is destined not to reproduce Nature literally, but to suggest an idea of nature. . . .[17] So-called imitative music does not imitate, it suggests. . . . Nevertheless, it is from the sounds of nature, the sounds produced by the wind blowing through the reeds, and more particularly from the utterance of the human voice, that music had its birth.[18]

D'Indy, letter to Saint-Saëns, letterhead of the Schola Cantorum, Director, Paris, 10 April 1919.[19]

Yes, my dear colleague, I do enjoy having numerous disciples to whom I try to teach what I consider healthy ideas about Art. . . . In your little book [*planquette*], you outline principles that I would have signed my name to as well, and very accurate observations that seem to prove that, when it comes to elevated art, at least, we think the same way—a notion that might seem unbelievable to those around us. . . . I don't need to go over what we share, you know it as well as I, but permit me to respond in a few words to what divides us, or seems to divide us. . . . I'll begin then and try to be brief.

1. I don't think it's possible to deny art its religious origin. The *features*, the *design*, the construction, however *useful*, are only aspects of an artistic achievement, aspects that become art works only through their *form*, as you explain perfectly. And what determines this form, in principle, if not the influence of religion, and no other?

The ordinary house (a work of utility) only becomes a temple or cathedral (a work of art) when its purpose is to shelter worship of a divine being, whether Pallas-Athénée or Notre-Dame. Likewise, the "reindeer" of the caves, decorative babbling, had *artistic value* only once it was turned into a Venus by Praxitèle or frescoes by Fra Angelico. This at any rate was what I meant to say.

Saint-Saëns to d'Indy, ca. 11 April 1919 or soon thereafter.[20]

If we don't agree on the origin of art it's because I consider it in its totality, down to its roots, and you don't go that far. This includes decorative art. For me art begins with the era of polished stone when prehistoric men, turning away from their stone fragments, gave their stone axes the elegant form we're familiar with. . . . Art took shape as it became religious; but its origin comes earlier.

Musical Expression

Saint-Saëns, from Les Idées de M. Vincent d'Indy *(1919), 4–6.*

It is perfectly clear that Art in general, especially music, lends itself wonderfully well to expression, and that is all the music lover [*amateur*] expects. It is quite different with the artist, however. The artist who does not feel thoroughly satisfied with elegant lines, harmonious colors, or a fine series of chords, does not understand Art. When beautiful forms accompany powerful expression, we are filled with admiration, and rightly so. . . . Art is capable of existing apart from the slightest trace of emotion or passion.

During the entire 16th century, admirable works were produced entirely devoid of emotion (with the exception notably of Palestrina's *Stabat Mater*). Their truer purpose is thwarted when an attempt is made to render them expressive. Wherein does the Kyrie of the famous *Missa Papae Marcelli* express supplication? Here there is absolutely nothing else but form. . . .

True, these forms exist only in the imagination, and yet, does Art as a whole exist in any other way? These forms are but imperfectly reproduced by musical notation, though sufficiently to suggest it.

D'Indy to Saint-Saëns, 10 April 1919.

2. According to you, "there is no emotion in the music of the 15th and 16th centuries"? Coming from you, this opinion surprises me profoundly, as it suggests you don't know any of the thousands of admirable motets from this period, which express feeling a lot more gripping than Palestrina's *Stabat*, a work that is rather cold and conventional. So I refuse to believe this gap in your knowledge about art. . . .

How can you not have felt your heart vibrate in sight-reading the masterpieces of Josquin, Lassus, Vittoria, Ingenieri [*sic*]??? How can your artist's soul not have been moved, not by the form, but by the intense expressivity of *O vos omnes*, *Nos qui sumus*, and *Pulvis et umbra*, to cite only names that come to me at this moment, as it can and should be moved in the presence of the expressive accents in Bach's *Agnus Dei* (which are exactly the same), in Beethoven's opus 110 or his Quartet no. 12, the final scene of *Armide*, or the death of *Tristan*? I'll never understand this in an artist such as you!

Saint-Saëns to d'Indy, ca. 11 April 1919 or soon thereafter.

I know 16th-century music better than you think. I've had in my possession the huge collection, *Musica divina*. . . . In Rome when I was twenty, I heard the famous Sistine Chapel chorus sing in full voice and without any nuance or expression, and I'm inclined to believe they were following the old tradition. Since then, people sing differently; modern ideas have been introduced into music. . . . Where might expression have come from in an exclusively diatonic music? It must have come when harmony became more complicated by the use of dissonant chords; nuance must have been arbitrary and unimportant. As I see it, its importance came later and little by little. At least, that's my hypothesis.

Musical Progress

Saint-Saëns, from Les Idées de M. Vincent d'Indy *(1919), 6–9.*

In the introduction to his book, M. d'Indy says the most excellent things about artistic consciousness, the necessity of acquiring talent as the result of hard work, and of not relying solely on one's natural endowments. Horace had said the same thing long ago; still, it cannot be repeated too often at a time like the present, when so many artists reject all rules and restrictions, declare that they mean "to be laws unto themselves," and reply to the most justifiable criticism by the one peremptory argument—that they "will do as they please." Assuredly, art is the home of freedom, but freedom is not anarchy, and it is anarchy that is now fashionable both in literature and in the arts.[21] Why do poets not see that, in throwing down the barriers, they merely give free access to mediocrity, and that their vaunted progress is but a reversion to primitive barbarism? . . .

Fétis foresaw the coming of the "omnitonic" system. . . . He could not predict the birth of cacophony, or pure *charivari*. Berlioz speaks somewhere of atrocious modulations that introduce a new key in one section of the orchestra while another section is playing in the old one. At the present time as many as three different tonalities can be heard simultaneously.

Everything is relative, we are told. That is true, though only within certain limits, which cannot be overstepped. After a severe frost, a temperature of twelve degrees above zero seems stiflingly hot; on returning from the tropics, you shiver with cold at eighteen degrees above zero. There comes a limit, however, beyond which both cold and heat disrupt [*désorganisent*] the tissues and render life impossible.

The dissonance of yesterday, we are also told, will be the consonance of tomorrow; one can grow accustomed to anything. Still, there are such things in life as bad habits, and those who get accustomed to crime, come to a bad end. . . .

It is impossible for me to regard scorn of all rules as being equivalent to progress, by which word we generally mean improvement. The true meaning of the word—*progressus*—is a going forward, but the end or object is not stated. There is such a thing as the progress of a disease, and this is anything but improvement.

The more civilization advances, the more the artistic sense seems to decline: a grave symptom. . . . The need to know is being substituted for the need to believe and to admire; and since what we know is insignificant compared with what we do not know, there is an immense field open to the human intellect. Nothing will ever again check the march of Science: this is deadly to Faith and Art. . . .

[The following passage was omitted from the English translation:] The principle on which so many illusory hopes have been based, "Love one another!" [*Aimez-vous les uns les autres!*], pales before another, as old as the world itself, "Exterminate one another!" [*Exterminez-vous les uns les autres!*]. This war, they tell us, will be the last one. . . . If Science, diverted from its purpose, put into men's hands such means of destruction that entire cities would disappear as in a dream . . . the Earth, devastated, depopulated, would continue to turn in its orbit until it lost its air and its water, its volcanoes extinct, a dead star like its companion the Moon.

Elements of Music

Saint-Saëns, from Les Idées de M. Vincent d'Indy *(1919), 9–13.*

In dividing music into its three essential parts, *Rhythm, Melody,* and *Harmony,* M. d'Indy very judiciously accords the first place to Rhythm. Let us therefore see what interpretation he puts on it. . . . He himself confesses these ideas are very frequently not his own at all, but rather those of Hugo Riemann, a German. . . .

According to d'Indy, Measure would appear to be the enemy of Rhythm "and it is not unreasonable to think that, untrammeled in the future as it was in the past, *rhythm* will again hold sovereign sway over music, and free it from the servitude in which it has been kept, for nearly three centuries, by the usurping and depressing domination of misunderstood *measure.*"[22]

Hitherto, however, it had seemed as though the invention of measure was a step in advance. I appeal for confirmation of this view to all who have undertaken the task of deciphering old musical manuscripts from which the bar line was absent. Did it not create syncopation? Has it ever prevented the emphasis or accent from falling where it pleased? M. d'Indy claims that the first beat of the bar is more frequently than not a rhythmically feeble beat. I have not noticed this, but rather the contrary. It would prove, however, that measure does not follow rhythm. Shall we have to return to the time when Measure was not indicated? . . . Perhaps it is the same with Rhythm as with so many things about which it is impossible to come to an understanding because different meanings are given to the same word.[23]

D'Indy to Saint-Saëns, 10 April 1919.

> 3. We cannot agree on rhythm because we do not conceive of it in the same manner. To come to an agreement we first need, as has been noted, a *common* definition of the word *rhythm*, whereas our definitions are, I believe, *opposed*. I'll move on, therefore . . . until there is agreement.

Saint-Saëns, from Les Idées de M. Vincent d'Indy *(1919), 13–14.*

Let us pass on to melody. In all melody, M. d'Indy (or is it Riemann?) assures us, there is a *preparation*, designated, I know not why, by the Greek word *anacrusis*. . . . But what are we to say of the following way of presenting the famous phrase of the Symphony no. 9:

The first bar, then, is nothing more than a preparation, and the melody really begins only at the second bar! Do not the first and third bars belong to the tonic, the second and fourth to the dominant? When the tonic and dominant are both present, is it not to the former that importance is attached? My entire musical sense rebels against the contrary interpretation, which seems to me a serious error of style.

D'Indy to Saint-Saëns, 10 April 1919.

> 4. Melody. Anacrusis—in my mind the key to every melodic period—is part of the melody itself. It prepares not the melody, because it is an integral part of that, but *the arrival of the accent*, the linchpin of any melody. Perhaps I explained myself poorly above and in the treatise, or you are confused a bit about this subject? I suspect that we would easily agree on the primordial importance of anacruistic preparation.

Saint-Saëns to d'Indy, ca. 11 April 1919 or soon thereafter.

The anacrusis determines the accent. Thus you hold that the accent in the finale of the Ninth Symphony should be not on the first and third measures, but on the second and fourth ones. As I said, all my musical intuition rejects this assertion.

Saint-Saëns, from Les Idées de M. Vincent d'Indy *(1919), 16–19.*

Harmony! In these times, it is the flesh and blood of music. Rhythm is the ossature on which it is built, Melody its epidermis.

Harmony, we are told, is born of Melody. This is a widespread opinion, though it is not my own. Harmony was developed after Melody, seeing that an advanced musical culture is necessary for appreciating the interest and charm of simultaneous sounds. Harmony, however, previously existed in the sonorous body that makes its harmonics heard, forming a chord over the fundamental. More particularly is this phenomenon perceptible in bells which often give forth a chord consisting entirely of harmonic sounds, the fundamental being scarcely perceptible.

One night, thanks to the absolute silence of the countryside, I heard an immense chord of extreme delicacy [*tenuité*]. This chord increased in intensity and resolved itself into a single note produced by the flight of a mosquito. Subsequently, in Cochinchina, I heard a powerful chord produced by the flight of an enormous beetle [*coléoptère*], resounding in the vast sonorous rooms open to every wind —one of those insects that are so common in these wonderful countries. What an enchanted fairyland are these tropical regions! . . .

No, Melody does not produce Harmony. If such were the case, Gregorian chants and folksongs composed without any accompaniment would benefit from being accompanied. The contrary is the case; accompanied they lose their entire character and charm. On the other hand, harmony may produce melody. This is what happens in the ballad "Ange si pur" from *La Favorita*. . . .

Harmony is based on the chords made by harmonics; it is a product of nature, antecedent to the human race. Melody is the creation of man.

Musical Editions

Saint-Saëns, from Les Idées de M. Vincent d'Indy *(1919), 30–34.*

The chapter devoted to harmony and the following chapters to the end of the first book of *Cours de composition* are full of excellent things. Practically my only regret is the superfluous indications and nuances added onto old madrigals, indications perhaps necessary for the actual performance of the pieces, but very undesirable in a treatise, which should sacrifice everything to purity of text. . . .

When the Breitkopf firm conceived the idea of publishing a complete edition of Mozart's music . . . unfortunately they entrusted the revision of the piano concertos to Reinecke, who, instead of aiming at textual purity alone, treated these wonderful concertos according to current fashion. Consequently, we find everywhere such indications as *legato, molto legato, sempre legato,* frequently running counter to the author's purpose. And he did even worse than this: but to go into this more would carry us beyond the present scope. Germany, alas, was destined to go even further in distorting its masterpieces. . . .[24]

How comes it that M. d'Indy, attentive as he is to the slightest details, did not more successfully resist the contagion of bad example? He protests quite rightly against the superfluous indications, notably the *rallentando* inflicted on the old masters in modern editions. And yet he, too, in the first part of his book, cites a fragment of Sebastian Bach containing a *rallentando* that the author has not indicated. A strange contradiction!

D'Indy to Saint-Saëns, 10 April 1919.

> 5. You criticize my indication of a *rall.[entando]* in an example from Bach, not called for by the composer. Yet, you are not oblivious to the role of the *mora vocis* at the end of all Gregorian *distinctiones*, a usage upheld until the time of Bach and even later (Mozart, Beethoven, and many others) without the author even needing to mention it, so common was the practice. Thus I don't think I've been an unfaithful translator in noting . . . a mode of performance confirmed definitively by documents.

Saint-Saëns to d'Indy, ca. 11 April 1919 or soon thereafter.

> What I said and here repeat is that the indication *rall.*, admissible in an edition for performance, has no place in a treatise on composi-

tion. It's not a serious matter. But what you indicate for the theme of the *Pastoral* Symphony, on the contrary, is extremely so. . . .

Saint-Saëns, from Les Idées de M. Vincent d'Indy *(1919), 34.*

In the musical quotations from the second book, we find hypothetical indications, arbitrary ties in which the influence of the Westphalian ideas too frequently make itself felt.[25]

D'Indy to Saint-Saëns, 10 April 1919.

6. Here I must confess that you're right. Many articulations in the examples I cite are false or erroneous. Thus I must apologize. . . . To save time, I simply cut them out of an edition, of course a *German* one [*boche*], since our French publishers had not yet decided to publish the classics. . . . I was wrong in doing this, I admit.

Fugues

Saint-Saëns, from Les Idées de M. Vincent d'Indy *(1919), 37–44.*

One day I was utterly stupefied to hear Gevaert, the famous director of the Brussels Conservatoire, declare that the study of the fugue was unnecessary. . . . M. d'Indy is not of Gevaert's opinion. He devotes a long chapter to the fugue, admirably documented and detailed, addressing its origin, formation, and elements. . . . D'Indy acknowledges that, in spite of the great changes that have taken place in music, the fugue, which has a great deal of vitality, still exists and has its admirers. The only thing is that it is less frequently used. . . .

Nevertheless, the fugue has not altogether disappeared from modern compositions. He honors me by including my name among those who have kept it alive, though he finds fault with my fugues for being somewhat cold and conventional. . . . Frequently in his *Cours* he praises my works and for this I am sincerely and deeply grateful, as he is not lavish with his favors. . . .

With reference to dance airs, I am not sure that the author has been sufficiently informed as in regard to the pavane, which he simply mentions in passing as an air in duple time.[26] . . . I'm very pleased to find that M. d'Indy attaches great importance to Haydn's sonatas. These are not known to the youth of today, who remain ignorant of their beauty.

The Rust Question

Saint-Saëns, from Les Idées de M. Vincent d'Indy *(1919), 45.*

M. d'Indy has a high opinion of the sonatas of F. W. Rust [1739–1796] upon which he dwells at length, regarding them as superior to those of Haydn.[27] It would be wise to proceed warily as regarding Rust's compositions, concerning the authenticity of which there has been much dispute. These sonatas have been considerably altered. Probably M. d'Indy was not aware that musical "faking"[*truquage*] is a common practice in Germany. . . . Rust's grandson [Wilhelm, 1822–1892] has protested against the authenticity of the famous sonatas, but to no purpose. M. d'Indy has caught his great composer and was unwilling to let him go.

D'Indy to Saint-Saëns, 10 April 1919.

7. You don't seem to be informed on this question, since you allege that the grandson of Rust would have objected to the authenticity of these sonatas. On the contrary it was he who miserably revised and ruined the works of his grandfather by completely changing the original writing, of such interest, and even interspersing some of his own compositions! Having always doubted the authenticity of these texts, I copied the sonatas myself from the manuscripts in the Berlin library. . . .[28]

Saint-Saëns to d'Indy, ca. 11 April 1919 or soon thereafter.

As for the Rust question, I guess I was poorly informed. If it's true, then I regret that I wrongly accused you.

César Franck

Saint-Saëns, from Les Idées de M. Vincent d'Indy *(1919), 45–50.*

We may wonder at the inordinate height of the pedestal upon which he has erected the statue of César Franck . . . "the greatest creator of musical form along with Beethoven and Wagner." It would be ungracious for me to dispute the merit of his works, as I was one of the first to give them a hearing, and at my own risk, when the public knew them little. Furthermore, when Jules Simon, then Minister of Public Instruction, consulted me on the choice of an organ professor at the Conservatoire, I strongly recommended Franck.

At the same time, though I esteem his works, I cannot see them on the same level as those of the great masters. . . . Franck was more of a musician than an artist; he was not a poet. I do not find in his works that latent warmth, that irresistible charm which makes us forget everything else and transports us into the unknown. . . . At one moment we come up against an ill-timed modulation, as in his Sonata for piano and violin . . . at another we have a construction in which something is lacking, as in the *Prélude, choral, et fugue.* . . . His much vaunted work, *Les Béatitudes*, is very unequal. . . . Generally speaking, we are more likely to find in him a violent and meritorious aspiration toward Beauty than true Beauty itself. . . . His emotion is seldom communicative. . . . At times a gloomy sadness hangs over his work. . . . His teaching did not meet with brilliant results . . . one of them called on me for advice. . . . His religious music, though eminently deserving of respect, calls to mind the austerities of the cloister rather than the perfumed splendors of the sanctuary.

There can be no doubt that M. d'Indy is the favorite disciple. . . . The same feeling makes me regret that Liszt does not occupy a more important place in the *Cours.* . . .

With this brief study, I hope to draw attention to this very fine work and increase the number of its readers.

D'Indy to Saint-Saëns, 10 April 1919.

8. Here our disagreement is serious. Putting aside my gratefulness toward the Maître to whom I owe just about everything I know, it seems that you are being unjust. . . . For me, I find in the music of Franck an intense poetry, a brilliantly communicative warmth, an irresistible charm. You can say that this is a personal appreciation and I won't deny it. But what I do not understand, is that you condemn as an "untimely modulation" a tonal state that is perfectly logical. In the development of the finale of the Violin Sonata, the key of B-flat minor (= A minor) becomes, with the addition of the note C (D-flat) a neighbor to the principal tonality, A major. In any case, this modulation, this tonal situation, is much less shocking than that of the Adagio in D-flat major of your Symphony in C Minor. These two tonalities are terrible enemies, harmonic material incapable of constituting a solid structure. None of the classics—neither Bach, nor Beethoven, nor even Wagner—used this kind of construction, which is truly . . . adventurous. I know of only one example from the eighteenth century, a Haydn sonata. . . . As for the *Prélude, choral, et fugue* . . . the fugue is perfectly regular, infinitely more musical than the very learned—and very empty—rantings of Cherubini. . . .

When it comes to our disagreements, some of which are more apparent than real, let me thank you, my dear colleague, to have devoted time—time that is so precious to both of us—to reading and examining my *Cours de composition*, which I hardly consider a perfect work.

Saint-Saëns to d'Indy, ca. 11 April 1919 or soon thereafter.

When it comes to César Franck, it's not my fault if I don't find in his works the intense poetry you find there, which I really would like to find there. Except for a few rare and wonderful exceptions, I find his music without grace and without charm. It bores me. It's not my fault, I assure you.

All the arguments in the world can do nothing to affect one's feelings [*sensation*]. Modulation in Franck's sonata may be logical, but it's unpleasant. The arrival of the key of D-flat in the Adagio of my symphony is only one of its main attractions. Besides, the only established tonality before this is F-sharp minor, a cousin of C-sharp, which is synonymous with D-flat.

Try as I may, it's impossible for me to find something to praise in the architecture of the *Prélude, choral, et fugue* and to see in the fugue something other than an exposition. . . .

So I end this connecting link bringing us together by regretting our differences, which will change nothing, I hope, in the cordiality of our relations and in the good humor of those relations when music reunites us, as is probable.

With feelings of high esteem,
C. Saint-Saëns

NOTES

Besides selecting and editing the excerpts from Saint-Saëns's book and the letters between the two composers, I have also amended Fred Rothwell's 1922 translation, and added some sections of the originals he left out. All other translations are my own.

1. See Michael Strasser's essay on the Société nationale de musique in this volume.
2. On 19 February 1887, d'Indy performed the Overture to the *Princesse jaune* in a transcription for two pianos, four hands, with Fauré, Messager, and Raymonde Blanc. Saint-Saëns's music was also performed at the Société nationale on 8 January 1887, 5 February 1887, 7 January 1888, 15 February 1890, 7 February 1891, and 4 February 1893 (with Marie Jaëll at the piano).

3. Jann Pasler, "Deconstructing d'Indy," in *Writing Through Music: Essays on Music, Culture, and Politics* (New York and Oxford: Oxford University Press, 2008), 101–39.

4. See Katharine Ellis's essay on Rameau in this volume.

5. See Saint-Saëns's essay, "Their Majesties," in his *Musical Memories*, trans. Edwin Gile Rich (Boston: Small, Maynard, 1919), 262–72.

6. See Sabina Ratner's essay on the *Organ* Symphony in this volume.

7. Jann Pasler, *Composing the Citizen: Music as Public Utility in Third Republic France* (Berkeley and Los Angeles: University of California Press, 2009), 501–7, 631–33. For the context of these compositions, see also my essays on Saint-Saëns and Durand and "Saint-Saëns and the Ancient World" in this volume.

8. See Stéphane Leteuré's essay on Saint-Saëns's traveling in this volume.

9. Compare Vincent d'Indy, "Du Sort de la musique religieuse en France devant les lois actuelles," preface to Charles Bordes, *La Schola Cantorum* (1905) with Camille Saint-Saëns, "Musique religieuse," in *École buissonière* (Paris: Pierre Laffite, 1913), 159–68, and "La Prononciation du latin: Discussion entre Saint-Saëns et d'Indy," *Tablettes de la Schola* (June 1912)—the latter appearing later in *École buissonière*, 177–86. On Gluck, compare d'Indy's essay in *Comœdia*, 19 January 1908, with Saint-Saëns's letter in *Comœdia*, 19 January 1908, reproduced in *Guide musical*, 26 January 1908, as discussed in Léon Vallas, *Vincent d'Indy* (Paris: Alban Michel, 1950), 2:74n1.

10. Cited in "Saint-Saëns Denies Being Germanophile," *New York Times*, 4 March 1917.

11. Georges Jean-Aubry, *Musical Times* (January 1917), cited in Stephen Studd, *Saint-Saëns: A Critical Biography* (London: Cygnus Arts, 1999), 267–68.

12. See, for example, Vincent d'Indy, "Se libérer soi-meme de la domination musicale allemande," *Courrier musical*, 27 April 1916.

13. For example, Saint-Saëns's "L'Honneur à l'Amérique" (1917), *Vers la Victoire* (1918), and "Hymne à la paix" (1919), as well as d'Indy's *Sinfonia brevis (de bello gallico)* (1916–18).

14. Jane Fulcher, *The Composer as Intellectual: Music and Ideology in France, 1914–1940* (Oxford and New York: Oxford University Press, 2005), 31.

15. Collection J.-G. d'Harcourt, reproduced in Léon Vallas, "Une Discussion Saint-Saëns et d'Indy," *Revue musicale* (February 1947): 79.

16. Saint-Saëns visited Pompeii in 1884. See also his writings on ancient lyres in Marie-Gabrielle Soret's essay on the subject in this volume.

17. With this idea, Saint-Saëns recalls symbolist aesthetics.

18. Camille Saint-Saëns , *Les Idées de M. Vincent d'Indy* (Paris: Pierre Laffitte, 1919); published in English as "The Ideas of M. Vincent d'Indy," in *Outspoken Essays on Music*, trans. Fred Rothwell (1922; repr. Freeport, NY: Books for Libraries Press, 1969).

19. Written on Schola Cantorum Director letterhead. Reproduced in *Lettres de compositeurs à Camille Saint-Saëns*, ed. Eurydice Jousse and Yves Gérard (Lyon: Symmétrie, 2009), 310–16.

20. Reproduced in Vallas, "Une Discussion Saint-Saëns et d'Indy," 84–87.

21. See also his essay that revisits these issues, "L'Anarchie musicale," in English in *Musical Memories*, 94–95.

22. Note here that Saint-Saëns uses capital letters for the musical elements and other concepts, whereas d'Indy does not.

23. The last paragraph in this selection was omitted from Rothwell's English translation.

24. Here Saint-Saëns takes particular aim at Westphal's approaches.

25. Saint-Saëns gives examples from Bach, Rameau, Scarlatti, Haydn, Beethoven, and Clementi.

26. Saint-Saëns then mentions his own use of the form in several operas.

27. See Vincent d'Indy, "Le Cas Rust," letter to *Le Temps* (April 1913), reproduced in *Guide musical*, 27 April 1913.

28. D'Indy published a few of these based on the autograph manuscripts.

PART V

SAINT-SAËNS IN THE
THE 20TH CENTURY

Saint-Saëns's Advocacy of Music Education

in Elementary School

JANN PASLER

Debussy thought musical education for the masses was a complete waste of time—"useless," he called it.

> Neither is it useful as a means of expression for an elite—often more stupid than the aforesaid masses. . . . The masses can no more be ordered to love beauty than they can be persuaded to walk around on their hands. And in passing we should remember that Berlioz really did win the approval of the masses without anyone having prepared the way.[1]

Saint-Saëns strongly disagreed. Like Gounod, he believed that everyone should have a musical education. He had worked with amateurs from the upper and lower classes, writing for and conducting their ensembles.[2] Moreover, he ardently believed in music's civilizing capacity.

When republicans won a majority in the senate and the presidency in January 1879, they had three goals: to break down class differences, to reduce the influence of the Catholic Church, and to lay the foundations for a lasting democracy by taking steps to ensure more liberty, equality, and fraternity. After the first law (6 December 1879) requiring elementary schools to include "moral and civic education," Jules Ferry, minister of public instruction and fine arts,[3] turned to pedagogical reform, inclusion of women in *écoles normales* (teacher-training schools), and construction of new schools. Inspired by study of the American public school system and intent on wresting control of education away from the religious orders, he pushed for new laws (1881, 1883) creating free, mandatory, secular public schools for children from ages six to thirteen.

As part of rethinking their curriculum, republicans also pressed for reform of basic music education in order that it contribute to the realization of republican ideals. If drawing, added to school curricula in 1877, teaches students to observe the world around them—analyze parts and the relationship of parts to a whole—and encourages them to organize their thoughts and perceptions in coherent ways, then singing, as republicans understood it, teaches rhetoric, aids memorization, leads to a taste for discipline, and instills "an instinctive feeling for order, measure, grandeur, and *beauty.*" From this, they believed, would come "love of school . . . of study."[4] Moreover, singing gives people the opportunity to tune their expression to that of others and enjoy the pleasure of reaching collective harmony. After the huge concerts at the Trocadéro during the 1878 Universal Exhibition, choral music became "the most important manifestation of a popular classical music."[5] Amateur choruses—whether bringing together fathers, uncles, sons, and neighbors in *orphéons* (a specific kind of French chorus for working-class and petit-bourgeois men, sometimes including children), or husbands, wives, and daughters in upper-class ensembles—strengthened ties to family, profession, neighborhood, region, and class, encouraging a sense of responsibility to something beyond oneself, which was needed in the nation.

In September 1880 Ferry asked Saint-Saëns for help in thinking about how to introduce the study of singing into elementary schools and *écoles normales.* The composer asked to put together a committee.[6] Seven colleagues joined him in writing reports to the minister. Saint-Saëns's essay, written on 6 November 1880 and reproduced below, established the tone and the rationale.[7] This was followed with not only supportive statements but also a range of points of view. In other words, rather than decide in advance the direction music instruction should take in the nation, the minister should hear from two representatives of the Conservatoire—Louis Bourgault-Ducoudray, music historian and himself director of an amateur chorus in the early 1870s, and Gustave Chouquet, music historian and director of its musical instrument collection; as well as the proponents of two diametrically opposed singing methods—Adolphe-Léopold Danhauser, author of a conventional solfège method, and E. Mercadier, physicist and teacher of the Galin-Paris-Chevé technique; and, to ensure that both religious and secular perspectives were considered, also the inspector of religious music in the 1870s, Charles Vervoitte, choir director at Notre Dame de Paris (1876–84), as well as two inspectors of singing in elementary schools, Danhauser and Albert Dupaigne.

Saint-Saëns began with three beliefs. First, music is an emblem of not only civilization but also the level that a culture has achieved. It demonstrates to the world the evolutionary stage a nation has reached. Second, everyone can learn music, not just those with specialized talent. It should not be associated with the privileges of a certain (aristocratic or upper-class) heritage. Third, knowledge of music can increase one's intelligence, as suggested above. The country, therefore, needed to take it seriously, get it to children early so music is not so difficult to learn, and make it accessible to all. Also, beginners needed good music to elevate their taste in order to appreciate more than "coarse" popular songs.

Several reports, including that of Saint-Saëns, bemoaned the inadequate results of thinking that "the formation and encouragement of choral societies," especially male *orphéons*, had been "enough to get everyone involved in music."[8] They agreed that making singing obligatory in elementary schools and training teachers in music should be republicans' first two priorities, with Bourgault-Ducoudray further insisting that singing begin in nursery schools. Chouquet raised a fundamental question: Should one start with theory or practice, the elements of "musical grammar" or "the education of the ear and the voice"? As he saw it, everyone had the capacity to understand basic theory, but only those with good voices could become good singers.[9] Others, pointing to how singing preceded theory in America, argued for the merits of learning music orally and by heart before turning to notation. Bourgault-Ducoudray pointed out that, when it comes to singing, recreation should play as great a role, or even greater, than pedagogy. In singing, the student needs to enjoy the process and take pleasure in it—"se faire plaisir à lui-même."[10]

The group concurred that all singing should begin with songs in unison, evolving to choral music, "for this alone can produce this warmth of soul and this spirit of cohesion that together produce the vigor and moral well-being of a country." Choosing the right singing method, however, was not obvious nor without controversy. Saint-Saëns, like many of his colleagues, preferred traditional solfège—learning notes with syllables (do, re, mi);[11] others argued for sight-singing with numbers (1 to 7) and dots, a system proposed by Rousseau in 1742 and popularized by Galin, Paris, and Chevé. Bourgault-Ducoudray saw the Galin-Paris-Chevé method as an insufficient replacement for learning musical comprehension (*le sens musical*), so why not acquire a universal musical language that would make all the great masterpieces available to students and "open their minds to infinite horizons"?[12] Verviotte and even Danhauser, who had the most to gain or lose, advocated imposing no one method on schoolteachers, but rather giving them the freedom to choose among a committee-approved list.

But what music to sing? If art was still "too often an object of luxury . . . a commodity that varied according to one's purse—an art for the poor and an art for the rich," and if "the purpose of great art is to unite the heart of a nation" *(faire l'unité dans le coeur d'une nation)*,[13] then one way schools could bring the classes together was by having their pupils sing the same repertoire. Here republican political agendas could have driven the discussion.

Since much elementary education had been controlled by the religious orders, one way to secularize schools would be to replace the study of plainchant used to prepare singing in the church, with solfège— the basics applicable to all music—especially in the teacher-training schools. Yet, unlike Saint-Saëns, Verviotte and Dupaigne both wanted to find a way for religious chant to continue to be sung in school. Verviotte noted that the only difference between it and other kinds of music was its notation in square neumes, and students could sing plainchant from transcription in traditional musical notation, used in most of the dioceses. Dupaigne, the only *rapporteur* to promote a specific aesthetic—simplicity—pointed out that plainsong embodies the essence of simplicity. As such, it is an excellent place to start.[14] Including plainsong would have been a compromise typical of officials working during the conservative, monarchist-led 1870s.

In addition to the need for age-appropriate songs, Dupaigne called for the composition of new songs. This was particularly important since, thinking that Germans knew how to teach music, those who assembled songbooks for French children often included many German songs with French texts. Dupaigne and others also saw particular "utility" in having children sing old folk tunes from the French provinces and encouraged instructors to collect them. From shared local pride might come shared national pride. Just as importantly, songs from or about the provinces would "serve to perpetuate the diversity and the variety of temperaments and characters that make up our beautiful country"—echoing Saint-Saëns's belief that music is emblematic of these.[15]

If music education was to be part of the formation of French citizens, lyrics would also need to be considered. Song texts related to subject matter taught in other classes, such as history and geography, could be sung throughout the day to reinforce other kinds of teaching. Songs about "Socrates, Galileo, Gutenberg" or "Vercingetorix, Roland, Joan of Arc," Bourgault-Ducoudray suggested, might inspire children and make them passionate about the country's past.[16]

These reports led to Minister Ferry's creation of an official commission in January 1882 that expanded membership to include Massenet, the Opéra director, an advertising specialist, and more administrators involved with elementary education. Their 200-page publication of 1884 republishes the initial reports, adds a long defense and explanation of the Galin-Paris-Chevé singing method by Amand Chevé, the minutes of their meetings beginning in November 1882, their final report, and the documents signed into law by Jules Ferry between August 1881 and July 1883.

In this 1884 document the authors dealt primarily with the problems of (1) creating *moeurs musicales*—nationwide musical practices growing out of everyone's ability able to read and write music as they read and wrote

French; (2) teaching *humanités musicales,* "the study of beautiful works, the feeling for nuance, in order to give students a taste for music and, if possible, a passion for it"; and (3) involving music in all events associated with the nation or locality so that its role and "public utility" were clear to all.[17] Regular music lessons, two to four hours per week, were seen as essential to achieving this, with singing to be taught before any theory. Piano should be preferred to harmoniums in the classroom and the organ allowed in performance venues. Wind bands, however popular they were everywhere, were not seen to be as important in the educational process as singing. Piano and strings should be encouraged over brass instruments—the former better able to instill "the taste for beautiful and good music in all genres, which is becoming a veritable social necessity given the demoralizing influence of café-concert music and the like."[18] Teachers, who would be required to take down a simple musical dictation as part of their training, were free to choose their singing method and manual. But the committee was concerned that they know masterpieces from all periods, which, in many French towns, would be helped by government support for the *concerts populaires,* orchestral concerts with many inexpensive seats.

If the Commission did not address Saint-Saëns's suggestion to create competitions to encourage new serious music for the schools, music teaching manuals nevertheless soon began to respond to the new conditions.[19] Danhauser's *Les Chants de l'école* (1881–83), in ten volumes, includes folksongs from the French regions as well as foreign countries, short simple pieces by Mozart, Beethoven, Schubert, Donizetti, and Meyerbeer, as well as music from the French past (Grétry, Lully) and present (Théodore Dubois and Henri Maréchal—both Prix de Rome winners, plus the organist Alexandre Guilmant). Like other textbooks of the time, this one tried to instill love of country and other republican values with their upbeat, joyful feelings. It became so popular that the City of Paris eventually distributed free copies to local schools. *La Première Année de musique, solfège, et chants* (1885), by the Conservatoire piano professor, Antoine Marmontel, followed. Going well beyond what Saint-Saëns had originally envisaged, Marmontel solved the problem of separate instruction in singing and solfège by including both, along with music from all periods of music history, arranged systematically according to the interval, rhythm, timbre, modulation, or technique taught. To help students understand what kind of expression was appropriate, Marmontel added explanations about the context in which the music was composed or performed. Through performance, students would come to know much of the operatic repertoire, including excerpts from new works such as Saint-Saëns's *Henri VIII* (1883). Later in *La Deuxième Année de musique, solfège, et chants* (1891), Marmontel included a music history since the Greeks, a description of musical instruments, and an analysis of musical genres. These volumes became immensely popular. Marmontel's first volume appeared in its 83rd edition in 1952, and Danhauser's solfège exercises, also published by Schirmer New York since 1891, were still going strong in the most recent edition of 1998, shaping the musical training of students and their teachers up through the present.

Report of M. Saint-Saëns
From *Rapports sur l'enseignement du chant dans les écoles primaires* (1881)

Mr. Minister:

The introduction of compulsory music study in elementary school, for which Your Excellency has taken the initiative, is a measure likely to have immense consequences in elevating the level of intelligence in our country. The development of musical culture is the clear sign of a superior civilization; one has only to grasp this truth to understand the need to work toward such a development as energetically as possible.

Until now, people thought that the formation and encouragement of choral societies was enough to get everyone involved in music. This method was certainly good, but insufficient. The reason is that choral societies, made up of adults, take men at an age already too advanced for them to profit from music study. What's more, since women are excluded from choral societies,[20] they find themselves limited to a restricted repertoire from which it is impossible for them to depart.

You, Mr. Minister, have decided that something else ought to be done. Study of the basic elements of music, which can sometimes present insurmountable difficulties to adults, is, for children, like a game. By introducing such study into elementary school, as you suggest, we will easily produce generations of young people of both sexes who, once their voices are trained, are well prepared for singing or, should their inclinations and aptitudes lead them there, for studying instruments. Sometime in the future, then, we will have at our disposal a veritable army of singers and instrumentalists, not to mention a gradual elevation of musical taste—the inevitable consequence of this state of affairs. This will lead the masses to prefer the pure and elevated enjoyment of ensemble music over the coarse songs with which they too often content themselves.

In my opinion, the study of music in elementary school should be confined to solfège for one or several voices—until the new order at least, and until experience has shined indispensable light on the question.[21] This study should begin as soon as children know how to read fluently. The Commission will have to examine which methods should be used for this teaching; the simplest will be the best. The excellent system of Batiste,[22] or perhaps even older, more basic methods, could be chosen. On this question the Commission will have a wealth of choices.

And who will give this instruction? Here a serious difficulty arises, demanding the Commission's full attention. In a country where musical instruction should be spread universally, the task should be the schoolteacher's responsibility. We should assume that a considerable number of schoolteachers are already capable of taking on this function. But an investigation should be initiated to enlighten the Commission on this point. In cities where a schoolteacher is lacking, it will always be easy to find a solfège teacher for the children. In villages this will be more difficult, sometimes impossible. Only time, as it gradually improves the situation, can resolve this challenge.

To secure the future, it is absolutely necessary to ensure that all schoolteachers are able to give solfège lessons themselves. This means replacing the study of plainsong in teacher-training schools with the study of music as a whole. For students who have already learned solfège before entering school, study should include the basic elements of harmony. We must also add to the faculty of every teacher-training school a music instructor appointed by the government or chosen through a competition whose program would be outlined by the Commission.

The Commission will study the question of incentives to be offered schoolteachers in compensation for their increased workload.

Should the study of solfège in schools give rapid positive results, as we anticipate, a competition could be instituted for the composition of choral music that would help students appreciate the practical results of their studies. Prizes given in these competitions should be of a sort to encourage even the most distinguished composers to participate.

Very sincerely yours, Mr. Minister, etc.

C. SAINT-SAËNS

6 November 1880

—*Translated by Jann Pasler*

NOTES

1. Claude Debussy, "À propos of Charles Gounod," from *Musica* (1906), in *Debussy on Music*, ed. and trans. Richard Langham Smith (London: Secker & Warburg, 1977), 224.

2. For example, Saint-Saëns conducted the amateur orchestra Société philharmonique de Paris in 1872 and performed with working-class and aristocratic choral societies on the Concert-Danbé (22 January 1874) as well as with the amateur chorus Concordia in their Bach festival (1885). He wrote works for *orphéon* competitions and other unaccompanied

male choruses, such as *Les Soldats de Gédéon*, *Les Marins de Kermor*, *Saltarelle*, *Aux Aviateurs*, *Aux Mineurs*, and *Hymne aux travailleurs*, in addition to those dedicated to such choruses in Paris and the regions. Through his friend Augé de Lassus, his music was often performed by Guillot de Sainbris's choral society of amateurs from the upper classes.

3. Ferry was minister of public instruction and fine arts from February 1879 to November 1881, again from January 1882 to August 1882, and from February to November 1883. When he was not in this position, between 1880 and 1885 Ferry served as prime minister.

4. Albert Dupaigne, "Mémoire" (1878), in Ministère de l'instruction publique et des beaux-arts, *Rapports sur l'enseignement du chant dans les écoles primaires* (Paris: Imprimerie Nationale, 1881), 68.

5. Ibid., 75.

6. Saint-Saëns discusses this in his letter no. 204 to Théodore Dubois, 21 September 1880. Rés F. 1644(2), Bibliothèque nationale de France, Musique.

7. *Enseignement du chant*, 5–6; repr. in Ministère de l'instruction publique et des beaux-arts, *Enseignement du chant: Travaux de la commission: Rapports et programmes* (Paris: Imprimerie nationale, 1884), 7–9.

8. See the document reproduced below.

9. "Rapport de M. Gustave Chouquet," 3 January 1881, in *Enseignement du chant*, 31–32.

10. "Rapport de M. Bourgault-Ducoudray," 6 November 1880, in ibid., 13, 15.

11. Solfège is not only theoretical study of the basics of music, it is also learning how to sing the notes and rhythms in various clefs, at first in unison and gradually in multiple parts.

12. "Rapport de M. Bourgault-Ducoudray," 9.

13. Ibid., 26.

14. Dupaigne, "Mémoire," 78.

15. "Rapport de M. Bourgault-Ducoudray," 28.

16. Ibid., 27.

17. Georges Guéroult, "Rapport sur le projet de programme d'études musicales dans les écoles primaires et les écoles normales d'instituteurs," in *Enseignement du chant* (1884), 147.

18. Albert Dupaigne, "Rapport presenté au nom de la sous-commission du chant," in ibid.,181.

19. For a discussion of the music manuals written for this purpose, see Jann Pasler, *Composing the Citizen: Music as Public Utility in Third Republic France* (Berkeley and Los Angeles: University of California Press, 2009), 320–23, 443–47.

20. It is not exactly accurate that women were not in choral societies. Women workers (*ouvrières*) did not have their own choral societies, but women employees at the Bon Marché department store, for example, were regular members of the store's mixed choral society. Furthermore, beginning in the late 1860s, upper-class women, whether aristocratic or bourgeoise, together with their daughters, sang in mixed choral societies such as Concordia and those directed by Bourgault-Ducoudray and Sainbris. In his "Rapport," Bourgault-Ducoudray also called for creating female *orphéons* to "introduce the same aspirations and beliefs in the two sexes" and prepare future mothers (27).

21. Saint-Saëns is most likely here referring to the new laws that would take effect after these reports.

22. See, for example, Edouard Batiste, *Petit Solfège méthodique: À la portée des plus jeunes voix* (Paris: Heugel, 1878); and *Solfèges du Conservatoire* (Paris: Heugel, 1865).

Saint-Saëns and the Future of Music

BYRON ADAMS AND JANN PASLER

Much was at stake in music when Saint-Saëns assembled his thoughts on musical evolution in an essay published in *Ménestrel* (24 June 1906). To warn his contemporaries about the risks of what he called here the limits of tolerable change and elsewhere "musical anarchy," he reflected on the nature of physical and human evolution, the idea of progress as a spiral, and the essence of art. Virtuosic in his references to a wide range of Western art, literature, and music from the Greeks to the present, he elaborated on his ideas in poetic, evocative detail. This was a subtle rather than shrill call for his contemporaries to acknowledge that they are part of human history: full of revolutions, innovations, and the excesses they had caused, only later to be reversed. The only way through this, he implied, is to understand fundamentals, the laws "whose roots plunge deep into human nature."

The playful, almost teasing, tone of Saint-Saëns's essay is evocative of the *feuilleton*, a literary genre particular to France that spread throughout the continent. Derived from the word *feuillet*, which refers to a folio or leaf of a book, the literary genre of the *feuilleton* was first popularized in Parisian newspapers in the early nineteenth century. The tone of a *feuilleton* was meant to be lightly ironic, humorous, opinionated, and subjective—but informative as well. Readers would peruse the weekly music journal *Ménestrel* over breakfast, sipping their café au lait, or sitting in the shade of the Luxembourg Gardens, waiting for a performance of Beethoven by the Garde républicaine and later Berlioz by the military band of the Eighty-ninth Infantry Regiment, as was the case for Raymond Bouyer, another *feuilleton* writer for *Ménestrel*.[1] The *feuilleton* reached its height during the fin de siècle with the essays of such luminaries as the novelist Marcel Proust.

The tone of the *feuilleton* pervaded music criticism of the time: the critiques of Colette's first husband, Henri Gauthier-Villars, who wrote under the pseudonym "Willy," and those of Claude Debussy, who styled himself

"M. Croche, Anti-Dilettante," were *feuilletons* in all but name. (In contrast, the reviews of Pierre Lalo and Saint-Saëns's former pupil Gabriel Fauré were more overtly serious in tone and intent.) In "L'Evolution musicale," Saint-Saëns demonstrated how effortlessly he had assimilated the tone of the *feuilleton*, which he uses with skill to present a complex topic rife with sophisticated ideas to a non-specialist reader. The polished clarity of this *feuilleton* is counterbalanced by the profound thoughts at its core, suggesting that Saint-Saëns would have agreed with the eighteenth-century author, the Marquis de Vauvenargues (1715–1747), who wrote, "Clarity is the counterbalance of profound thoughts."[2]

Underlying the essay is the composer's deep faith in science. In correspondence with the philosopher and race theorist Gustave LeBon, a "genius" for whom he had enormous respect, Saint-Saëns took great pleasure in communicating with someone "so logical and rational" in his thinking. He even saw himself in LeBon and "what would have been my intelligence if it had been developed." Saint-Saëns explained that, though he had been "dominated" by mystical logic in his youth, he had also come to understand "its destructive effect on rational logic." For him, "A society built on religion is destined to disappear with it." LeBon and he had both substituted "the need to believe" with "the need to know" and Saint-Saëns hoped that in the future this way of thinking would become widely embraced.[3]

The book Saint-Saëns and LeBon most discussed was the latter's *Les Opinions et les croyances: Genèse, évolution* (1911), but the philosopher also republished that year *Les Premières Civilizations* (1889), and was known for his *L'Homme et les sociétés: Leurs origines et leur histoire* (1881) and *Lois psychologiques de l'évolution des peuples* (1895), later translated as *The Psychology of Peoples* (1924).[4] Race strangely doesn't enter this correspondence, but Saint-Saëns admits to not understanding LeBon's "three types of society, irreconcilable among themselves": "I cannot accept the simultaneous existence of truths that are mutually exclusive." Is this a veiled attack on polygenism, essential to LeBon's categorization of peoples as primitive, inferior, average, and superior? If LeBon believed that the arts, the manifestation of the soul of a civilization, only change in accord with its racial dispositions, which are fixed, not alterable by education or intelligence, how did Saint-Saëns reconcile this with the monogenism embraced by most republicans, together with its related philosophy, evolution? Going to the heart of the matter, while avoiding the concept of race, Saint-Saëns focused instead on their differences over the notion of "certitude." For the composer, certitude is not "truth," but the sense that one "possesses truth."[5]

Saint-Saëns's essay on musical evolution appeared just after LeBon's *L'Évolution de la matière* (1905) and amid wide use of the concept. Others, too, used this concept to think about music. In addition to his 1906 review of Saint-Saëns's article, calling the importance the composer ascribed to science "very modern," Bouyer published essays in *Ménestrel* on the evolution of Italian music, singing, and the orchestra.[6] Saint-Saëns alludes to evolution in both its biological and historical senses. He was a keen amateur scientist who, like many French intellectuals of the time, espoused the evolutionary theories of Charles Darwin. In 1921, the elderly composer lauded Prince Albert of Monaco for creating a museum devoted to paleontology. For some, his *Carnaval des animaux* was a commentary on what people share with animals: Charles Lecocq, after attending a performance, exclaimed, "Cuvier himself would have been satisfied."[7] There was also the idea that much could be learned about human origins from music, especially that of "less advanced" people.[8] What is less clear, especially given his correspondence with LeBon, are Saint-Saëns's attitudes toward social Darwinism, a system of racial hierarchies such as those posited by François-Joseph Fétis in his *Histoire générale de la musique depuis les temps les plus anciens jusqu'à nos jours* (1869) and Joseph Deniker in his celebrated volume *Races et peuples de la terre: Éléments d'anthropologie et d'enthnographie* (1900).[9] Saint-Saëns refers to Fétis's "broad outlines of musical evolution" in his article "Musical Anarchy," but only in reference to Western music— "music, as we know it today," which began with the earliest harmony in the Middle Ages—and to say that even Fétis had not foreseen atonal music.[10] In *École buissonière*, if he proposes that "civilization marches from East to West"—from Asia, to Europe, to America, ending up in California— this hardly suggests a racial hierarchy, which would have Americans more evolved than Europeans.[11]

Saint-Saëns's understanding of "oriental" music is particularly relevant here. He was fascinated by the music of the Middle and Far East, as is reflected in such works as the Fifth Piano Concerto, op. 103, subtitled *L'Égyptien* as its second movement quotes a Nubian folk melody that he heard on a journey down the Nile; he also composed many other works inspired by these regions. Perspicaciously, Saint-Saëns recognized differences in the ways in which non-Western musical traditions developed. As Gaston Knosp put it, if "progress was forbidden to exotic music," it was both because progress implied "transgression," because it was defined as "synonymous with Europeanization, if not complete decadence."[12] As Saint-Saëns notes in his article on musical evolution, "Although slow in the Orient, especially in the Far East, artistic evolution in Europe is swift." When it came to music, Saint-Saëns believed that the development of the systems of harmony and counterpoint placed Western traditions in the vanguard of musical evolution, just as Deniker and others placed the Nordic races atop their pyramid of races. However, he viewed the very immobility he associated with oriental music as a productive critique of Western musicians preoccupied with constant change, with "the obsession for seeking the new at all cost, without aim or reason." "It's fashionable in Europe to mock oriental immobility," he writes elsewhere, but Orientals "could do the same to us, making fun of our instability; in the place of perfection, we prefer change, forgetting that all movement is not necessarily the path to something better."[13] Through holding fast to their traditions, oriental music, moreover, escaped periods of decadence, one of Saint-Saëns's deepest concerns about the music of his time and an underlying theme of his essay.

Despite the complexities in his thinking beneath the amiable veneer of this article, one can detect an unwavering belief in evolutionary determinism that led Saint-Saëns to declare, "The evolution of humanity, in all its manifestations, is inevitable, even fateful. Geniuses seem to lead the march and create revolutions, but they only succeed provided that they come at the right time." What follows does not deny this, but complicates his statement substantially: much great art is the result of crisis, innovation, and even reaction. Still, he argues, "The resistance met by any innovation in art never stops its progress; it only serves to slow it down, and sometimes that is a good thing. Without this brake, evolution would often be too rapid, and new forms that may have been too hastily abandoned would not have had time to develop and reach their full efflorescence." Saint-Saëns opines that the notion of "free will" is chimerical at best, a necessary psychological denial of cold deterministic reality that allows the artist to entertain an empowering illusion of agency: "The artist who creates is always unaware that he is part of an evolution: he relies on this ignorance. Belief in his free will, in the power of his genius, is indispensable to him."

Given these opinions, it is hardly surprising that Saint-Saëns views history, and especially music history, as a hermeneutic circle in a manner reminiscent of Hegel and other nineteenth-century German philosophers: history is posited as a series of cycles, simplicity followed by complexity with an inevitable return to simplicity after decadent implosion. But Saint-Saëns's historicism is also strikingly reminiscent of the metahistorical theories of the twentieth-century British historian, Arnold J. Toynbee, and Saint-Saëns's historicism allows for variation. Like Toynbee and Vincent d'Indy, he views history as a spiral that can never return to its point of origin. To clinch his argument, Saint-Saëns employs an astronomical analogy to expand upon the historiography of an admired author: "As Victor Hugo suggested, humanity follows the trajectory of a spiral—so does the polar Earth in space." A spiral also implies an ongoing relationship between the present and the past, something central to his aesthetics as well as those of d'Indy.

Arguably the most important past for Saint-Saëns was ancient Greece, with its classics of both music and literature from periods he considered "golden ages." He reveals his true colors as a classicist when he exults in "the literary glory of the Augustan age, with Virgil, Horace, and Lucretius," and elsewhere, in Pompeii and the lyres and citharas of Greece and Rome.[14] Admiring the ideal of Hellenic poise espoused by the Parnassian poets of his youth, Saint-Saëns also exalts Haydn, Mozart, and Beethoven as aesthetic kin of Corneille, Molière, and Racine, all of whom expressed "the beauty of language and the purity of the style—attributes of great artistic eras."

Saint-Saëns was keenly aware that, according to his own tenets, decadence was the problematic underbelly of progress and his own era was one of artistic decadence. As he reiterated, "Progress doesn't mean improvement, but progression, marching forward," which entails losses as well as gains. Like Knosp in his study of non-Western music, Saint-Saëns recognized that the arrival of Western progress—whether to the ruins of Karnak, the urban architecture of Algiers, or Indochinese music—can destroy a certain kind of beauty.[15] Progress, he felt, has not always been a positive force in the West either: "Our European civilization is marching in an anti-artistic direction" all the while thinking it is "cultivating Art."[16] Even science has not always been a positive force in the arts: photography has shown us "truth," as he and Gerôme used to point out, but "the truth of painting is not that of science."[17] Nonetheless, pointing to one of his favorite tropes, the leaning towers of Italy that "negate the fundamental laws of art: a monument, above all, should convey stability," he writes, "Decadence, in art, is not synonymous with inferiority." Like Bouyer, who points out that what was once audacious and even decadent can later become classical, such as Berlioz's *Symphonie fantastique*, Wagner's late works may be decadent, but they are still great.[18] To clarify, then, Saint-Saëns cautions that "inferiority" comes only in the final stage of decadence, "when the fruit is spoiled."

Saint-Saëns found his examples uniquely in German music—the Viennese classics to Wagner, ignoring Rameau, Berlioz, and his French contemporaries—but Ricciotto Canudo, perhaps writing in response to Saint-Saëns's article that same year, took a much closer look at the history of music from the perspective of evolution. For him, music documents how the Western soul evolved through innovations and crises, its "great conquests" indicating the "great stages of the history of mankind." Beginning with the origins of dance and singing, the birth of tragedy, then the revolt of Luther and Palestrina, he proposes a theory about three stages of musical drama. In his focus on "human passion," Monteverdi represented the "soul of the seventeenth century"; Wagner instigated a second phase, with "human thought" as "subspecies of metaphysics," and Debussy a third one, with his drama on "animist ideas." Canudo's aim is quite different from that of Saint-Saëns. Holding forth on the "French soul," both "Mediterranean and barbarian," he aspires, like Nietzsche, to "reconstitute" a certain "myth," "the glory of the 'Mediterranean race,'" the "cradle of the modern world." Like Saint-Saëns, Canudo recognized that innovators often go too far in "the necessity to repudiate" the past and thus critiqued much music along the way. However, for him, "the question of decadence" is "absurd," as the future is always contained in the past, every moment both "sums up and prepares." Defending Debussy and the advent of "musical atmosphere," the "conquest of the most vast and subtle areas of life," Bouyer deems him a "precursor" of a new art. Moreover, Canudo indirectly answers Saint-Saëns's critique of too much change in contemporary music by pointing to the "dynamic monotony" and the "search for meaningful immobility" in both Maeterlinck's tragedy and Debussy's opera, *Pelléas et Mélisande*. Canudo may agree with Saint-Saëns on the importance of melody, arguing that "the evolution of music itself is contained in the evolution of melody." But evolution, in his view, allows a place for the increasingly "supple and nuanced" melodies of Debussy in music history, "infinite melody."[19]

Such a context prepared Saint-Saëns to declare his own aesthetic credo: "Over time, only works in which beauty unites with simplicity rise to the top; those, therefore, are the most perfect." He proceeds to clarify this point by drawing on his understanding of Darwinian theory, observing, "In nature, it is not this way, and the most perfect organisms are those that stray more from simplicity; but art is not nature." In doing so, he differs from his younger contemporary, Debussy, who once stated, seemingly without irony, that Bach's music was "subject to laws of beauty inscribed in Nature herself."[20]

Saint-Saëns's interest in evolution, though different, calls to mind the ideas of other European composers of his time, such as his British contemporary Sir C. Hubert Hastings Parry, whose *The Evolution of the Art of Music* was first published in 1896 as a volume in the "International Scientific Series." Viewed as a radical during his lifetime, Parry adapted evolutionary theory, especially the ideas promulgated by the British philosopher Herbert Spencer, to the history of music. Like LeBon, Parry categorized the music of various ethnic groups according to their sophistication based on racial stereotypes.[21] Other contemporaries linked evolutionary science with aesthetics: Nikolai Rimsky-Korsakov was one of the first to realize the potential that new experiments in acoustics held for the technique of orchestration; Sir Edward Elgar was fascinated with chemistry and used chemical metaphors to describe his creative process; and Sir Charles Villiers Stanford sought to argue for the primacy of both diatonicism and "pure scales" by recourse to the harmonic series he claimed was found in nature.[22]

Unlike Ferruccio Busoni, who completed his essay "Entwurf einer neuen Aesthetik der Tonkunst" ("Sketch of a New Esthetic of Music") in 1907, a year after the publication of "Musical Evolution," Saint-Saëns was not tempted to play the role of prophet.[23] Yet he does make one prediction based on his own view of history. After "the chaotic polyphony of certain modern orchestras," he states unequivocally, "if the lessons of the past do not lie, a reaction is near"—a clarion call for neoclassicism, if you will. He further hopes that "a powerful genius will condense the chaos into a vast synthesis where the voice—that living, divine instrument—will resume the place it is owed." Saint-Saëns died before the advent of neoclassical aesthetics in music, the return to the simplicity of the past that he foresaw with such prescience. Although he would have been stunned by this ironic twist of the historical spiral, the "powerful genius" that would create a new synthesis, the aesthetic successor who came to value clarity, poise, and logic above all, would be Igor Stravinsky.

CAMILLE SAINT-SAËNS
Musical Evolution
From *Le Ménestrel*, 24 June 1906

As one advances in age, one seems to ascend to a high tower, from which increasingly vast horizons can be seen. Little by little, one becomes less interested in immediate concerns and more interested in observing the entirety of all facts, like the links of an immense chain—elements of a gradual, inevitable evolution. Whereas contemporary art still interests us, the whole of art interests us more, and we discover that in the history of art, as in that of humanity, similar causes have similar effects.

The evolution of humanity, in all its manifestations, is inevitable, even fateful. Geniuses seem to lead the march and create revolutions, but they only succeed provided that they come at the right time. Scientists—unaware of one another—often make the same discovery simultaneously. Turning to art, especially the art in question here, we see that the revolution brought on by Richard Wagner succeeded so well because it occurred at the right time. At the age of fifteen, I was incensed at seeing operas made up of uniformly molded pieces, a patchwork for which the drama served as pretext; I dreamed of operas divided no longer into *pieces*, but rather into *scenes*, with endlessly variable forms modeled on dramatic forms. At that very moment, Richard Wagner was writing *Lohengrin*.

The resistance met by any innovation in art never stops its progress; it only serves to slow it down, and sometimes that is a good thing. Without this brake, evolution would often be too rapid, and new forms that may have been too hastily abandoned would not have had time to develop and reach their full efflorescence.

The artist who creates is always unaware that he is part of an evolution: he relies on this ignorance. Belief in his free will, in the power of his genius, is indispensable to him. Moreover, he obeys an instinct stronger than his will, which he believes to be his will; the artist who lacks this instinct and who has only his will can never be a creator. Nevertheless, although he does not know it, and despite the influence of his personality, the artist is always more or less slave to a movement that carries him and leads him on, giving us those "eras," those "schools" so well known through the history of art.

Although slow in the Orient, especially in the Far East, artistic evolution in Europe is swift. One sees in architectural treatises how Romanesque art emerged from the debris of ancient art, destroyed by barbarians; this new art, influenced by Arabic art, in turn engendered the magnificent architectural and ornamental style of the thirteenth century. In the fourteenth century, ornaments became more numerous, only to reach such madness in the fifteenth that Gothic art, unable to stop itself in this race to the abyss, collapsed and gave way to the Renaissance, whose success threw us back for a long time into the arms of the Greeks and Romans. It is certain that fourteenth-century artists thought they had made advances over those of the thirteenth, and those of the fifteenth over those of the fourteenth. Although we cannot prevent ourselves from admiring the crazy wonders of the fifteenth century, now that we can see their works from a distance, we still look at the art of the thirteenth century as a type of pure style from which it would have been better not to stray.

Similarly, in antiquity, the riches of the Corinthian style never eclipsed the immortal beauty of Ictinus's radiantly simple Parthenon. And what of those leaning towers, which were once the pride of Italy? They negate the fundamental laws of art: a monument, above all, should convey stability, never sacrificing it to display a challenge overcome.

Closer to our own time, we have seen the severe styles of Louis XIII and Louis XIV styles followed by the affected art of Louis XV, which fled from the straight line as from something vulgar and detestable. It should be noted, though, that these exaggerations were invariably followed by a reaction that brought matters back to the point of departure, or rather to a neighboring point. As Victor Hugo suggested, humanity follows the trajectory of a spiral—so does polar Earth in space.

Music, too, has experienced these vicissitudes. After emerging from the trial and error of diaphonic writing, the laws of harmony and counterpoint were elucidated, and a well-organized polyphony was created, the resulting beauty dazzling its creators. Melody was abandoned to the everyday, was relegated to songs and dance tunes and scorned by church music and even the madrigal, noble secular music. For an entire century, artists cultivated ornate counterpoint, or something in an indecisive tonality approaching a sort of compromise between modality and tonality. The beauty of the writing rendered this art superior, albeit incomplete, and it is one we still admire today. In the seventeenth century people tired of the learned style; melody slipped like a mistress into the artistic world and soon reigned as despot there. Polyphony was abandoned, and was often replaced by a figured bass, indicating only harmony and meant to be realized *ad libitum* on the theorbo, harpsichord, or organ. Knowledgeable combinations, which earlier had constituted all of art, lost their importance. Polyphony then slipped under melody, resuming its place, and under the magic pen of Sebastian Bach reached such development that a new reaction was declared. Philipp Emanuel Bach, restorer of Italian tradition and unwitting founder of a new order, prepared the advent of the illustrious constellation in which Haydn, Mozart, and Beethoven are the glittering stars, a trinity occupying a place in music comparable to that held in French literature by Corneille, Molière, and Racine. The comparison is in no way comprehensive; but, on both sides, we admire the beauty of the language and the purity of style— attributes of great artistic eras. This was, in Roman antiquity, the literary glory of the Augustan Age, with Virgil, Horace, and Lucretius.

The most significant phenomenon of recent times is the emancipation of instrumental music. Born from dance music, as Richard Wagner rightly pointed out, it developed a certain need for abstraction and especially for color that seized hold of musicians, previously mostly concerned with line (melody and bass) and relief (polyphony). Impelled by Weber and especially Berlioz, the orchestra became an enchanting palette; color gradually stole all the attention, first pushing line into the background, then pattern [*modelé*] (after all, one can hardly call the chaotic polyphony of certain modern orchestras "pattern"). In the theater, the once-sovereign voice became enslaved, having compromised its sovereignty through shocking abuses of power. The consequence of this state of affairs is the negation of all the rules that had been elaborated over time, shaking the foundations of a 400-year-old musical edifice. It is a veritable state of anarchy. But one stops being shocked or even surprised when one sees the other arts and even literature going through a similar crisis. There is a general phenomenon here, no doubt due to inevitable causes. We are returning, in other forms, to stone filigree, to keystones crushing vaults instead of strengthening them, to the imbalance of leaning towers. If the lessons of the past do not lie, a reaction is near. What will it be? No one can say, but one can hope that a powerful genius will condense the chaos into a vast synthesis where the voice—that living, divine instrument—will resume the place it is owed, where line, pattern, and color will join together in perfect equilibrium, where tonalities, instead of dancing a mad, pointless round, will give one another mutual support, like pieces on a chessboard. Thus, a magnificent future is doubtless reserved for music, the modern art par excellence, the phoenix that never dies.

Happy are the artists born in a period of calm, when the laws of art seem immutable and are not questioned! Mozart had this good fortune. He found beneath his pen a completely formed style, spawned by the union of the Italian and German schools, a style that suited everything, symphonies as well as operas, tragedy and the most farcical comedies, the church as well as the theater, where a system reigned whose apparent despotism offered the musician immense resources and endless variety.

With Beethoven, music spread its broad wings, only to encounter the fate of Icarus: neither the symphony nor the sonata could maintain the height to which Beethoven's momentum had carried them. They flew too close to the sun and their wings were burned.

Extraordinary good luck befell Richard Wagner, who single-handedly effected an entire evolution and ended up surpassing even himself: his final works, like those of Beethoven, can be regarded as works of decadence, provided this word is given its true meaning. Decadence, in art, is not synonymous with inferiority. The woman who has lost her virginity, the first flower of her youth, or the fruit that has just surpassed perfect ripeness: are they less flavorful? Are they not often even more desirable? So it is with art, to which certain imperfections sometimes give a higher value.

Inferiority comes later, when the fruit is spoiled, when the woman grows old. Still there will always be those who love old women and mushy pears, and that is how the most degenerate forms of art find admirers. But these forms deprived of life cannot have a long existence. Over time, only the works in which beauty unites with simplicity rise to the top: those, therefore, are the most perfect.

In nature, it is not this way, and the most perfect organisms are those that stray more from simplicity; but art is not nature. Great minds have been mistaken about this. Victor Hugo, in one of his prefaces, puts order in a jungle and disorder in the classical gardens of Le Nôtre. Although it is true, he adds, that one encounters in the jungle fearsome and dangerous animals, "we would choose the crocodile over the toad." Here he puts his finger on the weak point in his own theory: there is no one who would not rather encounter the ugly but innocent toad than a crocodile or a panther.

No, art is not nature. And even if art were forced to draw upon nature as a matter of life or death, it would likely remain nature's antithesis. This is why art has its own laws whose roots plunge deep into human nature, into the obscure aesthetic sense, the sign and glory of our species. These laws can be broken, but not for long.

—Translated by Jann Pasler and Alice Teyssier

NOTES

1. Raymond Bouyer, "Petites notes sans portée: CIX: L'Évolution musicale et le grand art en plein air," *Ménestrel*, 8 July 1906, 209. This essay was dedicated to Saint-Saëns, philosopher of "Musical Evolution."

2. "La clarté orne les pensées profondes." Luc de Chapiers, Marquis de Vauvenargues, *Œuvres de Vauvenargues*, ed. D.-L. Gilbert (Paris: Furne, 1857), 374. Translation by Byron Adams.

3. Saint-Saëns's letters to Gustave LeBon that discuss belief and religion are from Monte Carlo, 22 March 1908 and 11 August 1911, Bibliothèque nationale de France (BnF), Manuscripts. The correspondence here begins on 14 March 1908.

4. LeBon, sent on an archaeological mission by France's ministère de l'instruction publique, had also written on Arab civilization (1884) and on Indian civilization (1887).

5. Saint-Saëns's letters to Gustave LeBon debating the meaning of the word "incertitude" are Paris, 10 May 1913; Algiers, 20 November 1913; Blida, 16 December 1913; and Paris, 7 March 1914, BnF, Manuscripts.

6. Raymond Bouyer was clearly fascinated by this topic, publishing numerous essays in his "Petites Notes sans portée" in *Ménestrel*, such as on the evolution of Italian influences on music (15, 29 November 1903); the evolution or decadence of singing (5 January 1907), a concern he also shared with Saint-Saëns; and the evolution of the orchestra (15 February and 7 March 1908). Others, too, used the concept in their analysis of music, including Albert Bertelin on the evolution of contemporary music (*Courrier musical*, 15 October 1912).

7. Camille Saint-Saëns, letters to Prince Albert of Monaco, 3 January 1921, and to Charles Lecocq, 1887, *Revue musicale*, 1 August 1924, 123–24, both quoted in Stéphane Leteuré, "Les Incursions musicales du compositeur Camille Saint-Saëns dans l'évolutionnisme," *Bulletin et mémoires de la Société d'anthropologie de Paris* (February 2011): 2–3.

8. "Music is as old as humanity. But which music? Savages can give us an idea." This idea opens Saint-Saëns's "L'Anarchie musicale," in *École buissonnière* (Paris: Lafitte, 1913), 121.

9. See also Jann Pasler, "Theorizing Race in Nineteenth-century France: Music as Emblem of Identity," *Musical Quarterly* 89/4 (Winter 2006): 459–504.

10. Saint-Saëns, "L'Anarchie musicale," 121–24.

11. Saint-Saëns, "Le Chevalier vert," in *École buissonnière*, 127.

12. Gaston Knosp "La Musique indo-chinoise," *Mercure musical*, 15 September 1907, 928.

13. Saint-Saëns, "L'Art decorative," in *École buissonnière*, 143; see also "Le Mouvement musical," *Revue de l'art ancien et moderne*, 12 November 1897, and also in *Portraits et souvenirs* (Paris: Société d'édition artistique, 1899).

14. See Marie-Gabrielle Soret's essay on the lyres and citharas in this volume.

15. Knosp, "La Musique indo-chinoise," 928; Saint-Saëns, "Egypte" and "Algérie," in *École buissonière*, 85, 90–91.

16. Saint-Saëns, "Egypte," 82.

17. Saint-Saëns, "Maïa," in *École buissonière*, 343.

18. Bouyer, "L'Évolution musicale," 209.

19. Ricciotto Canudo, *Le Livre de l'évolution: L'Homme: Psychologie musicale des civilisations* (Paris: Sansot, 1908), 8–9, 168, 289–96, 306. The preface is signed, "Paris, 1906."

20. Claude Debussy, *Debussy on Music: The Critical Writings of the Great French Composer*, ed. François Lesure and trans. Richard Langham Smith (Ithaca, NY: Cornell University Press, 1977), 84.

21. C. Hubert H. Parry, *The Evolution of the Art of Music*, 4th ed. (London: Kegan Paul, 1905), 60–61, 74.

22. Rimsky-Korsakov's readings in acoustics can be found in the preface to his *Principles of Orchestration* (1922; repr. Mineola, NY: Dover, 1964), vii. For Elgar's chemical experiments, see Jerrold Northrop Moore, *Edward Elgar: A Creative Life* (Oxford: Clarendon Press, 1984), 544. Stanford's obsession with the overtone series can be found in his *Musical Composition: A Short Treatise for Students* (London: Macmillan, 1911), 13 passim.

23. Ferruccio Busoni, *Sketch of a New Aesthetic of Music*, trans. Theodore Baker (New York: G. Schirmer, 1911).

The Fox in the Henhouse, or

Saint-Saëns at the SMI

MICHEL DUCHESNEAU

When the Société musicale indépendante (SMI) was founded in April 1910, the first concerts were probably among the most important of the 1909–10 Paris musical season. After almost a year of heated debate in music journals, the new organization symbolized a power move in the concert world by a group of young musicians defying previous generations associated with the Société nationale de musique (SN).[1] Their first season was short but intense, and the programming gives some very interesting examples of the musical diversity its founders aimed to provide. That diversity attests not only to their aesthetic orientations and artistic heritage but also to the constraints inherent in the music world of the time. Significantly, the second program of the SMI featured a Prelude and Fugue by Camille Saint-Saëns, not exactly known for supporting young avant-garde musicians.[2]

The founding committee of the SMI, whose principal members were Maurice Ravel, Florent Schmitt, Émile Vuillermoz, Alfredo Casella, and Charles Koechlin, had firmly resolved to demonstrate the open-mindedness of the new society. Their objective was to allow performance of pre-classical works (*œuvres anciennes*), considered the pillars of music, alongside modern works that might enable both audience and musicians to broaden their musical horizons. One concert in particular, on 4 May 1910 at the Salle Gaveau (see Figure 1), drew attention to these concerns, although old works (Henry Purcell and John Bull, played by Wanda Landowska on the harpsichord) and modern works (principally by Manuel de Falla and Charles Koechlin) were scattered throughout a series of lesser works (Maurice Le Boucher, Joseph Bonnet, Raoul Bardac, Marguerite Debrie), or at least so they seem from our perspective. Regardless, the society's open-mindedness signified as well an open attitude toward less well-known composers, often students or friends of SMI members. Seeking to build links between the masters of the past and present while promoting the interests of young musicians, both French and foreign, the society aimed to play the role of incubator for young musicians. This meant that the programming committee of the SMI, like that of the SN, would accept some works for which this might be the only performance. As such, the concerts were wildly eclectic, with music by quite famous composers often played alongside that of beginners or amateurs.

From the very first concerts, the committee tried to create a balance while carving out its position in the field of French music. Two important works by Fauré and Debussy were played on the first program: Fauré's "La Chanson d'Ève" and Debussy's *D'un Cahier d'esquisses*, thereby affirming a close relationship between the two masters. Saint-Saëns, Fauré's teacher at the École Niedermeyer, appeared on the second program. Fauré, consulted by his former students when the society was founded, possibly made this suggestion.[3] But why, when Saint-Saëns was shamelessly lambasting the founders of the SMI? As Koechlin takes pleasure in recalling many years later: "[Saint-Saëns] bluntly dismissed us (Ravel, Schmitt, and all of us on the committee of the SMI), when he told our president, Fauré, 'I hope you're going to let go of that band of Apaches.'"[4] An answer may be found through an analysis of SMI's second concert, which included Saint-Saëns's music.

We do not have enough information to be sure which of Saint-Saëns's preludes and fugues were performed in this concert. In 1910 the composer had already published two series of preludes and fugues: Opus 99 (1894) and Opus 109 (1898). The program notes indicate that this one was unpublished. However, there were many errors in SMI's programs at the time. Nevertheless, let us risk a hypothesis. Joseph Bonnet, who was playing three of his own organ pieces (*Dédicace*, *Matin provençal*, *Clair de lune*), performed the Saint-Saëns compositions. Bonnet, a pupil of Alexandre Guilmant, to whom Saint-Saëns dedicated the second Preludes and Fugues, op. 99, was not associated with one faction or another. He had studied at the Conservatoire, where he was named organist of the Société des Concerts du Conservatoire and, despite competition between the two schools, was published by Édition Mutuelle of the Schola Cantorum.[5] Possibly through his teacher Guilmant, Bonnet had in his possession the *Praeludium et Fuga* in C (dating from 1870), which seems not to have been performed publicly at that time. This work may be the one played at the SMI, unless it was one of the preludes from Opus 99 or Opus 109, which few people knew. Whichever the case, Joseph Bonnet's presence at the SMI concert as both composer and performer is not insignificant, as it demonstrates a clear link between independent composers and Scholists as well as among musicians who were less involved in the musical quar-

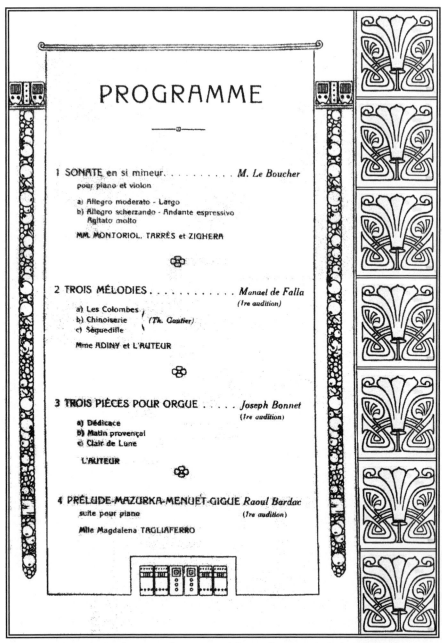

Figure 1. Program of the second concert of the Société musicale indépendante at the Salle Gaveau, on 4 May 1910.

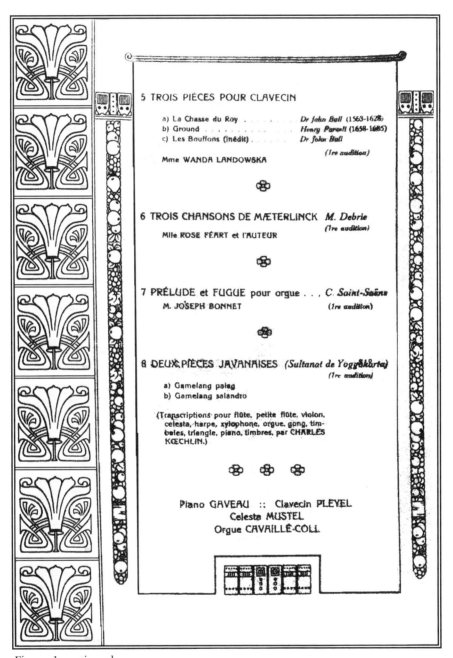

5 TROIS PIÈCES POUR CLAVECIN

    a) La Chasse du Roy . . . . Dr John Bull (1563-1628)
    b) Ground . . . . Henry Purcell (1658-1685)
    c) Les Bouffons (Inédit) . . . . . . Dr John Bull

                                 (1re audition)

Mme WANDA LANDOWSKA

6 TROIS CHANSONS DE MÆTERLINCK *M. Debrie*
                                      (1re audition)

Mlle ROSE FÉART et l'AUTEUR

7 PRÉLUDE et FUGUE pour orgue . . . *C. Saint-Saëns*

M. JOSEPH BONNET   *(1re audition)*

8 DEUX PIÈCES JAVANAISES *(Sultanat de Yogyakarta)*
                                    (1re audition)

    a) Gamelang palag
    b) Gamelang salandro

(Transcriptions pour flûte, petite flûte, violon,
  celesta, harpe, xylophone, orgue, gong, tim-
  bales, triangle, piano, timbres, par CHARLES
  KŒCHLIN.)

Piano GAVEAU :: Clavecin PLEYEL
Celesta MUSTEL
Orgue CAVAILLÉ-COLL

Figure 1 continued

rels of the time. For though the SMI was founded in opposition to the SN (considered after 1900 to be the stronghold of the Schola Cantorum), it is difficult to allocate clear allegiances to one or the other: a high number of musicians defected. The organizing committees drew from the same pool of musicians, and the SMI committee probably considered it important to show openness by including the works of Scholists or close friends of the school. Accusing the older society's committee members of resistance to new musical tendencies, Ravel left the SN. To program works by Bonnet and Saint-Saëns is unquestionably an example of the SMI's eclecticism and open-mindedness.

Thus a number of factors coalesced to inspire the SMI committee to include Saint-Saëns on this program: the desire to feature the names of great composers, stylistic and aesthetic open-mindedness, probable encouragement from Fauré, and possibly a proposal by Bonnet. But could it also be an ironic nod from committee members toward those who thought that the new generation of musicians were "returning to the savage beginnings of music"?[6] This is not impossible. There may also have been some deceitfulness on the part of the committee, wanting to prove that to revitalize the programs of Paris concerts, it was necessary to make room for modern rules of composition. Is this what they meant by juxtaposing a second-rate work of a master with a new work bursting with modernity and exoticism by a composer from the new generation? As Koechlin remarks in another context, the committee may have wanted to show "that certain works [by Saint-Saëns] are academic, even boring, having only on their side logical construction and impeccable technique."[7] Such comments were essentially those SMI members made in criticizing the Scholists: architectural mastery and solid writing technique are not enough to sustain a work of art, which necessitates inspiration and sensitivity.[8] What could provide a more vibrant demonstration of this than to have a Prelude and Fugue by Saint-Saëns on the same program as Koechlin's *Pièces javanaises*, whose "Temples," the first of his *Études antiques* for orchestra, had already been refused by the SN's committee in 1909?[9]

But the game of comparisons does not end there. The *Pièces javanaises*— "Gamelang Palag (Sultanat de Yogyakarta)" and "Gamelang Salandro (Sultanat de Yogyakarta)"—are the first two pieces of a *Suite javanaise* (op. 44 bis), the third one never completed. In fact, they were transcriptions of music assembled by Louis Laloy, musicologist and collaborator for the *Revue musicale SIM*.[10] It was in this magazine that the suite's second piece would be published in October 1910. Saint-Saëns, an indefatigable globe-trotter, had the reputation of being an Orientalist and was interested in Balinese music, though he had never visited Indonesia. But Saint-Saëns's Orientalism is not the same as that applied to works that received so much opposition from the SN—works that draw more directly from music heard at the *expositions universelles* or from early research of music ethnographers or the travels of musicians like Delage.[11] It is less about drawing on and adapting a melody, a rhythm, or a timbre to give a touch of exoticism to a work than trying to reconstitute a work and its sound in its entirety. To put side by side a work that symbolizes one of the most evolved forms of the Western musical language—the fugue—and one that adopts a structure completely foreign to Western music is not merely an act of rebellion. It is a demonstration of the importance of different musical approaches.

The relationship between Saint-Saëns and SMI musicians is, therefore, full of nuance. Let us recall that even if Ravel was ambivalent about Saint-Saëns's work, he admired the master's technique, particularly the formal construction of his works.[12] He also appreciated the composer's sense of melody. This is what led Ravel to declare in 1931 that his own concertos were written "in the spirit of Mozart and Saint-Saëns."[13] But he also could not restrain himself from placing a limit on Saint-Saëns's impact by declaring that "what Mozart wrote for the ear's pleasure is perfect, in my opinion, and even Saint-Saëns managed to do the same, although at a much lower level."[14]

As far as Florent Schmitt is concerned, the relationship was one of respect. In his memoirs, Schmitt acknowledges Saint-Saëns as one of those who supported him for the Prix de Rome in 1900: "And if finally I wasn't deserted, it was thanks to Gabriel Fauré, my dearly missed late teacher, who, though no longer at the Institut, was able to obtain for me among the sculptors and painters enough votes to counterbalance the animosity of the musicians. For apart from Massenet, Reyer, and Saint-Saëns, the musicians had it in for me."[15] A letter from Saint-Saëns to Schmitt confirms the former's support: "Thank you, dear friend, for the confidence you have shown in me; but permit me to tell you that from what I have seen of your work, . . . you have the necessary foundations and are at the point where you should only listen to yourself and the experience that time brings. Finish the instrumentation as you began it and all will be well." In a November 1900 letter, Saint-Saëns wrote to him, "I know of nothing more delightful than to watch young birds take flight toward the sun.[. . .] For you personally, my cordial friendship."[16] If we believe Koechlin's comments, Saint-Saëns must have changed his mind about Schmitt's music when he presented his Psaume XLVII from Rome in 1904 because Massenet had to support it in the face of Saint-Saëns's opposition.[17]

Koechlin never ceased to defend Saint-Saëns's work, particularly his operas (*Samson et Dalila*, *Ascanio*, *Proserpine*) and his symphonic poems (*La*

Lyre et la harpe, Le Rouet d'Omphale), but he drew a clear distinction between the musician's work and his opinions:

> It may be worthwhile to mention that when he was young, he worked at the front lines and did much for the evolution of French music, especially for the symphony. The classes he gave at the École Niedermeyer were some of the best and most useful, for he revealed J. S. Bach to his disciples; he was also one of the first to understand what our art stood to gain from reviving the admirable modes of early music.[. . .] If we cannot affirm that Saint-Saëns, as some have believed, is the best of modern French musicians, he is still a major figure in our history: a craftsman of the highest order, with an accomplished technique; an upright artist whose moral physiognomy, seriousness, and honesty should be presented as a model for many others.[18]

Koechlin's judgment becomes even more nuanced when he attempts to situate Saint-Saëns in the context of his contemporaries and advancement of the musical language. Although Koechlin cannot resist pointing out a certain "narrowness of mind," he is careful to explain the different positions adopted by Saint-Saëns with regard to Wagner and Debussy. He goes so far as to establish an interesting parallel between the classicism of Saint-Saëns and that of Stravinsky:

> At one time, when he was writing *Harmonie et mélodie* (a really wonderful book that should be reread!) he decidedly supported Wagner, going so far as to allow certain atonalities (Mime's terror in the first act of *Siegfried*). But *Harmonie et mélodie* dates from the happy period in Saint-Saëns's youth, when he *strode boldly toward the future*. Back then he was predicting (without indignity) the use of quarter tones! As for Wagner, he soon abandoned him: "There are," he wrote, "some works that we fall in love with at first and we allow them every indulgence. But later we get over them." And if, at Béziers (but this was before *Pelléas*) he seemed to accept Debussy (on the condition "that we don't play *only* his music"), his attitude shortly turned *nasty*, and distressingly unfair. For Ravel as well.[. . .] Only the *young*, thus attacked, got their revenge. Cruelly. Except for Ravel, they agreed that Saint-Saëns was an unimportant *epigone*. However, their opinion should be understood with caution. In some ways, their enemy was not so different from the most recent Stravinsky (about which I will say more); the attitude of these young people does not impress me in the least. . . . Today other musicians go even further. For

Stravinsky, music "can express nothing." So here we are surprised and somewhat glad to see Camille Saint-Saëns as a sort of precursor to Stravinsky in his search for the *abstract* perfection of Form. But why then should a Form be perfect, except to realize better than anything else this *something that must be said*.[19]

After the 1910 concert at the SMI, Saint-Saëns continued to vigorously resist the syntactical advances of the musical avant-garde. In "L'Anarchie musicale" (1913), a chapter of *L'École buissonnière*, Saint-Saëns writes that the atonal system

> is not a question of adding new rules to the existent rules, which took form naturally through time and experience, but of eliminating all rules and constraints. Everyone must make his own rules. Music is free, has found endless liberty; there are no perfect chords, no dissonant chords, no off-key [*faux*] chords; any aggregation of notes is legitimate. That's called—believe it or not—the development of taste [*sensibilité*]. In this case, a developed *sensibilité* does not refer to the person who, in sipping a great wine, can tell you the vintage and the year: it refers to one who indifferently drinks down a great wine, a cheap wine, cognac, and whiskey, preferring the one that most scratches his gullet on the way down.[20]

For Saint-Saëns, Ravel and his associates were without a doubt these drinkers of plonk and whiskey. Koechlin tackled this question when, in 1915, presenting a series of conferences on French music, he held forth at length on Saint-Saëns's criticisms of young musicians.[21] Saint-Saëns's reflections attest to the generational conflict that existed between Saint-Saëns and Ravel's contemporaries, more perhaps than a simple aesthetic difference since, as Koechlin pertinently remarks, Saint-Saëns, like the younger musicians, wished above all to be free.

In 1910, this did not prevent the SMI programming committee from making some strategic calculations and electing not to reject Saint-Saëns. As Koechlin noted years later, "In spite of Saint-Saëns's narrow-mindedness in his later years, [we must remember] the sympathy he had in his youth for all kinds of new music."[22] Probably referring to Saint-Saëns's activities in the 1870s with the newly founded SN, Koechlin pointed out that the elderly master had once been an avant-garde musician. And some of his works, like his first trio, "are charming."[23] In 1912 this trio would be, then, the second work by Saint-Saëns played at the SMI.[24]

Besides Fauré's probable urging, what probably convinced the SMI to program a work by Saint-Saëns on the second SMI concert can thus be summarized in two ways. On the one hand, Joseph Bonnet's participation gave the planning committee an unexpected chance to program Saint-Saëns as he deserved, given his place in the music world. The presence of the organ and Bonnet's proposal were well timed, even more so given that the work was of secondary importance, and contrasted strongly with Koechlin's *Pièces javanaises*. This juxtaposition underlined the intense aural gap between the two works, marking the borders between tradition and musical modernity, as conceived by the musicians around Ravel. On the other hand, to solidify the reputation of the SMI, the committee could not afford to pass over works by such well-known musicians. They thus scheduled Debussy and Fauré for the first concert, and Saint-Saëns for the second. The French tradition was thereby inscribed in the genes of the SMI. Committee members were aware of the value of certain Saint-Saëns works, but also of what he represented, symbolically, in the eyes of the public and other French musicians. Given Koechlin's intellectual steadfastness, his views of 1939 are likely to be the same as those he and his colleagues shared in 1910: it was impossible to exclude Saint-Saëns's music from the SMI concerts because he had helped create a French musical tradition that generations to come would build on.

—Translated by Lauren Elkin and Jann Pasler

NOTES

1. For more details, see Michel Duchesneau, *L'Avant-garde musicale et ses sociétés à Paris de 1870 à 1939* (Sprimont, Belgium: Mardaga, 1997), 65–122.
2. This would not be the only work by Saint-Saëns performed at the SMI. On 27 January 1912, his Trio no. 1, op. 18, was performed at the Salle Gaveau.
3. Koechlin wrote of Saint-Saëns in 1939: "I wouldn't say he was the *greatest* of French musicians. Such, nevertheless, was the opinion of Fauré, who was always faithful to him." Charles Koechlin, "Camille Saint-Saëns," radio presentation (Paris-Mondial), written 10–12 December 1939 and read 9 January 1940. Unpublished text, Archives Charles Koechlin, Médiathèque Musicale Mahler, Paris.
4. Charles Koechlin, "À propos de Camille Saint-Saëns," *La Pensée*, 24, May–June 1949, 31. Note that Apaches was also the name this group used for themselves. See Jann Pasler, "A Sociology of the Apaches: Sacred Battalion for Pelléas," in *Berlioz and Debussy: Sources, Contexts and Legacies*, ed. Barbara Kelly and Kerry Murphy (London: Ashgate, 2007), 148–66.
5. His Opus 2, an *Ave Maria* for voice and organ, was published in 1908 by Édition Mutuelle, founded in 1902 to publish Scholist composers by the secretary of the Schola Cantorum, René de Castera.
6. Camille Saint-Saëns, "L'Illusion wagnérienne," in *Portraits et souvenirs* (Paris: Société d'Édition artistique, 1899), 219.
7. Koechlin, "Camille Saint-Saëns."

8. In his script for Paris-Mondial radio, Koechlin writes: "[Saint-Saëns] did not deny the importance of sensitivity, but he judged it to be secondary; perhaps it even seemed to him, on occasion, unnecessary."

9. The SN also refused on this occasion Maurice Delage's *Conté par la mer*, another work that makes reference to an even more radical Orientalism.

10. *Revue musicale SIM*. See Robert Orledge, *Charles Koechlin (1867–1950): His Life and Works* (Chur, Switzerland, and New York: Harwood Academic Publishers, 1989), 345.

11. See Jann Pasler, "Reinterpreting Indian Music: Maurice Delage and Albert Roussel," in *Music-Cultures in Contact, Convergences and Collisions*, ed. Margaret Kartomi and Stephen Blum (Sydney: Currency Press, 1994), 122–57; and Pasler, "Race, Orientalism, and Distinction in the Wake of the Yellow Peril," in *Western Music and Its Others: Difference, Representation, and Appropriation in Music*, ed. Georgina Born and David Hesmondhalgh (Berkeley: University of California Press, 2000), 86–118.

12. For the connection between Ravel and Saint-Saëns, see Maurice Ravel, *Lettres, écrits et entretiens*, ed. and annotated by Arbie Orenstein (Paris: Flammarion, 1989), 35. Koechlin confirmed the importance of Saint-Saëns for Ravel in these terms: "For it is in Saint-Saëns's work that Ravel found the best lessons in orchestral balance and symphonic duration; it is also in Saint-Saëns that Ravel discovered the sovereign logic thanks to which, in one year of work, he endowed our French musical tradition with the astonishing and inimitable 'Bacchanale' in *Daphnis et Chloé*." Koechlin, "À propos de Camille Saint-Saëns," 31.

13. "Monsieur Ravel parle de son œuvre," *Daily Telegraph*, 11 July 1931, cited in Koechlin, "À propos de Camille Saint-Saëns," 364. See also Michael J. Puri's essay in this volume.

14. "Une visite chez Maurice Ravel," *De Telegraaf*, 31 March 1931, cited in ibid., 361.

15. Florent Schmitt, "Autour de Rome," in *Cinquante Ans de musique française (1874–1925)*, ed. Louis Rohozinski (Paris: Éditions musicales de la Librairie de France, 1925), 2:401.

16. Camille Saint-Saëns to Florent Schmitt, 17 July 1900, Bibliothèque nationale de France, l.a.154, and 30 November 1900, l.a.155. I would like to thank Jann Pasler for having been kind enough to provide for me these two documents.

17. Charles Koechlin, "Considérations générales sur la musique moderne et sur l'école française," in *Esthétique et langage musical*, ed. and ann. by Michel Duchesneau (Sprimont, Belgium: Mardaga, 2006), 41.

18. Koechlin, "Camille Saint-Saëns."

19. Koechlin, "À propos de Camille Saint-Saëns," 29.

20. Camille Saint-Saëns, *L'École buissonnière* (Paris: P. Lafitte, 1913), 124.

21. In his talks on the First World War, Koechlin mentions several times the severe judgments of Saint-Saëns. See Koechlin, "Considérations générales," 41–47.

22. Koechlin, "Camille Saint-Saëns."

23. Koechlin, "Considérations générales," 43.

24. As mentioned above, this Trio—no. 1, op. 18—was performed at the Salle Gaveau on 27 January. The performers were Albert Geloso (violin), Jules Tergis (viola), and Léon Moreau (piano). On 28 January 1915, the SMI programmed his Scherzo op. 87 and *Marche militaire* (a transcription of "Marche militaire française" from the *Suite algérienne* op. 60) for two pianos.

Saint-Saëns, Ravel, and Their Piano

Concertos: Sounding Out a Legacy

MICHAEL J. PURI

Along with Gabriel Fauré, Maurice Ravel (1875–1937) would be a top can-didate on anyone's list of major composers to have extended Saint-Saëns's musical legacy into the twentieth century. To be sure, significant differ-ences separate the one from the other: Saint-Saëns was Ravel's senior by forty years, composed far more music, wrote in a greater variety of gen-res, and generally preferred a more conservative approach to harmony. Both were republicans, but Saint-Saëns supported an initiative during World War One that Ravel refused to sign—the effort by the National League for the Defense of French Music to ban from French soil the per-formance of contemporary Austro-German works that had not yet fallen into the public domain. Yet Saint-Saëns is an indispensable point of ref-erence for Ravel's life and music. As the student of Gabriel Fauré, a lifelong friend and student of Saint-Saëns, Ravel was the latter's direct artistic descendant. He also learned a lot about form and orchestration from studying Saint-Saëns's music, praised the composer for his achieve-ments in these two areas, held many of his pieces in his personal library, and later recommended to his own students, such as Maurice Delage, that they also study his music. Further, Ravel explicitly acknowledged a debt to Saint-Saëns in the composition of his Trio and his two concertos. More generally, both composers embraced exoticism (of a Spanish variety in Saint-Saëns's *La Jota aragonese*, op. 64, and Ravel's *Rapsodie espagnole*, and of a more Eastern strain in Saint-Saëns's *Suite algérienne*, op. 60, and Ravel's *Shéhérazade*), revived the Baroque (as in Saint-Saëns's Suite, op. 90, and Ravel's *Le Tombeau de Couperin*), and engaged in pastiche (as in Saint-Saëns's *Le Carnaval des animaux* and Ravel's *Valses nobles et sentimentales*). In light of these numerous points of intersection and affinity between the two composers, it is only natural that they have been frequently evaluated in similar terms as impeccable stylists whose adherence to tonality and form express, in the midst of other alternatives during the late nineteenth and early twentieth centuries, their unshakable devotion to tradition.

The most promising genre in which to explore the relation between the respective musics of Saint-Saëns and Ravel is the piano concerto. One justification for this choice is Ravel's study of Saint-Saëns's piano concertos in preparation for the 1929–31 simultaneous creation of both the *Concerto pour la main gauche* and the *Concerto pour piano et orchestre*.[1] (We will henceforth refer to these concertos as the Left-hand Concerto and the G-major Concerto, respectively). Another is the commentary Ravel provided for his concertos, in which he mentions the importance of Saint-Saëns's music for his own, which is treated in detail below. A third is more historical and takes into account that in creating these concertos Ravel did not simply add two more to the French repertoire but significantly helped to revive the genre after it had fallen into neglect shortly after the turn of the twentieth century due to its perceived obsolescence as a nineteenth-century artifact.[2] Before we delve into Ravel's concertos we must first analyze those of Saint-Saëns to determine which of their aspects might have been attractive to a fellow composer and connoisseur of form.

Saint-Saëns's Piano Concertos

The piano concertos by Saint-Saëns are generally understood to be his most accomplished writing for piano.[3] Nevertheless, for some twentieth-century critics who were invested in the international reputation of French classical music these accomplishments were too limited to deserve the fame they received. In a 1930 essay on the piano music of Saint-Saëns Alfred Cortot avers that he does not wish to "insinuate that the success of Saint-Saëns's concertos abroad has done a disservice to the cause of French artists," but nonetheless goes on to argue that it kept focus away from "more penetrating or daring expressions" of the French musical imagination and has fostered the perception of French music as being merely "piquant."[4] Norman Demuth puts an even sharper point on the same argument, contending that the worldwide success of Saint-Saëns's piano concertos "did untold harm to French music in foreign ears, for . . . the spirit of the music was taken as representing the genuine French aestheticism, and French music earned the reputation of being frivolous and frothy, light and ephemeral."[5] Both authors may be correct about the reception of these concertos, but they fail to fulfill their scholarly duty to the extent that they let these superficial generalizations stand, instead of investigating and even challenging them. Consideration of the musical detail in these pieces actually reveals a wealth of compositional techniques that lend subtle complexity to apparently clear and simple forms. From this array of techniques I have chosen a representative three, whose terminology and procedures I explain in due course and whose potential importance to Saint-Saëns's legacy will also be revealed in the subsequent section on Ravel: ambiguation, double negation, and parody. In order to facilitate comparison among the musical examples I focus mainly, but not exclusively, on first-movement sonata forms.

"Ambiguation," a word I have formed on the model of "disambiguation" (the elimination of ambiguity), refers here to the indeterminacy of formal identity, whether as the result of underdetermination (no clear options) or overdetermination (too many options). Several good examples of this technique appear in the first movement of the Second Piano Concerto, op. 22. Most sections of this sonata-form movement are easy to identify, as shown in Table 1: an introduction by the solo piano (I), a primary area articulated by two closely related themes (P1, P2), an agitated transition (Tr), a secondary area with a single theme (S), the recapitulation of the primary area, transition, and introduction, and a short coda that repeats the first primary theme. At first, the framing of the movement on both ends by a substantial introduction and a coda, the gesture toward a monothematicism linking S to P, and the rough equivalence in length between the exposition and recapitulation all seem to contribute to a symmetrical sonata-form design. However, interspersed among these recognizable and symmetrical elements are three sections with a more ambiguous identity that are marked by the letters X, Y, and Z and whose opening measures are reproduced in Examples 1, 2, and 3, respectively.

Table 1. Form of the First Movement of
Saint-Saëns's Piano Concerto no. 2.

SECTION	I	P1	P2	Tr	S	Z	P2	Tr	X	Tr	Y	S'(P2')	I	P1-based Coda
STARTS AT MEASURE	1	4	11	16	29	41	61	65	70	75	89	94	99	112

X is a cadenza for solo piano that halts the progression of the sonata form in order to dwell on a motive from P2 and prolong a dissonant harmony (a diminished seventh chord). Although X ultimately yields to the transition, nevertheless for its duration we do not know whether the sonata form will continue or whether X will preempt it by returning to the fantasy for solo piano that began the movement. Y further unsettles the recapitulation by combining four elements with different formal associations: a dominant bass apparently belonging to the cadence that ends the

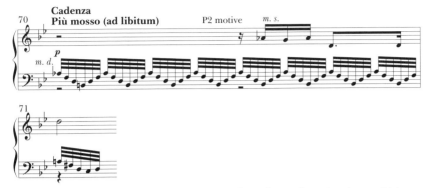

Example 1. X, mm. 70–71, the beginning of a cadenza for solo piano within the recapitulation of the first movement of Saint-Saëns's Second Piano Concerto, op. 22.

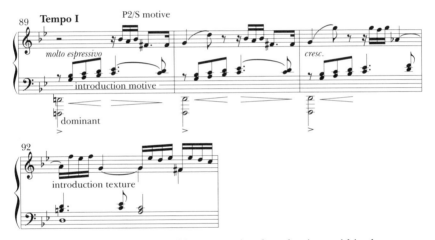

Example 2. Y, mm. 89–92, an ambiguous section for solo piano within the recapitulation of the first movement of Saint-Saëns's Second Piano Concerto, op. 22.

Example 3. Z, mm. 41–42, a passage for piano linking the exposition and the recapitulation of Saint-Saëns's Second Piano Concerto, op. 22.

transition (in Sonata Theory parlance, the "medial caesura"), a motive in the treble belonging to either P2 or S, a contrapuntal texture in the right hand that harks back to the introduction, and a motive in the tenor range that derives from a cadence in the introduction. Like X, Y is a Bermuda Triangle that does not allow us to get our bearings within the sonata form until we move onto the next recognizable element—here, a monothematic S that "resolves" the dominant bass of Y to the tonic, reintroduces the orchestra, and prepares for the reprise of the introduction by incorporating Y's introductory motive and texture.[6] In retrospect, we can analyze Y as akin to an "expanded caesura-fill" that combines elements from all four sections of the recapitulation: P, Tr, S, and the introduction.[7]

The final aspect of formal ambiguation in this movement is Z, a *dolcissimo*, "un poco animato" passage occurring immediately after a perfect authentic cadence in B-flat major that concludes S.[8] Z begins as a coda luxuriating in the key attained by S—the relative major of the tonic G minor—but gradually assumes, by almost imperceptible degrees, a more menacing aspect. Over the course of Z's twenty measures our understanding of its role in the sonata form changes from a coda into a retransition as the piano's continuous stream of thirty-second notes metamorphoses from leisurely ornamentation into furious virtuosity.[9] The more Z appears to be a retransition, rather than a coda, the less it is likely to return at the end of the recapitulation, and indeed it does not. However, there is an indication that Saint-Saëns was aware of the possibility for Z to remain unresolved in the ears and minds of his listeners. As shown in Example 4, the primary theme of the finale to Saint-Saëns's Second Piano Concerto is the slightly altered tonal resolution of Z that we missed in the first movement: both themes leap up an octave

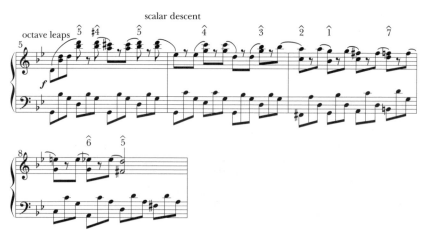

Example 4. The primary theme, mm. 5–8, of the finale of Saint-Saëns's Second Piano Concerto, op. 22.

or two on the dominant scale degree before returning to the dominant by a scalar descent interrupted by leaps and alighting noticeably on the raised subdominant scale degree. Despite the strong resemblance between these two themes, it would be difficult to make this association, were the finale theme not to appear transposed almost immediately into B-flat major (mm. 17–20), the key in which Z begins.

Another example of formal ambiguation in Saint-Saëns can be found in the first movement of the First Piano Concerto, op. 17. By breaking this movement down into its component sections, Table 2 shows that a lengthy introduction—one that maintains a consistent sequence of motives from one appearance to the next—precedes P in both the exposition and the recapitulation. Example 5 reproduces the artful transition that uses parsimonious voice leading to cadence from the mediant to the tonic at the moment the development dovetails into the (re)introduction; the quiet dynamic and tonal obliquity of this gesture presumably reflect the composer's intent to draw attention away from this preliminary tonic return and emphasize instead the structural downbeat at the *fortissimo* onset of P (measure 241), but it also masks, if only momentarily, the recurrence of the introduction. An equally extensive recurrence of the introduction does not appear in Table 2, since it is woven into S. To understand how this works, we will need to refer to two additional tables. Table 3 parses the initial introduction into its motivic components, as listed in the table's second row: a horn call, a string tremolo, a flourish, and an extended version

Table 2. Form of the First Movement of
Saint-Saëns's Piano Concerto no. 1.

SECTION	I	P	Tr	S	Dev	I	P	Tr	S	P-based Coda
STARTS AT MEASURE	1	25	57	84	144	217	241	261	290	350

Table 3. Form of the Introduction to the First Movement
of Saint-Saëns's Piano Concerto no. 1.

MOTIVE	I1	I2	I3	I1'	I2	I3	I1'	I3	I1'	I3	I1'	I3
TYPE	Horn call	Tremolo	Flourish	Horn call extended		as before						
STARTS AT MEASURE	1	9	11	13	15	17	19	21	21	22	22	23
ROTATION	1			2			3		4		5	

of the horn call. The bottom row of Table 3 groups these motives into five "rotations," each of which begins with a horn call before progressing through one or both of the other motives; as befits an intensification, the rotations grow shorter and more compact as the introduction nears its arrival at P. If we compare the design of the introduction with the format of

Table 4. Form of the Secondary Area (S) in the Exposition of the First Movement of Saint-Saëns's Piano Concerto no. 1.

MOTIVE	S1	S2	I1'	I1'	I2	I3'	I1'	I2	I3	I1'	I2	I3	I2'	I3'
TYPE	Leaps	Runs	as in Table 3											
STARTS AT MEASURE	84	96	102	117	119	120	121	121	122	123	123	124	125	133
ROTATION	n/a	n/a	1				2			3				

Example 5. The retransition, mm. 214–18, to the introduction in the development of Saint-Saëns's First Piano Concerto, op. 17.

Example 5 continued

S, as laid out in Table 4, we will note the unexpected recurrence of the introduction in its three I1'/I2/I3 rotations, whose elements compress together as we approach the midpoint and subsequently expand in a virtuosic intensification toward the climactic beginning of the development. The formal ambiguation that governs each iteration of the introduction—at the end of S and the end of the development—generally lies in the fact that the introduction is not essential to the sonata form. Thus each time the music places us back into the introduction it threatens to disrupt our orientation within the sonata form. More specifically, the strong association between I1' (the extended horn theme) and P raises doubts about the autonomy of S, which seems unable to reach a cadence without the intercession of outside material. It is ironic that I1' performs this rescue operation, since it is itself unstable, due to its setting by an inverted harmony. Similar to his solution in the Second Piano Concerto, Saint-Saëns responds to the unresolved tendencies of I1' by bringing it back *tutta forza* (as loud as possible) in the coda of the finale and harmonizing it at last with a root-position chord, the global tonic of D major.

The second technique that concerns us here is double negation, which I define as two consecutive contraventions of norms that end up realigning the piece with conventional behavior—a rebuttal to the adage that two wrongs don't make a right. A salient application of this technique among the piano concertos appears in the first movement of the Third Piano Concerto, op. 29, whose exposition (plus the onset of the development) is diagrammed in Table 5. The P theme, reproduced in Example 6, seems at first to be wholly secure, not only because of its monumental affect but also because of its buttressing on either side; the "Equal to" row in Table 5 shows that both the preceding introduction and the following transition feature P. However, an agitated Tr2 soon takes over and leads to a medial caesura that introduces both the key and the initial theme of S. Just as the key of S, D major, bears a minimal tonal relation to the key of P, E-flat major—the first marked aberration from normative sonata-form behavior—so too does the tranquillo S1 (Example 7) bear a minimal resemblance to the monolithic P.[10] After a few measures the piano begins S2, a solo improvisation on P whose gentle presentation underlines the affective

Table 5. Form of the Exposition of the First Movement of Saint-Saëns's Piano Concerto no. 3.

MOTIVE	P	Tr1	Tr2	MC	S1	S2	S3	S4	Dev
EQUAL TO	I	P	—	—	MC	P	—	—	P
STARTS AT MEASURE	32	45	54	77	92	96	106	111	127
KEY	I		iii	VII	VII		vi/VII	VII	VII (DC!)

Più mosso (allegro maestoso)

Example 6. The primary theme, mm. 32–36, of the first movement of Saint-Saëns's Third Piano Concerto, op. 29.

Example 7. The secondary theme, mm. 92–94, of the first movement of Saint-Saëns's Third Piano Concerto, op. 29.

distance between P and S. S2 lasts briefly before it yields to S3, an even dreamier, angelic theme with *pianissimo*-rolled chords high in the treble. The final segment, S4, is a virtuosic intensification whose endpoint completes the double negation: by coordinating the arrival of P at the beginning of the development (measure 127) with a deceptive cadence in the key of S, Saint-Saëns has reestablished normative sonata-form behavior—the development beginning with P in the key of the dominant (here, B-flat major)—by negating the negation of P that S represented in both affect and tonality. At the moment the development begins we recognize where we are in the sonata form, but unless we conscientiously retrace the steps that led us through the exposition, as we have just done, we will hardly know how we got there.

The third and final technique is parody, which refers to the general modeling of one stretch of music on another, as well as the specific transformation that makes sport of the model and thus usually lightens its affect. Although Saint-Saëns is well known for having parodied the music of composers such as Offenbach, Berlioz, and Rossini in *Le Carnaval des animaux*, we are concerned here with self-parody within a single work. A subtle but marked instance of self-parody on the small scale appears in the first movement of the First Piano Concerto. The transition from P to S is controlled by a single theme that is partially reproduced in Example 8 and evokes ballet with its delicate scoring—melody in high strings and winds, supported by horns and pizzicato strings—and melodic contour, whose slow scalar descent is interspersed with gentle leaps. With minimal fanfare Tr passes into S (Example 9), which parodies the preceding theme by transforming its innocence and grace into a more nervous, capricious, and mischievous version of itself: the anapestic rhythm is accelerated from two quarters and a half note to two eighths and a quarter; neighbor notes replace passing tones; and an additional mid-range motive in staccato eighth notes enriches the texture. Although the parody lightens the tone, the many changes that compose it suggest that the music has just gained a new depth and psychological complexity.

Example 8. The transition theme, mm. 57–61, of the first movement of Saint-Saëns's First Piano Concerto, op. 17.

Example 9. The secondary theme, mm. 84–86, of the first movement of Saint-Saëns's First Piano Concerto, op. 17.

Whereas parody may operate only within a single movement in the First Piano Concerto, it appears across separate movements in the Fourth Piano Concerto, op. 44. Table 6 sets into relief large-scale modeling in this two-movement work by stacking the first movement onto the second and vertically aligning their corresponding sections. The row Layer 1 tells us that both movements feature an Allegro section in C minor followed (without interruption) by an Andante, and the row Layer 2 indicates that four of

Table 6. Comparison of Formal Layering in the Two Movements of Saint-Saëns's Piano Concerto no. 4.

MOVEMENT 1

LAYER 1	1a: Allegro moderato C minor	1b: Andante A♭ major	
LAYER 2 (measure)	1 34 66	130 149 167	

MOVEMENT 2

LAYER 1	2a: Allegro vivace C minor	2b: Andante C minor	2c: Allegro C major
LAYER 2 (measure)	1 75 163	258	294 397 541

the five sections in both movements—except for the second Andante (2b)—divide into three parts, each of which begins with a complete statement of its main theme. Reference to the score supplements this list of similarities by revealing that the first Allegro/Andante pair supplies the primary themes for the second, even though these themes were only secondary in the first movement—a particular approach to thematic cyclicism that makes the repetition less direct. Table 6 also highlights major differences between the two movements: the Allegro vivace in the second movement (2a) is twice as large as the Allegro moderato (1a); the second Andante (2b) is smaller and simpler than its counterpart in the first movement (1b); and the second movement has an extensive final Allegro (2c) that the first does not.[11] Although 2c may seem to upset the symmetry created by all these correspondences, it actually bolsters this symmetry by providing a counterpart to both 1a (across movements) and 2a (within the second movement). Further, as the final section in an ABABA that spans both movements, it replicates the tripartite design of most sections at the level of the entire concerto.[12] Finally, it completes the tonal trajectory of the concerto by shifting C minor into C major and transposing the main theme of 1b from a non-tonic key (♭VI) into the major tonic.

If the modeling that generates 2c from previous materials charts a trajectory toward an apotheosis, there are also instances of a more typical parody in the Fourth Piano Concerto. Cortot, for one, senses a strong shift in this direction at the beginning of the second movement, where the "Scherzo [2a] brings to this gently melancholic serenity [of 1b] the lively contrast of its sarcastic rhythms and bantering irony." He further asserts that the orchestral return of the opening theme of the concerto (measure 34 in the second movement), "now enlivened by a mocking impulse," acts as a "riposte to the caustic insinuations of the piano."[13] Elsewhere, he specifies that the primary theme of 2a derives from "an episodic chromatic motive" appearing at the end of 1a (mm. 101–7),[14] but he does not seem to have noticed an aspect of this motive that is crucial to its parodic effect: it does not merely form a subset of the chromatic scale, but rather is a variant of the opening theme of 1a that compresses the pitch-class collection of the latter (Example 10) into two chromatic tetrachords ({8,7,6,5}, {3,2,1,0}), as shown in Example 11.[15] Note as well that the chromatic motive is the culmination of a long passage for piano in 1a marked *non legato* (mm. 90–107). The combination of chromatic transformation, rhythmic acceleration, sharp accentuation, and detached articulation lends this motive a somewhat grotesque character, as if it were diabolical laughter. If we happen to overlook this thematic relation, Saint-Saëns underlines it by effectively substituting the primary theme of 1a for the chromatic motive at the moment we expect the latter to return within "a

Example 10. The primary theme, mm. 1–9, of the Allegro moderato in the first movement of Saint-Saëns's Fourth Piano Concerto, op. 44.

Example 11. The primary theme, piano part, mm. 2–6, of the Allegro vivace in the second movement of Saint-Saëns's Fourth Piano Concerto, op. 44.

rondo structure" (measure 34). We should hardly be surprised to discover so many instances of modeling and parody in this piece—after all, the concerto is nothing if not a virtuosic display of variation technique, which pervades almost every section.[16]

Ravel's Concertos

In multiple interviews given shortly after finishing the G-major and Left-hand concertos, Ravel asserted that the "genuine" piano concerto, as exemplified by those of Saint-Saëns and Mozart, should be "lighthearted and brilliant, and not aim at profundity or at dramatic effects."[17] Ravel is clearly overgeneralizing here. Just as there are lighthearted and brilliant moments in more "profound" and "dramatic" piano concertos such as those by Brahms—most notably the jovial fourth movement of the Second—so too are there profound and dramatic moments in the piano concertos by Saint-Saëns and Ravel. Examples in Saint-Saëns's concertos include the outer movements of the Second, the Allegro maestoso theme of the Third, the fugue and chorale in the finale of the Fourth, and examples in Ravel's concertos include the searingly nostalgic second movement of the G-major and the outer sections of the Left-hand, among others. Notwithstanding these exceptions, however, Ravel's statement makes his aesthetic preferences sufficiently clear and provides a good point of departure for investigating continuity between the concertos by Saint-Saëns and the two by Ravel, especially the G-major.

The most immediately audible element of this continuity in the G-major Concerto is the brilliance of its piano writing: short-duration passagework for the right hand in the double-stroke octave or higher, which appears even in the ornamental passages of the more subdued second movement.[18] Throughout the G-major Concerto we find quick runs that unfold in various registers—sometimes in octaves doubled between the hands, as in the first movement's retransition (R17), and sometimes split between alternating hands to create a single line, as in the finale (R12). A touchstone for textural imagination in music, the latter movement is remarkable not only for its toccata figuration—repeated notes, interlocking hands, and hand crossings—but also its coruscating arpeggiations up and down the keyboard (R16). Counterparts to all these elements abound in the concertos by Saint-Saëns: note the brilliant riffs in the middle movement of the Second, the octave runs in the second movement of the Fourth, the relays and hand crossings in the third movement of the First, and the broad and extensive arpeggiation in the toccata finale of the Fifth (R36), which illustrates well what Ravel described as "the ingenious, facile and limpid development of Saint-Saëns."[19]

These numerous similarities strengthen the G-major Concerto's claim to having inherited Saint-Saëns's legacy more strongly than the Left-hand Concerto—as scholars have hitherto assumed—but we can also make striking claims on behalf of the latter. Since Ravel himself acknowledged Saint-Saëns's set of piano etudes for the left hand, op. 135, we might assume that Ravel's debt to Saint-Saëns lies primarily in the concerto's solo part, but this assumption is questionable. For one reason, the thick, sonorous writing for the soloist in the concerto bears little resemblance to Saint-Saëns's more streamlined etudes, which actually compose a neo-Baroque suite. For another, Ravel dismissed these pieces for being too "brief" and "sectionalized" to help him solve the main compositional challenge of the Left-hand Concerto: "to maintain interest in a work of extended scope while utilizing such limited means."[20] At first glance this comment may seem to indicate that Ravel was seeking merely to extract from these etudes some idiomatic figuration for the left hand, but I would argue that he was looking to Saint-Saëns, here as elsewhere, for innovative approaches to *form*, and was frustrated when he failed to find them in the etudes. It is true that Ravel esteemed Saint-Saëns for the "mostly superb" orchestration of his music,[21] but he also associated the elder composer with a "constant preoccupation" with form that resulted in "new processes of development."[22] Due to Ravel's own preoccupation with form throughout his compositional career, we find in the Left-hand Concerto not only new processes of development but also the ambiguation and parody we earlier discovered in Saint-Saëns's concertos.

The Left-hand Concerto is in one movement with multiple articulations at various levels of form that we will refer to as layers, just as we did in the Saint-Saëns analysis. In the first layer the Left-hand breaks down into an ABA', capped off by a coda that briefly reprises the B section. With respect to topic and tempo, the A section is a Lento overture (in the French Baroque style, at least initially) and the B section is an Allegro hybrid of a scherzo and a march.[23] In this layer it is not yet clear how the two sections interrelate: the B section could be either a sonata form development, or an independent, contrasting middle section, or an unexpected interpolation that interrupts a large-scale form unfolding across the two A sections. To sort through these possibilities, we must proceed to the second layer.

As shown in Table 7, Layer 2 of the A section falls into five subsections that follow the first two-thirds of a normative sonata form: an introduction (I, mm. 1–36), a primary area for solo piano (P, mm. 37–58), a dependent transition for orchestra leading to a half-cadential medial caesura in the relative minor (Tr + MC, mm. 59–82),[24] a secondary area for solo piano (S, mm. 83–96), and a development (Dev, mm. 97–120).[25] Two articulations at Layer 3 are worth mentioning for the clarity they bring to this particular sonata form. The onset of I2 (measure 33, a cadenza for solo piano) divides the introduction in half, allowing the orchestra and solo piano to make separate debuts.[26] The I2 cadenza is of particular interest for allowing the composer's persona to vault out from the preceding orchestral fog: note its many Ravelian hallmarks, including the serrated contour of the opening Spanish rhapsody, the exotic pentatonic underpinning the rhapsody, the final cadence that blends together the dominant and the sub-dominant, and the virtuosic bravado, which proudly sets aside any notion of "disability" associated with either the concerto or its commissioning per-former, the one-armed pianist Paul Wittgenstein. In addition, the onset of the retransition (measure 113) divides the development in half and marks the moment at which the bass ends its long circle of descending fifths and locks onto E (the dominant of the subsequent A of the piano cadenza), a long crescendo begins, and the bluesy theme in the orchestral introduc-tion that I will call "Q" (horns, mm. 8–14) returns for the first time since the beginning of the concerto. Example 12 reproduces the initial meas-ures of the primary themes of the A and B sections, as well as the X theme.

Section B differs from section A in many respects other than topic and tempo: it is in duple rather than triple meter; it is in E major, not D major;

Table 7. Form and Content in the First A Section of Ravel's Concerto for the Left Hand.

LAYER 1	A (Lento)								
LAYER 2	I (1)		P (37)			Tr + MC (59)	S (83)	Dev (97)	
LAYER 3	I1 (1)	I2 (33)	P1 (37)	P2 (46)	P3 (57)			D1 (97)	Retr (113)

(a)

(b)

(c)

Example 12. Several themes from Ravel's Left-Hand Concerto: the Lento P1 (a), the Allegro P1 (b), and the bluesy Q theme from the orchestral introduction (c).

it has many more measures. However, like section A it is articulated at Layer 2 into the subsections of a sonata form, albeit a more abbreviated bipartite type that Sonata Theory has recently identified as a "Type 2" sonata form. Among other features, this sonata form substitutes a development section for the recapitulation of the primary area; other examples of this form in Ravel include the first movement of the Trio and "Ondine" from *Gaspard de la nuit*.[27] As a Type 2 sonata form, section B divides in half (at measure 269), and each half divides again at the inceptions of S (mm. 246 and 417) to generate four subsections in total. Layers 3 and 4 of section B, as shown in Tables 8 and 9, set into relief the difference between the first and second parts of each half: whereas both P and Dev are long and internally repetitive—featuring three thematic rotations in the first half (beginning at mm. 121, 177, and 216) and five in the second (beginning at mm. 269, 315, 326, 357, and 373)—S is shorter and less internally varied, although of no lesser significance within the sonata form, since its return (measure 417) is the tonal resolution that transposes it from the relative minor (an Aeolian-inflected C-sharp) back into the tonic of E major.[28] As befits its greater length and complexity, the development receives the most attention in the program notes Ravel wrote for the Paris premiere of the Left-hand Concerto on 17 January 1933. He notes how the Q theme from the A section "suddenly appears" as an "ostinato figure extending over several measures which are indefinitely repeated but constantly varied in their underlying harmony, and over which innumerable rhythmic patterns are introduced which become increasingly compact."[29] The combination of repetition and variation within this subsection is another excellent example of "the ingenious, facile and limpid development" that Ravel identified in Saint-Saëns.[30] More specifically, the multi-rotational format that governs both the P and Development sections in the Allegro of Ravel's Left-hand Concerto is strongly reminiscent of the multi-rotational format that governs four of the five sections in Saint-Saëns's Fourth Piano Concerto, as previously discussed.

The Lento A' section in the Left-hand Concerto supplies the missing recapitulation to the exposition and development of the initial A section, but it diverges from the latter in several respects. In addition to the transposition of S into the tonic, the major difference between the two sections is that the overture in A' begins in the midst of the primary theme (at P2), thereby bypassing the orchestral introduction (I1), the piano cadenza (I2), and the initial section of P (P1). Ravel partially compensates for this elision by devoting the lion's share of the A' section to a passage he marks as the official "cadenza" (measure 475) for solo piano. This cadenza subsumes Tr, ornaments S with a more rapid accompaniment, and penetrates deep into Dev before the orchestra finally joins in (measure 515). But as the solo piano part is proceeding dutifully through the sonata form, it is simultaneously eroding the Lento's claim to formal autonomy by framing its sonata-form components within a cadenza—a section often considered improvisatory and parenthetical to a piece, rather than predetermined and essential. Here, again, we encounter a technique of ambiguation that would have made Saint-Saëns smile.

By raising the issue of autonomy, this subtle contradiction begs the larger question whether the A sections have formal priority over the B section, or vice versa. In other words, is the Allegro merely an interpolation into the Lento, or is the Lento a merely decorative frame for the Allegro? On behalf of the Lento's primacy, we reiterate that it is a self-sufficient sonata form. In addition, there are at least four reasons for asserting that the Allegro is an interpolation: it begins precisely at the moment we expect the primary theme of the Lento to be recapitulated (measure 121); when the Lento resurfaces (measure 460), it starts in the middle of P (P2, with measure 460 equal to measure 46), as if to confirm the violence inherent in the act of interruption; the subsection that immediately precedes the Allegro seeds the expectation of a recapitulation by emulating the orchestral introduction; in similar fashion, the appearance of the Q theme in the middle of the Allegro (measure 269) can be interpreted as a harbinger for the Lento's return, as if the latter were preparing to reassert its dominance over the interrupting Allegro. On the other hand, there is a resemblance between the primary themes of the Lento and Allegro that counteracts the sense of interruption: both feature a Lydian upper neighbor (♯4) to the mediant scale degree and are saturated with iambs—short offbeats leading to longer onbeats.[31] Ravel seems to confirm this resemblance in an interview:

> A special feature is that after a first part in this traditional style, a sudden change occurs and the jazz music begins. Only later does it become evident that this jazz music is really built on the same theme as the opening part.[32]

Thus the Allegro parodies the Lento, just like S parodied Tr in the first movement of Saint-Saëns's First Piano Concerto and the Allegro vivace parodied the Allegro moderato in his Fourth Piano Concerto. The parody really gets rolling midway through the sonata form when Ravel brings Q and the Allegro's P into a round dance that eventually culminates in the frenzied bacchanale of the stretto linking the Allegro to the Lento reprise (measure 437; L in Table 9). From this perspective, the Allegro provides an opportunity for recreation—a bit of high-spirited profanity in the midst of the Lento's grandeur and pathos, a Saturnalian celebration during sa-

Table 8. Form and Content in the First Half of the B Section of Ravel's Concerto for the Left Hand.

LAYER 1	B (Allegro; first half)								
LAYER 2	P/Tr (121)								S (246)
LAYER 3	1 (121)			2 (177)			3 (216)		
LAYER 4	P0 (121)	P1 (152)	P2 (168)	P0 (177)	P1 (191)	P2 (207)	P0 (216)	P3 (217)	

Table 9. Form and Content in the Second Half of the B Section of Ravel's Concerto for the Left Hand.

LAYER 1	B (Allegro; second half)											L
LAYER 2	Dev (269)										S (417)	
LAYER 3	1 (269)		2 (315)		3 (326)		4 (357)		5 (373)			
LAYER 4	Q (269)	P1 (303)	Q (315)	P1 (325)	Q (336)	P1 (346)	Q (357)	P3 (357)	Q (373)	P1 (373)	P3 (395)	

cred holidays. Or perhaps Ravel's instruction in the Allegro for the piano to play *spiccato*—a marking more appropriate to stringed instruments than the piano—is a clue to a hidden program in which Mephistopheles strikes up the fiddle to engage the folk in a *danse macabre*, a genre close to Saint-Saëns's heart.

The opposing point of view—that the Allegro is primary and the Lento secondary—is also defensible. By assuming a French Baroque overture as its primary theme the Lento invites us to interpret it as an introduction. Further, both Lento sections actually do function as introductions to the two Allegros (the B section and the B-based coda). Thus the Allegro sections are not only focal points for the Left-hand Concerto but also have the last word.[33] Moreover, as a sonata form the Allegro is just as substantial as the Lento and, lacking an internal caesura, has more integrity. Consequently, when the second Lento begins, it is equally possible to feel that the Lento has interrupted the Allegro as it is to sense that the Allegro interruption has finally come to an end.

Michael J. Puri

In the Left-hand Concerto Ravel shapes the framing Lento and the interior Allegro in such a way that we are invited to determine the priority of one over the other but are ultimately prevented from doing so.[34] So too do the piano concertos by Saint-Saëns often invite us to experience musical form as a delicious quandary in which we often lose our bearings, despite the abundance of landmarks to guide us through the form. Equal in their mastery of ambiguation, parody, and similar techniques, Saint-Saëns and Ravel both demonstrate—in ways peculiar to their own styles and eras—that traditional forms such as the sonata or the ABA can be made complex, dynamic, and surprising without sacrificing the basic clarity of their presentation.

NOTES

1. Arbie Orenstein, *Ravel: Man and Musician* (New York: Dover, 1991), 202n51.

2. Michael Stegemann makes this point in discussing the French piano concerto from 1891 to 1921 in his *Camille Saint-Saëns and the French Solo Concerto from 1850 to 1920*, trans. Ann C. Sherwin (Portland, OR: Amadeus, 1991), 211–22.

3. For example, in her survey of Saint-Saëns's piano music Sabina Ratner claims that his "most significant and enduring contribution to piano literature has been his five piano concertos." Sabina Teller Ratner, "The Piano Works of Camille Saint-Saëns" (PhD diss., University of Michigan, 1972), 87.

4. Alfred Cortot, *La Musique française de piano* (Paris: Presses universitaires de France, 1981), 335.

5. Norman Demuth, *French Piano Music: A Survey With Notes on Its Performance* (London: Museum Press, 1959), 32.

6. I place the notion of resolution here in scare quotes because tonal theory today locates structural cadences at the end of S, rather than between S and its immediately preceding medial caesura.

7. The "expanded caesura-fill" and its typical characteristics within eighteenth-century music are discussed in James A. Hepokoski and Warren Darcy, *Elements of Sonata Theory: Norms, Types, and Deformations in the Late Eighteenth-Century Sonata* (Oxford: Oxford University Press, 2006), 40–45.

8. Michael Stegemann locates the beginning of the development at C (measure 38), but this is inaccurate for two reasons: the harmonic progression from mm. 37 to 38 is an evaded cadence (V7–I6) that prompts a repetition of the three-measure cadential approach in order to attain the perfect authentic cadence across measures mm. 40 to 41. Further, I would not label X as a sonata-form development because it lacks the typical content and proportions of this formal element. Stegemann, *Camille Saint-Saëns*, 81. For a survey of this common compositional technique, see Janet Schmalfeldt, "Cadential Processes: The Evaded Cadence and the 'One More Time' Technique," *Journal of Musicological Research* 12/1–2 (1992): 1–52.

9. Although the piano descends into sixteenth-note, double-octave runs during the retransition's final four measures (57–60), the rhythmic staggering of the two hands by a thirty-second-note duration preserves the thirty-second-note attack stream.

10. Although such tonal relations may seem bizarre to us—especially when they are applied to the primary and secondary areas in a sonata form—Saint-Saëns is particularly fond of them. As Ratner has noted, "Saint-Saëns shows a special predilection for keys a semitone above or below the tonic." Ratner, "The Piano Works of Camille Saint-Saëns," 208.

11. Ratner reasons that the second Andante is smaller in order to keep the two movements roughly equivalent in length despite the addition of the Allegro. Ibid., 115.

12. My proposal of an intermovemental ABABA is supported by Cortot's assertion that the Fourth Piano Concerto "is of one piece and should be played without stopping [between the movements]." Cortot, La Musique française, 320.

13. Ibid., 323: "Le Scherzo apporte à cette sérénité doucement mélancolique le vif contraste de ses rythmes sarcastiques, de son ironie persifleuse. L'orchestre utilise comme riposte aux mordantes insinuations du piano, le thème initial de l'Allegro, avivé d'un élan moqueur."

14. Ibid., 321: "Un motif chromatique épisodique."

15. Ratner observes correctly that the primary theme of 1a uses all twelve pitch classes of the chromatic scale in "The Piano Works of Camille Saint-Saëns" (108). However, this observation is slightly oblique to my own: the connection that I am asserting between the primary themes of 1a and 2a depends only on the chromatic octachord that we find in the antecedent phrase of the 1a theme, whereas we would need both subphrases (antecedent and consequent) of the theme of 1a to complete the chromatic aggregate.

16. Stegemann claims: "At the time that op. 44 was written, variation was a totally new concept in the solo concerto context." According to Stegemann, what distinguishes this concerto from previous concertos featuring variation is that it uses this technique throughout the piece, rather than confining it to a single movement. Stegemann, Camille Saint-Saëns, 91.

17. M. D. Calvocoressi, "M. Ravel Discusses His Own Work," Daily Telegraph, 11 July 1931, repr. in Maurice Ravel, A Ravel Reader: Correspondence, Articles, Interviews, ed. and trans. Arbie Orenstein (New York: Columbia University Press, 1990), 476–78, at 477.

18. The brilliance of the writing in the G-major Concerto partially reflects Ravel's intention to perform it himself; although he never did so, he stated his intention many times before the premiere in London on 25 February 1932, at which Marguerite Long was the soloist and Ravel conducted the Royal Philharmonic Orchestra. For an example of such statements, see ibid., 477.

19. Maurice Ravel, "Concert Lamoureux," Revue musicale de la S.I.M. (15 February 1912): 62–63, trans. as "The Lamoureux Orchestra Concerts," in Orenstein, A Ravel Reader, 340–42, at 341. A comment by Hélène Jourdan-Morhange suggests that Ravel may have associated the genre of the toccata with Saint-Saëns: "[Ravel] liked to demonstrate to us that the ending of his Toccata [in Le Tombeau de Couperin] was pure Saint-Saëns!" Vlado Perlemuter and Hélène Jourdan-Morhange, Ravel According to Ravel, trans. Frances Tanner, ed. Harold Taylor (London: Kahn & Averill, 1988), 78.

20. Maurice Ravel, "Concert [sic] pour la main gauche," Le Journal, 14 January 1933, trans. as "Concerto for the Left Hand," in Orenstein, A Ravel Reader, 396–97, at 396.

21. "Ten Opinions of Mr. Ravel On Compositions and Composers," De Telegraaf, 6 April 1932, repr. in Orenstein, A Ravel Reader, 492–94, at 493: "Only Saint-Saëns orchestrated even better [than Franck] in his customary manner: mostly superb."

22. Maurice Ravel, "Les Mélodies de Gabriel Fauré," La Revue musicale 3 (October 1922): 22–27, trans. as "The Songs of Gabriel Fauré," in Orenstein, A Ravel Reader, 384–87, at 385: "Fauré, who studied with Saint-Saëns, appears to have been more attracted to the obvious Gounod-like color of certain works by his young professor, than to his research with respect to form, which for Saint-Saëns was a constant preoccupation. Fauré's songs do not bear the slightest imprint of the continual pursuit of architectural design found in the shortest works of Saint-Saëns, who truly created new techniques of development." It seems clear that Ravel's "development" alludes to much more than the middle section of

a typical sonata form. Apropos development in Saint-Saëns's symphonic poems—works Ravel knew well—Daniel Fallon makes a suggestion that makes more sense: "In a symphonic poem, 'development' is not neatly relegated to a specific part of the piece. In fact, one might claim that the degree to which composers 'develop' their material in the exposition or recapitulation of a sonata form movement—i.e., somewhere other than the development section proper—to the same degree do they anticipate thematic transformation which is often characterized by continuous unfolding or 'development' in a free form." Daniel Martin Fallon, "The Symphonies and Symphonic Poems of Camille Saint-Saëns," 2 vols. (PhD diss., Yale University, 1973), 1:242.

23. Henri Gil-Marchex famously described P1 as a theme "construit sur le rythme d'un sarabande" (constructed on the rhythm of a sarabande). Although I find it more useful to describe P as a French Baroque overture, due to its profusion of dotted rhythms and its introductory position within the concerto, I do not object to his interpretation. Gil-Marchex, "Les Concertos de Ravel," in *Maurice Ravel: Qui êtes-vous? L'Hommage de La Revue musicale, décembre 1938*, introduction, notes, and additions by Marcel Marnat (Lyon: La Manufacture, 1987), 145–68, at 162.

24. Daphne Leong and David Korevaar assert that the exposition of the Lento begins at measure 59, despite the lengthy exposition of P in the previous solo piano passage. Instead, I think it is more plausibly interpreted as a dependent transition, especially since it leads without interruption to the medial caesura (measure 71). See Daphne Leong and David Korevaar, "The Performer's Voice: Performance and Analysis in Ravel's *Concerto pour la main gauche*," *Music Theory Online* 11/3 (2005); http://mto.societymusictheory.org/issues/mto.05.11.3/toc.11.3.html. Incidentally, a medial caesura that prepares an S in the relative minor is rather typical for Ravel; other examples include the first movement of the String Quartet and the *Introduction et allegro*. Sigrun Heinzelmann interprets this tonal pairing in Ravel as a double-tonic complex. See Heinzelmann, "Playing with Models: Sonata Form in Ravel's String Quartet and Piano Trio," in *Unmasking Ravel: New Perspectives on the Music*, ed. Peter Kaminsky (Rochester, NY: University of Rochester Press, 2011), 143–79.

25. In Table 7 it is also possible to place the main sonata-form sections (exposition, development, recapitulation) into Layer 2 and their subsections (P, Tr, S) into Layer 3, rather than combining them into Layer 2. However, the type of formal articulation that interests me here is relatively blind to the rather abstract divisions of sonata form and therefore does not allow a clear distinction between the development and the subsections of the exposition, since they are all roughly equivalent to each other in length. Another advantage of this methodology is its ability to eliminate an additional layer that would further complicate Table 7 and make it more difficult to compare the individual layers across Tables 7, 8, and 9. The latter two have no need to distinguish among exposition, development, and recapitulation, since the B section is not a typical tripartite sonata form and each of its halves receives its own table.

26. Daphne Leong and David Korevaar dub the entire solo piano part a "cadenza," but since it also fulfills an official function within the Lento sonata form—exposing P— I have chosen to separate it from the opening cadenza and ascribe the latter to the introduction. Nevertheless, their segmentation of the solo passage into a frame and an interior— comprising an Opening Gesture (my I2), Theme 1 (my P1), Theme 2 (my P2), and a Closing Gesture (my P3)—helps to bring out the same technique of ambiguation that I find in the concerto as a whole: the design of a form in such a way as to make it impossible to determine which part is subordinate to which, despite the usual connotation of the "frame" as a subordinate element. In this case, the solo piano passage invites listeners to ask whether they have just heard a cadenza that stands outside the sonata form, or an exposition framed by a cadenza. See Leong and Korevaar, "The Performer's Voice."

27. Hepokoski and Darcy explain the Type 2 sonata form as a binary variant of the typical three-part sonata form in which "the second rotation [of the exposition's P/Tr/S, or some subset thereof] begins as a developmental space; only in the second half—often from S onward—does it take on 'recapitulatory' characteristics." Hepokoski and Darcy, *Elements of Sonata Theory*, 353. For an analysis of another Type 2 sonata form in Ravel (the first movement of the Trio), see Heinzelmann, "Playing with Models," 143–79.

28. Marie-Noëlle Masson, who produced the most detailed analysis of the Left-hand Concerto of which I am aware, identifies S as the trio of the Allegro scherzo. While I recognize the musical contrast between P and S that might suggest S to be a trio, her analysis of the Allegro's form seems less convincing to me than the Type 2 sonata-form interpretation, which accounts perfectly for both the initial key of S (relative minor, a common default choice in Ravel's sonata forms) and its resolution in the tonic upon its return in the second half. Marie-Noëlle Masson, "Ravel: Le *Concerto pour la main gauche* ou les enjeux d'un néo-classicisme," *Musurgia* 5/3/4 (1998): 37–52, at 45.

29. Ravel, "*Concert* [sic] *pour la main gauche*," 397.

30. One of Ravel's peers, Charles Koechlin, makes a connection between Ravel and Saint-Saëns that, at least to my mind, implicates the developmental techniques in both: "In his musical sensibility, Saint-Saëns is closer to the Ravel he did not want to understand, and what an injustice, and what a shame! For it's from Saint-Saëns that Ravel learned the best lessons about equilibrium in orchestral values and symphonic durations: it's from Saint-Saëns that he discovered the sovereign logic which allowed him, after a whole year of work, to contribute to our French music the stunning, inimitable Bacchanale of *Daphnis et Chloé*." Charles Koechlin, "À propos de Camille Saint-Saëns," *La Pensée* 24 (May–June 1949): 27–34, at 31.

31. It is also possible to derive the E major of the B section from the metrically stressed second chord of P1, an E-major triad over a D tonic pedal that occurs on the downbeat of the first measure.

32. Calvocoressi, "M. Ravel Discusses His Own Work," 477, says "seems to confirm" because Ravel's claim is vague, raising more questions than it answers. Consequently, we are left to wonder whether "later" occurs within the Allegro or the Lento, which aspect of the music is supposed to precipitate the observation of this thematic similarity, and whether the Lento theme to which he alludes includes only the Baroque overture P, or only the bluesy melody Q, or both, since the Allegro allows all three possibilities.

33. In case we are tempted to disregard the second Allegro as a mere coda snippet, we should note its significance as a large-scale tonal resolution that transposes the Allegro from E major in the B section into the global tonic of D major.

34. The interaction between the Q and P themes in the development of the Allegro gives rise to yet another experience of formal indeterminacy, as is apparent in this comment by Masson: "The ear situates itself at an equal distance from the one [theme] and the other, hesitant to locate one in the foreground and the other in the background." Masson, "Ravel: Le *Concerto pour la main gauche*," 47. She also argues that S is a thematic transformation of P2; if this relation is both plausible and audible (which I think it is), I would describe it as another instance of parody. Ibid., 49.

Saint-Saëns and Silent Film /
Sound Film and Saint-Saëns

MARTIN MARKS

Yesterday evening Monsieur Saint-Saëns added another plume to his chapeau. Our most eminent composer, having written masterworks in every classical form, has now shown his brilliance in a burgeoning field, *la musique du cinéma*. At the Salle Charras a new "Film d'Art" was projected, *L'Assassinat du duc de Guise*, accompanied by the composer's original score, played by an orchestra under the capable baton of Fernand LeBorne. Like the film, the score is a masterpiece and will surely live forever. If only younger French composers will follow the master's lead, and further advance this novel genre!

—From an imaginary news bulletin, Paris, 18 November 1908

By many accounts the Parisian premiere of *L'Assassinat du duc de Guise* caused a sensation.[1] The film dramatized a violent episode in French monarchical history: the murder, in 1588, of the powerful Duke Henri de Guise at the behest of King Henri III.[2] In addition to the somewhat lurid story, factors contributing to the film's success included the actors' nuanced performances, the elaborate mise-en-scène, the careful editing, and not least, the fine music by Saint-Saëns.

The event marked a milestone in the annals of film music—the first live performance of an original film score by a composer of such eminence; yet curiously, for all the composer's wide-ranging essays, reminiscences, interviews, and letters, we have yet to find any record of his thoughts about moving pictures or this project in particular. Also apparently lacking are any autograph scores or sketches. However, shortly after the premiere Durand published the printed score in a piano reduction, and the company preserved copies of the orchestral parts in its archive.[3] The film, too, has survived, albeit in rare copies, as has the original scenario.[4] Of equal interest, there is now a fine French recording of the ensemble score.[5] The surviving materials make one thing abundantly clear: at the ripe age of seventy-three, Saint-Saëns responded to this challenging new assignment with unflagging ingenuity and vigor. His *L'Assassinat* score combines a characteristic clarity and richness of formal design with singular ways of interpreting the historical drama that unfolds on screen.[6]

Like the film, the score is divided into a series of discrete tableaux linked into a multi-movement whole, suggestive of a pantomime score or ballet.[7] Dance comes to the fore in Tableau 1, which begins with a kind of minuet, followed by a brief passage recalling a French overture—the latter being lightly ironic, since it underscores the entrance of a minor character, a youthful page. Though not historically precise, these allusions to France's musical past, borrowed from the time when the monarchy reigned supreme, are meant to reinforce the period detail in sets and costumes. (Use of the minuet to evoke the aristocratic past became the custom in countless film scores for decades to follow.) In Tableau 4 Saint-Saëns incorporates another dance-like segment: a funeral march, based on music from his early Symphony in F Major (*Urbs Roma*).[8] This resurrected music cleverly suits the scene following the Duke's murder, when the King inspects the corpse (Figure 1); its mordant tone is enhanced by newly refined scoring and supple harmonies in keeping with Saint-Saëns's later style.[9]

Figure 1. A crucial moment from Tableau 4 of *L'Assassinat du duc de Guise* (1908): King Henri III emerges from behind his bed curtain and peers down at the murdered duke.

Besides his attention to the film's tableau structure, Saint-Saëns responded carefully to its dramatic arc by giving the score two unmistakable climaxes—each time bringing back the opening theme, though in different guises. In Tableau 4, when the murderers pounce, it returns in dissonant fragments, sequenced in wild developmental fashion. The music sweeps forward in a rush, just like the action—for visually, too, this tableau is climactic. Although each of the other tableaux plays out on a single set and in a single shot, the murder sequence unfolds in five consecutive shots, following the Duke as he moves from room to room, until his struggle to fight off the assassins ends in collapse. It is as if the violence on screen demanded something new—such "continuity editing" was still unusual at this time—and Saint-Saëns matched the fluidity of the shots perfectly. He found a different way to complement the film's conclusion. Soldiers lay the Duke's corpse in the huge Guard Room fireplace and set the body ablaze. Enter the King, who has come to gloat, followed soon after by the Marquise de Noirmoutiers, the Duke's mistress. Dramatically, her entrance marks a rounding of the narrative, since she has not been seen since the opening tableau. Accordingly, at the start of Tableau 5, Saint-Saëns brings back the opening theme, in its original quiet orchestration and dark key (F-sharp minor). But at the very end, for the final confrontation between King and Marquise, he has it played in thunderous unisons and faster rhythm. A *presto* coda accelerates still further, until the tonic chords come to rest on *fortissimo* repetitions of F♯ in bare multiple octaves. *Fin!*

The ending is emphatic to the point of melodramatic excess, yet it is what the drama ordered, and necessary from theatrical and psychological standpoints—especially since the previous tableaux all end quietly, in keys other than the tonic. After fifteen-plus minutes of thwarted cadences, harmonic deflections, and unsettling modulations (dependent upon French-style chromatic voice leading and enharmonic sleight of hand), a little tonic-thumping can't hurt.

· · ·

My best memory of the cinema? The sensation given me twelve years ago by a marvelous film, *L'Assassinat du duc de Guise*. It was a complete revelation.

—D. W. Griffith to Robert Florey, 1922[10]

In 1908, the theatrical elements of *L'Assassinat* were considered virtues. The production company Studio Film d'Art had been established the year before to make polished dramas on high-toned subjects, and hired leading professionals to work behind and in front of the camera. Scenarist Henri Lavedan was a successful playwright and member of the Académie française. Charles

Le Bargy, a co-director and the actor who played Henri III, took many lead-ing roles at the Comédie française, from which he recruited fellow actors to fill out the cast.[11] As for Saint-Saëns, though we do not know who invited him to compose the score, he was a logical choice due both to his prestige (good for publicity) and experience with dramatic genres. By then eight of his operas had been staged in Paris, and he had written incidental music for a like num-ber of plays in the city's theaters, including two at the Comédie française.

No matter the celebrated roster and the critical acclaim: the film and score did not remain in the limelight for long, at home or abroad. In the United States , the film was released in a truncated version, shorn of Saint-Saëns's music.[12] A few years later it was re-released in France (retitled *La Mort du duc de Guise*), and there is no sign that the score was played with the film at that time. By 1922, as evidenced by Griffith's words, the film and score lived on at best as distant memories.[13] Indeed, it has been claimed that by the 1920s the film was laughed at for its dated qualities on the rare occasions it was screened at all.[14] But given the very rapid pace of change in film production and exhibition practices during the first half of the silent period, it is hardly surprising that the film was disparaged and the score mostly forgotten. What is more surprising is the manner in which several other compositions by Saint-Saëns were subsequently at-tached to films, through acts of appropriation. The story of his posthumous career as a "film composer" is one he could never have foreseen.

· · ·

> Let us recall that during the silent film period . . . all the large inter-national cinema houses had orchestras . . . [and that] the bits and pieces of music they performed were taken from works by Saint-Saëns more than 20 percent of the time.
> —Albert Richard, 1983, director, *La Revue musicale*[15]

More than one-fifth of all orchestral music heard in "international" silent cinemas was by Saint-Saëns? If this was so, historians of film music have a good deal of explaining to do. Simply put, there is not much hard evi-dence to back up the claim, at least outside France.

In America, Saint-Saëns's music is certainly present within sources used by cinema musicians—including compiled scores, anthologies, cue sheets, instruction manuals for cinema musicians, and indexes—but not in the proportion estimated above by Albert Richard.[16] We can gain a more ac-curate sense of how the composer's music fit into the overall picture by examining two key artifacts from the mid-1920s, a decade when scores for feature films (especially dramas) normally included works from the clas-sical repertoire. In the large piano anthology *Motion Picture Moods* (1924)

compiled by Erno Rapée there is not a single work by Saint-Saëns.[17] One
might explain the lack with interlocking hypotheses: first, that his contributions to the solo piano repertoire were not widely known (unlike those
of Mendelssohn and Grieg, who are each represented by several pieces);
second, that many of his concerted works for piano were difficult to play;
third, that his most familiar orchestral pieces do not sit gracefully under
the fingers in piano transcription. By contrast, Erno Rapée's second major
film music publication, the *Encyclopedia of Music for Pictures* (1925) lists altogether thirteen works by Saint-Saëns, some under multiple categories,
both as mood music and as concert works.[18] This is a significant number,
but other statistics provide a broader perspective: the *Encyclopedia* has
more than a hundred subject headings, lists over a thousand pieces, and
includes several other major nineteenth-century composers with a greater
number of pieces than Saint-Saëns.[19]

How do we explain the composer's invisibility in one other grandly sys-
tematic source from the late silent period, the German *General Handbook
of Film-Music* (1927)?[20] All other important French composers from the
mid-nineteenth to the early twentieth century can be found there, some
in multiple entries (including Thomas, Gounod, Massenet, Chaminade,
Dukas, and Debussy). Perhaps the exclusion was a case of revenge on the
French composer, who took an extremely anti-German stance during
the First World War. In various writings (see especially *Germanophilie,*
1916) he called for a ban of German music from the stage and concert hall:
even Mozart and Beethoven had to go. That leaders of German film music
were only too happy to return the favor seems likely. (Perhaps Rapée as
well, since he spent some of those years working as a silent film composer
and conductor in Berlin.) In any case, since the *Handbook*'s index was
keyed to numerous published series of incidental pieces for movie playing, the implication is that Saint-Saëns's music was not made easily available
to cinema musicians in Germany.

In France at least, even if Richard may have exaggerated, we can be
reasonably sure that Saint-Saëns's music was heard in *salles de projection*
with some frequency. Particularly suggestive "evidence" appears within
Au Revoir les enfants, the beautiful film memoir written and directed by
Louis Malle in 1987. It tells the story of Malle's boyhood experiences, se-
questered in a Catholic boarding school during the Second World War.
The main character, Julien, befriends a newcomer to the school, "Jean
Bonnet"—and then learns that he is actually Jean Kippelstein, a Jewish
boy who has been given refuge by the school's priestly authorities. At the
end Nazis take Jean and several others away to almost certain death, while
Julien looks on helplessly. Within this tragedy one of the film's most heart-
warming moments comes when the boys gather to watch Charlie Chaplin's

1918 silent film *The Immigrant*. The town's female piano teacher and a male student violinist provide musical accompaniment, playing Saint-Saëns's *Introduction et Rondo capriccioso*—a surprising but inspired choice. Throughout the screening, the audience of boys and priests laugh again and again, delighted by everything they see, even while they pay no attention to the music. Yet Malle gives us several close-ups of the performers hard at work, watching the screen. We note their skillful playing and feel their concentration—the result being that we sense a deeper bond between music and picture than one might have thought possible. To the question, what does *this* music have to do with a comedy about poor European immigrants bound for the "New World," one answer lies in the action on screen: while the ship rolls up and down, Chaplin's Tramp finds ingenious ways to stand upright—and his acrobatics are mirrored by Saint-Saëns's virtuoso violin, which skitters and dances. A broader answer is that the music expresses what the audience of schoolchildren and teachers feel, a desperate need to keep *their* balance. One way it does so is by its very Frenchness, reinforcing their cultural identity during a period of shameful capitulation and collaboration. To be sure, this is not an overt act of musical patriotism, like the singing of "La Marseillaise" in *Casablanca*. But in this segment Malle has paid multiple homages: to bygone days of cinemusical practices; to the Tramp as the impulsive Everyman who thumbs his nose at authority; to Chaplin as an outspoken opponent of Hitler and friend to Jews; and to Saint-Saëns, an artist who embodied Gallic—"anti-Teutonic"—culture with irrepressible panache.

• • •

If I had words to make a day for you,
I'd sing you a morning golden and new.
— Farmer Hoggett to Babe

Au Revoir les enfants is one of 96 films and television titles listed (at this writing) on the Internet Movie database as having "soundtracks" by Saint-Saëns.[21] To trace patterns within this hodgepodge is not easy. We can start by setting to one side the cartoons and other pictures that contain only parodic quotations in passing—a frequent target being the composer's undying "Swan."[22] We can also put on the shelf several films containing more or less "straight" documentary concert performances, among them several that drew upon hackneyed highbrow-vs.-lowbrow plotting as a pretext for insertion of classical numbers.[23]

However, one of the queerest and most entertaining examples, *Goin' to Town* (1935), deserves a closer look.[24] Mae West stars as a western dance hall "queen" who later becomes an oil magnate and sets her eye on an

English earl. To attract his attention she stages a mini-production of *Samson et Dalila* for her new high-society friends. The sequence features an operatic tenor as Samson and West as temptress, singing the love duet from Act 2—and it stands the test of time as a quintessential example of camp. It almost seems as if West believes she's got the right kind of voice for the role and wants us to take the whole thing seriously; but even if (as seems more likely) she is consciously "vamping" the part with tongue in cheek and hips in motion, there is no mistaking the implicit attitude being expressed by the film. Through the 1930s, in Hollywood at least, music by Saint-Saëns was considered artistically *important*: it retained an aura of cultural prestige, combined with widespread audience appeal.

As presented by Jean Renoir within his masterpiece *La Règle du jeu* (1939), Saint-Saëns's *Danse macabre* brings more complex values into play, linked with the film's depiction of a society tilting toward the abyss. The locale is a magnificent baronial estate, set apart from the outside world. Plot, pacing, and several characters seem to have sprung from a Beaumarchais farce.[25] But midway the action begins to spin out of control and finally crashes to a halt with a senseless murder. When Saint-Saëns's music appears, it signals this turn toward tragedy; it also comes as something of a shock because the previous music has been innocuous, matching the film's seemingly frivolous tone.[26] *Danse macabre* enters as the climactic number within an evening of theatrical entertainments put on by the Baron's houseguests, who have devised a wild, *frisson*-laden dance of death: it is led by a man in skeleton costume, cavorting in the company of three white-sheeted "Spirits" who brandish skeletal umbrellas. At first confined to a little black-curtained stage (one shot has the dancers reflected in a mirror, like ghostly apparitions), the foursome soon runs into the audience, provoking mock terror—at which point the camera loses interest in their performance. While dance and music continue offscreen, we are directed to follow various characters as they spill out of the salon, chasing one another through adjacent rooms, in various futile "dances" of amorous flirtation, jealous rage, and comic frustration. The music seems to drive all of them with occult power, not least because four invisible hands play it on a mechanical piano.

There is historical irony at work here. Saint-Saëns had composed this piece in his thirties, as one of four energetically Lisztian symphonic poems. At that time they attested to his leading role in promoting a more advanced French musical culture, under the aegis of the newly formed Third Republic. As Jann Pasler has noted, aristocratic control during the Republic's first decade was still very strong, though the republicans were gaining strength.[27] It was a decade of sharp political contestation; just so the 1930s, the Republic's final decade, when Renoir became a cultural leader, too, closely associated with the Popular Front. With benefit of hindsight, we can see that in *La Règle du jeu*, appearing one year before the Republic's collapse, he refashioned *Danse macabre* into a poignant symbol of his world's impending collapse. Though as condemnatory of aristocratic folly as Beaumarchais, Renoir portrays all of the characters—aristocrats and servants, husbands and lovers, monarchists and republicans, heroes and bystanders alike—with an open frame and heart. His film is thus enriched by Mozartean compassion and subtlety. (Probably too much so for his politically sensitive audiences: the film was a major failure when first released.) The mechanized dance of death signals doom for all.

For Saint-Saëns the "film composer" there were happier days ahead. Even as versions of *Danse macabre*, "The Swan," and morsels from *Samson et Dalila* continued to pop up on film and television (all three have joined the Order of Perpetual Classical Icons), fresher material was also mined.[28] There is a particularly golden glitter to the composer's music as heard in the soundtracks for *Days of Heaven* (1978) and *Babe* (1995), two films of far-flung imagination in story and music alike.

In *Days of Heaven*, director Terence Malick uses "The Aquarium" from *Carnaval des animaux* during the film's opening title sequence, with remarkable effect.[29] The credits are superimposed over a dissolving montage of sepia-tinted photographs, each depicting a slice of American working-class life. Meaningful contexts are absent: we know nothing about these people, not even if they will be part of the story. This witty yet solemn music by Saint-Saëns adds a shimmery lacquer. Its glassy melody, rippling accompaniment, and strange harmonies impart to the sequence a mood of nostalgic fascination—as though we are peering through the camera lens at exotic specimens of ourselves from the past.[30] Although the piece never recurs within the film, the vivid impression lingers, due to Ennio Morricone's reworking of Saint-Saëns's theme within segments of his ensuing film score.[31] The first of these segments shows farmworkers gathered in a field for evening worship (the Bible is being read aloud)—to which Morricone responds by transforming Saint-Saëns's theme into what sounds like an old American hymn. In this version, now attached to the film's gorgeous landscape vistas, the theme evokes melancholy religious awe— fittingly so, since the film's tragic tale abounds in biblical symbolism.

Much more playful and endearing is the manner in which Nigel Westlake reworks another memorable theme by Saint-Saëns, the chorale from the Third Symphony (*Organ*), as a central component of his score for *Babe*. The tune shows up at many points, its textures and timbres varied but with the melody always firmly recognizable. In the main title it is played twice in succession: first on the celeste, with sugarplum-sweet rolled chords reminiscent of Papageno's magic bells, then in a full wind-band orchestration, punctuated by exultant brass fanfares. The dichotomy indicates the story's emotional range, from tender intimacy to blissful grandeur—that is, from scenes of Babe as a childlike innocent, dependent upon the "adults" around him for love and affection, to the ultimate realization of his dream to become a champion sheep "dog." At the conclusion of the symphony, when this tune thunders from organ and orchestra, the feeling of an apotheosis in the post-Beethoven orchestral manner is unmistakable; surpassing this in *Babe*, there are three diverse apotheoses, each quoting the tune with tongue in cheek and heart in throat. The sweetest is Hoggett's unaccompanied song to Babe, which begins with the lyrical lines quoted above (a pivotal moment in the narrative—the music lifts both farmer and pig from deep despair); the grandest is at the film's climax, after Babe has demonstrated his mastery and the stupefied audience erupts in cheers, with the non-diegetic orchestra chiming in; *sans doute* the goofiest is the pop vocal version sung by the film's chorus of mice during the end credits. How fresh and witty it was of the film's creators to hit upon the idea of using this tune! For those who recognize it, it seems as though the *Carnaval des animaux* has expanded to include several more denizens (including a pig, dogs, and sheep).

Figure 2. A scene from the 1995 film, *Babe*.

Should we take these instances as golden portents, and look forward to more examples of appropriate appropriations by filmmakers? The answer requires too much foresight. What we know for certain is that, as demonstrated by *L'Assassinat*, Saint-Saëns remained a dramatic composer of considerable skill and imagination well into old age; more important, that even if this score will not "live forever," many of his other works have shown great vitality, *Rondo capriccioso*, *Danse macabre*, *Carnaval des animaux*, and the *Organ* Symphony certainly among them. As concert works they remain popular favorites, but from time to time these and other pieces have sprung to new life due to their roles in film—a medium that both honors concert music and twists its meanings in all directions. We are left to wonder hopefully what Saint-Saëns's many beguiling works might have to offer the ear, the eye, and the imagination, during the next hundred years of multimedia.

NOTES

1. See Richard Abel, *The Ciné Goes to Town: French Cinema, 1896–1914*, rev. ed. (Berkeley and Los Angeles: University of California Press, 1994; repr. 1998), 39, together with the reviews cited in 475n174. Abel discusses the film in greater detail on 243–53, and he gives a translation of one of the most laudatory reviews, by Adolphe Brisson, in *French Film Theory and Criticism: A History/Anthology, 1907–1939*, vol. 1: *1907–1929* (Princeton: Princeton University Press, 1988), 50–52. Other important sources on the film include Georges Sadoul, *Histoire générale du cinéma*, vol. 2, *Les Pionniers du cinéma (de Méliès à Pathé), 1897–1909* (Paris: Denoël, [1948]), "Le Film d'Art (France 1908)," chap. 31; and vol. 3: *Le Cinéma deviant un art (1909–1920)*, "Les Séries d'art en France (1909–1914)," chap. 1; Ben Brewster, "Deep Staging in French Films, 1900–1914," in *Early Cinema: Space Frame Narrative*, ed. Thomas Elsaesser, with Adam Barker (London: British Film Institute and Bloomington, IN: Indiana University Press, 1990), 45–55; and Roland Cosandey, "Wo ist die große Treppe hingekommen? *L'Assassinat du duc de Guise* (1908): Raum, Tableau, Einstellung—eine Variation," *Cinema* (Basel) 40 (1994): 51–74 (trans. from the French by Margarit Tröbler).

2. Abel calls attention to the resonance of the story with contemporary French politics in *French Film Theory and Criticism*, 52n2.

3. The score was published with this title page: *Le Film d'Art / L'ASSASSINAT / DU DUC DE GUISE / Scénario d'HENRI LAVEDAN / Musique de / C. SAINT-SAËNS / (Opus 128) / Partition pour piano à deux mains* (Paris: A. Durand et fils, 1908). Piano reduction by Léon Roques. A full version of the score has yet to be published. I visited Durand in 1978 and examined the parts, which exist for flute, oboe, clarinet, bassoon, horn, piano, harmonium, and the usual five-part string ensemble.

4. The film is catalogued and may be consulted in the collection of the Centre national du cinéma et de l'image animée (CNC)) at Bois d'Arcy. Copies of the abridged version that was released in the United States in 1909 are available at select American film archives, including MoMA and UCLA. For the original film script, see Henri Lavedan, "*L'Assassinat du duc de Guise*: Scénario en six tableaux," *La Revue du cinéma* 3/15 (July 1948): 16–32. For a detailed shot analysis of the finished film (a conflation of different surviving copies), see

Pierre Jenn and Michel Nagard, *"L'Assassinat du duc de Guise* (1908)," *L'Avant-scène cinéma* 334 (November 1984): 57–72.

5. Ensemble Musique Oblique recorded Saint-Saëns's *Le Carnaval des animaux* (title track), Quintette, op. 14, and *L'Assassinat du duc de Guise* in France in 1993 (Harmonia Mundi, HMC 901472), with liner notes by Gilles Thieblot. Reissued in 2003 in an English-language edition by Harmonia Mundi (HCX 3951472).

6. For a detailed study of the score, see Martin Marks, *Music and the Silent Film: Contexts and Case Studies, 1895–1924* (New York: Oxford University Press, 1997), 50–61, 187–89, and 252–55. See also the valuable study by Michael Stegemann, "Der Mord als schöne Kunst betrachtet: Camille Saint-Saëns und die Anfänge der Filmmusik," *Neue Zeitschrift für Musik* 146/10 (October 1985): 10–14.

7. Lavedan's scenario divides the film into six tableaux, but Saint-Saens's score reduced these to five by combining the original fourth and fifth into a single tableau. In the scenario, Tableau 4 is concerned with the actual murder and Tableau 5 with the King's inspection of the Duke's corpse. These variations of formal layout, and the mystery of the score's reference to a missing "staircase" shot, are discussed by Cosandey in "Wo ist die große Treppe hingekommen?"

8. As noted by Brian Rees in *Camille Saint-Saëns: A Life* (London: Chatto & Windus, 1999), 382. See Saint-Saëns, *Symphonie en fa, "Urbs Roma"* (Paris: Éditions françaises de musique, Technisonor, 1974), 137ff.; and compare *L'Assassinat*, Tableau 4, mm. 86–126. The March theme in the symphony pervades the "A" sections of a large movement in ABABA form; the B sections, in F major, provide sweeter music, meant to console. As others have noted, there are resemblances between this and the slow movements of Beethoven's Symphony no. 3 ("Eroica").

9. In *Music and the Silent Film* I called attention to this passage (though I was unaware of its derivation from the symphony), suggesting its resemblance to such grotesqueries as Gounod's *Funeral March of a Marionette*.

10. Georges Sadoul, *Dictionary of Films*, ed., trans., and updated by Peter Morris (Berkeley and Los Angeles: University of California Press, 1972): see entry for *"Assassinat, L."* (I am grateful to Russell Merritt for calling my attention to this passage.) Thus far I have been unable to find independent confirmation of this anecdotal comment in any sources pertaining to Florey, nor in anything written directly by or about Griffith in the 1920s.

11. The other co-director was a more obscure figure, André Calmettes. A French Internet entry on him states that it was his idea to have a score, "to cover up the noise of the spectators." Such a rationale is unconvincing—it amounts to a discredited cliché, long used to account for silent film music in general. Moreover, the Film d'Art enterprise was one of several in those years that were tied to the creation of special scores, partly for purposes of promotion.

12. Marks, *Music and the Silent Film*, 64.

13. Various biographers of Saint-Saëns have relied on Griffith's comments as proof of the film's impact on the director's style and on film history more generally: see, for example, James Harding, *Saint-Saëns and His Circle* (London: Chapman & Hall, 1965), 204. This idea can be traced back to Sadoul, *Histoire générale*, 2:541n2, where he asserts that *L'Assassinat* was "greeted by the whole world as a masterpiece, above all by Griffith." Sadoul in turn refers the reader to *When the Movies Were Young*, a memoir by the director's first wife, Linda Arvidson Griffith (1925; repr. New York: Dover, 1969). The relevant passage in her book (65–66) is rather vague, though it does mention the film as an example of the "high-class pictures that Pathé and Gaumont were then putting out." For careful study of the relation between style in Griffith's films and various *"films d'art,"* see Tom Gunning, *D. W. Griffith and the Origins of American Narrative Film: The Early Years at Biograph* (Urbana and Chicago: University of Illinois Press, 1991), esp. 38–39 and 172–75.

14. See Henri Langlois, "French Cinema: Origins," in *Cinema: A Critical Dictionary; The Major Filmmakers*, ed. Richard Roud (New York: Viking Press, 1980), 1:400–401; also, for

a good historiographical overview of the film's reception, see Ian Christie, "Forms: 1890–1930: The Shifting Boundaries of Art and Industry," in *The French Cinema Book*, ed. Michael Temple and Michael Witt (London: British Film Institute, 2004), 56–57.

15. Albert Richard, "Au lecteur," *Camille Saint-Saëns 1835–1921: Correspondance inédite* (Paris: La Revue Musicale, 1983), 5 (my translation). The seventy-nine letters in this volume contain no references to *L'Assassinat*. My thanks to Jann Pasler for calling my attention to this source.

16. Here are three examples, each from a different kind of source material. (1) In the elaborate compiled score prepared by Louis Gottschalk for Douglas Fairbanks's version of *The Three Musketeers* (1921), he included music by ten nineteenth-century French composers, among them one piece by Saint-Saëns, the orchestral prelude to his oratorio *Le Déluge*, op. 45: it appears four times within a score comprising sixty-two numbered segments. (2) In the "Thematic Music Cue Sheet" compiled by James C. Bradford for *Sorrows of Satan* (1926, directed by Griffith), cue 6 in the list of sixty-three calls for "The Swan," as "Mavis Theme," and six subsequent cues call for the same theme to be repeated. (3) George Beynon's manual, *Musical Presentation of Motion Pictures* (New York and Boston: G. Schirmer, 1921), 35–36, offers a list of sixty-eight "standard overtures" that the author recommends for inclusion in every theater's orchestral library. Some composers are represented by several pieces (for example, Suppé and Mendelssohn); by Saint-Saëns there is one work, the aforementioned oratorio prelude. No other reference to the composer appears in this text.

17. *Motion Picture Moods for Pianist and Organists: A Rapid Reference Collection of Selected Pieces*, comp. Erno Rapée (New York: G. Schirmer; 1924; repr. New York: Arno Press, 1974).

18. Erno Rapée, *Encyclopedia of Music for Pictures: As Essential as the Picture, in One Volume* (New York: Belwin, 1925; repr. New York: Arno Press / New York Times, 1970). As the wide-ranging functionality of Rapée's categories indicates, the musical repertoire could take on strange associations, and the programs in many theaters encompassed much more than the movies alone within an afternoon's or evening's entertainment. To cite one example, the tone poem *Le Rouet d'Omphale* appears not only (as one might expect) under SPINNING WHEEL and SYMPHONIES AND SYMPHONIC MOVEMENTS, but also (as one might not) under AEROPLANE, BIRDS, and MYSTERIOSOS. Here are the other references to Saint-Saëns's music, listed in alphabetical order by musical titles (in the *Encyclopedia*, the order is by categories): *Danse macabre* under GRUESOME, MYSTERIOSOS, and SKELETON; *Henry VIII Ballet Divertissement* under AGITATO EXTRACTS FROM STANDARD WORKS; *Le Déluge* prelude (again!) under ANDANTES (NEUTRAL) and RELIGIOUS MUSIC; *Marche militaire française* under FESTIVAL MUSIC and MARCH—PROCESSIONAL; *La Princesse jaune* Overture, under COMEDY PICTURES and OVERTURES (each time misspelled "Princess June"); *Samson and Delilah* under GRAND OPERA, plus "My Heart at Thy Sweet Voice" and the "Bacchanale" under OPERATIC EXTRACTS and FESTIVAL MUSIC, respectively; *Suite algérienne*, movements 3 and 4, under SUITES, MISCELLANEOUS, plus movement 3 ("Rêverie du soir") under HAPPY CONTENT and PASTORALE; "The Swan" under ANDANTES (NEUTRAL); Symphony no. 2, movement 4 (Prestissimo) under AGITATO EXTRACTS FROM STANDARD WORKS and QUICK ACTION.

19. Some key composers whose listings are by rough count more numerous than Saint-Saëns include Bizet (more than 20), Délibes (22), Gounod (22), Grieg (60), Massenet (35), Mendelssohn (18), and Tchaikovsky (65). Alongside these are many more composers who specialized in writing incidental pieces for movies during the silent period (Bergé, Breil, Borch, Lake, Langey, Levy, Minot, Zamecnik, etc.), as well as others whose popular light-classical or salon music became cinema repertory staples (Chaminade, Herbert, Sousa, and Tobani).

20. Hans Erdmann and Giuseppe Becce, assisted by Ludwig Brav, *Allgemeines Handbuch der Film-Musik*, 2 vols. (Berlin-Lichterfelde and Leipzig: Schlesinger'sche Buch und Musik-handlung/Rob. Lienau, 1927).

21. The oldest film on the list (after *L'Assassinat*) is *The Last Days of Pompeii* (1913), included because a recent DVD version has a compiled piano score with some pieces by Saint-Saëns. IMdb also lists *Ceux de chez nous*, a silent documentary made by Sasha Guitry in 1916 to show

off France's great artists. In this the composer is seen both at the piano and conducting. (Guitry reissued the film in 1952, adding anecdotal commentaries about the footage.)

22. As the one piece from *Carnaval des animaux* that Saint-Saëns allowed to be published during his lifetime, "Le Cygne" glided into the silent film musical repertoire and from there into sound films, ripe for parody. It is briefly mocked, for example, in the 1932 cartoon *The Wizard of Oz* (based very loosely on the book), and in two early Warner Bros. musicals, *Dames* (1934) and *Gold Diggers of 1935*.

23. A prime example is *They Shall Have Music* (1939). Within this fictional story several concert staples are played, including five works featuring violin solos by Heifetz—a standout being his version of the *Rondo capriccioso*. As opposed to *Au Revoir les enfants*, in which the performance per se is not the focus, *They Shall Have Music* gives us a record of Heifetz in his prime.

24. *Goin' to Town* has been released on DVD as part of *Mae West: The Glamour Collection* (Universal Studios, 2006), a two-disc collection of five of her films.

25. The allusion to Beaumarchais is made explicit at the beginning by the singing of a roundelay, with the text printed on screen, from his play *The Marriage of Figaro* (Act 4, scene 10: "Coeurs sensibles," etc.).

26. Within the opening titles (in the restored version available from Criterion on DVD), the only composers listed are Mozart and Monsigny, as well as Roger Désormière (implicitly as arranger and conductor). Mozart's contribution is the Dance no. 1 in D Major, from *Three German Dances*, K. 605, heard complete during the opening credits. In the booklet that accompanies the DVD, Joseph Kosma is also credited as an arranger, and several more pieces are listed. An interesting discussion of some of the music is found in Michael Litle, "Sound Track: *The Rules of the Game*," *Cinema Journal* 13/1 (Autumn 1973): 35–44.

27. See Jann Pasler, *Composing the Citizen: Music as Public Utility in Third Republic France* (Berkeley and Los Angeles: University of California Press, 2009), esp. chaps. 3 and 4. *Danse macabre* is mentioned in varied contexts, 54, 228, 243, 261, 365n, 513n, and 700. The last reference is particularly striking, for comparing the effects of this piece to Ravel's *La Valse*. See also 295–96, which notes the paradoxical values of "republican" composers Saint-Saëns, Massenet, and Delibes.

28. Actually, even these pieces can still sound fresh when handled carefully. In *Hugo*, the 2011 film directed by Martin Scorsese, *Danse macabre* is played as an accompaniment to Méliès's *Voyage à la lune*, creating a delightfully surreal effect. It is as if Scorsese and his musicians have opted to confirm the assertion by Albert Richard cited above, by demonstrating that the composer's music was adaptable to all kinds of silent films regardless of direct correlation.

29. In the film's end credits, the performance of "The Aquarium" is credited to the Vienna Philharmonic; no conductor is listed, but as per the IMdb this performance was conducted by Karl Böhm in 1975. It thus would be the version released that year by Deutsche Grammophon, coupled with Prokofiev's *Peter and the Wolf*, for which the piano parts are played by Aloys and Alfons Kontarsky.

30. For a similar use of the piece, see the opening montage in the documentary *Visions of Light* (1992), co-directed by Arnold Glassman and Todd McCarthy. The recurrence seems anything but accidental, since the film traces the history of innovative styles of cinematography, with Nestor Almendros's camerawork on *Days of Heaven* given close attention.

31. Malick's treatment of Morricone's score for *Days of Heaven* caused considerable strain between director and composer, starting with the decision not to use the latter's newly composed title music, because the director had become "married" to Saint-Saëns's piece from the time it had been used as a temp track. (I am grateful to Dan Carlin, the film's music editor, for sharing this information with me in a personal communication.) In July 2011, a 2-CD issue of the complete score for *Days of Heaven* was issued by *Film Score Monthly*, containing the film's final music tracks as they stand, as well as all of Morricone's cues in their original order.

Beyond the Conceits of the Avant-Garde:

Saint-Saëns, Romain Rolland, and the

Musical Culture of the Nineteenth Century

LEON BOTSTEIN

Saint-Saëns and the Legacy of Modernism

Camille Saint-Saëns possessed extraordinary musical gifts: daunting range, versatility, and spectacular craftsmanship as a composer, not to speak of his virtuosity as a pianist and organist. Yet in his lifetime his music elicited a relatively restrained enthusiasm. The contrast eludes facile explanation. Famous, admired, and respected as Saint-Saëns was through-out his career, his place in the repertoire since his death in 1921 has weakened considerably. A great deal of his music has disappeared from view; a few works, mostly concertos (including the *Introduction et Rondo capriccioso*, op. 28), are played often, and one miniature, "The Swan," has become an indelible icon.[1] Saint-Saëns's music has consistently garnered admiration as elegant and expert even if it rarely if ever inspires deep attachment as compelling and original.[2] The transcendence, emotional intensity, and disarming distinctiveness many listeners have come to expect of truly "great" music seem absent.

In a 1899 volume on Saint-Saëns by Otto Neitzel—the sixth in the extensive and successful series of popular German-language biographies edited by Heinrich Riemann, itself evidence of Saint-Saëns's stature as a living composer—the paradox of Saint-Saëns's career framed the book's argument. In the art of music, Neitzel claimed, two basic categories of great "heroes" existed: conservatives and progressives. These categories mirrored a distinction between craft and originality. By way of explanation, Neitzel availed himself of an explanatory economic metaphor well suited to his readers. The "heroic" conservatives were comparable to investors who relied on massive, accumulated capital that they expanded by accruing interest. The great progressives resembled entrepreneurs who startled the world by creating, as if out of nothing, new sources of wealth.[3]

In the narrative of French nineteenth-century music Saint-Saëns was the leading conservative. Georges Bizet earned the distinction as France's leading progressive. Neitzel assumed that his reading public—amateurs and concert-goers—would not hold a prejudice against any heroic conservative, or view him as less worthy or admirable. His extensive and laudatory monograph closed with the enthusiastic expectation that more wonderful and welcome music would come from Saint-Saëns's pen, particularly "a beautiful string quartet."[4]

Neitzel's assumptions about the prejudices of the public turned out to be wrong. Posterity has relegated Neitzel's great "conservatives" from the nineteenth century to the margins, not only in music but in painting and literature as well. Instead the verdict of the fin-de-siècle modernist generation has triumphed. Typical of this critical consensus is Richard Strauss's opinion that Saint-Saëns's most successful opera, *Samson et Dalila,* was exceptionally well written, and superlative in terms of craft (which is why Strauss himself conducted it), but in the end it had "nothing to say." With real reluctance, the Nobel Prize–winning writer, activist, and prolific music critic, Romain Rolland (1866–1944), concluded in 1901 that Saint-Saëns's music was ultimately without real "interest"; the composer was an "excellent musician" but a "mediocre" artist. The music was too controlled, it lacked passion and the demonic; it revealed too much good sense. It would not be remembered as part of France's distinctive cultural legacy.[5]

Does Saint-Saëns's music merit the neglect it has received? In what sense can the composer legitimately be regarded as a conservative? Saint-Saëns may not exhibit characteristics dear to late-Romantic and early twentieth-century conceits about art and the character of artists (consider the views of Oscar Wilde and Thomas Mann)—that greatness demands extremes, the sacrifice of respectability, balance, and reason. But by the same token, the music cannot be dismissed. Even Glenn Gould "admired" Saint-Saëns (that is, all but his music for the piano).[6] The sophistication and refinement of such works as the less famous concertos, the Beethoven Variations, op. 35, and the oratorio *Le Déluge* show why Saint-Saëns succeeded in becoming among the most famous and popular composers of the nineteenth century, a "classic" in his own time, as Rolland put it.[7]

Nonetheless, the reputation Saint-Saëns achieved—the paradoxical combination of exceptional craft, lack of compelling surface novelty and persuasive spiritual or emotional content—coheres entirely with the composer's explicit aspirations and commitments. Saint-Saëns enthusiastically assumed the mantle of an eclectic and synthetic artist. He stood firm, beginning in the 1860s and 1870s and particularly in his later years, as an opponent to exorbitant claims on behalf of art (in the manner of Wagner) and to novelty, and most of all to the "illusion" of "progress" in the arts. As Marcel Proust observed in 1895, Saint-Saëns wished to "confer through archaism his noble credentials to modernity; to give, bit by bit, to a common cause the value of an original imagination the masterly, singular, sublime quality of expression, to create from an archaism a flash of wit, a general idea, a summary of civilization."[8] Saint-Saëns's outspoken defense of the inextinguishable vitality of tradition earned him the reputation, by the end of his career, as a reactionary. Even his most sympathetic biographers feel compelled to apologize for his polemical excesses and his denigration of and disregard for Debussy, Strauss, and Stravinsky.

Saint-Saëns's project was, in effect, to write new music for a wide public he believed capable of locating and appreciating normative standards in musical aesthetics—beauty, nobility, form, and clarity. He evolved a method of creative historicism. Proust put it this way: "He understands how to rejuvenate a formula by using it in its old sense, and to take each musical phrase, so to speak, in its etymological sense. He borrows their charms from Beethoven and Bach, or rather, as in one his most beautiful transcriptions, bestows on Bach charms that were not his before." Saint-Saëns was a "musical humanist." With "expert, disconcerting, diabolic and divine games," he "at every moment instills bursts of inventiveness and genius into what seemed to be a field bound by tradition, imitation and knowledge."[9]

In the first phase of his career in Paris, Saint-Saëns earned a reputation as a defender of new, controversial trends in music—of Schumann, Liszt, Berlioz, and even Wagner (and a few of his struggling French contemporaries, Bizet among them). Saint-Saëns's advocacy represented an attack on an endemic superficiality in taste and criticism and the sterile and rigid classicist academicism prevalent in Parisian musical circles in the 1840s and early 1850s. His defense in the 1860s of Wagner took courage, since many established figures, including Ambroise Thomas and Gounod (whom Saint-Saëns revered), were staunch anti-Wagnerians. Nonetheless, from the very start Saint-Saëns formed a self-image as a contemporary representative of a noble but malleable tradition. As the century progressed he fought to protect the integrity of tradition and musical culture against the specter of a decline in standards of taste that accompanied the dramatic social and material changes of the mid-nineteenth century, including the spread of literacy.

For Saint-Saëns, music was, in its essential aesthetic character, an aristocratic art, one of refinement, sensibility, and cultivation, endowed with a noble legacy and inexhaustible riches. The composer enthusiastically embraced the task of spreading the capacity for refined aesthetic discernment and reaching a broader public eager for music, especially in Paris after 1871. Politically, he was a staunch republican who believed in the potential reconciliation of democracy and the elevation of taste. He was persuaded that art could be part of a civilizing process and that the historic cultural achievements of the past, if properly preserved and renewed, could be passed on to future generations as a vital national patrimony.[10]

Saint-Saëns's music is in this sense the realization, through music, of an explicit project: the celebration of continuity within the aesthetic traditions of history. This, in turn, reflected the conviction that resistance, through art, against the corrosive dynamics of modern history was essential. Progress in taste and judgment could not be taken for granted as an inevitable outcome of the expansion of the literate audience. Saint-Saëns's ambition revealed a nuanced optimism—a sympathetic response to a wide-ranging cultural debate framed by a polemical worldview famously articulated in 1869 by Matthew Arnold in *Culture and Anarchy*, and subsequently by Max Nordau, in three separate volumes between 1883 and 1896.[11]

Rolland expressed a pointedly French version of this fear of a decline. He spoke of "artistic degradation," a "vice" or "secret sore eating away" at art and culture. The struggle was between health, chastity, and purity and debauchery and a "neurasthenic" sensibility characteristic of modernity. In 1911 Rolland defined the challenge facing art as the erosion of any civic virtue in the aesthetic sensibilities of the Parisian public: "The emptiness . . . the idleness, the moral impotence, the neurasthenia, its aimless, point-less, self-devouring hypercriticism . . . how people could live in such a stagnant atmosphere of art for art's sake and pleasure for pleasure's sake. And yet the French did live in it: they had been a great nation and still cut something of a figure in the world . . . but where were the springs of their life? They believed in nothing, nothing but pleasure."[12] In contrast to Saint-Saëns, Rolland, before World War I, already suspected that the remedy to this moral crisis of modernity required more than an aesthetic renewal, particularly one based in music. As Rolland observed, "Music is one of the great modern dissolvents. Its languorous warmth, like the heat of a stove, or the enervating air of autumn, excites the senses but destroys the will."[13]

Oblivious to such doubts, Saint-Saëns by the mid-1890s saw his work as an explicit act of defiance against the evisceration, in the name of progress and historical necessity, of normative aesthetic standards of "form," "balance," and "style" rooted in classicism. The enemy was a progressive philosophical historicism in the arts that led to a misplaced obsession with fashion brought on by the "continual progress" of modern civilization in industry, commerce, science, and the politics of mass society. Saint-Saëns's intuitions were more aligned with the eighteenth-century philosophical belief that there were rational normative truth-values in ethics and aesthetics. His approach to composition reflected a stubborn resistance to the idea that with history fundamental cultural norms inevitably changed. He believed that tradition reflected and vindicated essential stable values and practices. Understood properly, tradition adapted to history in a valid, disciplined, self-correcting manner. Therefore it was an indispensable bulwark against the rapid turns in fashion that had come to dominate modern cultural life. In Debussy's slightly ironic words, "We seem to forget that Saint-Saëns, going right against the grain, makes a point of taking no liberties; when others demolish everything, he sees all the more reason to conserve it. . . . He has a gift of artistic clairvoyance rare in these times, for many merely change the name of things, nothing deeper. Such conscientious workmanship must be proof of artistic worth."[14]

Saint-Saëns was on the losing side of a culture war that spanned his lifetime. The losers were not necessarily either conservatives or reactionaries, but defenders of a vision of classicism that took into account the demands of the present. Saint-Saëns studiously avoided closed systems and doctrinaire, imitative academicism. The victors were the artistic movements that embraced what they saw as the overwhelming and concrete imperatives of modern life. These inspired late Romanticism, realism, and naturalism and a succession of avant-gardes, the first of which developed in the late 1880s and emerged in the mid-1890s, and the last of which made its appearance immediately after World War I.

The rhetoric of a May 1914 *Paris-Journal* review by Apollinaire of a concert by Giorgio De Chirico's polymath younger brother Alberto Savinio is characteristic of that which prevailed and that which Saint-Saëns opposed. Savinio was a Max Reger student, an early experimentalist, and a proto-surrealist. Apollinaire averred, "People who have followed and participated in today's heroic art movements make a very clear distinction between the adjectives *modern* and *new*; and I hasten to say that only the latter is used in speaking of an artist whose work is genuinely new and daring, stunning and powerful. . . . We had become used to considering music as an outmoded, practically stagnating art. Everything in it was a slave to *aesthetics* and *beauty*, two abstractions to which we no longer attach any importance. . . . Admittedly, Savinio has not brought out a renewal of music . . . however . . . he has never indulged in those orgies of good taste to which our so-called modern composers have accustomed us. . . . I am not referring to composers like Erik Satie . . . who, although they have blazed no new trails, have at least helped to discredit in the minds of young people that melancholy good taste whose effects were so disastrous." Apollinaire concluded that Savinio's purpose in music was "to restore to it the chaste sentiment, the natural poetry, and the heroic . . . the spirit of fatality and eternity that breathes in the music of Modest Musorgsky."[15]

The construct of the "new," extending well beyond the notion of the modern, shaped a decisive, progressive, and rebellious facet of twentieth-century modernism. Saint-Saëns exemplified the musical culture anchored in "good taste" and tradition against which Apollinaire's "new" took aim. Insofar as the early twentieth-century avant-garde irrevocably altered the criteria of judgment in art, it has made developing empathy, attachment to, and admiration for the music of Saint-Saëns extraordinarily difficult. Any attempt to rehabilitate Saint-Saëns's reputation remains hampered by prejudices that emerged from the late nineteenth-century debate and were bequeathed, largely unchallenged, by the twentieth century to the twenty-first.

Saint-Saëns does not represent an isolated case. The mid-nineteenth century witnessed a proliferation of composers, writers, and painters of superlative gifts in whose work the requisite qualities of novelty, originality, and an overt adequacy to modernity seem absent, despite unmistakable virtues of craft, complexity, refinement, and elegance. Compare the contemporary reputations of Stendhal and Flaubert with that of Victor Hugo, Saint-Saëns's favorite author. The confrontation between mastery, defined in traditional terms, the appeal to normative "abstractions" of beauty and aesthetics, and a failure to establish a persuasive originality adequate to historical progress or the "modern" (from the standpoint of post-Wagnerian musical aesthetics) can be found in the work of two composers: Max Bruch (1838–1920), an exact contemporary of Saint-Saëns, and the somewhat younger Alexander Glazunov (1865–1936). Each produced, as did Saint-Saëns, an extensive varied catalogue of superbly written works, earned worldwide reputations, a loyal following, and wielded a powerful influence within the musical and cultural world of their respective nations, Germany and Russia, comparable to the role Saint-Saëns played in France.

The victory of the fin-de-siècle avant-garde against the cultural conceits and practices audible in Saint-Saëns, Bruch, and Glazunov was trenchantly articulated in philosophical terms after World War I. Theodor W. Adorno was persuaded that in modernity art "may be the only remaining medium of truth in an age of incomprehensible terror and suffering."[16] Authenticity was thus understood as a valid metaphysical quality of any work of art, mirroring some notion of truth in history. Even though Saint-Saëns's project was propelled by a combative historical stance directed against the ravages of "modernity," it is not surprising that Adorno remained deaf to Saint-Saëns. Saint-Saëns's conception of art defied the immanent logic of history, which disqualified his music from achieving the ethical qualities essential to aesthetic greatness. Adorno cited Saint-Saëns only in passing (on the issue of Debussy's "mannerist" tendency) and dismissed a piano concerto (played by Alfred Cortot) as "unsalvageable." It is as if Saint-Saëns had never existed. His status as one of the most admired, celebrated, and performed composers and musicians of Europe for over half a century was seen as a symptom of a discredited culture and aesthetic.[17]

Why then did Saint-Saëns, an exemplar of a cultural taste and practice that defined and embraced the notion of a normative legacy and standards bequeathed by the past, win the unqualified admiration not only of the public at large but of luminaries from Liszt to Fauré and Ravel? The answer lies, ironically, precisely in the distinctive synthesis he achieved between tradition and modernity. Ravel, in particular, pursued a comparable strategy. But Ravel's music has eluded the epithet "conservative." It is not clear that Saint-Saëns deserves that label, either. His most often played works, such as the Symphony no. 3, the *Organ* (1886), display melodic and harmonic usages explicitly reflective of current practice. But they also signal an overt debt to preexisting models. For Symphony no. 3, the model was a relatively recent one, Liszt's *Faust* Symphony. "Genius" was not to be found in novelty per se. Rather, it resided, in the process of imitating the masters, in the gift of being "unable not to be oneself."[18] Subjectivity and individuality, the historical present, demanded expression in art only within a classicist trajectory, one that included Liszt's generation. The limits to the neoclassicist composer Henri Reber's (1807–1880) achievement, in Saint-Saëns's view, lay in his lack of the "power and fecundity" to express himself uniquely. By contrast, in Saint-Saëns's view, a painter such as Ingres could never resist being himself, even when he sought to imitate Raphael.

During his career Saint-Saëns witnessed a shift in expectations concerning musical experience. In his early years what passed for tradition in musical form, communication, and expression was increasingly under siege as academic, old-fashioned, and sterile. At the same time, up-to-date fashion in France seemed patently artificial and superficial. The young composer went against the grain of a reigning but facile early nineteenth-century theatrical romanticism. His benchmark became Mozart. Mozart represented the ideal balance between "conforming" to public taste and originality, between a respect for conventions and traditions and the pursuit of novelty.[19] Saint-Saëns's classicist impulse was tempered further by nineteenth-century Romanticism, a welcome concession to public taste. It would be subsequently refined by incorporating the midcentury intersection of music, narration, and nationalism that was particularly audible in the work of Wagner.

The phenomenal success Saint-Saëns experienced as a prodigy encouraged the composer's bent toward absorbing and assimilating contrary tendencies in art. By the mid-1850s, when Saint-Saëns was in his early twenties, he had achieved a self-confidence characteristic of many prodigies, effortless assurance bolstered by adulation of the public and the admiration of older established contemporaries. It took the form, in Rolland's terms, of an "intellectual moderation" that prevented him from being "tortured by any passion." The "lucidity" of his "reason" protected Saint-Saëns from falling prey to any rigid adherence to a school or style. He possessed an enviable equilibrium based in an astonishing imitative facility that was catholic in its integration of "heterogeneity."[20]

Saint-Saëns was therefore the voice of reason, the musical Voltaire of the nineteenth century (not its Rousseau), a paragon of "perfect" French lucidity achieved through a sense of personal independence that was tied to a unique French commitment to "the great classical spirit, an encyclopedic 'high culture' of music." Saint-Saëns was the French master of a musical classicism that derived, however, primarily from German-speaking Europe. His historical contribution, for Rolland, was international and synthetic. He took music, viewed as a decorative luxury art form in France, and transformed it, using German models, into poetry with a special French sense of clarity, thereby making music a potent medium for national self-expression. His musical achievement bridged the gap between Berlioz and César Franck. By championing Liszt, Saint-Saëns opened the way for French instrumental music to connect with the other arts and to aspire to the philosophical and poetic, even though in his own works he refused to do so. But for Rolland (as for many of his contemporaries), and much to Saint-Saëns's dismay, the creator of a truly original new French tradition was not Saint-Saëns but César Franck. As Rolland put it, Franck fashioned the "victory" of the "new French music" Saint-Saëns helped prepare.[21]

By the time Saint-Saëns died, critics and audiences had become irretrievably contaminated by post-Wagnerian demands, particularly the call for an unmistakably recognizable national voice. The followers of Franck responded not only to this call—but to expectations that such music would bring with it the shock of the new, subjective, radical individualism, and a measure of spiritual transformation. Such expectations in the twentieth century rendered forging a connection to Saint-Saëns's achievement nearly impossible. To admire Saint-Saëns was to reveal one's own philistinism and superficiality—a matter of irony, given Saint-Saëns's attempt to combat both phenomena.

Even the defense of the composer as elder statesman and the most "complete" musician by his loyal pupil Fauré, as well as the respect for Saint-Saëns's craft and method admitted by Poulenc and Ravel, revealed a certain defensiveness, a distinct reserve, and restraint.[22] Rolland captured the overwhelming aspect of a nostalgic historicism that would ultimately define the work of Saint-Saëns. The music was, in the end, "often pale, a bit consciously self-effacing, except when suddenly, on a page, or in a phrase, in certain harmonies, the clear gaze of the past shines clearly."[23]

Painting and the Redefinition of Classicism

In 1897, Saint-Saëns expressed his own views on the extraordinary transformation and expansion of musical culture that had taken place since 1848. Music now reached a far wider public, all over the world. The printing press had spurred this spread, privileging instrumental music as "literature." Music alone, without narrative or illustration, "becomes a book, universal and indestructible. People of every country read it and understand it, whatever their language and race, and future generations will receive it intact." Music, through notation, had broken free of performance. It was no longer an art of mere "sensation" requiring a crowd. "Serious" music, Saint-Saëns insisted, blossomed only once it could be read alone, in solitude, like a book. This elevated a Beethoven symphony to the status of a tragedy by Racine. Neither of them "needs to be played to exist." The spread of literacy secured the autonomy of musical discourse and the centrality of the art of music as a universal human achievement. These in turn made a widespread musical culture in a modern democratic social order plausible.[24]

Since the future of music as more than entertainment and ambient temporal decoration was contingent on literacy, for Saint-Saëns the grammar, syntax, and formal procedures that justified its status as a public language and the peer of the written arts—poetry and philosophy—represented indispensable foundations. These had developed first in the eighteenth century and rightly turned out to be regarded as the "classical" foundations of musical art. The composer's innumerable reworkings of historical music for domestic use at the piano represented modern translations of music's past for music's new literate audience. He was intent on using literacy and amateurism to reach a broad audience so that refined judgment and taste might be cultivated and disseminated.[25]

The struggle to elevate musical culture in France, to emancipate music from its social and utilitarian entertainment functions, was well under way when Saint-Saëns came of age in the 1840s. Yet the gulf between academic classicists and pioneering Romantics—Chopin, Schumann, Liszt, and Berlioz in particular—appeared wide. Much like Mendelssohn (with whom he was continually compared), Saint-Saëns sought to reconcile these two seemingly irreconcilable trends. He knew that even Rossini, let alone the younger generation from around 1810, all recognized a common debt to Beethoven, if not Mozart. The young Saint-Saëns took it upon himself to forge a synthesis between classicism and the Romantic movement, seeking to redeem the principles of classicism—the pursuit of formal beauty—in a modern fashion.[26]

Saint-Saëns's construction of his own ambitions suggests a parallelism between music and painting. During the first half of the nineteenth century a tension existed between the traditions of classicism and the claims of Romanticism. Indeed, one of the most eloquent witnesses of the aesthetic ideals of a new French musical culture at midcentury that Saint-Saëns embraced was the painter Eugène Delacroix. Delacroix was an avid music enthusiast, for whom music was "higher than the other arts." His explanation echoed Saint-Saëns's conviction that music held something in common with the printed word, since for Delacroix music, "although completely in a convention of its own . . . is also a complete language. All we need do is enter into its kingdom."[27]

Delacroix rose to fame in the 1820s as the exemplary Romantic artist, the polar opposite of Jean-Auguste-Dominique Ingres. Although Delacroix insisted that art take on a "modern form," like Ingres he remained skeptical of fashions and derided any mere turn to contemporaneity and any rejection of classical models. For Delacroix, as for Saint-Saëns, "Mozart is undoubtedly the creator—I will not say of modern art, since there is none being produced at the present time—but of art carried to its highest point, beyond which no further perfection is possible."[28] Friendly as Delacroix had been with Chopin, both Chopin and Berlioz seemed flawed and too concerned with effect, a view Saint-Saëns shared. Delacroix revered not only Mozart but also Haydn and Rossini. He admired Beethoven, albeit with reservations. Delacroix held on to a notion of normative "excellence"; he applied his highest praise to Raphael (much like Ingres), Shakespeare, and Mozart. In 1855 he expressed his annoyance at the "ridiculous infatuation" with Wagner (whose most recent work was *Lohengrin*), declaring that, out of excessive self-regard, the German composer "suppresses many of the musical conventions believing that they are not based on any law of necessity."[29]

If Saint-Saëns feared the possibility that the spread of literacy in modern times, for all its fundamental potential, might bring a debasement of public taste, Delacroix was contemptuous of the public, the "mass of stupid people who, because they have neither taste nor discernment, are always having to find something new to get excited about." Excessive disregard for the past, for the "laws" of art, or too great an allegiance to tradition were "ridiculous preferences and aversions" that Mozart, for example, would not have shared.[30]

The judicious integration of a midcentury Romantic vocabulary with the veneration of Mozart, as articulated by Delacroix in the mid-1850s, expresses fairly the resilient foundation of Saint-Saëns's aesthetic. Delacroix described cogently the peculiarly French character of the aesthetic "eclecticism" of which Saint-Saëns was so consistently proud. Writing in 1857, he observed, with some irony, that "one might say that *eclecticism* is the particular banner of the French in the arts of drawing and music. The Germans and Italians had clear-cut qualities in their arts, some of which were mutually antipathetic; the French, in every age, seem to have attempted to reconcile such extremes by softening what appeared discordant. Thus their works are less striking. They are addressed more to the intellect than to the emotions. In music and painting they are inferior to all other schools through their practice of injecting into their work, in small doses, a collection of qualities which other schools find incompatible, but which the French temperament contrives to harmonize."[31]

Saint-Saëns remained true to this ideal of an intellectually refined French syncretic tradition, but without Delacroix's sense of its limitations. He resisted Franck and Vincent d' Indy's development of a radical effort to define a French musical vocabulary, just as he resisted the extreme enthusiasm for Wagner after 1871.[32] In the end, as Rolland observed, Saint-Saëns's somewhat reductive patriotism was never expressed stylistically in music beyond the formal criterion of intellectual clarity. Conspicuous patriotism led him to oppose the inclusion of foreign composers in the concerts of the Société nationale as engineered by d'Indy in 1886.[33] But Saint-Saëns's patriotism focused on a distinctly French gift for aesthetic judgment, one rooted in a unique confidence regarding form and taste that made explicit borrowings from the German and the Italian—and indeed from non-Western sources—a matter of pride and superiority.

The habit of appropriation that leads to eclecticism represented an aesthetic virtue, not a limitation. Giving way to fashion and modernity by sacrificing normative practices represented by Mozart (who had not invented a novel style, Delacroix proudly asserted) constituted a violation of the highest excellence. Saint-Saëns's A-Major Symphony, written at the age of fifteen, is astonishing in its command of form and counterpoint; its material is in no way banal and dull. It draws explicitly from Mozart's *Jupiter* Symphony. It may be reminiscent of models in terms of style, but it is every bit as distinctive as the Symphony in C (1855) written by Bizet, whom Saint-Saëns deeply admired at age seventeen.

Saint-Saëns maintained an intense lifelong interest in painting. He was proud of his personal associations with four painters, three of whom were avid musical amateurs. Among these amateurs was Ingres, as well as an artist nearer in age to the composer, as famous in his lifetime as Saint-Saëns and comparably dismissed and forgotten in the wake of modernism: Gustave Doré (1832–1883). The two others, close friends of Saint-Saëns, were once well regarded but are now considered minor figures: Henri Regnault (1843–1871) and Georges Clairin (1843–1919). Regnault, Clairin, and Doré each exhibit a syncretic mix of French Romanticism and classicism. Doré was world-famous, not only as an illustrator; he, like Saint-Saëns, had a significant following, particularly in America. Clairin, remembered most for his portraits of Sarah Bernhardt, also designed some costumes for the 1875 premiere of *Carmen*. Of the four, he was perhaps closest to the composer.

Although Delacroix's work remains understood as innovative and distinctive in its Romanticism, his thinking about art and art making ran parallel to that of Ingres. As early as 1821 Ingres declared, "I am then a conservator of good doctrines, and not an innovator. I am not, any longer, as my detractors pretend, a servile imitator of the schools of the thirteenth and fourteenth centuries, even though I know how to avail myself of them more fruitfully that they know how to see."[34] Writing in 1822 Ingres declared, "The great study is to be directed by reason and tact to distinguish the true from the false, and one can only achieve it by learning to become exclusive, and that is to be instructed, if I dare say so, by the continual frequenting of beauty alone."[35] The task was to judge beauty "intelligently" through the study of Raphael and Velasquez.

Like Ingres, Saint-Saëns became an idiosyncratic classicist, an outsider within a movement. Ingres had been closer to the vaunted contemporary Romanticism associated with Delacroix than contemporaries suspected. Similarly Saint-Saëns, despite a reputation as inclined to classicism, sought to integrate the sensibilities and ambitions of Liszt and Berlioz within the conventions developed by Mozart and Beethoven. It is therefore not surprising that early in his career he was criticized by conservative critics for stylistic innovations and distortions, just as Ingres has been throughout his career by conservative critics. Ingres's 1862 masterpiece *The Turkish Bath* is a visual equivalent of Saint-Saëns's finest works—the symphonic poems, the Third Symphony, and especially, *Samson et Dalila*. In all these works there is a keen appropriation of new trends, particularly the realist naturalism ascendant in midcentury painting exemplified by Gustave Courbet and its moral equivalent in music: narrative, programmatic music.[36]

Ingres's attachment to playing the violin became a French colloquial phrase: a *violon d'Ingres* became a synonym for any kind of hobby. This was a just verdict, according to Saint-Saëns. Doré was the far superior violinist, even though his musical imagination, much to Saint-Saëns's dismay, was too easily satisfied by the concerti of Bériot. Saint-Saëns befriended Doré who confided in him his battles with depression and his anger at his critical reception.[37] Saint-Saëns's empathy for Doré may have been rooted in a dimension of the composer's own personality that Rolland characterized as a "weary melancholy": a "quite bitter sense of nothingness" often camouflaged by a nervous gaiety and humor.[38] But more likely the composer was sympathetic to the scale, variety, and ambition of an output that paralleled his own. Doré's incredible range and skill as illustrator and painter were virtuosic achievements on a par with those of Saint-Saëns.

Doré's work, regarded with skepticism in France in a manner resembling that which hindered Saint-Saëns in getting his operas produced, ranges from small Daumier-like caricatures and his highly popular book illustrations, to large canvases, mostly landscapes, realist portraits, genre scenes, and a few monumental religious paintings. Doré utilized the full range of nineteenth-century styles from naturalism and mystic Romanticism to stark polemical realism. His techniques were equally historicist and eclectic, ranging from neoclassical drawing to evocations of Rembrandt and Renaissance compositional strategies, to a nearly impressionist brushwork in his later landscapes. Such virtuosity served Doré well in his lifetime, but earned him contempt posthumously. His enormous popularity, like that of Saint-Saëns, provoked a negative critical reaction that aligned itself with the progressive painterly tradition central to modernism. These biases continue to obscure Doré's achievement.[39]

Regnault and Clairin shared with Saint-Saëns an obsession with the Oriental, a dimension of French painting already present in Delacroix. Regnault's two most famous canvases, *Salomé* (1870) and *Execution Without a Hearing* (1870), directly reveal the painter's debt to both Delacroix and Ingres. Saint-Saëns mourned the premature death of his friend, the most musical of all the painters he knew (Regnault was killed during the hostilities of 1871).[40] The composer's 1871 *Marche héroïque*, op. 34, was dedicated to his memory. Clairin traveled with Saint-Saëns and lived nearly as long (he died in 1919). They shared an important mutual friend, the composer Augusta Holmès, with whom Saint-Saëns was infatuated and whose relationship with César Franck made cordiality between the two composers impossible. Regnault and Clairin displayed far less eclecticism than Doré, but they perfected the merger of classicist painterly skill, the illusionism of realism, and the Romantic fascination for their Orientalist subject matter. Their canvases suggest Saint-Saëns's own appropriations, within traditional forms, not only of oriental evocations but of narrative conventions in musical rhetoric developed during the nineteenth century.[41]

Although Saint-Saëns argued on behalf of the autonomy of music, he learned, first from Schumann and then from Liszt and Wagner, to use musical time in instrumental music (especially in many of the concerti) in a manner that was implicitly suggestive of a program, or a theatrical scene. Saint-Saëns understood keenly that Chopin's popularity derived from the capacity of the performer and listener to infer in the structure and rhetoric of the music a story line, or an emotional state. The forms Saint-Saëns adhered to may have invoked a classical tradition that resisted too great a causal link between musical aesthetics and emotion, but in Saint-Saëns's actual realization, the content and execution in the music were distinctly if not explicitly up to date in terms of melodic construction and elaboration, harmonic usage, instrumentation, and dramatic pacing. This is particularly audible, notwithstanding the explicit historicist sources and references in, for example, his opera *Henry VIII*.[42]

This synthesis was evocative of Regnault and Clairin. The Romantics in music had expanded the power of music to weave the illusion of prose realism, of illustration and correspondence through musical means. The work of Doré, Regnault, and Clairin, in their achievement of a disarming and provocative visual representation and illustration without decisive innovations in painterly strategies, suggest Saint-Saëns's appropriation of the narrative potential of music in his instrumental compositions, a concession to contemporary taste and a veritable key to the immediate affections of the musical public.

Saint-Saëns's self-conscious use of Romantic narrative procedures within a classical framework constituted a direct appeal to the legibility of refinement and craftsmanship within the rapidly growing educated public. This public was, for Saint-Saëns, central to the task of creating a distinct French contemporary equivalent to the German classical musical tradition. Saint-Saëns's ambition and success offer a revealing contrast to that of Brahms. It is ironic that the French—including Saint-Saëns and Rolland—had little good to say about the German composer. To them, Brahms was an "insipid" neoclassicist. Brahms, whose commitment to classical procedures and the legacy of tradition paralleled that of Saint-Saëns, and who, like Saint-Saëns, emulated Schumann, was considered in France as the epitome of sterile conservatism (this was also the view held by Tchaikovsky).[43] If for Saint-Saëns the French adulation for Wagner carried the danger of vulgarity and anarchy in music, Brahms represented a forced, unnatural, stilted, and pedantic allegiance to classicism. Rolland defined this fatal shortcoming as lacking the ability "to live, to live too much! . . . A man who does not feel within himself this intoxication of strength, this jubilation in living—even in the depths of misery—is not an artist. True greatness is shown in this power of rejoicing through joy and sorrow. A Mendelssohn or a Brahms, gods of the mists of October, and of fine rain, has never known this divine power."[44]

Saint-Saëns fared better, in Rolland's view. He embraced nineteenth-century theatricality, the flair for the dramatic, virtuosity, and the lighthearted. Saint-Saëns admired Liszt and Anton Rubinstein, for whose music Brahms had little respect. Both Saint-Saëns and Brahms shared an almost exactly identical view of Wagner, however.[45] They viewed him as brilliant in terms of compositional practice, but pernicious as a model and object of emulation and ideology. Neither had sympathy with virulent anti-Wagnerians. The difference was that Saint-Saëns was a polemicist like Wagner, and reveled in publishing his own prose. Brahms never assumed the mantle of critic or public commentator.

These similarities notwithstanding, the post-Wagnerian and modernist judgments in ascendancy since the end of the nineteenth century have accommodated a sharp reversal in the view of Brahms as a "conservative." Partly owing to Schoenberg's revisionist assessment, Brahms's posthumous standing has risen just as the fin-de-siècle opinion of Brahms as "unnatural" (vis-à-vis his contemporaries) has disappeared. Despite Saint-Saëns's parallel achievements, aesthetic commitments, and distinctive adaptations of classical practice, no comparable reevaluation seems imminent.

Prodigies, Tradition, and Musical Culture

In the history of music Saint-Saëns's two rivals in terms of talent and precocity as a composer were Mozart, whom he revered, and Mendelssohn, to whom he was compared. As a virtuoso performer he had just as few equals—Liszt, on the piano, and J. S. Bach, on the organ. As interpreter and improviser, he was regarded in France as being in a class by himself. The differences between the post-prodigy careers of Mozart and Mendelssohn on the one hand and Saint-Saëns on the other are telling. Leopold Mozart, once having grasped the talents of his children, exploited them. He understood the context of survival. A musician's livelihood depended on the reputation made in an international circuit within the aristocracy. Success with this elite public led to patronage, starting with the monarchy. Patronage and public were largely overlapping categories in a class structure in which the musician was distinctly not an equal. Leopold and later his son used their prodigious musical gifts to cater to a well-informed enthusiasm among aristocratic amateurs who shared in the near monopoly of political, social, and economic power in the ancien régime.

Musicians and patrons in the late eighteenth century recognized that there existed within the established rhetorical and formal conventions of instrumental musical entertainment an interior space, an opacity that defied easy description. Music was understood as possessing emotional power, significance, sentiment, and beauty that transcended its formal structure, the conventions of language, and its utility in terms of social function at court or in church. Instrumental music cloaked a capacity to suggest, if not articulate, the intimate, the philosophical, and the spiritual. Music in the era of Mozart was understood as Janus-like: it had its public function, an affirmative place in terms of public rituals. Music's capacity to amuse and even illustrate, with tone painting, enabled a composer to earn a livelihood. But it possessed the evident disruptive power of penetrating well beyond the respectable and mundane. This in part rendered it particularly alluring to its privileged patrons. Leopold Mozart communicated to his son that in order to survive, he had to go well beyond public utility and an imitative and affirmative competence and attain a craft and originality at the level of Johann Christian Bach and Haydn, both of whom commanded the coded interior and the visible exterior dimensions of musical communication.

Beethoven lived out his career under a modified version of the same system. Conditions had changed decisively by the time Mendelssohn made his appearance as a prodigy. In Berlin, Paris, and Vienna a new elite had emerged out of the chaos of the Napoleonic era—an urban, non-aristocratic audience that resembled the one Haydn had encountered in the 1790s in London. With the Restoration in France and the reimposition of monarchical control on the Continent, including censorship and an effective policing system, the twin attractions of musical practice—public and private—took on a new prestige and urgency. Of particular interest to this new public was precisely the indeterminacy and opacity of meaning in instrumental music.

Aristocratic patronage continued, but in greatly reduced form. The non-aristocratic public moved into the vacuum left by the decline in aristocratic patronage. They eagerly emulated the tastes of the nobility. Musical culture expanded, but through modified structures of public institutions. By the time of Mendelssohn's youth, choral and instrumental amateurism had made its signal appearance in numbers large enough to support music publishing, music education, and music journalism. Furthermore, whereas civic associations in most areas of endeavor were viewed as subversive, in music they were comparatively exempt from censorship and even encouraged after 1815, owing to music's apparent ideological neutrality and abstract nature, its connection to religious practice, compatibility with domestic life, and civilizing function. Between 1815 and 1848, music gained momentum among the educated classes as a unique form of life in which the freedoms of expression and movement could be exercised without fear.

The new civic associations and their offshoots—concert societies and conservatories—fashioned a public life for music. The continued participation by the landed aristocracy in musical life was now sustained by an open collaboration with the urban bourgeoisie. This alliance of elites helped secure the social prestige of the cultivation of music. It led to the transposition of private palace entertainments of the eighteenth century into the urban salon, at which a mix of aristocrats and haute bourgeoisie gathered on a common ground of cultural taste. This was the setting in which the young Mendelssohn first stepped into public view, conveniently, in his parental home in Berlin. Mendelssohn, however, had the double misfortune of being both Jewish and born to parvenu, non-aristocratic wealth.

Twenty-five years later, the context in which a composer could make a career had evolved even further. A robust urban public economy of musical culture had come into being. As a result, the young Saint-Saëns had to gain the attention of three constituencies to achieve success: 1) the remnants of the old aristocratic patronage class, such as the Prince of Monte Carlo; 2) the haute bourgeoisie of Paris, with its fashionable elite, including critics and colleagues in music; and 3) a burgeoning spectator public. This third group demanded and supported an extensive concert life. It was with this third constituency, the urban spectator public, which experienced enormous growth in France after 1870, that Saint-Saëns experienced his greatest success.[46]

Public culture may have been of keen interest during the reign of Napoleon III as a matter of policy and patronage, but during the Third Republic music evolved into a crucial shared ground between the state and the populace, a fertile arena for national self-definition and the assertion of democratic values. Particularly after 1880, a varied, diverse, and rich populist cultural life was encouraged. Especially in Paris, the traditions of classical music came to play a vital part. An ever more complex and byzantine web of politicians, publishers, critics, and promoters—key actors in a burgeoning music business—became a fixture of musical culture. Saint-Saëns was popular with all three constituencies from the very start of his career. He understood that the tastes and prejudices of the urban spectator public were particularly vulnerable to the influence of journalism.

But Saint-Saëns's early success in Paris was more comparable to Mendelssohn's experience than to the post-1870 context he encountered later. Saint-Saëns the prodigy was still dependent on a limited elite that controlled a semi-public arena as well as public recognition. This elite included a learned class—the leading musicians and pedagogues of the day—and critics, whose press accounts depended as much on public appearances as on rumors and a social network linked to the expanded patronage class that made up the audiences of the salons.

The prestige of music on the European continent before 1848 was only in part the result of its opacity and subjectivity of meaning, and thus its aura as the personal Romantic art form par excellence. The opera, too—that merger of words and music—had become a defining public cultural genre, especially in France. The expressive conventions of instrumental music, the seemingly inherent "Romantic" character of music as mirroring the infinite, the sublime, the ineffable, the interior self, and the divine, had been transferred to the theater to create a popular public form of entertainment that still benefited from music's protected status as a coded pseudo-language.

When Saint-Saëns came of age, he encountered in both the worlds of domestic and public music a consensus that the art form's capacity to communicate meaning derived from its formal essence, evident in the conventions of eighteenth-century musical classicism. Commanding, honoring, and emulating those practices was an essential precondition of success. Mendelssohn, more than Mozart, provided the model for how a prodigy could succeed. The teenage Mendelssohn secured his status as a composer by impressing the older generation (figures such as Goethe) by astonishing feats of imitation and emulation, evoking the power of music by using models from history. Mendelssohn found a way to realize his individuality within established traditions of form and conventions of expression developed between the eras of Bach and Beethoven. Both Mendelssohn and Saint-Saëns experienced public exposure and fame at an early age. For both, the demands of that experience led them to cultivate a historical self-consciousness that came to dominate their careers not only in terms of aesthetic ideals—the Romantic ambition to express subjectivity in a striking and original manner, but within the framework of classicism—but civic ones as well.

Mendelssohn's gifts enabled him to establish prominence and stability not merely with the limited public of the aristocracy but with the burgeoning urban amateur and spectator class, the literate reading public, that dominated the religious revival of the first half of the nineteenth century. Ironically, Mendelssohn's anxieties over his pariah status as a Jew led him to develop a strong sense of the civic and spiritual power of music. This, in turn, influenced the shape and character of his large-scale works. Historicism was an effective framework for reaching the expanding audience for the oratorio and symphony.[47] It flourished in conjunction with the explicit intent to communicate with the reading public, whose enthusiasm for the Romantic in literature and art Mendelssohn's generation understood well.

The assumption of classicism as a guiding framework for new music prior to 1848 underscored music's status as an affirmative, rather than a subversive medium. Aesthetic education through music led to civility in shared public space and the cultivation of invented civic memories and traditions. The public success of music after 1870 was an outgrowth of this aspect in the perception of music cultivated before 1848; the aesthetic sensibilities that merited dissemination after 1870 had been defined earlier in the century and carried the seductive imprimatur of a legacy of aristocratic patronage. A claim of cultural continuity in the face of political and social change made the integration of the classical and the Romantic an ideal basis for the invention of a national tradition in the arts. The appeal to a normative musical syntax and style lent legitimacy to the nineteenth-century distillation of historical continuity. It validated tradition—a notion dear to both Mendelssohn and Saint-Saëns.

The importance of virtuosic emulation and imitation was even greater in Saint-Saëns's youth than in Mendelssohn's. Saint-Saëns faced a far more robust infrastructure in Paris, one that included conservatories, concert societies, and journalism. Saint-Saëns successfully negotiated the private and public aspects of patronage and concert life and, like Mendelssohn, involved himself in the evolution of new institutional frameworks. His facility in all things musical made imitative eclecticism an effective stratagem (as it would be to three subsequent prodigy composers—Erich Wolfgang Korngold, Leonard Bernstein, and Lukas Foss). Referencing past models secured quick enthusiasm and affirmation, without much controversy from the public, particularly those newcomers to the art form eager to display refined judgment.

Saint-Saëns's prominence and centrality in French musical life reached new heights in the 1880s. If the composer expressed bitterness at disappointments, notably around the astonishing delays he encountered in mounting opera productions, it was owing to exaggerated expectations developed as a prodigy, the sense that he would always continue to elicit the same high measure of astonishment, and that there would be, in adulthood, few if any contemporary competitors, only older masters who assumed the role of eager supporters. Saint-Saëns's envy of Massenet's success can be understood in this light.[48] When the cheering remembered from his prodigy years ceased, Mendelssohn became increasingly self-critical. But in Saint-Saëns the triumphs of youth bred an unshakable confidence and resistance to self-criticism—a cocky sense, entirely legitimate, of an essential superiority that derived from his undiminished and unrivaled facility. That facility and ease may have been his undoing, as they have proven to be in many extraordinary prodigies who grow up without exposure to the terrors of obscurity, competition, and self-doubt of the sort that plagued Brahms and Paul Dukas.[49]

By the time *Samson et Dalila* reached the Paris Opera in 1892, Saint-Saëns's public success as a prolific performer and composer were at their peak. His career, in the context of music as a politically significant civic art consistent with republican ideals, confirmed the merit of his adaptive syncretic approach. The aristocracy, the urban bourgeoisie, and the broad citizenry all responded with a collective allegiance, lionizing him. His insistence that all music be written within a normative framework of style and form reassured the expanded listening public. Relying on shared stable criteria of judgment, value, and tradition that incorporated new sources of influence, new music could be properly and confidently vetted. Saint-Saëns's success with large-scale public works, from the 1881 *Hymne à Victor Hugo*, op. 69, to *Le Feu céleste*, op. 115, from 1900, made him the representative of the musical culture of the age. As Rolland noted in his characterization of the Parisian public at the end of the century, in Saint-Saëns's music one could see how "the music reflected the audience, the audience reflected the music."[50]

By the mid-1890s, Saint-Saëns's role as a representative figure extended to the mundane aspects of a modern career. Material prosperity and the assertion of normative aesthetic premises were mutually reinforcing. From the perspective of publishers, Saint-Saëns was a success. He was sought after as a concert performer. He wielded influence in the leading educational and cultural institutions, sacred and secular. In the expanded civic arena of the nation, his fame extended well beyond Paris. He was an international figure, arguably France's leading musical personality, having attained a status not dissimilar to that of Mendelssohn in German-speaking Europe in the 1840s.

With incomparable brilliance and enthusiasm, Saint-Saëns expressed through music the historicist self-confidence of nineteenth-century aesthetic taste.[51] He animated the inherited classical traditions of musical craftsmanship and form by bending them, so to speak, to fit the expectations created by midcentury Romanticism. He then accommodated the growing allure of exoticism and Orientalism and finally adapted into his own music the narrative realist strategies and sonorities of the pioneers of instrumental program music in a manner that contributed to the formation of French nationalism during the Third Republic. Yet his patriotism was oddly without partisanship. Saint-Saëns never revealed his views on the Dreyfus case. He cultivated an ideal of French cultural solidarity and pride that sought to rise above divisive politics and social strife.[52]

This ambition itself was a symptom of Saint-Saëns's roots in the political culture of pre-1848 Europe. Music had to be seen as politically benign. His allegiance to the concept of music as a fundamentally self-referential medium provided a framework of resistance against what he perceived as the ideological appropriation of the art after 1871. For Saint-Saëns, d'Indy's premise that expression and passion were essential purposes and goals of musical communication was fundamentally not only wrong, but pernicious. If music could convey translatable sentiments of emotion, it could also become a medium of political persuasion.[53]

Music, for Saint-Saëns, was self-sufficient—neutral with respect to specific emotions and ideas. Historicist and realist techniques in music were subsumed into neoclassical formalist norms that helped construct a shared French national heritage. Such a notion of music vindicated the cultural alliance cemented before the fall of Napoleon III between the aristocratic remnants of the ancien régime (supplemented by Napoleon I, Louis Philippe, and ultimately Napoleon III), and the ascendant urban bourgeoisie. Indeed, the music of Saint-Saëns was celebrated in the palaces of those with titles from England to Monte-Carlo, in the salons of the wealthy, and in the ateliers of writers and painters. In the last decades of the century, as music took its place in the entertainments of the broad national public, Saint-Saëns's disparate network of relationships, level of recognition, the range of his output, and his brilliance made him a defining presence in French music. Beloved by the wider public, Saint-Saëns became to music what Victor Hugo, his favorite author, had become in letters.[54]

Saint-Saëns therefore became the exemplary target of the parody, ridicule, and rebellion chosen by the generation of Alfred Jarry, whose *Ubu Roi* premiered in Paris in 1896. This avant-garde sought the inversion of established norms. It challenged the conventions of style and the rhetoric of justification. A de-legitimation of the reigning conceits of art and culture was under way, notably its cozy connection to authority and power.[55] An alternate aesthetic aristocracy and reality was in the making, one that seemed purely and perversely anarchic. As Pa Ubu exclaims in Act 3, scene 2: "My lords, I have the honor to inform you that as a gesture to the economic welfare of my kingdom, I have resolved to liquidate the entire nobility and confiscate their goods."[56] Apollinaire's era of the "new" was ushered in. Its definition of art centered on the defiance of history and the rejection of historicism. Jarry and his contemporaries expressed contempt for the very ambition and commitments Saint-Saëns had come to represent.

Among musicians, Saint-Saëns stood for the status quo, an oligarchy of taste, power, and respectability mediated through the aesthetics of restrained refinement reminiscent of artificiality. Debussy and Satie, as well as disciples of Vincent d'Indy, suspected in Saint-Saëns's detachment, ease, and confidence in a delusional aesthetics of mere beauty, a formalist art for art's sake, distant from nature and reality. Saint-Saëns held, for example, that prose, in the end, could not truly rise to the level of art. Such an attitude seemed to place music as an art in the role of an abstract, detached affirmation of reason, science, and progress (the conceits of the age), something utterly supplemental and divorced from ethics, politics, and the human. As Saint-Saëns summarized his position in 1913: "Just as morality has no business being artistic, so Art has no business to be moral. . . . The end purpose of morality is morality: the end purpose of Art is Art, and nothing more."[57] This smug sense of self-satisfaction provoked the satirical radicalism of the avant-garde rebellion of the 1890s. Despite Stravinsky's essential agreement with Saint-Saëns on the nature of music, the modernism that took center stage during the last decade of Saint-Saëns's life, well represented by the 1913 premiere of *The Rite of Spring*, only deepened the radicalism of the later 1890s, rendering Saint-Saëns's music irretrievably reactionary and regressive.

This critique of late nineteenth-century mainstream cultural taste in music, the de-legitimation of the conventions, habits, and norms to which Saint-Saëns catered and adhered—calls out for revision. The manner in which we have assigned value to music since 1900—with expectations that we will gain from the musical experience a dimension of social and ethical criticism—is suspect. Must we still take sides in the modernist quarrels of the twentieth century? Must we obtain satisfaction from the assignment of responsibility for corruption, exploitation (imperialism), alienation, inequality—injustice in general—to the tastes of the ruling elites who were, circa 1890, the patrons and the audience of Saint-Saëns? Such an attitude constitutes a barrier to historical understanding. A more differentiated and empathetic historical understanding of the status of music in France and Europe toward the end of Saint-Saëns's career might clear the way to a new receptivity to the composer's music.

Jean-Christophe and Saint-Saëns

A neglected source on musical culture in France at the end of the nineteenth century from a perspective located squarely in between the progressive (Debussy) and the conservative (Saint-Saëns) is Rolland's massive Bildungsroman, *Jean-Christophe*, completed and published in 1913. It is a *locus classicus* regarding the perception of the place and significance of music. The novel is remembered but unread. It is unloved on account of its florid, overbearing prose, its smugness, its lack of artifice or drama, and its tedious surface of pretentious philosophizing. Perhaps its fame and success were based on dazzling qualities to which we have become blind, just as many may have lost the capacity for deep affection for Saint-Saëns's aesthetic achievement. The novel was a major factor behind Rolland's receipt of the Nobel Prize in 1915.[58]

The novel takes the form of a biography of a composer, Jean-Christophe Krafft, a German born in the Rhineland who ultimately makes his career in Paris, where he dies (after more than 1,200 pages). Although nominally set in the present (that is, the early years of the twentieth century), the first volume, depicting the hero's early life, reads like a fictionalized biography of the young Beethoven in surroundings much like the world of the late eighteenth, not the mid-nineteenth century: an anachronistic context that is peculiarly jarring.

That dissonant detail aside, the basic outlines of Jean-Christophe's character and family (father and brothers) come to resemble a popular version of Beethoven's. Rolland wrote extensively and admiringly about Beethoven. The ways Beethoven is understood—as bizarre, rebellious, resistant to authority, hypersensitive, awkward with women yet hopelessly smitten for much of the time, irascible yet loyal, overcome with inspiration, and also deeply despondent, rude and outspoken yet tender, and overcome with a sense of justice—were well-worn clichés within the musical public, routinely underscored by Rolland's published music criticism.[59]

Yet Rolland, by transposing this Romantic icon of the volcanic artistic genius with roots in the eighteenth century into the late nineteenth century, created a framework for reconciling the claims for music asserted by progressives and conservatives at the turn of the century. Rolland shed his own particular philosophical light on the history and future of musical culture. To achieve this, he made Jean-Christophe an amalgam. The framework is Beethoven, but Christophe exhibits biographical elements of Hugo Wolf and others, even Saint-Saëns. An ironic link between the fictional and historical occurs late in the novel. Jean-Christophe, at the very end of his life, composes a choral symphony on a text of a protégé of his deceased friend (the writer Olivier), titled *The Promised Land*. In the year Rolland finished the final chapters, 1913, Saint-Saëns collaborated with his English friend Hermann Klein on an oratorio titled *The Promised Land*. The novel features a smattering of thinly veiled portraits, including a character, Cecile, based on Augusta Holmès, as well as other recognizable contemporaries of Saint-Saëns, such as Richard Strauss (a character in the book named Hassler) and Hans Pfitzner. At the same time the novel is filled with references to real works of music and historical events.[60]

Saint-Saëns's presence hovers over the novel. He informs Rolland's admiration for Christophe, who readily concedes the superiority of the German tradition and refuses, as did Saint-Saëns, to join his French colleagues in disavowing the achievements and models of Mozart, Haydn, Beethoven, and Bach (although, Saint-Saëns claimed to prefer Rameau, a view Rolland satirizes: "Quite distinguished men extolled Rameau in mysterious terms").[61] Rolland shared with Saint-Saëns a mixture of awe and envy of the musical traditions of France's national rival.[62]

The novel challenges the extreme "art for art's sake" philosophical underpinnings of Saint-Saëns's aesthetic. Rolland, following Rousseau, understands music as ultimately tied to the spiritual essence of nature, though it cannot be truly imitative. Early on, the prodigy Jean-Christophe is chastised for wanting to write something "pretty" in a manner that suggests a critique of Saint-Saëns's ambition to please his public's taste with sounds that are easy to listen to: "There you are! You wrote for the sake of writing. You wrote because you wanted to be a great musician, and to be admired. You have been proud; you have been a liar . . . a man is always punished when he is proud and a liar in music. Music must be modest and sincere—or else, what is it?"[63]

At the same time Rolland fashions his lead character's development as if he wished to see him develop precisely in the manner in which Saint-Saëns did, but with greater ambition. Rolland challenges the dangers inherent in Saint-Saëns's conception of music as autonomous in its logic and conventions, hinting at the toll taken by not forging a fundamental connection between music and emotions or ideas. Rolland writes of his main character: "During the years when the character is formed he [Jean-Christophe] came to consider music as an exact language, in which every sound has a meaning, and at the same time he came to loathe those musicians who talk without saying anything."[64] In contrast to Saint-Saëns, Christophe possessed "passion for strength" that "was the very opposite of the French genius for subtlety and moderation." Rolland's hero "scorned style for the sake of style and art for art's sake. The best French artists seemed to him to be no more than pleasure mongers."[65]

Saint-Saëns's traditionalism protected him from falling prey to short-comings that had come to define French composers in modern times. Rolland, no doubt referring to Debussy, wrote: "What they most lacked was willpower, force: they had all the gifts save one—vigor and life. And all their multifarious efforts were confusedly directed, and were lost on the road. It was only rarely that these artists became conscious of the na-ture of their efforts, and could join forces to a common and a given end. It was the usual result of French anarchy, which wastes the enormous wealth of talent and good intentions through the paralyzing influence of its uncertainty and contradictions."[66]

Nonetheless, classicism and formalism alone, as the case of Saint-Saëns showed, did not offer an adequate solution in the French context:

With hardly an exception, all the great French musicians, like Berlioz and Saint-Saëns—to mention only the most recent—have been hopelessly muddled, self-destructive, and forsworn, for want of energy, want of faith, and, above all, for want of an inward guide. . . . They never seemed to consider anything but form. Feeling, char-acter, life—never a word of these. . . . It never seemed to occur to them that every living musician lives in a world of sound, as other men live in a visible world, and that his days are lived in and borne onward by a flood of music. Music is in the air he breathes, the sky above him. Nature wakes answering music in his soul. His soul itself is music: music is in all that it loves, hates, suffers, fears, hopes. And when the soul of a musician loves a beautiful body, it sees music in that, too. The beloved eyes are not blue, brown, or grey: they are music: their tenderness is like caressing notes, like a delicious chord. That inward music is a thousand times richer than the music that finds expression, and the instrument is inferior to the player. Genius is measured by the power of life, by the power of evoking life through the imperfect instrument of art. But to how many men in

France does that ever occur? To these chemists music seems to be no more then the art of resolving sounds. They mistake the alphabet for the book.[67]

For Rolland, more was needed. The rational had to be tied to the natural, in the sense of Rousseau's notion that human perfectibility and reason have to draw their strength in society from man's essentially compassionate nature. Rolland suspected that Saint-Saëns's facility showed an absence of the spontaneous inspiration that had to precede reason. Inspiration as a criterion of aesthetic judgment in music became fashionable in part as a result of Hans Pfitzner's polemical crusade against modernism.[68] Inspiration was understood as a natural, nonrational experience and not, as Saint-Saëns saw it, as a function of intellect that must exhibit order and refined, clear judgment. Rolland observes: "This delight in inspiration was so vivid that Christophe was disgusted by everything else. The experienced artist knows that inspiration is rare and that intelligence is left to complete the work of intuition: he puts his ideas under the press and squeezes out of them the last drop of the divine juices that are in them— (and if need be sometimes he does not shrink from diluting them with clear water). Christophe was too young and too sure of himself not to despise such contemptible practices. He dreamed impossibly of producing nothing that was not absolutely spontaneous."[69]

Yet Rolland was not without admiration for Saint-Saëns's use of order, intellect, and craft to avoid producing mundane, imitative, and forgettable music. Consider this thinly veiled assessment from Jean-Christophe's first sojourn in Paris, where he found among the leading French "contemporary" composers a "lack of freedom: almost all of their works were 'constructed.' Sometimes an emotion was filled out with all of the commonplaces of musical rhetoric, sometimes with a simple rhythm, an ornamental design, repeated, turned upside down, combined in every conceivable way in a mechanical fashion. These symmetrical and twaddling constructions— classical and neoclassical sonatas and symphonies—exasperated Christophe, who, at that time, was not very sensible of the beauty of order, and vast and well-conceived plans. That seemed to him to be rather masons' work than musicians.'"[70]

Rolland shared Saint-Saëns's suspicion of the conceits of post-Wagnerian composers regarding music's connection to emotion and ideas. Christophe, Rolland writes,

was no less severe with the romantics. It was a strange thing, and he was more surprised by it than anybody—but no musicians irritated him more than those who had pretended to be—and had actually

been—the most free, the most spontaneous. . . . In truth, the candid
Schumann could not be taxed with falsity: he hardly ever said anything that he had not felt. But that was just it: his example made
Christophe understand that the worse falsity in German art came
into it not when the artists tried to express something which they
had not felt, but rather when they tried to express the feelings which
they did in fact feel—*feelings which were false.* Music is an implacable
mirror of the soul. The more a German musician is naïve and in
good faith, the more he displays the weaknesses of the German soul,
its uncertain depths, its soft tenderness, its want of frankness, its
rather sly idealism, its incapacity for seeing itself, for daring to come
face to face with itself. That false idealism is the secret sore even of
the greatest—of Wagner.[71]

Rolland chose to distort the conditions of Parisian concert life during
the time Saint-Saëns made his career in order to highlight the narrowness
of taste of the early 1900s, which was for Rolland a consequence of too
great an emphasis on surface style and fashion:

The same pieces at every concert. Their copious programs moved
in a circle. Practically nothing earlier than Beethoven. Practically
nothing later than Wagner. . . . It seemed as though music were reduced to five or six great German names, three or four French
names, and, since the Franco-Russian alliance, half a dozen Muscovites.
None of the old French Masters. None of the great Italians. None of
the German giants of the seventeenth and eighteenth centuries. No
contemporary German music, with the single exception of Richard
Strauss, who was more acute than the rest, and came once a year to
plant his new works on the Parisian public. No Belgian music. No
Czech music. But most surprising of all, practically no contemporary
French music. And yet everybody was talking about it mysteriously
as a thing that would revolutionize the world.[72]

In the novel it becomes clear that Rolland's ambivalence toward Saint-
Saëns possessed political roots. Saint-Saëns's aesthetic derived from
and cohered with the composer's sense of ease with his aristocratic public and
patrons, despite his allegiance to the Republic. Furthermore, Saint-Saëns's
"art for art's sake" formalism fit conveniently with the cultural prejudices
of the reigning economic and political elite. The separation of nature,
emotion, and expression from the essence of music while cloaking it in
neutrality also forced upon it a fundamental insularity.

But Rolland admired Saint-Saëns for writing for working-class audiences, children, and students. Saint-Saëns's enthusiasm for composing music along classicist lines for the masses inspired the argument Rolland chose to make at the end of the novel. Here, Rolland directly challenges the Wagnerian premises about realist music of illustration, narration, and emotional correspondence. He asserts, rather, that the dominant criterion for music to reach the masses needed to be formal beauty—an aesthetic logic rooted in traditions of instrumental music and immune to ideological exploitation. The traditions of instrumental musical discourse suggested the link between music and democracy, and defined the benefit of music for all classes. A "pure" music was required for the aesthetic education of the masses. Rolland, inspired by Saint-Saëns's career, sought to replicate the eighteenth-century link between the good and the beautiful as rational categories, but in a manner appropriate to contemporary circumstances. The aesthetic behind Rolland's political hopes lay closer to Saint-Saëns than to Strauss, Rolland's friend, whose virtuosic use of instrumental music revealed a radical realism in music, and furthest from Debussy.

Rolland placed the following exhortation in his hero's voice:

Music everywhere, music in everything! If you were musicians you would have music for every one of your public holidays, for your official ceremonies, for the trade unions, for the student associations, for your family festivals. . . . But above all, above all, if you were musicians, you would make pure music, music which has no definite meaning, music which has no definite use, save only to give warmth, and air, and life. Make sunlight for yourselves! . . . The public is sick of your crepuscular art, your harmonized neurasthenia, your contrapuntal pedantry. The public goes where it can find life, however coarse and gross. Why do you run away from life? Your Debussy is a bad man, however great he may be as an artist. He aids and abets you in your torpor. You want roughly waking up.[73]

The core of Rolland's critique of Saint-Saëns, in the end, was less strictly aesthetic or musical than it was philosophical and political. If there were a justification for stressing the formal aspects of musical art and retaining an allegiance to classical norms, it was that those norms created a binding objective throughout humankind, a platform for human progress based on universal truth. What Rolland objected to was Saint-Saëns's willingness to be content with public approbation and a narrow patriotism. Despite the attempt to write large-scale works for civic consumption, the composer appeared immune to any higher idealism, and was absent a sufficient commitment to the role of art in the creation of peace and justice. It was precisely the modesty and the ethical neutrality of his music—its clarity and emotional restraint—that rendered Saint-Saëns's vigorous and appropriate defense of aesthetic standards ultimately impotent. Nevertheless, this fundamental aesthetic and the command of classical procedures, harnessed to higher political ideals rather than taken in the direction of Richard Strauss and the post-Wagnerians, held the most promise for preventing the looming decline of musical culture in a modern democracy.

As Jean-Christophe grows old in the novel he comes to a realization that eluded Saint-Saëns, despite his fame and success. Christophe

> lost all interest in music which was a monologue, a soliloquy, and even more so in music which was a scientific structure built entirely for the interest of the profession. He wished his music to be an act of communion with other men. There is no vital art save that which is linked with the rest of humanity. Johann Sebastian Bach, even in his darkest hours of isolation, was linked with the rest of humanity by his religious faith, which he expressed in his art. Handel and Mozart, by dint of circumstances, wrote for an audience, and not for themselves. Even Beethoven had to reckon with the multitude. It is salutary. It is good for humanity to remind genius every now and then. "What is there for us in your art? If there is nothing, out you go!"... It was by returning to the musical language of all men that the art of the German classics of the eighteenth century came into being.[74]

Emulation of the eighteenth century provided, for both Jean-Christophe and Saint-Saëns, an antidote to what they regarded as the undisciplined narcissism of modern music attributable directly to the influence of Wagner. In the novel, we read:

> Modern music, which is so loquaciously introspective, dragging in indiscreet confidences at every turn, is immodest and lacking in taste. It is like those invalids who can think of nothing but their illnesses, and never weary of discussing them with other people and going into repulsive petty details. This travesty of art has been growing more and more prevalent for the last century. . . . Modern Europe had no common book: no poem, no prayer, no act of faith which was the property of all. Only Beethoven has left a few pages of a new Gospel of consolation and brotherhood: but only musicians can read it, and the majority of men will never hear it. Wagner, on the hill at Bayreuth, has tried to build a religious art to bind all men

together. But his great soul had too little simplicity and too many of the blemishes of the decadent music and thought of his time.[75]

Rolland's critique of Wagner, his skepticism with respect to radical innovations, and his disappointment with Saint-Saëns all derived from his vision of what authentic art needed to be in the context of modernity. First, music had to reconcile sounds and words, but not in Wagner's manner. Rolland understood the potential of Wagner's synthesis of the linguistic and musical: it had made the expansion of the audience for music possible and provided a stable rhetorical vocabulary for musical culture in a democracy. Beyond this, the music of modernity needed, in its naturalness, to confront the present. These criteria rendered the restrained classicism of Saint-Saëns inadequate, since the right kind of music could be achieved only with a synthesis of words and music that mirrored the material and spiritual course of history. Rolland has his aged protagonist return to the home of his childhood for inspiration: "The changes that had been in the making . . . were now fully accomplished: the little town had become a great industrial city. The old houses had disappeared. The century also was gone . . . the river had washed away the meadows where Christophe had played as a child."[76]

Nostalgia and restoration were not possible. The artist of modernity had to bear witness to the present. Rolland, assuming his own voice as the novel's author, described that present to his reader: "The tragedy of a generation is nearing its end. I have sought to conceal neither its vices nor its virtues, its profound sadness, its chaotic pride, its heroic efforts, its despondency beneath the overwhelming burden of a super-human task, the burden of the whole world, the reconstruction of the world's morality, its esthetic principles, its faith, the forging of a new humanity.—Such we have been."[77]

In the novel, Rolland attempts to locate how music and the aesthetic realm might offer a clear path out of the seeming bankruptcy and collapse of rationality at the end of the nineteenth century. At the end of the novel Rolland laments the collapse at the fin de siècle of the eighteenth-century traditions of rationality in the arts and sciences, traditions with which Saint-Saëns so closely identified himself: "The reason of humanity was exhausted. It had just made a gigantic effort. It was overcome with sleep, and like a child worn out by a long day, before going to sleep, it was saying its prayers. The gate of dreams had reopened; in the train of religion came little puffs of theosophy, mysticism, esoteric faiths, occultism to visit the chambers of the Western mind. Even philosophy was wavering. Their gods of thought, Bergson and William James, were tottering."[78]

Despite his limitations, Saint-Saëns's disciplined adherence to norms of musical form and argument was admirable, particularly his effort to find a modern rational means for making great music. He resisted the use of music "as an amusement—or rather as a palliative of boredom, or as another sort of boredom—in the theaters, or in fashionable drawing-rooms, to an audience of snobs and worn-out intellectuals." Likewise, Christophe needed to seek out "the real public, the public that believes in the emotions of art as in those of life, and feels them with a virgin soul . . . the new promised world—the people."[79] Saint-Saëns may not have thought that emotions were the subject of music, but his emotional connection to music paralleled the deepest connection to life.

But a core conviction of Rolland's contradicted one of Saint-Saëns's basic beliefs. Rolland was entirely persuaded of the possibility of objective progress in the arts over time. Rolland echoed the cult of Raphael among artists at midcentury in his hope that "music has not yet had its Raphael." Indeed, Rolland has his hero enter "into the sovereign serenity of Raphael and Titan . . . the imperial splendor of the classic genius, which, like a lion, reigns over the universe of form conquered and mastered; . . . Raphael filled Christophe's heart with music richer than Wagner's, the music of serene lives, noble architecture, harmonious grouping, the music that shines forth from the perfect beauty of face, hands, feet, draperies, and gestures. Intelligence. Love."[80]

The composer of modernity idealized in Rolland's novel would honor, with intimacy, "the order in harmony of the free passions and the free will" and "maintain the just balance between the forces of life."[81] The result would offer new musical sounds within "clear symphonies" and "the union of the most beautiful forces of the music" of the age: "the affectionate and wise thought of Germany with all its shadowy windings, the clear passionate melody of Italy, and the quick mind of France, rich in subtle rhythms and variegated harmonies."[82]

This description of a syncretic and eclectic achievement rooted in a normative tradition bears considerable resemblance to Saint-Saëns's music. Yet Rolland and Saint-Saëns diverge. In Rolland's dream of a modern synthesis of classicism and the post-Wagnerian, a political, ethical ideology takes center stage. Rolland was fascinated with Strauss's synthesis of formal conventions and contemporary imperatives. Strauss, however, lacked the requisite utopian humanist fervor. His music was at one and the same time ironic and bombastic, and without sufficient clarity and lightness, French virtues apparent in Saint-Saëns. Yet Saint-Saëns did not have that extra measure of inspiration, idealism, and intensity Rolland invested in his fictional hero, his modern Beethoven. Nonetheless Saint-Saëns came close enough to offer Rolland a model of how his ideal composer might develop his craft and adapt classicism to the radically changing demands of modernity.

Once one dispenses with Rolland's hyperbolic quasi-mystical humanism (which mesmerized Stefan Zweig and repelled Sigmund Freud), the core of the issue becomes clear.[83] When we relieve music, and indeed the arts in general, of the burdens of politics, and take away expectations that perhaps are unreasonable—such as moral betterment—we are left with a vision of a synthetic, eclectic body of work that resembles the achievement of Saint-Saëns. Saint-Saëns was no political idealist or radical democrat, yet his music is supremely accessible and has all the requisite virtues Rolland attributes to the final masterpieces of Jean-Christophe. Rolland hoped for more. But must we emulate him by burdening music with the failure of politics to serve humankind?

Perhaps our historical moment requires a Raphael in music, not a tortured Michelangelo (who in Jacob Burckhardt's view was the polar opposite to Raphael). To date, the Michelangelo role, granted first to Beethoven after the composer's death in 1827, has been assigned to Gustav Mahler. Within the historical repertoire from the late nineteenth and early twentieth century, there are few masters other than Saint-Saëns who display a persuasive economy of means and form and are not overcome with the fin-de-siècle pessimism and sense of irony and nostalgia that suffuse the works not only of Mahler, but in different ways those of Brahms, Richard Strauss, Edward Elgar, and Charles Ives. Saint-Saëns's immunity to an underlying "extra-musical" idealism and metaphysical pretentions baffled Rolland. But it might well be construed as a redeeming virtue that could lead us away from our status as passive spectators to becoming engaged participants in musical culture.

A new look at the music of Saint-Saëns might inspire a return to musical thinking, musical literacy, and a deeper engagement with playing and reading music. The hypothesis behind this claim is that complex and refined musical arguments in themselves, spread broadly within the population, might advance democracy, civility, and peace far more readily than the inward, self-indulgent, and sprawling musical canvases of Mahler that have become clichés of contemporary concert life, and whose claims to meaning have been emptied of significance by routine repetition. The power of music, the power of participation in making music, the power of thinking musically may reveal themselves fully to future generations through music of a more disciplined, refined, and restrained manner—music more in the spirit of Saint-Saëns.

This all recommends Saint-Saëns to us, along with his heroes—Mozart, Haydn, Beethoven, Meyerbeer, Bizet, and Gounod—all staples of the alliance between aristocratic and bourgeois taste of the nineteenth century, a verdict shared by Tchaikovsky (although he would have left Beethoven off the list). Many of these composers fell victim too quickly and easily to the derision of modernist criticism. Perhaps a reversal is now in order. Perhaps it is a counterintuitive sign of the progress in which the composer never believed that, as Mahler predicted in his own case, Camille Saint-Saëns's time has or will come.

NOTES

I want to thank Jann Pasler, whose input was invaluable, as well as my colleagues at the Bard Music Festival Christopher H. Gibbs, Byron Adams, and Irene Zedlacher for their assistance.

1. The *Organ* Symphony, no. 3, remains a staple in the repertoire, as does the *Danse macabre*. That particular piece shows the presence of Saint-Saëns in popular culture. The 2011 movie *Hugo* uses *Danse macabre*. For further information see Sabina Teller Ratner's invaluable catalogue, *Camille Saint-Saëns, 1835–1921: A Thematic Catalogue of His Complete Works*, vol. 1: *The Instrumental Works* (Oxford: Oxford University Press, 2002).

2. The biographical background of this essay relies on the following works: James Harding, *Saint-Saëns and His Circle* (London: Chapman & Hall, 1965); Michael Stegemann, *Camille Saint-Saëns, mit Selbstzeugnissen und Bilddokumenten* (Frankfurt: Rowohlt, 1988); Stephen Studd, *Saint-Saëns: A Critical Biography* (London: Cygnus Arts, 1999); Brian Rees, *Camille Saint-Saëns: A Life* (London: Chatto & Windus, 1999); and Timothy S. Flynn, *Camille Saint-Saëns: A Guide to Research* (New York and London: Routledge, 2003). For more on the composer's musical education, see Jean Montagris, *Camille Saint-Saëns: L' Œuvre, l'artiste* (Paris: La Renaissance du livre, n.d.), 8–17.

3. Otto Neitzel, *Camille Saint-Saëns* (Berlin: Harmonie, 1899), 1.

4. Ibid., 87.

5. See *Richard Strauss and Romain Rolland: Correspondence, Diary, and Essays*, ed., annotated, and with a preface by Rollo Myers (Berkeley and Los Angeles: University of California Press, 1968), 158; Alain Corbellari, *Les Mots sous les notes: Musicologie littéraire et poétique musicale dans l'œuvre de Romain Rolland* (Geneva: Droz, 2010), 191–95.

6. "Of Mozart and Related Matters: Glenn Gould in Conversation with Bruno Monsaingeon," in *The Glenn Gould Reader*, ed. Tim Page (New York: Knopf, 1984), 33.

7 Romain Rolland, "Camille Saint-Saëns," in *Musiciens d'aujourd'hui* (Paris: Hachette, 1917), 84.

8. Marcel Proust, "Camille Saint-Saëns," originally published in *Le Gaulois*, 14 December 1895, is reproduced in *Contre Saint-Beuve: Pastiches et mélanges; Essais et articles* (Paris: Gallimard, 1971), 382–86. English version at http://www.yorktaylors.free-online.co.uk/ saens.htm.

9. Proust, "Camille Saint-Saëns," 385–86. See also Marcel Proust, "Camille Saint-Saëns, Pianist," in *Against Saint-Beuve and Other Essays*, trans. and with an introduction by John Sturrock (London: Penguin, 1988), 132–32. On Proust and Saint-Saëns, see Jean-Yves Tadié, *Marcel Proust: A Life*, trans. Evan Cameron (New York: Viking, 2000), 230–32.

10. The most significant work on the role of music in France in the late nineteenth century is the magisterial book by Jann Pasler, *Composing the Citizen: Music as Public Utility in*

Third Republic France (Berkeley: University of California Press, 2009). See also François Porcile, *La Belle Époque de la musique française, 1871–1940* (Paris: Fayard, 1999).

11. See Max Nordau, *Entartung*, 2 vols. (Berlin: Duncker, 1893); and Nordau, *Die conventionellen Lügen der Kulturmenschheit* (Leipzig: Elischer Nachfolge, n.d.).

12. Throughout this essay, citations from Rolland's novel will be cited in English from the contemporary translation by Gilbert Cannan, which although misleading and awkward, gives a sense of the character of Rolland's rhetoric and thought. Quotes from these volumes will be cited by volume and page number. The French edition used here is Romain Rolland, *Jean-Christophe*, 10 vols. (Paris: Albin Michel, 1934). The English edition is *Jean-Christophe*, vol. 1: *Dawn, Morning, Youth, Revolt*; vol. 2: *Jean-Christophe in Paris*; vol. 3: *Jean-Christophe: Journey's End*, trans. Gilbert Cannan (New York: Henry Holt, 1926), 2:116.

13. Ibid., 2:247. Rolland indeed turned from criticism to politics after 1914, largely abandoning writing about music.

14. *Debussy on Music*, collected and introduced by François Lesure, trans. and ed. Richard Langham Smith (New York: Knopf, 1977), 196–97. Debussy's views on Saint-Saëns communicated a mixture of admiration and disdain. See Hervé Lacombe, *Les Voies de l'opéra au XIXe siècle* (Paris: Fayard, 1997), 240.

15. Leroy C. Breunig, *Apollinaire on Art: Essays and Reviews, 1902–18*, trans. Susan Suleiman (New York: DaCapo, 1972), 391–93.

16. T. W. Adorno, *Aesthetic Theory*, trans. C. Lenhardt, ed. Grete Adorno and Rolf Tiedemann (London: Routledge, 1984), 27.

17. See a concert review from September 1927, repr. in T. W. Adorno, *Gesammelte Schriften*, vol. 19: *Musikalische Schriften VI* (Frankfurt: Suhrkamp, 1984), 114.

18. Camille Saint-Saëns, "Les Peintres musiciens," in *École buissonnière: Notes et souvenirs* (Paris: Pierre Lafitte, 1913), 349–55.

19. Camille Saint-Saëns, "Musical Trends," in *On Music and Musicans*, ed. and trans. Roger Nichols (New York: Oxford University Press, 2008), 44–45. See also "Don Giovanni," in *Portraits et souvenirs* (Paris: Calmann-Lévy, n.d.), 220–29.

20. Rolland, "Camille Saint-Saëns," 87–94.

21. Ibid.

22. *The Correspondence of Camille Saint-Saëns and Gabriel Fauré: Sixty Years of Friendship*, ed. Jean-Michel Nectoux, trans. J. Barrie Jones (Aldershot: Ashgate, 2004), 10. See also Jean Michel Nectoux, *Gabriel Fauré: A Musical Life*, trans. Roger Nichols (New York and Cambridge: Cambridge University Press, 1991); and Carlo Caballero, *Fauré and French Musical Aesthetics* (Cambridge: Cambridge University Press, 2001).

23. Rolland, "Camille Saint-Saëns," 96.

24. Quoted in Saint-Saëns, "Harmony and Melody," in *On Music and Musicians*, 25.

25. See the extensive list of reworkings by Saint-Saëns in Ratner, *Saint-Saëns Thematic Catalogue*, 1:429–506.

26. A useful survey of French thought on aesthetics can be found in William Knight, *The Philosophy of the Beautiful* (New York: Scribner's Sons, 1891), 113–42.

27. *The Journal of Eugène Delacroix*, ed. and with an introduction by Hubert Wellington, trans. Lucy Norton (London: Phaidon, 2010), 287. See also Nina Maria Athanassolgou-Kallmeyer, *Eugène Delacroix: Prints, Politics, and Satire 1814–1822* (New Haven: Yale University Press, 1991), 78–93, 108–16; and Gilles Neret, *Delacroix* (Cologne: Taschen, 1999), 11–20.

28. *Journal of Eugène Delacroix*, 118.

29. Ibid., 319.

30. Ibid., 290–91.

31. Ibid., 375–76.

32. See Camille Saint-Saëns, *Les Idées de M. Vincent d'Indy* (Paris: Lafitte, 1919).

33. See Michel Duchesneau, *L'Avant-garde musicale à Paris de 1871 à 1939* (Sprimont, Belgium: Mardaga, 1997), 244–81.

34. Susan L. Siegfried, *Ingres: Painting Reimagined* (New Haven: Yale University Press, 2009), 14; and Andrew Carlton Shelton, *Ingres* (New York: Phaidon, 2008), 16–21, 198–215.

35. Siegfried, *Ingres: Painting Reimagined*, 335

36. Ibid., 17. See also Linda Nochlin, *Realism* (London: Penguin, 1971).

37. Camille Saint-Saëns, "Les Peintres musiciens," 351–53.

38. Rolland, "Camille Saint-Saëns," 90–91.

39. See the following catalogues: Eric Zafran, ed., with Robert Rosenblum and Lisa Small, *Fantasy and Faith: The Art of Gustave Doré* (New York: Dahesh Museum of Art, and New Haven: Yale University Press, 2007); and Annie Renonciat, *La Vie et l'œuvre de Gustave Doré* (Paris: ACR Edition, 1983).

40. See Roger Marx, *Henri Regnault, 1843–1871* (Paris: Librairie de l'art, n.d.); Henri Cazalis, *Henri Regnault: Sa Vie et son oeuvre* (Paris: Lemerre, 1872); and Auguste Angellier, *Étude sur Henri Regnault* (Paris: Boulanger, 1879), 64–85.

41. See Rees, *Camille Saint-Saëns*, 152 and 159.

42. On *Henry VIII*, see Stephen Huebner, *French Opera at the Fin de Siècle* (New York: Oxford University Press, 2006).

43. See Rolland, "Camille Saint-Saëns," 87; and Rees, *Camille Saint-Saëns*, 72.

44. Rolland, *Jean-Christophe*, 1:380.

45. Saint-Saëns, "Introduction," in *On Music and Musicians*, 4–11; and "L'Illusion Wagnerienne," in *Portraits et souvenirs*, 281–88; and also "Antoine Rubinstein," in *Portraits et souvenirs*, 143–60.

46. See Christophe Charle, *Paris Fin de Siècle: Culture et politique* (Paris: Éditions du Seuil, 1998); James H. Johnson, *Listening in Paris: A Cultural History* (Berkeley: University of California Press, 1995); and Theodore Zeldin, *France 1848–1945*, vol. 2: *Intellect, Taste, and Anxiety* (Oxford: Clarendon Press, 1977).

47. See Leon Botstein, "Neoclassicism, Romanticism, and Emancipation: The Origins of Felix Mendelssohn's Aesthetic Outlook," in *The Mendelssohn Companion*, ed. Douglass Seaton (Westport, CT: Greenwood Press, 2001), 1–27; and Benedict Taylor, *Mendelssohn, Time and Memory: The Romantic Conception of Cyclical Form* (Cambridge: Cambridge University Press, 2011), 275–80.

48. Saint-Saëns, "Jules Massenet," in *École buissonière*, 269–76.

49. Self-criticism often is associated with the internalization of the weight of tradition—a sense of never quite meeting a standard established in the past. Mendelssohn is an example, particularly with respect to releasing work for publication. In Brahms's case the music he decided to destroy when he turned sixty, much of it apparently for string quartet, a genre he thought no one could ever write as well as Beethoven, Haydn, or Mozart, seemed not good enough. Clara Schumann disagreed but could not persuade Brahms. Dukas represents perhaps the most tragic circumstance. If Saint-Saëns felt that craftsmanship came easily, for Dukas it seemed to be a struggle. A perfectionist whose music is indeed elegantly and economically constructed, Dukas made sure that only a limited number of works survived his relentless scrutiny.

50. Rolland, *Jean-Christophe*, 3:348.

51. See Friedrich Meinecke, *Die Entstehung des Historismus*, ed. Carl Hinrichs (Munich: Oldenbourg, 1965), 2–3.

52. See Rees, *Camille Saint-Saëns*, 328–30. Also Jane Fulcher, *The Composer as Intellectual: Music and Ideology in France, 1914–1940* (New York: Oxford University Press, 2005), 48–50.

53. See Saint-Saëns's comment, in his essay "Jules Massenet," in *On Music and Musicians*, that an art of emotion is a "decadent" art (165).

54. See Jane F. Fulcher, *French Cultural Politics and Music: From the Dreyfus Affair to the First World War* (New York: Oxford University Press, 1999); and Fulcher, *The Composer as Intellectual*.

55. See Roger Shattuck, *The Banquet Years: The Origins of the Avant-Garde in France, 1885 to World War I*, rev. ed. (New York: Vintage Books, 1968); Alastair Brotchie, *Alfred Jarry: A*

Pataphysical Life (Cambridge, MA: MIT Press, 2011). See also Mary McAuliffe, *Dawn of the Belle Epoque: The Paris of Monet, Zola, Bernhardt, Eiffel, Debussy, Clemenceau, and Their Friends* (Lanham, MD: Rowman & Littlefield, 2011).

56. Alfred Jarry, *The Ubu Plays*, trans. Cyril Connelly and Simon Watson Taylor (New York: Grove, 1968), 39.

57. Saint-Saëns, "L'Art pour l'art," in *École buissonnière*, 140.

58. See David James Fisher, *Romain Rolland and the Politics of Intellectual Engagement* (New Brunswick, NJ: Transaction, 2005); R. A. Francis, *Romain Rolland* (Oxford: Berg, 1999) 64–89; Stefan Zweig, *Romain Rolland: The Man and His Work*, trans. Eden and Cedar Paul (New York: Thomas Seltzer, 1921).

59. See Rolland, *Beethoven the Creator*, trans. Ernest Newman (Garden City, NY: Garden City Publishing, n.d.).

60. Rolland, *Jean-Christophe*, 3:465

61. Ibid., 2:46.

62. Saint-Saëns was deeply invested in producing a modern edition of Rameau. What made Rameau significant was not only his potential as French rival to J. S. Bach in terms of reputation. Rameau exhibited qualities that would come to mark the French musical genius and spirit: clarity, lightness, refinement, and the dramatic.

63. Rolland, *Jean-Christophe*, 1:91.

64. Ibid., 1:136.

65. Ibid., 2:135.

66. Ibid., 2:54–55.

67. Ibid., 2:54–63.

68. See Hans Pfitzner, *Über musikalische Inspiration* (Berlin: Fuerstner, 1940), 6–7.

69. Rolland, *Jean-Christophe*, 1:365.

70. Ibid., 3:372–73.

71. Ibid.

72. Ibid., 2:44–45. See also Pasler, *Composing the Citizen*, 358–400.

73. Rolland, *Jean-Christophe*, 2:405–7.

74. Ibid., 3:52–53.

75. Ibid., 3:90–91.

76. Ibid., 3:489.

77. Ibid., 3:348.

78. Ibid., 3:482.

79. Ibid., 3:187.

80. Ibid., 3:380–81.

81. Ibid., 3:420.

82. Ibid., 3:470.

83. See Zweig, *Romain Rolland*, 52–53, 166–71; and Sigmund Freud, "Das Unbehagen in der Kultur," in *Studienausgabe*, vol. 9: *Fragen der Gesellschaft: Ursprünge der Religion* (Frankfurt: Fischer, 1982), 191–270. Freud begins his famous 1930 essay, known in English as "Civilization and Its Discontents," with a critique of Rolland's conception of an "oceanic" feeling in humanity—a sense of common destiny that justified Rolland's faith in pacifism, a faith Freud found incompatible with the facts of human psychology.

Index

Page numbers followed by n indicate notes; italicized page numbers indicate material in tables, figures, or musical examples.

Name and Subject Index

Notes on the Contributors

Byron Adams, composer, professor at the University of California, Riverside, and scholar-in-residence for the 2007 Bard Music Festival, edited *Edward Elgar and His World* and *Vaughan Williams Essays*. He has served as president of the North American British Music Studies Association and is an associate editor of *Musical Quarterly*.

Leon Botstein is president and Leon Levy Professor in the Arts of Bard College, author of several books and editor of *The Compleat Brahms* (1999) and *Musical Quarterly*. The music director of the American Symphony Orchestra and conductor laureate of the Jerusalem Symphony Orchestra, he has recorded works by, among others, Szymanowski, Hartmann, Bruch, Dukas, Foulds, Toch, Dohnányi, Bruckner, Chausson, Richard Strauss, Mendelssohn, Popov, Shostakovich, and Liszt.

Jean-Christophe Branger, maître de conférences at the Université de Saint-Étienne, has devoted most of his work to the history of music in France during the Third Republic, especially the life and music of Jules Massenet.

Mark DeVoto (translator) is a composer, writer, and professor emeritus of music at Tufts University. He edited the revised fourth (1978) and fifth (1987) editions of *Harmony* by his teacher Walter Piston and has written extensively on the music of Berg. His most recent book is *Schubert's Great C Major: Biography of a Symphony* (2011).

Michel Duchesneau is professor at the faculty of music of the Université de Montréal. He is currently director of the Observatoire interdisciplinaire de création et de recherche en musique, a research center for interdisciplinary musicology.

Lauren Elkin (translator) received her PhD in English from the Université de Paris VII and the Graduate Center, City University of New York. Her essays and translations have appeared in the *Guardian, Bookforum,* and the *Daily Beast*. She teaches at New York University in Paris.

Katharine Ellis is professor of music at Royal Holloway, University of London, and author of two monographs (on music criticism and on the French early music revival), an edited collection of essays on Berlioz (with David Charlton), and numerous essays on music's social and cultural significance.

Annegret Fauser is professor of music at the University of North Carolina at Chapel Hill. Her research engages with music in France and the U.S. in the nineteenth and twentieth centuries. The recipient of the 2011 Dent Medal of the Royal Musical Association, she is currently editor-in-chief of the *Journal of the American Musicological Society*.

Yves Gérard is emeritus professor of the Conservatoire de Paris for history of music and musicology. Most of his of publications deal with Boccherini (catalogue of the works), Berlioz (correspondence and music critic) and Saint-Saëns (biography and anthology of Saint-Saëns–Lecocq correspondence, in preparation).

Dana Gooley is associate professor of music at Brown University. His publications have centered on Franz Liszt, virtuoso performers, and public culture in the nineteenth century. He has also published on improvisation, music criticism, and jazz. He was coeditor, with Christopher H. Gibbs, of *Franz Liszt and His World* (2006).

Carolyn Guzski is assistant professor of musicology at the State University of New York / Buffalo State. A recipient of the Adrienne Fried Block Fellowship of the Society for American Music, she also holds degrees in music performance from Peabody Conservatory and the Juilliard School.

Anna Henderson (translator) holds a master's degree in translation from Kent State University and is a professional translator with a focus on French contract law and software localization. Her current projects include a translation of *Japanese Grammar: The Connecting Point*, by Kimihiko Nomura.

Carol A. Hess, professor at Michigan State University, has received the ASCAP-Deems Taylor Award, the Robert M. Stevenson Award, and has been a Fulbright Lecturer (Spain, Argentina). Her latest book is *Representing the Good Neighbor: Music, Difference, and the Pan American Dream* (Oxford University Press).

D. Kern Holoman is distinguished professor of music at the University of California, Davis. His most recent book, *Charles Munch*, was published by Oxford University Press in 2011; *The Orchestra: A Very Short Introduction* appears with the same publisher in late summer 2012.

Léo Houziaux was born in 1932. He studied astrophysics at Liège University (Belgium) and carried out post-doctoral research in the U.S. (California, Massachusetts). Starting in 1962 he was involved in the early developments of astronomical research from space vehicles in Europe. His leisure activities are organ playing and Renaissance choir music.

Florence Launay, with a doctorate in musicology from Rennes University (France), is the author of *Les Compositrices en France au XIXe siècle* (Fayard, 2006), articles on notable French women composers, and essays examining the access of women to musical careers. She is also a professional singer.

Stéphane Leteuré teaches history and geography. His dissertation "Le Drapeau et la lyre: Camille Saint-Saëns et le politique (1870– 1921)" (Tours, 2011) will be published by Vrin in 2013. His research concerns various political dimensions of French nineteenth-century music.

Martin Marks is a musicologist and senior lecturer in the music and theater arts department at MIT. A film music specialist, he was music curator for four DVD collections published by the National Film Preservation Foundation; the latest is *Treasures from American Film Archives 5: The West, 1898–1938* (2011).

Mitchell Morris teaches at UCLA. His specialties include opera; music, gender, sexuality; American popular song; music at the last fin de siècle; and ecomusicology. He has co-edited the *Oxford Handbook of the American Musical* and written *The Persistence of Sentiment: Display and Feeling in Popular Music of the 1970s*, forthcoming.

Jann Pasler, professor of music at University of California, San Diego, has recently published *Writing Through Music: Essays on Music, Culture, and Politics* (2008) and *Composing the Citizen: Music as Public Utility in Third Republic France* (ASCAP-Deems

Taylor Award, 2009). She is currently writing *Music, Race, and Colonialism in the French Empire, 1880s–1950s* and is editor of *AMS Studies in Music* (Oxford).

William Peterson, Thatcher Professor of Music and College Organist, Pomona College, is a scholar and performer. He is co-editor of *French Organ Music from the Revolution to Franck and Widor* (University of Rochester Press, 1995) and author of "Storm Fantasies for the Nineteenth-Century Organ in France" (*Keyboard Perspectives*, 2009).

Michael J. Puri is an associate professor in the McIntire Department of Music at the University of Virginia. His work performs detailed analysis within broader interpretive frameworks in order to create new approaches to music. A recent example is his monograph, *Ravel the Decadent: Memory, Sublimation, and Desire* (Oxford University Press, 2012).

Sabina Teller Ratner, associate professor at the Université de Montréal, is the author of *Camille Saint-Saëns (1835–1921): A Thematic Catalogue of his Complete Works*: Volume I *The Instrumental Works* and Volume II *The Dramatic Works*. Presently she is co-director of a new comprehensive edition of the works of Saint-Saëns.

Laure Schnapper, professor at the École des hautes études en sciences sociales (EHESS), Paris, has published many articles on nineteenth-century Parisian musical life and two books, *L'Ostinato, procédé musical universel* (1998) and *Henri Herz, magnat du piano: La vie musicale en France au XIXe siècle (1815–1870)* (2011).

Marie-Gabrielle Soret is a curator of music at the Bibliothèque nationale de France, in charge of processing large archival collections of performers, composers, and publishers of the nineteenth and twentieth century. She has a doctorate in musicology, and is currently preparing Camille Saint-Saëns's *Écrits sur la musique*.

Michael Stegemann studied composition with Messiaen and wrote his doctoral thesis on "Saint-Saëns and the French Solo Concerto" (1982). Since 2002, he has been chair for musicology at TU University, Dortmund, Germany. He has written books on Vivaldi, Mozart, Schubert, Liszt, Saint-Saëns, Ravel, and Glenn Gould and edited music by Chopin, Fauré, and Debussy.

Michael Strasser is a professor of musicology at Baldwin-Wallace College in Berea, Ohio. He has published articles on the intersection of musical life and politics in late nineteenth-century France and on Arnold Schoenberg. In addition, he has presented papers on colonial music in Mexico and New England.

Catherine Temerson (translator) has translated over twenty works of fiction and non-fiction. Her most recent translations, to be published in 2012, are Florence Noiville's *The Gift* and Elie Wiesel's *Hostage*.

Alice Teyssier (translator) has lived in Australia, the United States, France, and Germany and has been doing musicological translations since 2004. A professional singer and flutist whose repertoire spans six centuries, she is currently pursuing a doctorate at the University of California, San Diego.